D0713017

My Life

MY LIFE
Sir Oswald
MOSLEY

Arlington House   New Rochelle, N.Y.

To P.

Preface to the American Edition copyright © 1972 by Sir Oswald Mosley.

Library of Congress Catalog Card Number 78-179718
ISBN 0-87000-160-4

MANUFACTURED IN THE UNITED STATES OF AMERICA

Acknowledgements

My acknowledgements are chiefly due to the patience of the reader who may discover some errors of fact or quotation in a long work compiled almost entirely from memory. My papers were lost in the destruction of war, and throughout I have been remote from most of my library. The main facts have been checked by others, who have access to records. They proved correct to a degree which surprised me in the circumstances. Quotations may sometimes suffer from unaided memory introducing improvements to long-cherished passages of the classics which might not be so apparent to their distinguished authors.

My thanks are due to my wife, who has contributed both enthusiasm for this book and an acute and most critical intelligence, and to others who have been good enough to read the proofs in whole or in part. Sydney Potter was my friend during the political fight to win Birmingham in the twenties, and after a long interval has generously exercised his editorial experience in reading these pages in the sixties; younger literary friends—Desmond Stewart, Robert Skidelsky and David Ashton—have assisted with the same task; Jeffrey Hamm and Robert Row have combined research with supporting the heavy secretarial burden; Comte Jean de Baglion has helped by checking at least the grammar of some of the French quotations, and Princess Clary has similarly assisted with the German; my brothers, Ted and John, and my daughter Vivien have supplied some photographs; and Jerry Lehane's friendship and ever-ready help make possible all my work. I owe much to my friends.

My publishers, Thomas Nelson and Sons, in their generous assistance, have gone far beyond normal obligations in providing James Mitchell's searching and stimulating questions on a wide range of subjects, and James Shepherd's capacity for close co-operation in arduous and accurate work under pressure. My good fortune in these respects has enabled me to overcome some of my initial difficulties in sole reliance on my own memory.

Preface to the American Edition

War in our troubled times has often changed the life course of men and nations. This story needs some insight and sympathy for those who fight in wars, in this case the First World War which left a deep sense of dedication in the survivors. To lose nearly all your friends at the dawn of life is an event which either dissolves character in the cynicism of life despair or steels and inspires it to enduring resolution. For better or worse I owe the dynamism of my political impulse to the First World War.

We went to that vast test with an idealism which was betrayed so blatantly that this fine emotion has withered in the world. It was "the war to end war", "the war to make the world safe for democracy", and those who returned were promised by desk-bound politicians "a land fit for heroes to live in". It was this last solemn pledge which took some of us into politics; we dedicated our lives to building such a country as a monument to our fallen companions and as a recompense to the mass of ex-servicemen who must now live in the fair conditions which their exertion and suffering should have won. The comradeship born in Flanders must be extended into peace, we must give ourselves to doing something for our people. So I went into parliament and became active in the British Legion of Ex-Servicemen.

This book tells the story of my individual experience of fighting in the air and in the trenches, and of my efforts to make good the sacrifice of our generation. In the words of one of my later speeches: "Through and beyond the failure of men and of parties we of the war generation are marching on, and we shall march on until our end is achieved and our sacrifice atoned". Foremost in that purpose of course was the prevention of future war. Never again must men suffer as we had, the generation of our sons must be saved. So I worked first with the statesmen of liberal mind who built the League of Nations, and when that failed opposed with every risk of life, liberty and spirit the Second World War. My constructive policy to avert it is described in this book, together with my previous political campaigns to arouse the people in far the largest political meetings ever held in Britain. The continuance of this crusade through every vicissitude is recounted, until the development of detailed plans in the dangers of the present period to forestall a final world explosion. Thought must ever precede the deed, and at the end of this book an attempt is made to clarify confusion with a proposal to divide the world into spheres of influence where the success or failure of diverse systems in competitive co-existence may determine a constructive future as an alternative to the universal destruction of nuclear war. The purpose was, and is, peace.

Always in life we must work for the best, but prepare for the worst. If Europe or America should be attacked, or our vital interests threatened, we must stand true to our alliance, and we must be armed so long as others are. In this respect I believe always in a phrase of one of my old speeches reported in this book: "Stand by our friends, and stand up to our enemies". Yet we should always first give reason and peace every chance, and the best chance for peace is that a united and therefore powerful Europe should be not a satellite but a colleague of America. We should not be dragged into the orbit of American adventure, from which surely now the American people have learnt to refrain; I first said, "Hold Europe, leave Asia", in 1950.

My claim to have tried long and patiently to give reason and agreement a chance both abroad and at home may be judged in reading this book. When we were faced with the great betrayal of the war generation I worked for eleven years in parliament both in the old parties and in independence, to right the wrongs of the men who were promised "the land fit for heroes" and were given the slums and unemployment. Finally, when every other means had been exhausted, came the explosion of fascism. For explosion it was, against intolerable human conditions which modern science then, and still more now, could rapidly remedy, if statesmen had energy and vision. Long have I held that "statesmen should live and work with scientists as the Medicis lived and worked with artists". That creative union in high achievement has always been frustrated by the idle frivolity of current politics. Hence the explosion of fascism, from whose bitter errors we must learn in our maturity. After the war I wrote: "Already the thought and the act of the future take shape. We reconcile the old conflicts and begin to achieve, today in thought and tomorrow in deed, the union of authority with liberty, action with thought, decision with discussion, power with responsibility, vigour with duty, strength with kindness, and service of the people with the attainment of ever higher forms of life" (1950).

Fascism was in essence an intensely national creed and it therefore divided rather than united Europe, despite some thought and effort described in this book. Policy was therefore entirely different in each country in order to meet particular national needs. In addition to natural and moral feeling it was out of the question for me to be anti-semitic in a British policy which strove to maintain a multi-racial empire and to promote its gradual evolution. We might quarrel temporarily about the question of a Second World War, but not about race. My efforts to prevent division and to unite Europe began with my support of the League of Nations, continued even in the Fascist period, and finally came to full development and expression when I was the first to declare for "Europe a Nation" in 1948. It should never be forgotten that America not only proposed the League of Nations after the first war, but after the second war strove throughout to promote rather than to impede the union of Europe; an act of unprecedented generosity, because it was the first time in history that one great power assisted the creation of another.

The constructive economic and social policies which form a large part of this book can apply almost equally to Europe or America. It is one of the paradoxes of my life that my work as a young minister in the government of 1930 is now approved as an answer to the problems of that day by almost all economic authority, while my ideas of the last twenty years still await acceptance, although I regard them as a far greater contribution to economic and political thought. Yet the time may be near when we require the positive action of government to intervene in the present chaos with leadership rather than close control, and to link the problems of inflation and environment in a solution which more reasonably and realistically uses both resources and manpower. Always I insist that "we can only do great things in a great way", and to meet the social dangers of our age it will be necessary again to evoke the heroic mood; not for the universal destruction which war now threatens, but at last for the high purpose of a creative peace.

Oswald Mosley

Contents

Plates

Author and East London friends after a meeting (*John Warburton*)
With the audience after a meeting in Trafalgar Square (*John Warburton*)
Walking to an open-air meeting
The author today (*Mark Gerson*)
The Mosley's home near Paris (*Photo Connaissance des Arts*)
European journey (*Keystone*)

I
Ancestry and Childhood

WE began with 'Ernald, a Saxon', who lived in the reign of King John at Moseley, a hamlet in Staffordshire four miles from Wolverhampton. The descendants of this 'Ernald de Moseley' moved to Lancashire and other parts of Staffordshire, married Normans and later added a slight mixture of Scotch and Irish. The 'e' was dropped from the family name in deference to a Latin epigram of the erudite Queen Elizabeth when an ancestor defied the law and organised a privateer fleet against Spain. My own strong feeling that I am a European appears to have some foundation in ancestry and family experience.

I have never made a close study of the family lineage, which is on record in various books of reference, but in my youth I remember a great-uncle who was a considerable authority on the subject. Facts no doubt in the course of time had become freely embroidered. It seems clear, however, that our family played a fairly distinguished part in the Civil War, though I have never tested by the record their claim to have defended Tutbury Castle until it was the last Royalist stronghold to fall in that bitter conflict. The reliable witness of my grandfather and great-uncle assured me that they had seen letters written by Cromwell when he was besieging Tutbury, threatening to burn down the nearby family home at Rolleston if we did not surrender the castle. It was in this ancestral pride that I made the daily march of a mile and a half and back from my grandfather's house at Rolleston to Tutbury each afternoon of my Staffordshire childhood under the watchful eye of my first sergeant-major, a kindly nanny. Fortunately Cromwell did not fulfil his threat, but contented himself with removing all the lead from the Rolleston roof to make bullets. Yet the fate of this fine old Tudor house was only delayed, and it was burned down in the latter half of the last century, together with the Cromwell letters and many other treasures. I never saw it.

All that remains of the house is a drawing of the Georgian façade which had been added in the eighteenth century. The main feature was reputedly a long, oak-panelled gallery which contained the best pictures, including several Van Dycks; this may well be, as the period was an apogee of family fortune, though knowledge of the breeding of shorthorns and shire horses was more conspicuous in my immediate forbears. We still have a Stubbs, which must have been tucked away in some back room; a Mosley boy, holding his horse, is accompanied by his dogs on the slopes of Tutbury Castle, perennial scene of reverent recollection and pilgrimage. The Van Dycks have disappeared without trace, except for an odd freak of fate; it may possibly prove that fire gave back what it took away. We suffered a second fire in 1954 at a house we had at Clonfert in Ireland where some of the remaining family pictures were hung. A large portrait which we always believed to be a copy of one of the Van Dycks was badly singed. It was sent to Dublin for cleaning and excision of the unimpaired centre, and in the process was pronounced original by the Irish experts.

Because of the burning of Rolleston we have few relics of the Cavalier period. Still less have we any record of the next upheaval in which we were involved. It is in the manner of English families, and indeed of the British nation, that long, slumbering periods of quiet life are followed by moments of abrupt awakening and sometimes of dramatic action. There was always a tradition that we were much engaged in the 1745 rebellion of Prince Charles Edward Stuart. The only evidence of this produced to me in my youth was a pin-cushion embroidered by some ancestress with the words 'Down with the Rump and God bless Prince Charles'. We still possess this pin-cushion, but of course it clearly refers not to Prince Charles Edward of the '45, but to Charles II when he was 'on his travels' as a fugitive from the 'Rump' of the Cromwellian Parliament. I was, therefore, inclined to discount the tradition that in 1745 we were armed and ready to come out with the Young Pretender on his march south as soon as he reached our house at Rolleston. We were saved from the subsequent disaster because he and the Highlanders turned back at Derby, eleven miles to our north.

This topic revived vividly when I addressed a public dinner in the thirties at which as usual I expressed my loyalty to the Crown. Sir Compton Mackenzie was present, and subsequently put the teasing question whether this declaration had any reference to the fact that Prince Charles Edward had spent the night in our family house on his secret visit to England the year before the '45. He referred later to this historical incident in a book on the subject of Prince Charles's well-concealed survey of the field of action for the following year. I had never heard this, but it was not difficult to understand how careful the family had been to destroy all record of the period.

The romantic tradition of opposition and insurgence—embodied in the grace and charm of the Stuarts and their cause—evidently moved our family at this stage, but the reader would be mistaken in thinking this accounts for the course of my political career. A portentous change followed, when the Mosleys became the incarnation of contrary English qualities. Perhaps we had after all the happy quality, the redeeming grace, of learning from experience.

The culmination was my great-great-grandfather Sir Oswald Mosley whose fire-inviolate portrait gazes down on me in his red robes of learning with massive reassurance of English stability, albeit with a certain whimsical charm as if he almost admitted it was not quite so serious as he made out. With him we enter a very different period of the family history, an unaccounted metamorphosis from the Jacobite, romantic Tory tradition to the solid, stolid respectable Whig. We are surrounded not by emotional revolutionaries but by squires and parsons, and by professional soldiers of the orthodox variety, like my father's two first cousins who were killed in the First World War, and my own brother Ted, who spent his life in the army.

This very worthy person, my great-great-grandfather, was indeed a pillar of the State in the Midland counties. It was he who appears first to have established that our Saxon family could prove its ancestry to the thirteenth century and trace it to before the Norman conquest. It seems in any case that the family is of a respectable antiquity, for works of reference and public monuments show that it was playing some role at least in Elizabethan times. My great-great-grandfather fortified his Saxon lineage by marrying an Every from a neighbouring family of Norman descent; this desirable out-cross—in agricultural language—appears to have occurred more than once. Armed then with an imposing presence and a weighty erudition in his own sphere, he entered the House of Commons in the Whig cause during the Reform Bill period. Apart from this concession to progress he showed little sign of possessing a radical frame of mind.

I have often been reproached in my political life with the rough part the family played in repressing the Chartist riots in Manchester, although I was never able to understand why I should be held responsible for events so many years before I was born. After all, Peterloo was a mild exercise in violence compared with some of the British doings in India and elsewhere during subsequent years. For all they knew, my indignant interlocutors on the alleged performance of my ancestors might themselves have been able to trace descent from those who during the Indian mutiny bound Sepoys to the muzzles of guns for the purpose of blowing them into the next world in unidentifiable pieces, thus robbing them not only of life but of their chance of paradise. Many of us Europeans would be in for a thin time in this world or the next if we were held responsible for all the dark deeds which adorn our family trees. The real matter of regret and reproof is that our generation has not progressed beyond the wickedness of our antecedents, and has even regressed by comparison with some of mankind's more enlightened periods.

The offence of our family's more impetuous members in restoring order in Manchester by a yeomanry charge rather than by persuasion was, of course, aggravated by the ownership of considerable wealth in the area. This was derived from the agricultural land on which Manchester was built, not entirely by the direct exertions of the family. From my point of view they made one disastrous error when they sold leaseholds for 999 years instead of for 99. That extra nine unhappily made the difference between our wealth and, for example, that of the Grosvenor family, who occupied a similar position in the development of London, but granted shorter leases which fell in sooner. Reflecting upon what might have happened in British politics if I had had so much money to spend, my contemporaries may consider that they can count their blessings.

The virtual sale of this land cut both ways, for we lost control over it. It was therefore again wide of the mark when I was frequently attacked in my political life for the subsequent development of Manchester. Not only did this occur before I was born, but the family could not have altered the course of events once they had granted these careless ieases. Our last effective influence in Manchester ceased with the sale to the Corporation of the Lord of the Manor rights early in the nineteenth century, this time for quite a tidy sum in a shrewd bargain which left some resentment. These rights, strangely, we had shared from early times with the De La Warr family; strangely, because the present Lord De La Warr was a fellow-member of the 1929 Labour Government. When I last looked, our coats-of-arms were still side by side in the remnants of our old family house at Ancoats; a quaint premonition.

These events, and also the cavalier romance, seem well established by the research of forbears. It is difficult for us today to understand this obsession with family trees. I am glad to know that I come from an old English and British family, but there my interest ends. It was different in the last century, when my great-great-grandfather in particular appeared to have shown an inordinate pride in his lineage. During his time in Parliament he is reported to have refused a peerage with the observation that an ancient baronetcy was preferable to a mushroom peerage. Although he was evidently a man of some intellectual attainments and considerable personal prestige, what he had done to merit a peerage is not entirely clear. Still more dubious is the remark concerning the ancient baronetcy, for he was only the second in the line. It appears however that this was the third Mosley creation of a baronetcy, which in earlier years had lapsed because the succession was insufficiently direct. The first creation dated from the reign of James I, so to say it was ancient may have been moderately justified.

The story of our family in the Elizabethan period is for the most part clear. Sir Nicholas Mosley was Lord Mayor of London under Queen Elizabeth, and a fine monument testifying to this fact still stands in Didsbury Church near Manchester. A more beautiful monument to another member of the family in a slightly later period can also be found in Rolleston Church. This marks the division of the Mosleys at that time between the earlier Lancashire branch and the migrants to Rolleston, Staffordshire, in the late Elizabethan period. They all seemed to have joined together a little later for the Civil War in the Royalist cause.

Throughout, a certain diversity occurred between the Staffordshire owners of agricultural land with a substantial farming tradition and the remaining Lancashire family who seem to have been largely engaged in the early cotton trade. There remained however considerable interplay of interests, for the Rolleston branch derived most of their money from the land on which Manchester was built, and the Lancashire family still carried on farming in the Didsbury and Chorley area. The old family house at Houghend still stands, though in a very dilapidated condition. It was abandoned long before my time, no doubt on account of the approach of Manchester which disturbed the rural habits of these countrymen. When I rediscovered the house it was sadly deserted, open to the wind and rain and stripped of panelling, staircase and all decoration or suggestion of a home. I wandered through the deserted stables and outhouses, which evidently came right up to the front door in the style of the smaller French chateaux. The only living thing appeared to me in the dusk as a ghostly shadow of a peacock perched on a cow-stall. I came nearer, and thought the motionless bird was stuffed, the only remaining relic of the old family life. I stroked it, and the live head turned towards me with a steady, tragic gaze of faraway memories; perhaps we should never have left?

How Sir Nicholas Mosley's diverse energies and interests carried him from this quiet country background to the position of Lord Mayor of London is a matter of legend. The job seems to have required a considerable variety of function and of quality in the incumbent. He is reported to have fitted out a privateer fleet against the Spaniards at a time when Elizabeth was at peace with Spain. The Lord Mayor's flagrant breach of the prevailing law was said to have been forgiven to him when the fleet returned with considerable booty, a substantial proportion being placed at the disposal of the pacific queen. Again according to legend, when he appeared before her in some trepidation to explain the situation and to offer a share in the swag, she delivered to him a family motto instead of delivering him to the axe he had merited. The motto was *Mos legem regit*, which was understood to mean 'Our custom is above the law' and has been proudly held ever since.

If the legend is untrue, some explanation is required for this strange device which is, of course, so much at variance with my own habit as the present family representative, who not only keeps the law but has had frequent recurrence to the courts to require others to do the same. The legend is fortified by the Queen's considerable reputation for erudition and wit, which in those days was often expressed in Latin punning. Play on the family name of Mosley is reputed to have given her such satisfaction that she forgot to be angry. It may be that the material recompense of the booty reinforced the purely intellectual pleasure. Who knows? To what extent do truth and legend coincide? Perhaps the most that one can say is that there was probably something in it.

Family crest with the motto given by Queen Elizabeth I for breaking the law.

Memory over generations is likely to be even more distorted than memory in a single life. Some things in life as in literature are worth remembering, but many trivial things the mind does better to discard; it should not be a lost luggage depot in a railway station through which we passed long since. I have always consciously trained myself in this sense. The result is that I hardly ever forget a fact that seems to me important and is relevant to the given situation, but when it comes to remembering every irrelevant detail of past life and of tedious people who have flitted through the scene without mark or purpose, I am lost. I can remember a scene, a statistic, a turning-point of action, a quotation of prose or poetry which has moved me, but not life's minor irrelevancies.

With this mental training and habit it is not easy for me to remember my childhood except for vivid memories of dear people I so much loved, notably my mother and my paternal grandfather. Otherwise my childhood, for reasons I will explain later, seemed to me of little importance. Few things are more overrated than the effect of childish experiences on later life. However, I well recall some of the early contrasts of fortune and circumstance which became still more extreme in my later life. My home life was divided between my mother and my paternal grandfather who was called Sir Oswald Mosley and was the grandson of the Reform Bill M.P. of the same name. They were usually on the best of terms, and she accompanied me and my younger brothers to his Staffordshire home at Rolleston-on-Dove. Her own house was on the borders of Market Drayton in Shropshire, near her parents and brothers, who had country houses a few miles away.

My mother lived in relatively straitened circumstances; a continuous struggle to make ends meet worried her a great deal. I was very conscious of this, being her eldest son and much in her confidence. The problem was to pay the school fees of three boys at what were considered the best schools and to provide us with clothes and enough good healthy food in the holidays. Whatever the difficulty of the situation she always succeeded in doing these things. We were much better off in this respect than many of my contemporaries. Nevertheless, it was not easy for my mother, and we suspected that it involved doing without many of the things which her friends enjoyed. She was a remarkable woman to whom I owed everything in my early life, and to whom I was passionately devoted until she died at the age of seventy-six years.

She combined strict religious principles with a robust, realistic attitude to life. The tenets of the Church of England were possibly modified by the long-continuing influence of the pagan world which can still be observed in many countries. An absolute morality in personal conduct was combined with a sturdy maintenance of the values of her own kind; an exact reversal of many current attitudes. She was less than twenty-four years older than I, as I was born within a year of her marriage, and extremely beautiful. Yet I never observed any male influence in her life other than her family and an occasional preacher of exceptional gifts. She was a paragon of virtue, but as loyal and vigorous as a lioness in defence of her own. Conventional education, and appreciation of literature, the arts and music were almost entirely lacking, though she played Strauss waltzes on the piano in a way that entranced me as a child. Her natural shrewdness coupled with a clear head for figures and simple business made her an able woman by any standards.

She was popular in the country circles in which she moved, because of her evident good nature, high spirits and considerable humour. Our friends by reason of her background were almost entirely concerned with agriculture and sport, and this was perhaps her chief anxiety: to enable her sons to take part in the sports of the field which she and all her friends felt were the only possible training for a man, and to which almost from infancy we were ardently addicted. It may seem strange in retrospect that she should so have taxed her energies and resources to keep ponies in addition to three hungry boys, but hunting in that world was almost a religious observance; and let me freely admit in another age that some of the happiest moments of my life have been spent with horse and hound. Well do I remember as a small boy the night before returning to school, sitting all evening long in a manger weeping with one arm round the neck of some beloved pony while the other hand caressed a favourite fox-terrier. It was a ritual of the old country folk with roots deep in a remote past; roots too which gave a certain vitality and resolution for very different purposes. All now very strange and far away, but insistently real at that time.

The ponies, and a horse for my mother, were usually a gift of one or other of the grandfathers, but their upkeep was something of a problem even with the cheap oats, hay and straw available in the country. Rough shooting was also provided close at hand by my mother's father; and at Rolleston where my Mosley grandfather had some four thousand acres there was plenty of such shooting and coarse fishing. The holidays were simply a matter of horse, dog and gun. These were the happy crumbs which fell from the well-laden tables of two grandfathers. It may be asked why they did not do more in a regular way to help my mother in her daily struggle to keep going, for they were both kindly men. The answer is probably that it simply did not occur to them. The shy reticence of their kind would inhibit any enquiry unless they were asked; and to ask was out of the question to my mother's reserved pride. The result was that we experienced extremes of contrast in our way of life, particularly in our visits to the Rolleston grandfather.

Even my mother's father—Justinian Edwards Heathcote—lived in a very different way to us. Sunday luncheon with the family was a sumptuous occasion, presided over by the grand old matriarch, my grandmother, square in physique and in mind with clear-cut and determined features, who came from another Staffordshire family. Her principles were rigid, and she never risked their impairment. Someone gave her a book by R. H. Benson, which she put aside with the rebuke that he was a Roman Catholic: 'I am not going to have them converting me'. Nevertheless, within her narrow limits she was a fine woman, always occupied with deeds of Christian kindness from which wide and diverse circles benefited.

Rolleston visits provided even greater contrasts with our way of life at home. It was an abrupt transition in childhood from a wayside house with a few rooms, a patch of garden, and one maidservant fresh caught from the village green, to the massive edifice of Victorian comfort—which replaced the burnt Tudor house—set amid its park, lakes and gardens. About thirty gardeners outside and eleven menservants inside maintained this establishment, with a small army of housemaids and of cooks, supplemented by two still-room maids exclusively engaged in the making of cakes, which must considerably have contributed to the vast girth of senior members of the family. My great-grandfather, well named Sir Tonman Mosley, was always reputed to have jumped off the scales when they passed twenty stone; jumped, for he was still active, and lived to be seventy-seven in defiance of modern dietary theory. His way of living—he had a large area cut out of the table to accommodate his stomach while he reached for the surrounding supplies—deprived him of only nine years of life in comparison with the spare frame of his learned father, the Whig M.P. for North Staffordshire, who died at eighty-six.

My grandfather was a man of more moderate dimensions, and the meals were not quite so gargantuan. He died at sixty-seven after a rather heavy dinner, topped up with his favourite combination of port wine and walnuts; but his strong constitution had been undermined by diabetes in a period before the discovery of insulin. His two brothers lived in the usual family fashion in full possession of their faculties until well into the eighties. The elder of the two was created Lord Anslow by the Liberal Party, of which he was a pillar. I had to take evasive action in avoiding his efforts to make the peerage hereditary to me—which I do not think could in any case have succeeded—but we remained on good terms and I had a strong regard and affection for him despite every political divergence.

His younger brother, named Ernald after the founder, and nicknamed Uncle Tat, was a tiny little man of girth almost equal to his height, who lived in a medieval doll's house near Horsham. He was like a Beatrix Potter character, and I was devoted to him in early life, listening for hours to his history or legend of the family. He left his miniscule dwelling to my youngest brother John. This was appropriate because the house was in the middle of the stockbrokers' paradise, but inappropriate because John is six foot three, and its long garden fence facing the Brighton road could so easily be decorated with the words 'Up Mosley' by my passing supporters; my genial relations with my brother survived even this test.

In each generation it was the eldest son—with the exception of my great-great-grandfather—who tended to live in a rather immoderate fashion, and I became another exception to the rule. I have sometimes wondered why I live in such a different way, and the answer I suppose is that I have a powerful desire to keep myself fit in order to serve certain purposes in life; also in our time we have learned more of the art of living, what to eat and what not to eat to keep the physical form we desire. It is curious that these relatively simple discoveries were not made sooner; only in recent years has the question of diet been seriously studied.

Sleep, the second great need of humanity, was also neglected by scientific research until quite lately. Conclusions on that subject in my youth were the purely empirical deductions of practical men. I owe much to the chance that in my first year in the House of Commons two remarkable old gentlemen—as they appeared to the youngest member—gave me the same advice: always to sleep some time between the midday and the evening meal. One adviser was Lloyd George, and the other Churchill; I took their advice, and am convinced this is one of the chief reasons why I am now alive and very fit after such a strenuous life. Most modern doctors now take the same view.

Life at Rolleston was a matter of instinct rather than of science; we were very close to nature. My grandfather had a prize-winning shorthorn herd, and was one of the country's leading authorities on shorthorns and shire horses. I was saturated with the farming tradition, lived in it, enjoyed it, and I still do. We were of the earth earthy, and I am glad of it. It is one of my deepest convictions that these roots in the soil are a very fine start to life. This calm existence rolled on at a leisurely pace. Farming stock and method had been built over long years, and the skilled men had often been there for generations. They formed one of the established institutions which, short of disaster, are relatively easy to conduct; what is difficult is to create new things. Everything was well run in, and managed with a stately ritual. My grandfather must have done a lot of work in his little office in a quiet corner of the large house and in his frequent inspections, but to us children the highlight of his efforts and successes shone on Sunday mornings. After church came a visit to the home farm. The whole well-ordered parade must occur between church and luncheon, so a watch would be ostentatiously examined if the sermon continued long enough to keep the men one moment from the Sunday dinner or to risk turning our own beef from pink to brown. Life had its rules, and the Sunday beef was a very serious affair indeed. Placed in front of my grandfather on an enormous dish was always a sirloin of four-year-old beef, whose breadth still makes all modern fare look puny. Then came the solemn moment when —carving-knife poised in hand—my grandfather recited the pedigree and recounted the many virtues of the dual-purpose shorthorn breed.

It is perhaps not surprising in the light of these recollections that my grandfather looked the image of the traditional John Bull, which became his nickname in wide circles. He was in his way almost a national figure. Among his numerous contacts with the world outside this completely self-contained enclave of existence were a strangely assorted couple, King Edward VII and Lord Northcliffe. The King saw him sometimes at agricultural shows, and was evidently attracted and entertained by his sterling character. One of his letters expressed a desire to lean over a gate with my grandfather contemplating a rural scene—the King's tact was as diverse as his amusement—and an immense signed photograph was always displayed with loyal pride.

Lord Northcliffe's intrusion into the country paradise was not so much appreciated as the political support given to me many years later by his brother, Lord Rothermere. Wholemeal bread became a stunt in the *Daily Mail* under the name of Standard bread. The startling discovery that such a substance existed was made in the forgotten village of Rolleston, where John Bull himself had installed the old stone rollers. The story went like wildfire, but we were all much too slow-witted to make any money out of it. In fact, the whole family felt an acute embarrassment at the publicity, which I have seldom since experienced in this sphere; the exception was my grandfather who took things as they came in his robust fashion.

Otherwise Rolleston life was remote from the world, a remarkable, truly feudal survival. Like medieval life, the economy was practically self-contained. Farms, the garden, shooting and the large and well-stocked cellars satisfied most needs; the same wagon which took our produce a few miles to be sold in Burton-on-Trent would return well loaded with a fine variety of the best beers. There was little need to go outside the closed and charmed circle, and we children never did. Our time was divided between farms, gardens and carpenter's shop, where the bearded Pritchard presided over a corps of experts who kept all things going as their forbears had done for generations. I learnt then to work with my hands both in farming and carpentry, and must admit that I was better at shovelling muck than in the fine work of joinery; both aptitudes have their use in political life.

Again in feudal fashion, the warmest and most intimate friendships developed between us and these people, so characteristic of traditional England, not only in their daily occupations but in the strong bonds of mutual sympathy in life's events, birth, marriage, death, occasions sad and festive; this was really a classless society. This early development was one of the three very diverse experiences which wove me into the warp and woof of English life. The second was the army—not only in regimental life, though the relationships of officers and men in the great regiments developed an extraordinary intimacy—but still more in army athletics where an absolute equality prevailed between all ranks. The third experience was very different: when I joined the Labour Party I spent two months touring the country each autumn to make daily speeches. Every night was passed in the house of a different member, nearly all manual workers, from the mines, steel works, shipyards, farms and all the diverse industries and trades of English, Scotch and Welsh life. The wife cooked and looked after us, gave the very best they had, and I have never been better cared for and made to feel more warmly welcome and accepted into the intimacy of family life. I owe much in knowledge and in sentiment to that wide range of cherished memories.

These experiences helped me in the days of class to become a classless man, and later to devise a type of political organisation which at least eliminated that archaic nonsense. At Rolleston the class values only emerged strikingly at the strangest point; in church. The habit must have developed over generations or centuries that everybody waited until the family took communion; it afforded them no practical advantage, because in any case they had to wait until the service was over. This custom was probably never by their volition, but for some odd reason at some point in time they had established the principle of roping off an aisle of the church. It was peculiar, because they only used one or two pews and the aisle would accommodate two or three hundred people. It did not much matter as the church was never anything like full. Yet even to my childish eyes it looked rather an affront to man, and soon a new uncumbent took it as an affront to God. The clergyman was a Royal Chaplain, by name Canon Tyrrhitt. He was uncle of Lord Berners, the gifted writer, composer, artist and wit who was a friend of ours when my wife Diana and I were living in Wiltshire in the late forties. The Canon was of a very different type from the usual run of country parsons in those days.

My grandfather was landed in this bit of trouble by his Royal allegiance. King Edward had asked him to grant the particularly well-endowed living to the Royal Chaplain. All went well until the clerical eye with the wide and sophisticated glance of a larger world fell on the rope offending both earth and heaven. A peremptory demand for its removal followed; and was promptly rejected. Then followed a perfectly ridiculous and much publicised lawsuit, costing thousands of pounds, which the family rightly lost. It might have been better handled, for my grandfather had the warmest heart, and any appeal to his neighbourly feelings or religious duty would almost certainly have met with a spontaneous and generous response; but the Christian beatitude—blessed are the meek—had missed the Canon by as wide a mark as the grandfather. It was all very childish, and expensive.

My grandfather was in every sense a child of nature. Fearless and combative in face of any challenge, he was immediately and entirely disarmed by any appeal to compassion and suggestion of friendship. He was completely a man, and I greatly loved him. His simple and generous nature made him a most likeable person, and he evoked almost universal affection from all who met him in his small world or in wider circles, where he moved with the same unaffected friendship as he did among his tenants, work people, country neighbours or the larger agricultural shows and institutions in which he played a leading part. His life and being were rooted deep in English soil.

We had for each other a strong affection. Some time before he died I had developed intellectual and cultural interests which were strange to him, but this in no way impaired our relationship. We had so many interests in common, of the countryside, sport and all the many aspects of traditional English life. As an amateur boxer in his youth, he had been runner-up in the middle-weight championship of Britain; he was also a runner, swimmer and all-round athlete, a remarkable performer. In addition to sport, my grandfather's knowledge of horses, cattle and every aspect of agricultural life was exceptional, and was of enduring interest to me. We never lacked things to talk about, for we had many of the basic things of life in common. The same faculties and tastes later stood me in good stead in the army and enabled the development of close companionship with men to whom a whole range of my other interests were literally a closed book.

The only moment of difficulty in my intimacy with my grandfather was in the expression of emotion; the English inhibition, perhaps our curse. When I told him in the latter months of 1914 just after my eighteenth birthday that I had volunteered and been accepted temporarily to leave my regiment for service with the Royal Flying Corps in France, he burst into tears. It was astonishing in such a man; he explained that he had been told that this was the most dangerous of all war services, and that I was all he had. If we had been classic Greeks we would have fallen into each other's arms in a transport of mutual emotion; I should have explained in warm and passionate words all that I felt for him. But I was just a frozen young Englishman; I could not move, I could say nothing. That has been a regret my whole life long. He died soon afterwards, and I survived the experience he feared for me.

Why is it that we cannot overcome these barriers? They can upon occasion be surmounted by minds and characters at a certain level of common interest and attainment, but they too often arise between generations. My relations with my grandfather were certainly more intimate than his contacts with his own grandfather, before whom he was accustomed to stand to attention like a soldier on parade at the height of the Victorian era. Manners were formal and family discipline was strict in this earlier period at Rolleston.

That massive building, emblem of Victorian achievement and stability on which the sun was never to set, remains vivid in my memory as it can still journey through nearly every room—the entrance-hall heavy with black oak, leading to a wide staircase which branched gracefully at the halfway point and was adorned with family pictures on the lofty walls reaching right to the roof; the large dining-room, which was the only room to the left of the staircase because it supplied the contemporary need in a house to be near the kitchen; the long passage leading to the sequence of rooms on the right of the staircase and beginning with the man in armour, past whom we used to scurry in lively apprehension when sent at night from the protracted dinner to bed at a reasonable hour; then the fantastic Moorish room which my grandmother fondly believed to be in the most exotic mode of the moment; the adjoining stereotyped drawing-room of the period, which she conceived to be the complete expression of exquisite femininity; then the library, a most agreeable room, all leather and filled with beautiful books, from which I still preserve some three thousand; next the billiard room, again all leather and redolent of post-prandial male jollity; and finally conservatory and ballroom with well-polished floor, which in childhood added shine to the seat of the pants, with my grandfather's little quiet work sanctum lurking beyond. An equally large area in the other half of the house was occupied by the varied cohorts of housekeepers, butlers, footmen, cooks, scullions, still-room maids, housemaids, etc., who lived in almost equal style of victuals and material comforts —the butlers were almost as portly as their patrons—which the descendants of their employers would today regard as an existence of magnificence. Chiming clocks inside, sweeping lawns outside, forever recall me to Rolleston.

I was regarded as the heir to all this and was ostentatiously so treated by my grandfather, although my father was still alive and the entail through him still existed; so it was perhaps well that I had the constant correction of return with my mother to her really humble home. Psychological wiseacres will at once draw their conclusions when the separation of my father and mother is mentioned, together with the estrangement between father and grandfather; in due course we will examine their pretensions, on which I have at least clear views.

In early childhood I hardly knew my father, as a separation had occurred when I was five years old, and he was regarded as something of an ogre by my mother's family; but later I established with him a happy relationship over a long period. My grandfather suffered from no such apprehension concerning any man, but had a robust dislike for his son, who was the eldest of a family which included three good-looking daughters. The origin of the feud was rather obscure, as during my father's childhood they appear to have got on quite well. My grandfather in crisp summary used to say he could sometimes tolerate a merry blackguard, but he could not endure a gloomy blackguard. This word now has a quite different connotation; my grandfather did not mean anything to do with dishonesty. What he had in mind apparently were certain performances in my father's early manhood, when he had a tiff with my grandfather on some trivial matter and established himself in a local inn, the Dog and Partridge in Tutbury. There he had apparently set out in some degree to emulate the record of a remote ancestor who was reputedly known as the Tutbury Tup. These events on his own doorstep were regarded by my grandfather as an affront both to the proprieties and to the local reputation of the family; hence the 'blackguard'.

The adjective gloomy seemed even more inappropriate, for my father in my experience was the very reverse; in fact, to a degree which caused considerable embarrassment. No doubt when upbraided by his father he had adopted a sulky demeanour, as often occurs on such occasions in the young of all generations. My grandfather was no Puritan, but he felt strongly that affairs of this nature should be conducted with a remote discretion, far from the family home. He was himself estranged at that time in a quite agreeable fashion from his wife, and seldom saw her. From her stylised portraits in youth, she appears as a large and beautiful doll, with an exaggeration of white, blue and gold colouring. She introduced the red-head strain to the family, which appeared in my favourite Aunt Vi, emerged again in my niece Veronica, daughter of my brother Ted, and finally in my youngest son, Max. My grandmother was rumoured to be of a frigid disposition, which

did not suit my grandfather at all; but his recompense was always conducted with the utmost discretion and dignity. He expected a similar
reticence from all his family, and was therefore outraged by my father's local
bacchanalia.

These differences sometimes took a strenuous form. In a quarrel during the
early manhood of my father my grandfather ventured the opinion that he
could knock him out with one hand tied behind his back. My father accepted
the suggestion with alacrity; he was a slim young man of about five feet nine
inches, but had himself reached the semi-finals of the Amateur Boxing
Association as a feather-weight. He reckoned that he would stand quite a
chance against a more accomplished middle-weight in his early forties who
had one hand out of action; in any case he was incensed. They repaired to the
sombre oak hall, announcing the sporting event to all and sundry, who duly
assembled. At first my grandfather took considerable punishment, but he
tucked his chin into the protective left shoulder and bided his time. Eventually
he saw his opening and knocked my father out with a single right to the jaw,
to the warm applause of the assembled family and retainers. Poor Pa in the
parlance of The Fancy was as cold as a mackerel.

A more genial occasion of the same corinthian character occurred when I
was sixteen and my father thirty-eight, more appropriately in the happier
atmosphere of the ballroom. My father had some reports of my performance
at Winchester where I had been for some time entirely dedicated to boxing,
and he wished to see for himself. Happily I was able to waltz round him almost
as easily as I had waltzed on the same floor with the local maids and matrons
of the county. My legs were then in good working order and very practised;
they kept me out of all trouble. His girth and way of life had slowed him up
considerably, and the long-trained straight left jerked his head back frequently,
to the evident pleasure of the same convivial company of spectators in another
generation. It was an embarrassing situation, and his ever more strenuous
efforts were clearly exhausting him. However, I managed to bring the affair
to a laughing conclusion with a merry handshake before the debate had
developed any real asperity.

This incident happened when a short-lived reconciliation with his father
had temporarily placed the house at his disposal, some years after my first
reunion with him. He had previously obtained a Court order for his three sons
to visit him in the holidays. The arrangement was soon frustrated; with the
barbarous insensitivity of which small boys alone are capable, we sat around
the house in postures of gloom and despair until he could bear it no longer
and sent us back to my mother and her family. It must have been very
wounding to his feelings, for he was on the whole a jolly fellow and simply
wanted to show us affection. If you took him the right way, life could be quite
happy with father. This I learned to do later, and established a genial relationship by using our mutual love of horses; he rode superbly.

His faults were mostly of a superficial character, but led to some rather disastrous results. Abounding vitality and physical energy were wasted. All went well in his youth, when he had considerable success as an amateur jockey, but when years and weight brought this to an end he did not know what to do with himself. Art and music were certainly represented in his own little house. A picture over the fire was a contemporary drawing of an ample lady in a very tight skirt with a monocled dandy walking behind her; it bore the caption, 'Life is just one damn thing after another'—at this point father's philosophy coincided with his art form. A wheezy gramophone of early date wafted the stentorian tones of a music-hall tenor insistently reiterating his urgent demand: 'Put me among the girls, them with the rosy curls'. On less amorous but even more festive occasions, the same favourite tenor would enjoin: 'Come along now, for a few of the boys are kicking up the hell of a noise—let's go round the town'.

The short honeymoon between my father and grandfather did not last long, and the only practical effect was temporarily to make my mother's situation more difficult. My grandfather's affectionate and spontaneous nature suddenly led him to feel that he must both be reconciled with his son and promote a reconciliation between my parents. She felt she knew better, and a rift occurred. My father was duly installed at Rolleston with a considerable supply of extra cash, and my grandfather retired to a relatively modest house and farm at Abinger near Pulborough in Sussex.

Trouble was not long in coming. A prize bull failed to arrive from Rolleston on the due date to consummate its nuptials at Abinger. Dark rumours circulated of a restless and inconsequent energy draining all the lakes at Rolleston with no good reason, and losing in the reckless process most of the much valued stock of fish. Finally there was a disturbing tale about some of the extra money being used to buy the fastest car of the period—strong in the engine, but weak in the brake—with a flat-out trial spin in the evening light which, in mistake of the road home, ran smack through the closed park gates of a respected neighbour. My father landed, as usual in his innumerable accidents, on his feet and unhurt; just as when he inadvertently cut a corner and turned over a dogcart containing my pregnant mother shortly before the birth of one of my brothers. It was not these vagaries which disturbed their happy marriage; she only left him when she chanced to open a carelessly unlocked drawer and found it full of letters from other ladies. Then she packed her bags and departed the same day, for good; obtaining not a divorce which was against her principles, but a judicial separation, which included custody of the children and a meagre alimony.

After a brief sojourn at Rolleston, which was available to me throughout, my father was sent packing on his travels again. My grandfather returned and ran the estate until he died in 1915. My father then inherited, and we spent a short time there together after the war. I persuaded him to sell the house and the estate, foreseeing the ruin of agriculture which politics were bringing and feeling that I could best serve the country in a political life at Westminster based on my constituency at Harrow. Happily, it was easy to obtain good positions for our highly skilled staff, but it was a terrible uprooting, causing me much sorrow at the time, and I have sometimes regretted it since. I would certainly never have done it if the original Tudor house had not been burnt before I was born, but it appeared then a mistake to maintain in post-war circumstances an unmanageable pile of a Victorian house together with a way of life which seemed gone for ever. Survival of the Tudor house for better or worse might have changed the course of my life.

My relationship with my father remained good until I joined the Labour Party in 1924. It was assisted perhaps by my complete independence of him, because my grandfather had left me some free money and in negotiation with my father had so managed the entail that I should never be completely in his hands. This arrangement probably rankled with him, but he never referred to it except at necessary business meetings with the Public Trustee. Our tranquil relations exploded when in his view I entered the devil's service by becoming a socialist. He knew no more about politics than higher mathematics, but he had the strongest Tory sentiment and prejudices. He at once published an attack upon me to the effect that I was born with a gold spoon in my mouth and had never done a day's work in my life. He meant, of course, manual work, for like many peasants he felt that only labour with the hands could be described as work. It was true that I had never done manual labour, beyond my early farm work under my grandfather's direction, and the later necessity sometimes to dig trenches under fire, but my young reaction was that in other ways I had worked throughout my adult life at high pressure. I also felt these were no terms in which an older generation should address someone who had fought in the war.

I was hurt and angry; but said little. The gold-spoon jibe was constantly used by my enemies and gave to the adroit cartoonist of the Conservative papers in Birmingham an opportunity to depict me reclining in a large gold spoon which was hoisted on the shoulders of the enthusiastic workers. I felt that men should not be assailed by their family in this fashion, and it led to an estrangement which lasted during the short remaining period of my father's life. The final explosion was probably due in part to his constantly increasing drinking. He died of sclerosis of the liver at La Baule in France in 1928, at the early age of fifty-four. I was still fond of him, for he had many good and endearing qualities.

Lord Horder was doctor to three generations of our family, which he told me had the strongest natural constitution he had ever come across; adding that my father's excesses were enough to have killed several men. I can claim no virtue for not following the same path, for drink has never been the least temptation to me. Nor could my two brothers or any other members of the family I have known possibly be described as alcoholics. The only other addict was apparently a great-great-uncle, also named Oswald, elder brother of great-grandfather Tonman, who had something of my father's disposition and also died young. For my part, I was to drink water most of my life, varied once or twice a week with wine or beer. Then I went to live in France and the agreeable continental habit developed in our house of drinking light wine. In recent times I have modified this by mixing an Alsatian wine with Perrier water; the hock and seltzer habit which was shared by an incongruous couple, Oscar Wilde and Prince Bismarck. I follow the classic world in believing that an occasional feast does good rather than harm, or as a French doctor put it: 'Il faut quelque fois étonner l'estomac'.

There was no tendency to excess in the Heathcote family; they were spare, tall people who earned their health. They were by nature much more respectable than the Mosleys, who always rather shocked them. They were more respectable in the sense that the middle class used to be more respectable than the aristocracy; not that any class difference existed between them, for they were two neighbouring country families with exactly the same background, which at that time used to be called the landed interest. Their attitude to life was different; not different in the sense of Cavalier and Roundhead, for the Heathcotes could not be described as Puritans, but they had not the almost complete freedom from inhibitions which was a characteristic many Mosleys shared both with much of the aristocracy and much of the working class. Lord Randolph Churchill, during his Tory democracy days, claimed: 'the aristocracy and the working class are united in the indissoluble bonds of a common immorality'.

The Heathcotes were a strongly united family, with a vital gaiety in each other's company. My mother had an elder sister who married a Life Guard, Sir Lionel Darrell, two younger brothers and a much younger sister, who was only twelve years older than I was and whom I loved as a favourite companion in sport and in a wide variety of young happiness; she married a Lees-Milne, who handled a salmon rod almost as well as his nephew was to manage the National Trust. Also cherished with affection was the wife of my Uncle Jack, the daughter of Lord Hill; she looked better on a horse than almost any woman I ever saw. There was plenty of health, life and affection in that circle. They all lived in houses near to each other; a closely knit community with its own attitude, vernacular and jokes, but with no tendency to be severed by the family from the wider life of the neighbourhood; they were very friendly people. The old couple were the centre, and were both remarkable. Justinian Heathcote, my grandfather, had been M.P. for the Stoke-on-Trent area, where on land long owned by the family some coal and steel interests had been developed.

They were Staffordshire people, who in my childhood had only recently migrated to neighbouring Shropshire because coal-mine land subsidence had affected their old home at Apedale near Stoke-on-Trent. They maintained close contact with their Staffordshire interests which were not far away. It is through this grandfather that I have my modicum of Scotch blood; his grandmother was a Lady Elizabeth Lindsay. She apparently claimed descent from the family of Robert the Bruce; hence perhaps my disposition always to try again even without example from a spider. The Irish blood came through my father's mother, who was the daughter of Sir Thomas White, sometime Mayor of Cork. Thus I can claim to be British as well as English, and through Saxon and Norman blood also European; the island freeze-up is really quite a recent invention.

The Heathcote grandfather was an imposing figure of commanding stature and demeanour, with a square-cut patriarchal beard of snowy white. He was kindly and affectionate and used to enthral my boyhood with tales of parliamentary life, its dramatic incidents and personalities. He was not a performer but a shrewd observer of the political scene; a typical Tory squire, but much less bigoted than his wife. He had considerable humour and delighted in such tales as Balfour's riposte to Parnell's obstreperous lieutenant, Mr. Biggar, by reference to 'the honourable member with the misplaced vowel'; a striking remark in debate, but in memory these anecdotes can all too easily be transferred from the smoking-room to the chamber. His favourites on different sides of the House were the radical Labouchére, who founded *Truth*, and Thomas Gibson Bowles, of most varied accomplishments on the Tory side. I had then no premonition that by marrying a Mitford I should acquire one of his granddaughters. It was the blending of Mr. Bowles with the Mitford and Stanley combination which produced that remarkable vintage. The merry sisters, as Evelyn Waugh called them, have together an unlimited capacity to blow bright bubbles of gay fantasy with peacock screams of ecstatic laughter which can transform and more than enliven any dull moment. The vivid esprit of Mr. Bowles undoubtedly made its contribution to this felicitous phenomenon.

My grandfather found Parnell by far the most fascinating personality of the period. In particular, he noted the contrast between the ice-cold Protestant landowner and his passionate, revolutionary Irish followers; his influence over them never ceased to astonish. It was the discipline he taught them which temporarily disrupted the English parliamentary system and would undoubtedly have won Irish freedom a generation earlier, except for his dark, personal tragedy, a weakness strangely unaccountable in such a will and spirit. My grandfather told how Parnell would suddenly and unexpectedly enter the chamber—after protracted absence on business into which few dared to enquire—to find an Irish riot in full swing, every man on his feet and roaring insults with red faces of fury. Immediately he appeared at the bar everyone would sit down, and complete silence would fall. Parnell would walk slowly to his seat with his usual stiff dignity, and ask the Whip what it was all about.

If satisfied, a slight motion of his hand would bring every man to his feet again in an uproar which lifted the roof.

How did it all begin? My grandfather explained that Parnell arrived at Westminster as a comparatively young man to find a completely ineffective Irish party under the leadership of an amiable gentleman called Mr. Butt, who usually turned up rather late at night in full evening dress after dining with the Tories. Parnell decided to put a stop to all that and, with the assistance of the member who got his vowel wrong, he did so very quickly. The continual row led on occasion to his being physically removed by the Sergeant-at-Arms and his assistants, but it was a fight—a hell of a fight—which thrilled all Ireland. It made him the hero of the Irish people and through their enthusiasm the undisputed leader of the Irish Party. How could such a man at the moment he had won his struggle—for Gladstone was obliged to negotiate with him, even when he was in Kilmainham Gaol—have thrown away all he had done, and himself, for the sake of Mrs. O'Shea? He thought perhaps that he could get away with it, that both life and love, ambition and beauty could be served to the full. In approaching a more luminous sphere I had something of this nature in mind when I wrote in my introduction to a translation of Goethe's *Faust* a reference to the enchanted, Byronic child Euphorion: 'He aspires to both beauty and achievement. In his longing for the furthest flight he reaches for the forbidden wings. Disaster strikes down from heaven.'

My grandfather's description of Parnell was not so dramatic as Disraeli's account of the shadows darkening round Canning—when he witnessed 'the tumult of that ethereal brow'—but I was always glad to have seen through the eyes of an acute and a sympathetic observer something of the astonishing interplay of personal frailty and great events. In later life I have often reflected how beneficially the course of history might have been changed if human weakness had not perverted destiny. Would the first war ever have occurred —if Parnell had settled the Irish problem without the delay of a generation and the protracted troubles which were at least a contributory factor in persuading the Germans that Britain could play no effective part in the war of 1914?—if Dilke, who stood firm against the division of Europe into rigid alignments of entente and triple alliance, had not fallen through an escapade or frame-up?—if the tragedy at Mayerling had not engulfed Crown Prince Rudolf, who for all his feeble character had considerable influence in resisting the same tendency from the other side? How much is history influenced by the vagaries of character? The truth probably lies somewhere between Marx's materialist conception of history and the view that it really made a difference to Europe when the Duke of Buckingham fell in love with the Queen of France. Both men and opportunity are needed to change history. It is the fiery contact of great men and great events which gives destiny the light of birth.

Thus was my childhood divided between two very different families. Does our life course derive inevitably from childhood background and influence, or is it true that the world is character?—basic, original character? How strong is environment, and how strong is nature? We need not be driven into the controversy between Lysenko and his victorious opponents, but it is tempting to take a passing glance at the psychologists, who claim in some degree to read our fate in our childhood years. Some opportunity was afforded me to study them during a protracted period more entirely dedicated to reading than is usually possible in middle life. Plato's requirement of withdrawal from life for a considerable period of study and reflection before entering on the final phase of action was fulfilled in my case, though not by my own volition.

The results at least gave me some chance to examine my own childhood in the light of analytical psychology. The broken home, the atmosphere of strife between preceding generations, some of the classic factors were present. At the end of it all, what effect did they have on me? The only evident result I will concede at once is really very trivial. I have a tendency to rely on some obliging woman to do small things for me which I feel she can do as well or better than I can, and are a waste of time for me to do; a conceit which obliging women are happily quite tolerant about. It arises clearly from being the man of the house too soon, and having had a fondly devoted mother, whose help in such respect I repaid from the earliest age by gratuitous advice and virile assertion on every subject under the sun. I had no father in the house to chase me around, to make me do little things for myself and keep my mouth shut until my contribution was opportune; but these are not failings to take too tragically.

In general, I did not suffer from lack of male influence. The company of one or other grandfather was constant, and no one could have been more male than these two. My uncles too were always at hand, two hearty, jolly country squires of the best sort. I was sent to the barracks which were then called the schools of the well-to-do, and a little later came in contact with the finest products of the real barrack life. This early contact with the athletic flower of the regular army was to exercise a profound, lasting and in my view most beneficent influence on my permanent attitude to life. A broken home certainly did not result in my becoming a mother's boy, deep as was my devotion to her. The wiseacres of psychological science may ascribe to this background some political tendencies in my later life which they dislike, but after a considerable study of the subject I am convinced they are talking nonsense.

There are certain things which at this stage may be noted about the study of psychology: it is in its infancy, and its protagonists are acutely divided. It is still in the period of research, with much more work to be done. Yet every sob-sister in the popular press feels she is competent in a breathless little article of slipshod appraisal and spiteful disapprobation to analyse the alleged

complexes of every giant or dwarf who traverses the world scene. Far more
serious people were long ago rightly taken to task by Jung in his *Psychologie
der Unbewussten Prozessen* for their pretentious impertinence in analysing
great figures of religion and philosophy, but lesser clowns in smaller circuses
still do not hesitate to show the same effrontery to all and sundry. There is
more nonsense, often ridiculous nonsense, written on this subject than on
almost any other.

Part of the trouble is that even the serious practitioners have few opportunities to study anything but disease. Those who find their way to the
psychiatrist's couch are not always good subjects for studying the daily
problems of abounding health and vitality. Everyone in childhood or youth
must invariably suffer again and again the shocks and disabilities which in
later life lead some to the psychiatrists' couch, just as everyone experiences the
cuts and bruises which later in life lead some to the surgeon's operating
theatre. The healthy psyche throws off the injury which in the weak becomes
a complex, just as easily as the healthy body throws off the bruise which in the
weak becomes a tumour. It is possible to go even further, and to say that
additional strength can come from early injury. I have seen extraordinary
experiments in botany where trees seriously injured early in their growth
develop a protective resistance which later results in far greater strength than
a more sheltered environment produces. 'What fails to destroy us makes us
stronger' is a proverb of a people with some experience of such tests of fate.
'Having seen the little world, let us now see the great.' Toynbee's theory of
challenge and response illustrates in the great spheres of nations the working
of the same nature principle which stimulates and develops the injured tree.
Jung must have had something of the same truth in mind when he wrote that
possibly we 'owe all to our neuroses'; although again it seems that the quality
of strong natures—the power to resist adversity—should be regarded not as a
neurosis but as a gift of character. In short, the whole subject is not quite so
simple as some amateurs think. Much more serious work should be done
before the potential of this infant science can be realised, and before it can
with confidence be transferred from the laboratory to the clinic.

I write this criticism of certain current tendencies in science while claiming
to have a more consistent record in support of science than anyone who has
spent his life in politics. In theory and in the practice of government I have
battled for science, to provide it with means, to encourage and to honour its
work. Years ago I wrote that modern statesmen should live and work with
scientists as the Medici lived and worked with artists. The glories of the
Renaissance were made possible by statesmen really given to art, and the
redeeming wonders of modern science and technology will be realised by
statesmen really given to science. Yet if they love science and appreciate its
vast possibilities they will never allow any branch of it to be prostituted by
the craft of a witch-doctor smelling out opponents of the existing regime and

ascribing to them the evil spells which are today called complexes. These things are serious matters, not the stunts of politics.

After my long general interest in science over a wide range, and continual reading of its latest, provisional conclusions, I doubt whether at this stage the science of psychology has sufficient data to justify practical application, particularly for children. When in the light of my studies I ask myself whether my reverses or successes in childhood and boyhood affected my life course, whether I should have been another man if my childhood had been different, I can only reply, I think not. Some odd combination of the genes in this strong country stock made me, for better or worse, what I am. The basic constitution is given to us like a strong or weak body. Afterwards the development or atrophy of the constitution depends on continual exertion of the will, just as the increase or diminution of a muscle rests on constant exercise. Then enters into the question of will the indefinable element of the spirit, but this is beyond the range of childhood.

2
School and Sandhurst

I WAS always in too much of a hurry. This tendency began at school; I was concerned to get on with it and to grow up. School to me was not a happy interlude before facing the harsh responsibilities of adult life. It was a necessary but tedious progress through which we had to pass before the wide life of opportunity, adventure and great experience could begin. This was a fault, but I sometimes feel nowadays it was a fault on the right side. The intense desire to become a man is surely preferable to the yearning for a lingering childhood. The hurry to embrace life is better than the flight from life. To me, childhood was just a nuisance; now it has become a blessed cult. Growing up must be delayed in early life, and old age welcomed in later life. Manhood with its responsibilities is the awkward and unpleasant time to be shortened as far as possible. The tendency is to flight from the world, back to the womb or on to the tomb. To play young in early life and old in late life is an exercise of the great escape mechanism. For better or worse my generation was the extreme opposite. We rushed towards life with arms outstretched to embrace the sunshine, and even the darkness, the light and shade which is the essence of existence, every varied enchantment of a glittering, wonderful world; a life rush, to be consummated.

It was a deep difference in attitude and approach, which has had far-reaching effects. If too much is made of a cult of childhood its values tend to be unduly exalted; the action proper to manhood can become inhibited, and its natural dynamism wasted. We are told in early life that we are too young to do anything, and in later life that we are too old to do anything; the peddlers of these inhibitions really mean that they are always against anything being done. The achievements of manhood are replaced by the fantasies of child-hood; Peter Pan mounts on the reversal of values established by nature and proven by history. Strangest paradox of all, just as science considerably extends the effective life-span it has become the fashion to shorten it by the cult of protracted infancy and premature senility. Therefore I admit to error in being always in too much of a hurry and usually driving things too hard, but I prefer the errors of dynamism to the religion of lethargy.

I arrived at my first school, West Downs, Winchester, just after my ninth birthday. It had an enlightened headmaster, Lionel Helbert, who had given up being a clerk in the House of Lords to found a small boys' school. He made a genuine effort to understand his pupils; he ascribed to me at an early age certain qualities of leadership, and wished me to join the navy, of which he was passionately fond. I arrived at nine as quite a bright boy, after the home tuition of the excellent Miss Gandy, an intelligent woman and kindly guide, but I rapidly became a very stupid boy, not by lack of school teaching but by stress of growth, which I am now convinced was responsible for my backwardness; at the age of fourteen I had reached my full height of six-foot-two and was broad in proportion. Roughly my rhythm was, clever from nine to eleven, half-witted from eleven to around sixteen, from sixteen to nineteen a gradual recovery of my faculties, and from nineteen onwards the achieve-ment of my capacities for what they have since been worth. All this makes me look rather askance at such things as the 11-plus exam, and other primitive tests which may at an early stage finally decide or at least influence a boy's future.

In later life I teased public schoolmasters with the remark that in my generation and the two preceding generations they had failed to discover at school any of the men outstanding in political life; exceptions were the father-in-law of my first marriage, Lord Curzon, and one or two others, while the list of those found stupid at school but brilliant in later life was long. I got an intelligent answer from Mr. Roxburgh, the remarkable first head-master of Stowe, a school I used to visit frequently at one time for a fencing match in the afternoon and a debate in the evening. He retorted that it was not the fault of the schools but of nature, because such men are usually slow to develop and the schoolmasters were probably right when they thought them stupid at an early age; another reason it seems to me for devising a system of progressive tests in education rather than to stake all on some arbitrary and abrupt line for the division of talents.

At West Downs my most unpleasant memory is of the intense cold; it was before the days of central heating and the long stone and wooden corridors were as bitter as the draughty dormitories where the sponges became rigid in the basin at any touch of frost. My brother, Ted, joined me there and seemed in danger of being frozen alive, despite the robust constitution of his adult life. My representations led to his removal to a less arctic spot. Chalk downs remain an aversion of mine; they surrounded West Downs and the neighbouring Winchester and were the scene of our compulsory walks. They always seemed to me hideous. Another of my dislikes at West Downs was swimming, which became one of the favourite pastimes and exercises of my later life. We all had to jump into the bath at the deep end whether we could swim or not. It was supposed to hasten the process of learning, but I always splashed somehow to the nearest side without much further effort. I had at that time a certain phobia about getting my head under water; due no doubt to arrival a fortnight late in the world, smothered and under painful necessity of being slapped until I filled my lungs with air for the first of those bellows which later resounded from so many platforms. This apprehension of smothering lasted for many years, and I did not learn to swim until I was grown up and persuaded by my first wife, Cimmie, on our honeymoon to join her in one of her chief delights. Otherwise I recognise no neurosis in myself except the dislike of an accumulation of papers, but that may be due to causes easily explicable; the ever present prospect of tedious work.

Life at West Downs was not too bad, but it was depressingly dull compared to life at home. I had none of that sense apparent in many modern children of moving into a wider life at school; home and school were just freedom and prison, it was as simple as that. Sport and games recompensed to some degree. Instinct and tradition of family took me at once to the gymnasium where boxing was well taught, and I won the light-weight championship soon after my arrival. In my opening fight I experienced for the first time incredulity that I could be winning. Later I won many elections, but could never believe in victory until the last ballot-paper was counted. Lloyd George was reputed to be the same in a larger sphere; he could not believe he was winning his landslide election of 1918, and in his unnecessary efforts to snatch victory made some speeches which were a subsequent liability he need not have incurred. Churchill on the other hand was usually confident of victory and was reputed not to have anticipated his defeat in 1945.

My tendency to be doubtful of success until it was proven carried me to remarkable lengths in this first athletic encounter of childhood at nine years old. After the opening clash the other boy took to his heels and ran as fast as his legs could carry him round the spacious gym—there were no ropes—hotly pursued as fast as my equally short legs could carry me. At length an insistent ringing of the bell terminated the farce, and we returned to our corners; breathlessly I enquired of our instructor, have I won? The last fight of the series in the final was my first endurance test. There was not much science, just slogging it out toe to toe with straight lefts and rights to the face. Gradually he gave ground and I won my first championship. Three years later I took a tremendous hiding from a boy in the final of the heavy-weight championship. My opponent was bigger, heavier, older and a better boxer. I should have had no trouble in winning if I had waited another year, but, as usual, was in too much of a hurry to go on to a public school and made this attempt, like everything else, prematurely.

Helbert, with rare insight, praised me more in defeat than in victory. When we left at the end of the term he selected two occasions to note in my school career. The first was the beating I took in this boxing final, because I had fought it out to a finish; it simply had not occurred to me to do anything else. The second was my performance in the school shooting championship, when again I did badly. I was captain of the miniature-rifle shooting team and could normally have expected to win the individual inter-schools champion-ship at the same time that the school team won the match. It was an off day for me and I shot so badly that I had no hope of the championship. Helbert remarked to the school audience that I had continued to do my best to the end of the day in order to contribute to the team's success; many boys apparently in his experience threw in their hands on such an occasion in a mood of petulant despair. Again I had not been at all conscious of any merit, because it did not occur to me to do anything else. Helbert however, rightly for a schoolmaster, was always on the look-out for early evidence of character. He noted in me that I was capable of the team spirit which has sometimes been denied; wrongly because I am a completely loyal colleague while a member of a team.

It has already been duly noted by analysts who induct from the trivial to the considerable that I was more attracted by individual sports like boxing, fencing and riding than by team games like cricket. Clarification of these turgid convolutions is often simple. I liked these sports better because I was better at them, and my background inclined me to the sports of the country rather than to the games of the town; individual ball games like golf and billiards seemed to me even more tedious. Was it also some complex that made me prefer conversation, reading or reflection to the playing of cards; extraordinary aberration of ardent time-killers?

My transition to the public school a year too early was one of the errors of my perpetual sense of haste. I persuaded parents and schoolmasters to let me go ahead for no good clear reason, just from a sense of urgency. I lacked at this point perhaps some calm, male influence to say: what is the hurry?— why not wait another year at the private school, be head boy, win the boxing, do all the things you like doing at the first school, and then take a higher place in the public school when you are a year older and better fitted to go there? But I was in a hurry, and this advice was not available.

I doubt if it mattered very much. I arrived at the public school a year younger than was normal, and my experience to that extent was tougher than the usual. As the chief merit of that education was supposed to be the toughen-ing process, it can even be argued that it was in this way an advantage. We were up early and to bed late, the food was meagre and the water cold, except once a week: we were at early school and enjoying the solace of religion in chapel before breakfast; the rest of the day was a hustling affair divided between lessons, compulsory games and fagging for the older boys. These prefects had almost the powers of life and death over the smaller boys without any effective check or supervision from a master; certainly the power to make their life a misery or reasonably tolerable. The power was on the whole exercised fairly and equally, according to a definite code. Junior boys were treated alike by these older boys in the affairs of everyday life, even the favourites. The strict discipline prevented any form of unauthorised bullying, and the ganging up of boys against each other which is often evident in smaller boys' schools was mostly absent from the public school. The main question, of course, is whether it is right to give boys of round eighteen years old a power over their fellow human beings which few would dream of according them in later life, however distinguished their career and however well founded and proven their reputation for kindly and humane dealings?

It is a strange system, which it does not occur to any other European people to employ. In France the general rule is to educate boys at day schools rather than boarding schools. The remarkable lycée system of State education can carry a boy from infancy to the final selective, technical and administrative academies which are among the chief assets of France. There are also schools equivalent to our public schools which are usually conducted directly or indirectly by religious orders. The reverend fathers know too much of the world to take any chances with original sin, and the boys are under constant supervision. It is entirely unobtrusive and the guiding hand is not noticed until something occurs. Yet on any scene of undue brutality or affection a firm gentleman in a beret appears very quickly, almost as if by magic; it is all well organised, and anything of that kind is simply stopped at once. In varying degrees most of the European countries rest their education on systems of this nature. The English idea seems to be unique.

The ideal system may lie as usual between the two extremes. But the English method—at least in earlier times—certainly achieved its apparent object by the toughening process. Its products had to be tough. They were to be fit to conduct a great Empire in arduous and often dangerous conditions. Even the boy who had been granted a power at eighteen which seemed absurd, was perhaps thus fitted to take charge at an early age of some large and rough area in an outpost of Empire. There was some method in this particularly English instinct, which seemed eccentric to other Europeans. Now that the Empire has gone, it would appear the prima facie reason for the public school system has also ceased to exist. The question arises: why maintain for the children of a small class of relatively rich people a system so tough that it would produce an immediate revolution if applied to the masses? Perhaps such self-questioning accounts for the present apparent loss of direction and self-confidence by the public schools.

This is not the place to discuss educational systems, and I would leave the subject here with some general and rather trite advice: give boys plenty to eat and plenty of sleep, some unobtrusive but adequate supervision, enough exercise to develop their bodies and enough interesting teaching to develop the particular bent of their minds, but not the superfluity which can stifle them with a burden of knowledge irrelevant to their tastes and capacities. Do not assume a boy is a fool because he is not clever when he is young and growing. Let the system of education be a progressive selection by power of merit alone, from the cradle to the chief executive posts of business, the highest chairs of the humanities, the innermost laboratories of science where the future of man can be decided.

In my personal story I cannot say that the public school experience did me any harm, and in some respects after the immense affection and tenderness of my home life it may have been a useful corrective. I was treated no better and no worse than anybody else. I did not suffer the particular brutalities at school which it appears Winston Churchill and others endured in an earlier generation. My election for the constituency of Harrow in 1918 gave me some insight into these matters, because the Chairman of the Conservative Association was a very old man who lived on the hill and had a long connection with the school. He told me that Winston Churchill—when a late-developing small boy—used to be called out in front of the class by his form master who invited his other pupils to look at the stupidest boy at Harrow who was the son of the cleverest man in England. Mr. Churchill once told me himself, still with some resentment, how certain little beasts used to flick him with wet towels. He did not appear to me in middle life to be much enamoured of his public school experience, but evidently in age developed an attachment of memory which led him often to sentimental journeys greeted by the red carpet rather than the wet towels of Harrow. Yet it seems likely that innate character rather than early vicissitudes selected for him the rough road of statesmanship in preference to the gentle paths of art.

The Wellington view about Waterloo being won on the playing fields of Eton is not the only opinion of the famous upon the practical results of that school. Chatham said that Eton could ruin a boy's intellect and spoil his spirit for half a century, and it does not appear to have done much good to Shelley. Lord Salisbury was approached to preside at a dinner to Lord Curzon and another young man he wished to favour, but refused when he learned it was under the auspices of Eton; even after all those years as Prime Minister the memory was still too bitter. May we at least congratulate the public schools on their failure to destroy the great, perhaps even on their success in evoking a strong response from the challenge of misunderstanding. Also it should always be admitted and affirmed that these institutions are regarded with strong affection by many good men; they are not made for the exceptions, but nature can look after them. In the modern age the public schools are unlikely to last long in their present form.

My relative immunity from the irks of public school life after the pains of initiation was possibly due to my athletics, which quite quickly won for me my own little niche in which I rested content and fairly happy. My intellectual life did not exist, and no one can be blamed for the lack of it, because at this point my intellect did not exist. A kind old schoolmaster was stating a self-evident fact when he took my hand one day in class and observed: 'How strange this hand can do anything with a sword, and nothing with a pen'. Not only was I incapable of thinking but my handwriting was illegible; the latter disability remains, as my friends and colleagues are painfully aware.

Physical life was then my whole being; certain spiritual experiences came a little later. I had finished growing by the time I was fourteen and my physical proficiency then developed rapidly, long before any mental development. Boxing was my first love and I only turned to fencing, in which my main successes were won, when competition boxing was forbidden to me. The headmaster of Winchester tolerated the sport within the school but would not allow any of us to go to the public schools competition, on which I had set my heart with some assurance of success from my instructor. Yet as so often in life, reverse and disappointment turn to success and happiness in the longer range of experience. Even disaster in great spheres has sometimes opened to me a vista of knowledge and achievement I would never otherwise have known. After the little world of boyhood sport I should never have continued boxing when I grew up; a reluctantly developing appreciation of my capacities would soon have led me to the conclusion that a head like mine was not for bashing. But international fencing, representing Britain in sport and entering into the camaraderies of the great *salles d'armes* throughout Europe was a joy of my manhood, and in my intellectual maturity gave me some sense of the fullness of life in the Hellenic gymnasium; *et ego in Arcadia vixi*.

That life began at Winchester. Every afternoon was an escape into another world, the company of the regular army. By far the most potent influences in my young life were Sergeant-Major Adam and Sergeant Ryan; the latter in charge of boxing and the former of fencing. No schoolmaster had anything like the effect on me which was exercised by this remarkable pair. They were products of the regular army, to which I had always been attracted from childhood. It had never occurred to me to be anything else than a soldier. Now I was in daily contact with a fine expression of the spirit I had admired from afar, and began to absorb the attitude to life which has stood me in good stead in many different circumstances and countries. This *Haltung*, as the Germans call it, is indefinable, but you know it when you see it. It is one of my deepest convictions, which time has never eradicated, that no man can have a better start in life than the regular army.

It is true that I did not continue in the profession of arms, for reasons stated to me with his customary lucidity by F. E. Smith when as a very young man I first met him. He had a remarkable gift, often present in men of outstanding talents, of bridging the gulf of generations by talking to the young as a contemporary would. He said: 'If you were a Frenchman or a German your profession would clearly be the army, because in those countries it is the great profession. In England it must, of course, be politics or the Bar, or both.' The same point was put from a more professional angle by the brilliant C.I.G.S. Sir Henry Wilson to new arrivals at the Staff College during the period when he was a senior instructor. General Fuller told me how discouragement was tempered by entertainment at the opening words of the first lecture: 'Our funny little army has six divisions. Why has our funny little army got six divisions? Nobody knows, and nobody cares.'

The army was small, but perhaps by very reason of its limited size was composed of an élite which was at least the equal of any in the world. Even prejudice does not impel me to put it any higher, because now we are becoming Europeans we must learn not to brag in a fashion disagreeable to the ears of future partners. Never say, for example, as English politicians continually do, that Britain will lead Europe; say rather that Britain will play a vital part within Europe; in these large affairs he does most who boasts least. I will content myself with the claim that the British army has never had any superior. Yet I admit in the company of Sergeant-Major Adam and Sergeant Ryan I might as a boy have been tempted to any hyperbole, which their modesty would have deprecated.

There was no time wasted in talk on arrival at the gymnasium. Ryan would snatch you out of the lethargies of youth in a couple of minutes. Bayonet champion of the army and runner-up in the feather-weight boxing championship, he moved with extraordinary speed. A follower of the classic Jim Driscoll, he determined to give me the perfect straight left; for nearly two years I was not allowed to use the right at all. Weaving, swerving, ducking, dodging, he would come at me as it seemed like a flash of lightning. From the moment he was in distance I had to send the left as straight as a ram-rod to the chin, and every time in the last split second his glove would intercept it while he mimed like a ballet dancer the groggy effect of a good connection. A brilliant teacher, he took immense trouble with me.

Not until the workout had really gone to the limit, was rest permitted; then the interval was well used in stories of the ring. I lived in the epic of his tour of India as second to Tiger Smith, the redoubtable southpaw who knocked out every heavy-weight available within the first round. The saga only came to an end when the supply of contenders was exhausted, and the Tiger returned with his laurels to the regiment which had nurtured his manly qualities. It was training for the body and also, I still maintain, it provided some food for the mind and character. These fights were clean and fair, were soon forgotten and left no malice. Until human nature becomes pure spirit, is not this among the better disciplines for the animal within us?

At this stage, life for me was all sword and no gown. The sword quite literally occupied my daily life after I was forbidden to box at the public school competition. It was a bitter disappointment to young ambition, for the long army training had provided some hope that I might successfully face the formidable Etonian who at that time had been produced by naval training to rule the roost at my weight. For the moment purpose had gone out of life, but was soon happily restored by conversation with Sergeant-Major Adam. This outstanding athlete was in charge of the whole gymnasium and of fencing in particular. He reminded me that the good legs and fast footwork I had developed in boxing might help me to success with the sabre, which depended much on speed and agility of movement. He was right, for the Hungarian sabre champions I saw later in life used to bounce down the piste and back like india-rubber balls. Thus encouraged by Adam I set to work, and it was soon discovered that nature had added to my speed of foot a rapid reflex action and general aptitude for fencing. He persuaded me to take up foils as well, in which there were far more contestants at Winchester. The upshot was that I also won the foils competition against boys several years older, and at the age of fifteen years and four months was sent to the public schools competition to represent Winchester with both foil and sabre.

It was an exciting day for me and an anxious day for Sergeant-Major Adam, to whom by then I had become greatly attached. He had never yet had a pupil who had won the public schools competition with either weapon, although on his record both in army competition and as an instructor he might have reckoned to have done so long before. In the previous year his star performer—a long-trained colleger of nearly nineteen—had been surprisingly defeated in the final by an aggressive Harrovian, who to our disquiet was again a competitor. A few rapid whispered instructions from Adam on how to deal with the Harrovian, and we were at it. I was fortunate enough to beat him in an early round, and reached the final. There I came up against a boy of a most unorthodox and disconcerting action who upset all my classic preconceptions. I was down three hits to one, out of a total of five up. I then threw all text-book plans to the wind, and decided to mix it with him and rely on sheer speed and constant attack. I took the next four hits and won the championship. All these things are good lessons for life; never hold too long to methods which do not work, be firm and fixed in principles, but infinitely flexible and adaptable in method.

After the anxious moments in the foils championship, the sabre competition was not difficult. I won the sabre championship with ease and emerged with what was then claimed to be a triple record: the first boy to win with both weapons on the same day, and the youngest boy to win with either. My joy was enhanced by the radiant delight of my friend Adam. I was left with a sense that although still a very stupid boy, I had become something of a physical phenomenon. It never occurred to me at this stage that I could ever be anything else. As an intelligent and sensitive child I had experienced acutely what I suppose can only be described as a sense of destiny; but all such brooding presentiment of that strange blend of triumph and disaster inseparable from great experience was now submerged in the first exuberance of physical vitality.

It was all splendid for the time being. Even my ambition to compete successfully against the Etonians was also achieved by another route. We went to Eton to fight a match between two teams of three for five hits up each fight. I won each fight five hits to love, a total of fifteen hits to nil; it was a highlight of my young life. A member of their team was a magnificent specimen of some eighteen years old who rowed in the eight, as my brother John also did at Eton a few years later. His surprise was considerable to find that in the subtle business of the sword strength counted for nothing against speed and skill; one of the main charms of that fascinating sport.

Fencing certainly gripped my early life. I even contrived by long persuasion to induce my mother to allow me to leave Winchester at sixteen in the hope of pursuing it in a wider sphere. My argument was based on the general ground that I was wasting my time by staying any longer, and I certainly felt this was true as I had then done everything which interested me. However my plan first to enter the British championship and then to go on a fencing tour of Europe was frustrated for two reasons. My mother began to sense that the European tour might be a little gay, while my father's temporary reconciliation with my grandfather deprived her of the means of financing the venture with ease. The first point was an error, because the best chance of keeping any boy on the straight and narrow path of parental approval is to encourage him to pursue an interest to which he is wholly dedicated. He will not in these circumstances play the fool with either mind or body. The second was certainly not her fault, for without my grandfather's assistance for any special venture she was much too hard up. So I have been left wondering ever since what would have happened to me in the British championship of 1913, and if that competition had brought me any success, in the world championship of 1914. I should certainly have given it priority over such an early entry to the army by starting at Sandhurst in 1914, and would only just have completed my European experience when the First World War began.

This was my last serious chance at the world championship, for after that I was never again first-rate. At the end of the war the full use of my legs was gone for good. It was ten years before I returned to the sport at all, and then at first only for exercise. Gradually I discovered that by adapting my style to my new condition I could be quite effective with the epée, the heavy duelling sword, which required less mobility. I was twice to be runner-up to different champions with this weapon in the British championship, and was a member of our international team. The last time I represented Britain was in the 1937 world championship at Paris, but I had no chance then of winning:

the dream of great achievement in that young world was gone. Nevertheless, fencing took me all over Europe into the intimacies of other peoples which the *salles d'armes* so richly provide. Many happy memories remain of joyous companionship in Paris, Milan, Rome and all the chief centres of Europe; vivid among them is the vision of Sergeant-Major Adam walking with his springy step along the Winchester High Street, head erect, chest out, holding his cane with correct sabre grip between the thumb and the heel of the hand, the forearm moving like a steel spring to the parry as he fought again in memory his epic contest with the redoubtable Betts, eleven years champion of the army; entire oblivion in his unseeing eyes for all lesser things, which included the scurrying scholars who later in the day would be welcome in his gymnasium to taste of manhood. May he so walk proudly forever, through an Elysian *salle d'armes*.

Did Winchester then give me nothing except the physical experience, because I was intellectually incapable of appreciating any of the things which really interested me in later life? This is not altogether true, because before my full physical development I had a certain spiritual experience. I must have been confirmed just before my fourteenth birthday, certainly by wish of my mother and with my own willing consent. We were instructed by a sympathetic clergyman who was also one of the masters, a good man of sensitive mind and delicate spirit. Neither then nor at any time had I any sense of revelation, but I became immensely impressed by the doctrine of love and the extraordinary impact it had on a very different world. It may be that my abnormal speed of growth had left a certain physical weakness as in a man who has been fasting, which made me at that time particularly susceptible. This materialist explanation may have some force but it is by no means entirely valid, for an impression of the possible power of love has remained with me ever since. It fascinated me later in my preoccupation with a conceivable synthesis between some elements of Christian teaching and the Hellenism which influenced my maturity. Nineteenth-century thinking seemed to me laden with this potential, which might in some degree be realised in the thought and even in the action of our day. All this was remote from my consciousness at Winchester, but I look back to that gentle schoolmaster in recognition of a first impulse which was submerged for a time in the torrent of life but returned in some degree in the years of reflection and striving for creation.

I have often since wondered whether priests and schoolmasters are wise in their presentation of religion to the young. Anything more repulsive to the religious sense than being dragged to morning chapel between early lessons and breakfast is difficult to imagine. Systematic starvation over a protracted period may induce a state of holiness, but delaying his first meal of the day to a hungry boy evokes the contrary emotions. In some schools this noxious practice has been abandoned, but the question still remains whether the droning of the compulsory services, only occasionally relieved by some fine music in a beautiful old chapel at school or church at home, is really calculated to produce a regard for religion.

Perhaps the ancients were wiser in their concepts of the mysteries. Is more interest engendered by private and progressive initiation into the strange beauty of the great religions? What would be the effect on a boy if he were told that the revelation of Christianity could not be imparted to him until he was sufficiently developed to appreciate a story which at least is among the most beautiful in the world? The classic method was exactly the opposite of the modern, but it gradually dissolved in the age of reason when philosophy came with continual questions. From my own early experience I could only, with much diffidence, give the church leaders some limited advice: not to make religion too dull to the young, but also not to make it too silly by ineffective imitations of current crazes and absurdities with which they cannot hope to compete. Neither in religious practice, nor in royal ceremonial or in politics is any lasting advantage gained by playing the monkey on the barrel-organ of transient fashion. In the end, conversion depends on ability, sympathy, example and conviction.

My life was thus divided between school and army. Each afternoon I escaped into the world where I felt at home, the gymnasium and the company of soldiers. It was not merely that I was determined to go into the army, and that the gymnasium provided me with the sports for which I had a particular aptitude. I liked the army and everything about it; the training it gave at Winchester, the gay life it would offer at Sandhurst, and finally the companionship of the large and devoted family which is a great regiment. I did not like the public school, and disliked or disapproved most things about it. It seemed to me a trivial existence, 'cribbed, cabined and confined' by many of the silliest shibboleths of the bourgeois world. Although I had a number of friends at Winchester I had far more at Sandhurst.

Apart from games, the dreary waste of public school existence was only relieved by learning and homosexuality; at that time I had no capacity for the former and I never had any taste for the latter. My attitude to homosexuality was then much less tolerant than now, because I have long taken the view on basic ground of liberty that adults should be free to do what they wished in private, provided they do not interfere with others. However, I would deal much more severely than at present with the corruption of the young of either sex, and with obvious propaganda designed to that end.

Our understanding of these matters in the present period has progressed beyond the curt summary of the situation I heard in my early days in the House of Commons. Some of us were discussing the matter in the smoking-room with an eminent K.C. who had been singularly successful in the defence of alleged homosexuals in court. We questioned him on the secret of these forensic triumphs. He replied: 'Simple—with the jury system you know that most of them do not believe it exists and the rest of them do it themselves'. We should now recognise that we cannot eradicate or suppress a fact which has existed from the beginning of history, but we can keep it within the bounds of strict privacy and prevent it being spread as a fashionable cult to circles which it would otherwise not attract.

Life at school seemed to me not a period to protract, but just a prelude to real life; so my chief desire was to leave as soon as possible. It was probably this attitude which prompted my Housemaster, Mr. Bell, to agree with my mother's view when she wrote suggesting I should leave. He replied: 'He seems always rather too old for us'. I was certainly at that age a bit of a prig. Mr. Bell and I, however, got on well together, as he was heavy-weight boxing champion at his university. We were both sorry that because of my early departure we missed a long-standing engagement for a boxing match on my seventeenth birthday. 'British Bell', as the boys nicknamed him, was killed in the war of 1914, when he took the earliest opportunity of joining up.

This attitude to the public schools may in part have induced me to give our two youngest sons an altogether different education. My two eldest sons went to Eton; after a long discussion, it seemed to Cimmie and me the best plan at that time. They went to Eton rather than Winchester, as except for myself and my Heathcote grandfather, all our relations on both sides had gone there. It turned out well, as Nicholas was head of his house and Michael captain of the Oppidans, and the effects in later life have been good. Nicholas, after a distinguished military career in the Second World War, during which he won the Military Cross, has become a widely-appreciated novelist. He also wrote a book on a 'Father'; *Rains*, not *Sunshine*. Michael was soon an assiduous and accomplished social worker. Vivien, my only daughter and eldest of the family, after going to a boarding school where she was very happy and made lifelong friends, married Desmond Forbes-Adam. Like their mother, my grand-daughters seem to like their schools; on the other hand, the Mitfords tended not to last long at English girls' schools, and with Diana the risk was never taken.

Diana and I were not inhibited in sending the younger pair to Eton by our war unpopularity, as the elder two had been at Eton either during the war or soon after, and it says much for its remarkable quality of tolerance that they suffered neither disability nor unpopularity. We decided to give Alexander and Max another education because we hoped to make them good Europeans, and thought that a command of languages is a most desirable gift of parents to children. For some time they remained at home in Ireland where they were well taught and had the advantages of country life with horses and sport. Then they went to school in France and Germany, returning to England in time to take their A-levels. Max afterwards went to Oxford, where he took a physics degree and was Secretary of the Union, before being called to the Bar. Alexander took a degree in philosophy at the State University of

Ohio. I think on the whole it was a good education, and that our choice was right; so do our sons.

I would not send boys to a public school today, because I feel they should belong to a larger world. Winchester certainly deserved better than the run of bad luck it had in my time and in the preceding period; its best-known products were Stafford Cripps, D. N. Pritt, K.C., and myself. However, many of the leading figures of the Civil Service, combined with the sedate memory of Hugh Gaitskell and the erudite ebullience of R. H. S. Crossman, may now assist it to sustain the burden.

A rather dull interval followed between my departure from Winchester at the end of 1912 and my arrival at Sandhurst in the beginning of 1914. The frustration of the European fencing tour resulted in a dreary sojourn at Westgate-on-Sea and Buxton Spa, selected as health resorts which had adequate teaching available for the army exam. I strenuously resisted the only available game, which was golf, in discontent at the absence of fencing; it seemed to me a tedious substitute. Six weeks in the late summer of 1913 were well spent, as I was sent to France to learn the language. Brest was selected as a town remote from Paris and unlikely to be too lively. However, it turned out to be very agreeable. My host was the local *député*; he and his wife made me much at home in the good old French bourgeois style, which included an introduction to the best cooking. Something of eternal France was present in this remote provincial city; I still hear in that land of enduring enchantment the same tunes being played at country fairs which at sixteen first introduced me to the free life of the Continent.

As usual in French cities, a *salle d'armes* was available with some good performers to complete my happiness. In the thirties one of the most redoubtable members of their Olympic team came from another provincial city, Le Havre. Here too I was introduced to the quick-action sport of pistol duelling with wax bullets fired from a smooth bore, which catch you a hard crack but do not penetrate special protective clothing and a fencing-mask fitted with thick non-splinter glass over the eyes. Years later I revived this sport at my house near Denham at a time when my return to fencing was the subject of some comment. The *Daily Herald* one day contained a short leading article addressed to my 'childish delight in weapons'. One of my close political associates during that period, John Strachey, was rather inclined to agree with the *Daily Herald*.

The age of sixteen saw some revival of my mental faculties, which did not reach full development for another two or three years, but enabled me to pass the army exams with reasonable credit, and to enter the Royal Military College at Sandhurst when I was just seventeen, an earlier age than was usual. If my memory serves me, I was fifth on the cavalry list, and would by the calculation of my teachers have been top except for my execrable handwriting which lost me what they maintained was the record figure of 800 marks.

Some pundit may be able to confound my memory by looking up this record, which I have not bothered to check—irrelevant detail without permanent importance can be left to the scavengers of youth—but these are the figures which remained in my recollections after many wise admonitions to learn to write; an accomplishment I never achieved. I always claim my bad writing is due to my mind moving too fast for my hand; Diana ascribes it to my carelessness, impoliteness and indifference to the convenience of others. I retort that she could read my writing very well in the first fine flush of romance, but the habit of marriage has dulled her acute sensibilities; there the matter rests, as is the way with marital arguments.

I arrived at Sandhurst at the beginning of 1914 and found an atmosphere remote from any premonition of war. It was immensely gay, and there I spent some of the most vividly happy days of my life. We broke every rule, and off parade had not the least regard for discipline. Few changes could have been more dramatic than the complete reversal in our attitude at the outbreak of war, when the playboys of the summer became overnight completely serious and dedicated young soldiers. The convivial group was a fairly large minority in the R.M.C., where the orthodox majority pursued a more sedate way of life. It was drawn from every company in the two large buildings—old and new—and was recognised by a certain flamboyance of demeanour. I remember looking round the large mess hall on the first night of my arrival and picking out some fifty to a hundred boys who seemed to me particularly objectionable; within a month they were my best friends and closest associates. It is often a male reaction in youth to resist instinctively vitality in others at first impact which later, in intimacy, attracts close friendship. These responses are almost chemical in their selective affinity—as Goethe suggests in a very different context in his novel *Die Wahlverwandtschaften*—and in young men of very male characteristics lead naturally to a form of community or gang life. It was the habit at Sandhurst to spend all leisure with the same people, whatever company they belonged to.

Exuberance took the form of climbing out of the buildings at night or slipping through one of the numerous doors, with the clandestine objective of a journey to London. A mixed assortment of old cars used to carry a merry company the relatively short distance. Not much harm was done beyond a certain fatigue on early parade next morning after a night without sleep. The tendency was to stay with the gang and to engage in pranks rather than any form of vice. A pastime in true corinthian tradition was to see how long it would take the stout array of ex-pugilists who acted as chuckers-out at music halls like the Empire to execute their genial duties. There was not much drinking, but a lot of good-humoured fooling.

The only time I was well and truly drunk in my life was at Sandhurst, and I never felt any inclination to repeat the unattractive experience; it happened by accident rather than design. For some celebration we assembled a large and jolly dinner party in Skindle's Restaurant at Maidenhead. The scene was idyllic to young eyes as we looked across the noble sweep of lawn illumined by distant lighting of trees and flowers to the glistening stream of moon-lit Thames. I began to feel on top of the world as the wine circulated with a freedom which was novel to a boy of seventeen. Some more practised hand also supplied liqueurs, and the sense of being on top of the world was gradually transmuted into a certain reversal of roles; I felt there was some danger of the world being on top of me. Fate guided my footsteps toward the fresh air of the garden. I had a last moment of *joie de vivre* as I began to descend— airborne—the steps which led to the lawn, but the exquisite flower bed beneath rose then from every side to embrace me in a clasp of the gods. I awoke next morning in my bed at Sandhurst, feeling the world was very much on top of me.

I learnt later that my companions had raised me from my floral tomb and placed me in the car of a friend, who turned out to be almost as much the worse for wear as I was. He succeeded, however, in driving back to Sandhurst with me inert in the back, but unfortunately then forgot where either of us lived. The result was that he drove rapidly round the parade ground wrestling with these fugitive memories, and was eventually flagged down by the Sergeant of the Guard who was aroused by the noise. The sergeant was a kindly fellow who recognised us both and had us carried without a word said to our apartments. There would have been a great row if it had come out.

At Sandhurst I returned to my first love, horses. The year between leaving Winchester and arriving there, except for the brief interlude at Brest, had ruptured my relations with the fencing world and checked my interest. My Heathcote grandfather had celebrated the beginning of my military career by assisting me to get an old horse with a tube, who was unsuccessful in steeple-chases but might be good enough for local point-to-point; he also promised to help with one or two polo ponies. At the same time my father's short sojourn at Rolleston with a fair supply of money had enabled him to acquire a stable of magnificent horses which I had been allowed to ride with the Meynell hounds. My enthusiasm for the world of the horse was fired again, and fencing and boxing receded into the background.

The first spring was much preoccupied by point-to-points which were strictly forbidden to cadets, although participation in the local drag hunt was permitted. The problem of entry without revealing name and origin to the local press was overcome by pseudonyms like A. N. Other, or, anticipating a mishap at an early obstacle, Mr. R. S. Upward. On my first appearance I was confronted by one of my Company officers who was riding in the same race; a real good sort who said not a word. My efforts were unsuccessful; the old horse was nearly always lame and soon broke down completely. His name was Peter Simple, and I was much attached to him.

There were some outstanding horsemen at the R.M.C., but I was never among the best of them, and had nothing like the capacity for handling horses of my younger brother Ted, who later entered the 1st Royal Dragoons and became an instructor at Weedon Cavalry School. Riding is largely a matter of hands, and mine were better with the sword or in flying early aircraft—an experience near to riding—in which they may have saved my life in my last crash.

The best among these young masters of horsemanship was with me at the Curragh when we joined our respective regiments. I knew him well and liked him, but must admit that I never performed with him a feat which he later ascribed to me. It was a case of memory transferring experience from one character to another, which can happen easily when some among many afterwards become well known. It can happen for good or ill; we can easily in legend acquire both merit and demerit we do not deserve. On this occasion I would gladly have accepted a compliment which I had in no way earned; in fact, on this embarrassing occasion I am ashamed to say I did accept it. It was awkward to know what else to do. Not long ago at the Hotel Russell in Dublin I was warmly greeted by this Sandhurst friend, who was surrounded by a considerable company. In introducing me he described an epic ride by moonlight we had once made together from the Curragh to his country house; a considerable distance across country taking all obstacles as they came. Of course he had done it; he was a most daring and accomplished horseman. What he had forgotten was that his companion was not me but A. N. Other; some other young officer from the Curragh. My dilemma was whether to deny it was me, and spoil his generous story—or to wear the laurel wreath I had not won. I blushed in silence.

At Sandhurst horses in one sport or another claimed most of my attention. Our work hours at that time were not long or strenuous, apart from arduous early parades. As summer came I began to play polo, and showed enough early promise to get into our Sandhurst polo team, though I was a complete novice and never continued the game long enough to become good at it. I started again soon after the war, but parliamentary duties and general political work made it impossible in my view to continue either hunting or polo. However, polo lasted long enough to cause me my only bit of trouble during my time at Sandhurst.

The background was a certain state of feud, almost of gang war in an exuberant hearty fashion between many of my friends and various other groups of cadets. The alignment was by no means simply between cavalry cadets and the rest, although many of us were destined for the cavalry or similar regiments. Most of the scrapping was between gang and gang. There had recently been something of this kind in a tea-room of which our friends were inclined to disapprove. I had not been much involved, but shortly afterwards a few of us were observed in a corridor by a considerable number who regarded themselves as affronted by this or similar incidents. A rush like a rugger scrum brought us to the ground, but we were quickly rescued by other friends who were close at hand. I then invited any of our assailants to an individual fight, which was not the prevailing habit. My rather provocative challenge in the heat of the moment was soon accepted, and a large boy was produced from their side who was a familiar figure at the end of the rope in the R.M.C. tug-of-war team. He was certainly older, heavier and stronger than I was, so all depended on what remained of the boxing skill I had not practised since taking up fencing well over two years before. I had a lively apprehension that timing and accuracy of punches would be lacking, in which case I should be for it.

He started with a series of rushes and wild, swinging punches, which I avoided with footwork or ducked, without much trouble. It was evident he knew little of boxing, and the only remaining question was whether I could still connect with accurate punches. He became annoyed by my evasions and rushed me with much determination when he thought he had me against the wall. I side-stepped in the manner so often practised for emergence from the ropes with the good Ryan, and he crashed into the wall. Now really incensed he turned and came at me like a bull, but, happily, as became an officer and a gentleman, with his chin up. This time I did not side-step but stepped right into him with the long practised straight left which—*mirabile dictu*—connected plump on the point of the chin. He went down, and out; even before I could follow through with the usual right. He was really knocked out by his own weight and momentum. It was not at all difficult for anyone who had been made to practise this punch so often; fortunately it was still there.

This incident gained me surprisingly—for my opponent was only big, he lacked skill—a most disproportionate prestige as a pugilist. It was therefore unfortunate that I was involved in another incident directly afterwards, as it rather appeared I was always throwing this skill about. Our Sandhurst polo team had suffered its first defeat. We were inordinately proud of having managed to beat a few subaltern teams in Aldershot and the reverse was a big disappointment. We ascribed it to a shortage of ponies and I, in particular, was concerned to find out what could have happened to a pony which I was to have ridden; the arrangement was that it would be bought if suitable. It appeared to have been sent not to Aldershot, where we had our match, but to Wellington, the practice ground of the R.M.C., by instruction of another cadet who also thought of buying it. I went to see him in order to complain that he had contributed to Sandhurst losing the match. I was no doubt not very conciliatory, and he appeared to me in no way contrite; I thought, perhaps mistakenly, he was rude. An argument followed, and ended in a fight, which I won. It was considered by some of his friends an affront, because he was two years older than I was and in his last period at Sandhurst, while I was in my first term. Also in their view I should not have fought because I was likely to win. There was in my opinion no certainty whatever about this, as I maintained in subsequent discussion with an offer to fight anyone else. After some talk between the two sides the incident appeared closed and I parted from my friends to go to my room.

Later in the evening a fair number of the other side attacked my room, which they failed to enter; no one was in any way responsible for what then occurred, as no one was near me. I knew that a number of my friends were in an adjoining block, and decided to climb out, join them and take the attack in the rear. Normally a performance of this kind gave me little trouble, but on this occasion I missed my foothold and fell some way, injuring my leg. The injury was not severe, and about six weeks later I was passed A1., fit for active service, and was back at Sandhurst for hard training on the outbreak of war. Two years later, after serving in the Royal Flying Corps, with air crashes followed by trench service, I was out of the war for good with one leg an inch and a half shorter than the other, in the category C3.

The consequence of the Sandhurst affair was not serious as none of us incurred any loss of promotion, although we should have suffered the loss of a term but for the war. My chief regret was that two of my friends were also sent down with me for the few weeks which remained of the term. After news of my injury got around, a number of them from the two main buildings had assembled to deal with my assailants. It was then getting late at night and it was considered a breach of discipline to leave their quarters, particularly for the suspected purpose of fighting other people. I was sent down as initially responsible for the affair and they were sent down as leaders in the subsequent action on my behalf. Happily it appeared in no way to have affected their military careers, and one of them ended up as a general. It was all very foolish, and of course I should not have got into a fight about something so trivial; at seventeen you sometimes do things, in the period of early vitality when spirits are high, which you would not dream of doing a year or two later. I do not think that anyone was much to blame; but it was mostly my fault.

When highly garbled versions of this affair were circulated in my later life, I was consoled by the reflection that I must have a character and career of singular impeccability if the only ground for attack was an incident when I was seventeen. It was regrettable at the time, as even then I was becoming too adult for that kind of thing. Fighting for the fun of it had already ceased to amuse. I had been brought up in the corinthian tradition—as it was called in the previous century—which made men ever ready to fight as a sport, or at the least provocation; but already with the development of other interests and general intelligence I was beginning to grow out of it. I never perhaps learned to swallow insults, but I did at least learn to ignore them. To do otherwise is by definition too Latin, too un-English. A brilliant French politician put the point with wit when he said: 'If a Latin is walking down the street and feels a heavy kick on the bottom, he cannot resist at least turning his head to notice who has done it; but the genius of you English in these circumstances is that you just pass on, unnoticing and uncaring'.

It became my ever increasing conviction throughout life that we should do our utmost to avoid the use of force; it is the last and saddest necessity. Perhaps the biggest factor in my development of this sense was experience of the First War. For everyone who went through that war the fun went out of force for good. Also, a continually increasing distaste for the use of force is part of the process of growing up, both for individuals and for nations. It is the development of the adult mind which eliminates the passions and actions of childhood. It is impossible to imagine the 'ancients' of Shaw's farthest vision in *Back to Methuselah* indulging in a 'punch-up'.

Certainly from the first war onwards I had a repugnance for violence, and in particular for its brutal and unnecessary use. Later in politics I had to prove my capacity and determination to meet violence with force and by leadership and organisation to overcome it. The sad fact is that in human affairs this is sometimes necessary. Yet when all is said and the past is done, we have to face the modern fact that the world simply cannot survive a continuance of the habit of violence. It has been the way of men to settle their disputes in this manner from time immemorial, at a certain point to lose their temper and fight. Quite suddenly the forward spring of science makes it too dangerous. All our instincts, all our training, all our concepts of manhood and of courage must—far too quickly for the slow movement of nature—be adjusted to a corresponding change. We have to put away childish things and become adult. It is not surprising that soldiers and others who have most experience of violence are often the most ready for the change. The knowledge that it is horrible is added in their case to the plain sense that it is childish and ridiculous. We must do everything in the world to avoid violence short of abandoning our world; the values which are the heritage of three thousand years.

There is always a point of misery and humiliation at which life is not worth living and brave men prefer to die. This attitude was superbly stated by Shakespeare: 'What's brave, what's noble, let's do it after the high Roman fashion, and make death proud to take us'; by Racine: 'Est-ce un malheur si grand que de cesser de vivre?'; by Goethe in his Achilleus: 'Aus der Hand der Verzweiflung nimmt er den herrlichen Kranz eines unverwelklichen Sieges'. These classic thoughts are appropriate to a moment when mankind approaches suicide. Yet we shall not now reach the point either of despair or heroism in the affairs of nations, unless the world goes mad; because in such event the other side know, or can be made to realise, that they too will die. We now need the adult mind on each side, and shall find it. The arrangement of the world has become a matter for those who understand that force is the last, the saddest of necessities, and that between nations it is now doom.

3
Service in the First World War

THE outbreak of war in August 1914 brought us all back to Sandhurst in a hurry, several weeks before we were due to return. The purpose was a brief, hard spell of war training before being sent to join our regiments. On the way through London I had a glimpse of the cheering crowds round Buckingham Palace, and sensed the air of general enthusiasm which since the Boer War had been called the Mafeking spirit. Everyone seemed to think it would be all over in a few weeks. The reason for this belief was not quite clear, but we were all gripped by it. Our one great fear was that the war would be over before we got there. A cartoon in *Punch* or some such journal showed a cavalry subalterns' mess discussing the outbreak of war; there would just be time to beat them between the polo and the hunting—or was it between the polo and the grouse? These brilliant troops had more reason for their optimism in the conditions of 1914 than some of the club experts of 1939, who were remarking that the Polish cavalry would have an easy ride to Berlin because the German tanks were really made of cardboard. There is always much nonsense talked at the outbreak of war, even after experience.

How much tragedy loomed if we could have looked into the future. We had to report to Sandhurst the next day, so in London I went to the Palace Theatre where a young actor called Basil Hallam, a friend of the previous summer, was having an unparalleled success in the company of a glittering actress called Elsie Janis, who was one of the wittiest and most brilliant of the hostesses and entertainers we have welcomed from America. He asked me how long I thought the war would last—a most hopeful question, because I was much less qualified to judge this than the man in the moon. With a crashing lack of tact, a truly wooden-headed display of youthful obtuseness, I indicated that what really mattered was that it should last long enough for us to get into it. His face saddened, and even then I had sensibility enough to realise what a tragedy it was for a young man just at the height of his first success, so recently won, to give it all up and go to the war, as he would feel impelled to do if it went on for long. It was quite soon afterwards that Basil Hallam's parachute failed to open when his observation balloon was shot down by attacking aircraft and he had to jump out in a hurry. It was a rough job, you had to get out fast to avoid the burning balloon coming on top of you. They had parachutes—which we had not in my days in the Royal Flying Corps—but the chivalrous rule of not shooting at a man going down in a parachute was not always observed in the case of someone jumping from an observation balloon; perhaps the German airmen did not regard them as belonging to the same fraternity. Another friend of mine in that corps was followed all the way down by two German aircraft plastering him with machine-gun bullets; he always said that he never gave a thought to being hit himself but had his eyes anxiously glued on the cord by which he was dangling for fear it would be severed.

The Army legend was that Basil Hallam's body hit the ground not far from the Guards band playing his smash-hit song of the 1914 summer, 'Good-bye girls, I'm through'; I do not know if it was true; these rumours and legends always circulate in an army, often in highly romantic form. The British private soldier under his rough exterior is much given to sentiment and imaginative credulity. Some believed that Field-Marshal Mackensen, one of the most distinguished German commanders of the First World War, was in reality Hector Macdonald, a general of the Boer War who was reputed to have committed suicide in time of peace after some dark event. There were no grounds for believing this story.

The tragedy of war was remote from our consciousness as we assembled at Sandhurst, only the excitement was present. The training now was certainly arduous, and most eagerly accepted. Discipline was absolute, everyone was a dedicated soldier. We were at it day and night, on foot and on horse in continual training. Still I never cross the Hartford Flats in the comfort of a modern car without recalling those footsore and saddlesore days. It was soon all over for the happy and hardworking band who were now gathered together as cavalry cadets in the old building. After a few weeks we were dispersed, and sent to our respective regiments.

I arrived at the Curragh Camp some thirty miles from Dublin with a commission in the regular army to join my regiment, the 16th Lancers. The Curragh was a depot for two of the great regiments of the British Army, the 16th and 17th Lancers, which were sister regiments. I had switched my choice between these two at the last moment by persuasion of a grand old figure of the 16th Lancers, Major Sir Lovelace Stamer, who was a neighbour and friend of my mother's family. Previously I had been intended for the 17th Lancers, because some of their officers had stayed at Rolleston for a local polo match during my father's brief sojourn just before the war. Among them was Vivyan Lockett, a member of the British polo team who defeated in America the celebrated American team led by Milburn; he was a distant cousin of ours. They had been good enough to invite me to join them, and apart from the attraction of their company the idea of wearing the famous badge—Death or Glory under a skull and crossbones, won at Balaclava—had a strong appeal. But the immense prestige of the 16th Lancers coupled with the kindness of our old family friend led me on the spur of the moment to state a preference for the 16th.

I arrived at the Curragh with the sense that it was a privilege to be accepted by either of these brilliant regiments, but in some trepidation that my slight change of direction had given offence. However, nothing happened except a little friendly banter, and I quickly felt that the question which regiment I joined was not quite so war-determining as I might have imagined. They were all extremely kind, and the necessary moral deflation was applied with a far gentler hand than that of the British Treasury in any equivalent economic situation.

It was the tradition of the regular army to assume that at Sandhurst we had learned nothing at all. We had to go through the whole business again, barrack square included, exactly like the last recruit who arrived as a private soldier fresh from making hay or from the factory bench. Above all we must take command of nothing until we had 'passed out'. One day we were out on a ride in charge of a rather pliable sergeant, a few simple manoeuvres on horseback which by then I felt I knew from A to Z. With his consent I took charge of the party, as I felt it would do me more good to develop the habit of command than to ride around in the ranks doing things I had learned so well at Sandhurst that I could almost go to sleep on the horse.

Suddenly I was surprised by a stentorian rebuke in front of the whole parade by one of the Rolleston friends who was a senior officer in the 17th Lancers. What was an officer who had not yet 'passed out' doing in charge of a ride? The sudden transformation of an easy, charming friend into a fierce martinet was something of a shock, but half an hour later in the mess he reverted to his usual form and attitude. He was right, for that was the way of the regular army. On parade discipline was absolute, with the most meticulous regard for time-honoured rules vigorously enforced in a fashion quite adequately rough. But in the mess, with the complete relaxation of a club of intimate friends, we were even required at once on joining to call everyone except the Colonel by his christian name; a habit which the newcomer was inclined to adopt with some diffidence. This way of life had developed over generations, and it worked. The rigours of discipline were tempered and indeed sustained by the warm loyalty of dedicated friends.

The same attitude prevailed with other ranks, although we did not see much of them off duty, except in sport. But every man was made to feel that he was a member of a large family and would in all circumstances be looked after. The most intimate confidence was encouraged and freely given with complete trust. The officer must and would take the utmost trouble to assist any man in his troop or squadron in any difficulty, either in the regiment or in his private life. Not only was this relationship developed by encouragement to make application for assistance in orderly room on official occasions, but every man had the opportunity during the occasions of daily routine in the most casual way to ask an officer's help or advice.

Every morning we had a ceremony called 'stables', which consisted in the grooming, watering and feeding of horses; all performed with minute regard for a formal ritual which must never be varied. I learned there, as much later in such a very different institution as the Foreign Office, that these rigid rules for redressing the carelessness and fallibility of human nature have their considerable practical uses. If doing a thing properly becomes a fixed habit, with dire consequences if it is disregarded, fatal or less serious errors are in practice reduced to a minimum. The stables ceremony, whether in barracks or in the field, had to precede any human care; horses came first, and we could neither look after ourselves nor others until this care was complete. Again without this fixed rule occasions of stress would clearly arise in which the horses would be forgotten, and on them depended not only the success but the very life of the whole corps. There was a natural logic in this business, for the army was composed of practical people whose methods had been evolved in a long experience; there was no question of sentiment.

At this morning ceremony of stables opportunity was provided for the most intimate relationship to be established between officer and men. The horses would be discussed during the work, together with the previous day's events and coming exercises. A man would also discuss with an officer his private affairs and ask advice in the most informal manner. This approach was often tactfully reversed, for the old soldier frequently knew far more about much of the military business than the young officer. His attitude was invariably protective towards his technical superior in a good regiment, and he would never let his young man make a mug of himself if he could possibly help it. Many were the friendly warnings quietly given and gratefully accepted, without the least impairment of the rigid hierarchy of discipline which maintained the whole steel structure. Such advice from an experienced troop sergeant to a young officer in all the intricacies of daily military formalities established between them almost the relationship of a mother and child. But the relations could in some cases be suddenly and sharply reversed when nature replaced ritual and the troop came under heavy fire in a dangerous situation.

The habit of discipline in those circumstances became more than ever valuable. The varying performances of regiments in the supreme test of war could always be traced to their discipline and leadership. Regiments would acquire through this means a collective character so individual that you could almost calculate with precision what in given circumstances they would do. To take an example almost unbelievably crude and simple: it was possible in support trenches in dry conditions to allow everyone to take off their boots if certain regiments were in the front line, because you knew they would hold long enough if attacked to give those in support plenty of time to move up. But this was not advisable in all cases.

This collective character of regiments, this intimate relationship between ranks and these practical working methods, can only be created over a long period of time. It can be found in varying degrees in all the great institutions of this world, where men have slowly evolved a pride in their ways and traditions in the manner of a natural and true aristocracy, the sense of belonging to an élite of service and achievement. The spirit of a regiment or an army always depends greatly on its leadership, and it can be destroyed very quickly—it has sometimes been done in the modern world—but it requires generations, even centuries to create it. And when you have lived with it you realise it is something unique, one of the wonders of human nature.

Those days at the Curragh in the autumn of 1914 confirmed the impression of the regular army which I had originally derived from Sergeant-Major Adam and Sergeant Ryan at school, and I became deeply attached to that way of life. Some years later, in the light duties of convalescence, I was to know very happy and relatively relaxed days at the Curragh. But in those early days of the war all was serious and arduous training. To 'pass out' and become a fully fledged officer did not take long. We new arrivals since the war began were then fully trained and prepared to go to the front. But the war of mobility for the time being was over, and the cavalry in Flanders were held back from the front in reserve. Trench war had begun and there appeared no immediate prospect of the cavalry being used. The casualties were not then occurring which we sadly realised would alone call us to the front as replacements, yet still the idea prevailed that the war would not last long. Impatience grew with the apprehension that we should miss the adventure of a lifetime. Men but a little older than ourselves would be able for ever to address us in some more prosaic English equivalent of Henri IV's gay and gallant words to one of his favourite friends: 'Pends-toi, brave Crillon, nous avons combattu à Arques et tu n'y étais pas'. Yet our English version was not always quite so prosaic after all: 'And gentlemen in England, now abed, shall think themselves accursed, they were not here'.

A condition approaching despair began to grip ardent young hearts; never had men appeared more eager to be killed. It was in retrospect perhaps a strange attitude, but it still seems to me healthier than the mood of a few clever young men who on the outbreak of the Second World War reached for the telephone to enquire what was going in Whitehall. Our generation was mad, perhaps, but it was the right kind of madness; some shade of the old George might have wished again these madmen might bite some of their successors.

How to get to the front was the burning question of that hour. One service alone supplied the answer: the Royal Flying Corps. It was prepared to take on completely untrained men as observers and send them straight to fight. I had never been up in an aircraft in my life, but I put in for the job at once. Directly I had sent in my application I remembered that in a gymnasium I had the greatest difficulty in making myself walk across a plank twenty feet above the ground; I had always much disliked heights. There was a considerable doubt about what would happen to me when I found myself several thousand feet above ground. Those were early days and it was not common knowledge that most people who dislike heights have no sensation whatever of that kind in an aircraft. In any case there was nothing for it now but to go and see what happened.

The sense of adventure into the unknown was certainly enhanced during the period of waiting by the most horrific drawings of aircraft being plastered by shell-fire which appeared in the illustrated weeklies. It turned out for once that the imagination of the artist had not greatly exceeded the bounds of fact, for during my time at the front with the R.F.C. I can rarely recall seeing any aircraft returning from crossing the lines without being hit. These early machines were flimsy contraptions, and precisely on that account could stand a lot of stuff going through them without fatality.

At last the wait was over and the order came to report for duty in France. I was joined by another young man from a Lancer regiment whom I had known at Sandhurst, and we understood we were the first two to go from the cavalry to the flying service in response to the appeal for observers. I had always liked him and we became close friends on the way over. I was just past my eighteenth birthday and he was a year or two older. The night before we parted to go to different squadrons he said to me, 'You know, we are much too young to die'. I warmly agreed. A few weeks later I heard he was dead.

My experience on the western front will be an entirely individual story; the reader must expect no history of even a small section of the war. I have always felt a clear choice existed between two states of mind, the writing of history and the making of history. He who is interested in the latter should only be detained by the former just long enough to absorb its lessons. In the case of the First World War a single idea existed for me: always to do my utmost in all circumstances to prevent it ever happening again. This thought was so burned into my consciousness by memory of the fate of my companions that it approached the obsessive far more closely than any other experience of my life. I was at that time too occupied to record anything, and afterwards I was not interested in registering any thought but the determination to prevent the fatal recurrence, if it were humanly possible. Even the colossal errors made during the war became irrelevant if the only task were to stop war in its entirety.

This attitude led me to take little further interest in the science of war, for war became something to be prevented at all costs. It was not until pure science in recent years entered the science of war as its complete determinant that this interest returned. For pure science in modern times offers the decisive choice of the ages, utter destruction or unlimited progress, the abyss or the heights. All politics are in this, and all the future. The problem of war and peace became one with the arrival of science; it was the problem of existence itself, the question of life or death. This was a new world, but from the old world I took one benefit which I shall never deny and always appreciate— a certain attitude of manhood which came from the regular army and helps much in the problems of life.

I am therefore not concerned with the weighty volumes which record the details of these vast events, but only to describe the personal experience of one individual who might have been any other of the millions who fought, and often died. What happened to us in our daily life then, and how did it affect our later life, if we survived? Most of our companions, of course, did not live, particularly in the Royal Flying Corps at that time. Memory is a parade of dead men.

We reckoned during that period at the end of 1914 that about sixty men, pilots and observers, actually flew; I have never checked the figure exactly. We were organised in two wings, the first under the command of Hugh Trenchard, who already had a high reputation and who became famous in later life. I was posted to the other wing which contained No. 6 Squadron, then under the command of Captain Beck; I spent most of my time with them. At the end of 1914 we were at Bailleul, and during most of my service we were either there or at Poperinghe, not far away.

At Bailleul the aerodrome, as we then called it, was alongside the lunatic asylum; a massive building reducing us to quite a narrow field which was awkward in some winds. It was there that my pilot said the day after my arrival, 'Well, let's make a start'. I went up in an aircraft for the first time in my life, and this valuable observer had not the least idea whether he was on his head or his heels, going or coming, for it was rather bumpy. That day we flew along the lines but did not cross them, just to get used to it. The pilot kindly pointed out all the landmarks which later became so familiar. For some time I never had the faintest notion where I was until I caught sight of the triangular pond at Zilibeke; I was never very quick or handy with compasses and map.

It was an odd idea to send completely untrained men to act as observers in the belief that they would see more than the highly-trained pilots. There was something in it, however, because in the degree of fire to which we were subjected on reconnaissance the pilot was usually fully occupied in taking what evasive action he could. All the same, his trained and experienced eye even then often took in more of what was happening on the ground than the unskilled observer. It was some time before the observer flying under actual war conditions became any use at all. Until then he was liable to be a dead-weight in the machine, and therefore to handicap rather than assist the pilot. Nevertheless, he probably learned more quickly under these conditions than in peaceful training at home; as Dr. Johnson said of the man who knows he is facing death, 'it concentrates his mind wonderfully'. The authorities were short of men, and naturally wanted to get things going quickly.

On my way to the squadron I met the most experienced airman alive, the holder of Pilot's certificate No. 1. I do not remember now whether it was at G.H.Q. or Wing H.Q. that I first met Ivan Moore-Brabazon, who later became a friend in many diverse circumstances. At that time I only saw him briefly, but we entered Parliament together in 1918 and were closely associated in the new members' group. Between the R.F.C. and Westminster I had learned to know him well in the company of mutual friends of his early days, who consequently called him Ivan, which he always remained to me in preference to the later Brab. He was a remarkable character, who combined with the most indolent demeanour an exceptional capacity for action. In his youth he was the first man to fly a mile, and in later life he won the Cresta race at St. Moritz at some incredibly advanced age for such a performance, varying these efforts with first-rate displays in sports as diverse as motor-racing and golf. Stranger still, he added to a continuing athletic capacity a first-rate mind; these gifts may succeed each other but they rarely coincide.

He was serving on the staff when I first met him, having ceased to fly before the war after witnessing the death-crash of his great friend, Charles Rolls. Apart from a pleasant interlude towards the end of the war, the next time I was to have a glimpse of him in effective action was in Parliament soon after my arrival. His immense experience and authority in aviation fitted him perfectly to be Parliamentary Private Secretary to Mr. Churchill when he became Air Minister. Ivan Moore-Brabazon was never a character who sus-tained easily the restrictive chains of office. During an air debate Mr. Churchill sought a little respite in the smoking-room, and engaged in conversation the circle in which I was sitting. Soon a Whip hurried in and said to him, 'You had better come back to the House, your P.P.S. is up and he is knocking hell out of the Ministry'. The exit from the smoking-room was portentous.

At the end of 1914 the work of the squadron was regular and arduous, and after the first trial flight along the lines I was launched straight into it. We did a reconnaissance at least once a day, and it usually took nearly three hours. It was normally a shallow reconnaissance over Courtrai to observe troop concentrations near the front line, but quite frequently we did a reconnaissance in depth which took us about seventy miles behind the German lines to observe their forces coming up. This further flight was much preferred to the observation sweep of about twenty miles behind the lines, and was regarded as quite a relief from the more exacting daily routine. The reason was that once you got through the first twenty miles you enjoyed relative tranquillity until reaching any of the main towns farther back, where they were again waiting with heavy fire.

The daily reconnaissance at short distance was a different matter. Their fire began directly the machine crossed the lines and did not let up for a moment during the whole flight until the line was recrossed to return home. The German method was to put guns in squares, with eight in each corner. Directly the aircraft was about the centre of the square they would open fire simultaneously, with cross-observation by telephone from each corner to the other corners with the usual gunners' information. The result was that thirty-two shells would be in the air at the first salvo, and they would continue firing at almost the rate of the French '75's, which then operated at greater speed than any other guns in the world. The moment we were out of one square we were into another, and so it continued throughout the convivial three hours. It is therefore not difficult to understand why our aircraft hardly ever crossed the lines without being hit.

The whole danger at that time was from ground-fire, as the fighting between machines had only just begun in a very rudimentary form. But the effect of the fire on aircraft which were flying at seventy to eighty miles an hour at a height of not more than 6,000 feet was naturally considerable. We were flying at that time BE2Cs, which were slow but reliable. They took off, flew and landed at about the same speed. No pilot could coax them much above their 6,000-feet ceiling. I was attached at one time to another flight using Morris Farman Shorthorns, the machines on which we used to learn to fly in those days. These machines were just as slow and even more clumsy, but popular with us at that time because they could reach a height of 12,000 feet. This by no means rendered them invulnerable to ground-fire, but at that height it was much less accurate. My pilot on the flight was the most brilliant the R.F.C. had produced in the handling of those machines. But he had two little habits which were highly disconcerting to the newcomer. The first was to zoom the machine on the take-off, which consisted of holding the nose down just above the ground for a considerable distance to get up maximum speed, and then to pull back the stick to send it up as it seemed almost vertically, finally straightening out just before the stall. The second form of playfulness was on returning from a disagreeable stretch of work to arrive 12,000 feet above his own aerodrome and then to stand the machine on one wing-tip and spiral all the way down; in effect, spinning it down like a top. His virtuosity impressed fellow-officers, riggers and mechanics—my word, some bird—but was an unpleasant surprise to his observer, if he had not been notified where to look.

For the secret was not to look straight ahead, or at the wing above, but along the wing below towards the ground to which you were spinning; otherwise the experience was a sure emetic.

He was a most charming man, and had the best hands I have ever felt operating one of those early machines; he had the touch of a pianist. Unfortunately he had an imitator in the flight who also had the best of natures but lacked the magic hands. He was the observer's dread, for every time it was anyone's guess whether the initial zoom would stall the machine or not, while extricating it from the final spiral just above the ground required an exquisite delicacy in the handling whose absence could result in a spinning nose-dive, generally fatal at that time. It was all endured with anxiety but without remonstrance, for he was such a good fellow and complaint would have hurt his feelings. He died heroically trying to fly his machine home to save his observer when he was mortally wounded in the chest, but he lost consciousness not far above the ground just before landing; they were both killed.

These machines even more than the BE2Cs sometimes involved a certain difficulty in crossing the lines with a following wind. When you turned to fly back, your progress was your flying speed less wind; say seventy miles per hour less forty. In extreme cases it would be impossible for an aircraft a long way behind the lines to get back without running out of petrol. There was only one way out of it, to put the nose down in a semi-dive and thus gain extra speed. This was impossible in the Morris Farman because it was believed it could not be put into a dive without risking the wings coming off. Consequently they were mostly used for gun-spotting, observing enemy batteries, and directing our fire upon them with morse signals.

The BE2C was a sturdy machine which could be put into a dive, but this had to be done with care. There was at that time a craze in design for what was called automatic stability which was embodied in the BE2C. If you stalled one of these machines it went into a dive from which it recovered automatically and bobbed up like a cork in water. All very excellent but it required elbow room to do it; if you made a mistake near the ground that was that. This capacity to withstand a dive, or rather a powered descent, was however very useful for returning against an adverse wind. The nose could be pushed down to give a speed of over 100 miles an hour, but this process, of course, brought the aircraft continually nearer to the ground, and after a long flight entailed crossing the trench zone very low indeed. Here the partridge on the wing enjoyed another sport. Intensive machine-gun and rifle fire at once began, and gave the bird the sensation of being at the wrong end of a rifle-range without the usual protection, as the bullets zipped through the wings. The only safeguard was the small wooden seat on which you were sitting, and the smack of a partly spent bullet could occasionally be felt upon it. The instinct of manhood in this disturbing situation was carefully to compress treasured possessions within this exiguous area of protection.

A rather similar sensation was afforded by the aerodrome at Poperinghe, because it was bordered by a field of hop-poles with a pond in one corner. In the event of an engine beginning to fail at take-off—which occurred fairly often—the pilot had sometimes to circle over the hop-poles to land against the wind. It was then interesting to look over the side and to speculate which of the hop-poles would strike home if the engine gave up completely. Poperinghe was an aerodrome of many hazards, as the golfers say of their more interesting courses. Returning from reconnaissance in poor visibility we once broke cloud for the first time just over the aerodrome. Immediately a French 75 battery which was stationed there for our protection opened fire and gave us a proper pasting. The pilot very skilfully dived in and pulled out just over the ground to land. The Frenchmen then saw at once we were an allied machine.

Justly incensed, I got out of the machine and walked toward the French battery. A figure advanced to meet me, holding some object under his arm. He was the French battery commander; as we approached each other he held out a shell-case and with a completely disarming smile said—'Souvenir'. It was the case of one of the French 75 shells he had fired at us, and to this day I still have it in the form of an old-fashioned dinner-gong. It took the place of the melodious cow-bells at Rolleston which used to be sounded in our childhood to summon us to the happy board.

Our relations with the French gunners, and with their flying squadron which shared the aerodrome with us, were usually of the happiest. Perhaps natural affinity was enhanced by fate's fortunate dispensation that the chauffeur of the French squadron commander, in the genial, democratic forms of French military organisation, was the head of one of the best-known brands of champagne in France. We tended afterwards in their mess to see through a roseate glow even the most trying incidents of the day, as when the two squadrons took a different view of the direction of the wind, with the result that two machines landing from opposite points just managed to avoid meeting head-on in the middle of the aerodrome and escaped with a mutual ripping of wings.

There was much improvisation in those early days among the French, who had that capacity to a degree of genius. But we English were able to make our contribution in the efforts of one of our most gifted members, who later passed into the immortality of heroism. L.G. Hawker was there in his early days with the squadron, very young, very inventive, always trying out new things and new methods. With much raillery we watched him tying onto his aircraft the first 100-lb bomb to reach the squadron (until then we had nothing heavier than 13-lb bombs) with a quaint contraption of string, wire and improvised pulleys to his pilot's seat, before he set out to deliver it to some German target of his particular dislike. We always maintained it had come off long before he reached the German lines, which he stoutly denied with his usual gay humour. However, he managed soon to arrange things as he wanted. He won the D.S.O. for destroying a Zeppelin on the ground with light weapons under very heavy fire and the V.C. for a successful battle against great odds in the air. Finally, he was shot down after a long air fight with the great German ace, Richthofen, who also died in the same way soon afterwards. They rest together in the Pantheon of heroism.

Hawker won his V.C. some time after I left the squadron. Another V.C. of the squadron, by name Liddell, was a very different type; he was as calm as Hawker was highly strung. He died superbly as a result of being mortally wounded in the air and flying back a long distance to save his observer and make his report. He succumbed to his wounds soon afterwards, and his V.C. was posthumous. Will and spirit in such deeds were exalted over the physical in a supreme degree. His was not the only case of men dying of wounds soon after landing, having flown their aircraft back a great distance. It seemed that the will alone held the spark of life until the task was done; it was extinguished as will relaxed.

Hawker was quicksilver compared to the steel of such natures. It would have been difficult to guess from his manner or appearance that he would be a V.C., yet he was one of the greatest of them all. He was very intelligent, nervous, and acutely sensitive to the conditions under which we were living. In the mess he would almost jump from his chair if someone dropped a plate. The continued noise during our daily flights had really affected him as, in different ways and varying degrees, it touched us all. Noise was to my mind the worst part of the war, whether on the ground or in the air. In the trenches the earth naturally received a great deal of the shock of shellfire, while it always seemed to me that explosions in the air were mostly absorbed by the aircraft and its occupants. I do not know if this sensation has any scientific basis; it may simply have been an illusion fostered by the greater loneliness of the air. You were up there by yourself while apparently the whole world shot at you, the hatred of mankind concentrated upon you. Certainly the whoof or crash of shells bursting round us continually during about three hours of the reconnaissance each day affected us all in various ways.

Hawker would never eat or drink before he flew, not even a cup of coffee. He would simply walk up and down while we were waiting in the morning, nerves on edge. This concerned me greatly during the considerable period I was his observer, because there was a belief then current that a pilot might faint in the air if he flew on an empty stomach. It had not much basis in fact, but in the early days of flying we were full of such legends; it was a new subject in a sphere new to man. Yet try as I would, I could never persuade him to eat anything. All was nerves until the take-off; then the man was transformed as the wheels left the ground. He was of all men I knew the boldest, perhaps the most reckless, certainly the most utterly indifferent to personal safety when a sense of duty was involved.

He would not play any of the tricks to avoid heavy fire, like zigzagging within the squares or turning the nose of the machine a point or two off the wind to cause a drift which deceived the gunner. He would go straight across the middle of the square of guns in case any evasive action impeded observation, and, worse still, if visibility was not clear, he would go down in the middle of the square to have a better look, thus presenting a closer and better target. This was one of the most trying operations to his observer, for he would throttle back the engine to descend and in a careless moment would sometimes lose it altogether. There was only one way to start these old engines again, which was to dive and thus make the air-rush swing the propeller. The most likely explanation of this sudden dive to the observer in front was that the pilot had been hit and had fallen forward on the joystick, as we used to call it. The only possible course of action then was to unfasten the seat-belt, struggle round in the narrow cockpit and try to lift the pilot in the rear seat off the stick. The reassuring climax was the grinning face of Hawker as he pulled the machine out of the dive with a triumphant roar of an engine re-started.

Fighting in the air was at that time not much developed because we had not yet got machine-guns and were simply supplied with the old short cavalry carbine. The nightmare of the pilot was that the observer would accidentally shoot through the propellor, so these rather ineffective combats were not very eagerly sought. But Hawker, even on a long reconnaissance, would turn round to engage several German machines at once miles behind the lines, even if to the hazard of the combat was added the risk of running out of petrol on the way back. The bundle of nerves before the take-off became berserk in the air. This contrast between previous nerves and subsequent action is a phenomenon to be observed in outstanding performance in very diverse circumstances; for example, in Lloyd George before a speech.

Hawker would take risks for fun, a rare characteristic in the middle of a war, and was always on the look-out for new sensations and experience of flying. Unfortunately I had spent some time as observer to an experienced pilot who was most expert in the trick then called tail-sliding, to which the BE2C was particularly well adapted. The pilot pulled back the stick as in the beginning of a loop until the machine was vertical with the nose pointing upwards: the aircraft would then slide tail first towards the ground, giving at any rate one occupant the sickening sensation of having left his stomach behind him a long way up in the air. The pilot would then throttle back the engine and the nose would come down, taking the machine into a dive from which the BE2C recovered in 2,000 feet, but not before. My old pilot used occasionally to perform this akward feat in sheer *joie de vivre* above the aerodrome to celebrate our return from some trying mission. I always felt that these performances might or might not be all right for the pilot who controlled the situation and had his own life in his hands, but they were not so entertaining for the observer, who had no effective say in the business.

However, I was unwisely persuaded by Hawker one day to go up with him for his first attempt at this trick in order to inform him if he did everything as correctly as the expert had done. Arriving at the necessary altitude, he stood the machine on its tail in proper form and we started the slide, but in his forgetful fashion he omitted to throttle the engine back at the right time. The consequence was that the nose of the BE2C remained in the air and we fell in this way much farther than usual. Again I had to struggle round in the narrow cockpit to indicate that the engine should be throttled back. When this was done we were unpleasantly near the ground, and the question arose acutely whether the BE2C would come out of its protracted dive before we hit it. We emerged just in time, skimming low over the aerodrome hangars. After a moment's pause for reflection I noticed that the aircraft was climbing once more and again I turned round. Hawker indicated that he was going up again to have another go. I equally firmly intimated not with me. He then put me down in the gathering dusk and a developing snowstorm. Nothing daunted, he went off alone, and did it to his own satisfaction. Such is the stuff that V.C.s are made of. Hawker's early death was a tragedy and a continuing loss to his country, for his gifts and qualities would through a long life have given it high and enduring service.

The tragedy was always masked by gaiety. The extreme, almost exaggerated gaiety of those who flew on each side has been noted recently in films which have skilfully reproduced much technical detail but have been less successful in their characterisation. It was perhaps necessary to live with those men to understand why this gaiety was a necessity, sustaining an attitude to life which has never yet been correctly portrayed. In short and crude expression, a dinner-party of intimate friends has to be merry if night after night there is a strong possibility that some of those present will not be there the following evening. In the trenches casualties could, of course, be terribly heavy, but, in a strange sense, death was more natural in those bleak and sinister surround-ings. We were like men having dinner together in a country house-party, knowing that some must soon leave us for ever; in the end, nearly all. This experience must also have been familiar to pilots and air crews in the Second World War.

An attitude later became clear to me which was at first incomprehensible and something of a shock. Soon after I arrived with the squadron, we were in a truck just starting a short journey into the town to lunch after the morning reconnaissance, when one of our machines came in to land obviously rather out of control after being badly shot up. It hit the ground, bounced and turned over on its back with a crash which smashed it badly; by a lucky chance it did not then catch fire in the usual fashion. I jumped out and started to run toward the machine to help pull out its occupants. Shouts came from the truck—'Where are you off to?—Come on, jump up—we are late for lunch—The men on duty will see to that lot'. Off we drove. The pilot and observer in the crashed machine were very popular, yet not a word was said about them. Suddenly they appeared in the doorway, very much the worse for wear, but—surprisingly—alive. Roars of laughter resounded through the little room—'Well, well, we thought we had got rid of you that time—never mind, have a drink'. Packets of back-chat ensued. That was the way of it, and it was the only way.

The R.F.C. celebrated the same spirit in its own macabre songs in the lugubrious, humorous tradition of the British army. These men were nearly all officers of the small regular army who had volunteered to fly in the early days, an élite of a *corps d'élite*. On a convivial occasion they would break into a long, sad but merry chant whose title was 'The Dying Aviator'. He was expressing his last wishes after a fatal crash, in which he had suffered multifarious mutilations described in bloody detail. A little depressing were some of the melancholy lines enjoining with much technical terminology the careful removal of various engine parts from the more delicate regions of the human frame. In fact, the legendary warrior was particularly fortunate, for he was not burned alive. We had in that period no parachutes, and men had to stay with the machine until it crashed. The flimsy contraption of wood and canvas would then almost invariably catch fire as the petrol exploded from the burst tank. The most fortunate were those killed instantly in the crash, or first shot dead.

My most interesting experience during the whole of this time had nothing directly to do with flying. At the beginning of the second battle of Ypres in April 1915, the Canadian Expeditionary Force had just arrived in the line for the first time, and we were detailed to work with them in spotting enemy guns and directing their fire upon the German batteries by morse signals. I was instructed to make contact with them and to take with me a wireless mast to receive these messages. On a calm spring day I set out in an R.F.C. truck and duly reached the Canadian guns at the usual distance behind the lines without incident. It was our habit to drive about in these trucks, often within enemy range, and as that part of the line happened to be quiet, it was rare for them to spot it or take the trouble to open fire. This had only happened once before, soon after my arrival with the R.F.C. and was the first time I came under fire. I stopped with the truck in a small wood where there were no marks of enemy fire, thinking we would be unnoticed, but we were spotted and heavily shelled. The little wood was in splinters but we escaped unscathed. I remember writing to my mother a delighted letter about the incident, because I experienced the common sensation of a great exhilaration at coming under fire for the first time, a peculiar ecstasy which soon wore off.

I reported to the Canadian guns that there was no particular reason for anticipating trouble that afternoon, although some rather abnormal troop concentrations on the other side had been noted from air reconnaissance. The work was soon finished by the corporal and two men accompanying me who were expert in the job, of which I knew little or nothing. Meantime, I had established genial relations with some of the Canadian officers, and having the rest of the day at my disposal, decided to send the truck home and stay with them a little longer. In these quiet conditions it would not be difficult to get a lift back to Poperinghe before nightfall for my usual work next morning.

All went well in the small, shallow dug-out where I was being generously entertained, until suddenly the Germans opened the heaviest barrage which the war had so far produced. Any movement appeared now to be out of the question; for the time being there was nothing for it but to sit tight in our little hole of earth and hope that we would not stop a direct hit. The barrage went on for what seemed to be an interminable period of time while the whole earth shook. This period of dull, tense waiting was eventually interrupted by something then completely novel. We noticed a curious acrid smell and at the same time a slight feeling of nausea. Someone said gas, and advised us all to urinate on our handkerchiefs and place them over our mouths and noses; above all we must make no movement which required deep breathing. It was the first gas attack of this war or any other. The advice we received was good, for this gas was not very lethal. The consequences were only severe to those who moved and breathed deeply, absorbing much of it into their lungs.

Shortly afterwards it became known that the combination of this exception-ally heavy barrage and the completely new experience of the gas attack had resulted in the entire exposure of our left flank, which had been held by French colonial troops. The Canadian commander was thus confronted with the hard choice of retreating to prevent the turning of his flank, or throwing in his reserve to cover the exposed position on his left; he chose to stand, and the order came to hold our line as it was. At this point it appeared highly probable that we would be encircled, and the commanding officer of our battery ordered me at once to make my way as best I could back to our unit at Poperinghe. It was useless to add fortuitously a Flying Corps officer to the possible loss, and on return to my squadron I could give some account of what had happened; the barrage by this time had rendered all communication very difficult.

I set out on foot, as no transport was available, and in any case it had no chance of survival under a fire of that intensity. From a small rise in the ground in the first stage of my return journey I looked back to see what was happen-ing. It was an unforgettable spectacle. As dusk descended there appeared to our left the blue-grey masses of the Germans advancing steadily behind their lifting curtain of fire, as steadily as if they had been on the parade ground at Potsdam. At that point it appeared there was nothing to stop them. Some of these extraordinary troops were already legendary to all on our side who could appreciate such values because they themselves were members of an outstanding *corps d'élite*, the British regular army.

We had heard the stories of the first battle of Ypres when the Prussian

Guard came out to attack, with the officers in front drawing on their white gloves as if they were walking towards a routine inspection. One of my fellow-officers—an observer of the Royal Flying Corps who had been in command of some British guns in that battle—described to me how some of them had exceeded their objective and came within a few hundred yards of his battery without support of any kind. A small party of them passed into a little declivity in the ground where they disappeared from view, but it was clear they were completely isolated and in a hopeless situation. So he sent over a few men with a white flag to require their surrender. They were found lying down in the small hollow. The young officer in charge said they could not surrender as that was against the principles of the Prussian Guard. They were exhausted, but when they recovered they would continue the advance; they were aware they had no chance. After a brief respite, they came out towards the guns, the young officer in front with his sword at the carry and all of them doing the ceremonial goose-step for the last time; they were all killed.

It was a performance utterly useless and incomprehensible to the layman, but the purpose was clear to any practitioner of the science of war; troops of that spirit can and will do things which most troops cannot do, and they did. Capacity to appreciate a great enemy is one of the characteristics of the true soldier, accounting quite simply for the mysterious fraternity of arms which some have regarded as blameworthy. This spirit was evinced when the airmen on each side sometimes dropped wreaths to mourn the death of a great opponent held in honour for his courage and chivalry. It is not to be regarded with suspicion as a sinister emanation of the military mind, but rather welcomed as a spark of hope for Europe, when in some future a transcendent spirit of youth, courage and natural nobility will surmount this period of bitter passions and dark revenges.

It is sad that in recent years it has been left to Russian rather than to Western films to portray the great enemy with truth, as he was; it is also dangerous to the cause which neglects it, because such art can influence in a high degree the minds and spirits of men. The communist state with all its detestation of Western values has often in its cinema approached with something near truth the force which inspires the other side. A notable example is the beginning of the remarkable Soviet film of Tolstoy's *War and Peace*; another is Eisenstein's extraordinary picture of the Teutonic knights coming out over the snow with the sun behind them to assail the motherland of Russia. When I saw it in later life in all the power of its order, dignity and dedicated purpose, my mind went back to that afternoon when I saw the élite German regiments advancing in the gathering dusk at Ypres. To understand men, and above all the highest motives within them—whether rightly or wrongly applied, that is another question—is to lay a true and durable foundation of the great reconciliation.

The aim now must be to take the noble inspirations which have been used on all sides for dark purposes of destruction and to unite them in the great synthesis which will make possible the creative future. Hegel in his *Philosophy of History* presents a brilliant image of the vast destructive powers of nature, fire, wind, water being finally harnessed to the purposes of man for creative achievement. So too in the European future the fierce passions which divided and destroyed us can be overcome, and the sublime spirit of duty, sacrifice and high endeavour then imprisoned within them and distorted to the service of war will be released in a union of all high things to make Europe and save mankind. The noble though inarticulate instincts of youth were of this nature, and all the squalor of a life in politics has not yet extinguished the spark which flew from the anvil of 1914.

I had little time for such reflection as I made my way through the barrage towards the Ypres–Menin road, which I knew from our work of reconnaissance was my shortest way home. Very soon on my journey I encountered some other extraordinary troops, the equal in their totally different fashion to the best of the Germans. It was the Canadian reserves moving up to occupy the empty section of the line. They were an astonishing spectacle to a regular soldier, for they were advancing apparently without any discipline at all under a fire so intense that by our standards any advance would have been impossible except by the finest troops under the most rigorous discipline. They were laughing and talking and walking along in any formation, while the heavy shells we called Jack Johnsons—after the Negro boxing champion: they were 5·9s and capable of wiping out a whole platoon with one explosion—were crashing among them in the most severe concentration of artillery fire men had yet known. They seemed not to care a damn, they just came on. Very soon after I passed through them—as we afterwards learned—they went right into the advancing Germans and that event very rare in war occurred, a bayonet fight in which both sides stood firm. Three days later the R.F.C. were engaged in trying to delineate the still indeterminate line after the changes brought about by the failed attack. I reported that the line went through a place called St. Julien where heavy fighting was taking place in what had been the little town. It turned out at that time to be considerably behind the actual line. Some two hundred of the Canadians had forced their way right through, and when surrounded, fought to the last rather than surrender. That spirit lived in both sides.

It was an awkward meeting with them on the way back to report to the squadron, for it was at least peculiar that an officer wearing the badges of the 16th Lancers and saying he was with the Flying Corps should be coming from the direction of the enemy advance. However, the English voice and possibly some incipient flair for politics soon convinced them. They told me that all troop movements through Ypres were forbidden that night, as a concentration of fire on the town had rendered it impossible. I decided to ignore the order, for I was then imbued with the fatalism of war, was dead tired and felt an obligation to rejoin the squadron as quickly as possible. I went straight through Ypres.

Then came the strangest experience. I found myself quite alone in the middle of the great square, spellbound for a moment by the enduring vision. Many of the glories of that architecture were already in ruins, and entirely in flames. Noble buildings collapsed in a sad fatigue born not of centuries but of a moment of bitterness, like a child's house of cards under a wanton hand, as heavy shells descended in direct hits. Too young for full consciousness, I yet felt some premonition of the sorrow: what the Europeans were capable of doing to each other; the waste, the tragic absurdity.

I went on, rejoined the squadron at Poperinghe, made my report and returned to my lodging and to bed, where I fell into the deepest sleep. An hour or two later I woke as a nearby house went up with a heavy explosion. The Germans had already advanced their guns and brought Poperinghe within shelling range. I hurried round to the mess and was told we had to get out at once, as there would soon be little left of the aerodrome or of our aircraft. The pilots flew out the machines at once and the observers were responsible for the loading of the lorries and the evacuation of all stores. I rode out under fairly heavy fire perched on a load of bombs.

Once the second battle of Ypres was over, the attack halted and a new line determined, the normal task of reconnaissance or working with guns was resumed. Boredom interrupted by terror, as someone well put it. The observers with some experience were now offered the opportunity of being trained as pilots. It seemed well worthwhile, for our lives would then at least to some degree be in our own hands. In desperate affairs there is always the desire to take action yourself, however great your confidence in the other man's decision and judgment. It is the natural desire of a back-seat driver to move to the front when it is a matter of life or death.

Another consideration was that by this time I had become quite a bit the worse for wear. During a reconnaissance a partly spent piece of shell had hit me on the head and knocked me unconscious; it had not penetrated my flying-helmet and must have struck flatly rather than with the sharp edge. But the blow was sufficient to leave me with slight concussion, manifest in nothing more serious than recurrent headaches which I never otherwise suffered. On another occasion return in a damaged machine had ended in the pond at the corner of Poperinghe aerodrome with a crash that threw me forward in the cockpit and damaged my knee; I walked with some difficulty. The opportunity to acquire the desired pilot's wings, coupled with these disabilities, decided me to accept the offer of a training course. After a visit to a skilful bone-setter in London who put the knee right, and a short spell of leave and rest at home, I reported for duty at the Flying School at Shoreham, near Brighton.

The aerodrome at Shoreham was small and badly placed, next to the river.

A take-off over the river was fairly frequent in the prevailing winds and resulted in a good bump soon after the wheels left the ground, when the nose of the machine was elevated and the flying speed low; the transition from land to water in these slow and clumsy machines always produced this shock. Early aircraft simply wallowed in these air pockets which might push the nose up, tail up, or one wing down, and needed instant correction to prevent a stall, a dive or a side-slip. It was not therefore a good idea to give beginners conditions in which a certain wind direction was bound to produce a severe land–water bump soon after take-off. In this position too an engine failure— which was frequent in early days—meant a descent in the river. However, these were war conditions and everything had to be arranged in a hurry. I noticed that in later years the position of the aerodrome was changed.

We lived in agreeable conditions in a bungalow town near the aerodrome. It was possible to hire a cheap and individual bungalow, and my mother came to stay with me for a time. Training was pushed ahead at a speed incredible to later generations. If I remember rightly, I had only about an hour and a half of instructional flying before my first solo flight. There was an advantage in having been an observer, for this gave one the flying sense. But it cut both ways, as it was liable to make a beginner over-confident. It was better in the early days to be a little nervous and on the look-out for mishaps. It was remarkable even in the case of experienced war pilots how many of them were killed in ordinary flying, apart from the war, through over-confidence and carelessness. You could not take any chances with early aircraft.

My training went smoothly and I took my pilot's test, which consisted of doing figures of eight over the aerodrome, and making a few reasonably good landings. I remember on that day I put up a particularly bad show by making some ill-judged and rough landings. However, I was awarded my certificate, which was marked something over 1200; the precious document was lost in my Irish house fire in the fifties.

Until then I had been in no serious difficulty, except on one occasion on a river take-off when I had forgotten to fasten my seat-belt. This was very foolish as in a bad bump in these machines you could easily be thrown right out, and we were strenuously warned never to forget to fasten ourselves in securely. Consequently, when I arrived over the river just after take-off and encountered the usual bump, I found myself shot from my seat and would have been thrown out if I had not been firmly holding the joy-stick, by which I quickly pulled myself back again. It was lucky that in the struggle the machine was not stalled. That was at least one mistake which I should never make again.

My flying was not bad, though I was weak on the mechanical side. We were not obliged to take it seriously, as there were no difficult exams on the subject, but we had to go through an engine and rigging course. My rather exaggerated pragmatism in never giving my energy to anything which has no practical use and does not interest me, led me to miss the opportunity to acquire some mechanical skill. My argument was that once in the air you could do nothing about it if anything went wrong, and on the ground the machine was looked after by our good friends the mechanics and riggers, who had years of experience and far more knowledge than I should have time to acquire, even if I had the aptitude, which I much doubted. Some of us were perhaps encouraged in this resistance to mechanical knowledge by the example of the most famous pre-war airman, Gustave Hamel, a genius at flying, who boasted his complete ignorance of mechanics.

At Shoreham I gave striking proof of a capacity to make mistakes soon after taking my pilot's certificate—though as usual in our errors in life, chance played its part. It was a day of normal routine flying with a fairly strong, gusty wind. The direction of the wind was indicated not by a wind-funnel sock, but by a T, a wood and canvas frame pivoted on the ground in the shape of a T with the cross-piece facing the wind. I may have been in the mood for some mild exhibition within the narrow limits of my knowledge and capacity as pilot, because my mother had come to watch and was standing at a corner of the hangar with my instructor, who was also a good friend. While I was up the wind changed direction so suddenly that there was not time to shift the T, which was on the far side of the ground and I failed to notice from smoke or other usually discernible signs what had happened. Consequently I made what I thought would be a rather fast, clean landing in the direction of the hangars—a direction which had previously been correct. But owing to the change of wind, the landing speed was considerably greater than I had intended. The machine hit the ground with a bang and was thrown high into the air. It was instantly clear to me that if I continued to attempt a landing I would crash into the hangars, so I opened the engine to full throttle, pulled back the stick and just cleared the hangars. My mother turned to express her admiration to my instructor for the skilful and pretty fashion in which her boy had bounced, but he was missing; for he was, of course, all too well aware of what was happening, and had gone to make ready for a probable disaster.

It was something of a miracle that the engine picked up quickly enough to lift the aircraft over the hangars, but the acute question then arose, what to do next? It was easy sitting out in front of a Morris Farman Longhorn to look down and see that the undercarriage was badly damaged. This meant that a normal landing might entail its collapse, with the result that the nose would enter the ground at speed and the engine would come on top of me; these machines with the engine behind involved this hazard, whereas an aircraft with the engine in front might offer nothing worse than standing up on its nose or turning over on its back.

I decided to turn round and attempt a slow, pancake landing. This meant coming in so slowly, yet without stalling, that the aircraft lost flying speed at exactly the right height and fell flat to the ground. If it lost speed too high above the ground the nose would go down and the fatal crash with engine in the back could occur. If it did not lose flying speed until too late, the under-carriage would make contact with the ground at speed in the way of a normal landing and would collapse with the same result.

With some difficulty, I managed to make a pancake landing, but from a considerable height and with a crash which was consequently severe, though the loss of flying speed did not occur high enough for the nose to come down and cause a disaster. It was a true pancake landing, but a heavy shock. My legs were driven hard into the floor of the cockpit and injured, one of them severely. Strangely enough, as sometimes happens with severe shock, I felt nothing much at the time as I was completely numb. I even managed to walk from the machine, and was unaware of the extent of the hurt until later, when the pain and swelling began. I got leave and went back to the bone-setter, but was informed that the injury was much more considerable this time. The treatment was not entirely successful; I could walk, but with some difficulty.

During this period I had news that my regiment required officers, because that spring they had suffered severe losses, particularly of officers, from the explosion of mines in the front line. I was in a dilemma, as I wanted to com-plete my training course and return to the R.F.C. as a pilot, but on the other hand felt that my first duty was to my regiment. This was the over-riding reason which decided me to return—it was not an order but a choice—yet I may have been influenced also by a desire to have the two experiences, air and the trenches. I was still moved in some degree by the strange desire to have all experience of this extraordinary and, as we believed, unique event. Duty and inclination therefore to some extent coincided. It was a sad fact that there was no longer any difficulty in getting to the front with the 16th Lancers.

First, I had to face a medical board to be pronounced fit again for war service. It was something of an ordeal, as the outcome was a bit dubious. Fortunately there was not much walking to be done, and they looked at everything except my leg. I calculated that there would not be all that walking in the trenches either, as it was mostly an affair of sitting tight—shooting and being shot at—and I had a reasonable hope that my condition would pro-gressively improve. I was right at first about the walking, as on my return to the Curragh we were nearly always on horseback, and this was also the case when I rejoined the regiment and found them at first behind the lines and with the horses.

Before long, in the early autumn of 1915, I was ordered to go in a troopship to France with a draft under the command of another 16th Lancer who was an old friend. We did not know, of course, where we would land, but to our happiness found ourselves going up the Seine and through the beautiful

Norman country; it was my first peaceful panorama of the France I have
come to love so much. We disembarked at Rouen, but I was either too hurried
or too ignorant on that occasion to see the cathedral or the other glories.
From Rouen we went by train to our destination, also unknown, and by some
skill of staff work came under shell-fire at a town near the front line—Béthune,
if I remember rightly. This exercise seemed to us redundant, as the regiment
at that time was quite a long way back—near Hazebrouk, again if I remember
rightly.

There we had the usual warm welcome, and found some old friends of the
first days at the Curragh. Colonel Eccles was commanding the regiment, and
the Adjutant was Lord Holmpatrick, who had the curious christian name for
an Irishman of Hans; he was one of the best-looking men I have ever seen
and was extremely efficient. My squadron was commanded by a distinguished
and kindly Indian Army officer by name Fraser, who had been attached to us.
He was distinguished because he had been decorated for his part in the
famous charge of the 9th Lancers when a Grenfell won the V.C. I was given
as charger a fine hunter, supplemented by a polo pony which was useful for
riding around the countryside trying to chase hares until they were exhausted;
a sport and a dinner. Life for the moment was agreeable. I was put in charge
of the squadron mess, but soon sacked for doing us too well; the fare was
appreciated but the bills were not.

These tranquil and happy days did not last long. An order came that all
officers who had no experience of the trenches should be attached for a period
to infantry. I had to report to a Welsh battalion, composed largely of
ex-miners. They were good troops, but they had been in the line a long time,
suffering heavy losses, and were generally feeling they had had more than
enough of that war. Men were suffering a good deal from what was called
trench-foot, a form of frostbite aggravated by damp and caused by standing
around too long in cold water.

Prevention was regarded by high authority as better than cure, but not all
the men took the same view. The orders were to seize every occasion to leave
the trench and do stamping exercises to promote circulation of blood in the
feet. This could only be done in foggy conditions, which were frequent at that
time of year, as our trench was not much more than fifty yards from the enemy
and in his full view. Life was depressing enough in these conditions in the fog
without scrambling out to do a lot of gymnastics. Such was the view of the
troops most forcibly expressed, and it took all the admirable tact of the officers
who understood them well and were on the best of terms with them to turn
the whole thing into a bit of a joke and thus to secure the fulfilment of the
orders without much ill humour.

At first life was reasonably quiet on the enemy side, but suddenly everything
came to life and day and night was one long strafe, as it was called. Old hands
knew at once from experience what had occurred: the Prussian Guard had

arrived. Being at close quarters with these remarkable troops, we responded to their continual mortar and grenade fire with rifle grenades. I took this habit with me to my troop in the regiment when we were next in the trenches, and it was good, except that these early grenades were liable on occasion to explode before they left the rifle.

The other grenades of the period were thrown by hand, and they were also a little tricky. They were called Mills bombs and operated by a spring once the safety-pin was withdrawn, which had to be held in place by the fingers until the bomb was thrown; the explosion followed five seconds after the spring was released. Wiseacres who did not mind the risk would release the spring and still hold the bomb for two or three seconds before throwing. This had two advantages, that it could thus be made to explode in the air above the enemy with more lethal effect, and would not be caught by some wide-awake athlete and thrown back before explosion. But it had the disadvantage that some Mills bombs exploded less than five seconds after the spring was released, with unpleasant results if still held. We were just too far to throw these weapons from our trench into a German trench, so they could only be used by crawling around no-man's-land at night. The rifle grenades on the other hand had a reasonable range and we could lob them over easily while comfortably ensconced in our own trench.

Life was always merry in the current fashion when confronted by the Prussian Guard, who believed in the principle of the perpetual initiative, which in this context meant continual fire varied with trench raids. Years later, after the Second World War, I discussed this idea with one of the best political intelligences Germany has produced. He said that the principle of the perpetual initiative was excellent in war and almost invariably paid off, but that in politics it could be a great mistake, as in this sphere it was sometimes better for a period just to sit tight.

Before this liveliness had continued very long, the Colonel came along the line to tell us that the arrival of the Prussian Guard usually meant something serious was afoot, and that he now had information from the Staff that they were likely to attack the following morning. He added for our encouragement that in this event he would recommend for the Military Cross any officer left alive and in the same position the following evening. I was left reflecting on the strange chances of these occasions; what option had I really got in this event, except to be killed or to win the Military Cross? It was life simplified. Clearly, if any of us had said: 'I think I prefer going home this evening to the winning of glory', it would not have been at all well received. In fact it would have had consequences—in the rough conditions of that war where psychology was not so deeply studied and political considerations were not so keenly appreciated—much more unpleasant and even more certainly fatal than staying in the trench. To surrender while still armed with a machine-gun and plenty of ammunition would clearly also be too ignoble to contemplate. So in simple practice there was nothing for it but to sit tight and shoot it out: result, therefore, death or Military Cross—it was as simple as that.

These reflections were finally curtailed by the eventually rather disappointing realisation that they were not going to attack. Nothing happened at all. They continued to make life very lively, but no more. The Prussian Guard were apparently there just to wake up this part of the line, which was one of their minor missions. The experience was most instructive, and in due course I returned to the regiment all the better for my sojourn with the infantry.

Soon the regiment was moved up to the scene of the Loos battle. We were in and out of the trenches for some time, alternating between a section which was disagreeable because we were often standing in water, and another sector which was on high ground and therefore dry, but with the disadvantage of suffering from a competition then prevalent in blowing each other up by means of mines. The regiment had considerable experience of this technique, having suffered terrible losses early in 1915 by enemy mines. The method was to tunnel under the opposing line, place a mine under their trench and explode it; then immediately to attack. By this time there was much expertise in the business; when one side began to make a tunnel, the other side would make a tunnel underneath it; tunnel would blow up tunnel. Even more finesse then entered the game. You would not tunnel but would make noises as if you were tunnelling beneath them, thus causing them to desist or to explode their mines prematurely. This was done crudely by pulling up and down a wet sack of sand with a dull thud in a hole dug sufficiently deep to make the sound realistic. The engineers had installed ingenious listening devices and instructed us in this whole technique. It was the war of moles supplemented by the most modern science then available. It was one of war's most disagreeable forms, because, if caught, you were liable to be buried alive.

I was more at home in the trenches than anywhere else, for a particular reason. The worst part of my life at that time was getting to and from the trenches. We moved up through communication trenches floored by duckboards to keep us out of the mud. Because these boards were much used they developed many holes, which could not be seen in the dark. My worst leg used to go through them with a result not only painful but temporarily disabling. The men on these occasions used to assist me with the most sympathetic friendship, and were, of course, enjoined not to say a word. Once installed in the trench I was quite all right, because any movement outside it was limited and in any case usually done on hands and knees.

At that time I developed a considerable sympathy with an act of indiscipline which it was my duty as an officer to prevent. The men always wanted to go up to the front line not through the squalid misery of the twisting communication trenches but over the top where the going was better. This risked losing one or two among us before we got to the front line, as a good deal of shooting was always going on. Yet it is an interesting fact of human psychology that at a certain degree of fatigue and boredom men lose all fear of death, just as people at the end of a long illness can be observed almost to embrace it. Rather than endure that long, weary tramp through the muddy communication trench, troops would prefer to risk death by marching over the relatively firm and easy open ground. There comes a limit to the nuisance of life in some conditions.

There was too a certain exhilaration in going up over the top at night. Lights fired into the air continually from each side illuminated the night sky, and the whistle of passing bullets contributed to the eerie beauty of the stark surroundings. There was a certain tragic loveliness in that unearthly desolation, the ultimate nihilism of man's failed spirit. Also, for many at that stage a wound could seem a release, and death was peace. Higher command naturally and rightly took another view: life must not be risked unnecessarily. Discipline had to be enforced, though I was particularly susceptible to the discomfort and pain of the tedious trudge below ground.

What mattered at that point of war was noise, whether in the air or in the trench. It was the constant, grinding shock of noise that wore men down. It was always said that all troops broke at a certain point of the bombardment, with the great regiments, of course, at a far higher degree than the lesser. I was always convinced that it was the sustained noise that did it, not the fear of death, which men at a certain point of weariness and war nausea almost entirely lost. That was why I always felt that absorbing the full shock of shell-fire during a three-hour reconnaissance in the air was even more trying than a much longer bombardment on the ground; it was such concentrated noise.

Men with the long habit of war hardly minded the rifle or machine-gun fire —that light, relatively agreeable zip past the ear—nothing would gravely affect them except the days-long ground-shattering roar of the bombardment which usually preceded an attack. Even the light whizz-bangs—as we called them—would not disturb them much, though they were more dangerous, because you could not hear them coming, than the heavy shells which signalled their arrival with a protracted whistle, and gave you time to scrabble in the mud. Noise, coupled with heavy concussion, most affected health and spirits.

The barrage I had experienced at the second battle of Ypres was worse than anything encountered at that time in the aftermath of the second battle of Loos, though it was a lively section of the line with a regular and severe morning and evening bombardment. The main pre-occupation, however, was the constant mining which required continual alertness. It was the explosion of a mine in the front line while we were in support trenches which exposed me to my most difficult physical test. My injured leg had been gradually deteriorating; it became more painful with movement and was much swollen.

Standing for long periods in water in one section of the line had done no good to the injured bones, which had not entirely set. In particular, it was difficult suddenly to move from a recumbent position. Like a lame horse, I would warm up when I got going, but if I had been asleep it was difficult to rest any weight on the leg directly I woke up.

I was asleep one night on the fire-step of a support trench when a mine exploded in the front line and we had to go up in a hurry. When I awoke, as usual I could put no weight on the leg at all. So it was a matter of hopping when the ground was firm, or going on hands and knees where it was too muddy for hopping. However, I kept up, and got there.

News of my condition eventually got around, and reached the ears of Colonel Eccles. There was a strong degree of paternalism in the colonels of these great regiments, which were conducted very like a large family. He sent for me and put me through some simple tests. I did not see him again until my wedding day in 1920, for the following morning I was on my way home by his arrangement and pursuant to his orders. A great surgeon, Sir Watson Cheyne, was on the point of retirement, but fortunately his son was a 16th Lancer and he took a special interest in my case. He warned me that only a fifty-fifty chance of saving the leg existed, which was in a sorry state after long neglect. He operated, and his skill saved the leg, though after a second operation towards the end of 1916 it was an inch and a half shorter. I had entered the war in the category A1, and left it in the category C3, fit for office work only.

The administrative and other experience which I gained from this exclusion from war belongs to another part of this story. I had seen enough in the air and in the trenches to be left with one resolve, some may say obsession: war must never happen again. We British, of these islands and the Empire, lost in that war 1,089,939 dead; over double the British losses in the Second World War, in which, in addition, at least 25,000,000 Europeans, military and civilian, lost their lives. There was no fun in our war; there was no fun in the Second World War for men or women who fought or suffered. The vast fact of such experience remains always with those who really know.

At the Armistice in 1918 I passed through the festive streets and entered one of London's largest and most fashionable hotels, interested by the sounds of revelry which echoed from it. Smooth, smug people, who had never fought or suffered, seemed to the eyes of youth—at that moment age-old with sadness, weariness and bitterness—to be eating, drinking, laughing on the graves of our companions. I stood aside from the delirious throng, silent and alone, ravaged by memory. Driving purpose had begun; there must be no more war. I dedicated myself to politics, with an instinctive resolution which came later to expression in my speeches: 'Through and beyond the failure of men and of parties, we of the war generation are marching on and we shall march on until our end is achieved and our sacrifice atoned'. What did it mean? What end? What atonement?—this sentiment of youth, which was then only instinct without shape? It meant surely that war must never happen again, that we must build a better land for our companions who still lived, that we must conceive a nobler world in memory of those who died. We later gave form to instinct, and clear will to passionate resolve; we failed once, but that purpose remains and will endure to the end.

4
The Gaining
of Experience

IT is easier to rise from a bed of thorns than from a bed of roses. I make this strange observation at this point because if any credit is due to me, it is on account of the deliberate choice of a hard life in pursuit of certain purposes rather than the altogether delightful existence which circumstances and my temperament offered to me. I had an unlimited capacity for enjoyment, and fortune had given me the means to indulge it. Moreover, once my war service was over there seemed no particular reason why I should not do so, provided my war companions received what they had been so firmly promised. In fact, I have sometimes wondered why I did not just relax and enjoy life. Why trouble so much with the attempt to make better a world which seemed quite content with the bad?

The question struck me years later, during a period of adversity, when a public official of ability and insight told me that he had always wanted to meet me to see whether I was mad or not; he was surprised to discover when he got to know me well that I was sane. He considered that any man must prima facie be mad if his whole career contradicted his own interest and comfort. It was easy to make the obvious reply that politics had come to a pretty pass if a sensible fellow like him thought a man must be mad if he did not put what he conceived to be the interest of his country and of humanity before his own interest. Yet it was inevitable that I myself should sometimes wonder if there were not better, more profitable and happier things to do than insist on saving people who were bent on drowning.

Let me not be misunderstood: I do not pretend to be a saint, let alone a Puritan. I always seized every opportunity to enjoy life to the full, provided it did not impede my purpose, and many opportunities came my way. But I gave a clear priority to purpose, an attitude which is simply commonsense. Any other course means that boundless capacity and considerable opportunity for enjoyment always win, or at least confront you with a continuing series of agonising choices between duty and pleasure. He who hesitates between the Grail and the Venusberg is lost. But happily there are moments of repose. Life should be a march toward great objectives, but with time to warm your hands before camp fires, a process which preserves both sanity and energy.

At first there was no conflict; purpose and pleasure entirely coincided. Clearly the way to getting things done was to enter politics, and I was offered a choice of the primrose paths with much classic tinkling of the lutes and flutes. This account will now be for many pages a success story. The summits of private happiness were balanced by the heights of public acclamation. It began directly I emerged from hospital in the war and continued for a good fifteen years. I enjoyed every moment of it. There was no conflict between purpose and happiness because during this period it still seemed possible to do what was necessary by normal and reasonable means. We, of the war generation, had not really believed all the guff turned out by the politicians —'a land fit for heroes to live in' and so forth—at least most of us had not. But we had thought that a decent home and living wage could be provided for our companions, who survived the war, because it seemed so relatively easy to do. Yet they had to wait until after a second world war for the precarious possession of a living wage, and many of them are waiting still for the decent homes. It was the slow realisation that the old world could not or would not give these elementary things, and was heading instead towards further and possibly irretrievable disaster, which finally brought the choice between purpose and the normal way of life which could have given me not only security but much happiness.

It might have been different in another age. There are periods in history when change is necessary, and other periods when it is better to keep everything for the time as it is. The art of life is to be in the rhythm of your age. This is clearly a great age when decisions can vitally effect the whole future of mankind, perhaps in this sense the greatest age the world has known. It is, therefore, a privilege to be alive at such a moment, but scarcely a happiness to those who are fully conscious of the potential of modern science and of the consequent politics. The necessity for effort is inherent in the age's sense of destiny. It had been evoked for me strongly by the experience of the war, and by the duty to make what recompense was possible.

I do not know whether in another epoch I would just have sustained the serene equilibrium of a tranquil world, and the enjoyment of private happiness, for I always feel urging me to effort the practical sense of the engineer who finds it difficult to leave by the wayside broken machines which he knows he is competent to mend, and in human affairs there are always plenty of defective machines inviting attention. Perhaps I was a little like the young Pontifex in Samuel Butler's *The Way of All Flesh*, who never said the times are out of joint, oh cursed spite, for he always knew that he was just the lad to put them right. But in other periods these things can be done quietly; the trouble in this age is that the job is too big to be done quietly. Men have to be persuaded of the necessity for action, and that is a noisy business.

My training for the part I had to play in life was partly conscious and partly fortuitous. Consciously it began as soon as I was out of the war and into hospital. My reading was omniverous and voracious directly I was capable of anything. I wondered if I had missed much by not going to university, and interrogated my Oxford and Cambridge contemporaries in order to discover if they knew much that I did not. The results were reasonably satisfactory, for though like all autodidacts I found gaps in my knowledge, I learned things the universities would not have taught me.

Otherwise my time until the end of the war was occupied by a plunge into social life, which began on crutches in London and was pursued with zest through the ample opportunities then provided; followed by a return in happy circumstances to the Curragh, a period as instructor to wounded officers at Eastbourne which gave me more opportunity for reading, relieved again by some London life, and finally administrative experience in the Ministry of Munitions and then in the Foreign Office. All contributed to my political education, not least the social life, whose value in some stages of experience should by no means be dismissed or even underrated. It can be a fatal malady to elderly statesmen who enjoy it for the first time in later life, just as measles is more dangerous to the old than the young; infantile diseases should be experienced early. Regarded with plain sense, social life can have a recurrent value throughout life to those who understand its uses.

Society of this kind is an 'exchange and mart'. People can meet quietly and without commitment to exchange ideas about everything from politics to business. Some people use it to exchange other things; the mart element only enters in case of the old and inadequate, and is usually confined to the outer fringes. For the young it can have considerable value because it enables them to know a diversity of gifted and interesting people very quickly. Even for the nation it has some purpose, because it can teach good manners. A British mistake is to send either oafs or dull clerks to represent us in various capacities in European capitals where manners are appreciated, a habit which unfortunately has increased in recent years.

Meeting other people always has its uses if it does not consume too much time—ask me anything but time, said Bonaparte—but the practical value of this society in recent years has declined, for a clear reason. The pressure of life has increased, and less and less are the men and women who think and do to be met in society. The function of society—in the sense the word is used in this limited context—is to provide a meeting-ground for an élite where they can know each other better and be amused; interesting and entertaining talk is the bait which draws them together. The interest is reduced when important people are too busy to attend, and entertainment also declines when the hostesses of a more leisured and resourceful period are lacking. Society does not long exist in a worthwhile form when it is divorced from the life of the nation. It belongs not to the café but to the private house, where those who *do* meet those who *think*—by no means, unfortunately, always the same people—and no confidence is ever betrayed.

The conditions of a true society in this sense were present after and even during the First World War. In London and to a large extent in Paris its vitality was due to a subtle blend of charm and dynamism in the American hostesses who played a large part in both these capitals. I was plunged into it even before I left hospital, as I was permitted to go out on my crutches to luncheon. How and when in exact point of time I met these various people I cannot remember, but it is easy to recall their personalities and the characteristic background of their houses. The range of this experience, of course, extends far beyond the war, right through the twenties and into the thirties, but it is possibly of some interest to regard together the glittering concourse of the notable hostesses of those days. Foremost among them in England was Lady Cunard, a bright little bird of paradise who, I understand, has often been described in recent books. Her contribution to the life of society rested on considerable wit and limitless effrontery. She made things go with a vengeance. If talk flagged and the taciturn great would not perform, she would wake the company up with a direct frontal attack. 'Lord Hugh, I cannot believe you are really a Christian,' she would say to the most devoted member of a great political family particularly dedicated to the service of the Church of England. This method usually evoked conversation at its liveliest, but the sheer, reckless force of her impact would on occasions produce only a shattered silence from which she would recover instantly by darting off in a totally different direction; the bird of paradise in pursuit of another glittering and distracting insect of thought, or rather of imagination.

She was American, and lived in a corner of Grosvenor Square, which has since been almost entirely occupied and rebuilt by her country of origin. Her life in England began as the wife of Sir Bache Cunard, a Leicestershire squire, who had disappeared from the scene before I knew her. Her serious life in London was entirely given to music and to the assistance of Sir Thomas Beecham. Her social life also sometimes served the same end, for the fun of her house drew money as well as wit and intelligence like a magnet. She herself had considerable erudition which erupted in conversation at the most unexpected points, but on the whole the ladies present were selected for their beauty rather than their intelligence. She understood that society should consist of conversation by brilliant men against a background of lovely

and appreciative women, a process well calculated continually to increase the
supply of such men. These beauties were often of character simpler than their
appearance and used to wilt beneath their hostess's vivid and indeed florid
descriptions of their charms and attributes as they entered the assembled
company. A word in rejoinder was only possible and permitted to the brightest,
among whom was my second wife, Diana. Lady Cunard always called her
Golden Corn and insisted she must be her successor in London society; a
hope which was frustrated by her marriage to me, consequent politics, war
and again politics.

Lady Cunard would announce your name and record with the clarity of a
toastmaster at the Lord Mayor's banquet, and in her whimsical and audacious
fashion would sometimes add a few imaginary attributes not usually discussed on such formal occasions. It could require a face of brass to stand up
to the barrage of badinage and comment, but it was all enormous fun. The
cleverest met together with the most beautiful, and that is what social life
should be. She died not long after the Second World War, during which she
went to live in a hotel: I last saw her in the late forties. After her death her
fascinating affairs were arranged with the utmost discretion by my friend,
Sir Robert Abdy, the art connoisseur, who rightly cherished her memory as
another work of art. I miss the bird of paradise among the sparrows round
Roosevelt's statue in Grosvenor Square.

It is strange that so many of the outstanding hostesses of this period were
Americans, because in the previous generation before my time they were
mostly English. In that epoch Lady Londonderry—not Ramsay MacDonald's
friend, but her mother-in-law—was the most prominent on the Conservative
side, balanced on the Liberal side by Margot Asquith, who was the match of
any woman in wit and more than a match in audacity, but lacked the resources
and the large houses necessary to the ambience of society in that phase. She
alone survived into my time, but, of course, was then without the citadel of
Downing Street. Many beautiful and distinguished English women still
possessed fine houses and considerable resources, but it was the American
energy which made the society of that period, and not only in England.
Among all the brilliant Americans the only equal in wit to Lady Cunard was
Princess Jane di San Faustino, who ruled Roman society in the twenties,
and ruled it in American, resolutely refusing for the best part of half a century
to learn Italian.

Soon after I left hospital I was taken to the house of Maxine Elliott, the
American actress, who lived at Hartsbourne Manor, a few miles from London.
Later she migrated to the Château de l'Horizon at Antibes in the South of
France, where I used to visit her in the twenties. A great classic beauty, she
looked like a Roman Empress should have looked; massive, at once sombre
and serene. She organised her life on an orderly and severely practical basis;
everything had its clear purpose and proper place. Her two chief friends were

Pierpoint Morgan, the financier, and Wilding the tennis champion. The young and innocent wondered what each was for.

It was in her house that I first met F. E. Smith, later Lord Birkenhead, and I think it was also there that I met Winston Churchill for the first time. F.E. was a frequent guest, and he then used to take me to luncheon at the Ritz while I was still on crutches. Lunch took a long time and was of course enlivened by his caustic wit which became legendary. About this time he invited me to a river party which left by boat from the House of Commons under the command of another M.P., his friend Commander Warden Chilcott. A gay debate had previously arisen in F.E.'s house concerning which ladies should be invited; F.E.'s views happily prevailed. Opposite each man was a magnum of champagne, which I had sadly to renounce under hospital orders. We arrived at Taggs Island, where we dined very well, and subsequently embarked to face the problem of navigation on the return journey, which the gallant Commander found much more difficult than the outward trip. We soon ran aground, and appeared to be stuck fast for the night. There was nothing for it but to return on foot to Taggs Island and find other transport to London. The tortoise on crutches had not much trouble in winning the race from the well-dined hares. F.E. soon turned up, full of charming contrition that I had had such a doing in my delicate condition. He got hold of a car and a driver, and said he would at once personally take me back. No doubt in recompense for my trying experience, he began to tell me a story which we of the younger generation were agog to hear; the details of the celebrated row during his visit to G.H.Q. in France. I woke with Big Ben booming midnight chimes in my ears, as we passed the House of Commons, and F.E.'s voice booming too with indignation at the culmination of a long account of his dramatic experience. After the fatigue of my crutch race I had fallen asleep at once, and to this day I do not know the intriguing ramifications of that famous tale.

At Hartsbourne F.E. would often sit up till three or four in the morning talking in fashion entrancing or combative according to the company, but his merry sounds could usually be heard on the tennis court by seven next morning; the candle was burning at both ends. At a rather later stage Winston Churchill used to come there too, and nocturnal debate became very lively. F.E. had the readier and quicker wit, but by next morning Churchill usually had a complete answer after a night's sleep on it. Another visitor from politics was Freddie Guest, a chief whip of the Lloyd George Liberals, an energetic and enterprising man who combined politics and air-racing until he reached quite an advanced age. He suggested that I should enter Parliament under their banner at the post-war election, but I already had some engagement to that other formidable Whip, Sir George Younger, the chief organiser of the Conservative party. These two efficient men had different views of their duties. Freddie Guest always used to say a Whip should not think too much

about politics—mooning around in other people's business—but should get
on with his own department of organising. Younger, on the other hand, was
always a busy intriguer and once made a spectacular entry into the political
scene. He retreated for good under F.E.'s crushing enquiry:'Since when has
the cabin boy mounted the bridge?'

The third American who played a considerable part in the political and
social life of London was, of course, Lady Astor; a far greater role before her
entry to Parliament than afterwards, because she was taken more seriously;
or perhaps it would be truer to say she was more appreciated. Her audacious
wit often passed all bounds, and was usually fun. However, such jokes sound
better in a drawing-room than in the lobbies of the House of Commons,
certainly to the ears of a pompous victim uneasily aware of the proximity of
the parliamentary correspondents. She often met her match in the wits of
the period, drawn from all sections of society. Most of these occasions are
probably apocryphal, such as that when a voice from the back of a temperance
meeting is supposed to have met her statement, 'I would rather commit
adultery than drink a glass of beer' with the penetrating query, 'Who
wouldn't?' But there is an authentic ring in my favourite tale of battle in her
own fortress, St. James's Square. As that celebrated wit and columnist
Lord Castlerosse, personally beloved and fashioned into a journalist by
Lord Beaverbrook, came up the stairs of St. James's Square during a glittering
reception, he was received by his hostess, Lady Astor, in characteristic
fashion. She leaned forward and patted his immense stomach with the
observation: 'If that was on a woman we should know what to think'. Came
the laconic reply: 'Well, it was last night, so what do you think?' The company
of anyone capable of such instant rejoinder was occasionally worthwhile, and
I sometimes enjoyed it while I still had the time, despite Max Beaverbrook's
remark reported by Harold Nicolson[1] that I should never have been seen at
Valentine's parties. This came oddly from him, because he himself found the
Castlerosse fun irresistible. Years later, Max and I talked of his long-dead
friend at his villa 'La Caponcina' in the South of France when I last saw him
just before his own death.

There is an old tradition of English wit in that robust vein, and may it
never cease on the appropriate occasion, despite any Puritan outcry. The best
repartee of all perhaps came from that other colourful and much more
disreputable figure, John Wilkes, and is well known. He was late for supper
with a heavy-handed peer who remarked on his arrival: 'We were debating
whether you would be hung before you died of the pox', and was met with the
immediate retort: 'That depends whether I embrace your principles or your
mistresses'. In English there is such a wide range of wit that it is difficult to
choose any brief anthology. In the opposite vein of the grand manner I

[1] Harold Nicolson, *Diaries and Letters, 1930–39*, edited by Nigel Nicolson
(Collins, 1966).

always like Peel's reply in Parliament to the Irishman who said he would as
soon see the devil as the Queen on the throne of England: 'When the sovereign
of his choice is seated on the throne of this realm, I trust he will enjoy, as I
know he will deserve, the confidence of the Crown'.

I myself heard in Parliament an engaging exchange between Lord Henry
Bentinck and Lord Hugh Cecil who, in the early stages of the Irish problem
after the First War, were taking different views of the question. The latter
was rallying the former on his seemingly abrupt change of opinion and saying
it would become him to give some account of his transition rather on the
lines of Newman's *Apologia*. Lord Henry rose with the interruption that the
principal factor in his conversion had been his unfortunate experience of
listening to Lord Hugh's speeches in the opposite sense. The rejoinder was:
'If it did not imply any offence to my noble friend, I should be tempted at
this stage of our discussion to make a transient reference to pearls'.

How much the character of people is reflected in their wit. It is amusing to
compare the English variety with the French: for example, Madame du
Deffand's reply to a tedious cleric who insisted on the miracle that a saint had
walked six leagues after his head had been cut off—il n'y a que le premier pas
qui coûte—made familiar to English readers by Lytton Strachey. Less well
known in the anti-clerical tradition still to be found within French life is
Clemenceau's letter to an abbé with whom he had a dispute about a tree
which cast a shadow into his garden. When the branches were finally cut back
he wrote a letter of thanks and appreciation which began: 'Mon père, je peux
enfin vous appeler mon père, car vous m'avez donné la lumière'. French wit
is not always so delicate and sometimes joins our robust English examples:
for instance, Henri IV, gallant and beloved King of France, relieving himself
in the garden when a beautiful lady of the court came suddenly round the
corner: 'Passe, ma belle, je le tiens'.

The leading English hostesses of those post-war days evoke different
memories; they were sedate, very sedate. Mrs. Ronnie Greville inherited a
brewer's fortune and lived in Charles Street, with a country house at Polesden
Lacey; appropriately she looked a rather blousy old barmaid, but she had an
intelligence acute enough to attract the diverse allegiance of the ascetic Sir
John Simon and the bucolic Sir Robert Horne. She mixed her company well
and also her dishes. Persistent of invitations to all well-known people was
Lady Colefax, who had a charming house in King's Road, Chelsea, with a
garden at the back, Argyll House. Endless were the jokes and stories about
her, authentic and invented. But she was a kind and agreeable woman, and a
provider of much fun to many people. Never has anyone hunted lions with
such persistence, and the chase was almost always triumphant. The gay and
learned head of the School of Oriental Languages, Sir Denison Ross, recounted that she asked him to lunch on a Monday, and, on his refusal,
continued to do so through each day of the week, compelling him to find

always a different excuse; finally he said, 'Dammit, I'll come, Monday'. Osbert Sitwell, whose wit I much appreciated, chose Lady Colefax for a favourite butt.

Practically everyone of interest in London life went to the house of this quiet bourgeois figure, presenting such a remarkable contrast to the sparkling Americans who in mind and character were in some curious fashion nearer to the aristocratic English hostesses of earlier periods—of the eighteenth century and the Regency—with their audacity, their wit and their vitality. The reason is perhaps that such expatriate American women develop an extraordinary capacity for assimilating themselves into other people's ways of life completely different from their own, and even into the manners of other epochs if the trend again makes them fashionable. Lady Colefax remained solidly and traditionally English. Harold Nicolson observed this quality one day acutely as we left her house together. She had upset with considerable mess the coffee cona in which she laboriously cooked the coffee of her guests. 'Dear me, I am a real Auntie Nervous,' she said. 'That moment,' said Harold, 'took us right back to the Simla nursery.'

Harold Nicolson was completely at home in that world, and should never have left it. His métier was diplomacy and the writing of belles lettres, to which he made charming and various contributions; in fact, his erudition went further and entered some really interesting ranges of thought. I remember him quoting a phrase I may in memory have improved—a foible of mine—'the only tears which mingled with the Hellenic waters were not for sins committed but for joys foregone'. He was one of the most civilised products of the London official and social world. Also he had considerable wit, he said good things. For instance: 'Lloyd George plays on an organ with many stops, Philip Kerr (Lord Lothian) is the *vox humana*'. I had some hope that H.N. might be such a stop in my organ, but he gradually insisted on becoming the *vox tremula*. He was quite unsuited to politics, as he appears to have recognised in his later diaries. He would have made an excellent ambassador and a possible Foreign Secretary in combination with a strong Prime Minister, but was unsuited to the rough and tumble of a new movement advancing novel ideas *contra mundum*. He was attracted by the thought, but repelled by the process; he loved the end, but could not bear the means.

I first met Harold Nicolson during the war in Leicestershire, where I used to escape from my hospital treatment in London to hunt each weekend directly I was allowed to ride again in leg-irons. Our brilliant hostess in a beautiful house believed in the sophisticated concept that the rigours of the chase should be softened in the evening by the imported company of London intellectuals, including the flower of the Foreign Office. The days were magical in this war-time continuance of hunting; the master of foxhounds was then the old Lord Lonsdale of yellow carriage fame; 'just to keep the foxes down'. This sport took the fortunate participants back to the life and spirit of the early nineteenth century, without crowds, only horses, hounds and the beautiful, weeping scenery. I can still never pass through it without emotion.

The great hostesses on the Continent really belong for me to a later stage in this story, the later twenties, but it is interesting to compare them with their London counterparts. Again, some of the most prominent were American, though in Paris and in Rome, as in London, exquisite and charming women also entertained in distinguished though less conspicuous fashion in their own cities. Comparable in wit with Lady Cunard was Princess Jane di San Faustino, who presided over a lively Italian and cosmopolitan gaiety in Rome and Venice. But the two styles differed sharply because Lady Cunard was almost a prude in conversation, while Princess Jane was outrageous. She would say anything, and the utterance was the more striking because it scintillated in clear loud American from an appearance of the utmost dignity, a Roman matron if ever there was one. Clad in the midday sun of the Lido at Venice in complete widow's weeds of white, in Rome corresponding clothes of black, relieved only by a slight border of white round her strong but clearly moulded features and snow-white hair, she mourned her husband with pious reverence and simultaneously regaled the fashion world with the extremities of scandal floodlit by her unfailing and eccentric humour. She occupied the central *capanna* of the classic beach where all newcomers must pass. A French friend said to me there only recently that after a long life and much experience he had never encountered anything more unnerving than the basilisk stare from that *capanna*, accompanied almost certainly by some searing comment to her fellow judges which youth might apprehend: 'mais quelle mechanceté', he sighed with nostalgic appreciation.

I once had an account of her long mourning which blended so incongruously with the sparkling sunshine of Rome and the even brighter sparkle of her conversation. She was in most expansive mood at a small dinner party which included Dora Labouchere—daughter of the English politician, and later married in a Roman series—Cole Porter, the song writer, was also present with his Yale friend, Monty Woolley, who later became familiar to cinema audiences. Both Princess Jane and Dora Labouchere reviewed their past lives. It is always difficult to determine at what points these outstanding entertainers retain contact with the truth, because art comes first, but the show was the thing and on its own stage it was some show. Princess Jane said she had lived with her distinguished husband for a long time in married bliss—eleven years I think, without a cloud on the horizon—until one day they were out driving in an open carriage. He then signalled to the coachman to stop, teed up on the kerbstone as for a golf-shot, and hit her as hard as he could over the head with his umbrella. After this first and abrupt indication of a marriage rift, he departed, and she never saw him again. She then explained in vast, uproarious and unprintably scandalous detail how her young American innocence had afterwards been surprised to learn just what arts she should have acquired to retain his affection. However, on his death she assumed her widow's weeds and wore them to the end. He must have been a man of considerable charm and parts, and his alleged habits were no doubt largely or even entirely imaginary. Invention came readily to the rich fecundity of her imagination.

Not to be outdone, Dora Labouchere described her marriage with Prince Rudini, who had regaled her as a young girl on her honeymoon with an extended tour of the seamier side of Paris night-life; the detail was profuse. The marriage ended in an annulment which cost her at least considerable trouble and time. Finally, in the dramatic recitation came the morning of the successful severance with the annulment complete, adorned by an enormous bunch of flowers and a note from Prince Rudini saying that he would have committed suicide by the time she received it; and he had. Dora Labouchere concluded her startling rhapsody delivered in a quaintly attractive voice which strangely blended the affectations of English and Italian society with the poignant phrase, 'I still treasure the damask stained with the peaches which Rudini threw at me'.

The tale was so good in the telling that truth became an irrelevance. As we went downstairs Monty Woolley, goggling the relative innocence of contemporary American university life, whispered in my ear: 'Say what they will, that Rudini was a swell guy'.

This Roman life was not only great fun, but in the unique beauty of the houses and the whole *mise-en-scène* and in the good looks and distinguished manners of the company it also gave at least the impression of a fine society. It was a university of charm, where a young man could encounter a refinement of sophistication whose acquisition could be some permanent passport in a varied and variable world. If he could stand up to the salon of Princess Jane, he could face much. In Rome her American sallies blended with the running commentary of a French barrack-room argot supplied by her long-lived parrot, which was believed to have belonged to Marshal Ney. From Venice emerged on to that classic strand a widow of statuesque dignity whose hand even in her old age Lord Byron would have dismounted to kiss on his morning ride along that same beach, because her conversation would have further enlivened—perhaps even have rendered unprintable—the stanzas of *Don Juan*.

Very different was life in Paris during this period in the company of the leading American hostess, because, particularly after her belated marriage, in her circle the world of action encountered the world of amusement. Elsie de Wolfe had herself made a considerable fortune in New York as an interior decorator, and much of American business life could be met in her house at Versailles, to which was added later a flat in the Avenue d'Iéna in Paris. Decorations in both houses were in her highly individual style and included immense golden panels by Drian of herself perched on the sweep of steps facing the pièce d'eau des Suisses at Versailles. Sunday there was usually lively with twenty or thirty people of all nationalities and professions to luncheon or dinner, in a setting which varied from a swimming-pool to a flood-lit garden; innovations in those days. This society presented a striking contrast with my other life in Paris at that time among French people. I was entranced by the varied company of the French in diverse situations, always entertained and often instructed by their conversation, which was and is perhaps the best in the world.

Miss de Wolfe's conversation was distinguished by immense vivacity rather than intellectual content. In fact, vitality was the keynote of her whole character. When nearly ninety she was still doing what she called her morning exercises, which consisted of being slung around by two powerful men of ballet-dancer physique. Her gentler entourage included two well-known characters of the period called Johnny and Tony who were always at her festive board, and had a more delicate appreciation of haute coûture than of high politics. However, the natural shrewdness of Johnny's Highland origin —the younger generation nicknamed him the Highlander—came out strong on one occasion. The American Election of 1932 was approaching, and the tycoons assembled at Elsie's dinner-table were covering Roosevelt with ridicule and obloquy, when up piped Johnny: 'I think Roosevelt is going to win'. 'Silly little Johnny,' echoed round the board in diverse tone and accent, 'What makes you think that?' 'Because all our friends think Hoover will win,' responded the Highlander. The demise of Tony was said in shadowy legend to have evoked Elsie's strongest qualities of spartan resolution: Tony is dead and we are a man short for dinner—the old guard might die, but Elsie did not surrender. Most of the tales were probably apocryphal, but she certainly combined the hard, cutting qualities of a good diamond with one of the most voluptuous settings it was possible to encounter. Consequently, into this delicate scene of beautiful women and young men, almost as exquisite as some of the specimens we see today, were continually intruded the toughest tycoons of Wall Street and American industry. It was a theatre of interest.

Elsie married my friend, Charles Mendl, whom I knew well after my first visit to Paris in 1920 and last saw there a few years ago just before he died, well in his eighties. It was a marriage as remarkable as it was unexpected, for both were getting on and she was some twelve years the senior; a marriage of scent and old brandy, as we called it. But he had considerable qualities in addition to being one of the outstanding bons vivants of our time. After a rough, cattle-punching youth in the Argentine—he was a most manly figure —he had turned up by some inexplicable process during the First World War as an official at the British Embassy in Paris responsible for dealing with the Press, and there he remained until the Second War. Sinister rumours attached to his activities, but I soon became convinced they were quite untrue. There was much talk of the *Chevalerie de St. George,* a reference to the old allegation that British diplomats abroad always tried to bribe the foreign Press and had ample funds available for this purpose.

Mendl had at his flat in the Avenue Montaigne one of the best cooks and was himself one of the best judges of wine in Paris. He invited me frequently, and as a young M.P. and later as a Minister I met there some of the most interesting personalities of France. One day he asked me to meet 'Pertinax' —his real name was Gérault—and to try to disarm some of the hostility he showed towards Britain in his newspaper articles. I found him charming, and we got on all too well, for when I was returned to Parliament at a by-election in 1926 he wrote a leading article entitled '*Le retour d'Alcibiades*' in a mood of hyperbole which ascribed to me among other more acceptable qualities capacities which would be more appreciated in French than in English politics. These thoughts no doubt occurred to him because we met in the house of Charles Mendl, who was preoccupied with this side of life. When I used to see Charles alone in his old age, his mind was still running to some extent on one of his chief life interests. He had an exchange one day with his doctor, who combined in true Gallic fashion a considerable professional capacity with much charm and wit: 'Doctor, I still think a good deal about women'—'You must keep on thinking, Sir Charles, keep on thinking.' Charles was a gay and lovable person, and I miss him with all the happy clamour of Versailles in those far-off days.

What was the purpose of it all, the object of going into society? Apart from fun, which is always worthwhile so long as you have the time, meeting people is clearly valuable, particularly people with influence in diverse spheres. It is better to meet them yourself, ask your own questions and form your own judgments. It can, of course, be done to some extent vicariously, in the manner of Sir William (later Lord) Tyrrell, a great ambassador in Paris and also a chief of the Foreign Office, who used Charles Mendl for this purpose. He did not go out much in Paris, and Mendl was his intermediary between the British Embassy and French life. I had the warmest regard for Tyrrell, whom I used often to see alone for long conversations and from whom I learned much. He was a masterpiece of diplomacy; after him Nature broke the mould, as Macaulay would have put it. Yet if you have the energy and the time, it is better to do it all yourself, to meet those who are most interesting and get to know them well personally.

This was by no means all that the society of those days could give to a young man. There too was the 'open sesame' to the world of culture, literature, music and art. True, you could buy an opera ticket, go to a gallery, and read great literature for yourself. The moment I was back from the war I did all these things in an almost frenzied desire to swallow all beauty in one gulp—it took years to establish a natural equilibrium of steadily and continuously extending knowledge and experience—but in society you could also hear the talk of the critics and meet creative people. While society is still what Spengler calls 'in form', it can give a great deal; it points in every direction of knowledge and beauty.

Naturally, just to live that life would have been entirely futile. If I had not had all the other experiences—war in air and trenches, my childhood among the people of the land, life in that very heart of manhood the regular army, and something almost the equivalent of a return to the Hellenic gymnasium in European athletics, the experience of administration in civil service, government and political organisation, intimate knowledge of the people's day to day bread and butter politics in the mass movement of the Labour Party, and later still the greatest experience of all in creating a new grass roots movement from the whole people—then my relatively trivial experience of society in the chief capitals of Europe would have deformed and isolated me as it did so many others. Added to this wide range of human experience, it was an advantage, a small but important ingredient to make a complete whole. *Ganzheit*, said Goethe, is the highest desideratum, the becoming of a complete man.

After my return from the war the process of development by experience went apace. Hospital treatment and convalescence were soon followed by entry into the administration, but two spells of light duty with the army came first. In 1917, the regimental depot at the Curragh was not quite so peaceful as usual because the Easter Rising had occurred the year before. The genial company of the hunting field by day was divided by the sniper's bullet at night. The Irish revolutionaries were much blamed by the army at that time for their method of fighting, but guerilla war was clearly the only possible means to carry on their struggle against an overwhelming military force; it was a method which became familiar all over the world at a later date. The military and political lessons of that period were considerable, but belong properly to later chapters where the politics and action of the time will be regarded more closely. Here we are concerned with the enforced relaxation which in my case followed the rigours of war, and the considerable contribution which it made to my complete life experience.

The element of charm was again provided in ample measure by the Dublin society of that time. Lord Wimborne was Viceroy and Sir Bryan Mahon was Commander-in-Chief. Both were married to remarkable and charming women —the first to a Grosvenor of exquisite manners, and the second to the widow of Sir John Milbanke, the Boer War V.C., and one of the most accomplished horsewomen Leicestershire had produced; both were outstanding as hostesses in their respective positions, though they did not get on well together. I had known both before, and found them in Dublin surrounded by my London and Leicestershire friends. As my duties at the Curragh were light, I was able to divide my time between the stimulating companies at Vice-Regal Lodge and G.H.Q., Ireland. All this did not last long, for I soon had to report to a more permanent location of light duty in the C3 category.

Life at Eastbourne as an instructor to wounded officers provided more opportunity for continuous reading. The duties were even lighter, as no one was fit for hard training, and the distractions were few. We lived on the chilly heights at the back of Eastbourne in canvas huts, which were not quite so cold as the trenches because we had the use of oil-stoves. It did not take me long with the friendships and associations I had now made to get transferred to administrative posts in London. The old boy or old girl network was working quite well even in those days, and I used it realistically and relentlessly while avoiding getting caught in the net. However, my first appointment was well outside its usual ambit, for I was sent to the Ministry of Munitions, where I had my first insight into industrial conditions and the negotiations with trade unions in which our department was continually engaged. At this stage I learned a lot but contributed little; it was then a new world to me.

My second sphere of operation was much more subject to social influence, for I was given an administrative post in the War Department of the Foreign Office, a very central situation. A few young men had to handle all the main telegrams which reached the government, and reply to many letters on instructions of the Secretary of State. I was the only outsider, as the rest were all professional diplomats who had entered the Foreign Service before the war. Strange to relate, my chief difficulty was my handwriting—strange because it seemed odd that in the Central Department of the Foreign Office in the middle of a war everything should be done by manuscript. The archaic forms in which letters were written at first also seemed to me peculiar, but I soon came to appreciate them because it was in practice easier and quicker to write letters in these set forms than to puzzle out various ways of address on each separate occasion. The rituals of the Foreign Office like those of the Army had a practical quality evolved over a long stretch of time.

The duties were in themselves extremely interesting, though I was, of course, at this stage very much the apprentice. The range of experience in foreign affairs was wide, as we covered practically the whole field. An additional advantage was meeting for the first time some of the politicians with whom I was later to be most closely associated. Aubrey Herbert drifted in one day with his subtle blend of charm and vagueness in manner which covered a very acute intelligence. If I remember rightly, he had just escaped from a German prison camp and was seeking Foreign Office advice in certain difficulties. He was a brother of Lord Carnarvon and very English, but became so involved in the affairs of the Balkans that he was offered the crown of Albania. After the war, during week-ends in his beautiful Adam house at Pixton, I used to combine shooting with speaking for him in his constituency at the neighbouring town of Yeovil. His adventurous nature was then calmer, but he had still on occasion to be restrained from diverting his guests by standing on one side of the balustrade at the top of the house which surrounded the deep well and jumping across to catch the opposite rail with his hands; a habit of his youth. His Albanian brigands were reputed to have enlivened the rural countryside before the war by galloping through the villages, shooting their revolvers in the air as a warning to their neighbours, because they suspected that a fusillade of guns from an adjacent shooting party was an ambush. Aubrey was reticent when rallied on these old stories.

He was a fine character and always on the right side in opposing all mean and cruel dealings, like the Coalition Government's treatment of the Irish after the war. Through him I met also my chief Conservative colleague in that early and tough fight of my parliamentary life, Henry Bentinck; a brother of the Duke of Portland, he was cast in the generous and courageous mould of traditional English statesmanship. He could afford to laugh when in the heat of an Irish debate Lloyd George, in reference to his ancestors coming over with King William, called him a 'bloody Dutchman' (Speaker Lowther, like all great occupants of the Chair, was often tactfully deaf), for it was one of his family, Lord George Bentinck, who advised the Conservatives to tolerate Disraeli on the ground that every gentleman's team required a professional bowler. Godfrey Locker-Lampson, the elder of two M.P. brothers, was one of the most industrious members of this group, which became attached to the two Cecils, Lord Robert and Lord Hugh, as we developed the Irish battle. It was the Foreign Office which first brought me into contact with these able men of fine instinct and character.

Other well-known figures were then also connected with this service, though our paths later diverged. George Lloyd was much occupied with the Foreign Office at that time, but only indirectly with our department; he was still an M.P. Mark Sykes spent much time in our company, which he invariably diverted as well as informed. Like most of these men, he was an expert on near-Eastern affairs, and his death through illness at the Peace Conference was a real national loss. He had exceptional charm and was an extremely gifted mimic. His chief turn was a charade of Mr. Churchill's expedition to Antwerp. It began with Churchill's alleged address from the steps of the Town Hall: 'Citizens of Antwerp, the might of the British Empire is at your disposal'—and ended with the alleged escape of Mr. Churchill's stepfather, George Cornwallis West, on a borrowed child's bicycle. These men were intermediate between me and an older generation, and their attitude was strikingly irreverent. The dramatic performances of Mr. Churchill evoked the liveliest sallies of their merriment, but their attitude to Mr. Lloyd George was much more severe. They detested him, and always called him the goat; a reference to his slight legs under the massive torso surmounted by a magnificent head which did in general effect rather suggest the great god Pan; but Pan at his best, using his most seductive pipes. I differed from them strongly in later years concerning the character and capacities of Lloyd George, for whom I had a warm regard when I got to know him well.

No account of the work in the Foreign Office during this period need be given, because it consisted chiefly of the routine fulfilment of duty at the centre of a war administration which now belongs to history. It was later that the rise of Russian power with the aid of British policy supplied a good quota of the professional traitors of communism to this classic department, which had long been a pride and distinction of British administration. An important and indeed essential ingredient in my experience was the know-ledge of administration and method gained at that time in two very different departments, the Ministry of Munitions and the Foreign Office, which touched British life and our relations with other countries at many diverse points. This was an opportunity to see the administrative machine from underneath: later, in my period within the Treasury as a Minister, I was to see it from on top. The combination of these administrative experiences added considerably to my equipment for political life, and helped me to understand the work of government as a whole.

5
Entry into Politics
The Centre Party
F.E.
Churchill

THE opportunity to enter politics soon came. There were two chances to be adopted as Conservative candidate, the first in the Stone Division of my native Staffordshire and the second in the Harrow Division of Middlesex. It seemed improbable that I should succeed in Harrow, as two strong local candidates were in the field and a third was a personal friend of Bonar Law, then leader of the party, who was understood to have indicated privately his hope that this candidate would be adopted. I knew no one in the constituency, but the Central Office was willing to put forward my name and it seemed worthwhile to try for a seat so near London. I was still in the army in 1918, though seconded to work at the Foreign Office, so my opportunities for political activity were limited, but it was not forbidden to stand in the post-war election.

I decided to see what could be done in Harrow before taking long and necessarily rare journeys to Stone, where I had many friends and a better chance of being adopted. Each evening I went by train to call on the dignitaries of the Harrow Conservative Association, mostly old men. They were amiable but not encouraging. However, they decided to have what was called a singing competition, to give the four prospective candidates a chance to show what they could do as speakers. This was for me an ominous occasion as I had never made a speech in my life. It was rather like my previous daunting experience of arriving on the Western Front as an accomplished aviator, having never before left the ground in an aircraft.

I decided to write out my fifteen-minute speech and learn it by heart. It was quite a good speech but shockingly bad in delivery. As one of the old politicians present said afterwards, good stuff, but badly chanted. I was far from having acquired the range of voice and variation in rhythm and tempo in which I later attained some competence. I did not even realise the necessity. To stand up and say something sensible seemed to me adequate. The speech consequently fell flat, though they applauded politely, possibly in sympathy with a very young man in uniform. Then came questions, and in that hour I was launched into politics. They were good, pointed, often expert questions, for Harrow was a dormitory of London where men and women lived who worked in the city and were versed in every intricate question of Britain and the Empire. I had by then read enormously and was vastly interested in politics; the fascination of the argument brought me alive and evoked some latent power of exposition. Questions ended in a scene of considerable enthusiasm. I was adopted as prospective candidate by over ninety per cent of the votes of those present.

Next arose the question of programme at the coming election. I knew little of Conservative sentiment, and cared less. I was going into the House of Commons as one of the representatives of the war generation, for that purpose alone. Yet Harrow was a traditional stronghold of the Conservative Party and among the older people there began to be much talk of far-off things, of pre-war politics. I had joined the Conservative Party because it seemed to me on its record in the war to be the party of patriotism, and that was the first principle, but patriotism to me was not something static, a sentiment of good things to be conserved. It was something dynamic and creative, seeking to build a better and more modern nation, constantly adapted to the development of the age and inspiring it. Particularly was this the case when so much needed to be done in providing a fair livelihood and above all good homes for our surviving companions of the war.

Already the national housing scheme appeared in my programme, as opposed to slow dealing through multitudinous local authorities. Munitions were produced like that in war, so why not houses in time of peace? Slums were to be abolished, and back-to-back houses. Land was to be taken for this and other social purposes by compulsory acquisition. The profiteer and jerry-builder were to have short shrift. Electricity and transport were to come under public control; already the debate between public and private ownership seemed to me irrelevant. It was just a question of which method suited best in circumstances which were constantly changing. In my programme health and child welfare schemes anticipated by many years anything effective being done in these spheres, and the chance of education from the cradle to university was to be provided for all who were capable of using it.

Finally, the home market was to be sustained by a high-wage system intended to produce an equilibrium between production and consumption. I was already aware that the cost of production depended not so much on the rate of wage as on the rate of production in mass-producing industries. It was thinking of this nature which more than forty years later sent two successive British governments blinking and shuffling toward the European Common Market, where mass production for an assured market is possible. In elementary form many of my later ideas were already born, and it is indeed surprising in retrospect that the Conservative Association of Harrow was at that time prepared to play the midwife.

The opportunity then was to keep and to develop the British Empire for constructive purposes, not only to preserve the Empire, but to make it capable of giving to our British people and to all its diverse races the good life which its latent wealth made possible. I expressed my chief principles of the 1918 election with the slogan 'socialistic imperialism'. It was an ugly phrase, but it was pregnant with the future. Let no one ever say that the combination of the socialist and nationalist ideas was a foreign invention copied by me. Neither I nor anyone else had ever heard at that time of obscure soldiers in the German and Italian front lines who afterwards built political parties. Nor, to do them justice, had they probably ever heard of the Conservative candidate for Harrow. Such thinking was in the very air of Europe, thrown high by the explosion of the war, yet by inherent reason of national character it later took completely different forms in the various countries. In other nations total collapse brought it to a rapid, rough and rude fruition.

Even in the tranquil air of Harrow the sober burgesses were able to support such novel thinking in the flash of post-war enthusiasm to meet the problems of peace. It was not, after all, so strange to them, for these roots were already in English soil through the combination of radicalism and imperialism in the Birmingham school of Joseph Chamberlain; also, in the continuing interplay of British and continental thinking during all creative periods, the same tendency had been reflected in Bismarck's advanced social programme under the aegis of the strongly nationalist state of Prussia.

The most irrational antithesis of our time always seemed to me to be the conflict between the progress of the Left and the stability of the Right. From this early stage my programme cut right across it. Later I was to express in far more conscious form the concept that progress was impossible without stability, and stability was impossible without progress. Synthesis, eternal synthesis, is the solution to many of the false dilemmas of our time. In an elementary form these ideas were present in my first election programme; they were combined with the urgent and practical demand for social reform —notably housing—to give ex-servicemen the land they deserved. I won by a large majority against an Independent Conservative whose chief argument was that I was much too young; a point easily countered by 'old enough for Flanders, old enough for Westminster'. So on the wave of post-war enthusiasm I was swept to the House of Commons at just twenty-two years of age as the youngest M.P., which I remained for some time.

The Air Navigation Bill provided an early and appropriate opportunity for my maiden speech. After quoting Chatham's celebrated reply to Horace Walpole concerning the 'atrocious crime of being a young man' and mentioning in becomingly modest terms my flying experience in the war, I launched into my main theme, which was the saving of the nation's air industry from the stranglehold of bureaucracy. Heavy penalties for negligence were preferable to the tender care of some government inspector who worked on the time system. It required no exercise of the imagination to see that the aircraft and the tank would soon supersede infantry as the decisive factor in war. The Secretary of State for War, Mr. Churchill, was falling into the same error as his predecessors at the War Office, who had refused to credit the possibilities of such a rapid extension of the activities of aircraft as had already occurred. The result of this quite lively assault was agreeably flattering to youthful vanity: among other references to the occasion was a cartoon in *Punch*, showing the young and dynamic airman painting Mr. Churchill as a doddering old man and urging him to bring his ideas up to date. It was our first encounter in debate, and I was on the perennially popular ground of the youth racket. It is entertaining in retrospect to see it used against Churchill when he was just forty-four years old; if the youth mania had then been in full swing he might have been retired from politics twenty-one years before he became Prime Minister in the Second World War.

It was a thin House, but a number of influential members were present, notably the distinguished Speaker Lowther, who was in the Chair. It was his praise of this first effort in the inner circles of Westminster which really made my early parliamentary reputation. I realised fully how much he had done for me in this respect some time later, after his retirement to the House of Lords as Lord Ullswater, when he devoted to my maiden speech his opening remarks from the Chair in presiding over a debate in which my opponent was the Duke of Northumberland, a man of 'die-hard' Conservative principles but engaging personality.

Lowther was an outstanding Speaker who had already become a legend on account of his firm character and penetrating wit. My favourite example was a pre-war tale of some pretentious bore making a speech of inordinate length and finally saying: 'Now, Mr. Speaker, I ask myself this question.' Both front benches distinctly heard a voice from the Chair replying: 'And you'll get a damned silly answer'. The secret of Lowther's success was a sense of the drama of the House of Commons. He would always, if possible, call the member, old, young or middling, who was most likely to make an effective reply to the previous speaker. He liked to heighten the tension of the debate in the confidence that his personality could maintain order, while less gifted Speakers sometimes try to diminish it and to reduce discussion to the commonplace. His decisions were clear and firm, but I was warned soon after arrival by the Cecil brothers—well versed in the subtleties of procedure and of human character—never to spring anything on him; this always entailed a

PORTRAIT OF WINSTON
BY MR. MOSLEY,
A PROMISING YOUNG ARTIST.

I trust that Mr. CHURCHILL, who is conducting the business of the War Office in Paris, will not read the Official Report of the debate on the Aerial Navigation Bill. For I am sure it would be as great a shock to him as it was to me to learn that Mr. MOSLEY (*ætat* twenty-two) considered him, in aviation affairs, as lacking in imagination. The idea of anyone regarding our WINSTON as a doddering old fossil!

(Reprinted by permission of *Punch*)

negative. The method was to notify him in advance that you were going to raise a point, and when he had had time to think it over he would allow it if it were at all reasonable. A real personality of that kind in the Chair is a big factor in maintaining the prestige of parliament.

After this maiden speech my part in debate was not noteworthy until the autumn of 1920. My divergence in the interval from the majority in that House of Commons on the subject of the Versailles Treaty will be discussed later. This period was spent in the intensive study of politics and all its related questions; also in learning to know better its leading figures. Particularly my association with the group of Henry Bentinck, Aubrey Herbert, Godfrey Locker-Lampson and their friends grew continuously closer, and a little later came my relationship with Lord Robert Cecil and his organisation, the League of Nations Union, and with both him and his brother Lord Hugh Cecil over the Irish question. Meantime, I was liquidating all my outside interests and distractions; the well-loved horses soon went, both hunters and polo ponies. Politics had become for me the overriding interest and required single-mindedness.

My maiden speech was delivered with impudent celerity, but it opened to me many doors and made me known to many people who had never heard of me. Back from the war and up from the country, I knew few people in public life, and still fewer in official circles, apart from my brief experience in the Foreign Office and Ministry of Munitions. I was invited to spend the weekend at the Asquiths' house, The Wharf, where I enjoyed at dinner the first evening all the exquisite embarrassment of Mrs. Asquith's gay enthusiasm for my effort. Earlier in the day I had arrived, very shy, among a large and seemingly distinguished company of whom I knew not a soul. Mr. Asquith was pacing the lawn, an imposing figure in all the majesty of remote reverie. 'Go and talk to him,' said Margot, yet the least appropriate action for an unknown new boy seemed to me the rousing of an ex-Prime Minister from more important thoughts. So she took me by the hand and led me up to him; all his deep kindness and subtle charm at once unfolded. I forget which of his friends described him as a 'small man with the beatific smile of one who has seen the heavens open', but I remembered it because it seemed to me true. His extraordinary serenity in adversity was perhaps due to his great scholarship; he rested on the sunlit heights of Hellenism, but nevertheless attended a Church of England service every Sunday morning, with only rare accompaniment of family.

That evening after dinner he invited me to play chess with him in another room, rather unexpectedly, as it was his habit to play bridge. It was quickly apparent that both of us had little capacity and less interest for the game. Soon he desisted and began to talk of the political past, magnificently. I listened entranced, and he long continued, as old men will when a young audience responds with a reasonable appreciation. Eventually, feeling selfish and socially apprehensive at this happy monopoly, I murmured some regard for his other guests. He replied: 'Generally I only play bridge to protect myself from the conversation of the people Margot brings to this house'. My awe at the other guests and my credulity of the less worthy Asquith legends simultaneously diminished. He was reputed to be unduly addicted to bridge and to drink, but I never saw him, or for that matter Mr. Churchill—another victim of the same rumour—in any way incapacitated by drink. Certainly they pursued the old English habit of living which reached its apogee in the eighteenth and nine-teenth centuries. They both did themselves well, but seemed none the worse for it.

Their way of life was very different from mine, which rested on the sound advice of the classic Greeks: 'Moderation in all things, especially in modera-tion'. I believed in an ascetic or rather athletic life, relieved by convivial occasions, rather than continual indulgence. Yet I was always resentful of the violent attacks upon these eminent men which derived apparently from the vicious disposition among the baser ranges of the Conservative Party to slander formidable opponents. I recall still some of the tales they used to circulate during my childhood about the man who has since become the tribal deity of their party as well as the hero of a large majority of the nation. The local dames of the sub-primrose variety in our county circles were avid to believe anything bad about Mr. Churchill during his Liberal days of the land campaign and the Ulster explosion. A house in a neighbouring county was burned down where he happened to be spending the night, and their verdict was clear and simple: naturally God sets fire to a house if the Devil enters it. I do not know who circulated the stories about his breaking his parole in the Boer War which were so conclusively refuted in numerous law-suits, but I only heard the truth when I arrived in the House of Commons and got to know him and his friends. It may be some such experience which moved Lady Churchill much later to say, according to a newspaper report: 'I can remember the time when my husband was more hated than Sir Oswald Mosley is today'. Men-dacious scurrilities and personal vendettas are chiefly revealed by history in periods of degeneracy, and they are no good portents for our national future; happily in our country they were confined to relatively small circles remote from the generous stream of English life.

It was also disgraceful that some Tories used to refer to Mr. Asquith as Squiffy and circulate rumours as filthy as they were fantastic about his wife. There appeared to be absolutely no foundation for these stories; their only conceivable justification was the entirely uninhibited character of her conver-sation, designed possibly to *épater les bourgeois*, in which she certainly suc-ceeded, and recompensing with a sparkling wit her almost complete disregard for facts. For instance, during my first dinner party at The Wharf she con-cluded her generous account of my maiden speech by fixing my hand with her claw-like grip and my eye with her ancient-mariner regard as she said:

'Your speech reminded me in some ways of my old friend Lord Randolph Churchill, but, dear boy, do not share his vices, never live with six women at once, it is so weakening'. This exotic friend of Rosebery and Balfour, and in her youth of Gladstone, certainly traversed in her wayward fashion a wide range of life experience.

Mr. Asquith moved serenely above all lesser things. He had no genius, but his own conduct recalled in some degree his fascinating phrase in another context: 'Genius alone on its golden wings soars beyond heredity and environment'. He clearly lacked the decisive and dynamic qualities necessary for a period of great action. He was rather the man for a Walpole period of protracted peace and relative tranquility, but he added to calm, poise and judgment a vision of the need for steady progress and embodied the finest English qualities of integrity and honour.

Mr. Balfour was another link with the more remote political past, and I met him first when I was just out of hospital in the war, even before entering Parliament where we were fellow-members for only a short time before he went to the House of Lords. In a happy and uninhibited early life, the opportunity to meet the great often comes by introduction of a bright and beautiful lady. Fate aided me in this way on more than one occasion and I met Mr. Balfour through a lady in whom he had a purely intellectual interest, and the reader will naturally conclude that at twenty-odd I followed reverently the statesman-philosopher's example. Strangely enough, we came together for the purpose of playing tennis at Queen's Club; Mr. Balfour's years were balanced by the leg-irons which I had to wear on leaving hospital and for some years afterwards. He brought another lady to make a fourth, whose name I forget. My partner in the intervals of playing tennis enhanced my impression of her mental and aesthetic qualities by observing: 'You have a precocious and unnatural facility in the combination of words'. This seemed to me at the time entirely just, as she was quoting something said of the younger Pitt. They were happy days in life-restoring contrast to the recent war experiences.

Mr. Balfour during my few meetings with him in this cursory fashion was an interesting study for a young man. He had great charm, and the appearance at least of absorbed interest in any companion of the moment, which is more often the attribute of successful hostesses than of distinguished politicians. Like so many famous men, he appeared to be proud of anything except his acknowledged accomplishments. At tennis his performance had a clear priority over his reputation for statesmanship and for an erudition in philosophy rare in politics. He had in reality or posture a complete detachment and indifference to all mundane things. He was clearly pleased when a little later in some slight clash in the House of Commons I described his conduct with the quotation, he 'handles all things mortal with cold immortal hands'.

The contrast between his languid demeanour and the steely resolution of his action as Irish Secretary is well known. Some sections of the bourgeois world were deceived by the gentleness of his manners. They misunderstand good manners, because they have none, and make the grave error of mistaking gentleness for weakness. H. G. Wells, for instance, called Balfour that 'damp Madonna Lily' (and Lenin called Mr. Wells 'that dreadful little bourgeois'). It would have been grimly entertaining to see the soft rotundity of H.G. summoning resolution to face the Irish gunmen with the calm of A.J.B. only five years after they had shot dead a predecessor in the broad daylight of Phoenix Park. Before he had been Irish Secretary for a few months the welkin of the Left was ringing with 'bloody Balfour'. His placid, almost drooping manner masked a tough and ruthless character; the same affectation often conceals outstanding capacity for action in the professional officer class of various armies.

Less well known than his Irish record is the account given by some of Mr. Balfour's contemporaries of the complete change in his Parliamentary method after the Conservative disaster in 1906, when he was elected as Leader of the Opposition to a very different House of Commons and with only a small minority behind him. It is a mark of the highest talent, particularly late in life, when a man can adapt his technique rapidly to a completely new situation. It appears that Mr. Balfour changed his make-up as dramatically as a wise women of advancing years will modify her appearance for the variations of sunshine and evening light. This capacity is a strength when the basic character remains firm. Which of the Scandinavians wrote: 'the future belongs to him who can assume as many shapes as Proteus'?

I was reminded again of this capacity in outstanding men to change their method as the situation requires when General de Gaulle found himself in ballotage during the French Presidential election of 1965. The sudden change from the portentous figure behind a writing table in the Elysée to the appearance on television of the *vieux bonhomme* in an armchair, generously answering even the most awkward questions of a young interlocutor, was indeed an abrupt change; but it worked. It is superfluous to add that no question arose of the General's basic character so suddenly changing.

Mr. Asquith was much less flexible. The Roman senator disdained any playing to the gallery and had, perhaps, a certain intellectual arrogance; hence some of his troubles. He ignored the basic rule to conceal contempt, for contempt is one of the things men never forgive. All this made him an attractive figure in his firm honesty, but he incurred unnecessary criticism. Nevertheless, he had a highly practical sense: '*Solvitur ambulando*' was one of his favourite sayings during discussions of parliamentary procedure. 'Does the right honourable gentleman mean by walking through the division lobby?' enquired Lord Hugh Cecil, as the Liberal Government had been using the guillotine. 'No, sir, by walking through the realm of reason in the light of truth,' replied the Prime Minister.

It is quite natural that throughout all the vicissitudes of politics Asquith should have retained a close friendship with Balfour, for they had so many friends and so many interests in common, quite apart from politics. Yet the friendship became apparently the object of profound suspicion to many people. In circles which should have known better it was suggested that politics were thereby rendered insincere; the lampoons of Belloc and Chesterton were largely directed at such relationships. The suspicion of the mass of the people sometimes took a robust English form in a native shrewdness misapplied. Dick Wallhead, one of the fine old pioneers of Labour when I first joined the Party, told me I must study the basic psychology of the movement, and recounted an anecdote of his youth. He was speaking in South Wales at a miners' meeting and was introduced by the local chairman of the Party in the following fashion: 'Why do we need a Labour Party? I will tell you why. Henry Asquith meets Arthur Balfour behind the Speaker's chair. Henry, says Arthur, come and have one. Henry says, Well Arthur, I don't mind if I do, and we'll see what we can do to dish the bloody workers.' There, observed the shrewd old Dick, you have the origin of the Labour Party.

Such suspicions were by no means confined to the working class, as it used to be called, but they were usually not well founded. These men were divided by great principles, but remained personal friends. This is perfectly possible, as I have found throughout my political life. There were great issues which divided the parties in those days, far more acutely than the main parties appear to be divided today. The land question, tariff reform, and particularly the Ulster problem not only created considerable differences of principle but also aroused the most violent emotion. Parliamentary rows extended from the Chamber even to the Ladies Gallery when on one occasion Speaker Lowther responded to an appeal to restore order there with the remark that he had enough to do with the devils below without occupying himself with the angels above.

How much better it is to hold great principles without personal animosity than to have no principles and yet to feel enmity. In those days they fought about their beliefs, but respected and even liked one another. In these days it appears they have no principles to quarrel about, or no principles which divide them, but on personal grounds they simply detest each other. Faith is replaced by spleen. The strangest parliamentary malady of modern times is that fundamentally the parties appear to agree about everything; when anything goes wrong they just adopt each other's policies, but abuse each other for doing it. All very practical perhaps, if it works, but disastrous to the practitioners when it ceases to work. They are left with nothing—except their mutual responsibility and mutual hatred, which can become a national danger, for the people are liable to believe in nothing if they have been deceived too long and too effectively by the central unanimity.

This is surely a perversion of the English tradition, which had so many virtues and for so long astonished other peoples. It is part of the English genius to stick to principles without incurring the bitterness which often racks other nations. The basis is far sounder if it becomes necessary to come together in time of national danger. Britain can then be saved by a tradition which is not often available to other countries.

This national idiosyncracy—as others regard it—has found effective expression in our time. References can be made to the Other Club because it has recently been the subject of comment both in books and newspapers. It was founded by Winston Churchill and F. E. Smith and was confined to some fifty members prominent in politics, business, science, literature and the arts. The purpose was simply to dine together during the parliamentary session, and one of its rules, if I remember rightly, laid down that nothing in the procedure should in any way 'mitigate the asperities of party politics'. It was always said that the Other Club was started as an answer to The Club, which was founded by Dr. Johnson and his circle, and in the early life of Winston Churchill and F. E. Smith was conducted chiefly by Asquith and Curzon. I was fortunate enough to be elected to the Other Club at a quite early stage in my parliamentary life, and remained a member until I felt it discourteous to the founder to attend in the bitter controversy which preceded the Second World War.

During the harsh controversy of these later years I was protected not so much by private friendship as by the public eulogies which had fallen like the gentle and refreshing dew of heaven in my orthodox period. It was impossible to give me the full treatment of most innovators. 'Thug' was just possible when other people attacked my meetings, and I had the impertinence to defend them with the aid of my gallant and devoted friends. 'Moron,' however, was out, because during considerable periods of my earlier parliamentary life I had been praised in a way which sometimes seemed even to my receptive ears a little exaggerated. The recent development of my thinking makes some of my earlier contributions appear immature to me now; nevertheless, the almost universal praise during certain periods of my early life saved me from the experience of most reformers. After this it was impossible to call me just a crank or an imbecile without my detractors appearing ridiculous, and such attacks were consequently confined to those circles in our country which are themselves imbecile and receive no consideration. Lately in these matters I have benefited by a variety of weighty judgments which I greatly appreciate.

This inhibition in my case no doubt caused the fury of the established world against my supporters to be redoubled. It is a mistake for the rulers of Britain to be moved by passion to persecute in such a bitter personal fashion the pioneers of new causes, to throw mud rather than to employ argument in the free debate which is so much advertised in public and so carefully suppressed in fact. Sharp reverses of fortune and treatment can embitter men. Some will seek revenge, and wait a lifetime to get it, though for my part I have always said that revenge is the hallmark of small minds. 'Stand by your friends, stand up to your enemies,' as I once put it, is a better principle than Roman Sulla's epitaph: 'Man never knew a truer friend or a more relentless foe'. Thus enmity must cease with the fight, and I am incapable of carrying it further. This is an English characteristic, and in my opinion desirable. When the hand is given and the struggle is ended, the rule of reconciliation should be held with fidelity.

It is of course far easier and better never to become embroiled in these bitter animosities, to be attacked and to reply without resentment, to fight truly for your belief when you are in the ring, but to feel no trace of bitterness when you leave it. Asquith is an example of a man who would congratulate as warmly what he considered a brilliant attack upon him as he would an able speaker in his defence. Such an attitude is sometimes considered to be detached from humanity, but it has at least the merit of avoiding some of the more egregious of contemporary errors.

It followed naturally from my general attitude that my first serious work in politics was an attempt to form a movement of the centre, which immediately received the benevolent interest of Winston Churchill and F. E. Smith and, over a decade later in more definite form, the active co-operation of Lloyd George. This second main impulse clearly derived from my first determination—to prevent a recurrence of war, to save the next generation from the fate of my friends, and to build a country worthy of their sacrifice. As we have seen, my whole political life was in a sense predetermined by this almost religious conviction, and it inevitably influenced me to seek a continuance of the national union of war for the purposes of peace, for construction instead of destruction.

It was evident in my election address and in the speeches of my first campaign in Harrow that my thinking and policies cut clean across the programmes and attitudes of existing parties. I was already a man not of the parties but of the centre, and there in terms of the truth underlying the superficial I have remained ever since, until in recent years I summarised my position in European debate as the 'centre dur contre le centre pourri'. Paradoxically, I feel obliged to offer apology not for inconsistency, which might be expected from my changes of parties, but for consistency in maintaining the same basic attitude through superficial changes. This should not necessarily be reckoned a virtue; to live a lifetime without changing an opinion is to live without learning and is the mark of a fool. In the unfolding of this story I am sometimes disturbed by my consistency, but though my ideas have not changed they have developed and grown with experience, reflection and the test of action.

It may also appear a paradox to claim to be of the centre when my policies must seem sometimes to be to the left of the Left and at other times to be to the right of the Right. It is an uncomfortable centre because it is in essence dynamic and not static, but the point of equilibrium in these fluent and progressive policies is undoubtedly the centre. To succeed in the continuing crisis of our time they must draw to the centre from left and right the best of the nation for the purpose of political action by all who are determined on survival and greatness. The seeming paradox arises because the policy is designed to evoke action from the whole nation. My attempted combination of 'socialism' and 'imperialism' in the election of 1918 was the first crude expression of this political synthesis, and it has continued to the present day not only in terms of synthesis but of fresh creation in larger spheres and with further vision.

Early in the Parliament of 1918 we formed an organisation called the New Members' Group, which was quickly nicknamed the Centre Party by the Press. It was composed mostly of members who had fought in the war, and numbered about one hundred and fifty. The Chairman was Oscar Guest, the brother of Lloyd George's Chief Whip, and the joint secretaries were Colin Coote, afterwards editor of the *Daily Telegraph*, and myself. None of my associates at that time have any responsibility for my further aims or subsequent life course, which were not yet apparent and indeed were not yet clear even to me. We met and we discussed, but not much more happened. The limitation was the power of the Party machine, which in the absence of grave crisis is always overwhelming in British politics.

These M.P.s of the war generation were very sincere and idealistic. What were their motives? Primarily to secure the fulfilment of the programme on which they were elected, an advanced policy of social reform declared in passionate and moving terms by Lloyd George. After the sacrifice of the war generation, the world was never to be the same again, and that Parliament in its social programme was to erect a monument to the fallen; at least, so I understood from the speeches of our leaders, and I think a good many others did too.

There quickly grew a sense that these aims were to be frustrated. It has never been for me quite true that this House of Commons was divided sharply between the war generation and the 'hard-faced men', as Keynes described them. The experience of that war was even more liable to harden the features than the process of making profit in business. The soldiers back from the war were not all idealists and the businessmen were not all war profiteers. Yet there was a certain psychological division which can perhaps best be expressed in the simple fact that the war generation was more disposed to take the 1918 programmes seriously.

I would not for a moment claim that many of them shared my ideas to the full. The combination of socialism and imperialism would have seemed quaint to most of them. My cross-party position was already finding some form in the political theory that you could neither have order and stability without progress, nor progress without order and stability. A synthesis of left and right was a practical requirement of political life. It is unlikely that they were thinking in these terms, and we did not hold discussions on these lines, but the Centre Party was a band of serious people believing that our programme of 1918 should be implemented. We felt in general and in particular that the organisation built in the war should not be sold for scrap. This soon tended in one detail to a certain friction, as some of our parliamentary colleagues were acquiring war stores at scrap prices.

Our group was filled with good intentions and with some incipient indignation. We were looking among the more experienced for leaders with the same feeling. It did not occur to me as baby of the House, aged twenty-two, or to any of the others that we could at that stage play leading parts. We were fresh from the discipline of the army hierarchy, and in any case felt that we were tyros at the political business, with everything to learn. We must look to the experienced generals of politics on their chosen battle-grounds; we invited them to dinner.

These dinners took place at the Criterion, and the first memorable occasion was when Mr. Churchill was our guest. I already had experience of his oratorical processes. After my maiden speech and in the early days of the Centre Party he seemed interested in me and developed a kindly flattery, seeking my opinion as typical of the new generation. In particular, he would try out his speeches on me, apparently a life-long habit of his, with many different auditors. In his Minister's room at the House of Commons he would walk up and down slowly collecting his thoughts and evolving them into speech, occasionally turning to his audience to see how it was going. At that time he was certainly not a ready speaker, it was all a considerable labour. I remember Mr. Asquith telling me that in his early days as a Minister Mr. Churchill had some difficulty in winding up a debate and had nothing like the natural gifts of impromptu speech possessed by his father, Lord Randolph. Nevertheless, as time went on he developed a remarkable aptitude for extempore repartee in the House of Commons, though sometimes an elaborate trap would be laid in advance for the intended victims into which they almost always fell. The really brilliant impromptu would seem to emerge from the depths of his being with the force of an explosion bursting through all the hesitations of his speech in seeking the *mot juste*; in fact, the impediment of his speech was finally developed with rare artifice into one of its chief attractions. He became a supreme parliamentary speaker, though he was always less pre-eminent in addressing mass audiences on the platform; but everywhere he was effective, both by reason of gift and personality.

I do not remember his speech at the Criterion, though it had almost certainly been tried out on me in advance. This was the first occasion of our Centre Party dealings; a recurring theme, reasonable and desirable but always frustrated. Mr. Churchill undoubtedly maintained a proper ministerial discretion, though it was not difficult to see what he was after. The drama that night was produced not so much by him as by his great friend, F. E. Smith. Whether or not this effect had been rehearsed between them I shall never know. They had long maintained a friendship which cut right across party alignments and was given practical expression in the institution of the Other Club. Churchill on the right of Liberalism and Smith on the left of Conservatism must have entertained from time to time some Centre Party thoughts, of which the older generation would be more aware. It had not occurred to the young and the innocent of the New Members' Group to invite them to our dinner together; or perhaps we felt it would look too much like a conspiracy.

We had no idea that F. E. Smith was in the same building, but a message was brought to Mr. Churchill directly after his speech. With gratified surprise he turned to me and said that his old friend was in the restaurant below and it would be a pleasure if he could be invited to our table. This was indeed a coup for the new members, and I hastened to execute my mission. I found the Lord Chancellor seated in a prominent position with the sole company of Lady Birkenhead. He appeared to be in an advanced condition of post-prandial content as he surveyed me indolently through the haze of his cigar smoke, countenance suffused but genial. I indicated that Mr. Churchill would be pleased if he would join our company upstairs, and looked enquiringly at his experienced partner. She said something to the effect that he was quite all right and I should take him along.

He rose with dignity to his feet and, leaning rather heavily on his guide, advanced in stately style to the door, with few words spoken. We proceeded, as the police say in difficult circumstances, to the field of action, where he sat heavily on a chair which was happily near the door. The symptoms were ominous, and I glanced enquiringly at Mr. Churchill, as previously at Lady Birkenhead, but his experienced eye immediately reflected an affirmative and he called at once on his old friend to speak, amid our resounding applause. Resting his full weight on his fists clenched on the table, Lord Birkenhead spoke like a bird for twenty minutes with little more than his customary lisp. It was astonishing, but both wife and friend had known the form.

Birkenhead was an extraordinary man and his way of life even in that generation was exceptional. He could support it without any apparent impairment of his faculties, but his imitators could not. The wayside became strewn with young men who thought that to be brilliant it was necessary to adopt his fashion. What was the secret of his Pied Piper appeal to the young? Wit and irreverence, always an irresistible combination to those who themselves combine brains with youth. Discussing his favourite butt, who happened to be his leader, Mr. Baldwin: 'The man has foot and mouth disease, every time he opens his mouth he puts his foot in it'. When approached by a conspiracy to replace Baldwin by Joynson-Hicks in a critical situation: 'Never swop donkeys when you are crossing a stream'. Looming, a sombre figure in his favourite corner table at the Ritz, when greeted after a good lunch by a much bemedalled general who had spent the war in the War Office: 'General, you have got a lot of medals'. 'Yes, Mr. Attorney, if I get any more I shall scarcely know where to put them.' 'Put them where you earned them, General, on your backside.' In F.E.'s company both Sandhurst and University could delight; eternal summer gilds him yet, in memory.

The long, leisurely luncheons and dinners, the drinking and the smoking of the best were all perhaps in the traditional manner of British politics at the end of the eighteenth and beginning of the nineteenth century, but the stress of life and particularly of administration was then far less. Yet even in a man so brilliant as F.E. I always had the impression that while the performance of youth could be indefinitely repeated, with almost greater effect in age, it was not so easy with such a habit of life to absorb new knowledge or to learn new tricks, equally difficult for old dogs and old drunks. There were plenty of people too in the classic world who lived in this way, but in that stressful and testing period they never achieved the heights of success by the arduous contemporary standards. As Cato said on the eve of his suicide: 'Only one man came sober to the overthrow of the State, but on that occasion the State was overthrown'.

It always seemed to me that such habits in varying degrees became the stock-in-trade of most of the statesmen during my early period in politics— an outstanding exception was Lloyd George—by reason of the extreme effort of mind and will necessary to start a great speech. It is a terrible thing to face a large audience, when both you and they are stone cold; yet once you make the painful effort of warming yourself up with your own exertion, your momentum soon develops effortlessly. I drink coffee before a big speech, but if you start on coffee, you end in another fashion almost as drunk as those who begin on alcohol. The choice is whether you start sober and end drunk, or start drunk and end sober. The former is much better, both for the health of the speaker and for the effect on the audience. The reason is that alcohol taken before a speech replaces the function of the endocrine system, and as the alcohol wears off at the end, the speech falls rather flat. If on the other hand you start cold, the exertion of speaking gradually floods your system with adrenalin and you end in a condition of excitement which is communicated to the audience. The effort of calming yourself later in order to sleep requires an almost equal exercise of the will; some have been prematurely exhausted by reason of their failure in this respect. I understand that science supports me to some extent in these reflections, which in my case are fortified by long and highly tested experience. I offer them for what they are worth to young speakers.

The recurrent theme of the Centre Party soon ended at this stage, so far as I was concerned, by reason of a rapidly increasing political divergence from Mr. Churchill. When it was resumed over a decade later, with far more vigorous impulse, Lloyd George was more in the picture than Churchill.

I had by then ceased to be a political infant because I had established my reputation with my speech of resignation from the Labour Government, and in the discussions of that later period had become competent to speak for the younger generation. Although the initiative from the older statesmen in this later stage of our story came mostly from Lloyd George, with the aid of Lord Rothermere, Mr. Churchill was certainly on occasion present at our discussions,[1] but he did not attend them all, or in the earlier phase play any leading part. The reason perhaps was that his relations were none too good in that period with all the young M.P.s with whom I became associated after my departure from the Labour Government, and in particular he had some personal friction with some of the younger Conservatives.

My own relations with Mr. Churchill remained reasonably good throughout, and were only intermittently interrupted by some spasm of passion at one of my more outrageous utterances. Even when he was moved on one occasion to shake his fist at me across the floor of the House, with a muttered 'You damned puppy', a welcoming grin in the lobby would follow a few days of scowling oblivion. He never bore malice. For my part, I always liked him and it was part of the 'tears of things' that deep differences in attitude to politics, though not to life, soon parted us and finally severed threads of fate which for a moment had been entwined.

Kaleidoscopic memories of Winston Churchill are reflected from many different occasions, happy, sad, passionate, but never mean or ignoble. Our clashes in debate were numerous and often ended in much gaiety, but never in prolonged ill-feeling. On one occasion he had wound up the debate after I had made a rather noisy, flashy speech for the Opposition, which had transmuted a dull and flat occasion into a lively and enjoyable uproar. He described in rolling periods how stricken and dismayed appeared the Opposition and how lost their cause, 'when forth sprang our young Astyanax, the hope of Troy'. There were roars of laughter at my expense and I was left wondering how he had managed it, for I was tolerably certain that he had never read a line of Homer. Later in the lobby he came rolling up to me, smiling broadly, and said with a dig in the ribs: 'Bartlett's Familiar Quotations, my boy, never be without them'. A large part of his charm was that he was completely devoid of humbug. He detested the goody-goodies, as he used to call them.

Churchill, with all his impulsive and emotional character, had a certain solid sense which traversed acute party divisions in a very English, no-nonsense manner, and made him normally and essentially a man of the centre. Typical of this quiet commonsense was his remark—'blood will only come from the nose in England'—said to me with a certain calm content when our Blackshirts were clashing with their Red challengers at our meetings all over Britain. He was frank in remarkable degree about himself and realistic about his prospects. 'What is the use of racing all your life if you never win the Derby,' he said to

---

[1] See Nicolson, *Diaries, 1930–39*, pp. 81–2.

me across the table at the Other Club a few years before the war; and on another occasion, 'The trouble is I have been on the placards too long'. He had then evidently despaired of ever becoming Prime Minister, and to all appearances it was a just appraisal.

What was the basic reason for that vast divergence of principle which separated me permanently in politics from a man I liked so much, Winston Churchill? The answer is clearly found in his son's biography, where a letter written by Winston Churchill in 1909 is quoted: 'Do you know, I would greatly like to have some practice in the handling of large forces . . . I am sure I have the root of the matter in me but never, I fear, in this state of existence will it have a chance of flowering . . . in bright red bloom'.[1] He had other moods, as his son points out, but it appeared to me that this attitude prevailed throughout the years which followed the First World War. It was noted in the Second by Lloyd George, who wrote to his wife: 'Winston likes wars, I don't'.[2]

This tendency of Mr. Churchill clearly rendered impossible a close political association with someone who returned from war with my passionate dedication to peace. This became evident at an early stage and was reflected throughout our relationship in all things, small and great. It began with his Russian adventure in 1919 and continued until the Second World War. He seemed to me constantly to risk war without good reason. I was only willing for Britain to fight again if our vital interests were at stake, whereas he appeared willing to engage in military adventures which risked lives and wasted our substance without that purpose. The main clash belongs to the later stage of this account, but the first encounters were sufficient to end our happy relationship in the incipient Centre Party.

My purpose here is not to write history, but to explain a personal course in life. I shall deal at a later stage with my case against the war of 1939; it is enough here to indicate my position in disputes which history will finally judge. My quarrel with Mr. Churchill soon after the First War related to three main issues: the Russian, Mesopotamian and Chanak adventures, as I regarded them. History may possibly hold Mr. Churchill guilty on the first two counts, but not on the third. Lord Snow quotes Lloyd George[3] as saying Churchill was responsible for the initiative in both Russia and Chanak. L.G. complained that in 1915 Churchill got out his map of the Dardanelles, and 'see where that landed us'. Then in describing his post-war government L.G. added: 'Before I could look round, he had got out his maps of Russia and we were making fools of ourselves in the Civil War. When that was over he got out his maps again—Greece and Turkey, and brought my tottering administration to a close.' Most students of the period will probably agree however with A. J. P. Taylor's view in his Oxford *English History* that Lloyd

---

[1] *Winston S. Churchill*, Randolph S. Churchill (Heinemann, 1967), Vol. 2.
[2] *The Years that are Past*, Frances Lloyd George (Hutchinson, 1967).
[3] *Sunday Telegraph*, February 5, 1967.

George himself was primarily responsible for the enterprise in Greece, and that Churchill was only a belated convert to the undertaking. For my part, I opposed all these adventures—Russia, Mesopotamia and Chanak—whoever was initially responsible, and I expressed myself on grounds of principle with a clarity which was adequate but with an invective which was perhaps exaggerated.

Lloyd George's general attitude to Churchill, described long afterwards by Lord Snow, that he was a dangerous and unsuccessful military adventurer—'a bit of an ass'—was certainly the view expressed in my speeches at the time. On one occasion in debate after observing that Mr. Churchill was 'borrowing his principles from Prussia to supply leadership to the National Liberal Party, which borrowed its name from Germany', I summarised my view of his performances: 'My complaint is that he is an inefficient Prussian; he is always beaten. Unfortunately for the tax-payer whose money is consumed in the maw of his omnivorous ambition, whenever he meets vigorous and determined opponents, such as Lenin and Michael Collins, his vaunted military genius appears impotent to effect a conclusion. And, at the end of an unsatisfactory and fluctuating combat maintained at the expense of English lives and money, upon the sheathing of his ineffective sabre, these enemies of his, whether they have been hailed as monsters on thrones of skulls or merely as chiefs of murder gangs, are received into his paternal embraces. We really do not get value for money. It is no good keeping a private Napoleon if he is always defeated. It is altogether too expensive a luxury. The Right Honourable gentleman has waded through blood to defeat in many adventures, he has often been compelled to surrender to force what he has previously refused to reason.'[1]

The charge was political profligacy and military incompetence. We had suffered the experiences of Antwerp, Gallipoli, Russia and Mesopotamia, as well as the bitter Irish events. This savagery of debate against a man who was then himself unbridled in his utterances—'monster on a throne of skulls' for the Russian leader and 'chief of the murder gangs' for the Irish leader, with whom he was shortly afterwards cracking jokes over a rifle in Downing Street during the peace negotiations—did not begin suddenly but developed gradually. I supported Mr. Churchill when government policy during a military operation was threatened by trade union action, although on practical grounds of the national interest I later opposed the policy as mistaken, and then urged withdrawal. We were in Russia as an operation of war, a fact demonstrated with much force in Mr. Churchill's speeches, and had to extricate Russian soldiers who had acted as our allies. It was therefore an outrage to everyone of my mind and temperament when Labour leaders threatened a general strike to enforce their political prejudice in favour of the Soviet power against which our troops were fighting.

There is no doubt about that threat. It was deprecated but explained by the

[1] *Hansard.*

moderate Mr. Clynes, then vice-chairman of the Labour Party, in a speech in Parliament on July 20, 1919: 'There has now been formed in this country so strong a feeling in the mind of organised labour that assurances can come only by a complete reversal of the policy so far formed in relation to Russia, and so strong is that feeling that it has been—I regret to say—deliberately resolved by a very formidable organisation known to the country as the Triple Alliance to take such steps as might lead to something in the nature of a national strike, unless we reverse our policy on this question . . . I should hope that the working classes in the use of the industrial weapon will neither now nor in the future commit an act which would supply to any other section of the community any excuse for the defiance of the law at some time or other.' The mild Mr. Clynes need not have feared a precedent, for such crimes were only permitted to the Left. Can we give a better definition of high treason than the calling of a general strike to enforce a change of policy by government, and in so doing to deny supplies and munitions to our troops fighting in the field?

While strongly supporting Mr. Churchill in the face of such threats, I nevertheless became convinced that we should extricate ourselves as quickly as possible from the Russian campaign. The parting came when the Russian expedition seemed to be in danger of becoming a crusade to crush Bolshevism. 'If we don't put our foot on the egg, we shall have to chase the chicken round the world's farmyard' was then reputed to be a Churchill phrase which has a genuine ring. I then began to oppose him, and successive governments pursuing the same policies, as part of consistent principles which I have pursued ever since.

It is pleasing to me today to observe that the motif of Europe was already running through my speeches. They all reiterated the same theme—eschew foreign adventures which are none of Britain's business, look after our own people, conserve our resources, guard our Empire, maintain our strength, develop our vital interests, which are in Europe, and ignore all distractions from these purposes in remote territories. Can I really be accused, when I opposed the 1939 war against a German driving through Poland towards Russia, of doing so because I was attracted by his political ideas rather than guided by my own deeply rooted concept of the interests of my country?

Aversion to wars I regarded as unnecessary swung my young allegiance in this decisive period from the side of Mr. Churchill to that of Lord Robert Cecil. The enterprise in Russia in 1919 seemed to me to risk British lives without British purpose, and in military terms it occurred to me that Mr. Churchill might not succeed where Napoleon had failed. Lord Robert Cecil, on the other hand, stated with great force the sensible and honourable theme that we must fulfil war-incurred obligations to allies, but extricate ourselves directly it was done from remote adventures which were no concern of Britain's.

Yet it was impossible not to feel some personal sympathy with Winston

Churchill, and this relationship endured many years after the parting of our political ways. From his side a warm and affectionate nature often moved him to gestures in private life which cost him considerable time and trouble. He was capable too of emotion in a degree unusual among the English, in this respect rather resembling Curzon. He came to some small private gathering to initiate a day nursery in memory of Cimmie some time after her death in 1933, and when he greeted me his eyes filled with tears. He was a genial host even to his prisoners and in the classic English tradition did what he could to mitigate our condition during the Second World War. Another vivid recollection of him as a charming host was at the twenty-first birthday party of his son Randolph, then a handsome and engaging lad. The present Lord Birkenhead also made a speech on that occasion, as a very young man with some of the wit and more than the charm of his father.

As many others have noted, Winston Churchill had no ungenerous qualities, a fact quite apart from his capacities as a statesman or the grave question of his policies. To the dismay and even to the disgust of some of my friends in several countries, I have never been able in personal as opposed to political terms to regard Churchill as a scoundrel or Roosevelt as a criminal. It should be possible, and it is possible in what we conceive to be the interests of our country and of our continent, to oppose men with every fibre of our being to the extreme of personal sacrifice, without treating as villains those who are personally honourable, even though, in our view, profoundly mistaken. To believe that all errors are diabolic shows a misunderstanding of the world, although if they threaten the ruin of our country we must combat them as if they were.

It is noteworthy too that even across all the bitterness of international divisions a certain regard, even admiration, for a great enemy is an imprimatur of the great periods of history. It was a moving moment in the surgent genius of the British when Napoleon came onto the bridge of the *Bellerophon* at Plymouth Sound by request, to show himself to the people in the fleet of small boats who had rowed out to see him, and every man in the crowd took off his hat. It must be conceded that he had committed no crime comparable with modern crimes. Yet since then we have travelled far down a road whose end was revealed in previous civilisations. Revenge today pursues not merely individuals but whole peoples, and the flames of animosity are stoked continuously with a propaganda hitherto confined to time of war.

It was not long in time from the luminous moment when Caesar wept by the bier of Pompey, although the death of his great rival made him master of the known world, to the dark hour when the execrable Octavia, wife of Antony, placed a golden coin in the mouth of the murdered Cicero with the squalid gibe: 'So much for your golden tongue'. Yet it marked a steep descent on the road to Avernus. When two great friends of intimate relation were thrown against each other by fate to fight for the world, it was a deep tragedy that one must die. The news of unparalleled victory was lost in sorrow as Caesar kissed the forehead of the fallen Pompey and then retired for several days, prostrated by grief. The extreme contrast with modern behaviour was not due to weakness, for never in the long history of action have the two essential qualities been so united in one man: the brain of ice and the heart of fire.

That is how I like to think of our Europe. I do not refer to the chivalrous wars when Frederick the Great and Maria Theresa fought for the exchange of a province, without any of the deliberate devastation of non-combatant life which returned to warfare with Stonewall Jackson in America. There is no need to revert to the moment depicted by Velasquez in the Prado, which shows the Spanish conqueror descending from his horse and bowing lower than the defeated Netherlander, before he embraces him to show that he honours a brave enemy. I refer to the young airmen who were my com companions in Flanders in the early days of the First War; they were of the modern age—its very flower—yet they felt the same high regard for the young enemies against whom they were thrown to death by the folly and failure of the old world.

If my generation felt in this way about the finer spirits among our enemies of the first war, it is surely right for me to retain no lesser sentiment about my chief opponent among my fellow-countrymen. With no bitterness and with some appreciation of the infinite variety of human existence in the tangled but brightly woven pattern of the fates, I recall one of the last evenings in the Other Club when I was sitting opposite Winston Churchill. He looked across the table and addressed to me a brief but prescient oration which I remember, and for good reason. It began with the simile that the river of history was flowing through a quiet and peaceful contemporary scene, so calm that it could even carry on its tranquil bosom the contemptible figures of Baldwin and MacDonald (his nominal leaders), but soon it would reach the falls, the cataract of destiny, the foam would sparkle, the spray would glitter in the sunshine of great opportunity and—leaning forward in poignant emphasis—'our time will come'. It did—with him in Downing Street, and me in jail.

Above left Lady Mosley, the author's mother. *Above right* Sir Oswald Mosley, the author's grandfather (nicknamed 'John Bull').

Below Monument in Didsbury church to Sir Nicholas Mosley, Lord Mayor of London, 1599.

Wedding group, May 1920, at Hackwood House, Basingstoke. *Front row* Earl of Athlone; Marcella Duggan; Marquis of Londonderry; Princess Alice, Countess of Athlone; King of the Belgians; Cynthia Curzon; the author; Queen of the Belgians; Alexandra Curzon; Marques de Soveral. *Second row (centre)* Marchioness Curzon; Marquis Curzon; Marchioness of Londonderry, Irene Curzon; Sir Charles Mendl.

Below left The author speaking at the dedication of the War Memorial in his Harrow constituency. General Ironside is standing on the right of the picture. *Below right* Cynthia with Michael.

The Labour Party Conference, 1929, with William Jowitt on the right. *Below left* Cynthia, the author and Lord Robert Cecil. *Below right* Holiday in Lossiemouth. *Left to right* Author, Ishbel MacDonald, Ramsay MacDonald, Alistair MacDonald, John Strachey.

The author with a member of the Swedish International team. The author last represented Britain in the world championship in Paris, 1937. *Below* The author aged twenty.

6
Marriage to
Cynthia Curzon
Curzon
India

My marriage to Cynthia Curzon was an event in my life of outstanding happiness and enduring influence. She was my steadfast, ever loyal and able colleague in the tough existence of politics, and my delightful companion in most of the charming occasions described in this book from that happy day in 1920 until her tragic death in 1933 at the age of thirty-four. She died of peritonitis following an appendix operation in a period before the discovery of the modern drug which would have saved her. Like most people, I have a great appreciation of real goodness of character, and I have never seen that finest of qualities in higher degree in any human being. She was a good woman in the true, natural sense of the word. In addition, she had an immense gaiety and *joie de vivre*, an enthusiasm alike for the fun of private life and the causes of public life, whose unreasonable frustrations would move her to the most intense indignation, but her enthusiasms were balanced by her calm and steady character.

When I met her she had advanced Liberal opinions, an instant, automatic sentiment in favour of the under-dog. She reacted strongly against the splendours of Conservatism, so faithfully reflected in her early surroundings, and this led her to seek close contact with the mass of the people and to prefer simplicity in her own home. She liked people, and her transparent sincerity and friendly approach enabled her to get on with them. Our house combined her welcome with these tastes, and made everyone feel at home.

We began married life with two small cottages at Ifold in the middle of the Sussex woods near Dunsfold; with their beams and low ceilings they were in extreme contrast with the lofty magnificence of her father's Hampshire house at Hackwood. We moved later to Savehay Farm, a Tudor house in about a hundred and twenty acres of land near the lovely village of Denham in Buckinghamshire. Again, the simplicity of style presented a challenge to the Regency glories of her father's tastes; a natural reaction which enlarged her experience, for happily she still retained her capacity to enjoy all spheres of life's diversity. Our London house at 8 Smith Square, with its roseate Queen Anne panelling, was a retreat from the busy political world, disturbed only by the harsh summons of the division bell. Our two elder children were born and brought up in these houses; Cimmie was a completely devoted mother, the life was domestic. Her real political interests came later, for she was at first given entirely to home life, relieved only by the gaiety of young parties in the country and the fun of London in the glittering twenties.

As Cimmie grew to political maturity she combined a passion to end avoidable suffering and unnecessary poverty with an urge towards the essential action and a hot impatience with its frustrations. It was not only her deep personal loyalty, but also her recognition that sentiment is not enough, which held her always in my political companionship. She recognised that we must will the means as well as the end, though the rough struggle was often detestable to her gentle nature. All ignoble means were excluded by such a character; if fight we must, our weapons must be clean, our victory magnanimous, or our defeat unflinching.

I met Cimmie first just after the war, and remember driving her home from parties to her father's house at No. 1 Carlton House Terrace. My first close association with her was in the by-election at Plymouth in March 1919, which followed Waldorf Astor's entry to the House of Lords on the death of his father. Lady Astor was the candidate and Cimmie was very fond of her; Cliveden, their house by the Thames, at that time played a considerable part in all our lives.

The by-election was as lively as all other events connected with Nancy Astor. I spent some time at Plymouth as a speaker, while Cimmie canvassed, and I vividly remember riding the storm caused by my attacks on the Labour leaders' war record at the large eve-of-poll meeting. It was here I met for the first time the Liberal M.P. for the neighbouring division, Isaac Foot, father of several distinguished sons, and formed a personal friendship which lasted through my parliamentary life. A great authority on Cromwell, he was a Radical who appreciated the character of action.

Cimmie and I continued to see much of each other for the rest of 1919, and in the early spring of 1920 we became engaged. She was the daughter of an enigmatic figure to the younger generation, Lord Curzon of Kedleston, who was then Foreign Secretary and had previously been a distinguished Viceroy of India. The stories of his dignity and pomp, of his archaic and affected manners were legion, and always include his old-world habit of giving words like grass a short 'a', as in bat. For instance, on his entry to the Secretary of

State's room at the Foreign Office, when, pointing at the inkpot, he commanded: 'Remove that object of gläss and bräss, and bring me alabäster'. I had never met him, but soon discovered that his real character was very different from his public image, as it would be called in these days. Cimmie, his second daughter, was on the best of terms with her father, though resistant to the exaggerated magnificence in which she had been brought up. His hobby was acquiring old castles for national preservation and doing them up in the grand style of his most discriminating taste. He was a snob—the theme of many of the stories—and she was not. He quietly observed to me one day: 'If you are the Leader of the House of Lords, it is your métier to be a snob'.

No doubt he apprehended that Cimmie's independent character might lead her to some marriage less desirable than the alliance with the eldest son of a prominent peer which he might have selected for her. She was a little uncertain of her reception when she entered his room in Carlton House Terrace to announce her engagement, and her entertaining account of his demeanour on this possibly trying occasion was long a cause of merriment to her friends. When she said, 'I'm engaged,' he rose and embraced her warmly; always affectionate and always correct. Then she thought she detected just the whisper of a sigh as his eye roved along the imposing array of finely bound books on his library shelf until it reached the humble reference books: for a moment it paused on *Debrett*, but moved on without hope to *Who's Who*. Then he spoke, in his curious, archaic accent with clipped, short 'a': 'Päss me that red book, and tell me his name'. Laughing, she passed over *Who's Who* and brought him instead *Debrett*: I was one of the lesser denizens, but still just inside the magic circle.

I liked him at once, from the first meeting. Lord Curzon was certainly a distinguished and imposing figure; his appearance was almost a parody of what a Leader of the House of Lords should be, but his dignity carried it without absurdity. God's butler, the young used to say, and it was a joke to which he referred with quiet appreciation; he was aware of most of the tales and quips at his expense. He collected them rather as Henry Ford gathered jokes about Ford cars, and would often analyse their degree of verity. Such stories as his alleged observation when he saw men just out of the trenches in a bath-house behind the lines—'I never knew before the lower clässes have such white skins'—would be laboriously dissected, with the conclusion that it was quite natural to note how remarkably clean these men had managed to keep themselves in these filthy conditions, yet—in the case of someone who had been haunted from Oxford days by the epithet 'superior person'—it had to be twisted into this absurdity.

He was much misrepresented, which to some extent was the fault of his rigid and frigid demeanour, though it was partly the result of shyness and partly due to a perpetual pain in his back for which he wore a support. He was almost always in pain, and anyone who knew him well must have felt sympathy for a man who sustained this affliction through incessant labour with gay good humour, only yielding occasionally to the petulance evoked by fatigue and suffering. He combined a sense of public duty with a zest for life, and though our conception both of the former and of the latter was deeply different, his apparent sympathy for me in our initial relationship may have rested on recognition of some corresponding motives. Cimmie said to me years later that my vitality took so much from life that I had a particular obligation to give much back. Lord Curzon in a more material sense took much from the world, and he certainly felt his obligation and laboured incessantly to repay it.

At our first meeting he had obviously decided it was his duty to ask me all the usual father-in-law questions, but found it embarrassing—too impolite; this basic shyness was one of the things never understood about him. The intense emotionalism also could never be detected behind the icy demeanour presented to the world. His manner and conduct in private life were more emotional than is usual in an Englishman. He was warm-hearted, and on all family occasions easily moved to tears. At the christening of our first child he made a little speech—toasting the trophy, as he called it—and then with tears on his cheeks embraced everybody. Margot Asquith gave the same event a more practical reception, visiting Cimmie in bed soon after the arrival. 'Dear child, you look very pale and must not have another baby for a long time. Henry always withdrew in time, such a noble man.' We were left pondering the effect of this private exercise on public affairs.

Lord Curzon could, of course, inadvertently be very intimidating to anyone outside his own circle. Billy Ormsby-Gore—later Lord Harlech—told me one of my favourite stories. He was on official duty at some meeting of a committee of the War Cabinet in Carlton House Terrace. Mr. Barnes, the estimable Labour member, the first to arrive, was clearly rather oppressed by the sombre pomp of the surroundings. Seeking relief, he pointed to an enormous photograph on the wall and enquired: 'Lord Curzon, what is that picture?' The crisp, short a's were prominent in the patient explanation: 'That, Mr. Barnes, is a photogrăph of myself and of my stăff, riding upon elephănts'. This ray of vice-regal sunshine did little to relieve the imperial gloom which was liable to settle on the Regency splendours of Carlton House Terrace on an occasion when unsuitable company was present.

The reaction to one of his own people who transgressed could be very sharp. The finer points of etiquette and dress were sustained with meticulous care when he gave dinners to the King and Queen at Carlton House Terrace. He had written, on the first occasion we were invited, a letter in his long flowing hand to the Palace, asking that I might be permitted to wear trousers instead of knee breeches; my smashed leg, of course, looked odd in the more formal dress. It is not therefore difficult to conceive that the sky was darkened and the earth shook when Sir Ronald Lindsay, of the Foreign Office, ambled up the stairs to shake hands with his chief and host standing at the top, clad in trousers. The hands were raised to heaven, the short 'a' was resonant, 'Lindsay!—I am aghăst'. It was doubly an outrage, as on two clear counts Lindsay should have known better. Firstly, he was already well on the way to his subsequent achievement of becoming head of the Foreign Office, and secondly he was brother to an earl of ancient lineage. Lord Curzon, however, in another context commented adversely on men of no personal significance who took undue pride in official uniforms, and concluded: 'If I walked naked down Piccadilly people would still look at me'.

There was quite a run of bad luck around these Royal dinners. We ourselves began very badly indeed. The formal invitation arrived and I carelessly handed it for acceptance to my secretary, who was a member of the Labour Party and unversed in the intricacies of these affairs; we will call him John Smith. The reply to Lord Curzon ran on the following lines. 'Dear Lord Curzon, Mr. Mosley asks me to say that he and the wife will be glad to dine with you and the King and Queen on the 15th prox. Yours sincerely, John Smith.' By return a letter arrived in the long, flowing hand. 'In the first place, your secretary should address me (if he must address me at all) as My Lord.' To those who knew him well, there was a world of weary resignation in that bracket. Then followed a complete social register, how and in what order of precedence every dignatory of the realm should be addressed and placed. It was most useful.

We were able to be a little helpful in return at an embarrassing moment on one of these regal occasions. George Robey had been invited to sing to the King and Queen after dinner; a sensible choice, for the royal taste was hearty, and Robey was finally knighted. He was going strong with his usual gaiety and effrontery, when he sudenly stopped. He gazed wildly around him, and then ran from the stage. Cimmie and I felt it was our duty to follow him and find out what was up. He was sweating profusely and in a state of perturbation. 'You see,' he explained, 'I suddenly remembered the next line was, "I feel just as good as a jolly old queen".' We felt that no prospect less formidable than the combined disapproval of Queen Mary and Lord Curzon could have broken the nerve of the great comedian.

Yet all this stately ritual was a part of Lord Curzon's practical sense. He belonged to that order, and it had to be supported with the long-proven means appropriate to it. My father-in-law showed himself a man of very different intellectual and moral stature from most of my opponents when he said to me that he could well imagine my period would be very different, requiring a different policy, attitude and way of life. He added suddenly and simply: 'I ask you one thing, not to become a good debater in the wilderness, a brilliant lone-wolf. That is all I ask. I don't mind if you join the Labour Party or come back, which I can arrange for you at once, to the Conservative

Party. I shall not blame you if you join Labour, but do not remain in ineffective isolation.' In retrospect this was prophetic, as I remembered when my attempt to found a new movement was frustrated by the Second World War and I was consequently thrown into a position of isolation. Although my instinct would have been to agree with his advice, fate confronted me with the dilemma of becoming a comfortable colleague in a journey to disaster or a lone challenger to a political world which was bringing ruin to my country.

Acute differences did not arise in our discussions of politics, for a clear reason. He represented in a high degree the qualities of order and stability without which the modern and complex state cannot survive. The dynamic progress which I sought to combine with order and stability in the creative synthesis necessary to secure either, was a concept which, for him, simply did not exist. He was profoundly familiar with every detail of imperial administration and concomitant questions of foreign policy, but a complete stranger to the economics of statecraft and to the lives of the people. Master of one subject in which I was interested, the other was a closed book to him; so we could only discuss subjects on which we had a certain measure of agreement.

Lord Curzon had a practical side in political judgments on his own ground which was more marked than in the organisation of his personal life and affairs. His method of life was obsolete, and he added to his ignorance of economics a lack of money sense in private life. I remember him showing in conversation, when he was Foreign Secretary, that he had not the least idea how the franc had moved during previous years, and his attitude in his personal affairs was the simple proposition that adequate money should be available to support his expensive tastes. He felt it a public duty to maintain in proper state the various fine establishments with which his exquisite and sophisticated judgment had endowed the national heritage; this led to some friction with his daughters, as most of the necessary money happened to belong to them.

When we married, the question arose of how Cimmie should deal with the money inherited from her American mother, who came from the Leiter family, which had amassed a considerable fortune in real estate. Years later they were stated by my political opponents to be Jewish, but when I was in America with Cimmie in 1924 this was never suggested. They were then reputed to be Dutch immigrants, and those I saw were big, blond, blue-eyed people. The rumour probably arose from the founder of the fortune being called Levi Leiter, but these Old Testament names are as common in the Welsh valleys as they are in Holland. The thought that they were Jews appeared in that period never to have occurred to anyone, but the story was freely circulated in England during the thirties, when I found myself in conflict with certain Jewish interests, for the clear but transient reason that I was trying to stop the outbreak of the Second World War. Needless to say, if

Cimmie had been half-Jewish it would not have made the slightest difference either in my attitude to her or in my political action in opposing anyone, Jew or Gentile, who in my view was agitating in favour of war.

Cimmie decided on our marriage to leave some of her money with Lord Curzon for a short time in order to tide him over a transition which might be awkward for him. He had little money of his own, but his second wife had a considerable fortune. Their expenditure was very large. Already his eldest daughter, Irene, had departed with most of her money, to his considerable indignation. It was therefore a difficult moment when Cimmie decided, with my support, to take the rest of her own. I insisted, and she agreed, that no detailed rejoinder should be made to his reproaches; it would have been all too easy, but would have created additional and unnecessary acrimony. It was a sad business which clouded a relationship otherwise invariably agreeable and happy.

Lord Curzon was difficult in money matters because he appeared to think that society owed him not merely a living but an existence of singular magnificence. He had the attitude of a spoilt child. This foible brought its nemesis, for his time was inordinately occupied with redundant domestic details. A man of considerable ability and immense industry, he became exhausted by attending to things which were quite unnecessary, a range of large establishments, and the staff required to conduct them. What Nature intended for politics was given to an interior decorating business. He had fine taste and knowledge which enabled him to acquire a valuable collection of pictures and objets d'art. Most of this collection was purchased by money supplied on his daughters' account, and they behaved generously in never attempting to deprive him of the results. He would have been wiser as well as more correct had he lived in a fashion more modest and less exacting, surrounded by a few objects whose beauty he rightly loved, leaving his time available for more serious considerations.

Lord Curzon's private life was indeed curiously organised, and in a manner which clearly exhausted him prematurely. I found him one day nailing down the stair carpet at Hackwood, and ventured to suggest that this was an inappropriate exercise for the Secretary of State for Foreign Affairs, as half-a-dozen footmen were available for the task. Could not one of them do it? Yes, but not so well, was the reply. He suffered from what I call the Bonaparte complex. A cherished possession was one of the best libraries in the country on the subject of Napoleon, which he afterwards bequeathed to the Bodleian at Oxford. He had firmly grasped the central fact of Bonapartism, that by working eighteen hours a day one of the ablest men who ever lived could personally supervise every detail of the working of his State and army; it was said down to the last button on the last gaiter of the last soldier. What my father-in-law never fully understood was that Napoleon's was the last epoch in which such a way of life was possible, even with such ability. The machine has become too big for such personal control by even the most gifted individual; in a later age even Caesarism has to be collective. The opposite method must be employed, which entails delegation, and rests, above all, on the choice of men. The ideal of modern organisation is that the ablest man in the central position should have only two functions: to initiate, and to repair when no one else can. He should be there to create ideas and to derive them from the whole nation—particularly from science—to launch them, and to drive them forward; also to act as a permanent breakdown gang in the event of disaster, which cracks the nerve of most men or passes beyond their capacities. That concept of modern method was not within the range of Lord Curzon.

Curzon was a great public servant who deserved better than the shabby treatment he received in the end. He was not in touch with the mass of the people as modern prime ministers must be, and he lacked the sensitive antennae which enable men to know what completely different people are thinking and feeling and so to devise their action. But as Prime Minister he would at least have saved the country from the squalid betrayal which led the nation toward war without providing the necessary armaments through fear of losing an election. In that sense was justified, after Curzon's defeat, his bitter jibe that Baldwin's appointment was the strangest event of its kind since Caligula had made his horse a consul. Curzon's limitations in the sphere of economics should not necessarily have inhibited his rise to the highest office of State, because others could then have taken adequate economic measures in spheres unfamiliar to the Prime Minister. He would, however, have been impossible as Prime Minister in the present period, because the intimate revelation of television immediately presents as a figure of fun any archaic aristocrat who is clearly as remote from the lives of the people as he is ignorant of the all-important subject of economics.

It is also unattractive to see a man destroyed through advice being given to the Crown by his best friends without a word of warning being conveyed to him. 'Then dear George will be Prime Minister?'—we understand his intimates enquired of Lord Balfour after the giving of crucial advice—'No, dear George will *not* be Prime Minister,' was the feline reply. Another old friend who intrigued against him on that occasion was St. John Brodrick, later Lord Midleton. Lord Curzon used to recite some lines about this contemporary of his which I think were of Oxford composition:

> Every dull complacent plodder
> Was meant by fate to be a Brodder.
> Then how did St. John learn to brod?
> Why by the special grace of God.

His early connections and friendships did not prevent, indeed, they possibly promoted Curzon's betrayal at the crisis of his career. Loyalty in the party which advertises loyalty is not always so apparent on these testing occasions as in the simpler homes of the mass of the people in their dealings with each other.

Lord Curzon did not deserve the trivial malice of some of the attacks made on him since his death. It is a modern fashion to ignore most of a man's public service and to publish instead any private scandal that can be raked from the ashes, but it does not give a true or complete picture. From some accounts it might be imagined that money and romance played a larger part in Lord Curzon's life than his service to the State. He certainly had an affair with Elinor Glyn which was subsequently much publicised; she spent a long period decorating his beautiful Elizabethan house at Montacute, where Cimmie as a young girl was often in her company. As a result, I met Elinor Glyn when we became engaged, then a most sedate lady without aid of tiger skin and full of good advice. She was more intelligent than her books; they clearly excluded marriage with a Foreign Secretary before tenure of that office became a comic turn.

If Elinor Glyn had never written a line she would have been an appropriate wife for an orthodox Foreign Secretary. She was a model of decorum, exceptionally well behaved; slightly prim for the aristocracy, but a good example of what the bourgeois world then believed a lady to be. She was also well educated and capable of discussing subjects with which few of her athletic heroes or exotic heroines would have been familiar. She knew what would touch the neo-romantic mood of the period and gave it to them, as others do today for a different market. Authors of this type are often not so silly as the books they write, but have sound money sense. When Curzon married again his relationship with Mrs. Glyn ended. Apparently he had omitted to tell her about his intended marriage; I knew little of the rights and wrongs of the matter, but would guess that the news broke sooner than Curzon anticipated. He was probably quite happily engaged on two fronts and felt no urgent necessity to withdraw from either. The exigencies of Venus in this situation differ from those of Mars. I doubt whether he meant to treat Mrs. Glyn unkindly or discourteously, for this was not in his character.

There is some reason to believe that the distinguished strategist was engaged at this time on yet a third front. After so much ill-nature in posthumous accounts of this side of his life, a more genial story can do Curzon no harm. A drawing-room in Grosvenor Square was rocked with laughter during successive luncheon parties because a letter had arrived beginning: 'My beautiful white swan'. Lord Curzon had inadvertently transposed two letters in their envelopes; one a formal refusal of an invitation from Lady Cunard and the other intended for Mrs. Astor, afterwards Lady Ribblesdale, who was a widow, rich, beautiful—and an American. Lady Cunard used to explain in exquisitely embroidered detail how touched she was by this unexpected attention.

Lord Curzon's policy and record in his various high offices can be left to history. The personal story of him can be left at my wedding day, a most trying occasion for one of his character and temperament, which illustrated his deep good nature. The trials were nearly all my fault, perhaps in one respect also Cimmie's. First, I was late. Lunching too happily at the Ritz with an old Sandhurst and army friend, who was my best man, I was approached by Lady Cunard with the apposite inquiry, 'Were you not being married five minutes ago?' We jumped up and hurried hatless down St. James's Street to the Chapel Royal, where Lord Curzon and the bride were waiting. He said not a word, but Cimmie afterwards teased me by saying he was obviously thinking I had run out at the last moment. It was also awkward because two kings and two queens were waiting—monarchs of Britain and Belgium, the latter had been at Hackwood during the war—and worse was to follow. Not realising the enormity of our youthful enthusiasms, we had arranged for a passage from *Tristan and Isolde* to be played at the end of the ceremony. It took far longer than we had realised, and all were standing throughout. To keep two kings and two queens standing while you played your favourite music was not included in Lord Curzon's social register, but it was the young people's day and their every whim must be satisfied. He took it all on the chin and never blinked an eyelid. That was good nature.

Our honeymoon was spent at Portofino, near Genoa, then an unspoilt fishing village. We lived in the Castello Brown, which belonged to the family of Francis Yeats-Brown, who wrote *Bengal Lancer*. History and beauty were there in rare combination. Both Dante and Napoleon had slept in the medieval fortress; across the lovely bay you could see at Spezia the tragic water, wine-dark with Shelley's drowning; along the heights which linked Portofino with Rapallo strode Nietzsche in the ecstasy of writing *Zarathustra*; Cimmie and I followed the same route more prosaically riding donkeys, and falling off them among the fireflies in the dusk. Every day we went through the orange groves to the sea, an enchantment which we recaptured the following year.

Travel in those early years engaged us much and some account of it belongs properly to this chapter of continuing life-experience and of the happiness of marriage, even if it means anticipating a little in time and leaving politics for a moment. The memory of Lord Curzon should always be joined to a journey through India, the land to which as Viceroy he gave so much. We went to India in the winter of 1924. If contrast is the essence of life, it was certainly present in the diversity of this extraordinary experience. Within India we found extremes of beauty and of ugliness, of flaunting wealth and abysmal poverty.

We determined to see everything, and we did—at that time some of the worst working conditions and the vilest slums in the world. In Bombay the great tenement blocks with four families often living in one quite small room, each group with its separate fire and the only egress for the smoke, one window; in Calcutta shanty towns worse than any I have seen anywhere else, with the main drain running down the centre of the street. Nothing could have prevented continual outbreaks of typhoid except the sterilising effect of the strong sun on the open cesspools. In the cotton mills they worked for a wage of five shillings a week, often with modern machinery supplied by Lancashire for its own suicide. It was no monument either to the humanity or to the intelligence of the British Raj. The contrast was the supreme beauty of India and the massive achievement of British administration in at least procuring with slender means peace, tranquility and life without bloodshed.

We went by P. & O. boat and stopped shortly in Cairo, where we combined seeing the wonders of Egyptian antiquity with a tour of the local slums; they were bad, though not so bad as those in India. I remember finding in a Port Said bookshop for the first time Shaw's book on Wagner; it had not yet appeared in his collected works. The sphinx should always be seen for the first time as Shaw's favourite hero saw it, by night. The same is true of most of the world's masterpieces, notably the Taj Mahal and the Piazza San Marco at Venice. We may arrange these moments, but chance brings often the most poignant emotion, as when suddenly and without forethought in the Protestant cemetery at Rome I read the words: 'Here lies one whose name was writ on water'. Sometimes the acute experience of beauty is due to the fortune of solitude, as lately in Greece when for over half-an-hour I found myself entirely alone in the Parthenon during the luminous sunshine of the afternoon, and felt that Goethe's pilgrimage was realised: 'Das Land der Griechen mit der Seele suchend'.

The journey to India by boat gave us the opportunity to read everything that could be found in London on the Vedas and the Upanishads; every aspect of Indian religion had to be studied. It was interesting in itself and it opened many doors which might otherwise have been closed. The combination of an effort to discover what Indians thought and felt with the Left-wing politics which suggested some sympathy with their aspirations, took us much deeper into Indian life than was customary for the English.

To arrive in Ceylon is the best way to start the Indian journey. After bathing in a sea of caressing warmth came the retreat to the hotel's swimming-pool when an Indian friend told us that sea-snakes were about, which were poisonous; perhaps he was inventing them, for we never saw any. Then came a tour of the island, at that time superbly organised for the few tourists. British administration was more concentrated here than in the rest of India, and the result was a high degree of efficiency. You could motor through primeval jungle on macadam roads and meet an extraordinary variety of wild animals. The butterflies are without parallel anywhere else I have visited in the world. Passing through a cloud of them with the sensations of the wings brushing against the face is described with pages of voluptuous French adjectives by Francis de Croisset in his little book, *La Féerie Cingalaise.*

Repose from these excitements was in the clean and well-arranged rest-houses in the middle of the jungle, where all was provided by a single capable and agreeable Sinhalese. Next morning an early start had to be made to see from the great rock the sun rising, and steam mounting in mysterious clouds towards the dawn from the vivid green sea of jungle.

Within this jungle were astonishing things. The vast black Buddha with the eternal lotus flowers placed by the big toe. The golden-robed monks moving through the jungle, glittering in the distance like fantastic insects against the sombre green of the interlacing trees. The lost cities, Anuradhaoura and Polunnaruwa, in those days partly buried in the oblivion of the all-embracing vegetation, were defended only by a vast pearl of water. A sense of man's ultimate destiny, of his interwoven inspiration rose from the exquisite moonstone designs of this superb civilisation as we learned that it was contemporary with the architecture of classic Greece. At that moment it was difficult to believe that mankind would not at some point in time be as one in a union of high achievement. Already across every physical division and without earthly consciousness of another presence, these two heights of human genius had reflected one another.

After a stay at Government House in Ceylon, and another in Madras, we went north to Calcutta, where the Governor was Lord Lytton; he was married to a woman of remarkable beauty and charm, one of whose daughters had been bridesmaid at our wedding. Lord Lytton had many contacts with Indian life, being a highly intelligent and sensitive man, while his sister, Lady Emily Lutyens, had penetrated into some of the inner circles in Madras. None of these officials placed any obstacle to our entry into the plenitude of Indian company and way of living; we were often guests in Indian houses, unusual at that time. Apart from the study of social conditions under the guidance of experts this gave us an insight into spheres not usually available to the English. For instance, on the way northwards we visited perhaps the most remarkable of all Indian temples, at Madura, in the company of an Indian authority whose exposition swiftly transmuted what appeared to European eyes as the barbaric obscenities of Hindu mythology into an elevated nature symbolism and remoter mysteries. We were sustained throughout our Indian journey by a subtle blend of official realism and Indian culture, which afforded us exceptional opportunities of understanding the country and the life of its people.

In Madras we entered the strange circle of Mrs. Besant and her friends. It was indeed a bizarre ensemble, for it occupied the house of Sir Edwin Lutyens, the architect; a complete non-believer in the theosophist cult. I knew a certain amount about it, for during my days in hospital I had read books by Blavatsky, Leadbetter and Mrs. Besant herself; kindergarten versions of theosophy have recently become popular. It appeared to be a quite logical religious theory—with less of the obvious contradictions which in some cases make metaphysical debates so easy to the experienced dialectician—but it was, of course, entirely lacking in proof for anyone who had not enjoyed these strange and felicitous experiences in dream journeys. The absent Leadbetter or the happily present Mrs. Besant could explain to you every detail of their journey in the astral or devechanic plane, but any request for evidence would be regarded as philistinism.

Sir Edwin Lutyens' hearty English character would burst through all this like an elephant through tissue paper. 'Annie'—he would say to Mrs. Besant at breakfast—'I have just dreamt that we were married in our last life, and you did not let me smoke in bed.' He was a most whimsical and engaging fellow of whom we were very fond. At that time he had just had his estimates drastically cut for the palace he had been commissioned to build at Delhi, and this threatened to spoil all his proportions. Among other things, the avenue for his ceremonial march of elephants had been shortened, and the hill was consequently too abrupt for their gait. His imitation of an elephant waddling in these conditions with a viceroy on top of him, was almost as diverting as his quick pencil distortions of the ceremonial coat of arms on official menu cards into the face and body of an angry pekinese dog, which made us laugh during pompous speeches at the Lord Mayor's banquet some years later. He was a great droll as well as a gifted architect, and got on strangely well with the brilliant band of Indian thinkers and mystics who surrounded Mrs. Besant and Lady Emily. Chief among them was Ramaswani Ayer— then responsible for law and order in Madras—who combined in a degree exceptional for those climes, the capacity for thought and action. This circle at least gave me a certain insight into Hindu thinking and character.

Unfortunately most English people in touch with Indian life belonged to freak cults of this kind. The rest seemed to be entirely cut off, although officials at the highest level were making painstaking efforts to understand. The mass of officialdom appeared to live entirely apart, particularly the women. They seemed conscious of little or nothing except the heat, which of course always affects Europeans more after a long sojourn than it does during the casual visit. Their manners to Indians for the most part left much to be desired. I remember commenting afterwards that India would be lost by bad manners. Some distinguished Englishmen—Lord Willingdon, for example—were loved, simply because they had the good manners which Indians appreciate. It was embarrassing a little later to sit next at dinner in Paris to one of the most beautiful and distinguished of the Indian princesses who had been educated in that city, and to have my enquiry why she never came to London met with the reply—'because in Paris I am treated like a lady'. Indians were then very sensitive, but they had cause to be.

It required, therefore, a certain degree of intelligence and sensitivity to get on with Indians at that time. They were full of complexes, well described in E. M. Forster's *A Passage to India*. This attitude contained both a sense of inferiority and superiority. We were staying with the Viceroy, Lord Reading—Rufus Isaacs of Mr. Asquith's Cabinet, a man of considerable capacity and of appropriately distinguished appearance—when the foremost orator among Indian statesmen came to dinner. 'Tell me, Mr. Sastri,' said the Viceroy, 'how did you acquire such a perfect command of the English language?' 'Your Excellency, I had the inestimable advantage of four years at Oxford University.' 'But many of our young men have had the same chance, without becoming orators like you.' 'Your Excellency, I had one very slight additional advantage, four thousand years of culture behind me.' My mind went back to the story of Disraeli's retort to the suggestion of Lord Malmesbury that he was an upstart. 'My ancestors were princes in the Temple of Solomon, while yours were running through your wet English woods with their backsides painted blue.'

Yet this arrogance could blend with the opposite complex. I had been up in the Rajput country staying in the magnificent dwellings of the Rajahs, and on returning observed to one of my best and most intelligent Indian friends that I had not seen a single painting by any of the European masters among all their wealth of possessions. At once came the shadow, and I knew he was thinking: the European feels that we are incapable of appreciating his art. It took me three days hard work to restore the old good relations; it was so absurd, because I should not have expected to find exquisite Persian miniatures in the country houses of England, and would not have been offended if an Indian had suggested that some should be acquired. I did not feel blameworthy for that, but a gaffe in the Rajput country made me feel guilty. It was in Udaipur, the lovely Venice of India, a city built on water. The Maharajah invited us to stay and arranged an elaborately organised tiger-shoot. We were placed in a high tower well out of harm's way while about a thousand retainers drove through the jungle; they were dressed in bright gold—as sunbeams—to emphasise the historic fact that the Maharajah was descended from the sun. The sunbeams converged on us from all sides, but no tiger; he had escaped. A small porcupine ran out, and I shot him; meaning to show that we were in no way put out by the failure of the tiger-shoot and that we still regarded it all as a jolly occasion. But my festive gesture was taken sadly amiss, as a sign of derision of the shoot provided for the Maharajah's guests. Again, it took some hard work to return to grace and favour.

One Englishman at least well understood India and the Indians: a clergyman, C. F. Andrews, who was an intimate friend of Gandhi's. This Englishman of saintly character introduced me to the Indian saint. I entered the room to find Gandhi in *kadda*—the cloth he used to spin—sitting cross-legged on the floor. I too sat down cross-legged opposite to him, instead of using the chair provided for the European, which seemed too pompous in the circumstances. He was a sympathetic personality of subtle intelligence who in appearance, mind and sense of humour reminded me irresistibly of Lord Hugh Cecil; perhaps because he was another ardent metaphysician with a sense of fun. He invited me to a private conference then being held between Hindus and Moslems to try to make a united front; he was Chairman. At the first session a roaring row developed between the Hindus and the Moslem Ali brothers, two mountainous men in flowing robes. Throughout the uproar Gandhi sat on his chair on a dais, dissolved in helpless laughter, overwhelmed by the comical absurdity of human nature. Not the intervention of the Chairman, but the sinking of the sun eventually restored order. At the ordained moment the Ali brothers stopped short, whirled round to face the appropriate direction and flopped down on their knees with their foreheads in the dust. After the specified interval, up they jumped and launched the row again, full roar, just where they had left off.

I later wrote a report on the Indian situation which was privately circulated among British politicians. It made two main points: the first that we could stay in India as long as we wished without so much trouble as some anticipated; Hindus and Moslems were hopelessly divided; never had *divide et impera* been so easy, for it had happened naturally. Further, if we did go, there would be bloodshed on a great scale. The first point was proved by the ultimate division of the country. The second was tragically proved when we left, and nearly a million were killed in the riot and massacre which followed.

I tried to put the economic problem in a nutshell with the phrase: India needs a mogul with a tractor and a deep plough. After a study of Indian agriculture and the land tenure system it was evident that starvation would be perennial until that great plain was deeply ploughed and sown with cereals, but every form of social and religious custom stood in the way. When a man died his holding was divided among his family into small plots surrounded by low banks. These *bunns* were sacred and must not be touched, so no plough could cross them. The peasants were scratching about inside their plots with the wooden instruments they had used for millenia. The system of *zeminder* land holding in Bengal was in some respects even worse. Add to this the problem of the large population of sacred cows—cows with free feeding range, even to eat vegetables off market stalls—and it is not difficult to observe the basic problem of Indian economics. Nor was it hard to deduce that a far stronger government would be required to cut through the tangle than anything the West at that time was able to produce. Hence my remark about the mogul with the tractor; it is all too easy to surmise who this may now be.

I studied Indian agriculture through the University of Rabindranath Tagore; it was called Santiniketan, the abode of peace. Situated in the middle of the great plain, the skyline encircled it on all sides like the inverted bowl of Persian poetry. Unfortunately the poet himself was in America, and

I never met him, but his family and assistants were there in full strength. The study of agriculture by day mingled agreeably in the evening with philosophic discussion. Indians were present who had graduated at Oxford, the Sorbonne and Heidelberg, in fact, at practically every university of Europe; European languages were fluently spoken. The discussions, sitting cross-legged under a huge tree, chiefly touched Sanskrit, and were conducted in English by a Swedish professor called Konnor, who had come specially for the purpose. After dark, philosophy would yield to music and dancing. Musical instruments of four-thousand-years-old design were played with a strangely haunting, plaintive appeal to far-away memories. Then came the young women of the Tagore family to dance, among them some of the most beautiful I have ever seen. Their faces, with perfect Greek features, were whiter than the Europeans', white as fine ivory, their figures sinuous perfection as they swayed to the rhythm of the age-old dance. There was no purdah among them, but we never saw them except on these occasions.

I met most of the Indian politicians in due course; Jinnah the Moslem leader, who seemed to me an able but cold and cynical lawyer: his long life dedicated to his cause later belied my judgment. Das, the early Congress leader, another lawyer without much regard for Hindu customs—he earned enormous sums, ate meat and drank alcohol—seemed sincere and forceful in his political views. In the Nehru family I met the distinguished father, Moltilal, but not the more famous son who later became Prime Minister. He was probably serving his long novitiate in British jails; an apparently indispensable preliminary to high office in the Commonwealth. These men were highly intelligent, and also reasonable. It should surely have been possible to arrange any necessary transition in due order, without the final panic-stricken evacuation which caused so much bloodshed and left so much bitterness, even if we had not the strength first to solve the economic question which is the real problem in India, the looming tragedy behind all the chatter and posture of the demagogues, both British and Indian.

This is not the place to discuss the present political and economic problems of India; they must either be solved from within, or else from without under the overwhelming pressure of material disaster. A truly Indian solution would require another Akbar, an extraordinary genius of thought and action of the supreme Caesarean category. Akbar had all the great qualities, the capacity for the most seductive persuasion linked to a reluctant ability for ruthless action when all else failed, the extremes of gentle sensitivity within the steel framework of statesmanship. His relations—as so often happens—separated and exaggerated all the qualities which in him found such exquisite harmony. The execrable Auraungzeb expressed his Moslem faith by cutting off the heads of Hindu monuments in the same wanton spirit of childish, vicious fanatacism which moved some early Christians to strike the heads from what they considered the pagan idols of classic Greece. The heavy paw of the ignorant, bigoted clown in not confined to one continent, the loutery is everywhere, always.

The other extreme in this same family was Shah Jehan, who created the Fort at Delhi, an abode of enchantment. Situated on top of a hill, it was surrounded by a wall roughly a mile long. Over the door the Shah had inscribed in Persian: 'If there be a paradise on earth, it is here, it is here, it is here,' in reiterative ecstacy. He spent his days in a pool containing forty niches in which he and thirty-nine wives sat neck-deep in warm water while over them were sprayed forty different scents, one for each; between their feet swam a glittering variety of oriental fish with jewels round their necks and tails, while into his hand was pressed wine in a goblet cut from a single ruby. Sparkling waterfalls—iridescent from various coloured lights placed behind them—rested their vision until dark, when boats of silver and golden hue conveyed them to love trysts in pagodas again surrounded by the eternally scented waters. It took just three generations of that way of life to turn the northern conquerors into drivelling incapables; the hard ice melted into the slush of the plain. It was Schiller who wrote that only the high gods could combine sensuous beauty of existence with spiritual peace, which in his neo-Hellenic thinking could come only from the striving of achievement and creation.[1]

I developed a deep and abiding affection for India, and resolved to help in its difficult problems if fate ever gave me the chance. Never has there been such a world of contrast; the terrible suffering of the masses in the slums of Bombay and Bengal; the abysmal poverty of millions gripped fast in old belief which denied the saving hand of modern science; the shock of incidents such as the dwarf, part animal, part human, tapping my leg when I was alone in the midst of a rather hostile Indian crowd, at the behest of his wealthy and humorous owner, who led him with a chain round his neck like a dog; the physical beauty of many Indian men and women, comparable with anything on earth and illumined by a combination of inner goodness and of high and fine intelligence; the Taj Mahal reflected in the water by moonlight—built by Shah Jehan and set in a cadre of cypresses by Lord Curzon—a symbol of Indian beauty rising from squalor and horror. India is a land of contrast, of ineffable beauty and of darkest sorrow, a jewel of the world, which challenges mankind to save it.

[1] Zwischen Sinnens Glück und Seelens Frieden bleibt den Menschen nur die bange Wahl, von der Stirn der hohen Uraniden leuchtet ihr vermählte Strahl.

7
Youth and Age
The Cecils
The League of Nations

My first burst into full publicity occurred soon after my marriage, when I exuberantly exploited the youth racket. It is true that I was tempted into it without quite realising what I was doing, nevertheless it was a silly business, and in the present period has become sillier still. I was invited to become the first president of the newly formed League of Youth and Social Progress. The founder was a smooth and smug little Liberal, an agreeable and seductive fellow but typical of the middle-aged politicians who in each generation exploit youth. They are particularly absurd when playing young with creaking joints, for the pretence is obvious in men who were never athletic even in their youth. I was not called upon to revive such performances, because at twenty-three I thought for a period the war had ended all that for me. My simple task was to deliver the inaugural address, and after the flattering invitation to become its president, I felt I must do the League of Youth and Social Progress well. In justice to my callow self I plead in mitigation that I had no idea of the publicity which the performance would incur.

Amid the splurge of youthful demagogy one phrase in particular hit the headlines: 'These old dead men with their old dead minds embalmed in the tombs of the past'. It was indeed silly, but at least a more striking phrase than some of the dreary drip which drifts at floodtide in the same direction nowadays. My entry into the House of Commons at question time next day was assailed on all sides by lively mummies indignantly flapping their funereal vestments. For the time being I had become highly unpopular with everyone who had reached the years of discretion, and that meant the great majority. I had become a pioneer of the modern racket, a champion of all whose sole moral or intellectual asset is youth; a rapidly diminishing asset, but temporarily protected and privileged by dubiety when time has not yet given opportunity to prove either capacity or incapacity.

What is the truth of the matter in the light of fact and history? Is youth an advantage or a disadvantage, or neither? I should at this point, of course, declare an interest, as they say in the House of Commons. At the time of writing these lines I am just seventy-one years of age. Yet I cannot say with Bernard Shaw: 'I am growing old and my powers are waning, but so much the better for those who found me unbearably brilliant when in my prime', because I am strongly conscious that my powers are not waning but still waxing. My most competent professional advisers support me with the information that my way of living and my family constitution should with ordinary luck give me many more years at the height of my powers. Yet I do not feel that my years separate me from youth. On the contrary my own life experience gives me the liveliest sympathy with the young. Some of my best years were wasted by the turgid suppression of elderly obscurantists who were generally proved wrong by subsequent events. If men and women have ability it will be evident and available at an early age, and should not only be encouraged but given full scope.

When Shaw wrote those ironic lines he was in process of conceiving by far the most brilliant and profound work of his life. Perhaps in this respect thinkers and artists are no guide to the life of action, for Goethe finished *Faust II* when he was over eighty and Titian was doing some of his best work at nearly ninety; Tolstoy, Balzac, Picasso and many other examples confound any claim to a monopoly of creative ability by youth. Shaw again in his acute observation of the life of action had something apposite to say on this subject. The answer to the question whether it is better to be young or old for the practical tasks of life depends mostly on your answer to the further question —what do you want to do? You are becoming too old to be a ping-pong champion at twenty, but in the view of Shaw you are much too young at eighty to be a statesman. Somerset Maugham added: politician at forty, statesman at eighty. As usual, Shaw's paradox contained and protected his underlying truth; the human tragedy is that we all die just as we are getting a little sense. His answer was to live longer and work later. But how? The answer still eludes us; yet we need not run away from life by retiring at the height of the powers which even our present life span affords.

It is clear that in certain specialised spheres of the mind, youth is as important as it is in sport. I have heard an eminent physicist say that you cannot easily use the language of modern electronics if you are over thirty, and for physics itself and the higher mathematics the supple qualities and mental flexibility of youth appear to be a considerable aid to invention. Yet the modern statesman who—in my own phrase—'should live and work with scientists as the Medici lived and worked with artists', requires altogether different qualities. His business is not to delve into the intricacies of the process, but to judge its effective results and to co-ordinate them with the results of other processes in a creative synthesis. This requires in supreme degree the qualities of balance, harmony, judgment, acquired authority by long proof of commanding capacity; attributes which are more usually associated with full maturity.

If we can see the organisation of the scientific state in the future as a pyramid in form, the lower layers of the edifice will be occupied by the most highly specialised departments and the apex by the most generally experienced intelligences which co-ordinate the whole. Between the base of extreme specialisation and the apex of general direction will be many layers, or storeys, of increasing co-ordination. At each stage will be minds which can co-ordinate the work of the separate, specialised departments immediately beneath, and their intelligence will become more general, more dependent on judgment rather than narrow, specialised knowledge, as the structure of organisation approaches the summit. This method of organisation, which I first suggested long ago in *The Alternative* (1947) may well be remote from the final form, but a world in which we overcome such absurdities as, for example, the complete division then prevailing between psychological and endocrine research, must surely evolve some such method of administration. When we contemplate these possibilities it is not difficult to conceive different but beneficial uses for the diverse qualities of youth and age at all levels.

In the present world this question of youth or age depends largely on whether opportunity comes early or late. A few kings of genius, like Frederick the Great or the two outstanding Swedes, had their opportunities early. Either heredity or revolution may give the early chance. Bonaparte had opportunity early, in a revolutionary situation which affords such men at all ages their opening. Yet it is not clear even then whether early opportunity is in fact an advantage. Napoleon at Waterloo appears in modern research to have been a burnt-out old man, although he was almost exactly the same age as politicians now recommended by the parties to head government and opposition as conspicuous examples of young statesmanship. It is comical to regard Bonaparte at Rivoli in his twenty-seventh year, and all the bright boys who were subsequently his marshals, and then to hear the present generation of heavily middle-aged politicians in Britain described as young. The youth cult they have done much to promote could so easily be used against them, who have neither the athletic appearance and quality of youth nor the dynamic capacities which in history have often been found in old men of outstanding quality.

Would Bonaparte have done better if his opportunity had come later? Would he then have avoided the egregious errors which destroyed him? There is much modern evidence which suggests an affirmative answer. The mysterious process of maturity appears in itself to achieve much. It is mysterious because it is indefinable; it is not just the acquisition of experience, but rather an almost physical process like the maturing of wine. Disraeli said: 'To the creative mind experience is less than nothing'. Ideas may occur at all ages and quite independently of experience, particularly in some spheres. But is it not equally true to say that experience aids the execution of ideas?

The ideal combination is clearly energy and experience. So long as men in later life retain their energy, the addition of experience or the strange process of maturity makes them better than when they were young; normally much better men. It is true in this event that a 'good old 'un is better than a good young 'un'. A man may either burn out or rust at a very early age; he can burn out like Napoleon or rust out like some of the drift we see around today. That depends on the stress of events or the way of life. Hence the phenomenon recently observed in America, that a man may be old at forty or be young at seventy-five; it is 'biological age', not 'chronological age' that counts.

It appears that very few modern statesmen can stand the strain of high office for more than a few years. I remember H. A. L. Fisher—then Minister of Education and later author of *A History of Europe*—saying to me that Lloyd George was the only man he knew who could physically remain on top of the volume of business flowing through Downing Street at the end of the First War. L.G. was an extraordinary man and he organised his life better than most politicians. They do not understand how to live under strain, and have not trained themselves for their task. Their way of life is mistaken, the nation's time and their health and energies are wasted in absurd trivialities. A man in high office should surely live like an athlete in light training, and should be completely dedicated to his mission. If he cannot even be serious for his few years of supreme duty, he is a poor fish.

Leaving theory to look at proved facts, at what has actually happened in the modern age, it is found that the old men have succeeded and the younger men have failed. For example, Chancellor Adenauer, General de Gaulle and Chairman Mao, all have in common only the factor of success. Adenauer was elected to high office for the first time at nearly seventy-four, he retired at the age of eighty-eight after fourteen years of power during which Germany rose from the depth to the height. Two years later at the age of ninety he again decided the fate of the German government and the political direction of his country. President de Gaulle at the time of writing is well advanced through the seventies after a period of power which has witnessed the French renaissance. Chairman Maó, also well into the seventies, at this point employs youth within the steel frame of a disciplined army for the fiery purpose of continuous revolution, and exhibits an extraordinary dynamism of age which for communist better or human worse has passed through a test of hard experience without parallel in the modern world.[1] In their totally different fashions and

---

[1] Two outstanding old men clashed in Paris, 1968. Maó exports chaos, but tries to import order. Anarchy was overcome by vote of the French people, which De Gaulle enabled for the first time in history during a crisis of the street.

extreme divergencies of policy these remarkable old men have all succeeded, though it should be freely conceded that they have been greatly assisted by the young teams which they selected. The recipe of success in the modern world has been a great old man, surrounded by a brilliant young team.

What of the relatively young men who in this period have arrived early in power? Two outstanding examples of completely different personalities and utterly divergent policies are President Kennedy and Chancellor Hitler. A study of their characters and methods belongs to history, but few will now claim that they succeeded in terms of achieving the aims they declared. Where is national socialism? Where is American power in its own hemisphere, which rested on the Monroe doctrine? Where is the 'new frontier'?—is it in Vietnam, where its author initiated large-scale military intervention?[1] These lives may or may not illustrate the German proverb—he who will live in legend, must succumb in life—but in terms of achieved aims, whether good or bad, neither of them can be compared with the older men just mentioned.

What of their immediate predecessors? Churchill was given power at a later age than the present youth racket would admit to be proper. After all the strain of war, he was generally reputed still to be going strong at eighty, and his way of life was certainly not conducive to long physical endurance. In the First World War Clemenceau formed his war-winning government at the age of seventy-six. On the other side, Hindenburg emerged from retirement to win the decisive battle of Tannenberg which temporarily saved his country, and died as the venerated President of Germany at the age of eighty-eight. Where were the young men in this picture?

Gladstone and Palmerston roared into their eighties in creative and dynamic policies. Lord Randolph Churchill's jibe that Gladstone was 'an old man in a hurry' turned out to be just the ineffective attempt to put a brake on age by youth which then itself failed. Gladstone was proved right in his drive for Irish Home Rule and other reforms at the end of his life; the myopic efforts of all the younger mediocrities of British politics to frustrate him cost Britain many years of bitter strife and incurred grave dangers. It is surprising too in the nineteenth century to discover the advanced ages of the three chief generals in the army which took Paris from the relatively youthful leadership of France. Louis Napoleon suffered the same defeat at the hands of age as his famous uncle in the campaign of 1812 when he was destroyed by Kutusov,[2] who was almost seventy.

[1] President Kennedy was inaugurated on January 20, 1961, and according to the report of Joseph Alsop 'considered that the "main theatre" was South Vietnam' and 'devoted all resources to the contest in this "main theatre" '. This report was confirmed in the same issue of the same paper by James Reston: 'We lost more men in Vietnam in 1967 than in all the other *five years* since our military intervention in that tragic country'. (*New York Herald Tribune*, Number 30, 1967.)

[2] His predecessor, Suvarov, was near seventy during his remarkable campaign against Napoleon's marshals in Italy. Radetsky, after years of exclusion and neglect, was eighty-three when victorious at Novara and then governed till he was ninety-one.

Wellington in the statesmanship of his fashion was effective to a fine old age, at least with physique and faculty entirely unimpaired by a strenuous but, by the standards of his period, sober life. One of the most striking examples of all was provided by his most valuable ally; Blücher at the age of seventy-three was down at the head of a cavalry charge at Quatre Bras and had a division of his Prussians gallop over him, only to rise and arrive two days later at the right time on the field of Waterloo. I was gratified to receive from Germany some friendly letters of comparison with old Blücher, when in a well-laid trap I went down under a Red mob in a street fight at the age of sixty-six, but managed to rise and go straight to the platform to make the speech they had intended to prevent. When we talk of the relative merits of youth and age it is well to begin with a study of the facts. Both have their uses; what we need are good men, old and young.

These men should be given their chance as soon as possible, old or young, early or late. It is another unfortunate fact of history and human nature that, apart from inheritance and revolution, good men tend to get their chance late rather than early. For example, a man much approved in age and much disapproved in youth was Sir Winston Churchill. An old friend and contemporary of his—the Irish-American sportsman, Ikey Bell—once said to me: 'The secret is to do what Winston did, live till all the men who hate you are dead'. It was a long march for Winston Churchill to become the tribal deity of the Tory Party from those early days when Lady Milner described him as 'half an alien, and wholly undesirable'. Certainly in many of his best years when he was generously inspired by some original ideas and had an ardent passion for social reform, Sir Winston Churchill was excluded from power by as tawdry an array of mediocrity as has ever dulled the English landscape. It would have been better to use that talent for creation rather than for destruction.

Chatham in his very different character and incomparably different achievement suffered the usual fate of great Englishmen. It was a long journey too from his classic reply to Horace Walpole in the report of Dr. Johnson—'the atrocious crime of being a young man which the Right Honourable gentleman has charged against me with such decency and spirit I will attempt neither to palliate nor deny, but will content myself with wishing that I may be of those

---

Our own Lord Roberts was hard on seventy when he became Commander-in-Chief in the Boer War and saved the situation; he died at eighty-two when visiting the Western Front in 1914. The Americans' own Syngman Rhee returned to Korea after over thirty years in exile at the age of seventy and ruled that country until he was eighty-five, winning all elections but resigning after the fourth victory, when his election methods were alleged to have fallen short of the standards required in American primaries. Diverse were the characters and achievements, but all were old. Finally do not let us forget Dandolo, Doge of Venice, who took Constantinople at the age of eighty-four, or Ho Chi Min, Doge of the Left, who took most of Vietnam at the age of seventy-eight. High politics seems no game for children.

whose follies cease with their youth and not of those who continue ignorant in spite of age and experience'—to the brief four years toward the end of his life when, with the firm support of the mass of the English people, he was permitted to save his country and to win for it a great Empire. Jonathan Swift's penetrating dictum certainly applied to him: you may observe the entry of a genius into the world when you see that 'all the dunces are in league against him'. The same tendency may be discovered in the dramatic and turbulent history of the classic world.

Personally I never found the least difficulty in dialogue with a different generation, and learn with no inhibition of years from anyone with anything to tell me. Young men and women should be consulted about their learning, which should relate to their future lives. They should be treated as adult by universities—and by the law. The present clash of age and youth seems to me one of the silliest misunderstandings in contemporary nonsense. The war of generations is more foolish than the war of class, for it has less reason. It is almost always the sign of some intellectual inadequacy on one side or the other; at a certain level of intelligence the clash of generations simply ceases to exist. Would two physicists at the age of twenty and fifty on the verge of a new discovery decide they could not work together on account of the difference of age? On the other hand, between complete illiterates the difference of a few years seems to be all important. Primitives live in narrow little age compartments.

When I was young some men in the older generation gave me the sense of being eternal contemporaries. Lloyd George was many years older than I, but he always made me feel we were of the same generation. Nowadays I feel contemporary with many of the young and the angry when I discuss subjects of mutual interest with them. At a certain level the difference in years makes no more difference than the colour of the hair. People without intellectual interest are divided by the most ephemeral things, like variations in contemporary fashion which in the course of a long life you see come and go half a dozen times. What does it all matter? Bonaparte when he rode alone across the bridge at Arcola was wearing hair down to his shoulders, but by the time of the Consulate he had it cropped short and brushed forward in pursuit of the Roman cult. I happen to prefer the latter vogue and would wager it will now soon return, but it does not much matter so long as men retain the qualities of manhood. The heroism of Thermopylae was not dimmed by the previous evening spent in the Spartan fashion of combing and even scenting their flowing locks. It was not long hair which made the Cavaliers lose to the Roundheads, but a certain change in life attitude resulting in an impetuous lack of discipline in the cavalry charge which rendered their action less effective than the balance, poise and resolution of their immediate and victorious predecessors, the Elizabethans.

What is wrong with our civilisation is that the best men are often either excluded altogether until they are needed in some catastrophe or kept waiting for their chance too long, which wastes not only their time but the vital assets of the nation. The remedy is to provide a system which gives all men of ability progressive opportunity from an early age, a chance which continues as long as their capacity endures. I suggested in *The Alternative* some methods which can at least be more effective to that end than the crude and wasteful process of setting the young against the old. There is always room at the top in a well-ordered society, because the supply of men with first-rate capacity is always too small. We must devise means to overcome the obstructive opposition of the league of dunces, who have existed ever since it was first suggested that men should leave the cave for the sunlight.

There seem two main reasons for the present cult of Peter Pan in politics. The first is envy, and that is as old as time. Heraclitus said that all the citizens of Ephesus should be hanged because through envy they prevented the saving of the state by the emergence of eminent men. Goethe in his wise and modern fashion combated the same vice of envy with the more effective weapon of wit in his epigram: 'the only consolation of the dunce is that genius is not immortal'. I would put it rather differently, and, of course, more modestly: old man, is the last gibe thrown by the sterile at the creative. They hope that age will reduce everyone to their own impotence. They are wrong; the great wines improve. Today we see the dull consoling themselves with the thought that the bright are not immortal, even while they seek to emulate them with the flattery of ineffective imitation. It was admiration rather than envy which was the mark of great ages—'*honneur aux maîtres d'armes*'; and still more in modern terms to the masters of intellect and character. The desire to tear down all excellence is the instinct of 'Silenus and his long-eared band', whose excesses in the last moments of decadence usually precede and even evoke renaissance among peoples still capable of great thought and action.

The second reason for the urge to seek ever younger statesmen, until the cradle itself is in danger of being ransacked, is surely due to the instinct to escape from a failing society. The older men and also the bogus young of the present period become discredited because they are trying to work policies doomed to failure. The remedy is not to make Peter Pan Prime Minister, but to change the system. The whole present process is particularly ridiculous at a moment when science is continually expanding the effective life-span. In face of the historic examples already quoted, why deny capacity to experienced men just at the moment when the scientific genius of the modern world is much prolonging that capacity? The nonsense will pass with the hour of crisis, and we shall return at least in serious matters to the Roman *gravitas* which has been the imprimatur of all great periods. May this brief and rather dogmatic digression be some expiation for the folly of my own youth, a libation poured on the statue of Peter Pan which was graciously and appropriately erected in Kensington Gardens at the beginning of this epoch, soon after the manly exposure of Achilles in Hyde Park had been decently veiled by petition of the ladies of Mayfair.

My young energies were soon given a more creative outlet by association with Lord Robert Cecil. The ablest son of an outstanding Prime Minister, Lord Salisbury, he embodied the mature, experienced and traditional wisdom of statesmanship, not only in mind but in the physical presence of an age-old eagle whose hooded eyes brooded on the follies of men, while they still held the light of a further and beneficent vision. I was first attracted to him by my sharp difference with the government of the day concerning the unnecessary risking of British lives in Russia. Cecil was also prominent in new ideas of social and industrial reform—such as co-partnership and profit-sharing—in which I warmly and actively supported him. Our policies in this sphere anticipated almost exactly in form and by some forty years in time proposals which were regarded as most revolutionary when advanced in the 1960s by the progressive thinkers who were announced as the young lions of Liberalism. 'Participation' is the latest version.

Most important of all to me were Lord Robert Cecil's constructive efforts to secure the peace of Europe and of the world in his advocacy of the League of Nations; early in 1920 I began actively to assist him in his work. Peace was throughout my overriding passion, and the League of Nations was the first and last effective and disinterested effort to secure peace by comprehensive international action. It was well conceived for that period, because the organisation consisted of similar peoples capable of acting together and voluntarily undertaking certain obligations of international law in accord with their own traditions. On the withdrawal of America it became in practical effect a European organisation for the maintenance of world peace. Finally we shall see that the League was wrecked by lack of will in statesmen rather than by defects in the machinery.

The first task which began in the company of Lord Robert remained the continuing struggle to extricate our country from Mr. Churchill's adventures. I could never be called a pacifist, because I was ready to meet the test of force in the First World War, and later when I believed it to be necessary to meet violence with self-defence in order to save free speech in Britain; I then organised the Blackshirt movement and achieved this object. But through my whole political life I have been strongly opposed to the sacrifice of British lives in any but a British quarrel. This attitude was clearly summarised in two of my speeches opposing the adventure in Mesopotamia, now called Iraq. They were made after Bonar Law's government was formed in 1922, by which time Mr. Churchill had lost his seat in Parliament; he had been the Ministerial champion of the policy when I had opposed it in the company of Lord Robert Cecil. I still opposed it when it was taken over by Bonar Law's government, of which Lord Robert became a member in circumstances which will be explained. The personal relations in that period were complex and variable, but my political themes were consistently pursued and these speeches were a typical example from a protracted controversy.

Though as always determined to extricate our country from military commitments which did not serve British or European interests, I should now take a more realistic view of oil necessities than I did then. It would in any case have been wiser to have developed the oil which was subsequently discovered in our own Empire, of which the geological survey had still been neglected even by 1939. My main charge against government in this period was that they were always running round the world looking after the business of every people except their own. When they finally woke to the importance of the British Empire which could have supplied all their needs with forethought and plan, they threw it away as a present to anarchy in a panic at the weakness to which their extraneous errors had reduced our country. My speeches at least attempted to call a halt to these adventures and to concentrate attention on the interests of our own people.

Speaking on February 15, 1923, I referred to our position in Iraq and observed that 'the matter has been flung, as all difficult and insoluble problems are flung, to the League of Nations. It is curious that the League of Nations is never invoked to stop the favourite wars of statesmen; it is only invoked to stop those wars of which they are getting rather tired.' I then developed one of my main themes, that if we allowed the matter to drift on we should be faced with the alternative of fighting a disastrous war, entailing immense expenditure in lives and money, or of withdrawing with grave loss of prestige.

I often reverted in later years to the argument that it was foolish to scatter universal pledges of support, and dishonourable then to honour only those which suited our own interest: the principle of a selective honouring of binding pledges. Many years later in the much larger sphere of the 1939 war with Germany I stated exactly the same principle and made the same charge: our statesmen had gone to war with Germany and sacrificed many lives to honour a pledge foolishly given to Poland, while later they sat back supinely while Russia permanently subjugated Poland. This tragedy could arise again in our time if we were called upon to fight a world war in support of pledges lightly given in Asia, which I have opposed for the same reasons in recent years.

When taunted in 1923 with advocating scuttle I retorted that recent experience had shown everyone was in favour of scuttle in the end. The question was when to scuttle, before or after the row began. There was nothing so detrimental to national prestige as being full of bluff and bluster until you got into a difficulty and then quietly climbing down. 'It is possible to walk downstairs with some grace and dignity of one's own free will, but it is impossible to be kicked downstairs with grace or dignity.' In the present recurrence of history these remarks apply to our situation East of Suez today.

I then drew attention to warnings from soldiers as eminent as Sir Henry Wilson and General Robertson and reminded the House of 'the fate of those

Empires which have endeavoured in the past to maintain enormous commitments in far-flung territories with inadequate force'. Our 'small and scattered forces in Iraq and throughout the world' were endangered by this policy and our home defence was jeopardised by the absence in Iraq of essential air squadrons. We were taking 'the gravest risk in this matter of our air defence' and in addition were squandering resources in these remote adventures which were urgently needed for education, health and housing at home.

I denounced statesmen 'whose eyes are averted from the destruction which their blunders since the war have caused in their own country, who can regard with tranquil gaze the seething cauldron of European politics'. Their eyes were 'fixed on eastern deserts' and they had scant sympathy with many of their fellow-countrymen who 'have to live with starvation' and are 'familiar with sorrow and anguish'. If they continued to 'burden industry with these colossal commitments' they would risk 'a collapse of the finances of the country'. In these parliamentary fights I first follow :d the lead of Lord Cecil, and later continued alone in support of principles whose consistent service has brought me many a battle and caused me many a trouble.

The principle object of our attack was always Mr. Churchill, main protagonist of these policies. This produced many vehement clashes between him and Lord Robert in which Mr. Churchill was usually victorious. However, on one occasion Lord Robert scored heavily with a slight adaptation of Dryden's well-known lines on Buckingham:

> Stiff in opinion, always in the wrong
> Was everything in turn, but nothing long
> And in the course of one revolving moon
> Was scribbler, painter, statesman and buffoon.

Even before my association with Lord Robert Cecil in the work of the League of Nations and the fight against Mr. Churchill's adventures, I had been invited by his elder brother Lord Salisbury to become Secretary of an organisation he had formed, called the 'People's League for Economy'. This was in 1919 and it brought me in close contact with this remarkable family. A number of visits to Hatfield were required at that time to further the people's cause. It was a sound concept by any standard, as the profligacy of the Coalition Government, both in the wild expenditure of public money and the sale of public assets at knock-down prices, often to dubious political characters, had become a public scandal. The day-to-day administration of this League, which was rapidly successful in a minor fashion, was too much to combine with my parliamentary duties, so I suggested to Lord Salisbury that it should have a whole-time salaried secretary under my general supervision. He concurred, and asked me to find a suitable man.

After a visit to the Oxford Union it occurred to me that its President was just the man. He was very bright indeed, and his name was Leslie Hore-

Belisha. During this period there was a succession of particularly brilliant Presidents of the Oxford Union, mostly derived from the war generation, culminating in the triumvirate of Guedalla, Hore-Belisha and Beverley Nichols. The last was eventually lost to politics down the garden path, after writing some charming things about me in some summer-house en route; the first was gained for literature after a period in the miasma of contemporary liberalism; Belisha alone went forward to a spectacular political career. Although he was some years older than I was, and a major returned from war service, he was younger in status, as I was an M.P. and he was still busy taking his degree and presiding at the Union. Directly he graduated I invited him to organise the People's League for Economy.

That staid organisation was an unsuitable frame for his volatile talents, for Belisha was in every respect the opposite of the cautious, calculating, steady and sober character which is supposed to be the attribute of his race; like several outstanding Jews, notably Lassalle and Trotsky, he was dashing to a degree, even reckless. At that time he lived well and hard, and in conversation was brilliantly amusing. His association with the Church and rectitude in the House of Cecil did not last long. The occasion of the break was my error in asking him to accept an invitation from the enterprising Vicar of the City Temple church to speak from his pulpit after lunch. It was reported to me afterwards by some of his young friends that he began with a side-splitting parody of the parsonic demeanour in the words: 'Rising as I do in this hallowed spot, my only regret is that I have neither the clerical voice nor yet the clerical manner'. The oration was interrupted at this point with a resounding hiccough and was necessarily brought to a premature conclusion. This did not go at all well with Lord Salisbury, and he departed from the People's League in a cloud of dust.

At this period of his life Hore-Belisha was 'living it up', a tendency which continued even after his entry into the House of Commons, where it marred some of his early speeches. It is greatly to his credit that he subsequently pulled himself together and drove forward with cool and sober will to achieve for a period the heights of political success. My last intimate discussion with him was due to a curious accident. We had taken a seaside house in Normandy, and went into neighbouring Deauville at the weekend. I visited the casino to see for the first time the celebrated Greek syndicate in action, and was surprised to find that their principal challenger at the big table was Hore-Belisha. He explained to me in the intervals of this desperate encounter that he had been left a considerable sum of money by some relation and meant for better or worse to put his whole fortune to the test that evening. He was quite sober.

I watched, fascinated by the drama, throughout the night. He invited me to supper at six o'clock in the morning, after rising from the table with three times the fortune he had staked. I urged him to leave Deauville next day and never to return. I never gamble myself, because I find so much in life more interesting, but the next weekend I returned to the casino to see if there were any comparable drama; there was, it was Hore-Belisha again. He emerged at dawn without a penny, and this time I invited him to supper. He was very cheerful, and explained that if he had retained that fortune he would have been tempted never to do a stroke of work and just to have a good time. Max Beaverbrook had offered him a job at a large salary as his chief political columnist, and now he was going to accept, it would be the making of him. I admired both his fortitude and his philosophy.

Our paths did not cross again until his disaster, when as Secretary of State for War he was driven from office by troubles in 1940. It was a personal sorrow to me that our organisation previously played a part in that assault, as years before I had much liked him, but it would have been a denial of public duty to prevent it. Afterwards I saw him only once again, and he looked at me with eyes of sad reproach. Public life is too often laden with these 'tears of things'. We were friends though we had a different attitude to life. He was always surprised and rather envious of my automatic decision in favour of purpose before pleasure in the bitter choice which is often necessary.

My mishap with the appointment of Hore-Belisha as Secretary to Lord Salisbury's People's League did not deter his brother Lord Robert Cecil from inviting me to act as Parliamentary Secretary to the League of Nations' Union, a large organisation which he had established with considerable financial assistance from Lord Cowdray to support his ideas for the promotion of the League of Nations. I accepted, and was much occupied with this task in the summer which followed my marriage and honeymoon in May 1920. We had rented the agreeable Downshire house at Roehampton, and I used to go up every day to the L.N.U. office at 15 Grosvenor Place in the morning and most evenings during the week to Parliament as well. Cimmie about the same time became active in the affairs of the English-Speaking Union. It was a happy summer.

I was attracted to Lord Robert Cecil by his fine character and by a rare combination of the practical and the ideal in his thinking. The concept of the League of Nations was well thought out. It sought peace by practical means, without any impairment of the national sovereignties which were still dominant, and provided a machinery not only to maintain peace but if necessary to enforce it. In addition to all the mechanism of conciliation and arbitration which could anticipate grave disputes and attempt settlement in the early stages, the decisive Article 16 provided very effective means for international action against any deliberate aggressor. The League of Nations was then not only a homogeneous body but also rested on the reality that every member was an established and a considerable country. Like all good ideas it could, of course, be made ridiculous by exaggeration to the point of absurdity, as we have seen after the Second World War in the United Nations, which in the General Assembly accords to a barbarous new country with a few hundred thousand inhabitants equal weight with Britain, France, America or Russia. The veto of the great countries in the Security Council is a purely negative power.

It is curious how many of the best ideas of the 1920s meet their *reductio ad absurdum* in the 1960s. This is perhaps characteristic of one of those recurrent periods of decadence from which happily the great peoples of Europe have always shown a striking capacity suddenly to recover in response to the challenge of necessity. In all things there is a just mean, and the League of Nations at that time held a fair equilibrium between falling into the dictatorship of a few great powers and the present relapse into a modern tower of Babel. It was a well-devised piece of machinery, but like all other mechanism depended on human operation. The essential ingredient of will in statesmanship was lacking from the League of Nations.

The League was eventually wrecked for all practical purposes in 1923 by Mussolini, who had a dangerous surplus of the quality which was so deficient in other statesmen. I remember then making an angry and most offensive speech about him to the effect that he had triumphed like a drunken motor-car driver, not by reason of his own skill but because all sober people had been concerned to get out of his way. In fact this bellicose utterance covered the retreat of pusillanimous supporters of the League. I had been all for action, and so to do him justice was Lord Robert Cecil. I do not know if Mussolini was aware of that speech at the time, as he followed debates in other countries fairly closely, but he was probably unaware of the action I desired to take, and we never discussed it when I subsequently knew him; by that time in any case it was an old story. To tell it we must again anticipate events a little. The consideration of subject is sometimes in conflict with strict chronology, but all these incidents happened within the first lustrum of the twenties.

After the election of 1922, when Lord Robert and I had parted, he to re-enter the Conservative Government and I to continue in opposition after refusing to accompany him, I remained on good terms with him and had some part in the remarkable events which virtually destroyed the League of Nations. It was in the summer of 1923 that Mussolini took a risk, when he had not the power to blow over a house of cards. He got away with it because those who had the power lacked courage. Mussolini shelled the island of Corfu and killed a number of people under the British flag. At that time Lord Robert was at a session of the League of Nations in Geneva, Mr. Baldwin was at Aix-les-Bains on his customary holiday to take the waters, and I was at my customary holiday in Venice to enjoy more varied fare. The Venetian scene was affected to some extent by the general atmosphere because some festive young Blackshirts had swum out to an English yacht in the harbour and affixed a bomb which did considerable damage, but by luck rather than precaution, injured none of the occupants. This is not the place to revive the origin of the quarrel—I knew then little and cared less about Mussolini, his

Blackshirts or Fascism—but to recall that for me as a young English M.P. the conduct of the Italian leader and his supporters appeared an outrage. This was the time, if ever, to move the application of Article 16 at Geneva and once and for all to establish the authority of the League.

I left Venice at once for Geneva, where I found Cecil in a considerable state of indignation and already disposed to take action. I added what fuel I could to the flame, for this seemed our best possible chance to affirm the rule of law in international affairs. Mussolini had only recently come to power and had no adequate armed forces, his finances were weak and the lira was tottering. If Article 16 had been applied it would probably not have been necessary to do more than to secure the return of his ambassadors from the country of every League member, which would at once have caused the crash of the Italian currency. In my contemporary judgment and in my subsequent appraisal of his character, after some opportunity to study it, he would have been much too realistic in a weak position to challenge overwhelming force once it firmly confronted him. For my part I was quite prepared to go further, and move for sanctions, which in those conditions would have been effective. We had every prospect of a rapid and spectacular victory for the League which would have justified this new machinery for the maintenance of world peace, to whose creation such long and arduous effort had been devoted. We had a rare opportunity firmly to establish the authority of the new institution and the rule of law. Nothing was needed except human will, but that was entirely lacking.

Cecil decided at once to travel to Aix-les-Bains, while I remained at Geneva. He was going to ask Baldwin for authority to move Article 16. Quickly he returned in much dejection. He had found the pitiful figure of the Conservative leader complacently immersed in the soothing waters, showing scant interest in international events. Damper even than usual, the feeble flame of that spirit had scarcely flickered at the news that people under the British flag had been killed by what appeared to us an act of international piracy. Baldwin made to Cecil the incredible reply that he must use his own judgment at Geneva and do what he thought fit. The Prime Minister of Britain would take no decision, and would bear no responsibility.

Lord Robert Cecil was not prepared to go ahead on his own, though the outcome of taking the risk might well have made him Prime Minister. His life work would have been crowned in the triumph of the League, which was more important to his honest nature, but inevitably his own political position would thereafter have been so impregnable that it must have rallied all who combined the desire for clean politics with the will to action.

This will was not available, because in such men it is only aroused by intense emotion. They were then reluctant to establish the authority of the League by an act of cold will fortified by the calm calculation that they had every prospect of victory and their opponent had none. Yet men of this kind in 1939 in a condition of white-hot emotion were prepared to risk their country, their Empire, the life of Europe and of world civilisation, when by any cool calculation all the odds were against them. They missed their chance when it was easy, and took it when it was desperate; but at what a cost. Strong moral feelings are certainly necessary to great action, but they should be exercised with realism. We need the heart of fire but the brain of ice.

All that mattered to me at the time was the maintenance of peace and the devising and establishment of practical machinery to serve that supreme end. My part was to fight for my cause, which was the League, to stand by my friends and play for my side. Lloyd George was my first target, because he abrogated the machinery of the League in favour of his own method of using the smaller and more mobile body of the Supreme Council of the great powers. It is, of course, always easier to decide and act in a small body of able men representing great powers, but in the long run it is not so effective in mobilising the opinion of mankind for peace. Lloyd George never had much grasp of deep principle and in practice had endured for years an extraordinary experience of obstruction in national and international affairs; consequently he favoured the Supreme Council in his feverish search for rapid action. This appeared to me to undermine the authority of the League. My object above all was to establish the comprehensive authority of the League in place of the old balance of power which divided Europe and risked recurrent war.

The particular mixture of reason and vitriol which was my recipe in that period is illustrated by a speech I made in the House in February 1922. I reinforced my argument in favour of the League and against Lloyd George's 'method of slipshod conference' in the Supreme Council with a satirical attack on the Prime Minister which evoked much laughter at his expense and much indignation at my impudence. I remarked on his 'state of a Roman emperor' at conferences in the villa of his millionaire Parliamentary Secretary, Sir Philip Sassoon, where he could be 'regaled in the evening with the frankincense of admiring friends', and the 'abrasions of controversy could be soothed' by a 'liberal application of precious ointment from the voluptuous Orient'.

In serious argument I agreed with the Prime Minister that some countries were 'threatening the peace of Europe, because they fear the aggression of others. Fear is the most potent factor today in the disturbance of peace. There are only two ways of alleviating that fear, one by a strong League of Nations which can guarantee the peace of the world and can guarantee countries against aggression, the other way by these entangling alliances to which the Rt. Hon. Gentleman is now about to commit the country.' I concluded by advocating that a comprehensive guarantee for all the principal powers in the League of Nations should be constituted under the Covenant of the League as an alternative to the old system of the balance of power which was responsible in large part for the catastrophe of the immediate past. We should move on to a 'new order and conception of the world which originated as the result of so great a sacrifice'.

My passion was peace, and I pursued it through any means which seemed the most effective. The way of the League was the opposite to the fatal division of Europe, caused by the traditional doctrine of the balance of power, which in my view had been deeply responsible for the First World War. This concept and its protagonists must be attacked with every weapon the debater carried. Some of these weapons of sarcasm and invective may seem inimical to the proper effect of the more reasoned and constructive passages in my speeches, but I had been educated in a tough school of debate. We shall see in the next chapter the origin of the development and ruthless use of these weapons, which alone won me a quiet hearing for my constructive argument. It was necessary by sarcasm and invective to establish among interrupters a certain fear of the retort, which was reinforced when they knew they would be selected personally for some wounding comments. I was not at fault in the beginning of this situation, for I had begun purely with the method of reason, but I was to blame in the flush of my youthful success for using these weapons too frequently and too roughly when I discovered their potency.

Sir Philip Sassoon was one of the butts of this speech in February 1922 because he was rather a joke among the younger generation for serving Lloyd George as Private Secretary in peace directly after he had served during the war in the same capacity to General Haig at G.H.Q. in France. Sassoon was in many ways a most engaging and obliging fellow whose amiable idiosyncracy was to entertain the great, the bright and the fashionable. I first saw my second wife Diana at a ball at his magnificent establishment in Park Lane several years after this speech. She looked wonderful among the rose-entwined pillars of the 'voluptuous Orient' as the music of the best of orchestras was wafted together with the best of scents through air heavy laden with all Sassoon's most hospitable artifices. Her starry blue eyes, golden hair and ineffable expression of a Gothic madonna seemed remote from the occasion, but strangely enough not entirely inappropriate.

The last occasion I saw Sassoon was one evening at supper at Lady Cunard's, years later in the thirties. I was alone with her in the drawing-room when the Prince of Wales entered, followed by Mrs. Simpson, Mr. Simpson and Sir Philip Sassoon. It was a little awkward because Sassoon himself was a Jew, and I was at that time engaged in a violent clash with certain Jewish interests. The quarrel had nothing to do with anti-semitism, it was concerned with the possibility of a second world war if a boycott of German trade were organised. The Sassoons were not connected with the agitation, and in any case both he and I knew how to be polite on delicate occasions. The superlative manners of the Prince was unconscious of all such things.

In this same speech of February 8, 1922, I baited Lloyd George for the failure of the conference at Cannes, when Briand fell from power immediately after playing golf with the British Prime Minister. This incident illustrated one of those occasions when English and French do not well understand each other. We are accustomed to the portly figures of elderly statesmen posturing in front of photographers in a pretence to play games at which they are obviously inept. The British may see through the pretence, but they feel it is endearing, a flattering tribute to our national idiosyncracies. The French take a sharper and more realistic view which, translated from their Latin urbanities into our Anglo-Saxon crudities, runs roughly as follows: 'We have paid these old fools to conduct the affairs of nations, not to lose time looking silly on the golf-links'. Briand was getting the worst of the game of golf—and of the conference—in the match with L.G. It was enough; he disappeared.

I also defended Lord Robert Cecil's alliance with the former Liberal Foreign Secretary, Lord Grey of Fallodon, who in private opinion I always found a singularly tedious and ineffective figure. It is true that I met him rarely; at the time he was being cast for a central part he was away bird-watching in Northumberland, and from my short experience of him I felt it was better that the birds rather than England should continue to enjoy his company. Lord Robert Cecil, however, liked him as much as he detested Lloyd George, and did all the work while Grey watched the birds. They may have fixed up some act between them of Cincinnatus Grey being recalled from the plough or the gulls which follow it, for the classic performance of the disinterested figure who has to be persuaded to return from the calm beauty of nature to the ugly turmoil of politics.

The intrigues became quite febrile, and Grey was certainly aware of them. I remember at the time a meeting being arranged in my house between Robert Cecil and Arthur Henderson to discuss a political combination under Grey for the defeat of the Coalition under Lloyd George. This meeting was of course never publicised, but the manoeuvres became well known and on one occasion were splashed in the Press under the headline: 'Grey Whigs on the green benches'. Henderson appeared interested, but Lansbury and others of the Labour Left were strongly against. Cecil by himself would have been much more generally acceptable than in the company of Grey. It seemed to me a strange complex that he should desire the shelter of this name, for he was in every respect ten times the man Grey was, and his relatively advanced ideas of social reform together with the considerable international standing acquired by his able and ardent advocacy of the League made a far wider appeal.

Lloyd George rather than Grey was the man who might have made the League work and have fulfilled all our hopes, if he had been won for the idea. I did not know him at that time, as I never met him until after he ceased to be Prime Minister. He was detested by all the outstanding Conservative, Liberal and Labour supporters of the League, and it may well be that he felt this solid block of hatred closed to him the door of League policies and impelled him to his own methods in the Supreme Council, which I felt so strongly at the time were destructive. Yet he could have made the League work, with his dynamic energy and consummate political skill.

Lloyd George evinced some emotion in domestic politics but gave scant indication of deep moral feeling, either in impulse or inhibition. It was this lack combined with the general incompatibility of temperament which separated him from men like Cecil, whose cause might have been brought to success if they had worked together. It has been one of the tragedies of our time that the good have so often been divorced from the dynamic. The ideal, of course, is the union of these qualities in one character, but that is rare. The English aristocracy in this period detested Lloyd George, who in tragic paradox was the only man who might have realised their fine ideals. This was true of all the men with whom I was then associated: the two Cecils, Henry Bentinck, Aubrey Herbert, Godfrey Locker-Lampson and, until his premature death, Mark Sykes.

Why did they so hate and distrust Lloyd George? His faults were obvious, and so to any insight were their origin. What did they matter in comparison with his extraordinary capacity to get things done, if he were under the right influence, aimed in the right direction? There was no doubt of his genuine desire to build an enduring peace, it was his methods which were in question. Yet it is surely possible in retrospect to realise a little of what he was up against, and to understand that he could never have achieved his results without methods somewhat foreign to their narrow rectitude, which was fortified by an established, an hereditary position. 'The little Welsh attorney' in the First World War often had the rigid obscurantism of an obsolete General Staff against him, sustained by the support of the Crown. He and the troops won the war in spite of them. Churchill in the Second World War came from a very different milieu and was aided by memories of the first; he had none of these disadvantages. He was not obliged to pass through the struggle of his ancestor of genius to attain his triumph.

Marlborough, like Lloyd George, had to make many bricks without straw, to manage the Crown with the aid of his wife, to manoeuvre an often hostile political situation at home, to handle obtuse and intractable allies, to intrigue by devious means in order to free his capable hands for great action. It is lamentable that such men should be placed in such a position, but this is a familiar situation in British history. Macaulay could write of Marlborough: 'At twenty he sold his vigour and his beauty, and at sixty his glory and his genius'. But it may be asked whether in the conditions of his time John Churchill would have emerged from obscurity, or the will of England would ever have been imposed on Louis XIV, if his methods had not been a trifle unorthodox. The rigid old Whig's ultimate understanding of life's realities may have led him finally to exclaim as he stood in front of Kneller's portrait of Marlborough after his terrific denunciation: 'Yet I can never gaze with equanimity into John Churchill's cold, sad eyes'. It was well that Marlborough's reputation in the end was so ably defended by his descendant Winston Churchill, who curiously at least to superficial observation differed from him in every particular of character. The descendant was in personal dealings conspicuously honest, warm of nature, impulsive, emotional, swayed by passion to a dangerous degree in his assessment of men and situations. The ancestor was ice-cold, realistic, coolly calculating, but deeply dedicated to great purposes of supreme benefit to his country. He was the Englishman who alone in the company of Chatham could match the two great Latins, Caesar and Napoleon, or the Teutonic genius of the two Fredericks, Hohenstaufen and Hohenzollern, on the dusty plain of action.

It is difficult even now to analyse what was the trouble between the best characters in English politics and Lloyd George. Probably it is true that at some point he sold honours, but he might have replied in his own terms that if the Huguenot King Henri IV could say 'Paris is worth a mass', he could be forgiven for tossing a few worthless plutocrats into a political museum he had always despised, if this could secure for him the means to break free from reaction and to solve the unemployment and housing problem. They shuddered when it was reported to them that Lloyd George's P.P.S., Sir William Sullivan, had walked into the Athenaeum after gaily performing a lightly delegated duty, observing that he had just 'made another two bloody bishops'; but they should have understood the fellow was a bit uncouth. There was already talk about the women, but some of the venerated pillars of the Constitution like Wellington and Palmerston had already forestalled L.G. in that sphere, and many of their favourite friends were at the same time quietly, unobtrusively surpassing him. Was it then just a question of manners, class, an attitude to life, a deep incompatibility of temperament? Whatever it was, it weighed with them more than all Lloyd George's dynamism and his potential of immense service to the cause of peace to which they were genuinely dedicated. They buttoned up their prim little overcoats against the chill of Lloyd George's methods, while their country and Europe caught pneumonia from the icy blast of the next war.

I may be unfair, and it may be true that they had previously made efforts to work with such men which had proved impossible; but I suspect that the emotions, complexes and personal prejudices of the old aristocracy cost this country dear in the days when their influence was still often decisive. They should have forgiven Lloyd George's minor faults, and have embraced his genius to use it for fine ends. Great affairs cannot afford the luxury of emotions. To be divided from men who can have value by reason of their imperfections is to misunderstand the world, which is imperfect.

The character of the Cecils was a strange and interesting phenomenon of English life. The subtle political wisdom of their Elizabethan ancestor still

lived in some degree among them, and I learnt much from the inner discussions of this association. Yet there was a febrile quality in their action
which must surely have been absent from the massive calm inherent in the
practical achievement of the Tudor period. Particularly was this noticeable in
Lord Hugh Cecil, who in some respects was the most brilliant among these
three sons of the great Prime Minister. His religious convictions traversed and
permeated his whole political being, and they were dragged into the most
inappropriate occasions. I never read a letter by him to *The Times*, illuminating
such a dry-as-dust subject as Free Trade, without apprehending that it would
conclude quite irrelevantly with 'To hell with the Pope', expressed, of course,
in his delicate and indeed exquisite phraseology. His intellect was entirely
mastered by his emotions, if someone inadvertently touched one of the key-
controlling buttons of his complex mechanism.

Lord Robert in his saintly personality and in the high endeavour of his
politics represented probably the last attempt for a long time to make the contemporary world sensible, humane and civilised, a world of well-arranged
peace. He was nearly a great man, and he was certainly a good man; possibly as
great a man as so good a man can be. There is something in a basic concept
of Greek thought, stressed by the neo-Hellenists, that an element of the
Dionysian is necessary as counter-point to the Apollonian in the perfect
harmony of creative nature. Lord Robert too suffered in some degree from the
inhibiting emotions which should never intrude in action. When the emotions
were touched, plain sense was liable to fly out of the window. It is always sad
to see such minds clouded by feelings irrelevant to great purpose, deflected
from practical achievement by the triviality of personal likes and dislikes.
It is a common condition in these delicate aristocratic constitutions which
cannot easily endure the dual strain of thought and action.

At the other extreme of politics Lord Russell's combination of clear vision
with a tendency to emotion dims the clarity of his thought in the moment
when effective action is possible. In so many cases of brilliant men the fine
motor of the intellect is wrecked directly it enters the rough field of action,
because the chassis of physical constitution and concomitant will-power is not
strong enough to sustain it. This is the basic reason why so few who can truly
be described as intellectuals are effective in the world of action. Calm deserts
them in the moment of decision when it is most required. Mr. Asquith was
nearly right in his telling epigram about the Cecils: 'They can never make up
their minds until they have lost their tempers'.

This psychology was the exact opposite of the character and temperament
of the masters of successful action. For instance, authoritative comment on the
nature of Julius Caesar notes the entire absence of feeling or passion in serving
his overriding purpose. He would sit calmly at dinner with a false friend who
he knew had recently been plotting against him—even to encompass his death
—if he could again be won over and could be used for present purpose.

Shaw's sensitive insight into such natures portrays this character in his fascinating play, which is surrealist in the true sense of the word. Caesar offers his arm to Cleopatra to escort her to a dinner party, knowing that the assassin she has prompted has already been quietly eliminated, and explains that there is no bad feeling because the point at which she would betray him had always been foreseen and was consequently forestalled. This extreme of icy, brutal but effective realism was the opposite pole to the temperament of the Cecils. They had little contact with the hard world of action, even in its relatively gentle, modern forms. The Elizabethan forebear must have been different, but those were rougher days.

In past and present we can see how big a part is played in these grave matters by the personal feelings and trivial emotions of statesmen. In my view the truth probably lies between Marx's materialist conception of history, in which economic forces alone are decisive, and the view that personal relations can be all-important. At this time it was certainly true that much might have happened if Cecil's dislike of the dynamic Lloyd George and liking for the ineffectual Grey had been reversed. These 'elective affinities' may be all very well in love affairs, but they are all wrong in statesmanship. Greater men, of more balanced character, further vision and firmer will would have overcome this incompatibility of temperament and used Lloyd George's driving force in service to their fine ideals. There have been men in history capable of this higher wisdom. The petulant passions of these nervous aristocrats divided them from all real possibility of attainment. When they looked at Lloyd George they should have ignored small things in the high Elizabethan fashion of their own tradition, and have said with Carlyle in his defence of Byron and Burns: 'When the ship returns to harbour with the hull battered and the rigging torn, before we assess the blame of the pilot, before we award the verdict of posterity, let us pause to enquire whether the voyage has been twice round the world or to Ramsgate and the Isle of Dogs'.

The immaculate state is easier for the sterile than for the creative.

8

The Irish Question Lloyd George's 'Reprisals'

MORAL feeling is essential but emotion is disastrous in great affairs: this was the sum of my early experience. Ireland in the autumn of 1920 evoked intense moral feeling. I felt that the name of Britain was being disgraced, every rule of good soldierly conduct disregarded, and every decent instinct of humanity outraged. These strong feelings can be judged on the facts presented to me at a time when I and my friends had advocated the granting of Home Rule to Ireland with Dominion status, and found instead that a special auxiliary force had been recruited, nominally to maintain order, but in reality—as we were soon convinced—to break the spirit of the Irish people by systematic terror reinforced with full licence to commit individual crimes.

Generally I had opposed government policies on practical grounds, in speeches which both preceded and followed this moral breaking point in 1920. My recurrent theme was that we should conserve our resources for the benefit of our own people and the development of our own country and Empire, and should refrain from extraneous adventures which exhausted our means and jeopardised those ends. This line I followed consistently until it brought me to the final clash in 1939. It was in origin an essentially practical viewpoint, a pragmatic concept of the interests of my own country. It entered the moral sphere only when the loss of British lives was threatened in addition to the dissipation of British substance, because this touched the deepest chord of my being after my experience of the First World War.

At that time no major war was imminent, and what appeared to me as the errors of government related rather to the exhaustion of the present and the jeopardy of the future than to any urgent moral issues. The Versailles Treaty deeply concerned me because it cast the shadow of future war. However, I did not feel competent nor justified as a complete newcomer in the sphere of foreign policy to break with my party and go into opposition on these grounds. The Versailles Treaty was certainly one of the main motives for my subsequent decision, but at this point my action concerning the Treaty was negative rather than positive in that I vigorously resisted all attempts to put pressure on Lloyd George for the destruction of Europe by the permanent pursuit of vengeance.

These efforts were organised at Westminster by an almost symbolic combination of decadence and dishonesty, Claude Lowther and Horatio Bottomley. The former's delicate claim to fame was the decoration of his fine Norman castle by placing multi-coloured fairy lights along its battlements and ensconcing rose-crowned cupids to relieve the severity of its internal alcoves. Bottomley was made of sterner stuff; he finally went to gaol for swindling ex-servicemen and old women, after claiming in the Sunday press that he received personal messages from Heaven. Lord Buckmaster, a former Lord Chancellor, told me he had seen a letter to Bottomley from an ex-serviceman dying of wounds asking to meet the author of these articles and be consoled in his entry to the after life, which was sent on by Bottomley to a local crony marked with the query 'Is there any money in this? H.B.' He had a demagogic success both as a journalist and speaker which was difficult to understand. His writing was clearly such blatant humbug that it should not have deceived a child. His style in speaking was peculiar, rocking from foot to foot like a captive elephant in the zoo while his hands see-sawed his spectacles in a monotonous motion, but he had a certain force of a revolting personality. He used to advocate a 'business government': some business!

My speeches in denunciation of the division of Europe and a return to the balance of power were inspired by my opposition to Versailles, but in point of time followed my move into Opposition, for which the Irish question was the actual occasion. I received the initial evidence on the Irish atrocities by pure chance. A young man came to see me who knew the Curzon children because he was their neighbour at Hackwood; Cimmie remembered him well. He told me a truly astonishing story. After the war he had knocked about the world, and eventually found himself rather hard up in one of the main cities of the British Dominions. There he had been approached by some form of recruiting official to join as an officer a new auxiliary force for use in Ireland. The conditions were good and he had had considerable military experience, so he accepted. Consequently, he soon found himself in a Black and Tan mess in Ireland, not only in the company of junior but of senior officers.

The first night a young officer entered the mess with blood on his clothing remarking: 'I can't make the swine talk'. This was his initiation. The methods employed were a commonplace of conversation among the officers concerned. The account which most remains in my memory was the use of thin steel rods to beat the victim into unconsciousness, when they were revived with eggs boiled till they were hot and placed under the armpits; this was stated to be a Chinese method of persuasion. It was affirmed that anyone would talk if the process were repeated often enough. These practitioners appeared to be under no constraint to use methods which left no mark; a consideration which apparently only occurred to later adepts in the art of torturing prisoners in other countries. My informant also provided evidence of the violent and undisciplined behaviour of those troops in the Irish countryside, which was a clear breach of all proper military conduct in treatment of the civilian population.

Following this interview I made enquiry in many different directions, and the evidence poured in. When I put down my first questions the parliamentary storm broke; yet as the evidence accumulated there was no possible doubt about the main charges. In the end they were sifted, and proved to the last degree, but still the government was obdurate and the Conservative majority greeted fact with nothing but noisy abuse.

I crossed the floor in October 1920 for a practical reason, though there was also a symbolic significance. It became impossible to get a hearing on my own side, so I preferred to face my enemies rather than be surrounded by them. It was better to confront what appeared to me as a charge of howling dervishes than to stand in the middle of it. I was astonished by the furious reception of my initial remarks on the Irish question from the Conservative benches. It was to me a plain duty to bring to the notice of the House facts whose redress I had vainly sought in private. Yet to the Conservative Party in revealing these things I was badly letting down the side, adding disloyalty to impudence.

To do these Conservatives justice, most of them probably did not believe a word I was saying. When I first received my information I went at once to Edward Wood, a senior for whom I had considerable regard; he was subsequently Viceroy of India and well known as Foreign Secretary under the name of Lord Halifax—in the jovial vernacular of the Churchill family, Lord Holy Fox. We were at that time on good terms and he listened to my account with kindness and patience. He then said quite clearly and definitely that agents of the British Crown did not behave as I had been informed. This was not the way of the British people and I could dismiss the whole incredible tale from my mind. He was the embodiment of the mandarin: 'See no evil, hear no evil, speak no evil'. Yet I was convinced that the alleged events were at least in part true, and urgently required investigation. I had no other recourse except to raise the matter in the House of Commons.

Then came the storm; they simply, crudely meant to put me down. I resisted, and used a method which soon won me a hearing again in the House of Commons. It was direct, often brutal personal attack with every available sarcasm, satire and invective. I became what Disraeli called a 'master of flouts and jibes and jeers'. They shut up because they were otherwise covered with personal ridicule. I picked out the noisiest and went for them direct until silence reigned. Sir Colin Coote has observed of me in this period that I could 'flay the skin off anybody inefficient in debate', but added in effect that I was then so intolerably insolent and arrogant in speech and in my whole demeanour that he apparently developed a life-long dislike of me. It was probably true that I appeared insupportable, but I was fighting for my parliamentary life and had to use the roughest weapons to survive. The modest mien of polite English society and the humble approach of the best parliamentary tradition would have been inappropriate.

Throughout this period I was sustained by the moral support of the upright, able, and experienced parliamentarians with whom I was then closely associated, and often assisted and sometimes led by their intervention in these debates. Henry Bentinck did not cross the floor of the House, but spoke with courage on the Irish issue from the Conservative benches. He obtained a hearing, albeit a rough one, because he had been there a long time and his vagaries in espousing moral causes had made him something of an established institution. His position was particularly delicate, as his beautiful and charming wife maintained throughout the stoutest Ulster convictions, which in no way impaired her relations either with her husband or his friends. The two Cecils went so far for a brief period as to speak from the front Opposition bench. They too had been licensed by time in their deviations from the Conservative norm, although they encountered much opposition in debate from their own party on this Irish issue. Hugh Cecil had been one of the ablest and most militant propagandists of the free trade cause when his party, under the auspices of Joseph Chamberlain, wholeheartedly embraced protection, and Robert Cecil's thought and policies at that time had only slight contact with true Conservative doctrine.

Our group soon found some affinity with Liberals who were moved by the moral issues of the Irish question. Foremost among them in the Irish fight was Wedgwood-Benn, who later joined the Labour Party.[1] He had a fine fighting record in the First World War, and in parliamentary debate combined courage with ability. He was a tremendous worker, to an almost obsessive extent, and even devised and daily charted a life graph on which he judged himself by the line of work accomplished to his own exacting standards. In addition to this novel preoccupation he had a clear mind, a tongue quick and ready in debate and a vast fund of moral passion which inspired his unflinching stand. He was a small man with an explosive personality who used

[1] Later Lord Stansgate and father of Anthony Wedgwood-Benn, Minister of Technology in the Labour Government at the time of writing.

to go for Winston Churchill like a fox-terrier at a badger, to be met on one hilarious occasion with the retort: 'the Honourable Member must really not develop more indignation than he can contain'. He was a splendid companion in a tough fight.

Another Liberal who stood firm and fought hard for the cause of justice in Ireland was Pringle, an experienced parliamentarian who died before his time. During the war he and his brother-in-arms of the Westminster variety —by name Hogg, but no relation either familial or political of the distinguished Conservative father and son—had been bitter thorns in the side of Lloyd George's government, as they were devoted Asquitheans. Pringle was a master of parliamentary procedure and, though no orator, of a caustic debating method. The Liberal Party was able to put into the Irish field a formidable team, occasionally with the massive support of Mr. Asquith. When jibed on one of the older statesman's frequent absences with the cry of 'Where's your leader?' Pringle continued his speech with the calm observation, 'the leadership of the Liberal Party is tonight in most capable hands'. He was never disconcerted.

It was natural that in the course of the Irish struggle I should have become closely associated and very friendly with some of the Liberals, but the story afterwards circulated that I accepted the Liberal Whip was untrue. The occasion of the tale was that in my years as an Independent I had none of the normal party information concerning parliamentary business, because, of course, I had no whip, and therefore a Liberal Whip, McKenzie Wood, arranged to let me see the notices sent out from the Liberal Whips' office. It was a purely personal arrangement with a close friend.

I was indeed often pressed at that time to join the Liberal Party, and refused on grounds of political conviction, but with personal regret as I much liked some of them. An agreeable memory of this period is that Lady Violet Bonham-Carter—now Lady Asquith—became god-mother to my son Nicholas; it is one of the few positions from which it is impossible to resign. We were in a small minority—Labour, Liberal and Conservative dissidents —against the massed ranks of the Conservative majority supporting the Coalition; this tended to draw the opposition together in a comradeship of arms during the savage debates on these events in Ireland.

The Liberals were quick to grasp and use against the government all available evidence on the Irish question, and some Labour leaders, such as Henderson, also came lumbering into the fray in their slow way. Conservatives like the Cecils were at first not so easy to convince. Robert Cecil was a K.C. with an acute legal mind, and had been one of the counsel in the Marconi enquiry, of which he retained vivid memories. He required exact evidence before moving, and Hugh Cecil was in this matter at first even predisposed against us. They were relations of Balfour, who had the toughest experience as Irish Secretary, and Lord Frederick Cavendish, assassinated in Phoenix Park, was another intimate associate of their older generation. The Cecils had long memories. Yet above all they were just men with an acute sensibility to moral issues. The necessary evidence was soon available in all too ample measure.

Finally the parliamentary battle against the Irish atrocities, or 'reprisals' as the other side preferred to call them, was successful to the point of securing peace with Ireland. This seems at first sight a high claim, but there is evidence to support it. We had stood throughout for Dominion status, which was in effect the final settlement, and in question and debate we had exposed facts which the British Government could not justify in face of world opinion. Even in Britain's much stronger situation of those days there were limits to the public odium which an administration could sustain, particularly in an issue which so closely touched America by reason of that country's large Irish population. The Irish insurgents were not only supported by funds from America but also by a highly organised world propaganda from the same source. Our fight in Parliament was conducted solely on the British stage, but it was regarded by a far wider audience.

My own opinion both at the time and in retrospect is that the decisive factor was our organisation of the Bryce Commission. Lord Bryce was then an old man and out of politics, but his name was particularly potent in this sphere because he had presided over the enquiry into the German atrocities in Belgium. Celebrated for his fine intellect and character in Liberal politics, he had become a world figure by reason of his chairmanship of a tribunal which set no precedent for modern times because it at least appeared to be conducted with conspicuous fairness. He was just the man for our purpose, and we soon persuaded him to act. An unofficial Bryce Commission was constituted with him as Chairman, myself as Parliamentary Secretary and a barrister as legal secretary. We set about collecting evidence, and did not lack for material. By that time facts reasonably established by local enquiry and presented without any adequate reply in parliamentary debate were available, such as the shooting of the pregnant Mrs. Quinn through the stomach as she sat in her doorway, and the firing on a crowd containing children at a football match. Our case was not difficult to establish. The scandal which would follow the publication of the Bryce report would rock the government. Peace followed instead.

How did these incredible events happen? How could I possibly in later years feel any regard for Lloyd George? They apparently happened, like most other brutal stupidities in British politics, almost by accident. The account given privately to us was that at a meeting between Lloyd George and Sir Henry Wilson—an Ulsterman, who was then C.I.G.S.—with some other ministers present, the soldier indicated that the troops were getting a little out of hand, as they were constantly being sniped by civilians—assassinated—so he did not think it mattered much if they hit back a bit. Lloyd

George was reported almost casually to have assented, and that was the beginning of reprisals. I tried to pin down L.G. by a question in Parliament, armed with our surprising knowledge of this meeting supplied from a very private source, and never saw him more embarrassed in debate. As he leaned on the box to reply it was observed that one of the notoriously short legs of the 'goat' was swinging in front of the other like the pendulum of a clock; this peculiar movement had long been legendary among us young Tories as a sure indication that he was lying. Naturally, I failed to extract any exact confession from such an experienced and accomplished performer, but he and his colleagues knew that we were really on to something.

Again it seems incredible that decisions of this magnitude can be taken in British government with this degree of casual frivolity; incredible unless you have been a member of such government. Apart from my own later experience in the period of pure harlequinade during MacDonald's second Labour Government, I was given accounts of the way business was conducted in the much abler administration of Lloyd George, whose absurdity, even when this sole executive genius in the politics of his generation was presiding, beggars credulity. During the First World War, while the War Cabinet was discussing sundry minor matters and L.G. was sitting at his desk writing, the theme was once the inordinate use of paper which needlessly taxed resources in wartime. Lord Curzon reminded the Cabinet that large quantities of paper for various publications were always wasted in periods of popular excitement, for example in the time of Titus Oates. Lloyd George jumped up with a bang of his fist on the desk—'Oats!—Curzon—you are quite right, the cavalry are far back with the horses eating their heads off and they are making no contribution to the war'. The Secretary, Sir Maurice Hankey, duly recorded: 'Cavalry to be dismounted and used in the trenches'. It was a poignant reflection that this haphazard decision was probably responsible for the deaths of most of my remaining friends.

It was apparently the peculiar custom of time-honoured usage for the upshot of such discussions to be recorded by the Secretary of the Cabinet. It seemed to me a strange method, though I had the greatest regard for the capacity of Lloyd George and of Sir Maurice Hankey. Probably in the first stage the Irish affair began in the usual slipshod, inconsequent fashion, but a point near national disaster was reached by the subsequent failure to grasp the situation and correct the mistake. The reason certainly was that Lloyd George himself was in the grip of powerful forces. A majority of the Conservative Party was fanatical on the Irish question, and so was the C.I.G.S. with his Ulster background. That formidable figure was the most brilliantly articulate soldier the army produced. When he later entered Parliament he immensely impressed me with a statement of the military case which rested on the simple but truly unanswerable theme: it is better to have no armed forces at all than an army which is just big enough to invite attack but not strong enough to win. Lord Hugh Cecil answered at least to the satisfaction of Mr. Churchill, who said in winding up the debate that the House had observed how easily the military argument could be circumvented and baffled by the thorny dilemmas of the experienced metaphysician; a jest which amused the House, but was no reply. Sir Henry Wilson was shortly afterwards assassinated by two Irish gunmen on his doorstep in Eaton Place.

Lloyd George after his initial error was held fast in the Irish bog because the army chief and the Conservative Party were against him. He could not extricate himself without risking the wreck of his government, until facts and parliamentary exposure convinced even those men that the game was up. I was glad and proud to have played some small part in these events, and still treasure the letter written to Cimmie by T. P. O'Connor—the grand old Nationalist M.P. for a Liverpool constituency, and at that time Father of the House of Commons:

> 5 Morpeth Mansions,
> Victoria Street, S.W.
>
> *December* 10, '23.

DEAR LADY CYNTHIA,

My going to Harrow for Oswald, was not only a pleasure but a duty. I regard him as the man who really began the break-up of the Black and Tan savagery; and I can never recall without admiration and wonder, the courage and self-sacrifice which such an attitude demanded on his part. So I said nothing on the platform which I had not said to myself many a time.

Both your husband and yourself will always be regarded by every good Irishman with appreciation and gratitude.

I may take this opportunity of saying to you that in presiding at the dinner to me, and in the wonderful speech he delivered, he put me under a debt of lasting and warm gratitude.

> Yours very sincerely,
> T. P. O'CONNOR.

The Lady Cynthia Mosley.

It was this fight too which brought me in contact with one of the outstanding journalists of my lifetime, H. W. Massingham, for whose character and capacity I developed a considerable veneration. I was therefore deeply touched when he wrote of me in the subsequent 1922 election: 'To me the most attractive personal element in the election is Mr. Mosley's "independent" candidature for Harrow. The force of events and Mr. Mosley's fine qualities have driven him to independence today, but he will be the subject of a brisk competition among the parties before many more years have gone over his head. He has attached himself a good deal to Lord Robert Cecil, but he is a figure of individual strength and purpose, a young man of genius, perhaps the most interesting in the late parliament. If character, a brilliant and searching mind, a sympathetic temperament and a repugnance for mean and cruel dealings fit men for the service of the State, Mr. Mosley should rise high in it. It is hardly a compliment in such days as these, to speak of him as a rising man. Yet I regard him as something of a star, and of no common brightness." [1]

It was tough going for a man of twenty-three when I began, but I had the impetus both of the revelations I had received and of my previous experience during a spell of nominal light duty in Ireland not long after the rising of 1916. We regulars then had our Irish experiences in the field, though most of the fighting was over by the time I got back to the Curragh.[2] The essence of the military events in Ireland was the competence of the regular troops and the incompetence of the irregulars. This accounted in my view for the difference between 1916 and 1920. Often in human affairs the origin of brutality is incapacity. Our people in the 1916 period also suffered the extreme irritation of soldiers on being sniped by civilians.

A man would be shot as they went through a village, and the subsequent search of houses would reveal nothing but women knitting and men digging the garden. The assassin—for so the sniper in plain clothes is regarded by troops—had disappeared under cover of the civilian population. Our men had the recompense of a complete mastery over the guerrillas in the field. They did not fall into ambushes or booby traps, because they advanced in the proper formation of trained troops. If a point or flanker were picked off, they would fan out and encircle the attackers in classic style at greater speed than the enemy's untrained and unequipped capacity for movement enabled him to achieve. At that time our people knew all about fighting, and the insurgents knew next to nothing. The Irish got very much the worst of it, and despite the exasperation caused by civilian sniping, these regular troops had not such a serious temptation to commit any unsoldierly act, which in any case their firm discipline prevented.

The end of effective fighting in this period was characteristic of the whole affair. The Irish held the Shelborne Hotel in the centre of the city and dug themselves in on St. Stephen's Green in front of the hotel. They omitted, however, to guard the back door of the hotel and the luggage lift, and an officer in my regiment, with a corporal, two men and a machine-gun entered quietly by the back door and used the luggage lift to reach the roof, which he found also unguarded. The Irish had also omitted one other essential precaution—to make traverses in the trench which they had dug on St. Stephen's Green in enfilade to the hotel. The rest was simple.

The situation was very different when the Black and Tans arrived on the

---

[1] *The Nation,* November 11, 1922.

[2] As the fighting was then over except for occasional sniping my account is not based on personal experience, but was derived on the spot from recent participants in these events.

field after the war. The Irish by then had learnt much about guerrilla fighting under the brilliant leadership of Michael Collins. They had the initial advantage of the capacity for secrecy acquired in century-long resistance to a strong military power, and all they needed was training and experience in this kind of fighting on a large scale. Their new opponents, on the other hand, were a scratch lot, recruited all over the place and thrown into the fray without discipline or training. Some of them had previous experience of warfare but few had any knowledge of that kind of fighting. Their lack of discipline was their fatality, and it lost them six hundred killed in six months. They did not move in the proper formation of regular troops, which is an arduous business requiring long training. They often drove around seated on open lorries, advertising their arrival in advance by firing their weapons into the air under the dual stimulus of alcohol and the desire to impress upon the Irish that the conqueror had at last arrived. Michael Collins and the boys would be waiting with a machine-gun behind one of the high banks at a corner of the road, where the open lorry on which the men were seated had to slow down. Once again, the rest was simple.

This account is, of course, an over-simplification, but I believe in a short compass it gives a fair view of what happened. The Black and Tans were up against a situation which is baffling and exasperating even to disciplined, trained and experienced troops. This was the beginning in modern Europe of the guerrilla tactic which has since been developed in many different spheres. In my essay, *The European Situation*, published in 1950, I foresaw that nuclear weapons would result in regular armies becoming the 'paralysed giants', and that future fighting, if it occurred, would be conducted in the way of the guerrillas. Particularly in cities, even regular troops, inhibited from the extreme of brutality by membership of a civilised nation, can be worsted by guerrillas who emerge from obscurity to strike and instantly retreat again into cover of the darkness which is provided by the support of the civilian population. At this point the struggle becomes as much political as military. The competent guerrilla is half soldier, half politician, for his first business is to win and retain the support of the civilian population which is his cover. In Ireland after the First World War that support was ready-made among the Irish people and was steadfast to an extraordinary degree.

The response of the Black and Tans was partly spontaneous and partly organised. The rage of men without training or discipline who feel unable to hit back while suffering heavy losses produced the stupid and brutal acts of individual violence which could have no effect except to swing opinion against them. But the attempt to break the morale of the civilians appeared to be systematic, and the object was clearly to prevent the Irish civilian population supporting the guerrillas.

Sir Hamar Greenwood was the Irish Secretary; a decent Canadian in private life, but Lloyd George's blustering bully boy in public. It was his business with much vituperation directed against the Irish and the Opposition to defend the policy of the government. My constant cross-examination of him at question time evoked the concentrated fury of the Conservative benches. For instance: 'In view of his discovery that "the murder gangs" never slept more than one night in the same place, has he yet discovered a more effective means of bringing them to justice than burning next day the houses of other people in the vicinity of their outrages?' Such questions floored the luckless Greenwood because he could not give the true answer: that the real object of the exercise was to create such a reign of terror among the civilian population that the guerrillas could find neither the food, nor the shelter or succour necessary to their existence. That was not an avowal possible in face of British, American and world opinion, but it would have been a statement of fact. For such reasons it was possible for the Parliamentary Opposition gradually to wear down the strength of the government and to induce peace. I do not think it will be found too high a claim by those with time and patience to study the whole story.

Why then were these irregular troops used at all? Why not use regular and trained troops, who at least would have suffered fewer losses and made a proper job of it? The short answer is that troops with real discipline and a great tradition cannot be used in the way the government required without destroying both, and no one knew this better than Sir Henry Wilson. To have made a proper job of it in the way of a regular army would have demanded a very large force. For instance, we reckoned that to drive efficiently the Wicklow Hills—always the main hideout of the guerrillas—would have needed at least 100,000 men. To complete the task as a regular military operation would have required more troops than were available and have been an open demonstration of military force, at once alerting and challenging world opinion. The force available was inadequate and world opinion was unpropitious for anything but an operation by stealth. Faced both with the limitations of their political situation and of the forces available, the government fell into the decision to use irregulars, who could fight in an altogether different way; the way not of a military operation against the guerrillas themselves but of terrorism to break the morale of the civilians who supported them. The Black and Tans were the arm created for their purpose, but it was an answer to the government's problem which in the end made things far worse.

The Irish as fighting men had become very good indeed. They were making monkeys not only of the Black and Tans but of the whole administration. It may not have been true that Michael Collins, dressed as a charwoman, was able to read the papers on the desk of Sir John Anderson, then Under-Secretary to the Lord-Lieutenant in Dublin Castle, but he was certainly better informed than his antagonist. This favourite son of the Home Office, later described by his admirers as the Tiger of Bengal, was finding the

Irish air not nearly so congenial as his later experience of the gentle clime of
India, where eventually he was able to play the strong man with more success.
Baffled and looking foolish, defeated and suffering heavy losses, the Black and
Tans faced a situation in which firmer characters and stronger discipline
have been known to break down in this modern world, which has so often
witnessed the tragic and the horrible. Confronted with triumphant guerrilla
tactics by a weaker force supported by a civilian population, the dominant
force is often tempted to employ two instruments: torture and terror. Torture
to obtain information—especially of coming ambushes—and terror to force
the civilians to betray the guerrillas, or at least to deny them assistance. The
Black and Tans were the first of many to succumb to that vile temptation, but
in the Irish they met a people of particular fortitude.

This most horrible phenomenon of the modern world—torture and
terrorism—the return of man's darkest ages which we thought would never
recur—has appeared in the last half century among many peoples. It is a
tragedy which requires close analysis, because it is essential to the health of
our continent and of the world that it should be brought to an end. Many
matters in the Irish story were simple, but this problem is never simple. The
terrible fact is that on both sides men who did vile things were often idealists.
There is, of course, always a small minority among all peoples who like being
brutal if they get the chance; the number may vary in different countries and
on diverse occasions, but it is always there. They are not the real problem,
because society can always deal with this sadistic criminal element if it has
the will. The real question is presented by those who do vile things for ideal
reasons. This is the stark challenge to leadership, for leadership bears the
prime responsibility by reason of the ideas formulated and the law, rule or
discipline enforced.

Among the Black and Tans were many idealists—as I later knew from
personal experience of some of them—who believed they were fighting for
their country and regarded the Irish as a treacherous enemy. It was a minority,
as always, who committed the outrages, and much was quite unknown to the
majority. They detested the Irish because they regarded their way of fighting
as immoral and blameworthy. Even among the regular army after 1916 I
often found this attitude. Another young officer would say to me out hunting:
'Look at them all, smiling at us and offering us drinks at the meet. Most of
them will be out with a rifle tonight to put a shot in our backs.' It was the
beginning of guerrilla warfare, and I remember even then having sufficient
insight to reply: 'How else can they fight our overwhelming force?—If they
stand up to us in the open they haven't got a chance.' But this kind of thing
is a great strain to discipline even in the best regular troops, and it turns
second-rate troops or irregulars into a vengeful rabble.

The large majority of the Irish guerrillas on the other side were idealists in
the highest degree, and few among them were there for any advantage of

plunder or ignoble motive of revenge. This was true even of those who committed the vilest crimes. How else can we regard the shooting of fourteen officers in one night while asleep in their beds, a crime which justly outraged English opinion and infuriated our troops? Yet the men who did this are credibly reported to have spent the previous evening praying together in a chapel like medieval knights on a vigil before battle. We come to the very crux of this matter when men who did such deeds, and who had foreknowledge of them, fell into the hands of British troops, who were aware that they knew what was going to happen. This terrible clash enters the dimension of classic tragedy when both sides are initially inspired not by base but by ideal motives.

This was the only occasion when I had first-hand information of such matters, but they have occurred in most of the great nations of Europe, and are now reported to be happening in Asia; the whole tragedy has been the subject of so much discussion, clouded by so much passion and blinded by so much partisanship, that it is difficult for anyone to take a clear view. In some political circles the point has now been reached where any atrocity is permitted to our own side, but not even a misdemeanour to the other. In truth, nearly everyone on every side has committed atrocities which have certainly varied greatly in degree and in extent, but possibly only on account of the degree of temptation and the extent of the occasion.

The killing or ill-treatment of prisoners or of anyone defenceless always seemed to me the most despicable crime known to man. It occurred on a great scale in the Second World War and will be considered in a later chapter. Whether large or small, I have always condemned such acts and attacked them in my political life whenever in a position to do so. Another incident of this kind in the 1920s involved me in another bitter controversy. In 1919 General Dyer at Amritsar in India opened rapid and protracted fire on an unarmed crowd which included women and children who had no immediate means of escape. He afterwards claimed his action 'had a moral effect throughout the Punjab'. I spoke on the subject in the Oxford or Cambridge Union —I forget which—in very strong terms. During this period I spoke frequently in university debates and I believe I was responsible for carrying the first motion in favour of socialism by twenty votes at one of them and just lost by four votes at about the same time in the other. My speech against General Dyer caused considerable excitement both at the university and at Westminster and evoked much controversy. One undergraduate paper attacked me fiercely and published a complete travesty of my speech, alleging that my peroration had 'amounted' to an appeal to the Indians 'to revolt against the English who have slaughtered your wives'. It is superfluous to state that I had said nothing of the kind.

It seemed to me unnecessary at the time to pursue a relatively obscure undergraduate journal for libel, but the matter became serious at the next

General Election in November 1922. Having crossed the floor of the House, I was then standing as an Independent in the same constituency of Harrow, and my Conservative opponent circulated the words—'revolt against the English who have slaughtered your wives'—in an aggravated form, because they were given, without any qualification, as my actual words. I immediately issued a writ for libel, but my opponent stood fast and challenged me to resign the seat if I lost the libel action. Foolishly I accepted the challenge, because it is really the business of the electorate and not of a jury to determine a seat in Parliament, but I was very confident of winning the action, and wanted first to ensure my electoral victory by calling my opponent's bluff.

I won by a large majority and went ahead with the libel case. Some weeks later my Conservative opponent sent in his card to see me at the House of Commons, and I went into the outer lobby to meet him. He told me that the Conservative Central Office had supplied him with his account of my speech as the actual words I had used, but on subsequent enquiry he had discovered that I had said nothing of the kind and he was now advised by his experienced solicitors that he risked damages so large he would be a ruined man. On enquiry at the Central Office he had been told he must look after himself. I was sorry for him and allowed him to escape with a public apology and pay-ment of a modest sum to a local charity. The opinion I then formed of the methods of the Conservative Party was confirmed at subsequent elections, and in other experiences.

I have a long record of opposition to the vile crime of killing or ill-treating the defenceless in various spheres, and it is one of the subjects on which I feel most strongly. It is sheer humbug to deny that these atrocities have been committed in different degrees by every side. If it rested with me, this practice would be abruptly and ruthlessly brought to an end with the utmost severity. That these things should occur even among Europeans is a dark stain upon the honour of our continent and a violation of every true instinct of humanity. We must resolve and ensure that they shall cease and that their end shall be followed by a deep *act of oblivion*. Then the wounds of Europe may be healed.

9
Elections 1922-4
Clydesiders
The I.L.P.
Birmingham

My second election in 1922 turned out to be a momentous affair for me. I had already passed through the fierce storm of the Irish controversy and other parliamentary battles already described; now I had to face the consequences. It was reckoned at the time that the Carlton Club alone supplied over two hundred cars on polling day to secure my defeat. Many of the big guns of the enemy were mobilised to fire in a constituency they found conveniently close to London. Happily, I had fortified my position with much local support. When the executive of the Harrow Association called on me to toe the party line, I appealed over their heads to the rank and file of the Association. It was a simple device which they bitterly called the card trick. A stamped postcard was sent to each member of the Association together with my statement of the issues involved, and he or she was invited to return the postcard to me with an affirmation of support. The postcards came back with an overwhelming majority in my favour. My good friend, Harry Miles, the agent, came too. Left high and dry, the executive met and adopted another Conservative candidate.

We formed another and more powerful association, and I issued a five-thousand-word election address stating in effect that I stood on the same programme of social reform as in 1918, to which I remained true in face of the renegade conservatism which had added various crimes like military adventures, the Irish atrocities and profligate expenditure to their general betrayal of the rights and the hopes of the war generation. I polled 15,290 votes to their 7,868, defeating them by nearly two to one. It was a remarkable result because I had to sustain alone the full weight and fury of the

Conservative assault, and Harrow was one of their traditional strongholds.

I was still associated with Lord Robert Cecil at the election of 1922 and he
came to Harrow to make a speech on my behalf. It was a bold and loyal
undertaking for him thus to support an Independent against the official
Conservative candidate in Harrow, for he remained the official candidate of
the Conservative Association in Hitchin. The situation was further complicated by his decision unofficially to sponsor a few other Independent candidates, chief among them Bernard Freyberg, V.C., who gave almost as dashing
a display in this election as on the field of war. Being a man of action, he did
not tamely submit to finding himself with a lack of cars on polling day, and
rang up almost every taxi and hire car in the neighbourhood to employ them
for the purpose of carrying his electors to the poll. This was, of course, a major
breach of election law of which he was superbly ignorant, and could carry
severe penalties. It was perhaps fortunate that he was not elected, though he
polled well, and the incident passed without notice or retribution.

Before the election Lord Robert Cecil sent me to see his friend the first
Lord Cowdray in Scotland and ask him for funds to support a few Independent candidates. It was my first experience of these magnates of industry,
which was repeated years later when I visited Lord Nuffield on similar
missions. Both were generous givers, but were concerned to impress on the
recipient that these large sums of money had not been easily gained. Lord
Cowdray had me met on the night train and took me for a walk in the morning,
discussing politics in general terms. He was an impressive personality, and I
was able to understand the reason for his remarkable achievements better than
in most such men. He was also a man of taste, and I observed in his Scotch
castle a fine collection of Impressionist pictures. Towards the end of the walk
he took me to the garage, where stood an array of expensive motors. His
purpose was to hold a discussion with the owner of the village garage concerning a repair to the exhaust of the humblest vehicle among them, the
shooting-brake. After hard and protracted bargaining, the deal was done at
fifteen shillings. Was this the way he had laid the foundation of his vast
fortune, or was he teaching me to value the coming gift? After an excellent
luncheon he quietly handed me a cheque for £10,000.

My sad parting from Lord Robert Cecil followed the 1922 election. He
decided to enter Bonar Law's Conservative government, and invited me to
accompany him into some post in that administration. This honourable man
and faithful friend said he felt an obligation to me and would not take office
unless I too was accepted, which would not have presented much difficulty,
as some time previously Bonar Law had spoken to Lord Curzon about me in
friendly and conciliatory terms. I had a considerable regard for Bonar Law as
Conservative leader because his outstanding abilities enabled him to substitute
argument for what I described in debate as 'zoological noises indicating the

first dumb aspirations to the flights of human speech' which were the only audible contributions to our discussions made by some of his supporters.

Bonar Law was a master of the art of winding up a debate. His method was simple in principle, but hard in practice. Speaking without notes, he would recapitulate the arguments of the other side often with greater force than their own capacities permitted. He would then demolish them *seriatim* in the same logical order he had stated them. His art extended even to the deliberate slip in order to extricate himself from difficulties. Defending himself once from a charge of undue subservience to Lloyd George he said: 'I was always a man to stand on my own bottom'. When the laughter subsided, he continued with his tired smile: 'The House always appreciates these occasions'. He knew both how to play on their infantilism and how to appeal to their good sense. It was not, therefore, any antipathy to the Conservative leadership at that time which induced me to refuse to accompany Lord Robert and remain on the Opposition benches. It was rather that the rift between me and Conservatism had then grown too wide, and that my sense of purpose led me toward far more positive action than it then presented.

I had something in common with Bonar Law because only three of us at that time could deliver a major speech in Parliament without notes: Bonar Law, Willie Graham whose premature death was a severe loss to the Labour Party, and myself. I used to speak in the House without notes, even winding up a debate on the Front Bench. My speech of resignation from the government lasted an hour and a quarter and covered a considerable complex of subjects and figures, but was delivered without notes. The trick with any adequate mental constitution is quite easily acquired. The mind can be trained to do abnormal things as a muscle can be trained to lift a weight. In early days I used to get someone to read me a *Times* leading article or a more complicated essay from a technical journal; then rise at once and reply to it, taking each point *seriatim* in the order read. The trouble was well worth while, for the delivery of a long complex speech in debate without notes is always regarded in Parliament as a rather admirable conjuring trick. It is quite essential on the platform to speak without notes, for anyone who aspires to first-rate performance with mass audiences; but that, of course, is far easier. Mr. Asquith used to regard speeches without notes as a rather show-off business, and perhaps he was right. He once explained to me that it was a 'superfluous efflux of cerebral energies', if I remember his words aright.

Lively debates followed in the Parliament of 1923 after my parting from Lord Robert, with me consequently attacking the government of which he was a member. I was already recorded as being among the twenty-five M.P.s most active in debate. Rent Restriction Acts and other measures on the domestic front occupied me increasingly, but any long review of these aspects of my work would overburden this book and frustrate its purpose of presenting a personal picture. As to housing and rent control, from that day to this I have taken the same line: control, until by drastic national action you have built enough houses. You cannot decontrol and place the tenant at the mercy of the landlord while there is still a housing shortage. That policy was continually developed, from my original proposal in 1918 for treating the housing problem as an operation of war, to my modern policy for surpassing the local authorities with a national plan.

Protection was made the main issue of the 1923 election by the Conservative government under Baldwin, after Bonar Law's retirement. Mr. Amery, the chief apostle of protection, came to Harrow with a great flourish to introduce a new Conservative candidate against me. We exchanged amities: he called me a 'Bolshevik', and I called him 'the busy little drummer boy in the jingo brass band'. Then followed a serious and well-reasoned debate on protection before a highly expert audience, for Harrow was inhabited by men and women working in most of the large trading and financial concerns of the country. Harrow had a strongly protectionist tradition, as the pre-war member had been one of the leading protagonists of this change in the fiscal system.

The question of free trade or protection was in those days to many people almost a religious issue. My approach to it was purely pragmatic. Whether you had one system or the other was a question of circumstance. If it was raining, you needed an umbrella, if the sun was shining, you did not. The wider considerations presented to me by certain subsequent experiences had not then occurred to me, but even at that early date my ideas were remote from the old-fashioned concept of Conservative tariffs. At the 1923 election I accepted the classic free trade argument, with an important addition or variation derived from the contemporary situation and extending to the present day, which I believe I was the first to note in debate. My novel argument was that fluctuations in the exchange rate of foreign countries made nonsense of any tariff barrier, and they were then continually occurring. Mr. Baldwin did not appear to understand these rather complicated arguments, though perhaps he was only 'playing stupid', at which he was as apt as some of our ambassadors. I had foreseen the era of competitive devaluation to gain an advantage in the export trade.[1] It is now well known that this benefit is secured through a manipulation of subsequent monetary policy to prevent the internal price level rising in proportion to the external devaluation, as it should in classic economic theory. The final triumph of this subtle method, of which the British Treasury became ultimately the most accomplished master, came with Sir Stafford Cripps's swingeing devaluation of our currency in 1949, which gave British export trade a substantial advantage for several years. In recent times everyone has begun to rumble the trick, and no one can now perpetrate a large devaluation without all the competitors threatening to do the same. But these were early days in this financial game of léger de main, and I was quite precocious to spot its possibilities.

[1] *Hansard.*

My stand against the Conservative policy of that time may seem a considerable inconsistency with my later advocacy of an Empire insulated from the fluctuations of world markets, and later still of a European economic system organised on the same basic principle, and it is true that this appears to be the main deviation from the usual straight line of my continually developing thinking. Yet protection in a small island which contains a few of the necessary foodstuffs and hardly any of its industrial raw materials is a very different thing from an empire containing nearly all of these requisites, or a united Europe which, together with its related overseas lands, can be in the same position. A certain degree of insulation from the world can be an advantage to an organism large enough to be capable of effective self-containment, but it is very difficult for a small economy bound to compete on world markets in order to buy what it lacks. However, the main influence which turned me from the classic economics to a more autarchic concept for the organisation of the British Empire—until that possibility was lost at the time of the Second World War—and subsequently to my later thinking on similar lines in relation to a united Europe, was undoubtedly my visit to America in 1925. This experience combined with the ruin of Lancashire and Yorkshire to inspire the concept of an economic system big enough to be viable, largely insulated from disruptive world competition, and by reason of that immunity permitting within its ample borders the undisturbed application of modern economics and monetary techniques. In a general form, this idea was perhaps anticipated in the phrase 'imperial socialism' during my first election of 1918.

These wider and deeper considerations were remote from Mr. Baldwin's plunge at the 1923 election into the old, crude Conservative protection of industrial inefficiency, which was accompanied as usual by still cruder forms of electioneering. My retorts to Conservative hecklers at the big meetings of those days still make lively reading, but I also attempted a fairly reasoned argument. Once again, however, the Conservatives brought up their big guns, and in the barrage and counter-fire the pale ghost of reason soon fled. The Conservative howitzer was Lord Birkenhead, and the shooting both ways soon became heavy. In the course of a somewhat intemperate oration in a local schoolroom, the former Lord Chancellor described me as the 'perfumed popinjay of scented boudoirs', who was consequently an unsuitable representative in Parliament for the matrons of Harrow and their respectable spouses. They might well have thought that Lord Birkenhead ought to know—although they did not accept his advice—for it was only a little later that the merry tale was running through the lobbies about someone approaching Mr. Baldwin with the suggestion that Lord Birkenhead should join his administration, only to be met with the sardonic rejoinder: 'F.E. says we are a ministry of faithful husbands, and I think we will remain one'.

I need not have been so surprised at this assault on me, because F.E. was previously reported—when visiting the constituency of Winston Churchill during their period of most intimate friendship—to have opened his speech with the remark: 'I learn from the *Dundee Advertiser*—the *journal*, not the *politician . . .*'. Yet in a surge of youthful indignation I took umbrage at this reference to me from a man much my senior, but whom I regarded as a friend. The 'scented boudoirs' was a supportable reflection, as for a period on my return from the war I had felt that such an ambiance was a legitimate relaxation for the warrior. But the 'perfumed popinjay' stuck in my gorge, as never by any stretch of the imagination could I have been described as of that company, and these seemed improper terms in which to describe the said warrior.

I bided a short time to seek revenge, and my opportunity soon came in the debate on the address on January 17, 1924. It was easy to stalk F.E. via Joynson-Hicks, who as Minister of Health and later as Home Secretary was a sublime figure of fun. They had both been involved in Sir Edward Carson's Ulster rebellion before the First World War, F.E. as 'Galloper Smith' in the role of A.D.C. to Carson, and 'Jix' as general fire-eater and blowhard. 'Jix' in this debate had raised a noisy alarm at the approach of a Labour Government, and after accusing him of 'trying to dress up the red bogey' and of suggesting that 'behind Labour members who made statesmanlike speeches there are great masses of subversive and bloodthirsty savages who want to deluge this land of ours in blood', I said: 'It is time that honourable Gentlemen opposite realised that any Government formed in this country will be composed of British men and women. The Government are posing as models of consti- tutional decorum, and they are holding themselves out as the one body which has never talked of violence or bloodshed in this country. The Minister of Health talked about the forces behind Labour. It might be of interest to inquire into some of the forces which he once claimed were behind him.

'He said: "Behind us is the Lord God of battle. In His name and our names"—a modest conjunction—"I say to the Prime Minister, let your armies and batteries fire. Fire if you dare, fire and be damned." The House will be relieved to learn that they did not fire, and that the heroic orator survived to occupy at present the position of Minister of Health. That is a quotation from a speech which the right honorable Gentleman delivered at Warrington on 6 December, 1913, as a responsible member of the Conservative party . . . . After the speeches we have heard from benches opposite, we feel that the fields of Ulster never resounded to the thundering hoofs and the doughty deeds of Galloper Smith, a man of war right up to the very moment the war begun. Now, after a seasonable interlude, in which he has indulged in more peaceful avocations, he is a man at war again.'

The sting was, of course, in the tail with its reference to F. E. Smith's war record. In retrospect I much regret this attack—despite the provocation I received—because it was completely unfair. F. E. Smith was a most gallant man, but the government was quite right to insist that his almost unique abilities in his own sphere should be used in administration rather than dissipated in the field. He often gave striking proof of his courage. However, by this time tempers were up, and I refused to withdraw when approached by our mutual friend Freddie Guest. I took the line that F.E. must also withdraw what he had said about me at the election, which was, of course, impossible for a man in his position, and was indeed an arrogant demand on my part. The attack caused considerable comment and widespread indignation among some of our friends, which surprised me at the time.

F. E. Smith, like Winston Churchill, was quite devoid of malice, and he greeted me in the old, genial way at a dinner party some time later. I last saw him in a bath-chair when he was very ill shortly before his death, and had a strong impulse to approach him and to express my warm regard for him, but suffered an inhibition I had known before in face of the gulf of generations. I say now what I would have liked to say then: he was a big-hearted, generous, brave and brilliant man; his faults were trivial in comparison with his gifts and his manly character, and may be left to the insignificant condemnation of the loutery and prudery which lack both wit and human understanding.

I won the election of 1923 by 14,079 votes to 9,433. The majority was reduced, but still substantial, and in face of the protectionist tradition of Harrow was something of a triumph, which confirmed my strong position as an Independent. The general result placed the Conservatives in a minority, with the Liberals under Mr. Asquith holding the balance between them and Labour. Speaking from the Opposition benches in the decisive debate on the address, I gave my reasons for voting to defeat the Conservative Government. Some passages from this speech in abbreviated and consequently disjointed form may be worth quoting, both as an illustration of my developing political position and as an example of a debating style which is dead and cold in print, but in the heat of controversy enabled a member in his twenties to fill the House to capacity on his rising.

Referring to the record of the Government I said: 'It can be very briefly summarised. They have lavished money on Mesopotamia, on Singapore, and on wild-cat schemes of adventure in all parts of the world. They have econo-mised to pay for these adventures on health, on education, and on every measure of social reform. They have financed the luxuries of Arab princes by starving physically and mentally the people of this country. They have made remissions of taxation to the rich, and they have paid for them by squeezing the poor. They have stood baffled and bewildered in front of the great housing problem, because they dare not face their friends in the great housing trusts which are controlling the building industry.'

We had experienced 'all that oppression of the poor and defenceless to which we are accustomed from reaction', but not the 'strength of administra-tion which theorists tell us is the advantage of a Conservative Government'.

At home, Mr. William Bridgeman, the Home Secretary, had been compelled to restore a hundred deported Irishmen 'to their distracted families and their weeping wives, and the Government once again was confronted with the painful reality that they were born to make men laugh, not women weep'. Abroad, 'they have done just enough to irritate everyone—not enough to achieve anything. That is the most fatal of all policies. . . . It reduces the authoritative accents of a great nation to the shrill railing of a bedridden old woman. . . . They could never bring us peace, but we were told that Conservative administration brought us prestige and honour among the nations.

'Let me take the one occasion on which the case for Britain and the case for humanity has been stated by the present Government—the Note of August last. A Note was written setting out our claims, urging the paramount necessity of a European settlement, saying that every day Europe was coming nearer to the brink of catastrophe, and threatening that Britain would take separate action unless something were done. Then what happened? The whole Cabinet broke up and went on their holidays for a month. The Prime Minister, in particular, went to Aix-les-Bains. After writing one pompous letter, they all went to bed for a month, so arduous was the exertion of maintaining so much dignity.' (This was a little *méchant*, as Lord Curzon was still Foreign Secretary.) 'The next act in that sad farce was the most lamentable and disgraceful of all—the drowsy return via Paris of the sleeping beauty of Aix-les-Bains. In Paris, our somnambulist was hypnotised afresh, and an astonished world learned, through a disgraceful communiqué, that where . . . a difference . . . between right and wrong had existed, now, in view of the changed situation, no divergence of view existed; and from that moment we have drifted on, helpless, impotent, and derided of the nations . . . while the Prime Minister assuaged our fears and those of mankind with little sanctimonious sermons about his duty, his admirable intentions, the policy that was always about to be initiated, which, in fact, was a policy of drift buoyed up by drivel.

'That is the record of this Government—a record which by insensate foreign policy and administrative blundering has added to our miseries of unemployment, a policy which leaves us a ghastly heritage of slums, starvation, and suffering in our midst. The handiwork of this Government is written all over the map of our country in the characters of human anguish. For my part, if I gave one vote to keep in power for one night such a Government, I should feel that I deserved to be drummed out with ignominy from the great army of progress. . . .

'Let us substitute another policy which does not wait in sycophantic adulation, punctuated by snarls, upon any individual or upon any country, but which defines a policy of our own, pro-British, pro-European, and pro-humanity. Let us be the enemies of no country, but the friends of all peoples, the unflinching opponents of any policy that is the enemy of mankind. . . . In all lands there is a revival of the progressive spirit today. In every country the forces of progress are looking to our land to give a lead. We shall achieve this not by quarrelling with any country, but by rallying those forces . . . in all the lands to the banner of progress, and that banner must be raised by some country and some people. There is the opportunity lying in the hands of this Parliament, in the overwhelming majority of this Parliament, of one of the greatest missions which historic destiny has ever imposed on the people of this country . . . of placing itself at the head of the peoples of Europe and leading them on the great march back from those dark lands of suffering and sorrow in which we have sojourned so long . . . to lead the peoples of the world in re-establishing a system of justice, of reconciliation, of peace upon earth.'

A fine Conservative character, Francis Curzon, the racing motorist, afterwards Lord Howe, followed me in the debate and observed that he was not surprised to find me making this speech from the bench next to two revolutionary members from the Clyde. He was right, for it was the Clydeside group under Maxton and Wheatley who almost alone among leading members of the Labour Party at that time were sincere in their determination to carry out the programme for which the rank and file of the party had worked so hard. He might well have expressed surprise at my ingenuousness in believing there was even a shadow of hope that these things could be done by a party under the leadership of Messrs. MacDonald, Snowden and Thomas.

My path now led inevitably to the Labour Party. 'Through and beyond the failure of men and of parties, we of the war generation are marching on,' and the only hope of implementing any of the pledges now lay in the party which had been thrown up by the mass of the people to right their wrongs. It is true that Lloyd George was my original leader on the Left, until he fell in 1922 and formed his own Liberal Party, but he was then in isolation and in no position to do anything creative. At that time I did not know him personally and it seemed more practical to ally myself with the party that had a mass revolutionary following. A surprise was the remarkably favourable reaction of the Labour Party when I joined them. The more I was attacked by the Conservative press, the greater the enthusiasm of the Left.

Doctrinaire socialism of the old school made only slight appeal to me, but socialism as I defined it two years later in the Birmingham proposals as 'the conscious control and direction of human resources for human needs', I could accept. This definition would still be acceptable to me with a slight change of emphasis: more reliance on general direction of the state rather than detailed control, and the substitution of purposes for needs in order to recognise that all achievement is the result only of intensive effort. The conscious direction of human resources for human purposes I should still regard as a good general principle.

It may well be an error to use the term socialism because it is an emotive word which repulses many people, and is capable of so many different interpretations that in the end it has come to mean almost nothing except a mild shock to complacent guardians of the status quo. Perhaps this view is too much the converse of Dr. Dalton's observation to his young admirers in some interval of discussing one of his forthcoming budgets with lobby correspondents: there may not be much in socialism, but a lot of people seem to want it. The just mean is surely to approach economic problems which are the subject of religious emotion with a method more practical and realistic; pragmatic, if the word were not now devalued by contemporary reduction of the language of action to the uses of absurdity.

My inclination in British politics was always toward the guild socialists—then represented by such thinkers and writers as G. D. H. Cole, Hobson and Orage—rather than to state socialism, whose exponents were the Webbs and the Fabians. The tradition of the medieval guilds in England, of the Hanseatic League and the syndicalism of the Latin countries was much nearer to my thinking at that time, and I returned to it in my European Socialism during the 1950s, when I proposed a workers' ownership of industries already nationalised, and, in the event of their success, the extension of the principle to other fully developed industries; measures accompanied both by vigorous encouragement of a completely emancipated private enterprise in all remaining industries and also by a reversion to private enterprise in cases where workers' ownership failed; a pragmatic method implementing the test of practical results. When I joined the Labour Party, and later, I was not closely in tune with the mandarin attitude of state-control which reached its summit in the thinking of the Webbs.

It was the dynamism of the Labour Party at that time which really attracted me, and this came mostly from the rank and file. The Clyde M.P.s represented the drive to reform, and they soon became some of my closest parliamentary associates. Before I joined Labour they had invited me to Glasgow and together we had seen the slums whose abolition had been promised in 1918 but which still existed in 1924, and in large areas of the country are still there in 1968. Similar visits to Liverpool with Jack Hayes, the ex-policeman and Labour Whip, and later intimate knowledge of Birmingham gave vivid proof in these execrable housing conditions that all the pledges given to the war generation had been betrayed. This perhaps more than any other single factor was the motive power which took me into the Labour Party. There were many intellectual arguments which I had already myself developed frequently in parliamentary debate, but here was the real impulse of vital feeling.

Joining Labour in March 1924 at once brought invitations to address mass meetings in Glasgow and throughout the Clydeside area. I was accompanied by Cimmie, who by then had become a very effective speaker, one of the best women I have ever heard on the platform, and the fact that she was Curzon's daughter further inflamed the fury of the Conservative press. Invitations poured in from all over the country to address mass meetings, and very soon I was invited to stand for Parliament by more than seventy local Labour constituency organisations. However, I took no immediate decision where to stand at the next election, although it could not be long delayed, and concentrated on getting my bearings and taking the best advice on that subject and other questions of procedure in my new party.

Membership of the main Labour Party and the Independent Labour Party was then permitted at the same time, so I joined them both. I was rapidly elected to the National Administrative Council of the Independent Labour Party, and at a later date was also elected to the National Executive of the Labour Party. MacDonald and Snowden by this time had fallen out badly with the I.L.P., which they had originally planned as a combined factory of ideas and of revolutionary spirit for the mass of the Labour Party with its dominant Trade Union influence. When MacDonald succeeded to the Labour leadership and developed an appropriately bourgeois outlook the effective leadership of the I.L.P. soon reverted to Maxton and the Clydeside group.

The colourful personality of Maxton has been described too often to require repetition. He was a most genuine person in all things, except in his French revolutionary make-up; I am always inclined to distrust men who require make-up in politics, whether it be the sansculotte self-consciously posturing in the shadow of a papier-maché guillotine on the Left, or the bucolic pig fancier, too honest to be true stuff, of the Baldwin school on the Right. The most remarkable man among the Clydesiders is not so well known to a later generation; he was then Minister of Health and the only member of that group to hold Cabinet office. Wheatley was the only man of Lenin quality the English Left ever produced. He had made a small fortune in business and sat for a Glasgow constituency. His method in debate was cold, incisive, steely, and contrasted completely with the emotionalism of his colleagues, particularly with Maxton, who was an orator of the John Bright school. Wheatley was a master of fact and figure, and far more than any other member of the Labour Party impressed me as a man who might get things done; it followed naturally that MacDonald detested him. Wheatley and I had an esteem for each other,[1] but the reader will by now have deduced that my path did not lie in the direction of the Lenin school. In any case, Wheatley died prematurely, and hope of effective action from the original Labour Party probably accompanied him to the grave.

Much of my early period in the Labour Party was spent in acting as intermediary between MacDonald and the Left wing, then represented chiefly by the I.L.P.; I must have been almost the only man on speaking terms with both except for the shadowy and sickly figure of Clifford Allen, who was also sadly doomed to early death. Later legend attached to me the reputation of being a

---

[1] Wheatley said of the author: 'A man who was bound to play a brilliant part in British political history . . . one of the greatest and most hopeful figures that the Socialist movement had thrown up during the thirty years of its history'. December 14, 1926.

difficult colleague, presumably because I found it difficult to condone the betrayal of every pledge given to the electorate. In fact, I am a loyal colleague as a member of a team, and when I find it impossible to be loyal I do not stay in the team to intrigue against colleagues, but leave it and challenge them openly. It is a simple principle, which in these days may be regarded as simpliste, but it seems to me the only honourable course. Before you leave, you should put up with much, and I certainly did in the Labour Party, with everything except the complete betrayal of the mass of the people who had trusted us.

It seemed to be my duty in the Labour Party to do what I could to keep the party together, as the only hope at that time of getting anything done in Britain, and to that end I associated with MacDonald while remaining an active member of the I.L.P. executive. However, my position in the party was in no way dependent on MacDonald. I had four sources of independent strength. The first was my election to the National Executive of the Labour Party by vote both of the constituency parties and of the trade unions. The second was my simultaneous membership of the National Administrative Council of the I.L.P. by election of its members; I believe I was the only member of both governing bodies. The third was my territorial strength in Birmingham, which I found a Conservative stronghold and which in five years under my leadership was turned into a Labour fortress throughout the central area. The fourth was my capacity as a parliamentary debater, combined with my ability to draw the largest platform audiences in the country. These four attributes in conjunction made me a power in the party independent of MacDonald or anyone else.

I was still too young to play a leading role myself, and was therefore constrained to work through established personalities and institutions. This was the only effective way of implementing the ideas which moved me, and to this end it was certainly necessary in some degree to accept the philosopher's advice: 'Harness to your chariot a conspicuous donkey, a most conspicuous donkey'. Yet the primary reason for my close association with MacDonald was party unity rather than any considerable hope that he personally would act as an executive instrument. He was an agreeable person but, as I found later in government, quite incapable of decision and action.

Striking evidence of this weakness in MacDonald was already provided in a conversation I had with him in the summer of 1924, which I well remember. He had recently had a considerable success in foreign affairs and, as the fear of any revolutionary conduct by the government had soon vanished, the Labour Party was on the crest of a little wave which might have carried it to a majority. I urged him to ask for a dissolution and an immediate election. 'No, my boy,' he replied, 'that is what Lloyd George would do, much too opportunist. I know a trick worth two of that; we will carry on and show them what we can do with a long spell of steady work.' He carried on, and six

months later the steady old moke in his proudly worn official uniform of blue
and gold harness, pulling his little cart of minor meddling in administrative
muddles, without a thought even of a larger opportunism, and certainly
without even a smoke dream of creative action, caught the harsh lash of a fate
contemptuous of easy complacency, right in his tenderest part, from the
Zinoviev letter which the Tories were much too innocent to know anything
about. At that moment I was reminded of one of the most tedious of his
seemingly interminable anecdotes. It was an account of riding donkeys up the
Himalayas, which wandered to some kind of conclusion with the words: 'So
on they went, on and on and up and up, indefatigable beasts'. It is not always
the most patient donkey which wins the race, though admittedly, as we in
Britain sometimes know to our cost, it can happen.

Six weeks before the election in November 1924 I entered the fight in
Birmingham. It seemed to me unfair to some of my old associates to fight in
Harrow, though with my firm roots in that constituency I might have had a
better chance of winning than in Birmingham. Also, I wanted to give some
striking service to the party which had so well received me. The Chamberlains
and their machine had ruled Birmingham for sixty years, first as Liberal-
Radicals and then as Conservative-Unionists. Their party machine was at that
time probably the strongest in the country. We had six weeks in which to
smash it.

I chose to fight Neville Chamberlain, who sat for the working-class constituency of Ladywood in the centre of the city; his brother Austen was the
neighbouring M.P. and their names and abilities made them a formidable
combination. Our own organisation had a paying membership of some two
hundred, but when we started the canvass only three elderly women and two
young men would accompany us. They were fine people, typical of the English
workers, and closely resembling the other pioneers later attached to our new
Movement before and after the Second World War. They were all manual
workers, and against them were the serried ranks of some of the ablest
businessmen in the country who with the aid of the massed middle class and
of many Conservative working men constituted the powerful machine of our
opponents.

My colleagues among the candidates we found on the spot were a rather
simple lot. A grand old pioneer of religious bent called Frank Smith was
fighting the neighbouring constituency against Austen Chamberlain. We held
a meeting together with Frank Smith in the chair, packed with our working-
class constituents, but with the front row occupied by prominent businessmen
who had come to see the new freak. The chairman began with what seemed an
interminable oration about his own peculiar brand of metaphysics, and just as
I was entertaining some transient hope of its conclusion, pulled out a football
referee's whistle, blew it and shouted 'Half-time'. He then called for prayers,
flopped down on his knees and said them. Soon he got up, blew his whistle

again, said 'Half-time is over' and continued his speech. After another thirty minutes of the best, he called on me. It was an inauspicious start.

However, my raging speaking campaign, both indoor and outdoor, and the superb work done by Cimmie in leading the canvassing team, eventually turned the scales. It was a joyous day when in the courtyards running back from the streets in the Birmingham slums we saw the blue window cards coming down and the red going up. The court leaders of some hundred people were usually dominant old women, and when mother turned they all turned. Mrs. Chamberlain worked magnificently on the other side in street canvass, but when it came to demagogy Neville was not in the ring. An able administrator—despite F.E.'s jibe that he was an adequate Mayor of Birmingham in a lean year—he had no great appeal to the masses. During the count he sat huddled in a corner, either exercising an iron self-control or in a state of near collapse; his agents did everything and he never moved.

The count was a drama: there were two re-counts. First Chamberlain was in by seven, then I was in by two, and finally he was in by seventy-seven. It was alleged by some of our people that votes had disappeared, and uproar broke out with men fighting in the crowded public gallery and people pointing to the floor as they bellowed—'That one's got 'em in his pocket'. It appeared from our enquiry that their allegations could not be sustained. Chamberlain was declared the winner, and we left the Town Hall at six o'clock in the morning to find an enormous crowd in the square outside which had waited up all night to hear the result; they were singing the Red Flag. They seized me and carried me around with an enthusiasm which deeply moved me. I decided to remain in Birmingham, and soon after the election turned down an invitation to stand in a by-election for a safe Labour seat at Forest of Dean. A splendid team of young men joined me in Birmingham as candidates and we built our organisation with the aid of a new organiser from the Clyde, Allan Young. Four years later Neville Chamberlain had deserted Ladywood for the safety of a middle-class stronghold in outlying Edgbaston, as the advance we had achieved in face of the wave of Conservative victory in the 1924 election made his position precarious. At the election of 1929 we took half the city from the Conservatives, and the tradition of sixty years was at an end. Labour had its chance.

10

Birmingham Proposals
Shaw and the
'Rich Socialists'
The General Strike

DURING the decade 1920 to 1930 I produced a series of constructive economic and administrative proposals; they have been generously recognised by eminent authorities in the present period. It is said now that I was a generation ahead of my time, and the validity of some of these policies seems to be widely admitted. My gratification at this belated recognition is only disturbed by the thought that I have done far more valuable creative work in recent years than I did then, but if it again takes thirty years for it to be understood I shall be exactly a hundred when time is ripe. However, the crisis which I believe to be inevitable can at any time bridge the gulf between thought and action, because it will render necessary new policies. The crisis of war interrupted and retarded the slow movement towards my thinking in the thirties, and conversely a crisis of the economy can accelerate the acceptance of new ideas at the present time.

The interval between 1924 and my return to Parliament in 1926 was valuable to the development of my political thinking. The General Election of November 1924 lifted Mr. Baldwin to power with a secure majority, while in Birmingham I was put out of Parliament by a narrow margin. I was free for intensive reading and reflection for the first time since my period in hospital and of quiet administrative work at the end of the war, and also able to travel through India and America and gain further valuable experience.

The background of my economic thinking was first developed by a study of Keynes—more in conversation with him than in reading his early writings, for he did not write *General Theory* until the thirties—and later by my American journey, which brought me in contact not only with the brilliant

economists of the Federal Reserve Board but also with the American technocrats, very practical people who were paid the enormous sums which the
United States even then accorded to its most valuable technicians.

Much of this constructive thinking remains relevant, *mutatis mutandis*, to
the situation facing our country in 1968. I published first a pamphlet sum-
marising the Birmingham proposals which I had stated in detail in a speech
at the I.L.P. Summer School in August 1925, and had discussed during
debates in the previous April at the I.L.P. Conference. At about the same
time I engaged in a controversy in *The Times* with the banker, Robert Brand.
My own chief contributions to the Birmingham proposals were (1) The
requirement of consumer credits in addition to producer credits and their
combination with national planning. (2) The recognition that banking and
credit were the key points of the economy and that their command was
essential to any effective planning by government. (3) The possibility of
maintaining an expanding island economy by monetary manipulation behind
a floating exchange rate.

The first point anticipated by many years and in a far more scientific
form the haphazard provision of hire purchase by private enterprise, which
had long existed on a petty scale almost at pawnbroker level, but was finally
expanded into a vast system in response to the necessity for creating an industrial market by placing purchasing power in the hands of the people.[1]
The second forestalled by thirty-four years Aneurin Bevan's speech about
'the commanding heights of economic power', regarded by the Labour Party
as a brilliant flash of insight a generation after its first statement in the
Birmingham proposals to which the party outside Birmingham had been
altogether blind. The third anticipated by twenty-four years the partial
application of this policy by Sir Stafford Cripps and the Treasury in 1949—
devaluation without a floating exchange rate—which chiefly enabled the
success of our export trade in the ensuing decade; also by forty-two years the
half-hearted attempt of another Labour administration in 1967 to follow in
Cripps's footsteps.

These policies went beyond the concepts of Keynes, from whom I and
others learnt our basic economics. It was in this period that I first put the
question: Is Keynes enough? My answer was, no: it was necessary to do more.
The present epoch has already seen the doctrine of Keynes fully implemented,
and before long we shall see the decision between these two opinions in the
coming economic situation. The difference between us in the sphere of
monetary policy at that time was stated in my speech on the Birmingham
proposals as follows: 'These facts of our recent experience are recognised by
modern monetary reformers. . . . They join with us in deprecating any fall in

---

[1] Instalment debt in the United States was estimated at 1,000,000,000 dollars in
1920, 3,000,000,000 dollars in 1929, and 40,000,000,000 dollars in 1960. (*Encyclopaedia
Britannica*.)

the general price-level, and aim, as we do, at stability of prices. Here arises the first difference between modern but non-socialist economists and the Birmingham proposals. At this point we carry modern monetary theory through a further stage to what I claim is its logical conclusion. . . . They say they will give extra purchasing power without recourse to the fatal expedient of the fall in the price-level by expanding credit as and when more goods are produced. Mr. Brand, the well-known banker and economist, said, in the course of our recent controversy in *The Times*: [1] "As the general wealth of the community increases, its purchasing power, represented by currency and bank deposits, will, under a proper currency system, be allowed to increase correspondingly in order to avoid falling prices".

'When the goods are produced he is prepared to supply more money to buy them, and consequently no fall in the price-level will result unless the generally accepted quantity theory of money be refuted. But we reply that the goods will not be produced unless manufacturers see markets ready to absorb them. Unemployment haunts us because industry will not produce without markets. Demand must precede supply. Our monetary reformers put the cart before the horse when they say that goods must be produced before the purchasing power to buy them has been created. The modernised bankers like Mr. Brand say to industry, in effect, "Produce more goods and then we will expand credit". Industry says to the bankers, "Show us first a market and then we will produce the goods." . . .

'We part company definitely with these monetary reformers when we advocate that State banks should give a clear lead by the bold and vigorous use of the national credit. We propose first to expand credit in order to create demand. That new and greater demand must, of course, be met by a new and greater supply of goods. Here our socialist planning must enter in. We must see that more goods are forthcoming to meet the new demand. If, by socialist planning, we can ensure a greater supply of goods corresponding to the greater supply of money, inflation and price rise cannot result. On the other hand, the new demand will have mobilised the service of men and machines now idle in the production of urgently wanted commodities. . . .

'The first essential of any successful socialist planning is to see that the new money goes into the right hands. . . .

'The ordinary method employed by our banks when they desire to expand credit is also a direct incentive to an inflationary result. The method is to lower the bank-rate and let anyone borrow who can give reasonable prospect of profits. The ordinary lowering of the bank-rate is not in itself an expansion of credit. It operates through the encouragement of borrowing, and it encourages the least desirable kind of borrower. . . . Most of it remains in the hands of speculators and new rich classes. . . . The new money would then be

[1] Mr. Brand was by then one of the bankers who had virtually become a Keynesian. The dates of the *Times* controversy were April 17, 20, 22 and 28, 1925.

employed for definitely anti-social purposes and would result in precisely those evils of inflation which our monetary reformers so deplore and which some of them have the audacity to impute to our proposals.

'We propose, in fact, to expand credit in a novel, scientific and socialist manner; to send our new emission of money direct to the spot where it is most required and will be used for the greatest economic and social advantage. As Socialists, we select for our medium of credit expansion the necessitous areas of poverty,[1] and propose to emit our new money in the shape of consumers' credits. These credits are an emergency measure to break the vicious circle of destitution and unemployment. The suggestion that they replace producers' credit is, of course, an absurd travesty of the plan. Producers' credits will naturally also be necessary for the production of the goods for which consumers' credits create the demand now lacking. Consumers' credits are a special expedient in time of industrial stagnation and collapse to stimulate effective demand in the right quarter and to re-start the dormant mechanism of production. . . .

'We propose to constitute an Economic Council vested with statutory powers. The business of this Council will be to estimate the difference between the actual and potential production of the country and to plan the stages by which that potential production can be evoked through the instrument of working-class demand. The constant care of the Economic Council must be to ensure that demand does not outstrip supply and thus cause a rise in price.

'It is evident that the new money must be issued gradually and that industry must be given time to respond to the new demand. . . . The Council would feel their way gradually to the maximum production. . . .

'When the maximum production of the nation is nearly reached, no new money must be created or inflation will follow. A point must be fixed at which all payments by the State must be balanced by taxation. Under the further machinery of these proposals, prosperous industry, producing to full capacity, must then shoulder its own wage bill, without further assistance for this purpose from State credit. . . .

'Let me now deal with the actual machinery by which our Economic Council would direct the major operation of creating fresh working-class demand to evoke our dormant capacity to produce. Alternative methods present themselves.'

I stated my preference for the following: 'The Economic Council would fix from time to time wages which individual firms or amalgamations were to pay. The State banks would then grant overdrafts for the payment of these wages until the Economic Council directed that the industry could shoulder its own wage bill by reason of its increased prosperity. No additional overdraft for wage purposes would then be granted.

'No question could arise of one firm being assisted as against another by

---

[1] Apparently the first suggestion for regional action.

the granting of these credits. Their present wage burden would remain the same, and their present competitive basis would be preserved. . . . The credits granted would be earmarked as assistance to wages, and could in no way be a subsidy to industry. . . . Wages could be forced up in the highly skilled trades as their production increased simultaneously with rises in the less-skilled and lower-paid occupations.'

These policies were accompanied by a considerable degree of socialist planning, such as import boards, for which I was not primarily responsible. The begetters of this method were two distinguished civil servants of the First World War—E. F. Wise and E. M. H. Lloyd—who at this later period were much associated with us.

It is not possible here to give more than a disjointed and crude summary of proposals which themselves were crude. Yet they contain *inter alia* a still valid idea for an effective reflation in a dirigiste economy. This attempt 'to see that new money goes into the right hands' and thereby to avoid the dangers of inflation and consequent collapse inherent in the present hire-purchase system still has some merit. It must be remembered that the whole concept of the creation of purchasing power to evoke production was at that time rejected out of hand; even Keynes went no further than urging on quantity-theory lines an adequate supply of credit to prevent a fall in the price-level, credit which would only be available to producers and general borrowers through the ordinary banking mechanism. Much later came hire-purchase on a great scale in a sporadic, almost convulsive effort of a failing system to furnish the market which the normal purchasing power of the people could not provide. Yet even today no effort has been made to meet the danger of a creation of credit without plan which the Birmingham proposals then foresaw. The point could come at which the hire-purchase system can collapse like a house of cards; it may be the first symptom of ultimate crisis.

Viewed against the background of Labour policy at that time, these proposals were essentially a challenge to the 'inevitability of gradualness', as the Webbs called it. They formed a revolutionary plan for action over the whole field of national life, and traversed completely the previous concept of the Labour Party that developing industries should be taken over one by one as they became ripe for nationalisation, or, as I later put it, that a Labour Government should hold the baby for capitalism by nationalising industries with full compensation just as they became obsolete.

It was clearly right for me to affirm in introducing the Birmingham proposals: 'We cannot say in face of the present situation, after a hundred years of evolutionary socialism all over the world, the starving worker of today need not worry because his great-grand-children will live in the millenium'. Yet it must be admitted that they were in some respects crude as well as revolutionary, and that they were based on a sectional rather than a national appeal. My thinking of today, both more advanced and more sophisticated, and devised to serve the whole nation rather than any section or faction, would condemn them as an elementary effort of an immature mind. In some respects they were superficial and marred by youthful exuberance and social passion, but even prejudiced judgment will find it difficult to deny to them a measure of creative thinking and a considerable anticipation of the future, certainly a more scientific approach than society ultimately accorded to dangers and problems which at that time we alone foresaw.

My speech on the Birmingham proposals in August 1925 concluded with an analysis of Mr. Churchill's policy of returning to the gold standard, which added something to Keynesian theory. Foreseeing the disastrous effect that the policy would have on the mining industry, which led nine months later to the General Strike, the speech included a stringent attack on Mr. Churchill's effort 'to base this gold standard upon pre-war parity with the dollar. This effort has involved the policy of drastic deflation which since the war has immensely increased the burden of the National Debt, and has proportionately benefited every idle rentier at the expense of the worker by hand or brain in productive industry. . . . Faced with the alternative of saying good-bye to the gold standard and therefore to his own employment, or good-bye to other people's employment, Mr. Churchill characteristically selected the latter course.' This was a reference to Mr. Churchill's recent return to the bosom of the Conservative Party as Chancellor of the Exchequer, which put him in a weak position to challenge the City of London, the Treasury view, or the Party in general by refusing to return to the gold standard.

I continued: 'A further dose of deflation followed, and the result is faithfully reflected in the unemployment figures, precisely as we foretold'—and then quoted Keynes saying that he estimated on this occasion the Conservative 'manipulation of the value of sterling is calculated to benefit the rentier class to the tune of £1,000,000,000 and to increase the real wealth of the owners of War Bonds by £750,000,000, which sum exactly wipes out our laborious efforts at debt redemption since the war'. I then added my own analysis of Mr. Churchill's 'defence of this policy, which he says *has no more to do with wages and unemployment than the Gulf Stream*'. This now historic pronouncement must surely rank with his father's question—'What are these damned dots?' when confronted for the first time with the mysteries of the decimal system—as the two most remarkable observations ever to issue from the Treasury through two Chancellors of the Exchequer. Across the gulf of years father and son were at one in their monumental ignorance.

However, my speech ignored the self-evident fact that these were the days of the amateur and went on to deal in detail with the effect of the Birmingham proposals on the export trade. The argument showed an acute awareness of the detrimental effect on exports produced by an artificial appreciation of the exchange, and of the stimulating effect of a depreciation accompanied by planning and executive action to prevent a corresponding rise in the internal price-level; points which were not generally grasped until a much later period. National planning based on a combination of monetary manipulation and executive action on a great scale was proposed, leaving the whole industrial field open to a stimulated private enterprise while it served the national interest in responding to a larger home market and to export opportunity. This policy challenged fundamentally the old socialist concept of the dead hand of bureaucracy taking over a few selected industries in step-by-step nationalisation.

In the same speech I suggested a floating exchange-rate combined with some of the executive measures already described, arguing its benefits in a passage which has considerable relevance to the modern situation of Britain.[1] 'If we still failed to find foreign markets for our exports and we continued to receive more imports, the exchange would tend to depreciate. If then our measures were successful in preventing a rise in domestic prices, imports would be automatically checked and exports would be stimulated in the manner already described. The correct trade balance would then tend to reassert itself through the automatic and justifiable movement of exchange, which now, by a curious paradox, is the only although least desirable object of State interference. [2]

'If still the situation was not remedied, industry would find a greater incentive to produce for the home than for the foreign market. A transfer of machinery and labour would then take place from production for the foreign market to production for the home market. (In any case some such transfer will probably be necessary in the not far distant future.) The new demand would thus be satisfied not by foreign production, but by home production for home need.

'This process might go very far without any danger to the import of necessary foodstuffs and raw materials. By no means all our present imports represent foodstuffs and raw materials. We import completely manufactured articles to the value of £300,000,000 per annum, most of which could be made at home. Our essential supplies can be purchased by far less exports than are at present sent abroad. The natural revulsion from the crude fallacies of Protection has resulted in a fetish worship of the present dimensions of our export trade by minds which have just succeeded in grasping the elementary fact that we must export in order to import certain necessaries which cannot be produced at home.' I concluded by saying that these were 'some of the

---

[1] 'I'm rather a floater myself' (Mr. Harold Wincott, *Financial Times*, May 7, 1968, discussing the Canadian experiment. Mr. Reginald Maudling discussed a floating exchange-rate as former Conservative Chancellor of the Exchequer in 1967.

[2] I had previously stated: 'The exchange is not the body of industry, but merely the thermometer which registers the condition of that body. The Conservatives have triumphantly "pegged" the thermometer, while leaving everything else to flux and chaos. They cry, "this is stability and health" when they have merely broken the instrument which records the state of the industrial body.'

consecrated bogeys with which high finance endeavours to browbeat' all reformers.

At that time I was surrounded by a brilliant group of young men, among whom I best remember John Strachey, Allan Young and Sydney Barnet Potter, who were all with me at Birmingham. I have already noted that the part of this constructive thinking which was not of my own creation—notably the Import Control Board system—was the work of E. F. Wise and E. M. H. Lloyd, who were close associates but not in the Birmingham group. John Strachey was with me as candidate for the Aston Division of Birmingham, which he won at the 1929 election: I had met him just before the 1924 election and suggested his adoption. He was my chief assistant in working out the Birmingham proposals, and had one of the best analytical and critical intelligences I have ever known; his subsequent writings on Marx introduced his method of thinking and working to an even larger audience. His mind was essentially analytical rather than creative; his earlier work described my thinking and his later work described the thinking of Marx and the neo-Marxians, but I am unaware that in either case he added any substantial invention. His excellent book on the Birmingham proposals was entitled *Revolution by Reason*, the name I had given to my pamphlet embodying and concentrating my study of the subject at the I.L.P. Summer School in August 1925; it was a lucid and admirable exposition. At every stage of this thinking I discussed its development with him—both in England and in journeys to France and Italy—and far more than any other of my companions he aided the slow evolution of the complete idea with the clear and acute understanding of his first-rate mind.

It was in America in the winter of 1925-6 that I was confronted with a challenge to derive new ideas from fresh facts. This journey developed and in a sense fundamentally changed my economic thinking. Hitherto my plans had been devised to make an island economy work in a highly competitive world. A new and more scientific method of expanding credit to secure full production for buoyant home market—with new demand based primarily on the necessitous regions—was the essence of the Birmingham proposals. External market relations were to be preserved and protected by a floating exchange-rate coupled with bulk purchase of foodstuffs and basic raw materials based on wartime experience, which not only aimed at buying advantageously but also at putting a strong bargaining power behind our exports. Concentrated buying of the biggest customer in the world could demand every kind of *quid pro quo* in other markets; this was a power which might lower barriers and open doors to our export trade. In short the whole plan envisaged an island economy battling for world, as markets Britain still does today.

In America the vast experience of my tour through the industrial regions opened my eyes to new processes, to tendencies and economic facts which were then in their infancy. I saw forces at work which years later would operate to the destruction of our island economy unless we were ready and willing to join in a larger economic unit. The immense productive power of American industry would eventually flood any existing home market unless measures were taken far beyond the thinking of Congress or prevailing orthodoxy, and would wash over to world markets and drown our struggling export trade; the rationalisation of industry would enable backward labour to be used in the simplified processes of the conveyor belt, and this evoked a prospect of the backward areas of the world being exploited to the jeopardy of the advanced; the further developnent of automation—already incipient— presented yet another awesome vision of industrial revolution going further to restore the balance, this time in favour of advanced labour to the ruin of the backward areas when automation had finally superseded rationalisation; in America it seemed to me I was present at the birth of a new age. With such complete dependence on world markets a free island economy would no longer be possible, however ingenious were the hands which manipulated its affairs. The idea arose of an economic unit large enough to be viable in relative independence of world markets, and in my new phrase capable of 'insulation' from the 'external factors' which subsequent British governments admitted to be the cause of their downfall. It was not enough to be an island: we could only live by being great. The answer was Empire or Europe, and I then said both. I journeyed between 1925 and 1929 from Birmingham toward a world idea. America had given me a vision, and I shall never forget the debt.

May I now define my personal position before citing the recognition my work of those days has since been accorded by authoritative opinion, and contrasting it with treatment at that time. The reader may well think it is immodest, unbecoming and un-English for me to quote praise of myself at various points of this book, and in any normal case I should be disposed to agree. Yet in my case I would ask consideration of the way I have been attacked before I am condemned for this method of reply; it is really necessary in my circumstance to redress the balance. Also it indicates possibly some lesson for the future when something subsequently acclaimed is assailed with such totally uninformed, merely foolish and destructive abuse at the time. Before presenting the verdict of others it may also be right for me to attempt some assessment of my work and to analyse the ingredients of whatever merit it possessed. Again I hope to be forgiven for being entirely frank without any false modesty in the normal and I feel attractive tradition of England, also to be judged free of exaggeration which could suggest the boastful character the Englishman so rightly dislikes. The mean between stultifying reticence and a suggestion of the vainglorious is always difficult to hold.

My policies were then produced firstly by my own capacity of creative thought, secondly by recognising quickly the value of new ideas produced by other people and by synthesising their thinking with my own, thirdly when it came to government by a dynamic drive for action, fourthly by patient but firm effort to secure team work and to get from each his best contribution. The capacity for creation and for synthesis are both essential qualities, and it is difficult to judge which is the more important. Sometimes I am almost inclined to follow Aristotle in according the highest merit to the ability to see a connection between phenomena which is not generally apparent, and this is essentially the process of synthesis. That the capacity to synthesise—to take ideas and weave them into a harmonious whole of effective action—is for a statesman even more important than creative thought is an arguable proposition. Yet the qualities of creation and of synthesis are by no means antithetical, and should be combined; add dynamism, and at the appropriate time we can have the action which a country or continent requires.

The familiar process of denying a man credit for his work is difficult in my case, because my creative thinking on different occasions has been assisted by entirely different teams. It is therefore only necessary to contrast the present recognition of my work with the treatment it received at the time. Our thinking was serious and our lives were dedicated during the 1920s, in striking contrast to the squalid frivolity of the attacks upon us; ideas and labours were alike greeted with sheer silliness. When such serious effort is simply assailed with the shrill squeals of cretinous children the country is heading for trouble; and today we have got it. The silliness of one period can produce the disaster of the next, and now that we are near disaster it may be interesting, and possibly instructive, not only to see what we were trying to do but to assess the dominant forces which were determined to prevent anything being done. They were described in my platform speeches of the period as King Bank and King Bunk; financier and Press Lord.

The following quotations mark the contrast between present recognition and past treatment. They relate more to the second phase of my constructive thinking, the Mosley Memorandum, and my subsequent resignation speech, than to the Birmingham proposals we are considering in this chapter. By 1929 I had the benefit both of the American experience and of my work as a Minister, with the help of the Civil Service. My developed policies at the later date were naturally more mature than the Birmingham proposals.

A. J. P. Taylor in his *English History, 1914–1945* wrote of me: 'His proposals were more creative than those of Lloyd George and offered a blueprint for most of the constructive advances in economic policy to the present day. It was impossible to say where Mosley got his ideas from. Perhaps he devised them himself. If so, they were an astonishing achievement . . . evidence of a superlative talent which was later to be wasted.' R. H. S. Crossman, when Chairman of the Labour Party and not yet burdened with the high office in government his talents later commanded, wrote of me in the *New Statesman* on October 27, 1961: 'Revealed as the outstanding politician of his generation.

. . . Mosley was spurned by Whitehall, Fleet Street and every party leader at Westminster, simply and solely because he was right. . . . Mosley was prepared to discard the orthodoxies of democratic politics and to break with the bankers of high finance in order to conquer unemployment . . . this brilliant Keynsian manifesto was a whole generation ahead of Labour thinking.' Many other authorities agreed with this view, and at the time of writing a new generation, struck by the close parallel between the politics of 1930 and today, has taken up the theme: for instance, *Blackwood's Magazine*, so long representative of staid and traditional opinion, wrote in January 1967: 'Mosley's genius soared and fell like a rocket for the saddest of reasons: he was in his ideas a generation too early . . . his economic ideas are now almost universally accepted'. The practical and pragmatic aspects of my work in the 1929–30 government were recognised by Mr. Harold Wincott, writing in the *Financial Times* on January 21, 1968: 'Even those of us who lived through those years can only marvel, re-reading the economic history books and the biographies and autobiographies, at the stupidities that were perpetrated— and hope that had we been in positions of authority and influence we would have been on the side of the small and oddly assorted band of angels who then had the right ideas. Keynes, Oswald Mosley and Lloyd George, for example'.

Yet in the twenties the answer to this thinking was a combination between parties and popular Press to smother the thought and action which might have averted the troubles of today. Throughout that period it was impossible outside Parliament, or certain party conferences, to get serious discussion of any subject except at the mass meetings I addressed continually throughout the country; and while popular enthusiasm can supply the necessary motive power to implement ideas, it is not the laboratory for their detailed examination and development. Both major party machines were in the power of conservative elements who lived completely in the past, and rejected modern ideas which they were generally incapable of understanding, even if they had been willing to make the effort. National newspapers at that time were the main instruments of forming opinion, and they were largely in the hands of Press lords who were masters of certain aspects of business and finance but almost entirely ignorant of serious politics. Support for any new idea depended more on their whims and predilections, personal likes and dislikes which varied fitfully and continuously, than on any understanding of national problems or sense of national responsibility. Their dream was to form governments of their cronies in the way that men form clubs, not serious parties supporting new ideas and clear courses. To do anything with them it was necessary to become a crony, and at a later stage I cronied myself with some result. The grinding of personal axes was the game, and the serious business was circulation. Keep it silly was the watch-word, and treat them rough if they get serious was the action.

It is a blessing of the present period that the Press has much improved, for the reason that it is mainly conducted by genuine businessmen. The new idea is gaining ground that Press proprietors should sell genuine news like other industrialists sell genuine goods. Over a large area of the Press slanted news is becoming a thing of the past. A certain sense of responsibility to the public replaces the peddling of interest and the pursuit of personal feuds. There is a serious attempt to present unbiased news, and even to preserve some right of reply. This is one of the few beneficent revolutions Britain has experienced in the modern age.

The same thing cannot be said, in my experience, of television. It is surely grotesque that an institution established by national charter should be able continually to attack an individual over a long period of time without according any right of reply. It can become a national danger that in a period of gathering crisis the public mind should be continually debauched with systematic silliness; for what was a whim to the old Press lords has become a system to the official masters of television. Keep it silly and stop them thinking is the general rule. When ideas are discussed they are confined to the prevailing and visibly failing orthodoxy. I may possibly, in the light of modern and authoritative comment, be forgiven for citing my own case as a man who in the economic sphere is now generally admitted to have been right in the last crisis, but has never at the time of writing been permitted by the BBC to put his view on the present crisis to a television audience.

The method of King Bunk in the twenties was to publish everything about us except our serious life and our constructive ideas. Our brief trips abroad during that period incurred the most trouble with the Press. Short visits to Paris were unnoticed; time was spent mostly in private houses, where we made friendships which have been a happiness to me throughout life. But each summer we used to go to the South of France or Italy for a holiday of a month, which we felt was well earned after a year of hard work in Parliament, supplemented by continual weekend meetings for the party and long autumn speaking tours, and this was regarded as a grave offence.

The Press at that time took the view that no one who was a Socialist was entitled ever to have a good time. We were pursued throughout our holiday to ensure that we should not. To take one ridiculous incident typical of the treatment, a sea-sport we used to enjoy was the predecessor of the modern water-skiing, not the old aquaplane but a free board, rather like the modern surf-board, with a rope from the motor-boat direct to the hand which enabled the playing of various tricks. This excited the Press, and reporters pursued us in motor-boats of their own to get snapshots of the 'rich Socialists' at play, published with captions suggesting that we spent our lives doing nothing else.

The largest meetings in the country, speeches that packed the House of Commons, policies which in the next generation were quoted by historians and economists as having offered a solution of the contemporary problems —all could pass without a mention—but every time that my backside hit the azure blue of the Mediterranean, a headline or photograph would ensue. King Bunk reigned, and he fed the people the dope of drivel which turns their stomach today in recurring economic crises. It is true that cinema stars now suffer the same treatment, but the difference is that we had something serious to say and they have not; our concern was the country, and theirs is the box-office.

The 'rich Socialists' line of attack soon became the chief stock-in-trade of Press and Party, and entered into every sphere of our life. Bernard Shaw came back with a strong counter-attack on our behalf; his article entitled 'The Yahoos' was a dialectical masterpiece. We took up the fight and got the best of the 'rich Socialists' argument, though the Tories as usual did not notice that until it came to the vote. Our theme was the confusion in their minds between Christianity and Socialism; we enquired why people who often paraded their religious views in politics had not yet obeyed the injunction: 'go sell whatsoever thou hast and give to the poor'. Our proposition was not to make everyone poor, but by a proper organisation of society to make everyone reasonably well-off. To stop the dog-fight of the capitalist world the first step was not to put ourselves under the dog-fight. Then and since I firmly decided to retain sufficient of my money to give me independence, and to maintain health and energy without which I should be of no use to anyone.

The Tories thought that the 'rich Socialists' attack was a real winner in a situation very different to the present affluent society, where such issues scarcely exist. When the neighbouring constituency to Ladywood in the Birmingham area became vacant and I was invited to stand, they made it virtually the whole issue of the Smethwick by-election in 1926. The theme was that I left my Rolls-Royce outside Birmingham and changed into a Ford, while Cimmie also removed her diamond-covered dress in favour of a more appropriate costume; this puzzled her until she remembered she had once appeared in Birmingham with a shawl covered with bits of glass bought in an Indian bazaar. In fact, of course, we turned up in our ordinary clothes and in our usual car, which I think was a Vauxhall. This business went so far that when Oliver Baldwin—the socialist son of the Prime Minister—came to speak for me and found us all eating fish and chips in the local pub, his jovial enquiry—'Where's the champagne?'—captured the headlines next morning: Baldwin asks Mosley for champagne. However, the only practical result was the embarrassing pursuit of the journalists in question with hat-pins by the local Amazons, strong arms which had never worn a black shirt.

The by-election caused much excitement and attracted considerable publicity. The result was to multiply the previous Labour majority nearly five times. The Tories got it all wrong, as they often do in their different background, for it is not the working-class but sometimes the middle-class which is envious. This was vividly illustrated the following May Day, when

I was invited as usual to head the customary procession through Birmingham
by the local Labour parties and trade unions. Members of the organising
committee approached me with a request that my much-advertised Rolls-
Royce should appear in the proceedings, as the boys wanted to show that
their man had a better car than Chamberlain. I had sadly to confess that I
had never owned such a masterpiece.

Health knows no envy. The Tories got it wrong because jealousy is a
disease, not a symptom of well-being. Abounding vitality may feel compassion, but not envy of the condition of others. Happily, this deep health is
still the quality of the British workers; they retain their original nature. They
fear no man, and they envy no man; this character endures and is one of the
chief hopes of the future. The Australians say: 'Dead fish rot from the head
down'. In Britain the rot has not yet reached and permeated the body of the
nation; action in time can forestall that disaster. Most people will get as much
as they can for as little effort as possible, if a society built on illusion provides
opportunity, or temptation. Yet the workers of our country still feel it is
unnatural to get something for nothing, and they have a basic contempt for
those who seek such an existence. That is why in a decadent society renaissance is most likely to come from the mass of the people.

Marx had some reason to stress his proletarian revolution when society
collapses because the ruling class is riddled with the disease of error and
indecision; in short, when it becomes decadent. A healthy people can then
produce new leadership to replace a clique which fails because it has surrendered to overwhelming opportunity for self-indulgence, though in
practice much of the leadership towards a new society has always come from
individuals with the character to resist the temptation of the old. This is
particularly true of England, where an aristocracy with roots in the soil has
hitherto provided at least sufficient leadership toward necessary reform to
avert the bloody upheavals of lands which lacked such quality in crisis. This
aspect of the original Whig tradition is never well appreciated by the bourgeois
Tory mind with its crude class divisions of the cities. When the tattered
remnants of the Whig tradition taunted me from the tawdry ranks of Toryism
with being a class traitor, because I had taken the side of the people in the
Labour Party, my reply was simple: it is you, not I who betray our very
English heritage, when you take the part of reaction against the people.
Toryism then seemed to me as bereft of the British spirit as it was ignorant
of English history. My view perhaps was coloured by the fact that the Conservatives never relaxed in their diverting inventions about our double lives.
The brilliant cartoonist of the *Birmingham Mail* made the most of it. After
one election victory, he depicted me handing in my working-man's clothes
and drawing out my top-hat and full dress from the cloakroom of a fancy-
dress party under the headline, 'After the bawl'.

By that time, the position of the party had been much fortified in the

Birmingham area by the General Strike. I was convinced for reasons which have been explained that the deflationary policy of the Conservative Government was entirely responsible for the strike, and I was passionately on the side of the workers, whose standard of life in my view was being directly attacked by an incompetent government in support of an obsolete and ultimately doomed system. We had already shown in unanswered arguments that the deflation and the consequent attack on wages was quite simply a gigantic transfer of wealth from those who lived by earning to those who lived by owning; no student of Keynesian economics would now venture to deny this. So I did my utmost to support the strike in every way, and this involved making about twenty speeches a day. The men did not lack spirit, but became deeply bored when they had nothing to do. The organised amusements of today were not the habit of the workers in that poorer period, and even now not many of rich or poor are happy if thrown on their own resources. Books, the wonderful boon of present civilisation which brings the best music to the home, quick transport to walks in the lovely countryside of England, not much of these things was available to the workers of Birmingham in 1926. The General Strike was in danger of collapsing through sheer boredom, and for that reason—strange only to those who did not understand how the people lived—I had to make twenty speeches a day.

The General Strike was called off by the General Council of the trade unions after nine days. Both sides were wrong: the Government in a policy of brutal stupidity and the trade unions in getting themselves into a position where they were in danger of challenging the Constitution and the power of the State. They were right to call it off and to rely instead on political action, and it was not their fault that they were later let down by the political leaders. During this period I formed more close friendships and a high regard for some of the trade union leaders, which I have always retained.

MacDonald on our return to London was bewailing that the discredit of the General Strike would mean a terrible set-back for Labour. We young men from Birmingham were convinced of the contrary, and went out to prove it. We threw ourselves with passion into the political fight, and at the first essay with a vigorous intervention in a Hammersmith by-election assisted in a big increase in the Labour majority. Smethwick soon followed and the victory of our view was complete. All this by no means endeared me to the middle-class leadership of the Labour Party. Despite every effort of the Press to turn the workers against me, it was from them and from some of the trade union leaders that my support came in the effort to get things done. They wanted action.

My ideas of the future were forming rapidly and I must have appeared more and more of a menace to the middle-class leaders of the Labour Party. It was their complacency, rooted in the ideas of the nineteenth century, and not the urge of the mass of the people toward the change they then found necessary, which moved Bernard Shaw to write: 'You will hear something more of Sir Oswald before you are through with him. I know you dislike him, because he looks like a man who has some physical courage and is going to do something; and that is a terrible thing. You instinctively hate him, because you do not know where he will land you.'

11

Roosevelt and
American Industry

WE went to America in 1926 to study industry and to meet those who create it. This was our main interest; American politics were then to me a secondary affair. Nevertheless, we were caught up immediately after our arrival in New York by politics and society, and although we soon extricated ourselves and were off on our industrial tour, it was interesting and hectic while it lasted. The chief contrast of these first acquaintances was the difference which divided F. D. Roosevelt from his brilliant relation, Alice Longworth. They moved in very different circles, and she was outspoken in her dislike of F.D.R. She remained very much the daughter of her father—the former President Roosevelt—and reminded us of Lady Violet Bonham-Carter, Asquith's daughter, both in her abilities and in her prejudices F. D. Roosevelt was in the opposite party and then on his way to becoming Governor of New York as a supporter of Al Smith, the attractive demagogue of 'Brown Derby' memory.

The invitation to meet Franklin D. Roosevelt came out of the blue, for we neither knew him nor had an introduction; he wrote to us at our hotel and invited us to his apartment in New York. It was characteristic of the warm-hearted, hospitable American way of doing things to be direct and informal instead of waiting to be introduced in our European fashion. Time is saved, and nothing is lost except false dignity. In a European phrase of the eighteenth century, Roosevelt had enough dignity to be able to throw away a little of it.

The meeting was both impressive and strange. He was alone in the room with his wife, seated on a chair from which he could not rise to greet us. He was completely paralysed below the waist, and by all accounts in a worse condition at that time than in his later years as President. What a contrast between this magnificent man with his fine head and massive torso, handsome as a classic Greek and radiating charm, though completely immobile, and the exceptionally ugly woman, all movement and vivacity with an aura of gentle kindness, but without even a reflection of his attraction. How did they come together? It was the first enigma which greeted us in America, and it remained a mystery until much later.

We got on well from the start, and before we left he invited us to join him in his house-boat in Florida for a long fishing trip at the end of our industrial tour. We accepted gladly for apart from the prospect of an agreeable journey in his company, he had warned us that a period of repose and relaxation was indicated after the exertion of a Press-accompanied industrial tour which might try the physique of a Hercules. Mrs. Roosevelt excused herself as she had other engagements at that time, and we never saw her again until many years later and in very different circumstances.

We visited Roosevelt several times before leaving New York, and on all subsequent occasions his mother was present. We saw in the older Mrs. Roosevelt some of the splendid looks she had bequeathed to her son. She had much of his charm, combined with the distinguished manners of a hostess of the old school. F.D.R. himself sometimes reminded me of the great hostesses of Europe, so solicitous of his guests, so active and imaginative in devising fresh amusements on the fishing trip. He had a lively sense of fun, which was never still; always active and vital, his company combined the dynamism of America with the manners of Europe. Life for him was clearly a paradise, but a demon had entered, the shadow of his affliction traversed the sunlight.

We naturally discussed politics much at this time, as well as later on the trip. In fact, he was interested in nothing else. He was thoroughly a liberal in the best sense of the word. He had compassion, the first requisite in a statesman of any opinion, he really cared about people and human suffering. He also had a deep respect for the individual and for liberty; another essential. In all these matters he was sensitive, even emotional. Yet this seemed to be about the limit of his political range; he had scarcely an inkling of the turmoil of creative thinking then beginning in America, which I discussed later in the technical sphere of money with the officials of the newly-formed Federal Reserve Board, and in the industrial regions with the vastly paid technicians of the mass-producing plants who already foresaw a productive potential which would eventually confront statesmanship with a problem to overwhelm all previous economic thinking. He was aware these things were happening, but his mind did not grapple with them. He was remote from the fascination of these problems.

Roosevelt was executive not constructive. Already this was clear to any discerning eye, for his vigour of character inevitably made him executive, but his limitations of mind with equal inevitability prevented him being constructive. He was an example of too much will and too little intellect; usually English politicians of any capacity reverse these qualities to make the opposite defect. It was easy to see that he would act rapidly and ruthlessly in an emergency. He had been an ardent under-secretary of the Navy and had participated to the full in its life. His family background also provided dynamic impulse and tradition; he had the right blend for action. I felt a strong sympathy with him in these qualities and with his urge to remedy human suffering. Recently an English journalist has written: 'It is no accident that it was an authoritarian aristocrat, Bismarck, who gave Germany its great socialistic Insurance Acts; Roosevelt, the authoritarian American aristocrat, who gave America its radical New Deal; and Sir Oswald Mosley, the authoritarian British aristocrat, then a Labour Minister, who was prepared to solve unemployment in the 1930s along genuinely socialist lines'.[1]

How can similar background and initial impulse lead to such different life courses? I will attempt a brief analysis of defects in Roosevelt's attitude and method which in my view later led to considerable catastrophe. Roosevelt lacked entirely the ultimate realism by which alone the durably great can be achieved. To achieve human happiness it is not enough to will the end unless the means can be grasped in a clear and ordered sequence of thought and action. Emotion without clarity and vision can end in disaster, and the hot, cloudy impulses of Roosevelt were a catastrophe not only to the British Empire but to all Europe, from which neither we nor mankind in general have yet recovered. The wrongs of life are not righted simply by turning the world upside down and putting what is underneath on top; in effect, just replacing the gentle tyranny of an old order with the harsher tyranny of communism. American liberalism had nothing to replace the system which it destroyed, and today we must rebuild on the ruins which it left. We acknowledge with gratitude that subsequent American statesmanship not only gave Europe in the period of consequent disaster material help which saved it, but also in an act of generosity unique in history willed the creation of Europe as another great power. It is European division, jealousy and pusillanimity which has hitherto impeded European union, not American inhibition. Other Americans have done much to remedy the ruin which Roosevelt, by inadequacy rather than malice, bequeathed to our continent. We will return both to his charming personality and to his mistaken policy.

Our arrival in New York was typical of America's warm-hearted welcome, even though we were already members of the Labour Party with its socialist policies. We were swept off to dine the first evening with Mrs. William Randolph Hearst, whom I had met previously at the parties she used to give in Paris. She had a large apartment in New York, while her husband, the newspaper proprietor and publicist, pursued other interests at his vast

[1] Peregrine Worsthorne, *Sunday Telegraph*, October 1, 1967.

domain in California. The dinner we were told was a little improvised affair to welcome us; it turned out to be for eighty people in a large baronial banqueting hall characteristic of Hearst reproductions of European period pieces. All went well at the dinner, but embarrassment came directly afterwards. A large cinema screen descended on one of the lofty walls, and to our considerable disquiet it showed giant figures of ourselves; I had given interviews before the cameras on the liner, and at the same time pictures were taken for the silent films of those days. It was the first time that I had ever seen myself on the screen, and I experienced the same shock that most people do. It was a heavy punch to sustain immediately after the mellow ending of such a dinner.

The evening finished in much gaiety, and was followed by a shower of kindly invitations. Then, as always, I liked Americans. There are some, of course, who are repulsive, but so are some Englishmen and other specimens of all our European people, as we have all felt when we have seen and heard a loud-mouthed fellow-countryman—who has probably just made a packet of money in some dubious enterprise—throwing his weight around in a French or Italian restaurant to the embarrassment of his compatriots and the detriment of his country. The longer I live the more I feel it is absurd to generalise about the European people, among whom the Americans must be included in friendship though not in political system. In each country there are people we love and others for whom we have a very different sentiment, just as in a family we prefer some to others. Among these close relations division is not of the soil but of the spirit.

It is difficult to remember after this lapse of time where I first met the gay American friends of this period, before, during or after this first tour of America in the spring of 1926. Some of them were well known at that time, others became famous at a much later date. The Barrymores for years played a considerable part in our life, but they must have been friends before the American tour, because I remember them staying with us at our little village of different cottages at Ifold in Sussex, which we called our country house when we were first married. Most of my memories of them were in Paris rather than in America. John and Blanche Barrymore were our friends; their sister Ethel and brother Lionel we knew only slightly. John and Blanche were certainly a scintillating couple, as beautiful as they were brilliant in their very individual fashions. I still maintain that he played Hamlet better than any other actor I have seen. No one has ever gazed so sardonically at the blood-stained fingers as they were slowly raised one by one after the duel scene. No one has ever spoken better the tragic, ineffable peace of the last line 'the rest is silence'. It is sad that drink and the exhausting diversity of his love affairs eventually reduced this fine actor and agreeable companion to a parody of his previous distinction in his last performances. His mind, too, might have been good if he had ever given it a chance.

The dark, flashing Hungarian beauty of his wife Blanche was a fitting background to her extraordinary qualities. She had reigned briefly in the orthodox society of New York before running away with John, and soon returned to sparkle in a world of more diversity in two continents. Their relationship was affectionate but hectic, because they clashed at many points. I once said to them: 'You both have the same occupation in life, each doing what you want and trying to stop the other doing the same thing: you both win on the first point but both flop on the second'. More trouble came when she also insisted on playing Hamlet; I did not see her performance, but understood the object was not quite achieved of improving on John's. She liked the role of romantic young men, playing l'Aiglon on the stage and writing poems about Greek boys running through the woods of Versailles; a conjunction which seemed to her quite natural. She was an amateur in art, but an artist in life, combining Central Europe and America at their most vital, wittiest and best. She died as she lived, putting on a tremendous show. I only know the details at second-hand, but understand they included a lying-in-state with continuous playing of Wagner's music. These outstanding American women attend to everything; another of our friends requested no flowers at her funeral, because she had arranged their sumptuous display herself in advance and did not want the colour scheme spoilt.

America at this point touched the more colourful and romantic periods of European history, when some people still had the courage to be flamboyant. Blanche Barrymore would have felt at home with some of the men and women of the Renaissance, perhaps, in their less extreme moments, even with the Borgias; in some moods she might even have been equal to their extremities. Yet very rich Americans have usually shown eccentricity rather than artistry in life. William Randolph Hearst, for instance, had an enormous property in California where his guests lived in various luxurious establishments often miles apart. We never got beyond being entertained by Mrs. Hearst in New York and Paris in a very different society. But the accounts of his life at that time often prompted in me the thought that a paradise of mind and body might have been created if any of these magnates had had a modicum of the taste and capacity for life displayed by Frederick the Great when, in his spare moments, he assembled Voltaire and the élite of Europe at Sans Souci; or of Shah Jehan in the fort of Delhi, where life perhaps inclined more to the voluptuous than intellect requires or the sororities of America would approve. The phenomenon of a very rich man who really knows how to live has yet to appear in America. A small society which taught the world how beautiful life could be might be justified when the full affluence of America is realised, and the still prevailing areas of poverty and degradation have been resolved.

The society we saw at that time varied between a rather stiff imitation of English aristocracy and the bohemian gaiety of artists. In the first category were the Vanderbilts, whom we had met with Lord Curzon at the time of our marriage. Mrs. Vanderbilt was at home in the Curzon milieu in London, and in America she appeared to live in much the same way, but in an even more exaggerated fashion. She stood up quite well to the shock of the socialist opinions we had acquired since meeting her in England. The lighter side of American life which later became so spectacular and so publicised was then only just beginning to appear. Cole Porter, a little dark elfin creature whom I always expected to find sitting on a mushroom, was singing his songs to us in private, but not yet in public. He and his beautiful wife Linda were more in our life later in Paris and Venice than at that time in America. So was Elsa Maxwell who in those days gave discreet parties, at least in Paris, without publicity of any kind. According to the legend she had recently emerged from playing the piano in some local cinema, but her simple and boisterous turn at the piano in these small parties had not yet been transmuted to a world-wide music hall with all participants displayed to the headlines in the grotesque acrobatics of superfluous wealth. The Vernon Castles floated through our lives, literally floated, for they were famous professional ballroom dancers, and later they entranced London as they had New York. This gay and varied world briefly arrested but did not long delay us in New York, for we had come in all the seriousness of our political mission for a different purpose.

Our main purpose in America was to tour the industrial areas, which was indeed an experience. We were accompanied throughout the whole journey by a large concourse of journalists of both sexes. Once we tried to shake them off by an elaborate manoeuvre and thought we had made a clear getaway, but they were waiting for us on the platform of our arrival. They were very agreeable and completely honourable; never on the whole tour was anything said off the record reported, and they were with us night and day. Down the coal mines we went, and the women journalists came too, in the silk dresses of the period. Wet and plastered with coal dust as we emerged, I would condole with them on their ruined dresses: 'That's all right, it is all on the paper,' they would reply. America even then did everything— large or small—on the grand scale.

We saw almost everything that was to be seen, beginning with the slums of New York and the virtual segregation of various communities. I had an astonishing experience which at that point in my life I could not begin to understand, and had never seen in Europe. The usual large team of journalists was accompanying me on foot through the slums of New York, where I was examining housing conditions, which at that time were very bad. Suddenly the journalists were missing, and I found myself surrounded by people who were immigrants and could hardly talk our language, but I spent some time among them and entered their houses on their friendly invitation. When eventually I emerged from this quarter into streets which were quite different, the journalists were there again. 'What happened to you?' I enquired, for it was the only time I had lost them on the whole tour. 'We were not going in there at any price,' was the reply. It was the first time I had ever encountered a strong anti-semitism, which at that time was to be found more in America than in Europe. As we shall see I had a quarrel years later with certain Jews for political reasons, but have not at any time been an anti-semite.

A Spanish friend of mine, the Marques de Valdeiglesias, told me of much the same experience when he went to America about that time. As a young man he made friends on the ship with a lady of dark and romantic beauty, and in New York was much in her company. One hot day he suggested they should go bathing together, and she replied: 'Certainly, but you must come to our beach'. He understood for the first time that she was a Jewess, and was astonished to learn that Jews were segregated in different beaches, as various communities are in South Africa today. Anti-semitism then appeared in various sections of American life from top to bottom. There were legends of Otto Kahn's exclusion from the opera and his vigorous action with weight of money to overcome it; stories in universal circulation which I never checked in detail.

Certainly this attitude was prevalent in Washington, in whose social life the family of Cimmie's mother, the Leiters, was prominent. This made the more curious the stories circulated years later that they were Jews. I never heard a word about this in America, and in retrospect it certainly appears to me impossible for them to have occupied that position in that atmosphere if it had been true. I reiterate that if Cimmie had been half-Jewish it would not have made the slightest difference in my attitude to her or in my political action in opposing anyone, Jew or Gentile, I thought was in favour of another war.

The industrial tour was one of the most interesting experiences of my life. It was in Detroit more than in any other centre that I found striking confirmation of one of the main points of my economic thinking from 1918 onwards. The Ford factory produced the cheapest article and paid the highest wage in the world; in terms of money value, nothing on earth could compare with that original Tin Lizzie. Mass production for a large and assured home market is the industrial key. It is not so much the rate of wage as the rate of production which determines the cost of production. Britain, turning slowly towards an assured European market, is beginning to grasp this forty years later; the time-lag is too long, and stubborn resistance to all new thinking has been a national danger.

Another new fact struck me in Detroit with a force which turned me away from the classic economic teaching, ranging from Adam Smith to Marshall. I watched men working at the conveyor belt in the Ford factory. Each performed some simple operation on the vehicle in the making as it reached him on the conveyor; a process which later became familiar, but these were early days. Even with my complete mechanical ignorance I could have stepped in at practically any point on the line and done the simple job of turning a screw or fixing a bolt; it was simplicity itself. The genius lay in the organisation which had evolved such easy tasks for the individual worker. Some of the workers were quite primitive types only recently come to America—a number of them, I was told, illiterates—and they were ideal for the job because normal labour was apt to find it too monotonous; during this period men were leaving the factory on account of the monotony at the rate of about a thousand a week.

This was a new world of industry with new problems. At once the thought occurred to me that the most backward labour could eventually be exploited in other countries by this method, to compete with the most advanced labour. Oriental and African labour does not mind monotony as much as the Europeans do, and could be trained quickly to do simple tasks on the conveyor belt under the minimum of skilled supervision, once the factory was installed. In India the previous year I had seen the beginning of the same tendency, which later ruined Lancashire with low-wage competition by using rational-ised industrial processes. Were the orthodox economics still valid if the backward and low paid could do the same thing as the advanced and well paid —and even for psychological reasons do it better? What became of the classic concept that skilled labour in open competition will always defeat unskilled labour? This question ultimately proved decisive in the fate of the cotton industry of Lancashire and the woollen trade of Yorkshire. India, Hong Kong, Japan and China knocked out our traditional trades with rationalised machinery, supplied by our English counties for their own destruction in open competition on the world and even on the British market.

The same process is now about to be repeated on a far greater scale in our present confusion of thinking and muddle of organisation. Emotion rules, and men learn slowly. They usually act only when they feel as well as see the facts. These problems are not insoluble and can be settled in a humane and decent way, but we have to sort the world out a bit. Facts I first observed in Detroit forty years ago can still be fatal if simply released to play havoc in conditions of world anarchy.

This book includes some answer to these dilemmas, which, however, as usual in human affairs, will soon be followed by new problems. My later visit to Pittsburg suggested the stage which would follow the period of exploiting backward labour; a renewed triumph of highly skilled labour, which in the end can again turn world industry upside down. I was learning a lot in America, and my thinking was beginning to leave Adam Smith far behind. In Pittsburg I saw the opposite quality, extreme of skill not only of design but of operation. The most highly developed steel works then in existence were already being operated in large-scale processes by relatively few men. In the huge shed was seated a man in something like a railway signal box, operating levers which controlled the movement on rollers of red-hot lengths of steel; already manual handling as a considerable factor was finished. There, in elementary form, was the further vision, the ultimate method in which very few skilled men would manipulate masses of machines. The final process of automation in which machines replace men, except for skilled supervisors, was not yet born, but at Pittsburg it was at least in the womb. For those with eyes to see, the future loomed in these American factories.

It was possible to foresee two stages in industrial development. The first would be rationalised industry in which unskilled labour would perform simple tasks served by a conveyor belt under a certain amount of skilled supervision. The second would be nearly automatic machinery in which highly skilled labour would manoeuvre machines doing nearly all the work which had been performed by unskilled labour. Classic economics would ultimately return in the victory of the skilled, but there would be chaos in the interval if all development were left to chance. First, the attraction of the unskilled all over the world from primitive, rural occupations to factories, and the devastating competition of the low-paid against the high-paid. Then the return in triumph of the skilled and the throwing into a vast unemployed scrap-heap of all the primitive labour thus exploited. One thing was clear: those grave problems could not be left to settle themselves.

Things happen far more slowly than we think, all culminations are delayed; my main errors have been not in fact, but in time. Everything took longer than I anticipated, but these things are now beginning to happen, and the facts must be faced. If we are not to fall into the tyranny of communism with its iron control of all human affairs, we must evolve a conscious dirigism by government in Britain, Europe, America, and ultimately the world, which with foresight will meet these events, and with State intervention will at least hold the ring while science, individual initiative and free industrial organisation, operating within the limits of an ordered society, win clarity and progress from confusion and chaos. This does not mean universal control by the State; it means the opposite, absolute freedom of industrial initiative within conditions which State action makes possible. It is not the duty of government to conduct industry, but rather to create a system which makes possible the free conduct of industry by private enterprise. This means the elimination of unfair competition by sweated labour which can be exploited through modern industrial processes with disastrous consequences to more advanced communities. It is in the sphere of wages and prices that government must intervene, not in management.

These things will not just sort themselves out through the classic economics, with the addition of a few built-in stabilisers of Keynesian theory, until the imagined happy ending with all the advanced peoples making computers and aircraft and the backward peoples performing the simpler tasks. A sane order of the world will not just happen, like a ripe plum falling into the open mouth of a man lying on his back. We must pay some attention to one of Bernard Shaw's favourite cracks: 'As the teacher said to the child who had written, "King Solomon had a thousand porcupines," "think child, think" '. As a young man in Detroit and Pittsburg, I had something to think about, and my subsequent, perhaps untimely insistence on action showed that at least I had some idea of what must be done.

We visited almost every industrial centre of America, except California and its celestial industry, the cinema. In Chicago it was the Armour meat factory, where the live pig entered at one end of the conveyor belt and emerged at the other end neatly packaged in a tin. 'Our business is not pretty, but it's useful,' said its efficient chief, 'we use everything except the squeal.' It seemed to be as humanely conducted as such an establishment can be. The intricacies of Sears Roebuck's mail-order business were also studied; it is almost true to say that we left nothing out.

The end was Palm Beach and the industry of pleasure which stretched along that enchanted coast to Miami. There we learnt to know the end product of American success, the fabulous millionaires; men like Josh Cosden, who was reputed to have started punching tickets on a tram and to have won, lost and won again three big fortunes before he was forty. He entertained us in his house on the sea, built by the architect Meisner; an establishment whose luxury baffles description, but yet was constructed with considerable taste in the Spanish style. A friend of his told me recently that the house was eventually sold for a record price even in America, but that Cosden himself died bankrupt.

We usually swam in this milk-warm sea from the private beaches of such friends, but we went on the first day to the public beach, where the dress of the women was supervised by an official carrying various pieces of coloured cloth slung from his waist. The year 1926 was before the bikini epoch and the rule in Florida on the public beach was that a woman must have no gap between her obligatory stockings and her ample bathing dress; the purpose of the coloured patterns worn by the beach bureaucrat was to match up the stockings if doubt arose that they were too near flesh colour. Naturally, most of the Europeans in our party failed to make the grade. Yet at a variety show that evening considerable beauties approached our supper table on a moving platform clad in practically nothing at all; at a time when such performances were unknown in the reputable establishments of Europe. Our surprised enquiries were met with the expert information that the beach was under State law and the theatre under Federal law; or vice versa, I forget which.

Shock followed shock for our innocents from the European garden of Eden, inflicted by American prudery which had tasted of the apple. Archie Sinclair swam round the pier of the public beach and found a small crowd awaiting his return to grasp his hand in an emotional welcome for a man who had just survived a mortal danger. They explained that if you swam out of your depth you were liable to be eaten by the barracuda; a fish about the size of a salmon but with an immense jaw and fiercer than the shark. He expostulated that he had seen many notices on the beach enjoining 'No Soliciting', but no warning of the barracuda. He was informed that to mention the chance of soliciting was good for business, but the bite of the barracuda was not. A practical folk, the Americans.

However, Europe made a strong come-back in the formidable person of Princesse Winnie de Polignac. She was born in America, a Singer sewing-machine heiress and aunt to the almost equally formidable Daisy Fellowes; the family had a large interest in the Everglades Club where we all lived. It was an agreeable establishment with comfortable little chalets surrounding the central club-house to which we walked in the morning for an excellent breakfast. We found the Princesse de Polignac one morning in this central hall addressing the management in commanding tones on the subject of her broken lavatory: 'What is the use of being as nasty as Americans, if you are as inefficient as Sicilians?' We had naturally to rally to her side, for she gave the best musical parties in Paris, which in festive seasons ended with the staff of the hunt entering to blow their horns; we had an affection for this extraordinary character who, in old age, blended the creative energy of America with the subtlest charms of Europe.

We were fortunate to find in Florida some of our most treasured friends from Paris, and were eventually tempted to linger too long. Interesting things too were happening in Florida, notably the exaggerated land boom. Plots were being bought and sold over and over again in frantic speculation, and prices were astronomical; rocks out in the sea were being acquired for some future mythical construction. Eventually more serious economists began to calculate that if almost the whole population of America spent its holidays there, supplied with a considerably larger income than it currently possessed, the place would still be oversold. The subsequent crash was a warning to similar tendencies in Europe today. Many of those speculations would come off in the long run, but, as oft-quoted Keynes observed, in the long run we are all dead. So the boom which centred round Tampa was left with America's favourite comedian, Ukulele Ike, singing: 'Oh, sunny Florida, why did I ever tamper with you?'

Dog-racing was then starting up for the first time in Florida, and, after seeing it, I was asked if it would be a success in England, and was offered the chance to get in on the ground floor. I replied that it would certainly be a great success with our sporting British public, but as an M.P. I felt it was my duty not to encourage gambling; so I could not participate. Two fortunes I missed in that period through rather absurd scruples. The other was a chance to bet on the election results of 1929. The British Stock Exchange had a system of betting on election results. As it had been my duty for some years previously to make the last speech for the Labour Party at practically every by-election, I knew all the chief agents of the party intimately, and was well aware from close experience what the result of the election was likely to be. The Stock Exchange had grossly under-estimated Labour's success, and with my information I should be betting on a certainty. I refrained, because I knew that I was likely to be in the following government, and thought it would be unbecoming for a Minister to have made a fortune on the previous election results.

Was I right to maintain this attitude of unequivocal rectitude?—or was I just a damned young prig? Human nature—particularly British nature—will gamble in any case—fools and their money will be parted in any case—money in the right hands can be used for beneficent purposes. I have spent a considerable proportion of my own fortune to support things in which I believe, and I might just as well have picked up more money for good causes from people who believed in nothing. Is that just the cynical judgment of later life? Should the older self salute the idealism of the younger self? Or should the younger self salute the wisdom of the older self? These are age-long questions which can only be determined by fusing the fiery resolve of idealistic youth and the cool, calm judgment brought by the years, into the tempered steel of maturity.

The studies and pleasures of Florida were curtailed by the arrival of F. D. Roosevelt in his boat, and the journey along the Keys began. The objects were fishing and talking. In the sport we met once more the savage barracuda, which was caught on the line as in trolling for salmon. His bite was severe and you had to watch his teeth during the landing. The best fun was going fast in a motor-boat over the shallow lagoons to get the sting-ray It would lie flat on the bottom, easily visible, and the business was to get the harpoon into it and to pass on at speed before the sting tail came lashing over to retaliate; thereafter you slowly exhausted it by playing the cord attached to the harpoon. We used to set bait for shark at night when the boat was at rest. Much commotion would then ensue during dinner, and I would climb down the ladder on the side of the boat to finish the shark with F.D.R.'s revolver, under the lights flashed by the coloured crew. Next day it was impossible to swim near the boat, for many sharks would be attracted by the blood.

F.D.R. himself, on account of his infirmity, only bathed sitting in shallow water off the beach, while we without much difficulty would beat off with wooden oars the relatively harmless little sand-sharks who would come wriggling in to have a look. The sail fishing and tarpon fishing—which were the main sports of Florida—were a more elaborate business which would have taken too much time, and belonged chiefly to another season. We were there for the interest and fun of a trip with F.D.R., for talk and good company.

These fine things we had in full measure, accompanied by all his gaiety in cooking waffles and other American dishes which were novelties to us.

Did I change my first impression of F.D.R. as a result of this journey in daily contact? He was, first and foremost, essentially the politician. It was a paradox that a man from his relatively gentle background should come through the rough-house of current American politics on his way to the top. But that kind of man, once he faces up to it, can be the toughest of the lot, as I had already learnt in the war. In the world of daily political manoeuvre it would be difficult to match him, but he showed no sign of far-reaching ideas, or even of any deep understanding of such matters. A good thing, according to the true politician, for ideas are liable to lose the vote tomorrow afternoon. Yet lack of far vision and consequent failure to find real direction can lead to final disaster. In those high qualities of politics F.D.R. was not comparable to the great Europeans. Still more notably, he lacked the clarity and grasp so often to be found in American businessmen and economists. The attraction of the best minds to business rather than to politics was at that time a menace to America, which now fortunately appears to be diminishing. F.D.R. remained to me just a consummate politician of the short-term variety, animated by genuine liberal principles and considerable emotionalism.

It was impossible not to like Roosevelt as a host, for his charm and evident good nature encompassed his guests. Yet this companionship did not suggest to me that he had the mental equipment or the stature of character requisite in the President of the most powerful country in the world, or in the subsequent arbiter of our European destiny, which he so slightly understood. We parted company on the best of terms, and remained in occasional, friendly correspondence for several years.[1] Our vast differences in a much later period did not arise because it seemed most unlikely that he had the capacity to reach a position where he could do such harm. Yet as we know from experience in our own country, the absence of all effective equipment can be not a detriment but a passport to success in the politics of normal times; they like them like that.

Through this and other friendly encounters—charming companionships with many different Americans—we had at least banished the pessimism expressed by the American ambassador, George Harvey. Cimmie had sat next to him at dinner one night, and extolled the virtues of the English-Speaking Union for bringing Englishmen and Americans together; she was

[1] I still have two letters written from Executive Mansion, Albany, New York, on December 12, 1932, and from the White House on March 27, 1933. In the December letter, written to Cimmie two months after I had launched the fascist movement in October 1932, Mr. Roosevelt refers to 'that fine husband of yours' and sends his 'warmest regards to you both'; an indication that prior to wartime propaganda even liberal opinion did not regard a man holding fascist opinions as necessarily a villain. In the same letter he writes, 'there will still be occasional chances for fishing and I hope we may have a repetition of that jolly trip some time soon'.

The author's American journey early in 1926 was to study American industry and technique. On arrival, he met F. D. Roosevelt in New York, and later accompanied him on a fishing trip off Florida. Mr. Roosevelt became President six years later. Here the author is with Cynthia and F.D.R.

In an American coal mine in 1926.

The Birmingham Rag Market during the General Election of 1931 after the ejection of the assailants and departure of most of the audience. Peter Howard, then captain of the English Rugby team and later the Moral Rearmament leader, is on the platform (fourth from left). Author in centre.

'The private army.' Author and staff in the uniform that, as he said later, 'was a mistake'. Francis-Hawkins is behind him.

A debate between the author and James Maxton at the Friends' Meeting House, Euston Road, in February 1933; Lloyd George is in the chair. This debate resulted in a libel action against the *Star* in which the author was awarded £5,000 damages.

Below left Mussolini and author at a Fascist parade in Rome, 1933. *Below right* Lloyd George teases the author with the Fascist salute as he leaves Churt.

At a Fascist meeting in Limehouse after the banning of the uniform.
Street march through East London.

one of the early moving spirits. 'My dear young lady'—he replied to her ingenuous enthusiasm—'I long ago came to the conclusion that the only hope of Anglo-American friendship is that Englishmen and Americans should never meet.' The dry damper of American wit is an interesting contrast to the dynamic efficiency which is born of their basic optimism.

This is a line of humour particularly American which I always find both entertaining and attractive. For instance, an American friend of the present day for whom I have warm regard and affection, told by Diana that our elder son had been given a grant from an American university for a tour of South America, said drily: 'They will pay anything to get rid of them'. Typical of their fun were the two men in a great hurry coming from opposite sides of the stage. 'How are you?'—'Not quite myself'—'Congratulations!' A line of snappy humour which makes their illustrated journals entertaining.

We returned from the languorous climate of Florida to the stimulus of New York, where I had some more interesting discussions. The effective operation of the Federal Reserve Board was in its early days, but its officials seemed to me among the best brains in America. They appeared to be fully abreast of the thinking of Keynes at that time, and were already wishing to apply such monetary techniques to the American economy. As intellects and executives they were far ahead of anyone I saw in American politics. How much of the background of my economic thinking and subsequent action I owe to them, and how much to Keynes, is difficult to determine in retrospect. At that time, he had published the *Economic Consequences of the Peace*, and his tract on *Monetary Reform* in 1923, but *General Theory* did not come out until much later, in 1936. Yet I had many conversations with Keynes during this period, and he was publishing many articles and reviews; the later excuses of the politicians that they could not have been aware of his thinking in 1929 because *General Theory* only appeared later was in no way valid. They could easily have learnt what they needed to know either by talking to Keynes or to the brilliant R. C. Hawtrey, who was then in the Treasury. They preferred to follow Montagu Norman, who was wont to explain that in economic affairs he followed his nose. I would roughly assess my debt on economic thinking about equally, fifty-fifty to Keynes and to the staff of the Federal Reserve Board in those early days. They already had the idea, but were inhibited from effective action by politicians who knew nothing of the subject, by the prejudice, vanity and archaic opinions which led to 1929.

Another interesting aspect of American life was the private enterprise corporation conducted on a non-profit making basis, which achieved extraordinary results. For instance, the Metropolitan Life Insurance Company of New York at that time had no apparent profit motive whatever. The principal executives were paid large salaries by our standards at that time, the Chief had £30,000 a year and his main assistants had £5,000 a year each, but they had no profit incentive, beyond drawing their salaries, in the success or failure of the concern. Its success was remarkable. Some twelve million policy holders derived extraordinary benefits. They came mostly from the population of the poorest immigrants, and were looked after from the time of their arrival in America until their well-provided funerals. They were even met at the boat and personally accompanied to their destination; thereafter they were cared for with a truly paternal solicitude. An extensive propaganda among them supervised their health and way of life in every detail. 'Swat that fly and clean that saucepan' and many other admonitions were their daily injunctions. Any British Minister of Health would have been sacked at once for wasting public money on such a scale.

Yet the hard dollar results of all this expenditure and effort was remarkable. The mortality line of the immigrants had been above the mortality average, but just before my arrival it had crossed the national average and beome less; the chief executive showed me the point of the transition on his graph with triumph. The result was therefore to spare the Corporation millions of dollars, for the saving of illness payments and deferment of death payments much exceeded the propaganda expenditure. Here was private enterprise achieving results in the most dramatic and beneficent fashion without any regard to profit motive. There was much for the European to learn in America.

Already was apparent a sense of service; *Ich dien* was passing to America. This people, who were supposed to care for nothing but grabbing money quickly, were already producing an élite which desired to serve its fellow men, a tendency which is developing and growing more rapidly now. Europeans may laugh or cry sometimes at their efforts in Asia or Africa, where we had some success for generations, or deplore their intervention, their errors and disasters which we could have avoided. The head may still be weak in those affairs, but the spirit is willing, and it is spirit in the end which counts. In this sphere character is yet more important than intelligence, for intellect can be bought but character cannot. Perhaps it is now partly true to say that America has too much character and too little intellect, but Europeans have too much intellect and too little character. Yet in these circumstances we will not join with Mr. Canning in bringing in the New World to redress the balance of the Old, but rather will summon once more from Europe the character, will and spirit which has been the inspiration of the world and can be again. Then we shall not forget our friends—prominent among whom have been the Americans—and in the great partnership of equals we can do much together.

It is necessary to know Europe, but it is also good to know America. There was a long interval between 1926 and 1964 when I returned there to give a university lecture. It seemed to me that Europe and America were now much closer together. The old sense of the European being centuries older than the American had passed. They were with us together, in a world which had contracted, and obliged this propinquity; their own war and post-war experience had advanced them an age in time. Strange link between these two worlds was a chance meeting in Paris with Mrs. Roosevelt, long after the death of her husband. In the house of a mutual friend we had a long conversation. The deep quarrel of our politics was bridged as memory travelled across the years to that first meeting in New York, when I entered the room where she was alone with F.D.R. and wondered at the mystery of the relationship which at this second meeting I began to understand.

The American journey had completed the period of experience in my early life. I had at this point seen much of the world and its leading personalities. The early impression remains that much goodness exists in mankind; it is stupidity far more than wickedness which is the present trouble of the world. Falstaffs are more common than Machiavellis, the clown is more frequent than the villain, in every continent. There I may leave the acquisition of wide-ranging experience, which makes the complete man only if it is accompanied by the capacity to see and to recognise facts. Then comes the test of action.

12

Parliament and the Labour Party Shaw the Seer

PARLIAMENT is the basis of the British tradition, and most people tell me that I should never have gone beyond Westminster. I give my proposals for reform later, but say now that I owe my whole start in life to the House of Commons, to which I consequently and naturally feel a debt of gratitude. Sir Donald Maclean put the point to me well one night, walking home from Westminster after one of my early speeches: 'There is only one royal road to success in the world: it is through the House of Commons. Nowhere else can an unknown young man challenge all the old men and their cherished beliefs, with the result, if he is good enough, that he rises to the top and at once becomes a national figure.' He was a most experienced parliamentarian, Deputy Speaker, Chairman of Ways and Means, and for a time Leader of the Liberal Party, who was kind and encouraging to me in my early days. It is strange to reflect that this name is remembered not for the distinguished father but for a son at present in Russia; symptomatic perhaps of this period.

Sir Donald was surely right, for if the House of Commons did not exist we should have to invent some other institution for the discovery and promotion of new ideas and new men. In *The Alternative* I suggested a 'proposer, opposer, assessor' procedure, in which new men and new ideas could be tested and brought to the notice of authority and the public. As I have suffered disadvantage in life from suggesting measures which are too far ahead of the time, I am content to leave this necessity of the scientific future to the age in which it belongs, and to rely for the present on the time-honoured method of discovering new talent which Maclean justly recommended.

These survivors of the Asquith tradition all had a lively interest in the promotion of ability, and would at once notice and befriend anyone who came fresh to Parliament and showed any gift for debate. The most conspicuous members of the pre-war Asquith administration in the Parliaments of my time were Lloyd George and Churchill. Others were Sir John Simon, leading lawyer of the age, Sir Alfred Mond, builder of Imperial Chemicals, and Sir Herbert Samuel, statesman and philosopher. I knew the last two less well, but had a high regard for their talents and character. The government of 1914 was reputed by experienced parliamentarians to be the most brilliant administration of the twentieth century. Fools were not suffered gladly, and did not long remain. Asquith, on the other hand, would always seek and promote the young and the able, and would put up with them even when they were a bit of a nuisance; an example was his toleration and encouragement of the young Churchill, who would not have found things so easy in the Conservative or Labour Party. The character and attitude of the leadership in such matters is all important.

Parliament is a judge of talent because it is a microcosm of the nation; every kind of intellectual gift and every attitude to life can there be found. Each great party contains a diversity of character and talent. The Labour Party in my day ranged from Philip Noel-Baker to Jack Jones the member for Silvertown. The former is now a Nobel Prize winner and has probably worked longer and more assiduously for world peace than any man alive. When I first knew him he was associated with Lord Robert Cecil in League of Nations work, long before his entry into Parliament. He was—in a sense incongruously —a famous runner and captain of the British Olympic Games team. I did not know him then, as he was seven years older and his achievements were much earlier than my humbler connection with international sport. According to legend, his diplomatic skill and Quaker patience had experienced the utmost strain of his career when he was called upon to arbitrate in the heavy-weight boxing, because the teeth of South America had happened to meet in the chest of North America. All lesser difficulties of politics and diplomacy his charm and skill surmounted with ease, until at last he was awarded the Nobel Prize. His knowledge of Europe and of foreign affairs in general can multiply by ten anything available to the Labour Party, yet he has only been employed in the lesser offices of state. The Labour Party wastes talent as well as promoting characters quite unsuitable to high office.

Jack Jones was distinguished in another direction, for he brought to an end in the House of Commons the habit of Latin quotation, which he would invariably greet with a stentorian roar: 'That is the winner of the two-thirty'. Sheridan in an earlier epoch had eliminated Greek with the actor's device of reciting gibberish in an apparently Homeric metre to the wisely nodded assent of the country squires, who were too irritated by this outsider's trick to be caught twice. Jack Jones was always at his best on the subject of drink, and followed a rather emotional speech from Walter Guinness with the opening

remark: 'Now that we've blown the froth off the stout . . .' His more scintillating interventions were in *sotto voce* asides which could not reach the
Speaker's ear, as his offer to Lady Astor—who had complained of the adverse
effect of alcohol on the human stomach—that as a life-long consumer he was
ready to put his stomach against the noble lady's any night she liked. His
clash with Sir Douglas Hogg did reach the Speaker's ear in crescendo. The
able and equable figure of the Attorney-General always irritated the member
for Silvertown, who on one occasion persisted in interrupting him from a high
perch beneath the side gallery, until ordered to leave the Chamber. During
his stately exit Mr. Jones paused at each supporting pillar of the gallery to
hurl a fresh insult, with answering roars of 'Order!' Finally, before disappear-
ing through the swing-door with an indignant crash, he delivered himself of
a brief but pointed allocution: ' 'Ogg's yer name and 'ogg yer are, 'ogg, 'ogg,
'ogg—bloody pig'.

I have only seen the House so convulsed on one other occasion, and for a
very different reason. The scene was the presentation of a Private Member's
Bill by Commander Kenworthy, ex-heavy-weight champion of the Navy, of
swarthy countenance and determined aspect. He entered the House of
Commons in the Liberal interest by defeating Lord Eustace Percy at Hull in a
sensational by-election. The House had long been prepared for the dramatic
occasion by the histrionic appearances of the Commander, who displayed a
brassy effrontery on every possible parliamentary opportunity where a noisy
persistence could claim the publicity sometimes denied to eloquence. The
generally risible effect of his orations was enhanced by this monster of virility
having an almost feminine lisp which turned every 'r' into a 'w'. This
peculiarity, coupled with a considerable sense of the dramatic, but none of the
incongruous, produced many happy occasions. Speaking on Africa he
declared: 'Now, Mr. Speaker, you see wising before you this gweat big black
pewil'; and on naval airships, with passion: 'Mr. Speaker, we have had
enough of these gweat gasbags'. Delighted cheers would greet these announce-
ments, but the loudest applause was reserved for his subtler occasions.
Speaking on the miserable lot of some refugees who had been forced to take
to the road he said: 'There they were, Mr. Speaker, carrying with them their
little household gods; yes Sir, holding in their hands their *penes* and *penates*'.
This, of course, brought down a House still versed in the elements of the
classics. His leader, Mr. Asquith, observed later in the debate: 'My honourable friend has illumined our discussion with an appropriate wealth of
classical allusion'.

We were thus well conditioned for the impressive occasion when our
colleague introduced a Private Member's Bill with all the stately ritual of
Parliament. Never before or since have I heard any man receive such an
ovation in the House of Commons. He stood at the bar with stiff dignity until
the Clerk of the Table announced his name and the title of the Bill—

Commander Kenworthy, the Prevention of Animals Performing in Public Bill —then advanced down the floor of the Chamber, bowing correctly with solemn mien at the regulation intervals until he reached the table and handed in his Bill. The House passed into an ecstacy.

As always in life, some are born funny and others mean to be. The Irish fell into the second category. Three brilliant members of the Nationalist Party remained: my old friend T. P. O'Connor, Father of the House; another good friend, Joe Devlin, one of the greatest parliamentary orators I ever heard; and Jerry McVeagh, whose wit was legendary. Before my day was his famous exploit of talking for a quarter of an hour on the Expiring Laws Continuance Bill and being out of order the whole time. He arrived in the Chamber with a large pile of *Hansards* from which he appeared to be reading extracts from past debates on this complicated referential legislation, passing rapidly through various topics. Finally came a learned disquisition on the habits of the peewit in Southern Ireland, which he was really reading from a scientific paper concealed in *Hansard*. At last the Speaker—who had sent messengers for a succession of *Hansards*—rose and said he could find nothing in the Bill or in reference to past occasions concerning the habits of the peewit in Southern Ireland. With a glance at the clock, Jerry McVeagh replied: 'Neither can I, Mr. Speaker, but I've won my bet'; and with a most courteous bow to the Chair he left the Chamber, carrying his load of *Hansards*.

It was Jerry McVeagh too who cried 'The prodigal son and the fatted calf' as Lord Winterton and Sir William Bull approached the table together as tellers in a division. The former was in trouble with the Whips, and the latter carried his success well in front of him. Winterton began as youngest member of the House and ended as its Father. In his early days he was apparently an obstreperous character, then known as Lord Turnour, who succeeded later as Lord Winterton to an Irish peerage which enabled him to remain in the House of Commons. The parliamentary legend ran that during his time as youngest M.P. he was being a nuisance during a speech of Sir Alfred Mond, who sharply replied: 'Silence in the nursery'. Winterton in reference to the well-known fact that the founders of a great British industry were in origin German Jews, shouted back: 'Silence in the ghetto'. A remark which would today for comprehensible reasons entail exclusion from public life, passed with cries of 'Order', and the imperturbable Mond continued. Soon came his revenge. At a Speaker's reception someone was tactless enough to introduce Sir Alfred Mond to Lord Winterton. 'Delighted,' purred Mond in his guttural tones as he extended his hand, 'for one dreadful moment I thought you were that ass Turnour.'

Mond's speech in debating capitalism versus socialism on a motion proposed by Snowden was one of the finest intellectual performances I have heard in the House of Commons. He had the advantage of really understanding Marx, almost unique among the Conservatives, whom he had then joined. It gave him too a pull in exact thinking over Snowden, who was better versed in Robert Owen and the English socialist tradition. Mond could speak with reason and with wit whose effect was enhanced by his peculiar voice and appearance. He would set elaborate traps for his opponents, and prepared one on this occasion. As gifted in intellect as he was deficient in looks, the orator affirmed that socialism was impracticable because of the diversity of human attainments: 'Some are beautiful, others are not'. When the cheers of the irreverent had subsided, he turned to them with an ingratiating leer which anticipated Groucho Marx by several years, and added: 'Some are clever, others are not'. Few men in this period have so combined intellectual, business and political acumen in such high degree; or the capacities of both branches of the Marx talent.

Such was the happy but inconsequent comedy of what MacDonald described in one of his letters which I still retain as 'this dear old place'. The real forces in the Labour Party were outside Parliament, as they are today. It was the great trade union leaders who really ruled; they held the purse strings, and the trade unions' massed membership was the basis of the Labour Party. Their votes settled all issues at party conferences, and secured the election not only of the trade union members of the National Executive but also of the constituency representatives as well. This method of electing Executive members has since been altered and the constituency parties alone elect their members to the National Executive. But I depended in my day on the votes of the trade unions to secure my election to the National Executive, as they outnumbered by an immense majority the vote of the constituency parties on which I could always count after my speaking campaigns throughout the country. My speaking also contributed much to the rank and file support for me within the trade unions, which must have overcome the prejudice of some of the leaders against me in order to secure my election to the National Executive.

My closest companion in the trade union world was A. J. Cook, the miners' leader, an English figure, a true product of England if ever there was one. It was not generally known that he was born the son of an English private soldier in a barracks in York, because he rose to fame through the Miners' Federation in Wales, by the simple process, as he so often told me, of turning up at miners' meetings and denouncing the existing and highly popular leader 'old Mabon' as a crook; his proudest exhibits were the scars on his head caused by the windows through which over a considerable period the miners used to throw him. Will, endurance and at least the partial justice of his complaints triumphed in the end; he was a living symbol of the peculiar process by which alone a reality achieves the final acceptance of the British people.

Arthur Cook was regarded as the most dangerous revolutionary in the country. In reality, he had one of the coolest and best heads among the Labour leaders. His methods, however, suggested the contrary. I got to know him well when we were elected to speak together by the miners at their immense meetings like the Durham Gala, he from the trade union side and I from the political side. On such occasions he appeared as the acme of demagogy. After the long march past of the miners with bands blaring and banners flaunting —which may have first suggested to an errant young man that colourful methods were not so inappropriate to British politics as some supposed—we repaired to a large field below the castle where A.J. put up his classic performances. Sometimes stripped to the waist on a hot August afternoon, he dealt in rhythmic slogans rather than in normal speech. Once, after a little recent trouble between unemployed miners and the police, a few of the familiar helmets appeared peacefully on the edge of the orderly crowd of some 100,000. A.J. started a chant of furious monotony like the beating of tom-toms —'Bloody Bluebottles, Bloody Bluebottles'—and it echoed back from the vast audience like the roar of the sea. No one was any the worse, and two hours later we were sitting calmly with other miners' leaders in the local pub with A. J. Cook discussing economics, of which he had a remarkable grasp. We became firm friends. He died prematurely, probably as a result of kicks on the legs by some cowardly louts who had once attacked him on a railway station. The Labour Party was haunted by such early mortality among their men of real resolution, for both Cook and Wheatley in their maturity might have combined mind and will and acquired an equilibrium which would have made their dynamism effective.

A very different personality was Mr. Ernest Bevin, who later became the favourite of Conservatism and the opponent of Europe. My speaking brought me advantages, but cut both ways, for I always attribute Bevin's life-long antipathy to an occasion when we spoke together at a large meeting of his dockers. He had been much publicised in the Press as the dockers' K.C., and the workers are inclined to be a little suspicious of leaders who are much lauded by their enemies. Also, he had so long been familiar to them that they may have become a little bored with his oratory, robust and trenchant though it was. Possibly for this reason my speech at the meeting got a rousing reception, while his fell rather flat; Mr. Bevin did not like it. We clashed continuously at conferences when he opposed my constructive economic policies of the late twenties and early thirties with the same bovine vehemence which marked his opposition to Britain's entry into Europe when he was Foreign Secretary in the forties. Finally, he continued to register his dislike not only of my policies but of my person by refusing us passports for four years after the war, despite the disapproval of both front benches of an attitude which in principle violated Magna Carta. He could hate; he could do everything but think.

The transport workers under Bevin and the miners under Cook at that time were usually in opposition on the main issues before the party. The third chief of the great triumvirate of trade unions was J. H. Thomas, with whom I was soon to be linked in government. He was always to be found on the side of Bevin rather than of Cook. These three together could have settled almost any issue within the party, but at that time they were rarely agreed. There was of course a large complex of other trade unions with considerable votes at party conferences; I was on good terms with most of the leaders, and together with the miners they could secure my election even if the railwaymen's and transport workers' votes were cast against me. At that time I was one of the few men coming from my background who had intimate contacts in the trade union world, and felt completely at home in the friendship of a number of its leaders.

The Webbs had considerable influence within the trade unions, though Beatrice Webb was always at pains to emphasise that she came from a totally different world. I had a considerable respect for the grand old couple, whose company with its extreme combination of high thinking and low living I used often to enjoy, and I was inclined to agree with G. D. H. Cole that at least the Webbs 'had the courage of their obsolescence'. Sidney Webb was an incongruous figure in the House of Commons, with his benign, academic demeanour and his short legs and goatee beard surmounted by large round shining spectacles. Yet on one occasion a speech of his from the front bench produced a first-rate row. The Tories became bored with an oration which was quite exceptionally tedious, and shouted at him: 'Lie down, nanny!' The Labour benches were at once ablaze with indignation, and it was a little difficult to understand the degree of their fury. Afterwards in the smoking-room, Walter Elliott—who apparently once practised medicine in a district where such points were well understood—explained that if the Conservatives had just shouted 'Sit down, nanny' it would have been accepted as a legitimate mode of address which merely suggested that a man looked like a goat. But to shout 'Lie down, nanny' was to address a man as if he was a goat, and that raised the sensitive question of *status*. Webb himself floated serenely above all untoward incidents, as when he observed, after accepting the seals of office from King George V, that he had heard a noise like a first-class railway carriage.

When he was elevated to the House of Lords with the title of Lord Passfield, his wife continued to be called Mrs. Sidney Webb; she minded about such things. Beatrice Webb was a personality, but entirely subjective in her judgment of men and events, a living caricature of the attitude sometimes described as feminine. She bestowed angels' wings or a tail and horns entirely according to her agreement or disagreement with the views of the person in question. I received both decorations on different occasions. It was Sidney who provided most of the brain and all of the judgment in that combination.

Four other prominent men in the party came from a different world to the normal Labour member. The two Buxtons came as I did from what used to be called the landed interest, but as they were also Quakers, their attitude and conduct differed considerably from the Mosley way of life. Noel Buxton was a tall and distinguished-looking man with a long lugubrious face and a pointed beard; romantic in appearance, like Montagu Norman. His delicacy of demeanour and sentiment was belied by the toughness of his experience; he had travelled far and wide, often in difficult and dangerous conditions, and was a considerable authority on foreign affairs and on the remoter regions of the Commonwealth.

His brother Charles Roden Buxton was another fine character, a really good man who yet remained human. He was always sucking a pipe, but never minded when my youthful impudence rallied him with the remark that this was truly immoral because this excess caused by neurosis could impair his intellect and undermine his physique, while more natural indulgences I could indicate might do him good and he would be inclined to stop when he had had enough. The attitude of the Buxtons in this respect rather resembled that of another dear old governess of the party, Susan Lawrence, also a Quaker. She said to me in the tea-room one day that she had long known that a spectacular financial crash was coming. The gigantic speculator in question had ruined thousands of shareholders, and I could not conceive how Miss Lawrence had been in the know throughout. Observing my surprise, she added that she had heard long since he was living with a mistress; that a love affair should lead inevitably to the robbery of shareholders seemed to me a *non sequitur*.

Charles Trevelyan also came from the background of the landed interest; he was a nephew of Macaulay and closely related to members of one of our most distinguished literary families. With him I formed a much closer friendship and he was my chief, certainly my most intelligent supporter in the Cabinet when it came to the crunch; as Minister of Education he was in a key position. Charles Trevelyan had a long, saturnine face and a fine head. He was very sincere and more forceful than the Buxtons, rather excitable, passionate, and devoted to his causes and his friends.

Arthur Ponsonby had been a page to Queen Victoria and his brother Fritz Ponsonby was a lynchpin of the Edwardian court. More than any other in this circle, Arthur Ponsonby had broken from the Establishment, outraging prevailing sentiment after the First World War with a short book which really changed opinion. He took three stories of German atrocities in that war, the nuns who had their breasts cut off, the children who had their hands hacked off, and the corpses which were boiled down to make soap. With long research he proved that all three stories were completely untrue.

The pendulum then swung very far the other way and nobody in the Labour Party ever believed again any German was anything but an angel, until the socialist leaders in that country, whom they resembled so closely, were swept from the political scene in the early thirties. Prominent among the Germanophiles was the honest and gifted E. D. Morel, who came from a middle-class family and spent his life exposing the injustices of the Versailles Treaty and prophesying the inevitability of an explosion. He was proved right, but by then the fears and prejudices of the Labour Party had stood his argument on its head, and reversed every principle for which the party had ever stood, in their drive toward a second world war for the destruction of their political enemies.

These aristocrats or landed proprietors of the Ponsonby-Trevelyan-Buxton type were a big disappointment to MacDonald, for they took the principles of the Labour Party seriously. He welcomed them all warmly as recruits to the Right who he hoped would give stability as well as respectability to the party; but to his consternation they all at once joined the Left and became the main motive power of progressive ideas and forward policies. They had not left their background, their interests and their friendships for the simple purpose of placing Messrs MacDonald, Snowden and Thomas comfortably and securely in the seats of office. They were determined to do something for the mass of the people whose conditions had moved them to a certain sacrifice, as well as for world peace, to which they were entirely dedicated. It was new-comers more typical of the middle class who proved reliable in support of the Labour Party hierarchy. Foremost among these was Dr. Dalton. The 'Dr.' was much emphasised in the party, for Labour loved a don like the Tories loved a lord.

There are few things more valuable than a first-rate don, e.g. Keynes; there are few things more disastrous than a third-rate don, e.g. Dalton. Both coming from Cambridge, they shared the friendship of Rupert Brooke, who is on record as finding Dalton rather fatiguing. Later in life, Dalton's courting was transferred to the trade union M.P.s, on whose support alone he could rely for his party eminence. Never a man of the first rank in debate, where he was loud of voice but flat of foot, he was a nimble and assiduous worker in the lobbies. He patrolled them continuously, his large wall eyes rolling in search of the trade union quarry round whose shoulders the avuncular arm would be placed with the query, 'How is the family?' It was almost as safe and effective as Disraeli's classic question as leader of the country squires—'How is the old complaint?'—except in the very rare case of a trade union bachelor. He had to lobby hard and I had to speak hard to secure our trade union support, but he was also elected to the National Executive. Like all third-rate dons, he was determined not to un-learn what he had learnt with such pains, and was consequently a model of orthodoxy. The middle layers of the great universities are as well conditioned as Pavlov's dogs. They are submerged in their information, while the first-rate dons move buoyantly on top of it as they survey the world's fresh facts and create new thought. Unhappily, few of this type have so far been attracted to parliamentary life.

Dalton went to the Foreign Office in 1929 as Under-Secretary when

Henderson was Foreign Secretary, after MacDonald's effort to make me Foreign Secretary had failed because Henderson so strongly objected. Kingsley Martin in his life of Laski wrote that 'MacDonald had sent for Laski and talked about the Government—they had argued about the Foreign Office, which MacDonald had first thought of giving to J. H. Thomas and then would have given to Sir Oswald Mosley had not Arthur Henderson stood out to bursting-point'. Henderson always appeared to me genuinely to believe in the Labour Party policy, though in a very woolly fashion. Certainly he held a watching brief for himself as next Prime Minister, if my forward drive were to succeed, and his personal relations with me (except in the Foreign Office dispute, of which I was unaware) were consequently good, because, being too young myself to become Prime Minister, probably in his view I had a chance to reverse the established applecart for his benefit. To give him his due, his main objective was to keep the party together and for this he really worked himself to death. A lay preacher, he was easily moved to moral indignation, and he often had good cause. Soon after joining the party I found him in his office in a state of near apoplexy. 'Look at this,' he groaned, as he handed me some local Tory leaflet which stated that the return of a Labour government would involve the nationalisation of all the women in the country, as they alleged had already happened in Russia. I gathered that this programme was not for the pleasure of Mr. Henderson.

The third main power in the party after MacDonald and Henderson was Snowden, but this was not immediately apparent, as the first impression of power in that quarter was Mrs. Snowden. A tremendous snob, she made a straight line for us when we joined, and soon exposed herself to Maxton's pointed jibe that her sole ambition in life was to occupy the position in society which Lady Cynthia Mosley had recently vacated. She was gradually disappointed in us, but she got on quickly in the outer circles of London society, where no sense of humour is required; some wit is necessary to penetrate further. An official fête was arranged for the Commonwealth at Hampton Court, the Royal Palace I have always most admired. Mrs. Snowden was there as a living advertisement for Commonwealth products in a plenitude of feathered finery. 'Mrs. Snowden,' I said, 'isn't this a lovely house?—after the revolution we must live here together.' She drew herself up coyly, but with loyal determination: 'Oh, Sir Oswald, this palace belongs to the King and Queen'.

It did not take us long to discover that not Mrs. but Mr. Snowden[1] was the real trouble. A truly gritty Yorkshireman, he lived completely in the economics of the previous century, not of Marx or even Owen, but of Adam Smith and Marshall. He said to me quite simply when we were struggling with the haunting problem of unemployment: 'One day Chinamen will wear their shirts

[1] Snowden himself was no snob. It was left to a later Labour Chancellor to combine the economics of Mr. Snowden with the social aspirations of Mrs. Snowden.

an inch or two longer, and then there will be no unemployment in Lancashire'. Events moved faster than changes of fashion in China, and our government is still finding difficulty in persuading Chairman Mao to wear his shirt longer for the benefit of Lancashire.

Snowden's appearance was interesting, because he had an impressive, splendid face, much cleaner cut and more determined than that of MacDonald. He had an intellectual contempt for MacDonald, since within his Gladstonian limits he had a lucid intellect and was a powerful debater. The result was that he could not think why MacDonald was leader instead of him. The reason was possibly an accident in youth which had crippled him, and he could only walk with the aid of two sticks. This did not appear to have embittered him at all, for his ascetic countenance would light up with a smile of extraordinary charm.

In politics he was completely imprisoned in the dichotomy of his type: there is heaven where we want to go, but this is the earth and this is what we have to do; heaven being a vague dream called socialism and the earth being the Treasury view of capitalism in the narrowest sense. It remains a common phenomenon within the Labour Party; the complete division of mind and spirit between some ideal world and the practical thing which has to be done tomorrow. Yet by reason of the precision and clarity of his mind, Snowden in practical affairs was always separated from MacDonald, who by then had become hopelessly woolly. As a result, the relations between them were always bad and this used to worry MacDonald. In expansive mood after dinner one evening he suddenly said: 'All might have been well if I had just thrrown my arrms arround Ethel yearrs ago'. This concept of the way to win a colleague on the distaff side was the only contact I ever observed between MacDonald and the classic world.

Snowden before my arrival had nothing more serious to knock over than the living wage policy of the I.L.P. He did not find this difficult because a minimum wage considerably in excess of prevailing wages in industries competing for world markets could easily be shown to cost us out of those markets, and to produce an instantaneous economic crash. The dilemma of attempting to move towards socialism in one small island entirely dependent on world markets was quickly exposed. My arrival confronted him with a completely new animal in the Labour Party, the pragmatic man. I was interested neither in the I.L.P.'s dreamy vision of a socialist world nor in nineteenth-century capitalism which was breaking down before our eyes. The Birmingham proposals for all their complexities said in effect: let us meet the unemployment problem, which is the crux of the whole matter, here and now; nothing matters immediately except that. We can meet it by a series of measures some of which are socialist while others are not, but which all mean the active, dynamic intervention of the State under government leadership. To Snowden and his advisers in the Treasury this view became anathema. In the living-wage policy he had a dummy to knock down, a pushover for any dialectician, but now he found a serious argument in a sphere of which he was entirely ignorant. He was familiar with Montagu Norman and the Treasury thinking of that time, but the thinking of Keynes, or the comparable thinking of the Federal Reserve Board economists, was a closed book to him. When I won the I.L.P. for the Birmingham policy he had a serious case to answer, and he did not like the author of his trouble, though we always remained in a reasonably polite personal relationship.

Clifford Allen, the Chairman of the I.L.P., also did not care to abrogate the idealistic fabric of policy he had so long and carefully woven in favour of policies which sought results without dogma. He was sincere and clear-headed, but his health had been ruined during his imprisonment as a conscientious objector in the First World War. Essentially the type of *éminence grise*, he worked assiduously behind the scenes and was expert in personal relations. As Chairman of the I.L.P., he was more successful than Maxton in keeping the ebullient and pertinacious Emanuel Shinwell within the bounds of order, when we were fellow-members of the National Administrative Council. Shinwell was then a prickly customer in debate and in the council chamber, but a man of complete integrity who in private life had charm as well as intelligence. I remember with pleasure that he and his wife came to stay at our Denham house with Maxton and other I.L.P. colleagues. Clifford Allen was more priest than king in Pareto's dichotomy of statecraft. He presided with skill over the I.L.P. summer schools which produced serious thinking and discussion, and at the end of the day's debate took tea with grace in the drawing-room of Lady Warwick, surrounded by signed photographs of her royal lover. The grounds of Easton Lodge were then as freely accorded to socialism as her previous favours to Edward VII.

My relations with Clifford Allen were reasonably good, although I was a cuckoo in the nest of his comfortable theories. There was no rivalry between us because he was no platform speaker. Maxton was the only man who then drew comparable audiences, but it was impossible to have any sense of rivalry with someone of such sincerity and deep good nature. I delighted in his company; he always concluded summer schools with his immensely popular rendering of 'The Pirate King', followed by 'I feel, I feel, I feel just like the morning star'. It was sad indeed that the morning star rose and sank in the 'love-ins' of Easton Lodge, as they would now be called; I mean the I.L.P.'s, not King Edward's. The assertive novelties of today seem in some respects merely to underline traditional latin wisdom: 'Plus ça change, plus c'est la même chose'.

There is sadness in this end result of generations of socialist struggle; the pathos of it all after the bright hopes that were excited. So many members of the I.L.P. and the trade unions were such sincere, splendid people, who had sacrificed so much. George Lansbury was an example; 'Dear old George, heart of gold, head of feathers,' as they used to say. He was the member for Poplar and for years a hero to all East London, particularly when he went to jail with his fellow Labour councillors over some municipal dispute. His origins were lower middle class, but he looked like an Old Testament prophet; perhaps a cross between a prophet and a dairy-farmer. As he came rolling in with his mutton-chop whiskers, you would say, here's a man up from the country who has just milked the cows.

When he started speaking the farmer would be transformed into a prophet; he was that blend of the earthy and the visionary which the English rightly love. He was suspicious of me when I first joined the party in 1924, and rather annoyed because the Clydesiders, who were more revolutionary than he was, made such a fuss of me. It was not until we were teamed together on unemployment and he saw that I was really out to get something done that he moved to my side. Then he was magnificent, he backed me throughout and fought like a tiger, almost to the point of resigning with me. At our parting he was practically in tears and said: 'I have been with the party all my life, and this can split the party. I can't go with you, but I'm with you in spirit.'

Lansbury was of course a very emotional man, but he also had a streak of realism. His influence in the party was enormous; so much so that, after the collapse of Labour, when the National Government was formed in 1931, he was for a time made party leader. He had no original ideas, but he would not give way on things he really believed in; even if he did not see clearly he felt strongly, and that is a considerable motive force; faith and clarity are a rare and more powerful combination.

Clement Attlee succeeded Lansbury as leader of the Labour Party, and later became Prime Minister. I never knew him well, although he was offered and accepted my office as Chancellor of the Duchy of Lancaster when I resigned. He certainly made no effective contribution to the solution of the unemployment problem while he held that post, and therefore must be reckoned as content to join a government visibly breaking the pledges on which it was elected. He was apparently employed in assisting MacDonald in other matters. Nevertheless, there was more to him than Churchill's epigram: 'a modest little man, with plenty to be modest about'. He had a clear, incisive and honest mind within the limits of his range, and was apparently a competent chairman of committee in preserving the balance between conflicting forces within the party; a quality which the Labour Party always prefers in its leader either to vision or to dynamism.

Far more important than the politicians in that period were the thinkers and writers, for in that age of failure they were the seers of the future. The clear thought of one age can and should become the action of the next. I met most of the intellectuals and knew some of them well; foremost among them was Bernard Shaw, who entered and influenced my life in the twenties and thirties.

Memories of him stretch from the early meetings in the Mediterranean to the memorable days at Cliveden when he was writing *St. Joan*, and include his encouragement of my break with the Labour Party followed by his last-moment attempt to persuade me not to leave the party.

One summer holiday when I was a young M.P., we used to meet on the sun-swept rocks of Antibes and swim together in the Mediterranean. Cimmie and I stayed at an hotel, and Shaw with a rich man of similar opinions who owned the spacious Château des Enfants, so called because he had adopted over thirty children and brought them up with a truly inspiring combination of socialist and millionaire principles. When the bus stopped at the gate of the Château, the conductor almost invariably observed: '*Ce monsieur a trente enfants*', and the appreciative passengers with almost equal regularity responded: '*Quelle fécondité*'. It was a relaxed atmosphere, but I never put the questions to G.B.S. I would give anything to ask him now. It was probably not so much a matter of inhibitions between generations as immaturity in my own mind; I was not yet ready. At the time of Shaw's centenary I wrote an essay about his study of Wagner in which I said how much I wished that in youth I had asked him all the questions I would like to ask him now. When we met beside the Mediterranean I had just read his book on Wagner, which then, as now, impressed me in range and suggestive profundity of thought as ranking next to his *Methuselah*. It was a much better chance than previous, more formal occasions with the Webbs, or in his flat at the Adelphi, or later at Cliveden. How often men entering the door of life must have passed old men leaving, and have afterwards regretted they were not yet ready to talk with them.

At Cliveden he read to us each evening what he had written during the day, and answered our admiration with the engaging deprecation that he was only acting as a reporter; he had been studying the trial of St. Joan and was simply recording what she had actually said. Shaw's strange relations with the Cliveden hostess, Lady Astor, can perhaps only be explained by a paradox, for she was rather like one of those impossible women in some of his plays who obviously never existed in real life. He wrote much about women, only to demonstrate that it was the one subject he knew absolutely nothing about, and even the best efforts of Mrs. Patrick Campbell could hardly bring them to life.

Where Shaw was supreme was in his understanding of the great men of action and in his adumbration of what men might one day become. It was this which first fascinated me in him. It was not that he was himself a man of action, for he lacked that decisive character; though in his early days of advocating an unpopular socialism in the rough house of Trafalgar Square he had more contact with action than any other intellectual of his time and faced up to it manfully. Yet he understood men of action—very different from himself because they were in some respects as cold and ruthless as he was kind, warm and human—by some extraordinary intuitive process, and was able to present them in moments of decision in an almost photographic likeness which can sometimes reveal more than all the tomes written about them; his mind was like the sensitive lens of a first-rate camera.

Toward men engaged in great affairs he had three distinct attitudes; a complete contempt for contemporary politicians, of whom he had much experience, which emerges in his plays through the caricatures almost amounting to burlesque; a realisation that a far higher type had already appeared on the human stage, far more capable of effective action but doomed to be surpassed because of the ruthlessness of their natures, which was possibly a contemporary necessity; and a concept of a future man combining the capacity for government with wisdom and compassion. The first type is seen in Burge-Lubin and all the other parodies of politicians; the second appears in *Caesar and Cleopatra* and in his profound observations on the character of Caesar in his work on Wagner, also in his short but incisive sketch of Bonaparte in *The Man of Destiny*; the third is revealed in shadowy outline through the 'ancients' of his *Methuselah*, 'as far as thought can see'.

His conscious derivations from the history and philosophy of the last century are clear, and he added much to them. It is less clear how conscious was his derivation from the whole sequence of this European thinking which stems from Heraclitus even more than from Plato, but his erudition was wide and deep. He realised the essential truth that nothing conceived by man can be entirely original when he said that he could see farther than Shakespeare because he was standing on Shakespeare's shoulders. Rosebery grasped something of the same fact when he remarked that an entirely original speech would be understood by no one. Shaw derived but also added, and will more and more be regarded as a considerable creative thinker.

What Shaw desired for the world was the adult mind, and how right he was. Are not many of mankind's troubles simply due to the behaviour of spoilt brats? His cure for this bother in *Methuselah* was to live longer, until we can grow up. As this is not yet attainable, we must rely on the slower processes of evolution, and meantime must make do with a study of the highest types which have yet existed with a view to finding or producing more of them. For this purpose he turned primarily to the character of Julius Caesar, because he was attracted by the combination of an extraordinary capacity for thought and action with qualities conspicuously humane by the standards of that epoch. In his admiration of Caesar he went so far as to say that if there were now enough of men like him on earth, 'all our political, moral and ecclesiastic institutions would vanish to make way for a higher order'.

This theme interested me, for if we desire to practise any art we should study its leading exponents. If a man wants to play tennis well, he should go to Wimbledon and watch the style of the contemporary champion. If he enters politics, he should read history and study the form of the great masters of action. For this purpose Julius Caesar had always seemed to me the supreme example. In my early days in politics I thought of writing about him, but was put off by one of the foolish inhibitions of youth which fears to appear pretentious; so I continued these studies in silence and once again saluted Shaw.

There were several remarkable writers at this time, but—outside the professional philosophers and scientific writers who much influenced me—none of those who could be described as artists or thinkers seemed to me the equal of Shaw in their insight or capacity for creative thought. He was essentially a thinker, and most of the others were story-tellers or translators; what the French call *vulgarisateurs*: those who translate into relatively simple language the abstruse thoughts of more distinguished thinkers.

Among the writers I then met was Lytton Strachey, whose delightful style to my taste was at its best in his essay on Racine. My acquaintance with him was slight and my most vivid memory remains an occasion when we were both invited to a wine-tasting party. He greeted me with the words: 'Thank goodness you have arrived, I was convinced that I had been lured here to be murdered'. He had been the first arrival at the given address, which turned out to be an underground cellar hung with duelling swords. His high voice emerging from his strange appearance must have startled the tribunal which interrogated him on his conscientious objection to the First World War with the question: 'What would you do if you saw a Prussian officer raping your sister?' only to be met with the alleged reply: 'I should try to come between them'. I prefer this version which I heard long ago, to another account of the same incident in a recent biography.

Aldous Huxley sitting on his shoulders, like some of the Cecils, is another recollection of that period. It has been said, in France even more than in England, that I was one of the characters in *Point Counter Point*, but in fact he only knew me slightly and the characterisation, if it exists, related entirely to my public appearances, which he had apparently studied to some extent. I suffered a good deal in this period from appearance in novels which ascribed to me in private life the qualities which had been observed solely from my performances in public life. My passion on the platform was all too easily transmuted to most private occasions in the bright imagining of these artists who had only seen me in contact with crowds.

Wyndham Lewis, Roy Campbell and others who were supposed, sometimes incorrectly, to represent my point of view in literature, I got to know at a later stage. Wyndham Lewis used to come to see me in most conspiratorial fashion, at dead of night with his coat collar turned up. He suggested that he was in fear of assassination, but the unkind said he was avoiding his creditors. I found him agreeable but touchy. He showed me one day two drawings, of Stafford Cripps and of myself, and was displeased when I commented: 'The governess and the gorilla'. Apparently it was fatal to befriend him, for his savage satire,

The Apes of God, was full of characters who were mutual friends and who I knew had done him some kindness.

Roy Campbell was an altogether more robust character, full of he-man postures, bronco-busting and similar exploits; a type which I usually rather suspect, but much in him was genuine. These gifted men will undoubtedly get the recognition they deserve when their opinions cease to be unpopular. How contemptible it is to denounce any work of art on account of the artist's political beliefs, and how often has history held up the mirror of ridicule to the perpetrators of this philistine absurdity. Ezra Pound I met when I was just forty, and found him exactly the opposite of what I expected from the abstruse genius of his poetry, which has so enthralled the younger generation of the present period. He appeared as a vivacious, bustling and practical person, making the shrewd observation that Englishmen of my class never grew up until they were forty. I never met D. H. Lawrence, who is sometimes said to have an occasional affinity in his writing with my political action. Neither did I meet nor have any communication with T. E. Lawrence, despite many later rumours to the contrary. Two distinguished writers, my great friend Henry Williamson and another friend Richard Aldington, took diametrically opposed views of this enigmatic character. I do not really feel qualified to express an opinion as I knew nothing of him apart from reading the *Seven Pillars of Wisdom*.

H. G. Wells seemed to me essentially a translator of science to a large public, a story-teller rather than a thinker, but some of his stories reveal a sense of beauty which was not evident in meeting him, except possibly in his curiously veiled eyes. We missed each other in discussion, as at our first meeting we joined in playing his childish but most enjoyable ball game in his house near Easton Lodge, and on the second I was engaged in the equally youthful but necessary occupation of listening to marching songs for the new movement. Chance, or our obstinacy in our oddities, deprived us of any intellectual contact. I did not seek to go further with him because from my information on his previous interventions in politics he appeared as a colleague to be as full of complexes as a hedgehog of prickles. He detested other literary figures like Shaw whom I admired, and anyone who physically was an entirely different type to himself; some hefty lad in the local rugger fifteen must have lifted one of his lady-friends during his shop-assistant days in one of the sexual encounters with which he was unduly preoccupied.

Shaw, by contrast, combined the highest flights of intellect with a noble character; he was devoid of all small, mean qualities. If he had a fault, it was the really exaggerated modesty which underlay a public posture of the opposite extreme. He was afraid of being laughed at, and when there was any risk of this, always resolved to get the laugh in first. Great men of action, on the other hand, never mind on occasion being ridiculous; in a sense it is part of their job, and at times they all are. A prophet or an achiever must never mind an occasional absurdity, it is an occupational risk. Even Shaw's warmest admirers must admit that all those defence mechanisms of involved paradox sometimes amounted to sheer silliness, which he sought at all costs to avoid. The origin seems partly timidity and partly—despite his innate kindness and compassion —an underlying contempt for his audience. The man who worshipped the adult mind felt that he must play down to the children. It was both a weakness and an arrogance, for which one of the sources of his thought had already provided a possible justification: 'I love the great despisers, for their souls are the arrows which are yearning for the further shore'.

The same tendency can be seen in Goethe: the concealment of truths for which the world is not ready to protect the prophet from the fury which is the consequence of premature revelation.

> The few, who something therefore really learned,
> Unwisely frank, with hearts that spurned concealing,
> And to the mob laid bare each thought and feeling,
> Have evermore been crucified and burned.[1]

This is certainly intellectual support for the modern school of statesmanship in several countries, which clearly believes that the real objectives should always be concealed from the people. I, on the contrary, still believe that to achieve great ends it is necessary to take the risk of clearly declaring high objectives and facing the storm until finally, with the aid of events, mind and will can persuade the people to attain them. Quite simply, I do not believe that in a great age government by small tricks will work for long, and always maintain that great things can only be done in a great way.

Goethe in the limitations and also in the dangers of his epoch always stopped short before he said too much: for instance, in his poem *Die Geheimnisse*. Shaw never stopped short, but when he saw trouble looming, adopted the defensive attitude of standing on his head and twinkling his toes. The maddening result of this peculiarity was to rob some of the finest passages of English literature, when a giggle was substituted for the last chord of a great orchestra; Shaw then lost his strength and betrayed his genius. I experienced in him this characteristic of always withdrawing before a conclusion when he urged me to break with the Labour Party and to start a new movement. He had even invented a name for it; he suggested we should call our people The Activists. Yet just before the new party was launched, he suddenly insisted that I must remain in the Labour Party, on the grounds that I was bound to succeed MacDonald, who could not last long. Cimmie and I never knew exactly what made him so suddenly and belatedly changed his mind, but it always amused us later to imagine that he went round to see his old friends

---

[1] Discussed by the author in his introduction to the Euphorion edition of *Faust* on Goethe's bi-centenary.

the Webbs in one of his most puckish moods to impart the chuckling information that he had planted a real squib under the Fabian chair, and had met
with a stern rebuke from his grand old schoolmistress, who told him it was
most improper behaviour after a life-time spent in building the Labour Party,
and that he must pick it up at once. Like many other great artists, he could
portray action but he could not participate.

13
Office in MacDonald's
1929 Administration

OPINIONS may vary about the policies for which I was responsible during the decade 1920 to 1930, but it would be difficult to deny that they were a serious attempt to meet the problems of the day. Many of us in that period dedicated ourselves to the cause of doing something for our country and its people at a time when human suffering and national danger alike demanded action. I had entered politics with simple objectives: to prevent any recurrence of the war which had inflicted such losses on my generation, and in place of that senseless destruction to build a fair way of life. I felt with ever increasing force that modern science not only provided the means to give everyone at least a good house and a living wage, but, with competent political direction, steadily to increase the standard of life. After eleven years, experience of politics I had complete confidence in my own capacity to solve any problem confronting the nation; that confidence has not diminished but has grown with the years.

Labour at last had the great opportunity in the victory of 1929,[1] because we could be sure enough of Liberal support at least to deal with the immediate unemployment problem. Here was the chance to do what we had promised after long years of effort.[2] What then was the result of all these exertions, requiring some personal sacrifice in leading an arduous existence of incessant struggle in a storm of abuse instead of the good life we so much enjoyed and

[1] Labour had 287 seats in Parliament, and the Liberals had 59.
[2] I was again elected for Smethwick, the neighbouring constituency to Ladywood, and Cynthia Mosley was returned for another Midlands constituency at Stoke-on-Trent in my native Staffordshire.

for which we had ample means? The answer presents a degree of frivolity and indeed of absurdity which it is difficult to credit. Before I became a Minister I used to say that Bernard Shaw's caricatures of the mind, character and behaviour of politicians were hardly funny because they were too remote from reality. After a year in office I felt inclined to say: Shaw's plays are an understatement.

Pride of place in the riotous burlesque of politics provided by Ramsay MacDonald's second Labour Government must be awarded to J. H. Thomas, but before discussing my relations with him against the general political and parliamentary background, I should describe the means at my disposal, and the men who assisted me in producing the creative ideas which will later be discussed. In 1929 I had the assistance of what was then and still remains the most brilliant executive team in the world, the staff of the British Treasury. Ramsay MacDonald formed his second Labour Government after the election in May, and invited me to become Chancellor of the Duchy of Lancaster, a post which left me free as a Minister virtually without Portfolio to undertake a special task. I became one of four Ministers charged with the unemployment problem, with a room in the Treasury and an official of that department as whole-time secretary. J. H. Thomas was the Minister primarily responsible, and he also had a room in the same building. The other two Ministers, Lansbury and Johnston, were housed elsewhere, as they were responsible for the Office of Works and the Scottish Office.

It must be clear to anyone who is good enough to study it in detail that my short-term policy of meeting the unemployment problem of 1929–30 could only have been produced with the aid of the Civil Service; the long-term policy proposed at the same time is in another category, but again the knowledge and assistance of the Civil Service made an immense contribution. This is not to say by any means that all the Treasury officials were in agreement with these policies, for that would be remote from the truth. It is a tribute to the integrity of the department that its officials work with equal loyalty to a Minister whether they agree with him or not, provided the Minister knows his own mind. That proviso is vital, for if an incompetent Minister in an inept administration wanders into the Treasury or any other department asking—'What do we do next?'—the answer is likely to be a negative, a reply indicating their estimate of the government's capacity. If the Minister defines clearly what he wants to do after listening carefully to everything they have to say, and gives clear instructions, he may count on their entire loyalty in executing government policy even when they completely disagree with it. More often than not most of them disagreed with me, but they always helped me, and I shall always be grateful to them. The same willing assistance came from other departments. I had a task rare to the point of being unique in government administration, having direct access to all the main departments of State and the right personally to consult their Civil Servants on any subject. From this experience I derived a lasting benefit.

My method was to wrestle out practical policy in continual conference with various departments. For this purpose I had little personal assistance, in fact only the Treasury Secretary, Donald Wardley. John Strachey was my Parliamentary Private Secretary and Allan Young remained with me as a private secretary, but as they could not attend the departmental conferences where everything was done, they could not be of much assistance in this work. Donald Wardley, who always accompanied me, was a tower of strength. A splendid character, much decorated for bravery in the First World War, he was always calm, clear-headed and helpful. His personality was charming and his interests were diverse; he was afterwards responsible for Treasury work with the national art treasures.

We were charged with the task of assisting a man who was entirely incapable of understanding the subject, J. H. Thomas. It was impossible to dislike Jimmy, as he required all the world to call him, for he had many endearing qualities. A man was indeed disarming who at a meeting of the railwaymen he had led for so many years could reply to angry shouts of, 'You have sold us, Jimmy,' with the jovial rejoinder: 'Well, I've been trying bloody 'ard, but I'm darned if I can find a buyer'. He was also by no means a fool and proved himself a shrewd negotiator for the railwaymen whom— with the usual reservation of a chance to make money—he served well for most of his working life. Oliver Stanley once remarked to me from his vantage-point in the city that Jimmy was finding it more difficult to move in and out of the market in the 1929–30 period than previously, when he was selling a bear on railway stock before a strike he called or threatened himself; he would no doubt have claimed among his cronies that this was a little perquisite of office which his abilities and services justified.

However, in the 1929 Government the truth was soon obvious; Thomas found himself in a sea of new problems completely out of his depth. It was one thing to manoeuvre skilfully with all his natural cunning in railway negotiations on a set of facts and figures which a lifetime of slowly acquired experience had enabled him to master. It was another to deal rapidly with novel problems and multitudinous difficulties covering the whole area of State and industry in a pressing and menacing situation. An able K.C. would probably have grasped in a weekend the basic facts and figures which were Thomas's armoury in railway negotiations, and he was certainly familiar with them after that progress through life which he once celebrated in the striking phrase: 'To think that I was once a carriage councillor and am now a privy cleaner'. But in the unemployment problem he was faced every day with the necessity of decision on a fresh set of facts whose mastery would have given an able K.C. a hard night's work; and Jimmy's nights were differently occupied. He had a job in which he simply did not know if he was going or coming. All the little tricks of personality and bonhomie availed him no longer—Beatrice Webb used to say he dropped his aitches as carefully as a beautiful woman puts on her make-up—he was really up against the facts of life at last.

Every week he and I used to meet the heads of all departments in the Civil Service to review progress with the unemployment problem. These admirable people listened with patience to the trivial absurdities with which J. H. Thomas sought to mask his complete failure to understand the real subject. They turned down his more grotesque suggestions as gently as possible, but his reverses incensed him and he was continually seeking outside evidence with which to confound them. One morning I went into his room as usual to accompany him to our weekly meeting, and also to try to make him understand a rather complicated point at issue between me and the able chief of one of the ministries which was on the agenda for the meeting. He was sitting at his table with his head on his hands, and, on my entry complained: 'Oh Tom, I've the 'ell of an 'ead this morning'. My ambition to clarify a difficult subject was clearly out of place. After desultory conversation on the bitterness of the morning after the night before, he brightened a little to say that he really was going to show up the Post Office this time—the gentle sarcasms of its gifted chief had sometimes rankled—but the messenger entered to say the meeting was waiting before we got far with the pending exposure.

As the Lord Privy Seal preceded me down the passage I observed with curiosity that he held one hand behind his back and that his coat tails bulged ominously. He entered the room still in the same posture and seated himself with care at the head of the table, only one hand available for the free gesticulation which usually accompanied his eloquence. He said at once that he had a subject of urgency and importance to discuss which must take precedence over the whole agenda; that was good-bye to any hope of a real discussion of the serious subject I had set down. Turning at once to the Post Office he enquired with a minatory glare: 'Did you tell me that box cost fifteen shillings to make?'—and he pointed an accusing finger at the small wooden container on the wall below the telephone, which in those days held its works. The answer was in the affirmative, and at once the mystery was revealed. With a triumphant flourish, out from beneath his coat tails came a precisely similar box which he banged proudly on the table. 'There you are, made of tin, and our boys did it here in Britain; none of your mahogany imported from abroad, and'—he surveyed the table with a roving glance of triumph—'it cost four bob'. We then had some minutes of the best on economy in general and the time-honoured theme of buy British and be proud of it. At the first pause in the flow of his robust oratory, there came a still, small voice from the Post Office: the actual box on the wall cost only three shillings, it is the things inside which cost the other twelve.

Those were the days indeed, with the Post Office usually the object of hot pursuit. Much departmental time was occupied with the Lord Privy Seal's insistence that wooden telegraph poles should be replaced by concrete poles made in Britain. Reams of paper were circulated from the department to prove what a disaster this would be, and the chiefs of the whole Civil Service were regaled for long periods of our precious weekly meeting by the consequent debates. The head of the Post Office at that time added a certain charm of personality to literary gifts which were known in wider circles, and may have derived more amusement from the exercise than the rest of us. His theme in brief was that concrete poles were more expensive and more dangerous. But Jimmy's bulldog qualities were not so easily frustrated. He wrote to a trade union friend in Australia and got the desired reply that telegraph poles in that country were made of concrete. The air at our weekly meeting was once again charged with the pending ministerial triumph, as the letter was read with all the dramatic effect of the parliamentary artist. Then came the rather languid reply: in Australia they must have concrete poles because the white ants immediately eat wooden poles. A long pause was at length interrupted by a pawky voice from the Scottish Office: clearly the only solution for our economic problems is to import the white ant.

The Dominions were more directly involved when Thomas went on a journey of several weeks to Canada with the object of developing export markets. Nothing serious was done, it was just a gas and booze tour, and on his return this was soon revealed in the usual farcical fashion. Industrialists were invited to meet us in solemn conclave to hear all that he had accomplished on their behalf; notably on that of the coal chiefs. They assembled, impressed and gratified that a Minister of the Crown should have spent so much of his time and the public money acting as their commercial traveller, and were rewarded by a resounding oration informing them in general terms that as a result of his protracted exertions the Canadian market was theirs for the asking.

After flowery expressions of gratitude for such an achievement, amounting at first almost to acclamation, some tactless brute of a soldier, who had been a prominent and successful member of the General Staff in the war and had since retired to perform equally valuable service to the coal industry, ventured to raise the delicate question of price, which had not hitherto been discussed. At what price would they have to deliver their coal in the Canadian market which Mr. Thomas had been so good as to obtain for them? The reply was that the Minister had fixed all that and that they would find it was quite all right. Question and evasion continued for some time; and at length the industrialist put his point with military precision. America is not only highly mechanised but has a short haul to Canada, while Britain has a long haul; that is why in straight competition the Americans have always been able to beat us there. Does the Minister mean he has persuaded the Canadians to pay more for their coal in order to buy British? If so, what is the price?—I must insist on an answer. Mr. Thomas in a condition verging on apoplexy shouted: 'That is a most impertinent question'. The gathering dissolved in considerable confusion.

So it continued, 'on and on and up and up' in the MacDonald terminology, without any intervention from that 'indefatigable beast' who was supposed to be conducting the government. I remained on good terms with him and was able sometimes to see him privately with opportunity to inform him, but was then translated straight into a Shavian comedy with the Prime Minister ready to discuss anything under the sun—preferably the gorse at Lossiemouth, which, he would recall with nostalgia, was then in bloom—everything except the relevant subject on which the life of his government depended. The other two Ministers who were supposed to be dealing with unemployment, George Lansbury and Tom Johnston, had even less access to MacDonald, and in any case were usually too occupied with their own departments even to attend our weekly meetings at the Treasury. They appeared to realise quickly that with Thomas we should get nowhere at all, but they always gave me loyal support in my efforts; particularly Lansbury, who was the less busy of the two.

Eventually I saw no more of Thomas than was necessary, and got on with the job of working out, within the departments, what seemed to me the real policy necessary to deal with unemployment. Contact with Thomas merely brought further difficulty and embarrassment. For instance, on one occasion he suddenly asked me to announce in the House of Commons that he had just approved expenditure of £70,000,000 to provide employment. I queried the figure, which had appeared in no discussion and no minute, but was informed it was an urgent instruction to announce it from the Cabinet, which had approved it and required the publicity to ease the parliamentary situation. It was the only time in my life I ever gave to the House of Commons a fact or figure which was not valid, or could even be challenged, and I did not forgive the deception. My relations with Thomas deteriorated.

I summarised my series of proposals for dealing with unemployment in a document which became known as the Mosley Memorandum. It was circulated to Thomas and the Cabinet. If I recollect rightly, I notified him in proper form that I intended to do this, but he complained that I should first have discussed it with him. I had done this for the best part of a year without result and the time had come for action; also, I was on strong and legitimate ground. An unfortunate incident then occurred for which I was not responsible, but which gave my enemies a weapon to use against me within the Government. John Strachey took the Memorandum home, and an unauthorised person was reputed to have seen it lying about. The gist of it got into the Press, and Thomas was quick, with some support from Snowden, to accuse me of leaking it. This was a lucky chance for the old gang, of which they took full advantage. They could ride off in high tantrum on an issue of

ministerial propriety and thus avoid all discussion of the real subject in which
their incompetence, indecision and procrastination were to destroy the
Government little more than a year later. MacDonald was always superb in
the injured role of the old queen suffering an attack of lèse majesté, and
Thomas in a dispute on the level of who pinched the beer money in a local
trade union branch was as clever as a monkey getting away with a coconut.
We had a lot of trouble but escaped unscathed, except for poor John, whose
invariable failure to conceal his intellectual contempt had already got him in
badly with the lot of them.

John Strachey was an adumbration of later difficulties between the trade
union side of the labour movement and those who were called intellectuals;
sometimes a misnomer, as the pretention to intellect is often in inverse ratio
to the fact. A real intellectual, of robust constitution and with goodwill in
all human relations, is perfectly capable of acquiring the equipment necessary
to success in a mass movement. He must really like people, and have the
physique to stand the racket of learning to know well a considerable diversity
of human beings. He must be at home everywhere; in every sphere of British
life in those days, and also of European life in these days. In many intellectuals
the fine but delicate motor of the intellect lacks a chassis sufficiently sturdy
to carry it far on the rough road of experience; the machine soon breaks, or
is withdrawn to some quiet garage of the mind. John Strachey had the
necessary robustness of physique and character, but nausea overwhelmed him
when his cold intellectual eye surveyed a familiar spectacle: the Labour leader
engaged in keeping his party together by importing to high office a strange
assortment which was quite unsuited to any place in the government of a
great country. Some of the trade union leaders were among the best practical
minds of the nation, and would be of value to any administration. Yet not
only trade union leaders, but key party figures, were selected by party
exigencies rather than their abilities.

It is part of the fatality of Labour that the leader is always dependent on a
balance of forces which inhibit action. The prisoner leader is an invariable
result of the whole structure, psychology and character of the party.
MacDonald simply could not afford to dispense either with Thomas or
Morrison, who chiefly obstructed action—Thomas because he understood
nothing and Morrison because he was a narrow, rigid, vain little bureaucrat,
devoid of vision and incapable of movement beyond his office stool. As
Minister of Transport he rejected the schemes for national roads which
thirty years later had to be put through in a hurry, with all the difficulty of
such a task in a period of full employment, while at that time they could have
anticipated the coming breakdown of the English road system and have
provided work for the unemployed. There were then thirty different road
surfaces between London and Birmingham—an inconvenient arrangement
even for the stage coaches when these roads were designed—but Morrison

strenuously resisted all proposals for a national road system; he was the man of the local authorities which had nurtured his career. That is why a new generation of young Englishmen spending weekends in their splendid cars have had a better view of the backside of the car leading them in a large, coiling queue than of the glorious countryside of England; even now the national road system I then advocated is far from complete.

No persuasion would make Morrison move as Minister of Transport, and MacDonald had to protect him because he was the party chief and organiser of London, the local Mrs. Fix-it. An excellent adjuster of local disputes within conflicting constituency organisations, he was totally unfitted by natural aptitude or experience for national administration. He had considerable gifts as a propagandist, and in the Second World War made a stirring appeal to the young 'to go to it'—an exercise from which he was unfortunately inhibited in the First World War when young himself—but must then have been as incapable of an executive task as he proved himself earlier at the Ministry of Transport. He was an expert on the parish pump, who was later translated by the domestic exigencies of the Labour Party not only to the highest offices of State but even to the Foreign Office when 'Europe' was in in the making.[1] He was in the Home Office at the time of my release from detention in the war, and is sometimes given credit for that event. I have always understood it was only the heavy pressure of Churchill which obliged him to release me; but Morrison showed a certain courage in facing the communist-led agitation to put me back.

Morrison had a shrewd instinct from his point of view when he wrote to MacDonald rebutting the Mosley Memorandum to the Cabinet: he complained that it would appear to involve such an overlordship of his executive responsibilities that a Minister's life would not have been worth living. He would certainly have shifted uneasily on his well-padded office stool if I had had the power to tell him to get on or get out. No wonder people of that kind resent the entry and action of any dynamic character within the Labour Party. The trouble is that they have the power to obstruct because their removal can bring the party down, and a Labour Prime Minister is consequently not an executive but an equilibrist. His only necessary quality is the capacity to balance on the tight-rope until the whole crazy show falls off.

Worse even than the obstructive bureaucrat is the Thomas type within the party. The Prime Minister is always liable to have imposed on him a drunken clown as a candidate for high office of vital importance to the whole nation. Soon this freak imported to serious affairs by party exigencies will cut his own throat as surely as the piglet venturing to swim in deep water; this was

---

[1] Mr. Morrison crowned his career by presiding over the Foreign Office during the departure of Burgess and Maclean. He was no doubt as unconscious of their activities as his predecessor Mr. Bevin, who ineptly remarked: 'Left can talk to Left'.

the inevitable end of the Thomas case, and in the process much damage was done to the national interest. Yet the Prime Minister in his cage of party interest and sentiment cannot resist without breaking the party, until nature has taken its course and the harm has been done. The reasons inhibiting MacDonald from sacking Thomas were his power in the trade unions and his backing in a strong section of the parliamentary party. MacDonald's own position depended on the Thomas element in the party, and although they were so different in character, they were also united by old and strong bonds of friendship and mutual interest. Why should MacDonald break these ties and risk his position on account of an internal debate on economics, of which he understood all too little? Better to retreat like a cuttle fish behind an ink-screen of indignation about the Memorandum and thus avoid all decision.

Thomas too at almost every weekly meeting had been faced with the painful necessity of giving a decision in a discussion of which he understood nothing. Almost invariably there was a point at issue between me and the brilliant Civil Servant who was his chief assistant, an able but in my view very conservative gentleman. At the end of the debate the adviser would turn to Thomas and say in effect: may we then take it, sir, that your decision is so and so? Thomas then had the choice of playing safe and awarding the palm to the Civil Service, taking a risk and backing the wild man with his Birmingham and I.L.P. ideas, or telling the truth and saying in his vernacular: 'I ain't understood a bloody word'. He always played safe. So did MacDonald, with the inevitable result not only of my resignation but of the ultimate doom of his government. For my part I felt quite simply that if I lent myself any longer to this cynical harlequinade I should be betraying completely the people to whom we had given such solemn pledges to deal with the unemployment problem. I resigned in May 1930, and explained my proposals to deal with unemployment in the House of Commons on May 28.

I was not just the young man in a hurry, as they tried to pretend, or the advocate of 'wild-cat finance', in the phrase of Snowden. My plans were based on the new orthodoxy, of which they understood nothing, and had the backing not only of the dynamic genius of the older generation, Lloyd George—with all the immense authority of his peacetime achievement in office and of his wartime administration—but of the master of the new economic thinking himself, J. Maynard Keynes. As all my papers were destroyed by war action while I was in prison, I have to rely on memory for the writing of these memoirs; happily, however, extensive checking has proved it reliable even in events of many years ago. In the matter of Keynes I am indebted to Robert Skidelsky.[1] He wrote that I sent the Memorandum to Keynes for his comments—I presume this was in order, because he was in a semi-official position and the document had not yet gone to the Cabinet: —Keynes then 'with Mosley's permission, showed it to Hubert Henderson

[1] *Politicians and the Slump* (Macmillan, 1967).

they both agreed "it was a very able document and illuminating" '. Keynes supported me throughout this period, and even later went so far as to say to Harold Nicolson he would have voted for the New Party.[1] My own memories of this brilliant and charming person with the gentle manner and razor-keen intelligence, consist mostly of lunches in his house, sometimes alone and sometimes with the occasion decorated by the exquisite presence of his wife, Lydia Lopokova, of the Russian ballet.

A formidable array stood for action, but it was thwarted by the machines the parties had created over years and still more by the type of men the parties produced. The rank and file of Labour, like the rank and file of the Conservative Party, were the salt of the earth, but it was the nemesis of their complacency in a relatively quiet period that they could only produce leaders capable of misleading them. Bonaparte's jibe that the English are lions led by donkeys has often been true of the Labour and Tory rank and file. Those leaders would have disappeared and the machines would have consented to action or have crumpled if the crisis had become graver, as it did in other countries; but it was only just sufficient in England to break Labour and to install in its place a combination of MacDonald and Baldwin: it was that multiplication of zero by zero which finally produced the great nullity of Britain's present condition.

After Thomas's convivial tour through Canada it was at least clear that he was not going to persuade the main capitalist countries to accept our goods as a favour to Britain, and few things appeared more improbable than the bureaucrats conducting nationalised industries in Whitehall or thereabouts making them more competitive on world markets than they were under private enterprise. In any case, the first hesitant steps in this step-by-step socialism had yet to be taken. Labour was therefore thrown back on its original theory—most remote of all from any reality—of effective action through international socialism. There I had already seen not only in depressing theory but in deadly fact what the prospects were. I had been sent as a representative of the Labour Party to a meeting of the Second International in Brussels some time before we took office.

The fact that some of the other Europeans were of an altogether different order intellectually from the leaders of the Labour Party at that time in no way affected the basic situation that it would at best take centuries to achieve anything through international socialism. The Frenchmen were interesting to meet, Léon Blum, in particular, a highly intelligent Jew; but even in the much stronger position of a French economy, which in comparison with our top-heavy island was relatively self-contained, neither his intellectual attainments nor his international affiliations saved him from short shrift at the hands of the bankers a few years later when he became Prime Minister of France. Vincent Auriol, afterwards President of France, spoke at these

---

[1] See Nicolson, *Diaries*, 1930–39, p. 72.

meetings on finance and economics with singular lucidity. Listening to his exposition, I wondered with youthful and still partly insular curiosity, whether his performance would reinforce Curzon's description to me of a French statesman, stating with irrefutable logic a case which was afterwards invariably disproved by facts. The one thing clear at the Second International was that no action of that august and well-intentioned assembly was going to solve the immediate problem of unemployment in Britain.

This view of the Second International was emphasised by a visit to Berlin in the company of MacDonald shortly before he formed his second Labour Government, early in 1929. We had a discussion with the leaders of the German socialist movement who were affiliated to our party in the Second International, but the concentrated talk in the German fashion soon became too serious for the taste of MacDonald. At length, leaning back from the table with his favourite act of the grand seigneur who was a distinguished patron of the arts, he enquired what the current opinion of Van Gogh was in Berlin. Van Gogh? Van Gogh? ran the puzzled query round the table until someone with a flash of light ejaculated—a painter! Then my favourite character at the meeting, a fine old sweat of a Prussian drill-sergeant, rose to his feet with a click of heels and said: 'We ring up the museum, we enquire'. MacDonald gave up.

So far I had only noted in MacDonald his foolish and ridiculous way of life which wasted the time of the Prime Minister and consequently the time of the nation. The deep element of hysteria in his character only emerged after this European tour. I was then to observe the basic character of these men of double-talking and double-dealing. They were entirely different animals in all things, great and small, to the masters of action whom history has revealed to our judgment. They are unfortunately a recurrent type in our country during periods when the river of history is passing through the quiet and peaceful contemporary scene of Winston Churchill's description: 'so calm that it can even carry on its tranquil bosom the contemptible figures of Baldwin and MacDonald'. The Baldwins and MacDonalds are always present in those circumstances, continually changed and adapted in superficial appearance, with new presentation and make-up to suit the always transient fashion, but in underlying reality they are the same men. They are the 'goody-goodies', the figures of infinite worthiness, the models of public virtue and private decorum. They are the products of the Puritan tradition, and most faithfully they follow the form of that tradition. Limitless has been the damage they have done to England until now the destruction reaches its climax in the inevitable reaction from Puritan repression.

The last direct and notable injury inflicted on the English people by the squalid curse of Puritanism was the Abdication, for which Baldwin was primarily responsible. Now comes the inevitable reaction into the contrary absurdity and possible fatality which it had always invited. A generation on the run from its inhibited past will soon find that even the relief of drugs cannot shelter it from the fact of living. The curse of Puritanism may be lost when England enters Europe and a wider consciousness, where an equilibrium can be found again. Meanwhile, the land so respectable as to reject Edward VIII now presents a hilarious spectacle for the diversion of the sophisticated Europeans; the steady old mare which for generations just dragged the milk-bottles from door to door on the domestic round has suddenly run away with the cart and smashed the lot.

Personally, I am as much against licence as I am against repression; we need a return to the sanity and balance of the main European tradition. To revert to Puritanism would be merely to reverse the medal and in the end to lead back to the present disaster in a cycle of inevitability. I deal with these matters to emphasise the catastrophe of Puritanism, both in primary and secondary result, and to advocate a more rational, European outlook. I write also in order to urge my view that an altogether different kind of man is required for the conduct of great affairs. This type has appeared before on the stage of history, and in lesser degree during our own period in the person of Lloyd George. He and other less important contemporaries were rejected largely on bogus moral values by men who were often themselves humbugs, whited sepulchres in the old biblical phrase, whose private lives sharply contradicted their public standards, with the result that a dual morality, and a consequent anxiety neurosis, produced a hysteria which was a danger to the nation's business. We must guard against a reversion to Puritanism whose denial of nature produced these personal catastrophes as well as the present repulsive orgy of licence, from which happily the mass of the English people are still free, and aim in the future at producing a new kind of man in states-manship, who has been adumbrated in the highest prototypes of the past; men of calm and balanced character, of freedom yet of self-control, of dis-criminating taste rather than of inhibition. This is why I deal briefly with topics which could not be justified entirely by any amusement they may cause, for the jokes are in a sense too tragic and the personal issues involved are too bitter. It is necessary to blow the lid off humbug so that new values and new men may emerge.

I am far from suggesting that the present position of Britain is due to the sexual repression of its Prime Ministers, for A. J. P. Taylor probably under-estimated when he wrote that six relatively recent Prime Ministers had committed adultery. Yet an acute difference between public protestations and private standards, and the consequent habit of humbug, can be an underlying cause of disaster, particularly when accompanied by a way of life which is in conflict with nature itself. Basic character can undoubtedly survive all life's vicissitudes if it be strong enough. Yet weakness of character can be aggravated by experience, just as the weak body further deteriorates in wrong living. Character can best be judged by the way men handle situations of all kinds.

MacDonald's conduct in private affairs was all too similar to his action in public affairs. It is to illustrate this point that I follow briefly this by-way of history.

MacDonald in this sphere was a strange case. He was at that time most handsome, as old men go, with good features, fine hair and a superb voice which was his greatest asset on the platform and in Parliament. Possibly the reason why he became leader rather than the crippled Snowden was that he was so much better looking. F.E. once said to me that in England no man gets far at the bar or in politics unless he is good looking, since the English care about looks. This is not altogether true, I have known some very ugly men who have been a success in politics, but there is something in it and MacDonald owed much to his physical appearance. Allied to these looks was a very sentimental temperament. Many comical tales used to be told about him. A man who journeyed in the lower ranges of the Himalayas with him and lived in the next room of a chalet with a fine view, told us that MacDonald came out in the morning, just before the sun was rising, and throwing wide his arms exclaimed in his rolling Scottish voice: 'The day belongs to the worrld, but the dawn belongs to me'. Such stories made him rather a joke to the younger generation, as they were supported by his obvious vanity and emotional character.

MacDonald was in principle a moral man of Puritan antecedent and instinct; in company with many of his colleagues, he would regard a love affair as a fall from grace rather than a fulfilment of life. Yet strangely enough the wittiest thing he ever said to me indicated a wider view of these matters. An old man, who was a well-known supporter and a large subscriber to the party, became involved in a scandalous divorce case. I said to MacDonald, in the lobby: 'This may do some harm'. 'Not at all,' he replied. 'If the old chap was your age, the public would be indignant because they would know he had enjoyed it; but at his age they know it wouldn't give him much pleasure.' MacDonald must have been thinking of Macaulay's analysis of the puritan opposition to bear-baiting: not on account of the pain it gave to the bear, but of the pleasure it gave to the spectators.

It was not love affairs but his absurd fashion of life which exhausted him. He had a mass of papers to read, people to see all day long and speeches to make, and on top of this he liked to go out to dinner parties; being a great snob, the dinners were usually in circles so remote from the party that the Webbs were shocked. In particular, his delight was to sit up all night talking to Lady Londonderry—grandmother of the present Lord Londonderry—they were surely linked only by her curiosity and his snobbery. She was a woman of character, though not very clever, and had a splendid house in Park Lane, the old Londonderry House which was then the scene of the official Tory receptions; when he spent his evenings in these surroundings the Lossie Loon—as MacDonald sometimes described his young self with nostalgic affection—no doubt felt he had made it at last.

It was observing the conduct of MacDonald at this time which possibly gave me my strongly held opinion that men in office ought to live like athletes, not dine out, go to banquets and dinners, but only see people relevant to business. If an athlete lives like that before a world championship, why should not a Prime Minister live in the same way? Must we English always play at work, and only work at play? It seems to me that statesmen are poor fish if even for the few years at the height of their responsibilities they cannot be serious. Yet they were nearly all frivolous in this way to the last degree, except Lloyd George, who lost little time in his pleasures. As a result, MacDonald was in a state of permanent exhaustion, *non compos mentis* when it came to discussing serious matters. Yet he was not really a stupid man, for Robert Cecil used to tell me that in his early days he made good speeches. Even as Prime Minister he was still capable of making a fair speech after a few days of fresh air and reasonable food and sleep. He could have done his work well enough if he had led a sensible life, but his social existence made a monkey of him and reduced him to a condition approaching imbecility.

What politicians call relaxation is almost always escapism, and there is no escape from supreme responsibility. MacDonald sitting up all night talking to Lady Londonderry, not because he was amorous but because he was a snob and liked idle talk; world leaders at the height of their responsibility losing a day in chasing a ball instead of taking their exercise walking in a wood or a garden and thinking at the same time; statesmen running around public and private dinner parties boozing and gassing until they reach a state of physical and mental exhaustion; the better type in politics seeking diversion by filling the mind with detective stories and rambling Victorian novels as some fill a tired stomach with sweets, instead of resting with eyes covered for the few minutes which can work an almost miraculous physical restoration once the habit is acquired, or reading a classic of enduring beauty which elevates the spirit, or seeking the repose and inspiration of immortal music, now readily available. These may be the real immoralists, guiltier than the men who follow Nature but allow no diversion from life's serious purpose. No one can enjoy life more than I do, few at times have enjoyed it so much, but I repeat that a Prime Minister who cannot be serious, entirely dedicated for the few years of his supreme responsibility, is a poor fish. The capacity to be serious also requires long training, a habit of living designed for such a life. Wanted, the adult mind: Shaw was right.

It was events after our European journey together which finally revealed the deep hysteria of MacDonald's nature. His speech to the Reichstag was the main purpose of our journey and it had a considerable success, for he was living a more reasonable life than usual and getting some rest. Surrounded by plump young Conservative M.P.s, to whom MacDonald talked quite lucidly, I never heard the name of Adolf Hitler, and did not even know the Nazi Party existed in the spring of 1929. The Embassy suggested that we should invite Frau Stresemann, the wife of the German Chancellor, out to dinner. We were informed that she was a lady in the middle fifties, very young for her age and very gay, and were tipped off that it meant a tour of the night resorts of Berlin. MacDonald behaved seriously, because he thought this a less suitable occasion for the coming Prime Minister than an evening spent in Londonderry House, so he detailed us for the job, with the assistance of our old friend Harold Nicolson, who was Counsellor at the Embassy.

Cimmie and I had never seen anything like that night in our lives. In several of the many resorts to which we were taken, the sexes had simply exchanged clothes, make-up and the habits of Nature in crudest form. Scenes of decadence and depravity suggested a nation sunk so deep that it could never rise again. Yet within two or three years men in brown shirts were goose-stepping down these same streets around the Kurfürstendamm. The Germans in some respects are a rather exaggerated people; as Carlyle observed, 'there is a nimiety, a too-muchness' in them. Aldous Huxley added acutely: 'The Germans dive deeper and come up muddier than any other people'. What we then saw in Berlin was of course no more characteristic of the mass of the German people than some excesses in London today are typical of the British people. Yet Apollo and Dionysus are both represented in the vast energy of the German nature, both elements are inherent in the character and a part of its genius. When they fall, the Germans rest like Atlas on the earth, and when the giant rises much depends on what voice is whispering in his ear.

My last memory of that evening in Berlin is of poor Harold dropping to sleep at six o'clock in the morning while vigorous ladies waltzed with red roses behind their ears and roses drooping from their mouths—and not only ladies—until one of those terrible paper balls in use in German night clubs hit our counsellor a blow in the eye severe enough to wake him up, and with fresh access of official zeal he swept us off to bed.

MacDonald did not participate in the festivities of Berlin, but after our return to England suffered some embarrassment from involvement in a romantic relationship which was brought to my notice by others. Most people in the modern world will at least agree that no reason exists in morality or honour why an elderly widower should not have such a liason. I feel that MacDonald himself was quite unconscious of anything in this affair except his personal emotions; he ran true to the form of Puritanism relapsing into hysteria. The poor man was just another illustration of nature's requirement —sung by the poets—that romance belongs to youth rather than to age. If the habit must become life-long, at least experience should be acquired early. Elderly statesmen should either know much about love, or refrain from it. Certainly in a position of high responsibility, time and energy should be conserved for the task alone.

Such stories are really no subject for laughter, because this pathos of the

wreckage of Puritanism has become the tragedy of England today. I do not
desire to tell them, because my only purpose is to draw the lesson, not to
rule out a Lloyd George in favour of either a MacDonald or the immaculate
Baldwin. No doubt one of the main features in the exclusion of Lloyd George
was the dislike of 'the goodies' in the Conservative and Liberal Parties for
his free way of living, though his private life should have been irrelevant to
his public career. His love affairs have been so widely publicised by others
that it can now do him no harm to discuss the subject. My only contact
with this aspect of his nature was when Lloyd George gave a dinner in a
private room in a good and most respectable hotel long since pulled down.
I arrived first and he showed me the list of guests, which not only included
politicians supposed to be at some enmity with each other, but also names
drawn from very different spheres. I said: 'This will lift the roof if it gets
out'. Lloyd George replied with his ineffable dimpling expression: 'My dear
boy, if everything I have done in this hotel during the last forty years had
got out, you have no idea how many times I would have had to retire from
politics'. Entire absence of humbug was part of his charm to the younger
generation; it has been a common feature of the few really great men I have
known.

He said to me once: 'Love is all right, if you lose no time'. I understood it
was always his practice to go straight to the point and to press for a decision
one way or the other. He did not, of course, go so far as Bonaparte in the
celebrated story of a lady arriving to meet him during a Council meeting
which began quietly but became difficult and increasingly engaged his
passionate energy. The A.D.C. is reported to have whispered in his ear,
'Madame est arrivée'; Napoleon, 'Que Madame attende'; A.D.C., 'Madame
attende'; Napoleon, 'Que Madame se déshabille'; A.D.C., 'Madame est
déshabillée'; Napoleon, 'Que Madame se couche'; A.D.C. 'Madame est
couchée'; Napoleon, 'Que Madame s'en aille'. Such methods may save time,
but they scarcely savour the subtler moments of romance.

Some of the great masters of action gave more time to this art, and can
consequently be charged with some loss of time, but their balanced characters
were devoid of hysteria. There is a note of reproach in one phrase of
Mommsen which can be found in his great passage on Julius Caesar
beginning: 'It is not often given to mortals to contemplate perfection'. The
sentence in my translation runs: 'It was not until he had passed the meridian
of his years and the torrent of his passions had subsided that this remarkable
man attained the acme of his powers as the instrument of action and of
destiny'. His experiences in early life certainly gave him more practice in
handling all situations, both delicate and dangerous, than had the less fortunate MacDonald

Modern biography delights to deal in trivial scandal rather than in large
events, and would often do better to discuss the thought and action of the

subject. Yet some of these occasions can illustrate a man's way of handling situations. Caesar's calm character and cool method in all things grave and gay, were well displayed when he was suspected by Cato of being an accomplice of Catiline and of winning time for the approach of the rebel army to Rome by protracting debate in the Senate. When a messenger brought him a note, Cato demanded it should, in modern parlance, be placed on the table, but was met with a refusal. On Cato's further insistence, Caesar threw him the note, observing that he could read it, but no one else could. It was a passionate love letter from Cato's sister, Servilia, mother of Brutus. That is why in the final scene Caesar is credibly reputed to have said: 'Kai su teknon', rather than 'Et tu Brute'; the habit of such Romans was to talk Greek with intimates, in rather the same way as French was used in the circle of Frederick the Great.

There we can observe even in this limited sphere an altogether different kind of man, a type which is certainly more appropriate to a period when action is required. Men in the classic European tradition showed not only a profoundly different attitude to some of the basic facts of life, but an altogether different character in the handling of situations of all kinds. Hysteria was excluded, all was ruled by purpose served by character. We need in England today a return to character with neither the hysteria of repression nor of licence, in harmony with life, nature and purpose reaching ever higher. 'The world is character.'

It is at present too much to hope that we may secure a plenitude of the men in politics of whom Shaw wrote that if enough of them appeared on earth, 'all our political, ecclesiastical and moral institutions would vanish to make way for a higher order'. Yet we might, if not in politics at any rate in art, come nearer to the ideal described in a view of the moral future written in one of Nietzsche's moments of inspiration from which Shaw and some of the best of his contemporaries derived so much:

'The work of such poets—poets that is, whose vision of man is exemplary—would be distinguished by the fact that they appear immune from the glow and blast of the passions. The fatal touch of the wrong note, the pleasure taken in smashing the whole instrument on which the music of humanity has been played, the scornful laughter and the gnashing of teeth, and all that is tragic and comic in the old conventional sense, would be felt in the vicinity of this new art as an awkward, archaic crudeness and a distortion of the image of man. Strength, goodness, gentleness, purity, and that innate and spontaneous sense of measure and balance shown in persons and their actions in a clear sky reflected on faces and events, knowledge and art at one; the mind without arrogance and jealousy, dwelling together with the soul, drawing from the opposites of life the grace of seriousness, not the impatience of conflict: all this would make the background of gold on which to set up the real portrait of man, the picture of his increasing nobleness.'

The knowledge given by modern science can help in choosing men today, and in training them tomorrow. I seemed perhaps too crude, too ambitious, and too fantastic, when I once wrote that mankind with the aid of modern science could now play the midwife to destiny, in accelerating evolution. Yet history and science together can at least point to the kind of men required when action is needed.

For the immediate purpose of realising new values in a failing society, I believe we should look not to Puritanism but rather to the classic Greeks and to our own Elizabethans. There is a real danger that a 'biological revulsion'—in the acute Muggeridge phrase—from the crude disgust which our present situation evokes may lead back to Puritanism, setting in motion another cycle of fatality ending again in decadence. I am at this stage concerned chiefly with economics and practical action, and considerations of ethics and philosophy belong to the conclusion of this book. Meantime, I suggest as a principle adequate to the present question: not back to Puritanism and forward with hysteria; but back to Hellas and forward with science.

14
Resignation
The Fight at Labour
Party Conference

In the emergency of 1929 I was able to combine immediate action with long-term plan, tactics with strategy in military terms. I knew by then quite clearly where I was going, and immediate action could therefore serve ultimate purpose. Years of study, and journeys to examine world-wide conditions had brought this clarity. Yet in government I was met with urgent and menacing facts in which theory availed me little. I had to act, and quickly, yet to retain my sense of direction and final objective.

Any plan of action should deal with the immediate and the ultimate, with present facts and long-term objectives. Particularly in a national emergency, we have to act quickly with any means to hand, sometimes without regard to further considerations. The first need is to live; then we can plan the future.

My resignation speech and the whole policy on which I resigned from the Government in May 1930 were therefore sharply divided between a short-term and a long-term programme. This dichotomy is not always clearly understood. For example, the unemployment proposals which Lloyd George produced with the assistance of Keynes and other economists resembled closely the short-term emergency programme which I produced with the aid of the Civil Service. Yet the long-term programme in the second half of my speech went far beyond anything which Lloyd George or even Keynes were then suggesting. It was not until 1933[1] that Keynes began to approach this position.

---

[1] Keynes wrote two articles on national self-sufficiency in the *New Statesman* on July 8 and 15, 1933; they jettisoned entirely the classic free trade position and in effect were a lucid exposition of the basic economic conclusions I had reached in government. When I wrote to congratulate him, he replied with his customary charm,

Liberal thinkers today begin to recognise a need for new and fundamental measures which Liberal leaders were far from appreciating in 1930. For instance, Mr. Grimond stated recently that in 1930 I possibly understood better than anyone that 'wage regulation and world-wide changes in the pattern of trade undermined the case for a continuing free trade by one country alone'.[1] This indicates a considerable advance in Liberal thinking since that period, and is at least partial recognition of the facts which moved me to produce the second half of my programme, the long-term reconstruction. That the traditional basis of Britain's island trade was gone for ever and that we must seek entry into a wider economic community largely insulated from the chaos of world markets, are facts now generally recognised; they are admitted in Britain's attempt to enter the Common Market. My policy in the thirties was a developed Empire market, and my policy in 1948 was a united Europe, including the Dominions and other European overseas territories. The short and long-term programme in my resignation speech were two entirely different things, but they coincided rather than conflicted because the short-term programme could gain time for long-term reconstruction.

The long-term policies were direct heresy in terms of that period, although my resignation speech secured very wide support. It must therefore have been the short-term programme, the urgent sense that something must be done and that this was a real effort to do it, which evoked the favourable reaction. It was indeed a wide response which cut clean across all parties. There was a real consensus in support of these emergency measures which is shown in the letters and Press support I then received. People do not applaud a speech just for the manner of it; they applaud because they are in agreement with its contents. Few are as capable as Mr. Asquith of appreciating the merits of a performance which entirely contravenes their opinions.

The reception of this speech by Lloyd George, Churchill and other speakers in the subsequent debate is well known, but a selection of letters I received from members of all parties may add something. They have never been published before, though none of them was marked private. They reveal the welcome from all sides of the House to an effort at action after years of drift.

'Your speech was the best I have ever heard in the House, and I imagine must be one of the best of parliamentary performances.'—Brendan Bracken.
'It was much the best speech I have heard in Parliament since the war . . . with L.G.'s assistance you will now put your policy through . . . gratitude from

---

but added that the purpose of the articles was to save the country from me, not to embrace me! Two years before he had told Harold Nicolson he would vote for the New Party, (Nicolson *Diaries*, April 29, 1931), but the start of fascism in 1932 then alarmed him and most of the intellectuals. Yet in 1933 he had definitely abandoned the Liberal position and adopted the basis of our economic thinking.

[1] Review in *The Spectator*, December 15, 1967, of Skidelsky's *Politicians and the Slump* (Macmillan, 1967).

us all . . . it was superbly done. I cannot put into words what I think of its skill and power.'—Philip Noel-Baker.

'The best and most constructive speech I have heard in the House. It was fair and it was splendid.'—Clement Davies.

'It was, I suppose, the greatest parliamentary *tour de force* this generation will hear.'—Robert Boothby.

'A really great parliamentary performance . . . I was enormously impressed by it . . . I don't believe there is anyone else in this House who could have done it.'—Violet Bonham-Carter.

'May a great admirer express his great admiration.'—John Simon.

Finally, the letter which pleased the speaker most came from his mother in the gallery, saying that 'people of all shades of opinion' thought it 'the finest speech heard in the House for twenty years'.

It was possibly this experience which contrasted more strikingly than any other with the later course of my life, and provided the high test postulated by Kipling: 'If you can meet with triumph and disaster, and treat those two imposters just the same', a phrase, like much of the writing of that notable author, verging on the grotesque but containing also in the manner of genius something of a noble truth. Eulogy pelted me with the rose petals of praise like wedding guests a bridegroom, when no one knows what foreboding of future felicity or sorrow time already holds. To present the contrasts which have been the essence of my life it is necessary to show both sides of the medal, the praise and the abuse. During these recent years the view has been mostly of one side, and to give a balanced picture I depart from the usual practice, to which we English rightly adhere, for reasons I gave in Chapter 10; the whole requires an occasional immodesty. Certainly my life was abruptly changed, at least for a happy interval, by the effect of that speech. I had now moved from the left to the centre of British politics, where in underlying though sometimes unrecognised truth I have remained ever since. The sunshine of almost universal approval dispersed for a time the encompassing shadows. As the *Observer* wrote later: 'Men and women went to Mosley because something had to be invented to save society' (October 8, 1961). The centre and even the right looked towards me, as well as all the more realistic and ardent spirits of the Labour Party.

The strength of the support in the Labour Party was soon afterwards openly expressed in the document which came to be known as the Mosley Manifesto; it supported the entire policy and was published in the following July. This manifesto was signed not only by Labour M.P.s like John Strachey and W. J. Brown, who afterwards helped in the formation of the New Party, but also by the miners' leader, Arthur Cook, and by Aneurin Bevan and other influential Labour M.P.s, such as Philips Price.

The general attitude of the Press toward my resignation speech was summarised by the correspondent of the *Daily Herald* in his description of the debate: 'An insistent sense of national emergency breaking down party barriers seemed to sweep over members. . . . Sir Oswald Mosley entered a brilliant defence of his attitude followed by a vigorous and detailed offensive . . . when he sat down there was long and continued cheering from every section in the House. . . . Tory members discussing it with me afterwards seemed almost awed, such was the impression it made on them.' The national Press appeared to my astonished and gratified breakfast regard to be virtually unanimous.

The making of a short-term programme to meet the emergency of unemployment was essentially an administrative matter, and could only be achieved by a Minister in contact with all departments, who could get the facts and put them together into a whole of practical executive action. Theory was only touched at one point, the then novel concept of deficit financing; the rest was the synthesis of all available plans and the drive to execute them in a workable form with the maximum speed and minimum cost. To get the facts is the first test of administrative capacity. My method is to ask continual questions, probing and searching until the necessary data is available. When the evidence is conflicting, let the experts confront each other and argue it out, with the administrator stimulating the debate continually with fresh questions until truth emerges. The first requisites of effective executive action are clarity and precision; clarity in the ascertainment of facts, precision in the recording of the resulting decision.

As a young man and a junior Minister facing the emergency of unemployment, with access to all information but without the authority of the Prime Minister or even of the senior Minister in charge, I had to rely entirely on persuasion and the capacity to get on well with all the people concerned. I was far from being in a position to employ my favourite method of recording to a secretary at an executive conference the decisions taken, requesting anyone present to suggest corrections or raise objections, and then further recording clear responsibility for executive action on each point. This method always seems to me an elementary executive necessity. Very different were the methods necessary in my position as a Minister in the Labour Government; I had to walk warily through a labyrinth of time-consecrated departments, and to deal amiably with many agreeable gentlemen at not much more than the pace they were accustomed to travel, before I could collect my facts and piece them together in the plan of action which I recommended first to the Cabinet and then to the House of Commons.

My short-term programme immediately to put people to work was not in itself particularly original. Work was to be provided for 700,000 to 800,000 by three main measures: an emergency retirement pensions scheme opened places in industry for 280,000, raising the school age accounted for another 150,000, and a further 300,000 were to be found employment in constructive works.

In addition, my resignation speech made a novel suggestion for land drainage and slum clearance by 'a more direct intervention on the part of the State with a view to short-circuiting the local delays' and advocated 'something approaching a mobile labour corps under decent conditions of labour and wages'. So far as I am aware, this was the first time there was any proposal for a national approach to the housing and slum-clearance problems, superseding the slow-moving machinery of local authorities.

While the three main schemes to provide work for 700,000 to 800,000 people were not entirely original, the method and machinery for doing this was in those days not only novel, but a direct challenge to current thought, for it was to be done by loans. Even granting the Keynsian principle of deficit financing, which was then revolutionary, the detailed methods evolved with the aid of the departments had some ingenuity. The annual Exchequer charge incurred was the surprisingly low figure of £10,000,000 a year. Even today it may be quite interesting to study the contrivances for averaging and amortising the costs of the scheme over a period of years and reducing to a minimum the budgetary burden. These schemes rested for their success on a mass of detail which I explained in my resignation speech of an hour and a quarter, and the House was good enough to follow it closely and manifestly to understand.

Why then did the Government not welcome the provision of employment for 700,000 to 800,000 men at the remarkably low annual charge of £10,000,000 to the Exchequer, particularly when the detail of the financing was unchallenged by its spokesmen in debate? The answer is that the loan method, or deficit financing, during a depression, shocked to the very core the financial orthodoxy of this socialist administration; surprising, but a fact. When I asked: 'Is it wrong in days of depression to raise a loan on the revenue of the Road Fund for the provision of an emergency programme which in days of prosperity is repaid by a Sinking Fund from the Road Fund?'—the answer was that Mr. Snowden thought it very wrong indeed; in fact, the suggestion outraged him even more than it would have shocked Mr. Gladstone. The orthodoxy of the period utterly rejected such policies with a background of Keynsian economics, and both front benches were united in this negation. Mr. Churchill, while he was good enough to welcome the method and manner of my exposition, was equally with Mr. Snowden a prisoner of the old economics; they detested each other, but in finance shared the same opinions.

The argument on this crucial matter I stated as follows: 'It must be remembered that to set many men working for a year costs a great deal of money. It costs £1,000,000 to employ 4,000 men at work for a year, and £100,000,000 to employ 400,000 men for a year.[1] Therefore, if you are going to do this work on any large scale, large sums of money will have to be raised by the State or local authorities to carry it out. How is it to be raised, out of revenue or out of loans? £100,000,000 out of revenue! Who will suggest it in

[1] These figures, of course, relate to the value of the £ in 1930.

the present situation? It is 2s. on the Income Tax. It must be raised by loan. If the principle of a big loan is turned down then this kind of work must come to an end. . . . If this loan cannot be raised then unemployment, as an emergency and immediate problem, cannot be dealt with.

'I have no doubt that we shall hear from the right hon. Member for Epping [Mr. Churchill] in answer to this latter part of my case, what he has so often described as the Treasury view: the view that any money loans raised by the Government must be taken from other industrial activities and will put out of employment as many men as are put in employment. How far is that case supported by the present Government?' (I knew, of course, by then that Snowden in this matter completely agreed with Churchill.) 'I should like to have the views of the Chancellor of the Exchequer, for every argument with which I have been met seems to support that case.

'I admit that there is some force in that view in a period of acute deflation. If you are pursuing a deflationary policy, restricting the whole basis of credit, it is difficult to raise large loans for such purposes as this. . . . Given, however, a financial policy of stabilisation, that Treasury point of view cannot hold water. It would mean that every single new enterprise is going to put as many men out of employment as it will employ. That is a complete absurdity if you pursue that argument to its logical conclusion. If it is true, it means that nothing can ever be done by the Government or by Parliament. It means that no Government has any function or any purpose; it is a policy of complete surrender. It has been said rather curiously, in view of the modesty of my programme, that it is the policy of the "red flag". I might reply that what is known as the Treasury view is the policy of the "white flag". It is a policy of surrender, of negation, by which any policy can be frustrated and blocked in this country.'

The argument I advanced would now be almost universally accepted, but it was then rejected by both front benches and opposed by the whole weight of the party machines. The time-lag between the acceptance of new thinking, or even of new facts, is indeed disturbing in an age when facts continue to move so much faster than the minds of men.

I clinched this argument with a reference to the Government's faulty method of seeking conversion which included a quotation from the President of the Board of Trade speaking a few days earlier—'During the past fortnight alone £16,000,000 of new capital has been authorised or raised for overseas investment, and so I trust the process will continue'—and commented 'Why? Why is it so right and proper and desirable that capital should go overseas to equip factories to compete against us, to build roads and railways in the Argentine or in Timbuctoo, to provide employment for people in those countries, while it is supposed to shake the whole basis of our financial strength if anyone dares to suggest the raising of money by the Government of this country to provide employment?'

Here we see the beginning of the clash between a producers' and a financiers' policy, between my desire to develop a home market based on the purchasing power of our own people, accompanied by the concentration of our resources for the development of this system, and the traditional view that we should lend money abroad and encourage a swollen export trade for the purpose of building a strong position in international finance. The initial inspiration of this large development of policy certainly goes back to my speech at my first election in 1918 when I used the phrase 'imperial socialism'. It emerged again in 1929 in the developed form of a viable economic area under the general direction of a strong central government.

The key word *insulation* enters the political vocabulary in the following passage: 'I want now to suggest that the policy of controlled imports can and should be extended to other trades, for this reason: that if we are to build up a home market it must be agreed that this nation must to some extent be insulated from the electric shocks of present world conditions. You cannot build a higher civilisation and a standard of life which can absorb the great forces of modern production if you are subject to price fluctuation from the rest of the world which dislocates your industry at every turn, and to the sport of competition from virtually slave conditions in other countries. What prospects have we, except the home market, of absorbing modern production?'

I had already established the premise of this argument in the following passage: 'We must always, of course, export sufficient to buy our essential foodstuffs and raw materials, but we need not export enough to build up a favourable trade balance for foreign investment of £100,000,000 a year, or to pay for the import of so many manufactured luxury articles as today come into the country. We have to get away from the belief that the only criterion of British prosperity is how many goods we can send abroad for foreigners to consume. Whatever may be said for or against the recovery of the swollen export trade that we had before the war, the fact remains that it is most difficult ever to restore that condition again, and facts have to be faced if we are to find any outlet for our present production.'

I was now fairly launched into a long-term programme which took me beyond Keynes and all the thinking of that period. It becomes even clearer at this point of the speech that the whole policy on which I resigned was sharply divided between an *ad hoc* emergency programme to meet the immediate unemployment crisis and a long-term policy to reconstruct the whole basis of our industrial life, changing our economy from a financiers' to a producers' system.

The long-term policy went far beyond the short-term programme, and some way beyond the Birmingham proposals. The only sharp clash between the old thinking and my new thinking in the short-term lay in the concept of deficit financing, and there I had the massive support of Keynes, not only in his theory but as already noted in his personal intervention. The long-term policy on the other hand entered seas which were then completely uncharted, whose tidal force all these years later drives Britain to recognise the basic justice of that economic analysis in seeking entry to the largely insulated area of the Common Market. For to create a system insulated from the world shocks which have rendered increasingly difficult our industrial position and were described in detail for the first time in that speech, it was necessary to discover and develop a viable economic area, and that could only be found either in the Empire or in Europe. When the Empire was lost Europe became the only possibility for Britain to enter a system containing the two necessities : internal planning, and insulation from the disruption of external factors. The dangers which have now arisen and the needs which are now agreed were foreseen and presented in that speech, but they were then denied by the full force of orthodox opinion and obstructed by the full weight of the party machines.

My long-term policy also went beyond the Birmingham proposals, because in essence they were an ingenious method for the management of an expansionary home market in an island economy with the aid of a floating exchange rate, a possibility still relevant in 1968. They added to Labour policy the necessary ingredient of modern monetary thinking—which was entirely lacking—and certain other devices which went beyond Keynes. But in this speech of 1930 I went further, and envisaged an economy insulated from the disruptive world forces; competition of cheap labour supplied by finance with modern rationalised machinery, deliberate dumping below production costs, price fluctuations and collapse of world markets; and also from other countries' exchange manipulations to secure an artificial advantage for their exports of which I had given warning long previously in parliamentary speeches.

The insulation concept led inevitably to the idea first of an Empire and then of an European economy which I developed later in full detail. Imperial socialism then grew up and became adult in a greater sphere. The only possibility of making this idea effective was to develop an area large enough to be viable, containing its own market and with access to sufficient raw materials and foodstuffs.

Two experiences had intervened between the Birmingham proposals in April and August 1925 and my resignation speech in 1930: my American journey, and the information I obtained from the departments in my year of office. In America I had seen the developing industrial processes already described. In the government departments I had been able to examine in practical detail the continually increasing difficulties our export trades were encountering. Consequently, I had reached the conclusion that our traditional trading and financial system, resting on a large export surplus, could not continue indefinitely, and that the day would come when we would find considerable difficulty in selling sufficient exports in open competition on world markets even to pay for the essential foodstuffs and raw materials without which our island economy could not survive. In other words, our present balance of payments problem was bound in the end to arise.

The main theme which I stated in 1930 is now proved true, and is recognised in the attempts of all British parties to enter a larger and considerably insulated economic unit. Mr. Macmillan as Prime Minister stated when speaking in America on foreign trade: 'Your trade is only 7 per cent of your gross national product, whereas ours is 32 per cent of our comparable figures'.[1] The implication of this speech, and of all subsequent speeches and actions by responsible statesmen, is that this disproportion could not indefinitely be maintained. The validity of my main theme is now recognised in all present policies, but was then rejected by all parties. They were united in the belief that we could only solve our problems by still further increasing our export trade to world markets. It is true that since then we have increased our exports in absolute terms by means for which the country has no politicians to thank; but we have not solved our problem because our relative share of world trade has progressively declined to the point where we are confronted with recurrent balance of payments crises.

Our absolute increase in export trade has been achieved by science and industrial technique alone. Only the remarkable diversification of our industries has saved us, and this has been entirely due to scientific discoveries and technological developments. If we had been obliged to rely on the traditional trades of that period we should long since have been insolvent; for instance, the vast dimensions of our cotton and woollen trades have shrunk to the negligible in terms of balance of payments statistics, for precisely the reasons I then gave.

It is one of the most notable facts of the post-war period that the politicians have twice been saved from the results of their egregious errors by the discoveries of the scientists. If it had not been for the diversification of British industry through new inventions and techniques, we should have been bankrupt long ago; if it had not been for the discovery of nuclear fission the triumphant armies of Russian communism would have overrun Europe two decades back. In the most diverse spheres the frenzied politicians have attempted to commit national suicide, but have been pulled out of the morass into which they plunged by the saving hand of science. Completely unabashed, the talkers continue to claim the credit without one word of thanks to the doers, and worse still without even providing them with sufficient funds to prevent the drain to America of brains which have hitherto been the only salvation of Britain.

It may be complacently contended that natural luck and the ability of our scientists and technicians can always assure that fresh discovery arrives at just the right moment, and that consequently the politicians had nothing to worry

---

[1] *The Times*, April 27, 1962. Monsieur Raymond Aron writing in *Le Figaro* on January 4, 1968 stated that America's imports and exports amounted to only 4 per cent of her national production.

about at the time I was analysing the demise of our traditional trades on account of factors then easily observable and since proved to be correct. Yet surely statesmen can only deal with facts as they are, and it is criminal to rest the life of great nations on the arrival of these happy chances. The drunk may argue that if he has missed the lamp-post once on his way home he will always do so, but this cannot be the sober calculation of statesmanship. Britain has hitherto survived by astonishing luck, and it still faces a crisis which in the end can only be met by similar policies in the new context of Europe and of modern science.

When I resigned from the Government, in effect I staked my whole political life on two main issues. The first was that this top-heavy island cannot continue indefinitely to sell so large a proportion of its total production on the open markets of the world; this analysis is now recognised to be true in the search for another market arrangement. The second was that the purchasing power of the Western world could not indefinitely absorb the production of modern science without the devising by government of new economic policies of a totally different order to the ideas then prevailing; this was not only my view, it was stressed by many of the highest paid engineers of American industry, then known as technocrats. The validity of this second analysis was temporarily postponed by Roosevelt doubling the price of gold in the thirties, and by the sequence of armament boom and another world war.

Yet at present the same ominous symptoms begin to reappear, despite the higher purchasing power of the post-war affluent society reinforced by hire purchase. The situation is graver than before, because a large proportion of American production surplus to normal demand has been absorbed by minor wars, by the armament competition of the cold war, and by the related space programme. Temporary prosperity rests on the dangerous abnormalities of hire purchase and the cold war, in the continent on which depends the rest of the Western world under the present system. We approach the time when these grave issues may be put to the final test, but the measures now necessary to meet them are best dealt with later as a whole in a comprehensive study of my post-war thinking.

It may be argued against my position in 1930 and subsequently that my speeches were too alarmist and appeared to suggest a collapse which did not occur. Yet the collapse would already have occurred, but for the intervention of science and the Second World War. Also, in order to awaken a dormant country it may be necessary to speak in strident tones, though I believe it always best, in the long term, to tell the country the plain truth. I know this view separates me entirely from the modern school of statesmanship in more than one country, which believes that you must always tell the people the opposite of the truth, say you are going to the left if you mean to go to the right and vice versa. Yet government by small tricks may be all right in small periods when everything is more or less running itself, but in great periods when great action is necessary some voice must be raised which tells the people the whole truth and rouses in them a will to act, a passion for high achievement; particularly is this true of the British people.

I would plead guilty if at any time I exaggerated the case in order to get the people moving, but on the record it does not seem that I was much to blame on this score. My considered judgment in my resignation speech when I was speaking to my largest audience in Parliament and to the whole nation outside, was contained in the following passage: 'This nation has to be mobilised and rallied for a tremendous effort, and who can do that except the government of the day? If that effort is not made, we may soon come to crisis, to a real crisis. I do not fear that so much, for this reason: that in a crisis this nation is always at its best. This people knows how to handle a crisis, it cools their heads and steels their nerves. What I fear much more than a sudden crisis is a long, slow crumbling through the years until we sink to the level of a Spain, a gradual paralysis beneath which all the vigour and energy of this country will succumb. That is a far more dangerous thing, and far more likely to happen unless some effort is made.'

It is the tragedy of present Britain that in politics this is precisely what has occurred.

There have been a variety of reasons for this disaster to which I then and later drew attention, and will again consider in this book together with remedies for the present situation. We are now engaged with the clash of the thirties between the new economic thinking and the old methods which bear such heavy responsibility for present troubles. It led to a deep rift within the Labour Party between those who regarded the problem in national and those who saw it in international terms. We stood firmly on the ground that it was possible to solve the unemployment problem by purely national action, and our opponents took the traditional view that Britain was entirely dependent on an inflated export trade; on world markets and therefore on international finance. The division between international socialism and imperial socialism —as I called it years before anyone had ever heard of national socialism—was inevitable.

Internationalism and socialism were contradictions in terms. How could we make socialism in one small island, depending entirely on selling goods in open competition on the markets of the capitalist world? Was this to be done by nationalising industries one after another over a long period of time, and having them more effectively conducted by clerks in Whitehall than by the businessmen who had created them? Meantime, these industries were rapidly succumbing on world markets in face of ever-gathering difficulties, while unemployment mounted at home. Were we to wait while the propaganda of the Second International not only captured the great capitalist countries but slowly converted to socialism every dark corner of the earth? As I put it a little later, the most grotesque assumption in the political world was the basic belief of the old socialism that mankind's awkward squad would suddenly and simultaneously fall into line, and march off together in quick step to the millennium at the command of Blum and MacDonald.

It was an illusion which inhibited all effective action, because it meant that the advanced must always wait for the backward. The step of the fastest was automatically reduced to the pace of the slowest, and this psychology was deeply rooted in the Labour Party. If I am thought to be exaggerating to the point of the *reductio ad absurdum*—and it is true this method is sometimes the best to illuminate error—in what other terms can a wide range of phenomena be explained, stretching from the speeches of the quite shrewd and sensible J. H. Thomas, saying that our only salvation lay in our export trade, to the fervent singing of the Internationale at party conferences, whose idle dreams were the only reality of international socialism. It is possible at this point not only to understand the deep differences between nationalism and inter-nationalism in all socialist and progressive movements throughout Europe in the immediately ensuing period, but to discern as well the reasons which are today driving all British parties to abandon their international positions—whether socialist, or capitalist and financial—and to seek entry into a larger and considerably insulated economic unit, whether European or Atlantic. They may choose the European solution and reject the Atlantic as I do, or vice versa, but the one thing on which they all agree is that they cannot remain entirely at the mercy of international forces on world markets.

The reasons for this complete change of opinion are precisely those which I gave over thirty years ago. We are slowly learning not to blame each other but to condemn the system; hence the escape toward Europe by many who were far from loving Europe. We are not only faced with the competition of cheap, sweated labour which developed more slowly than I anticipated—though it was strong enough to ruin the traditional trades of Lancashire and Yorkshire—but far more mobile factors which can be used ruthlessly against us either for political or economic reasons. America, for example, with a margin of 7 per cent of its total production going in export trade, can always afford to undercut us below production costs in foreign markets if its home trade becomes inadequate; a process impossible for us when 32 per cent of our total trade is involved. Russia, with a self-contained communist economy, can always at a certain point decide for political reasons to put a proportion of its output on world markets well below any production costs. All the other factors which I visualised so long ago are still present, such as the collapse of primary producers and of world prices through over-production, and the failure of great combines, with consequent price collapse, which can be even more disastrous now than then. Finally, the cheap labour competition which developed gradually before the war is now accelerating with the entry of lower-wage countries into our traditional markets. The exploitation of the far cheaper African labour for competition on an open world market is now a live possibility when political corruption coincides with a complete absence of any trade union protection for the illiterate and helpless worker.

Stronger than all economic reasons in the conversion of so many inter-nationalists to the insulated continental economy is a psychological factor, which was one of the main themes of my speeches in the thirties; it is more than a psychological question because it goes to the very root of a great people's freedom. The international system of trade places a nation completely at the mercy of international finance, on which that trade rests. My analysis was soon proved correct: MacDonald's government was broken by the financiers in 1931, Léon Blum's government fell in the same way in 1937, and in 1966 Labour with this experience behind it did not wait to be broken; it quietly took over the policy of its opponents at the behest of the financiers in complete reversal of all Labour's principles. After being the creatures of Wall Street in 1931, and the creatures of Zurich in 1966, it began at length to occur to the Labour leaders that European partnership is better than financial servitude. The interval is thirty-five years, but the servitude is the same; it happened for precisely the reasons I gave then and have given ever since.

The last voices raised in the Labour Party against entry into Europe come from those who prefer the Empire now they have lost it; characteristically, they detested the live reality but now love the nostalgic memory. All creative opportunities like the development of Empire in the twenties and thirties were rejected until the real chance was gone; yet now the ghost of the departed is used for the usual purpose of negation and obstruction. In this negative policy they are joined again by those Conservatives who boldly stand for an Empire they have thrown away without noticing the loss. They remind me of a House of Commons debate long ago in which the monolithic figure of Ronald McNeill stood for a traditional Conservative policy in the twenties when all around him had deserted, and I pointed out that if a man stood alone on the battlefield when the whole army had fled, it could either mean that he was the bravest man in the army or just the only one who had not the wit to run with the rest.

I must resist at this point the temptation to be drawn into more modern, controversial subjects, such as my argument in the 1950s that Labour was then behaving in precisely the fashion which Marx had predicted for a failing capitalism. Their only policy was to discard into world markets the pro-duction which their international system did not permit their own people to consume, and their only hope—piously expressed by Labour leaders[1]—was

---

[1] America . . . has still to learn the full duties of a creditor nation. In the nineteenth century Britain was the creditor nation; we recognised our responsibilities in two ways. We kept an open door, in the shape of free trade, to the products of the rest of the world, and we invested capital abroad on a prodigious scale, without always seeking the security that it would be repaid. . . . The most important economic effects of the war were just those which disrupted the economies of Western Europe and made them more dependent on North America, not just for a year or two after the war, but it is now clear, for a generation to come.'—Harold Wilson in a BBC broadcast reprinted in *The Listener*, March 6, 1952.

that America in the twentieth century would take the place of Britain in the nineteenth century as the international moneylender of the financiers' system to which they were completely subject. Now at last certain facts are recognised; so let as many Englishmen as possible go together into an European economy which is insulated but not isolated.

Apart from the issues before the House of Commons and the party which were described in my resignation speech, I should give some account of the methods I and my friends employed to use all the machinery of the Labour Party to secure a change of policy. It was clearly our duty before making any further move to exhaust all possible means of action as loyal members of the party. Therefore, before making my speech in the House of Commons on May 28, I put the issue to the party in the same committee-room where Parnell fought for his political life. It is said that I made an error of judgment in forcing the issue to the vote. On the contrary, I had decided after deep reflection, coldly and deliberately in advance of the meeting, to bring the party to a decision or eventually to leave.

I was not ready to abandon millions of fellow-countrymen to unemployment and near starvation, to further years of suffering, while these comfortable people sat at Westminster in complacent betrayal of the pledges we had given. It was easy enough for them to say—young man wait, why such a hurry?— it was not so easy for people to wait in the slums of Birmingham while we drew our salaries and they drew the dole.

I was determined to have a decision between action and inaction, and if the party refused to take action, I felt it my obligation to seek other means to secure it. This was not a young man's impatience, it was a different concept of public life and duty. No one understands now better than I do the need often to wait and exercise patience in public affairs. I have shown some patience in these long years. It is sometimes necessary to delay in politics, to manoeuvre and to find other paths to arrive at desired objectives. Yet in addition to the ever-present urge of human suffering on a large scale, there was no logical reason at that time why our economy should not have gone quickly to a real collapse.

I said in the House of Commons on September 8, 1931: 'If we take the first seven months of this year and compare them with the first seven months of 1929, we find a 45 per cent drop in exports. . . .' If that process had continued, Britain would have been ruined, and this would have happened, but for the unforeseeable extraneous factors already discussed and to which the action of British government made no contribution whatever. If I had acquiesced in the indefinite delay of action, I should with the knowledge in my possession have been an accomplice to a real betrayal of my country. Britain survived once again by a series of lucky chances—in the long run possibly unlucky, because the deferment of crisis can make it worse—but to rest a policy on these shifting sands is to be a fortune-teller and not a statesman.

It was a situation in which no one who cared for Britain or its people could just sit back and take it quietly. That is why I rejected the appeal of Henderson, and even of my friend Trevelyan and of other good men, not to take the issue to the vote at the party meeting. Their argument was that the party was with me but was not yet prepared to act; I must play for time. Only twenty-nine voted with me. It remained my duty to try everything possible within the Labour Party before making any other move, to give the rank and file as well as the parliamentary party a chance to take action. This meant going to the Party Conference in October 1930.

I have already said that the machinery provided at the Party Conference did not give party workers—the devoted people who do the work in the constituencies and secure the return of Labour M.P.s—any real opportunity to express their will. Each constituency party had one vote at the Conference for every thousand members or less. This meant that one of the big trade unions could out-number the combined vote of the constituency parties, and in practice the trade union vote was in the pocket of a few big bosses. When the vote was taken on the unemployment issue, it was reckoned that the constituency parties voted ten to one in my favour. Yet a single man with the power of Mr. Bevin, who had the Transport Workers' vote in his pocket, could out-vote the lot of them; and he did. A story was in circulation directly after the Conference that A. J. Cook's taxi broke down, with the result that he arrived late and that the miners' vote went against us instead of for us. He was often late, but I was too busy at the time to verify whether it would on this occasion have made all that difference. The facts may be left to any historian interested, but it is certainly the kind of thing which could have happened.

Even so, the result was a fairly close thing: 1,046,000 votes for us and 1,251,000 votes against. The trade unions were divided. Some of their leaders were strongly in favour of action and I was on good terms with them. The trade unions and the constituency parties together sent me back to the National Executive, of which I had been a member for several years, and Thomas was voted out of the Executive. We did not directly clash, because I was on the constituency list and he was on the trade union. Yet it was a fair test of our relative positions, because the trade union vote in those days was decisive on both lists, and I was returned by trade union votes even more than by constituency party votes. It was remarkable, as some of the most powerful trade union leaders, like Bevin, were bitterly against me.

Much more notable, because it was a spontaneous demonstration by the rank and file, free from the control of both party and trade union bosses, was the reception I received from the Conference; it put me in a strong position which a few extracts from contemporary descriptions will illustrate. Fenner Brockway wrote of the reception given by the Conference to my speech: 'The delegates rose *en masse*, cheering for minutes on end. I have never seen or heard such an ovation at a Labour Party conference.' Emanuel Shinwell said: 'I shall never forget the occasion when Mosley was cheered to the echo at a Labour Party conference at Llandudno'. John Scanlon wrote in his book, *The Decline and Fall of the Labour Party*: 'By the time Sir Oswald rose to make his speech . . . the volume of cheering which greeted his rising showed the amazing hold he had acquired on the minds of the delegates. . . . Sir Oswald's vote was the biggest challenge ever delivered to the governing machine. . . .' John Hammond wrote in the *Socialist Leader*: '. . . The cheers echoed round him and he was hailed by wildly excited delegates as Labour's next Prime Minister'.[1]

Why then did I not hold on and play for time, in the confidence that the party would eventually come my way and I could do what was necessary? This course was strongly urged upon me, and I have been much blamed for not taking it. After all the Government was already near to defeat, and a few more votes that afternoon would have meant its reconstruction, probably under Henderson as Prime Minister and with me in ᴗ ᵻrge of economic policy. Was it not then madness not to have a little patien_e and to wait a bit? So ran the argument against me, and it had much force.

I was strongly, perhaps too bitterly conscious of the conditions of the unemployed who had trusted us, and I felt the betrayal of that trust was a dishonour. This admittedly was an emotional reaction and no one is more convinced than I am that emotion should not hold sway in great affairs. You may rightly feel the extreme of human compassion, but you should not allow yourself to be in a condition of nervous excitement when you have to operate. However, there was more to it than that; I had become convinced that the Labour Party was incapable of decisive action.

I had come to the deliberate conclusion that in real crisis Labour would always betray both its principles and the people who had trusted it. The whole structure of the party, the character and psychology formed over years made this inevitable. The Labour Party could not, by reason of its very nature, be the force the British people desperately needed to save them. A year later I was proved right in the first test of this opinion in the conditions of that time. As crisis developed, Labour simply broke and ran. The leaders went over to the enemy and the rank and file dissolved into fragments of discord and dismay. No party in that condition could be trusted by the country for any serious purpose. I felt that in crisis Labour would always crack.

Time may show in the quite near future whether the estimate I then formed of the character of the Labour Party will prove permanently true. It was not that I had a poor opinion of the rank and file of the party; on the contrary, I thought them the salt of the earth. Yet any body of men and women with such leadership and with the long habit of discordant chatter instead of collective

[1] Again I hope the reader will forgive these personal references, for reasons stated in Chapter 10.

action will break into futility in such a test. For many of the trade union leaders and some of my parliamentary colleagues I also had high regard. I simply thought that the leadership had built a party with a structure, character and psychology which was inadequate to great events. The individual character of the leadership over a long term has an enormous effect on the collective character of the party, and in the case of the Labour Party it seemed to me this influence had been fatal. I was deeply convinced that sooner or later a situation would arise in Britain which would require not only new policies but a different order of character and resolution.

The conduct of the Labour Party in the crisis of 1931 was one of the most extraordinary paradoxes known to history, as well as an almost unique record of personal incompetence and political cowardice. I gave my summary of the situation during a speech in Trafalgar Square on September 14, 1931: 'There was an element of farce in the tragedy. Spokesmen of the late Labour Government saw in the crisis that collapse of capitalism which they had prophesied with religious fervour. The crisis came in a lucky moment for them. Labour was in office, and had every resource of the State at its command. What happened? The great day dawned, and Labour resigned; cleared out just when they had the realisation of their greatest wish. What must we think of a Salvation Army which takes to its heels on the Day of Judgment?'

15
Consensus for National Action: 1930 and Today? The Formation of the New Party

ACTION, whether in 1930 or 1968, requires the means to act. I proposed a reform of parliamentary procedure, giving the Government power to act by order, subject to the right of Parliament to dismiss it at any time by vote of censure. This policy I gave in detail to the Select Committee on Procedure and Public Business on June 4, 1931. I had already proposed the reform of the machinery of government outlined in my resignation speech, which has not yet been implemented, and had previously submitted to a conference of Ministers in November 1929 a plan for a small Cabinet of action, as in time of war, assisted by an economic General Staff.[1]

At the time of my resignation I believed that all this could only be done by a national consensus of the most vital elements in the country, and I entered into close relations with Lloyd George and a number of the younger and abler men of all parties. The effort failed then because the degree of crisis was insufficient to secure so great a change; comparative figures of the economic position in Britain and other countries will illustrate the point. Our country never reached the same grave situation as had prevailed elsewhere in Europe.

The economic situation of the 1930s is now recurring, and it will be aggravated rather than ameliorated by the changes science has since brought and by the distortions wars have imposed on the economy of the world. Action of a drastic character will therefore again be required, and it may be of interest to consider not only my long-term policy, but still more the changes in parliamentary procedure and the reform of government machinery necessary to meet the parallel situation, because they remain completely relevant.

[1] Notes on an Economic General Staff, submitted to the Cabinet, November, 1929.

We may also do well to enquire why in 1930 every vital element in political life was frustrated in the attempt to secure action, why the dull lethargy of mediocrity triumphed in the coalition of Baldwin and MacDonald which commanded the Conservative Party machine.

There are only two ways to meet such a situation: a national consensus to secure action—which we first attempted—or a grass-roots movement of the people, which I set out to create when that attempt failed. It is right always to try with the utmost patience to secure action by the gentle, English method of national agreement. More drastic action which bitterly divides the nation should only be undertaken if without it the nation may die. This became necessary in my view in the early thirties because the danger was not apparent enough to secure a national consensus, and yet might at any time have become very grave indeed. What then occurred belongs to the rest of this story. I believe the danger this time will gradually become so apparent that a consensus for national action will be possible for the limited period which will be necessary. Indeed, at a certain point it will be inevitable. All great nations which retain vitality and the will to survive decide to save themselves by one method or another at a certain point.

That is why, for some time before writing this book, I advocated—and still do—a government drawn not only from politics but from business, the trade unions, the universities, the civil service, the fighting services, and other vigorous elements of national life. Since 1948 I have defined the objective as entry into a completely united Europe, and have proposed long-term measures of reconstruction to achieve and follow that entry. I have also suggested short-term measures, if necessary as strenuous as a wartime or siege economy.

No one would be so foolish as to suggest a wartime or siege economy for a permanent basis of British life—it can and should only be the short-term means to the long-term end—or to propose difficult measures if an easier way is available. My contention is that we should have contingency planning for a wartime economy, if all else fails. Even this, of course, will be resisted to the last by those who, over the years, have consistently underrated the seriousness of Britain's position, and have failed to meet any situation in time. Yet the British people would certainly respond to the appeal for a wartime basis of life for a short period in order to achieve great and clearly defined objectives. It should be explained that by this means we could not only live, but could win the position in the world we desire. What, for the time being, we refrained from consuming at home, could if necessary be dumped on world markets with disastrous effects to other economies. We could in the last extremity make ourselves such a nuisance that our reasonable proposals would before long be accepted. We could play the rogue elephant better than most, for the purpose of cleaning up the jungle. We have immense means in our scientists, our technicians, our skilled workers and our productive capacity. All is possible to Britain if the will of our people can be awakened by a government determined to act. The wind and water would be squeezed out of our economy in the process, and subsequent relaxation after this supreme effort could establish a more rational basis of national life.

If you take the steady view—as I now do more than ever—that much more needs to be done, the first essential is the means to do it. I believe the measures I previously suggested for the reform of parliamentary procedure and of the machinery of government are still the best to secure the necessary action by the democratic process in which I believed then and believe now. We shall see later that my deviation in the interval was not so considerable as is sometimes suggested, for throughout I have stood for the principle of regular and free elections to decide and control the life of the government.

There is now much loose talk of 'business government' without any clear definition of what this terms means. I gave a definition in a speech during the thirties: 'The proper relationship of government to Parliament is that of company directors to shareholders—the shareholders should decide broad policy and then give the directors complete freedom to carry it out'. If 'business government' means anything clear and practical, it means government given the power to act by the people's representatives in Parliament, in the same way as a board of directors is given that power by the shareholders, subject to their right to interrogate and if necessary dismiss the directors at a shareholders' meeting. This makes sense, it is precisely what I proposed to the Select Committee in 1931, and propose again today. I suggested that government should have the power to act by order, subject to the right of Parliament to dismiss it by a vote of censure. I would now add that M.P.s should have the right regularly and systematically, though not continually, to interrogate Ministers.

This makes a practical proposition of the term 'business government', which as a vague phrase is no aid to clear thinking. Otherwise, business government can only mean that government should itself conduct the whole country directly, as management conducts a business; namely, universal nationalisation or interference, the last thing the business world wants. The job of government is to make possible the job of industry, not to do it. This bedrock fact must stand out of the spate of nonsense now talked about government and industry.

The main passages of my opening statement before the Select Committee on June 4, 1931, ran as follows: 'These proposals are not advanced in the idle and mischievous desire to assail venerable institutions or time-honoured traditions. They are advanced as the minimum reforms which we believe to be necessary to meet the national emergency which begins to threaten the whole structure of the State. We hold that it is possible to reconcile the requirements of the modern world and of the present crisis with the preservation of popular liberty and the original and proper function of Parliament. This is the objective of our proposals for Parliamentary reconstruction.

'The original and, as we conceive it, the proper function of Parliament was to preserve liberty and to prevent abuse of power by the control of an elected Parliament over the executive. That essential function we propose to retain.

'Under these proposals Parliament would at any time have the power to dismiss the government of the day by vote of censure. While that power is retained, it is absurd to speak of dictatorship. No man or government can be a dictator who is subject always to instant dismissal by a higher authority. At the same time, however, we hold that it is necessary to afford government far wider powers of rapid action than it at present possesses, so long as the Executive retains the confidence of Parliament. In brief, we believe that while a government is entrusted with the task, it should be given a fair chance to do it. To that end we advance the following concrete proposals:

1. *General Powers Bill*

'The first act of a government of action should be the presentation of a General Powers Bill to Parliament. That Bill would confer on the government of the day wide powers of action, by order, in relation to the economic problem. Orders under the Act would be laid on the table of the House for a period of ten parliamentary days. If unchallenged during that period by a substantial body of members, they would have the force of law. If challenged, any orders would be discussed in a brief debate, and a "yes" or "no" decision would be given by Parliament. The House would have the power to accept or to reject an order, but not to amend it.

2. *Government*

'The power of government by order would be vested in an emergency Cabinet of no more than five Ministers, without portfolio, who would be charged with the unemployment and general economic problem. The normal Cabinet would be retained for less frequent meetings in order to ensure proper co-ordination and consultation between the departments of government.

3. *Budget and Supply*

'The main powers of legislation required by modern government would be vested in it under the foregoing proposals by a General Powers Bill. The problem of budget and supply still remains. It is recognised that the power to refuse supply and to reject taxation is one of the oldest of parliamentary rights, and constitutes a considerable power of Parliament over the executive. These rights would be retained by the allocation of supply days as at present, and by the preservation of Parliament's right to discuss and to vote on the details of a Budget.

'The power to abuse the latter right would, however, be removed, and every Budget would be introduced under a strict guillotine procedure.

4. *Argument*

'Argument and further detail in support of these proposals if desired can be advanced verbally before the Committee. It is only necessary here to observe that at most two or three main measures can be passed through Parliament in the course of a Session under the present procedure, and that consequently such procedure must be utterly inadequate to the necessities of an emergency situation. No other proposals have yet been advanced by which that situation can be materially altered. In fact, the view is often expressed that the present delay and check upon legislation and the action of government is in itself desirable. Such opinion differs fundamentally from the view here presented.

'We start from the premise that action is desirable; our opponents start from the premise that action is undesirable. There can be no reconciliation between these two opinions. All who believe that rapid and drastic action by government is necessary must first face the necessity for a fundamental revision of Parliament, whatever their opinions upon the nature of the action to be taken.

'Only those can reject the principle of profound changes in the parliamentary structure who believe that no necessity exists for such action in the present situation. The onus rests upon those who reject those proposals of showing either that alternative and preferable plans for securing rapid action by government can be adduced, or that no necessity for such action exists.'

Reading thirty-six years later the ensuing debate in the Committee, with the impartial eye which is time's gift to the partisan, it seems to me that this policy was unshaken by opposing argument to a quite remarkable degree. Far the ablest contributions came from the Liberal Chairman, Ernest Brown—afterwards well known as a wartime Minister—and his Liberal colleague, Leslie Hore-Belisha, who adduced a ripe Disraelian wisdom in his intimate knowledge of British constitutional traditions. The Conservative and Labour members had changed places in their attitude to me, for the former were relatively friendly and the latter hostile to a point which I found sad, as some of them were old friends; neither evinced the capacity to illuminate in any way our discussion of the subject.

I would today add a suggestion to those proposals which might in any situation be apposite. Any such plan for effective action by government or Parliament is liable to leave the private member with the feeling that he has nothing to do. In the modern situation, I believe a Prime Minister bent on action would be well advised to mobilise the M.P.'s desire for activity in a useful purpose. Why not a committee of all parties attached to each department for a continuous survey of detail? True, a special Minister and some Civil Servants would have to be detached to look after it, and that would cost time and money. Yet they would dig out facts of neglect and inefficiency which would be invaluable to a dynamic Prime Minister in his drive to get things done. Information is invaluable because it is the basis of action. A Prime Minister should not thwart, but should use the M.P.'s desire for activity, it could be a nuisance, but a useful nuisance. He should measure exactly and gradually ration the time given in direct access to himself against the benefit derived, and the consequent concentration of discussion would introduce a new business method and sense of executive urgency. Once again the forces of disruption might be canalised for the purpose of construction.

With this addition I would stand for these proposals today. I believe they would both make the work of Parliament more effective and shorten the time the House must sit wasting Ministers' time in ill-informed discussion. The right to question Ministers, to expose abuse and, if necessary, to dismiss government by vote of censure would be scrupulously preserved. In the long interval, I have formulated a number of more elaborate schemes, though none of these denied the basic democratic right of the people freely to elect and to dismiss their government by their votes. Yet for the practical purposes of getting things done smoothly, efficiently and fairly, in the view of rational men, I now think none were so good as these original proposals. We want something which will work with the minimum of friction, and these proposals for the reform of government and the revision of parliamentary procedure may yet meet the requirement of a period when action becomes a necessity. They were resisted by men who then could not see the first crash of their economic, financial and party system which was then just four months ahead. We had reached the great divide between the old world and the first effort of renaissance.

My struggle in office to secure an adequate machinery of government was continuous. It is now on public record that in 1929 I had advanced proposals for an 'economic general staff'. In my resignation speech a year later I went straight to the point: 'The first issue between the Government and myself arises in the purely administrative sphere of the machinery to be employed in dealing with the problem. I submit to the Committee that, if anyone starts in any business or enterprise, his first consideration must be the creation of a machine by which that business can be conducted; and, when a government comes into power to deal with unemployment, its first business is the creation of an efficient and effective machine. That machine, in my view, does not today exist, and I will say why.' I continued: 'My admiration for the Civil Service has vastly increased since I have been in office. But to achieve a policy of this nature it is absolutely necessary that the whole initiative and drive should rest in the hands of the Government themselves. The machine which I suggested ... was a central organisation armed with an adequate research and economic advisory department on the one hand, linked to an executive machine composed of some twelve higher officials on the other, operating under the direct control of the Prime Minister and the head of the Civil Service himself, and driving out from that central organisation the energy and initiative of the Government through every department which had to deal with the problem.

'It is admittedly a complex organisation. I was told that to carry such an organisation into effect would mean a revolution in the machinery of government. . . . To grapple with this problem it is necessary to have a revolution in the machinery of government. After all, it was done in the War; there were revolutions in the machinery of government one after the other, until the machine was devised and created by which the job could be done. Unless we treat the unemployment problem as a lesser problem, which I believe to be a fallacious view, we have to have a change in the machinery of government by which we can get that central drive and organisation by which alone this problem can be surmounted.'

I returned to this theme throughout the speech. 'These things should be the subject of consideration and research by the most powerful economic machine that the country can devise. That is the point of my request at the beginning of my speech for a Government machine for governmental thinking. We have all done our thinking in our various political parties. Governments, officially at any rate, have never done any thinking. It is very difficult to analyse and get at the facts of the modern situation unless you have at your disposal the information and the research which Government Departments alone can supply. That is why it is so essential to have at the centre of things machinery that can undertake that work. . . .

'There is a case for the Government taking a more effective control of the situation. The first duty of Government is—to govern. The worst thing that can happen to a government is to assume responsibility without control. . . . When you are setting out on an enterprise which means nothing less than the reorganisation of the industrial life of the country, you must have a system. You must, in a word, have a machine, and that machine has not even been created.' In this sphere I tried to stir them into action with the jibe: 'A great scientist said to me only a few months ago, "In the last thirty years the scientific and industrial capacity of the world has increased more than it did in the previous three hundred years", and rather unkindly he went on to add, "The only minds that have not registered that change are those of the politicians" '.

This was, I believe, the first occasion on which a power house for government was suggested. I understand there has been some talk of it again in recent times. According to one newspaper report, the power house began and ended with the addition of one Civil Servant and George Wigg to the Prime Minister's department. I have added in recent times to these proposals the suggestion that an expanded and consolidated Ministry both of Science and of Technology should be constructed, linked directly with the Prime Minister's department suggested in my original proposals. This would implement my long desire that 'statesmen should live and work with scientists as the Medicis lived and worked with artists'. In this way we could secure a continuous dynamic drive to implement the scientific revolution, an old struggle of mine within government and outside since I first clashed with

MacDonald on the National Executive of the Labour Party in an effort to secure adequate funds for science.[1]

My attempt to secure a national consensus after my resignation in 1930 did not extend beyond the House of Commons, because from that House it would have been possible to form not only an adequate but a brilliant administration. There were some absurd and many ineffectual characters in Parliament during the twenties and thirties, but there was also a considerable number of serious and able men drawn from all parties, who sensed the national danger and were in sufficient agreement, at least on the immediate emergency, to work effectively together. We shall see that this combination was not achieved because in Britain at that time the gravity of the economic crisis was never sufficient to break the power of the ruling politicians who commanded the party machines.

The natural instinct is to seek the easy way out in a combination of well-known figures who control the prevailing parties, and only to turn to more drastic measures and dynamic personalities when this fails to work, and it is seen that zero multiplied by zero is zero. In any really serious crisis a still vital and determined people turns to new men and new forms, and once the necessity is plain, no people is more capable of decisive action than the British. That this did not occur in 1931 was in no way due to the leaders of the National Government. Everything they did would, even in the quite short run, have made matters much worse by a system of 'stop'—as it would now be called—so drastic that it would have inhibited any subsequent 'go'.

Four events were responsible in the 1930s for the postponement of economic crisis: the devaluation of the pound in 1931, Roosevelt's doubling of the price of gold in 1934, the armament boom, and the Second World War. The British Government did not mean to devalue the pound, the old lady fell downstairs; she did it again in 1949, and repeated the performance at the end of 1967. For reasons I analysed in some of my earliest parliamentary speeches, the accidental devaluation gave a fillip to our export trade and temporarily reduced unemployment. Roosevelt's doubling of the price of gold was entirely fortuitous to the British Government; it had not even occurred to MacDonald at the world economic conference he called—appropriately—in the Geological Museum of South Kensington, and the liquidity problem was equally remote from the consciousness of Mr. Baldwin; but it had the same effect as the

[1] Before the election of 1929 there was a strenuous debate in the National Executive of the Labour Party concerning a draft I was asked to prepare for the election manifesto, after a draft by MacDonald had been turned down as too woolly. He objected strongly to a proposal I included for a fixed annual sum to be allocated to science for pure research in industry and medicine. He said it was against the principles of the Treasury to allocate money unless they knew exactly in advance what value they were getting for it, and wound up his argument with the query: What are your scientists going to discover? His further objection to the style of my draft, which he described as 'the hectic rattle of machine-gun prose', finally persuaded the executive to request R. H. Tawney to draft a compromise document.

discovery of new goldfields in the nineties—a boom which temporarily floated the world economy off the rocks on which Britain was stuck fast. The effect of Roosevelt's action had worn off by 1938; hence the rise in British unemployment from 1,456,000 in 1937 to 1,700,000 in 1938, a warning to all who believe that purely monetary measures can remedy a real economic crisis. However, the armament boom which preceded the Second World War then took over the care of the shipwrecked mariners who were called British Government, and the final outbreak of war swept both them and their economic troubles away in a maelstrom whose final result the modern world may shortly encounter. These were events unique to that period; a third world war is not now available to solve our economic problems without blowing up the world in the process.

Both the main parties had already proved themselves impotent to deal with the unemployment question, and indeed equally unconscious of the fundamental situation. Labour was then moved by the warmer human feelings, by a true compassion, but was even more fuddled and ineffective in method, and was betrayed by a cynical, arriviste leadership. Conservatism was a little less incompetent, but more coldly selfish in its service of particular rather than of national interests, more indifferent to mass suffering, more stubbornly unimaginative in resistance to new ideas, more dully resentful of dynamic measures and men, more inveterate in the search for mediocrity in leadership; Conservatives could only awake in a situation as desperate as war, which even induced them to accept Churchill, whom they had so long excluded. It seemed to them in the early thirties that the worst of the crisis had passed, and office was beckoning them across the ruins of the Labour Party. 'Danger gleams like sunshine to a brave man's eyes,' said Euripides, and office glitters like a neon light to the Tory eye in opposition, when Labour government fails.

Yet in a real crisis no serious person could for a moment believe that a Tory Government, or a coalition, could do much better than Labour. The basic errors and the end results are both the same. Tories believed in doing nothing —nothing real—and Labour in office was soon scared into the same position. Neither of the old parties could meet such a situation, although their rank and files are patriotic people who according to their beliefs give generous and disinterested service. Some national consensus not only of parties but of the whole people is necessary, in peace as in war, to meet a grave crisis. In 1930 the attempt failed because the sense of danger was insufficient. In 1931 I turned to other methods and measures when a consensus had failed, because I still felt deeply that we must prepare to meet a crisis which could destroy our country's position.

The failure to secure a consensus in 1930 was a tragedy, because nearly all the ablest men in British public life had in varying degree foreseen the coming crisis and the leading figures in all generations had come together. In broad outline they were in two groups, the old and the young. Once again I found myself to some extent the link between two communities. After my resignation speech, most of the young men in the House of Commons who counted for anything expressed to me a large measure of agreement with it. Harold Macmillan[1] was the boldest in that he wrote a letter to *The Times* which much assisted me, and was rebuked for his unorthodoxy by a subsequent letter signed by R. A. Butler and two other young Conservative M.P.s. I did not know Butler at all and he was inconspicuous at that time. Oliver Stanley was closer to me than any other Conservative M.P. and led the discussions with me. Macmillan, if I remember rightly, did not take part in the regular discussions, but met me from time to time, as he recounts in his memoirs.[2] It was always to me a mystery why Eden was so assiduously groomed for leadership by the Conservative Party, as his abilities were much inferior to the abilities of Stanley and Macmillan.

Mr. Anthony Eden had a fine war record, good looks and a generally distinguished appearance. In my early days in Parliament he delivered from the back benches, in the style of a sixth-form boy at the annual prize-giving, dull little set pieces which nobody noticed. Later, he was built up by the whole force of the machine into Conservatism's favourite son of the Baldwin epoch. As Foreign Secretary he was an architect of the division of Europe, and as Prime Minister he was the main opponent of the union of Europe, which he publicly stated he 'felt in his bones' Britain should not join. He owed nearly everything to his photogenic looks, which the Conservative managers may have thought would overcome the initial difficulties of their appeal to the housewife. This picture-postcard of the Tory slot-machine finally became a soggy piece of waste paper in the Suez Canal, after failing completely under the first test of his statesmanship in real action. Mr. Anthony Eden and I had no attraction for each other, and I leave him floating on the smooth waters of the Avon.

Walter Elliott, on the Conservative side, took part frequently in our discussions. He added to an exceptionally good war record and social experience as a doctor a wide erudition and a fascinating capacity for conversation. His power of exposition did not extend so successfully to debate, where he was too diffuse with an argument insufficiently concentrated, often a fault in those who delight others and themselves delight in conversation. Walter Elliott, too, wrote a letter to *The Times* which was helpful to me. Sir Colin Coote notes in his life of Elliott;[3] 'Baldwin was seriously annoyed. He administered what Walter called a "lambasting". A horrified Walter made his peace.' The incident showed just what we were up against in face of the still unshaken power of the party machines, and Macmillan in his memoirs records that similar

---

[1] See *Winds of Change*, Harold Macmillan, Vol. 1 (Macmillan, 1966).
[2] *Ibid*, p. 267.
[3] *A Companion of Honour* (Collins, 1965).

pressure was put on other Conservative M.P.s not to join in my effort to meet the unemployment problem.[1]

Bob Boothby, too, was much in our company. He combined a brilliant capacity for debate with the rare quality at that time of a real understanding of monetary theory and a grip of the Keynesian techniques. It appeared he was never entirely successful in imparting knowledge of these mysteries to his chief during his sojourn at the Treasury as Parliamentary Private Secretary to Chancellor Churchill—not even with the aid of the Treasury official, R. C. Hawtrey, who alone in the sphere of pure theory could encounter Keynes on equal terms—but in these discussions at a later date Boothby was of much assistance to us. When he was subject to concentrated attack I myself was out of action under 18B, but I surmise that the Tory team would have been unable permanently to exclude Boothby's outstanding abilities from high office if an Asquith or a Lloyd George had been his leader. Bob Boothby always was and still is the best of company, immense fun.

Foremost in the talks on the Labour side was Aneurin Bevan, and, of course, John Strachey, who had so long been associated with me. W. J. Brown also played an important part at this stage. The warm emotional appeal of the gifted Bevan contrasted strikingly with the cool calculation of the Civil Service trade union leader; Bevan was almost exactly my age, but had not yet developed his full debating prowess. Henry Mond—the son of the exceptionally able member of pre- and post-war governments, already described—was most active among the Liberals, with Archie Sinclair maintaining a friendly attitude in the background. A considerable number of M.P.s of all parties participated in these loose and non-committal discussions, which took place mostly in my house at Smith Square. When the talks began, I asked them at once to suggest any points of disagreement they had with my resignation speech. I was glad to accept their amendments, which were insubstantial and in my view were an improvement. We arrived in policy at a virtually complete agreement.

My tendency always is to drive things too hard, and when agreement was reached on policy, I began to ask for a date to be fixed for action, which is a very different thing. However, my usual insistence that action must follow a clear view of what should be done was not responsible for the break this time. Several things occurred which drastically altered the situation. Decisive was the fact that the crisis was developing more slowly than anticipated, and the sense of danger was relaxed, together with the call of duty to take risks in the national interest. Baldwin, as we have seen in Walter Elliott's case, was exercising enormous pressure, which was strengthened by the improved prospects of the party, and the party machine was able to threaten young Conservative members, not only with exclusion from the now probable Tory Government but also with the loss of their seats. These factors in combination were sufficient to deter them from further action, and I make no complaint of

[1] *Op. cit.* p. 267.

what then happened. The Tories went out quite fairly and honourably, for they were committed to nothing. Oliver Stanley said to a mutual friend that I would never trust them in any future action together because I would feel they had deserted. This was not so, I had no such feeling. At this stage of the discussions they were committed to nothing and they were quite entitled to withdraw.

The same was true of Aneurin Bevan, who owed his career and his seat to the Miners' Federation, which was far from being completely under the control of Arthur Cook. He went quite honourably and fairly at about the same time, and so did most of the other Labour M.P.s who had signed the 'Mosley Manifesto' we will later consider. The enterprise of going further, breaking with the party machines and taking their political lives in their hands, was becoming much too risky for most people on either side of the House in a situation which did not appear to be a really disastrous national crisis. Labour M.P.s were also quite entitled to withdraw, for they were committed to nothing. The same could not be said for W. J. Brown, who stayed on the field much longer. When the time came for action, only four other M.P.s, John Strachey, member for Aston Birmingham, Cynthia Mosley, member for Stoke-on-Trent, Dr. Robert Forgan, member for Renfrew, and from the Conservative side, W. E. D. Allen, member for West Belfast, remained of our impressive company. The rest had melted like snow upon the desert's dusty face, for the good reason that the sun was still shining. It was conclusively shown that a consensus of that kind for national action can only be effective in a far greater degree of national crisis. I was perhaps alone in the certainty that such a crisis would eventually occur, but the time was not yet.

The discussions with the older men in politics occupied a longer period. They began as purely social occasions before I was a member of the Government, and continued in serious form after my resignation until the eve of the National Government in 1931. Letters help sometimes to fix dates, but can only be published under the time-honoured rule to which I rigorously adhere, if they are not marked private. Two letters from Beaverbrook assist in this respect. The first, dated December 7, 1928, began: 'My dear Mosley, I do not usually write in the newspapers about those whose friendship I seek without communicating the material to them first to make sure they do not mind publication'. He went on to say that he had written about me in the *New York World* and hoped I would not find in what he had said 'anything to complain of or anything inconsistent with our personal relationship'. It was at that time certainly a personal relationship, as I did not enter into any form of political negotiations until after my resignation from the Labour Government in May 1930. His second letter, dated July 17, 1930, took things much further: 'My dear Tom, I congratulate you on your speech.[1] It was a very fine achievement. I am ready at any moment to make overtures in your direction in public, if

---

[1] A later speech, which followed the resignation speech.

you wish me to do so. On the other hand, I will be glad to organise a committee to work with you and your colleagues in the hope of hammering out an agreed policy.' I maintained close contact with Beaverbrook in this period but did not take up his suggestion of a committee; probably because I was closely engaged at that time, on the one hand with the group of young M.P.s, and on the other with Lloyd George and Lord Rothermere, who was usually on good terms with Lord Beaverbrook but was not always easy to harness with him.

Lloyd George was the moving spirit in the older group, more so than Churchill, who was sometimes but not always present when we met.[1] The situation was depicted with some accuracy by the cartoonist Low, who combined much inside information with an acute political sense, when he showed us setting out into the desert with the assistance of Lloyd George, while Churchill remains in the picture, but a little further withdrawn into the Tory background. It was during this period that I grew to know Lloyd George well and to appreciate gifts unique in his generation, which at this conjunction of events at home and abroad might again have been of immeasurable benefit to our country. This was not to be allowed in any situation short of the catastrophic. All the dull people combined to get Lloyd George down. They succeeded—but they got the country further down: the epitaph of an epoch.

Mr. Churchill had clearly considered the national consensus or Centre Party idea ever since our early meetings with him in the new members' group of 1919, and after many vicissitudes, at that time in the early 1930s, still thought it a possibility. His relations with the young Conservatives however were not good. Oliver Stanley in particular disliked him, partly perhaps by reason of some little trouble between Mr. Churchill and his father, Lord Derby. Lloyd George, on the other hand, was more completely a stranger to the young Conservatives, though no longer the object of the intense dislike he had been to their slightly older generation. Apart from individual encounters, the two groups, so far as I knew, never met. I alone appear at that time to have been present at the discussions with the older men as a representative of the younger generation. It was much easier to have a concentrated discussion in the younger than in the older group; a situation which I believe in a really healthy society would be reversed. I felt that if we could get the young to decide on definite action, that would be the moment to approach the old with a clear-cut proposal. This agreement among the younger men had been reached when all chance of their adhesion to a new combination was shattered by events. In addition to the favourable situation of the young Conservatives,

---

[1] Harold Nicolson, in his *Diaries*, 1930–39, p. 81, describes one of the occasions when Churchill was present with Lloyd George and the author at a meeting in the house of Sir Archibald Sinclair. The meetings with Lloyd George and the young Conservatives were much more frequent.

the simple mathematics of modern politics were operative; the degree of crisis was inadequate to secure decisive action.

The situation of the brilliant old men was different because they were already effectively excluded by their mediocre contemporaries, who commanded the party machines. Discussions with them continued over a considerable period, usually at dinners given by L.G., but sometimes by Lord Rothermere, who was much interested. L.G. on these occasions sparkled, revolved and coruscated with his sensitive antennae feeling in all directions. He knew what others were thinking and feeling, with the intuition supposed to be found in gifted women but usually rather the attribute of outstanding men. His wit and charm covered and mitigated the impact of a concentrated purpose almost unique in his generation. Sometimes it would go a little too far, but he would always quickly recover. On one occasion, at the end of a dinner party, he handed round imaginary posts in the government which must be formed, and concluded by turning to Lord Rothermere with a chuckling dig in the ribs: 'For you the Garter'. L.G. was so pleased with his little *double entendre* that he did not pause to enquire whether the Garter was the prerogative of the Crown or of the Prime Minister; he was never well versed in such niceties.

If Lloyd George had been able to form an administration, I do not think that any of the men who took part in these discussions would have refused to serve; neither the old nor the young. Churchill, as Chancellor, had taken a different line, which was obligatory for a newcomer to the Conservative Party in that position at the time, but he appeared subsequently to move nearer to Lloyd George and I felt their old relationship could easily be resumed. It was a formidable array, which included Lloyd George, Beaverbrook, Rothermere and most of the clever young men in all three parties, and to understand the reason for the success of the establishment and for our failure we must understand the logistics of politics. The question why we were frustrated is not puzzling to anyone who has been able to study the science of real politics in the modern world.

Normality always reigns until a real crisis occurs, and over long periods it can produce some very dull and mediocre statesmen. British history could always have been written in terms of Britain awake or Britain asleep, with alternating moods which summon to the head of affairs an entirely different type of man; this is even more valid in a world of fast-moving and decisive events. In other European countries nothing changed until things went badly wrong, either by reason of defeat in war or economic crisis, but then things happened very quickly. It would be possible to show on a graph in almost every case that the rise of unemployment coincided with major political change; the degree of crisis—either in terms of unemployment or social disintegration, or both—was much more severe than in Britain.

We shall see that the unemployment figures in Britain never reached half the crisis level prevailing in other countries where things happened, and then, for extraneous reasons already discussed, went sharply down from the high plateau of 1931 and 1932, when the nation was beginning to turn toward action. That is why the British, who always take it easy when they can—but are particularly determined and vigorous when they cannot—took the quiet way out through the National Government of 1931, which was a combination of parties controlling the extremely powerful party machines. The power of the party machines in Britain only yields to the storm of great events. The two wars brought to power leaders who were by no means favourites of the party machines and would almost certainly otherwise never have led the nation.

Unemployment in Britain stood at well over a million during most of the twenties. Thereafter it rose sharply to 2,642,000 in 1931, the year of my discussions with Lloyd George and others, a rapid rise which indicated that we were heading for a considerable national crisis. Yet it was nothing like sufficient to secure the major change we contemplated, and people were still inclined to think that quite normal measures could meet the situation. Unemployment reached its peak in the next year, 1932, when I launched the new movement, but by then it was clear that the rate of increase was slowing considerably. Things had temporarily taken a turn for the better, which reassured most people; but I remained convinced that crisis would eventually return in an aggravated form, for the basic reasons I have described and on which I rested my whole action.

Unemployment fell, except for one fluctuation, from 2,756,000 in 1932 to 1,408,000 in 1939—the opposite conditions to those which make possible either a national consensus or the arrival of a new movement in power obtained, for such events depend entirely on the economic situation. This invariable rule has become almost exaggerated in the modern world, where fluctuations in the popularity of governments, statesmen and parties, are shown to follow even in minute detail the oscillations of economics. So far no economic variation in the post-war world has been large enough to bring changes comparable to those of the twenties or thirties, but the more sensitive state of public opinion at the present time indicates an even more acute liability to change in any form of crisis. In the affluent society, a man who has a full plate whisked away from in front of him can be quicker to react than the down-and-out of the pre-war period who was accustomed to protracted conditions of unemployment and poverty. It is the ruined middle class which makes revolutions, and in pre-war terms nearly everyone is middle class now.

The rise of new parties on the Continent during the twenties and early thirties coincided exactly with the decline of economic prosperity. Both Germany and Italy suffered economic collapse, accompanied by an acute inflation which dislocated industry, caused widespread unemployment and ruined the middle class. The Italian disintegration, economic, political and psychological, was extreme, and brought Mussolini and the fascists to power in Italy almost as rapidly as the collapse of war brought Lenin and the communists to power in Russia. Can anyone think that any of these events would have occurred without collapse in war or economic catastrophe in peace?

Political fortune in terms of economics can be measured more exactly in the protracted German struggle. Unemployment in Germany was 1,355,000 in 1928, and the proportional representation of the Continent then gave the National Socialist Party 12 M.P.s, on a national average vote of 2·7 per cent. In 1930 unemployment had increased to 3,076,000 and the National Socialists then increased their M.P.s to 108, with a vote of 18 per cent. Less than three years later, in January 1933, the National Socialist Party came to power; unemployment had then risen to 6,014,000, and they had 196 M.P.s. There is not the slightest doubt that the rise in unemployment brought them to power. After years of intensive propaganda by Hitler, Goebbels and all the rest of them on the subject of the Versailles Treaty, the occupation, maltreatment and humiliation of their country, as well as their allegations against the Jews, and a skilful use of every social conflict, the net result in 1928 was 12 M.P.s and a vote of 2·7 per cent. Five years of rapidly increasing unemployment then brought them to power with an avalanche of electoral successes. When I look at that German economic situation in the light of my own experience, I sometimes wonder why they took as long as thirteen years to win power.

The circumstances we encountered in our British movement varied as widely from the experience of the German party as our policies differed from theirs. A comparable table of unemployment figures proves the point. From the foundation of our party in 1932 to the outbreak of war in 1939, unemployment in Britain was reduced by nearly 50 per cent. From 1927 until the Nazi movement gained power in January 1933, unemployment in Germany increased four and a half times. The German party was carried upwards on unemployment figures rising to a peak of catastrophe, which demanded a great change in government, while with an illusion of increasing prosperity, the rulers of Britain were saved from facing the results of their economic errors by external events, which ended in world war.

Can Britain, then, only return to greatness through catastrophe? Is what the French call *la politique du pire* valid? Can men who want to get things done be accused of wanting the worst because it is a prerequisite of action? If a doctor diagnoses a tumour and prescribes an operation, it does not mean that he desires the illness of the patient, but that he tells the truth as he sees it. He is then liable to be very unpopular if all the other physicians are prescribing a slight dose of salts and a little gentle massage for a passing malaise. Yet naturally a nation will not turn to the surgery of decisive action until all other remedies have been exhausted. This is very human, and it is what happened in 1931; after a long interval of many sweet and bitter drugs, we are now returning to reality, and truth, for better or for worse, will eventually emerge.

Action is possible in crisis because men of intelligence and realism are prepared to set dogma aside and to face facts as they exist. Noteworthy in 1930 was the acceptance by many good democrats and parliamentarians of the necessity for sweeping reforms in the structure of government and in parliamentary procedure. In a later period, when prejudice and passion inhibit action by clouding every issue, such measures might be denounced as fascism by those who use as a term of abuse a subject to which they have never devoted five minutes' serious study, but in fact such measures are nothing of the kind. Before this age of intellectual intimidation, experienced parliamentarians were quite convinced of the need for some such reforms of government method and parliamentary procedure as were outlined in my resignation speech and later crystallised in my detailed evidence to the Select Committee.

On December 8, 1930, a document with seventeen signatures was printed in the *Daily Telegraph* under the title of the *Mosley Manifesto* and extensively in most other papers. It was signed by sixteen Labour M.P.s—who included Aneurin Bevan, W. J. Brown, Secretary of the Civil Service Clerical Association, Oliver Baldwin, John Strachey, and myself—and by Arthur Cook, General Secretary of the Miners' Federation. The Manifesto followed closely the general line of my resignation speech, and today it is startling in its sharp departures from traditional Labour thinking and from the prevailing psychology of the party in recent years. It affirmed that 'an immediate policy is required, more drastic and determined than any policy yet formulated by any government in the House of Commons . . .', and suggested similar reforms in the machinery of government and in the parliamentary machine: 'It is impossible to meet the economic crisis with a nineteenth-century parliamentary machine. While the power to maintain or change the government must, of course, be retained by parliament, wide powers to deal with the present economic crisis must be vested in the government of the day for a stated period, subject only to the general control of parliament. The whole organisation of the executive machine, Cabinet, and departmental structure must be adapted to the needs of the present situation. An emergency Cabinet of not more than five Ministers, without portfolio, should be invested with power to carry through the emergency policy. The normal Cabinet or departmental chiefs should be retained for less frequent meetings to deal with normal business. . . .'

The Manifesto also accepted the insulated economy: 'The home market must be the future basis of British trade, and that home market depends on the high purchasing power of the people, which in turn depends on high wages. Purchasing power can only be maintained and increased if the wages and conditions of the workers are sheltered from the present crisis in world conditions, such as price fluctuations, organised dumping, and the competition of sweated labour. . . .' Import control boards and commodity boards were to be adopted for this purpose, with the additional use of tariffs accompanied by various safeguards. It was argued that 'centralised' purchase of our foodstuffs should give us powerful leverage to secure acceptance of our exports in return. 'Excellent opportunities clearly exist for the early conclusion of such agreements in the British Commonwealth. . . . The Dominions have for the most part foodstuffs and raw materials to sell, and we have manufactured goods to sell. This natural balance of trade should be developed under a Commonwealth plan of mutual advantage. . . . We should aim at building within the Commonwealth a civilisation high enough to absorb the production of modern machinery, which for this purpose must be largely insulated from wrecking forces in the rest of the world. . . .'

The concept of the insulated economy resting on the mutual development of Britain and the Dominions was accepted in full. To this complete departure from normal Labour Party policy was added a bulldozer to drive through their cherished, traditional network of local authority procedure: 'We believe that only the will and the power to cut through the intolerable network of governmental and municipal procedure are needed to make possible the early provision of work on schemes of urgent and immediate importance. In addition to constructive works already detailed in parliamentary debate, we suggest an attack by direct action on the great problems of slum clearance and rehousing. . . . Nothing should be allowed to stand in the way of using a very large number of our unemployed men on this vital task. . . .' Snowden, Churchill and the Treasury view suffered short shrift in the phrase: 'In finance we should pursue a producers' policy. The producer, whether manufacturer or worker, has been penalised for ten years by a financial policy which benefits the bond-holder and handicaps production. The first concern of financial policy must be the maintenance of industry, and this demands a stable price level. . . .'

The Manifesto concluded with a clear definition of the difference between the immediate necessity for action and long-term principle: 'In the advancement of this immediate policy we surrender nothing of our socialist faith. The immediate question is not a question of the ownership, but of the survival of British industry. Let us put through an emergency programme to meet the national danger; afterwards political debate on fundamental principle can be resumed. . . .'

Most men of sense would surely agree that in a moment of national crisis this was a realistic assessment of the position. The events and the pressures which prevented this remarkable company from pursuing to conclusion the policy in·which they expressed their belief, could be subject to a long analysis. Why did Aneurin Bevan retreat in filial fidelity and slumberous content between the twin bosoms of the Labour Party and trade union movement which had so long nurtured him, only to awaken again in 1959 to the realisation that nothing could be done to implement his ideals until the 'commanding heights'[1] of finance were assailed and occupied? He had seen the light then, but it faded from his eyes for the lifetime of a generation. His ultimate, belated, but again transient return, to that vision was then hailed as a flash of inspiration by the Labour Party, though he merely repeated the main theme held by the signatories of the Manifesto in 1930, which derived from the Birmingham proposals in 1925.

Why did John Strachey after giving so much time and energy to the development of a policy which rested the whole economic system of our country on a partnership between Britain and the Dominions in an insulated economy, suddenly present a memorandum to say that we must work with Russia instead of the Dominions, and then leave me on the nominal ground that I would not accept a change which made nonsense of the whole policy? Harold Nicolson recounts in his *Diaries* that Strachey was much offended by my description of his conduct as 'pathological',[2] which was indeed tactless; irritation should never intrude on these serious occasions. There were reasons, of course, in the deep psychological sphere; once again emotion destroyed purpose. What matters in life is to get things done that have to be done: things which were then necessary to reduce human suffering and to maintain the greatness of a great nation, and in this age may be necessary to prevent the destruction of the world. Mankind in my time has paid a sad price for personal feelings and emotions, and may yet pay more dearly still.

Yet I shall always remember with gratitude that four M.P.s accompanied me at first in the formation of the New Party, as well as Allan Young as organiser, after the atmosphere of crisis had been temporarily dissipated, and men could again convince themselves that normal measures without undue personal risk could meet the situation. Harold Nicolson too behaved splendidly in giving up a highly paid job on the Beaverbrook press to edit the paper supporting the New Party. *Action* was lavishly supported by Lord Nuffield, but suffered a fall in circulation from 160,000 to 16,000 in ten weeks. Our electoral defeat gave the competent professional staff no time to get it going. Later, some of our amateurs in fascist days gradually built it up to become a self-supporting paper.

Lloyd George remained acutely apprehensive and manoeuvred continually in private gatherings. He retained close and friendly relations with me, but he did not see the necessity for the long-term policy, and was unwilling to start a new party. Yet those of us who launched the new movement were convinced that crisis would return in an aggravated form and that a policy of long-term reconstruction was vitally necessary. We had failed to secure a national consensus, a warm and ardent agreement on action by the whole nation; it

[1] Aneurin Bevan in a speech at the Labour Party Conference at Blackpool on November 29, 1959.
[2] *Op. cit.*

remained our duty to act by means of the second best, a long, arduous and bitter process to arouse the nation before disaster. This view of our duty led us inevitably to the streets and the villages, to the homes of the people, where alone we could awaken the will to action in a new movement. In a continuing crisis it might be done with reasonable speed, for in such circumstances the British have a considerable capacity for improvisation. But I also stressed that it could mean a long, hard struggle over many years.

The New Party was launched on March 1, 1931. Then came one of those incidents which warn us against hubris by reminding that we are the playthings of fate, a moment when we can indeed 'say ditto to Mr. Burke' in his poignant apostrophe: 'What shadows we are, what shadows we pursue!' On the eve of the opening meeting I fell ill with pleurisy and pneumonia, quite a serious matter before the discovery of antibiotics. I could scarcely lift my head from the pillow. It was too late to postpone the party's inauguration, for the placards were out all over the country. I was advertised to speak at the opening meeting and was to have been seconded by W. J. Brown, M.P., who was experienced and effective both in the House and on the platform. It was decided that the meeting should continue with Brown as the main speaker, assisted by Cimmie and John Strachey. But a message came that Brown could not attend, and he was not available on the telephone.

I ordered an ambulance to take me to his house in the suburbs, where I found him at home. After being carried into his living-room on a stretcher, I asked his reasons for not attending the opening meeting. Then something occurred which I had only seen rarely before; his face seemed to be pulled down on one side like a man suffering a stroke and he burst into tears. He said he would lose his trade union job and his family would be ruined. His fears appeared to me exaggerated because he knew I had already obtained a guarantee from Lord Nuffield to cover his salary for several years. He had never previously voiced these apprehensions, and had always posed as a man of decision, of iron will and resolution. The very few men in whom previously I had observed this phenomenon had likewise usually rather emphasised their determination and courage before they found themselves averse to getting out of a trench when the time came. W. J. Brown was evidently experiencing the same sensations. I had myself carried back to the ambulance.

Cimmie and John Strachey got through the opening meeting, and then undertook the meetings in the country at which I was advertised to speak. They had a tough time, which foreshadowed to some extent the organised campaign of violence that broke out when I was back in action again, and which was particularly disgraceful as the main speaker was then a woman putting over a reasoned case in a gentle and charming style which not even the most embittered could describe as offensive. Our team of M.P.s had now been reduced to four. W. E. D. Allen was always a writer rather than a speaker, and Dr. Forgan was distinguished more for his agreeable manners and pleasing personality than for platform performance; he was neither a speaker nor an administrator, but excellent in public relations.

Directly I was through illness and convalescence, we launched into a by-election at Ashton-under-Lyne with Allan Young as candidate. It was a Labour seat, where the previous figures, at the 1929 election, had been 13,170 and 9,763. We had only a scratch organisation and the campaign was chiefly based on three big meetings in a local drill hall which held nearly four thousand. We polled just about the number who attended these meetings, for the by-election figures were Conservative 12,420, Labour 11,005 and New Party 4,472. Our intervention had split the Labour vote and put the Tory in. The size and enthusiasm of our meetings had caused rumours to circulate in London that we were winning, and some portentous figures loomed in the shadows of these stimulating gatherings. But on the day of the vote, the party machines, as usual, defeated the overt symptoms of incipient mass enthusiasm.

The vote was large enough to put us on the map and cause the New Party to be taken seriously. Our meetings had been orderly except for a lively heckling, which helps rather than hinders a speaker. But the climate changed completely when the figures came out after the election. It may be that the organisers of violence had decided to hold their hand because they did not want to excite sympathy for us. They had, in any case, a ready field for their activity after the vote, because Labour Party workers had come in the evening hours from all over Lancashire to hear the result and were naturally annoyed that our intervention had put their man out. Nevertheless, I base on two facts my view that the violence that night was led and to some extent organised by the usual communist experts; the first, that the whole atmosphere and situation was then totally different to anything seen in the election; the second, that in my long experience violence never occurs on a large scale in England unless it is deliberately organised and led.

The uproar outside reached us inside the hall. The senior agent of the Labour Party, representing their Headquarters, informed me with some gratification that I would be lynched if I went outside; a menace, not a warning. John Strachey reported afterwards that surveying the howling mob outside I said, 'This is the crowd which has prevented anything being done in England since the war'. This is true, but it is clear that I did not mean they were averse to change. What I meant then and mean now is that the long-experienced and entirely dedicated agents and warriors of communism always play on the anarchy inherent in the Left of Labour to secure confusion, disillusion and ultimately the violence which is essential to their long-term plan. In a crisis they will prevent any major reform or ordered progress through the medium of the Labour Party.

I went through the crowd with a few companions and we suffered no serious injury. There were few police about. For some time, demonstrators surrounded our hotel shouting, but eventually they went home. No harm was done, except to the psychology of John Strachey. I do not mean that he was frightened, for he was not. John Strachey was a man of courage. He quite suddenly formed the view after this occasion that the mass of the workers were against us, and that we were on the wrong side. From this opinion he never turned back, until his collaboration with the Communist Party. It then took him some time to evolve once more into a pillar of Labour orthodoxy. The reasons for his little tour of mind and spirit were not difficult to discern.

Intellectuals drawn to the Left, partly by mental and partly by emotional processes, are apt to form an entirely mythical image of the working class. I suspected then and knew later that such scenes of violence are nothing to do with the mass of the British workers, the people who had been to my meetings all over Britain when I toured the country speaking every evening and staying every night with a different manual worker. The whole thing was a put-up show by sophisticated communists playing on the emotions of a not very large number of Labour workers in a moment of disappointment and frustration. Most of the crowd, as usual, were just there to watch, and the row as usual only came from one or two front rows of agitators. If the whole crowd had really been so hostile, we must indeed have been lynched, for we were quite powerless.

The view that the mass of the British workers rise in their wrath against men and opinions they disapprove and will do violent and brutal things is simply invented nonsense. Such events are bogus from start to finish, for they are manufactured by the Communist Party. If a man is alone, a score of these roughs will make him appear a public enemy by surrounding him and kicking him, or a public hero by encircling him and cheering him. If police protect him, the communists say that he cannot come among the people without protection; this impression is the object of the whole exercise. We were soon to prove through the blackshirt movement that once you had seen off the bitter professionals on the other side, you would again find not only orderly but happy and jovial audiences among our friendly and good-natured British people. John Strachey and others like him were taken in by a front of plaster concealing an ugly visage, which happily is not yet in charge of England and certainly does not represent the mass of the British people. I believe it never will, unless all resolution deserts us and the character of the British is entirely changed.

The days of the New Party were now numbered. We had to develop a different character to meet an entirely new situation. New men came to us, who were ready to fight for their beliefs, in type the dedicated blackshirt. John Strachey left after putting in his strange memorandum contradicting directly the whole basis of the policy we had long agreed together, and he was accompanied by Allan Young and the philosopher, C. E. M. Joad, who was an intimate friend of Strachey's and afterwards well known as a broadcaster. Harold Nicolson held on longer, more in loyalty than out of conviction. He simply could not grasp that I had the stark choice of facing violence or of closing down. He did not approve the new men now necessary to our cause, and they did not appreciate his delicate thought in choosing a pretty little wayside flower as our party emblem, nor his literary artistry in writing an article entitled: 'Lift high the Marigold'.

All over the country we met a storm of organised violence. They were simply out to smother us, we were to be mobbed down by denying us our only resource, the spoken word; we were to be mobbed out of existence. The General Election, with the whole Press supporting the National Government, coupled with the smother tactics of the Left, led to our inevitable defeat, in which I polled 10,543 votes and the rest of the twenty-two New Party candidates polled an average of 1,036 votes apiece. We had to reform our organisation, but not our policy, to meet an entirely new situation.

Before the day of this renaissance I published the epitaph of the New Party and emphasised our enduring determination:

'Better the great adventure, better the great attempt for England's sake, better defeat, disaster, better far the end of that trivial thing called a political career, than stifling in a uniform of blue and gold, strutting and posturing on the stage of little England, amid the scenery of decadence, until history, in turning over an heroic page of the human story, writes of us the contemptuous postscript: "These were the men to whom was entrusted the Empire of Great Britain, and whose idleness, ignorance and cowardice left it a Spain". We shall win; or at least we shall return upon our shields.'

16
The Founding of the British Union of Fascists

Fascism was in essence a national creed, and therefore by definition took an entirely different form in different countries. In origin, it was an explosion against intolerable conditions, against remediable wrongs which the old world had failed to remedy. It was a movement to secure national renaissance by people who felt themselves threatened with decline into decadence and death and were determined to live, and live greatly. Without understanding these three basic facts it is possible to abuse fascism, but not to make a serious reply to its case and to its spirit. They can no more be smothered by abuse than they can finally be suppressed by force; an argument must be answered if it is to be defeated, and to be answered it must first be understood.

Fascism does not exist at present, not because it has been answered, but because it belongs to the epoch before the Second World War. Since that period science has presented us with a new set of facts, the errors of fascism have provided their lessons, and nationalism has been extended to a European patriotism. Those of us who were fascists can learn both from new facts and from our own mistakes; it is easy to learn from errors for which we were not ourselves responsible, particularly when we are confident that we personally would have avoided them. At my worst, I have never made any claim to infallibility, which I leave to those responsible for the present condition of the world. After the war I faced fresh facts, learnt from past mistakes, and felt free to become a European.

Why then, had I become a fascist? For an answer to this question we must return to the autumn of 1931. The victory of the National Government in the election of October that year crushed the New Party and gave complete power to men who we knew from bitter experience would do nothing except hasten the gradual decline of our country into the decadence of a second-rate power, even should they be saved by external factors of which they understood little from bringing its speedy ruin. The degree of crisis in Britain had been insufficient to secure the national consensus of every vital element necessary to save the country, and after the frustration of all our efforts within Parliament the continuing complacency of the electorate defeated the New Party in the landslide of 1931. Yet we were more than ever convinced that sooner or later a supreme effort must be made by the British people if the nation was to live in any form worthy of its greatness—still recognisable as the land we loved—or even to survive at all.

What were we to do?—Just give up? Lord Beaverbrook at this point made me an offer to write for his papers. He was always a good friend when you were down, but some said not so good when you were up. Lloyd George once said to me: 'Max always wants to cut the heads off the tall poppies. That is his whole psychology.' My head had been well and truly cut off by the election of 1931, and he at once made me this offer. I take it now, as I took it then, to be a gesture of friendship which should be appreciated, but I preferred to keep my complete independence. Siren voices also were not lacking to suggest that we had ample gifts and means still to enjoy life and that the deluge might come after us. Staid and influential voices answered in the conflict of conscience—coming curiously from the Right, to which I never belonged—advising that I should make a tour of the Empire and return as its expert to rally the forces of an imperial conservatism. I felt that my part was neither the voluptuary laughing on the ruins of his country's greatness, mocking his own ideals and the trust of his companions, nor the ideologue spinning idle dreams of imperial panoply for a people who had lost the will even to hold what their fathers had won. My duty was to awaken the will to live and to live greatly, to dedicate myself to a national renaissance.

At the point of this decision I was confronted by three facts. The first was that movements of national renaissance in the entirely different forms suited to the two countries in which they occurred had been founded years before in their disintegrating societies, and that one of these movements had long since won power and the other was clearly about to win it. The second fact was that precisely the same conditions had evoked these two movements as were present, though in far less acute degree, in our British situation; the origin might be defeat in war, or merely economic decline threatening collapse, but the results of unemployment and mass suffering in varying extent were the same. The third fact was that the response of the old world, and of communism in particular, to the foundation of these movements had been exactly similar to our New Party experience. When they emerged with new policies, they were not met by reasoned argument but by organised violence. In our case it was clear beyond a shadow of doubt that the initiative in violence came not from us but from our opponents. We assembled to hold peaceful meetings and to present a reasoned case, and others attacked our meetings for the purpose of breaking them up. They attacked and we defended.

Among all the profusion of falsehoods which these events generated, I most resented the imputation that I took pleasure in violence because I had to organise the blackshirt movement for protecting my meetings. It was almost suggested that at my great meetings I preferred a fight to a speech. The charge was obviously ridiculous—why on earth should I?—for the meetings attracted by far the largest audiences ever assembled in Britain. A politician who wanted to assault his audience rather than persuade them would clearly be certifiably insane.

Apart from what has been said and written about my capacity for speech, I have a proved statistical record of persuasion in most diverse places and conditions, to which my opponents have never yet produced an equal. The reader of this record will have observed that I became the youngest M.P. by winning Harrow with a majority of 11,000 as a Conservative, and in the two subsequent elections reversed this verdict by defeating the Conservative candidate in this stronghold of that party by large majorities. After that came the challenge to the Chamberlains' fortress in Birmingham, which they had held for sixty years, and the capture of every seat in the centre of the city for Labour after five years' intensive effort under my leadership. Then followed the two elections in the neighbouring constituency of Smethwick, with greatly increased Labour majorities; and finally the winning of over 10,000 votes at Stoke-on-Trent in face of the 1931 landslide, while the rest of the New Party candidates averaged about 1,000 votes apiece.

Why should a man with this electoral record suddenly take leave of his senses and with much trouble and some expense assemble the largest audiences seen in Britain, not for the purpose of persuading them, but of beating them up? For sheer absurdity this line of attack upon me was an easy winner among all the foolish and grotesque inventions I have known in politics. The whole allegation can be met with the two words which answer the sheer silliness of so many cretinous suggestions—what for?—*cui bono*?

A dishonest line of controversy in these circumstances, is that no one should mind a little heckling. Who does? Interruptions, heckling, can be the making of a speech, and any speaker of any experience can always score. What fun they were, all the old gags of the English platform, equally enjoyed by speaker and audience. When a persistent Marxian holds up question time:[1] 'I see, sir, that you are an authority on Marx, and have no doubt read

[1] Questions were always invited at my meetings. The usual allocation of time was 1¼ hours to the speech, a ¼ hour to collection and literature sale, 1 hour to questions. This procedure differed from continental practice, and the question period was a good training for modern television. Style was then conversational and intimate, quite different from the speech.

him carefully'. 'Yes, I have.' 'You have read all six volumes, I take it?' 'Yes, I have.' 'Then, sir, may I congratulate you both on your learning and on your industry, for he only wrote two.' The authority bobs away red-faced on a sea of laughter, until the audience can return to matters of more immediate interest to our pragmatic people. It is all good, old-time English fun. Rough but genial exchanges are always appreciated in the traditional strongholds of the British worker. A stentorian bellow from a burly but obviously bogus claimant: 'I would have this audience know that my jaw was broken in six places at one of your meetings'. 'We are all delighted to hear it working so well tonight.' Slightly subtler rejoinders would dissolve in laughter; undergraduate heckling at university meetings: 'Are you in favour of birth control?' 'Well, I was, but I am beginning to think it is about twenty years too late.'

When so much was said and written about my ability to deal with hecklers in my early days, why was I supposed to lose that capacity I so much enjoyed? Of course, what we were up against was nothing like ordinary heckling; it was organised shouting by dozens, or sometimes hundreds of men, accompanied by violence often prepared in semi-military fashion. I have probably now a larger experience of mass meetings than any man alive, and I can assure the reader that serious disorder never occurs at a meeting in Britain unless it is organised. The British people may love you or hate you (I have experienced a bit of both) but they will always give you a fair hearing. If they do not want to hear you, they will stay away; a simple and silent remedy.

When organised force is used against you, only two courses are open, if authority has already proved either unable or unwilling to keep order: to surrender, or to meet force with force and to win. After the New Party experience it was perfectly clear to me that I could blow the red roughs a kiss, pack up and go home, or, after due appeal and warning, eject them from my meetings. It should be remembered that I had no resource except the spoken word: no Press, no radio, and little money. Public meetings were our only way of putting over our case, and if our audiences were to hear it we must be prepared to fight for free speech.

We were faced at first with heavy odds, and to lose would mean the end of our movement. It soon became clear that to win we had to wear some distinctive dress, a uniform in order to recognise each other. That is why people obliged to fight have worn uniform of some kind or other from the earliest days of human history. We wore coloured shirts for the same reason, and black was chosen not only because it was the opposite to red but because at that time it was worn by no one else in this country. A shirt is the easiest and cheapest garment for the purpose of recognition, and the shirts had to be paid for by the men themselves, most of whom were poor, some even being on the dole. Others had already worn coloured shirts for the same reason, but this no more made our movement Italian, or German, than wearing uniform turns an English army into a German army. This particular jibe was easily answered.

Yet the other similarities remained; our movement was an explosion against intolerable conditions, an effort at renaissance, met by organised violence. Not only in Italy and Germany, but in almost every country in Europe, parties were springing up which had long since come to be known by the world in general as fascist. Was it either honest or practical to deny that we were a fascist movement? The honesty of denying we were fascist could be long debated, but the impractability was quite clear. When the bystanders see an elephant coming down the street, it is idle to tell them it is a pleasant Sunday afternoon outing organised by the Young Men's Christian Association. We were a distinctive British movement of intense national patriotism, but in the age of fascism it was clearly jejune and possibly dishonest to deny that we were fascists.

There is always of course a disadvantage in bearing a resemblance to foreign parties, however superficial, particularly if in essence you are a movement of ardent patriotism. It is easier for the parties of the Left, which were seldom notable for their patriotism until they had discarded the Empire, and then discovered the patriotism of little England as a handy instrument for use against the patriotism of great Europe. The parties of the Left have always been international in sentiment, and have been openly organised in this sense. Socialists belonged to the Second International, of which the Labour Party was an official member throughout this period; communists go further in being not merely members of the Third International, but in accepting the leadership of a foreign party and a foreign State.

Liberalism also had international derivations. The creed of the nineteenth century began effectively with the French Revolution, and the Liberal Party in Britain has enjoyed, indeed boasted of its European affiliations. Charles James Fox was far from approving the excesses of the French Revolution, but he admired its initial spirit and stood resolutely against its suppression by external force. No one on that account suspected for one moment that this English patriot would become a danger to his country when it was menaced by French Revolutionary armies under Napoleon, but that was before the introduction to Britain of dago values of mutual suspicion more suitable to the transatlantic climate of a banana republic.

No one in that period was so morally dishonest or so intellectually feeble as to impute to Fox, or to Grey and the Reform Bill leaders, all the crimes of the French Revolution, or to burden the Liberalism of the nineteenth century with the local excesses which were the responsibility of individual leaders such as Robespierre. Liberalism survived the mess in the bedroom when it was born, as many a fine man has done, and finally grew to adult form in Britain. It was our Reform Bill, not the initial explosion in France, which finally gave beneficent shape to the nineteenth century. My hope and confident conviction was that in Britain fascism would also find expression in its highest form, and would be destined to cast the mould of the twentieth century.

Members of fascist and national socialist movements in other countries no doubt felt the same, for it was both the strength and the weakness of fascism that it was an intensely national creed. This impulse gave it the strength of patriotism, but also the weakness of division. We were divided by our nationalism. This brought the danger that Europe would perish in the same tragic manner as the city states of classic Greece; united by the genius of their kind, by their philosophy, architecture and art born of this unique kinship, but divided by a nationalism which in the view of history must be regarded as artificial. It was the sin of fascism to repeat this error, with consequences of still enduring tragedy.

We were sometimes suspected of being organised in a fascist International. On the contrary, we were much too national; the view of history may well be that we were not nearly international enough. There were sporadic meetings between leaders, and occasional holiday parties touring each other's countries, but no form of systematic organisation. I myself met Mussolini about half a dozen times, and Hitler twice; neither of them after 1936. In those critical years I was much too busy at home to go abroad at all. Our fault was not union, but division. Yet it arose from the natural cause that we were different in our policies and outlook, by reason of the national characters of our movements.

More, not less, should in my view have been done to surmount these differences for the purpose of preserving peace. Fascism in each country was too busy serving its national interest. Confronted with a clear choice between pursuing national ambitions or promoting some form of European union through the universalism of fascism, the national socialist and fascist leaders invariably chose the former course. Whenever fascism was really beginning to succeed throughout Europe, it always received a knock-down blow from the leaders already in power prancing into some territory or other in service of purely national interests, often accompanied by boastful and menacing language which created the alarm of war and increased opposition. Even when the Axis leaders came together in the last phase, it was more on the basis of an old-fashioned alliance of mutual interest than of any union of the spirit. Never talk to me of a fascist International, for the peace of Europe might have been maintained if such an organisation had existed. If our continent had found a reasonable measure of union through a new European spirit, instead of division by the old nationalism, twenty-five million people might be alive today and Europe the greatest power in the world.

An exaggerated nationalism must be counted both the strength and the weakness of fascism. It was strong because nationalism is always a quick starter in popular favour, but it was weak because narrow nationalism has

the same short legs as lies, and is soon overtaken by facts. Another characteristic of fascism combined the same blend of merit and error in an almost
equal measure. The drive to action was right, it was an urgent need of the
period. Unemployment, bad housing, and poverty when science had already
virtually solved the problem of production in any well-organised community
—these were wrongs crying to Heaven for vigorous action. Yet one of the sad
lessons of history, which must be learnt, is that action can be too dearly
bought. Individual liberty is the basis of any civilised society, and we regress
to the chaos of the Dark Ages if this is not recognised. Individual rights should
not impede or blackmail the advance of the whole community; no man can
claim to set his rights above those of the whole nation, and no minority can
claim in effect the right to rule, but the right of the individual to suffer no
loss of liberty without trial must be inviolate. Personally, I maintained this
right before, during and after my long imprisonment without trial.

The rights of the individual were not preserved under fascism abroad, and
thereby more was lost, even in terms of action, than was gained. Even in the
eighteenth century and even in time of war, Bonaparte said that the moral to
the material was as three to one; in the twentieth century, in time of peace
the moral is far stronger still. Action and will are both necessary, but both
have their limits; action can be too dearly bought, and it was. To affirm this
truth is not to admit any shadow of justice in the case of those who, before
the war, condemned the crimes of fascism and condoned the crimes of Soviet
Russia, when it paid their squalid policies and sustained their European
crimes to strain at the gnat and swallow the camel.

There are more ways than one of killing liberty. Free expression of opinion
in any organised form was openly denied by the State in the fascist countries,
but to a large extent it was covertly denied by subtler means in Great Britain
before the war, and has been entirely denied for all effective purposes since
the war. It is possible either to kill freedom by force or to smother it by the
power of money with the connivance of the State. There is not much freedom
left to the individual with a new opinion, when the Press, radio and television
are denied to him; when public meetings are his only form of expression, and
the State, while denying him the right to keep order, refuses to keep order
itself. Complete the process with Labour majorities on local councils refusing
the use of public halls under their control, and a Conservative majority in
Parliament using the police, not to keep order at outdoor meetings, but to
ban the meeting and to stop the proceedings the moment organised opposition
threatens disorder; then the triumph of democracy in England has disposed
of what Mussolini called the rotting corpse of liberty even more effectively
because less blatantly. Hypocrisy rules in quiet triumph: 'the coward does it
with a kiss, the brave man with a sword'. Freedom of speech in face of the
established parties joins the economic freedom of the individual in face of the
capitalist combines, which in time-honoured definition long since granted

the 'liberty' to sleep on a bench in the park to a man who cannot afford a room at the Ritz.

We must start at the beginning of this development and cover the process in proper stages, before we contemplate in all its exquisite perfection the present system for the complete suppression of unorthodox opinion whenever it attains an effective, organised form. Disorder had often prevailed at public meetings in Britain for years before I was born. Our New Party experience showed that under the existing dispensation the police were unwilling to keep order. None of these things mattered to the established parties, which had a big Press to support them, and who in the case of the Conservative Party confined their large meetings to ticket-bearing supporters who dutifully assembled over large areas to hear their leaders. We were a new movement and we were entirely dependent upon the spoken word at public meetings to find the support which did not yet exist. It was perfectly clear that we were to be denied by organised violence this sole opportunity for political progress. What were we to do?—Pack up and go home?—Or organise ourselves to defend our meetings? A few of my valued associates chose the first alternative, I chose the second.

We had a programme slowly and laboriously created during my Labour Party days—no foreign invention—which we were convinced could save the country in condition of crisis that might at any time deteriorate into national disaster. It seemed to me an absolute duty to give our people the opportunity to understand it and support it. To be capable of thought, but not of action, would be to me contemptible, a denial of every principle. What I later described in *The Alternative* as the thought–deed man—the man capable of both thought and action—must become a living reality, an embodied truth essential to human survival. We had done the thinking, now came the time for action, to turn thought into deed.

We faced an experience similar to all who were disapproved by the organisers of red violence. Quotations from members of other parties need not be repeated extensively; a few will suffice. Mr. T. Howard, M.P. for South Islington, said: 'I challenge any leader of the Conservative Party, or of the Liberal Party, to organise a meeting in London . . . and to advertise the meeting as an open meeting and to get a hearing'. Mr. Cecil Pike, M.P. for the Attercliffe Division of Sheffield, said: 'I have seen in my Division meeting after meeting wilfully broken up, and I am perfectly convinced that every other member of this House has had the same experience'.[1] The *Manchester Guardian* reported on March 8, 1934: 'Lord Beaverbrook was shouted down last night at an eve-of-the-poll meeting at Camberwell. . . . When Lord Beaverbrook rose to speak, his words were inaudible beyond the front of the hall, owing to the stamping on the floor and persistent singing. It appeared at one time that the platform would be rushed, but there was a strong bodyguard

[1] *Hansard*, vol. 290, June 14, 1934.

of stewards. After a further attempt to make himself heard, Lord Beaverbrook sat down, amid opposition cheers. Later, he left the hall, after shaking hands with those on the platform. . . . Later several free fights took place in front of the platform. . . . Several stewards were knocked down in the rush, and afterwards one was carried out battered and bleeding. The police were called in, and the hall gradually cleared'.

A notorious case was Mr. Churchill's meeting during the 1922 election in his constituency at Dundee, when he had just undergone an operation for appendicitis and had to address the meeting from a bath-chair. *The Times* of October 14, 1922, reported the meeting under the heading: Mr. Churchill Shouted Down: 'Mr. Churchill who addressed an audience of 5,000 persons at the Drill Hall, Dundee, last night, met with so much interruption and disorder from the Labour element that the meeting was eventually abandoned. The hall was packed. Mr. Churchill was received with a storm of boos, hissing and cheers, and the chairman's remarks were greeted with the singing of "Tell me the old, old story". Mr. Churchill began his speech from a sitting position to the accompaniment of booing and cries. . . . He said, "If about a hundred young men and women choose to spoil a whole meeting, and a hundred of these young reptiles choose to deny to democracy the power to conduct a great assembly, the blame is with them. . . ." The meeting broke up in disorder.' Mr. Churchill was unable to put his case at open meetings throughout the election, which he lost.

Such cases can be multiplied many times, but enough has been said to show that I did not invent violence at British public meetings. Many others had the same experience, but as members of the old parties, they had the Press and the ticketed meetings of the party leaders. I had to hold open meetings and secure a hearing, if the large and fair-minded audiences who had come to listen were not to be denied the right of free speech by an organised minority. We had either to throw out 'the young reptiles', or to close down. I am no snake-fancier. We acted, we won: that was our offence. For some years there were fights at our meetings all over Britain, but never once were the meetings broken up. Even in that period, many meetings were orderly, but they would always have been liable to attack if I had not organised and led the blackshirt movement. These devoted young men saved free speech in Britain.

The proof is that for several years before the war our meetings were held all over the country in perfect order, and they were far the largest political meetings ever held in Britain. The culmination was the meeting in July 1939 at Earls Court—not at the Empress Hall but in the neighbouring hall, about three times larger, where the Ideal Home Exhibition and similar events are organised—which was claimed to be the largest indoor meeting ever held in the world. This hall was much larger than Madison Square Gardens in New York or the Deutschland Halle in Berlin, and no other party ever attempted to hold a meeting there. At Earls Court most of the audience had paid for their seats, and the sale of tickets at all my meetings was then one of our main sources of income; we at least owed to those who had paid that they should hear the speech. Opposition was entirely absent, and the meeting ended in extraordinary scenes of enthusiasm. All over the country we then had the same experience, because the British people were again able to hear the speech to which they chose to listen and the organised denial of free speech had ceased to exist.

The peak of organised violence had been reached and surmounted some years previously in June 1934 at Olympia, a meeting discussed ever since. There the victory for free speech was not won without bitter experience. We were not only up against the hooligans described by Mr. Churchill as 'reptiles' —often armed and under alien instigation—but also the support given to them by more respectable people. A pamphlet our movement issued after the Olympia meeting had a title which drew attention to this phenomenon, *Red Violence and Blue Lies*. It was always something of a mystery to me why a number of Conservatives took the side of the reds against us, and the only credible explanation I ever received was that the Right feared we might win, but did not believe the victory of communism in England was possible. Any stick was good enough to beat us with, even the red bludgeon used against the Conservatives themselves, until they retreated behind their Press and ticketed meetings.

It was, of course, perfectly possible to have genuine differences of opinion on a subject like the Olympia meeting without ulterior motive, and fair-minded members of the Conservative and other parties took different sides in the subsequent controversy. Most of them only saw what happened on the spot in the violent fighting which took place in the hall; they were unaware of what had occurred previously in the systematic organisation of disorder for attack on the meeting from outside the hall. Some Conservative M.P.s witnessed these happenings, and recorded them in the Press. Mr. Patrick Donner, M.P. wrote, for instance, in the *National Review*: '. . . that fact is that many of the Communists were armed with razors, stockings filled with broken glass, knuckle-dusters, and iron bars; that they marched from the East End, the police kindly escorting them, with the avowed purpose of wrecking the meeting. A friend of mine saw a woman Fascist with a razor-cut across her face, and with my own eyes I witnessed gangs of Communists (some of them dressed in black shirts to make identification of those responsible for the uproar more difficult) resisting ejection with the utmost violence. If then, as cannot be disputed, some of these hooligans were armed, can it in equity be argued that the stewards used their fists, when provoked in this manner, with more vigour than perhaps the situation required? I listened carefully to comments of those nearby, and noted that one woman present referred to the "restraint" shown by the stewards.'

A collection of weapons taken from the attackers was afterwards made and the photographs are still on record. Our stewards had to eject these armed men with their bare hands, for they were not only forbidden to carry weapons, but were often searched to ensure the order was obeyed. Our Constitution laid down precise rules for dealing with disorders at meetings: 'Interrupters will be ejected only on the instructions of the speaker as chairman of the meeting when the persistence of an interrupter prevents those in his vicinity from hearing the speech. Ejection will be carried out with the minimum of force necessary to secure the removal of the interrupter from the meeting.' Were our stewards really to be blamed if they punched with their fists men who attacked them with 'razors, knuckle-dusters and iron bars'? If they handled the opposition with such brutality, why was not a single case of that kind detained in London hospitals that night? At our own dressing-station, according to signed statements of highly qualified medical personnel: 'Sixty-three Blackshirts were treated for injuries, mostly abdominal, and injuries caused by blunt instruments'; the injuries included, 'Blackshirts kicked in the head and in the stomach and laid up for three weeks' . . . 'girl Fascist with a scratch, commencing under her eye and running down her cheek and neck and finishing on her back, between her shoulder blades. I do not think this scratch could have been done with a finger nail, but that some sharp instrument must have been used. While treating this case, another girl Fascist was brought in; she had been struck by a man and her glasses smashed in her face. She was bleeding from the region of the left eye.' A long list of these cases could be made, but no evidence was produced of similar injuries among the opposition or of any serious injuries at all.

Why then did we find it necessary to organise a dressing-station at Olympia, which we intended to be another political meeting to convert the British people to our cause, after a series of quiet meetings which had followed the effective organisation of the blackshirt movement? The answer is that the attack on the meeting was openly organised in advance. We knew all about it, and so did the authorities. For three weeks before the meeting, incitements to attack it were published, and maps were printed to show how to get to the meeting. For instance on May 17: 'The London District Committee of the Communist Party has decided to call upon the London workers to organise a counter-demonstration against the demonstration of Sir Oswald Mosley, which is advertised to take place at Olympia on Thursday, June 7th' —May 26: 'Marches will be organised from five different parts of London in the late afternoon to arrive in the Hammersmith Road in the vicinity of Olympia at 6.30 p.m. . . . Arrangements should be made in the localities for parties of workers to travel on the Underground to obtain cheap facilities for parties'—May 28: 'The Communist Party is confident the workers in the capital city will resist, with all means, the Fascist menace'—May 31: 'Every militant worker in London should put his whole energy into mobilising the

masses of London against Mosley on Thursday, June 7th'—June 1: 'The
workers are going to be all out at Olympia on Thursday week, June 7th,
when Oswald Mosley and his Blackshirts hold their monster demonstration'
—June 4: 'The workers at a debate decided to march against Mosley on
Thursday night. The anti-Fascist front grows every day. Thursday night
will see the London workers marching on Olympia. . . . The East End of
London is covered with huge slogans and everywhere are signs of widespread
initiative being displayed in this anti-Fascist fight. . . .' These extracts are
taken from various newspapers, and are on public record available to
anyone.

This attack was organised, so far as their limited experience would permit,
in the manner of a military operation. We had a legal and a moral right to
resist, if authority permitted the attack to take place. In the fair light of
history, can our men be blamed for defeating with their bare fists this armed
attack, which had the deliberate and declared purpose of suppressing free
speech in Britain?

I am content to accept the verdict of Lloyd George, who wrote in the
Sunday Pictorial on June 24, 1934: 'People began to ask themselves what was
the meaning of the Albert Hall[1] phenomenon: what might be the subterranean
strength of the Blackshirt Movement, and what its promise or menace for the
future government of the country. But still more startling was the summoning,
on June 7, of a meeting of this body at Olympia, for this is the biggest hall in
London,[2] only capable of being filled, if ever, in connection with some
stirring national crisis. Yet the Blackshirts secured an audience of 15,000
people to pack the huge exhibition hall, and to listen to an oration by their
leader which went on for more than two hours.

'Not all listened sympathetically; a considerable contingent of Communists
manoeuvred an entry into the building by dubious means, with a view to
organising such disturbance as would frustrate speech. Their failure to do so
was due to expulsory methods which several spectators have described as
brutal in the extreme. This statement is challenged by the promoters of the
meeting. It is difficult to explain why the fury of the champions of free speech
should be concentrated so exclusively, not on those who deliberately and
resolutely attempted to prevent the public expression of opinions, of which

---

[1] What Lloyd George called the Albert Hall phenomenon was that in the thirties I
addressed in the Albert Hall a series of crowded and enthusiastic meetings in quick
succession, an experience unknown to the old parties. The hall was refused to me
after the Second World War, but I then held similar meetings in other large halls
like the Free Trade Hall in Manchester and Birmingham Town Hall, until they too
were refused to me by Labour-controlled councils in 1962. After the war, in successive
years I held large and orderly meetings in Trafalgar Square until, in 1962, it was also
refused to me after a revival of organised disorder.

[2] Olympia was the largest hall available in 1934. The Exhibition Hall at Earls Court,
where my meeting was held five years later, is reckoned to be about twice the size of
Olympia.

they disapproved, but against those who fought, however roughly, for freedom of speech.

'Personally I have suffered as much as anyone in public life today from hostile interruptions by opponents determined to make it impossible for me to put my case before audiences. Naturally, therefore, I have an antipathy to that class of interruption, and I feel that men who enter meetings with the deliberate intention of suppressing free speech have no right to complain if an exasperated audience handles them rudely.'

The facts about the Olympia meeting, which are much in our favour, have been on record for many years, but have never been told; facts, too, are subject to the great smother. Legends of every kind are circulated about this meeting, bearing no relation to truth. For instance, in support of the ridiculous charge that I preferred a fight to making a speech, it is often stated that I stopped speaking for a considerable period and had the searchlights diverted from the platform to various fights which were taking place in the hall. If this were true, I should indeed have been an orator of unexpected modesty. In fact, the loudspeaker wires were cut, and for a period I was completely silenced until they could be repaired. As for the searchlights, they were nothing whatever to do with me and I had no control over them; they belonged to the newsreel companies, which were present in force. Directly I was silenced, they preferred to take pictures of the fighting. I had no means of obliging them to keep the lights directed on the platform, short of using force, which would indeed have been an outrage.

Was the speech I made after the blackshirt stewards had restored order, so provocative, so inflammatory, such a menace to the life of the State that a highly organised, virtually military operation could conceivably be justified to stop its utterance while authority looked the other way? The speech was almost entirely about economics. For instance: 'Between 1929 and 1933 the decline of our export trade amounted to no less than £200,000,000. We must set about systematic building of our home market.' It stressed the need for change: 'Our people are weary of socialism, which in the name of progress sets the interests of every country before its own. They are weary of conservative reaction, which keeps things as they are in the interests of the few. Today, they demand a new creed, a new spiritual movement which unites the principles of patriotism and progress, which loves king and country and is determined to build a country worthy of its people.'

Stories about what happened at Olympia are repeated over and over again and lose nothing as time goes on. For example, Mr. Philip Toynbee, well known to readers of the Sunday Press for his book reviews, broadcasting for the BBC on November 10, 1965, gave his memories of the Olympia meeting more than thirty years before, forgetting that he had already described them in *Friends Apart*: an excusable lapse in such a prolific writer. For in describing his impulsive and chivalrous intervention against the blackshirt stewards, he had clearly forgotten his previous visit to the 'ironmonger' and his 'seething' through the streets with the 'anti-fascist crowd'. Those events are vividly described in *Friends Apart*: 'Sir Oswald Mosley held a monster meeting at Olympia. In the afternoon we bought knuckle-dusters at a Drury Lane ironmonger, and I well remember the exaltation of trying them on. We flexed our fingers. "A bit too loose here. Not very comfortable on the thumb." We were expert knuckle-duster buyers. We seethed with the anti-fascist crowd down the cul-de-sac beside Addison Road station. . . . Later, we had somehow contrived to penetrate into the great auditorium itself. Olympia was nearly full—tier upon tier of the curious and the enthusiastic, and the enthusiastic in the great majority. . . .' Then an account of interrupters and 'A moment later the stewards had closed in on them. . . . We ran up the stairs and threw ourselves on the stewards' backs. . . . Tearful, bruised and broken, I was at last thrown out into the street.' Buy knuckle-dusters before a meeting —go there to have a row—jump on the stewards' backs—get thrown out roughly—have a good cry. Mr. Toynbee may well plead in mitigation that he was very young at the time; he may exclaim with Euripides, in words which will be familiar to a descendant of his grandfather: 'Ah, youth and the days that were!'

Olympia was a decisive battle. I regret having to write in such terms of a legitimate political meeting in our own country, but this was a fact. The most massive and seriously organised attempt ever made in Britain to smash a meeting by violence was heavily defeated. When the attackers had been ejected, the meeting continued to a normal conclusion in perfect order. I was able to deliver to the overwhelming majority of the audience the speech they had come to hear. Without the blackshirts, the meeting would have been a shambles. Why then, in concise repetition of Lloyd George's question, should the defenders rather than the assailants of free speech be blamed? At the time we received from some opponents in all the parties the reply of a vicious political prejudice, and I leave the final answer to history and to the fairer judgment of a new generation.

The meeting was decisive, not only by reason of the defeat suffered by the strongest attack which the opposition could mount, after open organisation for three weeks without hindrance of any kind from authority, whose plain duty it was to use the resources of the law against a publicly prepared breach of the peace. Sad though it was that these things should happen in England, the final effect was comic because the mind and character of the Left were so clearly revealed. Our opponents succeeded in frightening themselves out of their scanty wits with their own propaganda. In face of all evidence, which produced savage injuries to our people and only clean punches to the face on the other side, they launched an atrocity propaganda against us with the connivance of some members of the old parties who would use any means to discredit a new movement, whose rapid growth they feared. The allegation of our brutal behaviour certainly did us considerable harm, but it also helped to bring to a speedy end the attacks on our meetings. The 'reptiles' of Mr. Churchill's description saw now with certainty that they would be thrown out, and the snakehouse was rife with rumours that they might lose their fangs in the process. The opposition believed their own stories and were scared stiff. They were not the first politicians to fall victims to their own eloquence. Peace and order soon reigned; there was little further disorder at our meetings before the war, and they might have become like church services where the interruption which aids the speaker is impious, had it not been for the continually increasing enthusiasm of the audiences.

The blackshirt movement in the thirties was the only guarantee of free speech in Britain, and a spirit which was banished from our country, with results now all too plain, may merit some further examination. It all began in a characteristically English fashion, we improvised to meet attack, to meet an existing situation. When five hundred roughs were imported in coaches from all over the Midlands to smash a meeting of twelve thousand friendly people in the Birmingham stronghold my leadership had created for the Labour Party in five years, after sixty years of Conservative domination; when we were attacked on Ashley Green, Glasgow, by a similar force armed with razors after I had addressed an orderly crowd of sixty thousand; when we were threatened with lynching, after the count at Ashton, by a similar imported force after a three-week campaign of large and orderly meetings; when during my illness my wife's meetings were broken up in similar fashion all over the country, we felt quite simply that we had to do something about it. I began gradually to collect a regular body of stewards, young men in plain clothes who acted as chuckers-out in the traditional English fashion, as I had seen Tories thrown out of Liberal meetings when I was nine years old, and as when I was seventeen, I had often been thrown out myself with a merry band of my Sandhurst companions, when making ourselves a nuisance at such a time-honoured English institution as the Empire music hall.

Why then did we not leave it there? We always succeeded in holding our ground, but in the course of the fight the meeting would be smashed to pieces and the alarmed audience would vanish, as at Birmingham. We never lost the day, but it was always a Pyrrhic victory. We were facing what amounted to a military organisation with an amateur improvisation. We were fighting professionals, the communists who were past masters of organised violence, and we must ourselves become professionals. We had at that time a good scratch lot, some formidable fighters among them, but they were there, if necessary, to fight with their fists as individuals, and the reds were there for the express purpose of fighting as organised guerrillas with weapons. Our men were always forbidden to use weapons, but they were later trained to fight in organised units under clear command, and were practised in judo and boxing.

At first, we just had good amateurs like Peter Howard and Kid Lewis, an amateur in politics but not in the ring. Peter Howard was the Oxford University captain of the English rugger team. He was a friend of Harold Nicolson, who enjoyed his company in private, but not his companionship on these occasions. After the failure of the New Party, he became one of the leading figures of Dr. Buchman's moral rearmament movement, which had the money more fully to exercise his idealism. Ted Kid Lewis was ex-welter-weight boxing champion of the world, a Jew from Whitechapel, where he was New Party candidate in the 1931 election; my last appearance in that borough was in his support. I much appreciated Kid Lewis after seeing his fight with Carpentier, in which he conceded a lot of weight and gave one of the gamest displays I have ever seen in the ring. Like all the great professionals, he would never hit any man in private life for fear of killing him, but would go through a hostile crowd with his hands in his pockets, just barging with his shoulders. He was at the time keenly attracted to politics, but was bitterly disappointed by the result of his Whitechapel election and retired altogether. There were a number of colourful personalities among the New Party stewards, but they were essentially an amateur gathering.

After the defeat of the New Party, we began seriously to organise in the light of our sharp experience of organised violence. If we had to fight, we were determined to win. The first essential was the means to recognise each other quickly in a fight. It had become a military matter and we were up against the problem, which all armies have faced from the beginning of time. The first need is to recognise each other; the second, if possible, to recognise the enemy. This enemy in his long experience employed many artifices to prevent recognition, even going so far on some occasions as to use our dress. The communists after many years of fighting together had no need of uniforms, because they could recognise each other. After several years' experience we were in the same position, and our stewarding of indoor meetings was unimpaired when the uniform was finally removed, but in the early days it was a first essential for us in order to avoid fighting each other in the general mêlée.

I made one considerable mistake in the matter of uniform. We began well —I still think that at the time and in the conditions we faced it was right, and certainly necessary—with the simple black shirt, which anyone could buy or have made at home for a few shillings; private enterprise produced them in bulk. Soon our men developed the habit of cutting the shirt in the shape of a fencing-jacket, a kindly little tribute to my love of the sport; also this form had the practical advantage that it gave the opponent nothing to grasp, in particular no tie which he was wont to pull adroitly for purpose of strangulation. My mistake was in allowing the development of a full military uniform for certain men who qualified to wear it.

Technically, the matter had nothing to do with me, for I was divorced by

A Blackshirt rally in Hyde Park in 1934.

A Blackshirt club.

Violence in 1937 after the uniform ban. *Above left* Author opens a speech at Liverpool. *Above right* Hit by missiles. *Below left* Falls on to platform. *Below right* On the way to the hospital.

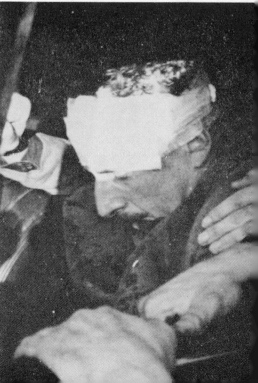

The Great Blackshirt meetings in the open air were effectively brought to an end by the Public Order Act, 1936, which removed both the uniform and the right to keep order at outdoor meetings. Indoor meetings continued to grow in size and enthusiasm, culminating at Earl's Court Exhibition Hall, July 1939, then reported to be the largest indoor meeting in the world.

Diana.

Author with Diana and Alexander on eve of his arrest, May 1940. She was arrested five weeks later, when her son Max was eleven weeks old.

our Constitution from the management of the financial side of the movement, and this was in origin a purely commercial matter. The company producing our supporting newspaper, *Action*, supplied the military uniform to any man who gave five nights' service a week to the party and sold a certain number of copies of the paper. I think even these men wearing the special uniform had to pay for it; but they were allowed to wear it on certificate of the party that they gave five nights' service, and of the journal that they sold the requisite number of papers. It was called the Action Press Uniform.

I was not therefore responsible for the uniform, but undoubtedly I could have used my influence to stop it and I did not; on the contrary, I accepted the invitation to wear it myself, in order to encourage others. The reason was that the men were desperately keen to wear it as a mark of distinction, a party honour. They were soldiers, good soldiers, and soldiers like a smart uniform. With my background I simply had not the heart to stop them, and so much to disappoint them. It was an error and a dereliction of duty, for I should have known that while we could have got away with the simple black shirt, the uniform made us much too military in appearance and would create prejudice. The old soldier in me got the better of the politician.

We created a real military organisation after the failure of the New Party, as the only way to defeat the highly-organised Communist guerrillas. Fortunately, many of us had some experience of it. I reverted to type and lived in the spirit of the professional army where I began; I was half soldier and half politician. Around me by then were men wearing every medal for gallantry the army had to offer. It is difficult to say exactly in retrospect how and when they came. As the sense of crisis in the mass of the people deepened and our struggle intensified, they seemed to appear from nowhere, from the limbo into which Britain all too often casts those who have served it well.

They were joined by others of similar type and character, who were too young to have fought in the previous war. We set about the job in a thoroughly professional manner. Another essential was to get a barracks where men could be concentrated and trained. This was provided by Whitelands College near to the Chelsea Barracks; it has since been pulled down and a block of flats built on the site. There were large sleeping-quarters and a drill or sports ground at the back for training. A mess and canteen were established, so that men could both live and sleep there. They paid for their keep, and the Whitelands barracks was practically self-supporting. Our administrative offices were in the same building, and I had a room overlooking the parade ground.

Another essential was mobility. We must be able to move rapidly about the country from the H.Q., particularly to areas where branches were newly formed and local members were not yet trained as stewards for meetings. The chances of disorder were always far less when the highly trained men from headquarters were present, because they were experts in the business, with all the patience it required, and never lost their heads in the excitable fashion of the neophyte. They would wait calmly through any uproar until the process of repeated warnings was exhausted and a clear, definite order given by the speaker to eject the assailants of the meeting; I was always both chairman and speaker at my own meetings, as the situation needed a firm and experienced control. The blackshirts were moved always by the slogan I gave them in the early days: 'We never start fights, we only finish them'.

Our means of mobility were ordinary vans used for moving furniture. They had thin tin sides and wire netting over the few glass windows, and this protection was sufficient to stop most of the missiles then in use. We were only fired on once, when a bullet went through the window of my car at Hull; I can vouch for the hole, but not for the incident, as I was not in the car at the time. Some witnesses said it was fired from a neighbouring roof. The vans used for transport quickly became known among our opponents as armoured cars and the wildest tales were circulated about them. We were always aided in our efforts to maintain order by the simple process of our opponents becoming scared by their own propaganda and thus losing prematurely their stomach for the fray.

All this meant money, though much less than was alleged. The men paid for everything themselves, from the black shirts to their accommodation. The movement only had to find money for its administrative staff, which never at any time exceeded one hundred and forty men or women, and that was at a later stage when the black house, as our barracks in Chelsea came to be called, was closed and we had ordinary political offices in Great Smith Street. We then had national inspectors or agents throughout the country, like all political parties. Having given the movement its spirit by centralisation, I had then decided to spread that spirit throughout the country by decentralisation. The change was introduced in 1935, sixteen months before the Public Order Act, which made the army illegal. I will deal later with the whole question of finance, though I was by my own volition, and consequently by our original Constitution, removed from that sphere.

My part was to declare policy and to assume the ultimate responsibility of decision and command. In practice, there was far more consultation with members before policy was published or decisions taken than in any other party. Not only did I always consult my colleagues at headquarters, but in my constant journeys throughout the country I consulted all members. This was done both in regular conferences and in the assembly of blackshirts after every meeting, when I not only addressed them but also moved among them talking to individual members. I felt deeply that we owed each other this friendship, and their companionship was one of the joys I have known in life. It was also an essential method for obtaining the vital information which produced efficiency, because it was difficult in these conditions for anything important to be kept from me. We were, admittedly, organised as an army, but it was an army with a difference, for our members were volunteers who could walk out any day they liked, telling me or anyone else to go to the devil. Strangely enough, very few of them did. Our discipline was voluntary, an act of devotion, without sanction of any kind. It had to be a new model army, and it was.

It has been said that this was the first time since the days of Cromwell that a 'private army' was created in Britain, and it is likely to be the last, for such an enterprise would today be a serious breach of the law. The question is often asked, how was it done? The answer is partly by force of necessity and partly by inspiration of the spirit we gave it. This spirit could not have been so fully and enduringly created without the community of the old black house The basis was that in a class-ridden society, our life together was entirely classless. In the black shirt, the traditional duke's son and dustman could meet in the mess with complete equality, scarcely aware of each other's origin. This was the second great advantage of the distinctive dress, which made our men all look the same.

The discipline on parade aspired to be up to Guards' standard, but did not exist in the mess, where all ranks met in equality and complete companionship. This was the basis of a new model army, with its new political idea, and a new ideal of life. 'Opportunity open to all, but privilege to none,' was intended to ring with the classic appeal of an army whose every soldier carried a baton in the knapsack. Our morality declared that all was permitted, provided an act did no harm to others; or to the man himself, thus impairing his dedicated service to the land he loved. It was designed to instil a renaissance of manhood. Such an attitude did, indeed, produce a new spirit. Deliberately, we willed the birth of a type who was half soldier and half politician, partly a tough warrior in hard and practical tests, and partly an inspired idealist who reached for the stars with his feet firmly on the ground. This was our dream of the blackshirt character and in many fine young men it was largely realised.

I am often pressed to answer more fully the question, what was my relationship with these men and what was the effect on me of the extraordinary life I led for seven years, between 1932 and 1939? My relationship with them was the companionship of a dedicated order. We were a band of companions wholly given to the saving of our country for purposes in which we passionately believed, and by methods which we became convinced were entirely necessary. In action, all command depended on me, but in the common rooms of headquarters, or in the local premises of something over four hundred branches throughout the country, I was just one of them. I joined in the free discussion of politics which always prevailed among us, in the sports to which our spare time was largely given, in the simple club-room gatherings where we would drink beer together or cups of tea prepared by women blackshirts.

This was the most complete companionship I have ever known, except in the old regular army in time of war, more complete even than my early days in the Labour Party, when I enjoyed every night the warm hospitality of a different working-class home. It was more complete because we were banded together by the common danger of our struggle and the savage animosity of the old world towards us. Most of them were very like members of the Labour Party in the days when I was first a member, when it still suffered ostracism and persecution. They liked dressing up and having bands and banners, just as the miners did at the Durham gala; symbols which were then anathema to the shy middle-class with its public school inhibitions, though recruits from their ranks were soon infected with the gay panache of which, in England, East London is the spiritual home. They were English people of the very soil of England, with their warm geniality, humour and ever-ready courage.

Panache is a French, a European word, while most of our members were very British, but it best describes the outward aspect of the blackshirt attitude. They certainly expected me, in spirit, to wear the white plume of Navarre. Great meetings under frequent attack over a long period resembled in some respects a battlefield, but with a difference. The task of a general is complicated if he never knows on arrival at the scene of action whether he will have to deliver a speech which convinces the audience with appeal to reason, and in conclusion moves some of them by the passionate appeal of idealism to the ardours and sacrifice of a new mission in life; or whether he will have to lead a fight to eject well-organised and armed hooligans before any argument can be addressed to the quiet and orderly British audience. The two performances require different moods, as even Bonaparte discovered, when Lucien pulled him out of the Assembly riot at the time of Brumaire; both capacities were often needed, for the speech still had to be made when the roughs had been thrown out.

We won these fights without exception, from the early days when, after repeated warnings and continued uproar, I used to come down from the platform myself to lead the fight, as in the first battle at Birmingham. Our assailants on that occasion subsequently had the effrontery to charge me with assault, but after hearing the evidence, it did not take the Birmingham stipendiary long to dismiss the case. Later, we were organised with groups of stewards each under an individual leader covering every section of the hall. The rule was never to move until I gave the order from the platform, on which I remained throughout at this stage of organisation. It was my habit to give three clear warnings before ordering the ejection of those causing disorder, with the minimum force necessary, and once we were properly organised the process did not take long. The audience who had come to hear the speech remained after the fight because they were witnesses of its necessity. So many people saw what happened at first hand throughout the country that the wild abuse of our alleged brutality did not in those days cut much ice outside the narrow and interested circles of its manufacture.

The effect on us all was very like a return to war conditions, with which many of us were familiar. For me, it was a sharp change from the normal politics to which I had become accustomed during the long interval, and I am often asked to describe my personal feelings on such an occasion as Olympia in 1934. After that meeting I was allowed to speak briefly over the BBC; the last occasion I was permitted to use the medium of that organisation which in recent years has so frequently employed other people to discuss me. Afterwards, one of their commentators said in effect that to him the most shocking part of the terrible occasion was that throughout the meeting and my subsequent talk over the radio I had been so inhumanly calm. This remark truly astonished me, for I could not see that the necessary business of throwing a bunch of roughs out of Olympia should have caused emotional disturbance to anyone who had experience of air and trench fighting in the previous war. Where did they think we came from? The men in local command could not be rattled then, and I saw less reason to be excited in the Olympia fight, even if the other side had razors and our men only had their fists. In fact, it is quite essential on such occasions to remain calm.

If you have a small command of a platoon, or troop, as it is called in our service, everyone looks to you if the balloon goes up in an attack, sudden bombardment, or other alarm. You develop the habit of remaining calm and giving clear orders. It was the same in the larger command of blackshirt politics. But there was an added test because spotlights were focused on the platform, and sometimes strong cinema lights for most of the time; if the speaker should lose command for a moment, it would be instantly communicated to the stewards in a loss of confidence and to the general audience in alarm and disturbance. I developed the habit of complete impassivity, while giving clear instructions to the stewards, and asking the audience to remain seated as it would soon be over. This was one of the occasions when above all the principal must be calm.

How then did I feel before, during and after; inside myself, as they say? Here again I was fortified by a diverse experience. Waiting in a small room before a meeting like Olympia, when I knew a battle long organised by opponents was bound to take place, was a strange experience, and similar though less exacting was waiting before the 1939 meeting at Earls Court. In the first case there was an audience which I had to convince, but first a fight which we had to win. In the second case, at Earls Court, all the fighting was over, but a huge audience was assembled, all of whom I must try to convince and some of whom I must lift to further heights of enthusiasm. It would be a tremendous effort of the mind, will and spirit for the sake of the cause in which I passionately believed. That period of waiting is a time of awe.

In the end, the moment comes and you go over the top. All the intellect, the faith, the preparation of the spirit, is then of no avail without the effort of the will. The act of starting is that of an automaton, moved by will alone. If you sit down in that little room with introspective questioning—can I really go on to the platform under those spotlights, speak for over two hours, convince them, move them to a passionate enthusiasm, possibly after keeping command through all the squalid necessity of a dirty, unpleasant fight? —clearly the answer is, no, it is quite impossible, out of the question.

These thoughts intrude in many situations, small and large. In the boxing-ring of youth, looking at that strong boy in the opposite corner, who is bound to beat you; then the bell, you are at him, and sometimes, to your astonish-ment, you win. Looking at that big fellow at the other end of the piste in a world fencing championship, introspection can quickly summon the same inhibitions. Sitting inertly in an early aeroplane while the engine is ticking over and the riggers and mechanics are giving their last attention, it is clearly impossible to take the flimsy contraption off the ground, through a long and difficult experience, and then to put it safely back on the same small patch of earth—if, that is, you question capacity closely and anxiously. Give all high tests the utmost preparation of mind and body, the closest attention to essential detail; yet the final act in all real things is will; you open the throttle as you swing it into the wind, you are off and the sky belongs to you.

Our whole situation was governed by the fact that for all practical purposes we were engaged in a military operation against the highly trained guerrillas of communism, who were prototypes of those who have since appeared in many different parts of the world. It was in one way a more exacting occupa-tion than ordinary war because the enemy was armed and we were not. He was allowed a strange latitude by the law, which he openly and obviously broke, while we had to be scrupulously careful to keep within it, as even a suspicion of stepping outside it brought immediate prosecution. Our final victory was no doubt confirmed and established by the death in the Spanish Civil War of some of the most redoubtable of our opponents, but we had won decisively before that. Many of the typically English characters among the communists had by then come over to us. Ever after those days, some of our best members were ex-communists, and some of them held important posts in the party. Communists are well versed in real politics and after the requisite period of test they often become valuable members.

It may be felt that throughout this period I much overrated the danger of communism in Britain. That is an easy view in the affluent society of the 1960s, but it misunderstands both the fluidity of the economic situation and the flexibility of communism. Modern experience indicates that the world economy can change for better or worse very quickly, and with it will change the tactics of the communists. At present, they are playing their hand very gently, and have assumed almost the appearance of a bourgeois party in the countries where they are strongest. Their organisation has been founded a long time and has an able and experienced leadership. Since 1848 the communists have learned much, and have developed an extraordinary variety of methods; the long training of their membership has achieved a complete discipline, based on a deep understanding of the ultimate objectives of the party and the need for continued manoeuvre to attain them. A party which aims not at the reform but at the overthrow of society cannot openly declare its objectives and must create a hard core of membership which understands the need for a constant change of tactic. The communists are also possessed by the belief that the end justifies the means to a far greater extent than any other practitioners of this pernicious and socially disruptive doctrine. Dedicated communists are highly-trained political soldiers, equally prepared to sing in the choir of churches open to their infiltration, or to use machine-guns in the streets, which are conveniently carried beneath surplices.

Admirable in communism is the power to endure, to return again and again from defeat, and to march through disaster to final victory. This quality was for generations unique in politics and comparable only with the morale of a great army. An example was the retreat of the German army in 1914 to positions prepared in advance against disaster on the Aisne, while their main force was advancing in the full flush of victory on Paris. That manoeuvre seemed to professional soldiers a superb performance; foresight in command and morale in the troops. In politics, the communists have done the equivalent over many generations, and as a result have won half the world. It seems a rule of history that real men and real movements who finally change the course of events must first pass through the ordeal of recurrent defeat and long disaster; a natural test of greatness in any cause. Communism is never a negligible force; it should be studied, as the great enemy should always be studied in every move of his method and in every fibre of his being.

Detestable in communism, and fortunately for us also laden with the seeds of its ultimate disaster, is the quality of its fanaticism which uses and justifies the vilest of means to achieve ends which it genuinely believes to be noble. It is finally disastrous because it inevitably destroys all honour and trust among men, even within the party. If you are ready to assassinate by some wretched trick an opponent[1] who impedes the ends of the party, you finally assassinate comrades when you become convinced they too are impeding the ends of the party. Hence the judicial murder of old bolsheviks under Stalin and all the long and horrible record of communism devouring its own. Communism can always be defeated by political forces with similar resolution which combine great beliefs with the basic values of honour and

---

[1] It is true that political assassination was banned by Lenin when he denounced the ineffectiveness of nihilism, in his *Infantile Diseases of the Left*, but character assassination was then practised with unprecedented vigour and with results which in the end were much the same, even physically.

fair dealing among men. Such movements only fail when they fall victim in some degree to the moral disease of communism.

The opponents of communism have a further strength in that their policies can be openly declared, because in due season of proved facts they are acceptable to European society, while the objectives of communism are not. This is the basis of my belief that in the end we can only do great things in the great way of declaring the truth, and that government by small tricks fails in great periods; it will then succumb to the larger and more practised villainies of communism. Meanwhile, let us not delude ourselves that communism has changed, or will easily change, its character. It was a long march from Siberia to the Kremlin, and it is an insult to communist leaders—with whom I am confident we can at least work out a system of competitive co-existence—to suggest they will sell the birthright won by that sacrifice for a mess of pottage prepared by corruption.

The great weakness of communism in the West is that it is obviously a party controlled and directed from abroad, and subject to influences which in some respects are Asiatic rather than European. We, on the other hand, were to any close observer clearly in whole essence and character a British movement, and it was this quality which attracted to us some genuine but patriotic revolutionaries who had previously been drawn to communism. We always felt ourselves European as well as British, but we have seen that our relationship with fascist movements in foreign countries was too slight to keep the peace rather than strong enough to jeopardise our own country; the truth was once again the opposite of imputation. We need lose no time in discussing the suggestion that we were in some mysterious way responsible for the atrocities committed in German concentration camps at the very time we ourselves were held in prisons or British concentration camps; this idea is confined to the moronic substratum of politics.

Our British movement achieved so much in face of steadily declining unemployment figures that it cannot be doubted we should have won in Britain if the crisis had deepened. Such conditions would have arisen when the effect of Roosevelt's doubling of the price of gold was exhausted, and unemployment began to rise in 1938, but for the hectic rearmament boom, followed by a world war. This was certainly the opinion of men well placed to answer this question. For instance, a leading journalist of the Left, Hannen Swaffer, wrote in *World Press News* on August 5, 1943, under the heading 'Saved by the War', that it was 'left to the war and 18B' (imprisonment without trial) 'to deal effectively with Mosley and his movement,' and concluded: 'Yes, but for the war we might today have been a Fascist country'.

The question remains, how in face of declining unemployment and improving economic conditions, we nevertheless made progress which appeared so spectacular. The evidence of membership figures I cannot disclose, for it was our rule never to publish them. It seemed to me that fluctuations were inevitable, and in a struggle of such intensity it would be an error to notify the opponent either of weakness or of strength; in real politics as in war it is better to keep him guessing. The overt evidence of progress between 1934 and 1939 is sufficiently shown in the difference between the Olympia and Earls Court meetings. This visual evidence controverted the assertion that we declined after the Public Order Act in 1936, for this was clearly not the case. At that time we were no doubt strengthened by the temporary decline in the economic situation reflected in the unemployment figures of 1938, but after that opposition to the war became the main issue and thrust even economics into the background. The rise of our movement continued throughout the full seven years until 1939 with only temporary fluctuations.

The active membership was not always the same; a very large number of men and women passed through our hands and were only temporarily active, but on the whole we did not lose them as the Communist Party did. We found that the few members who turned against us had usually some acute personal reason. Normally, men and women after intense activity would become inactive in a kind of moral exhaustion, but they nearly all remained with us always; complete and permanent loss was rare. It has been a saying of our movement, based on truth: once with us, always with us.

We lost a few leading figures in the inevitable shocks and trials which all new movements undergo, but the majority stood firm throughout. In May 1937 we had to dismiss one-hundred-and-one out of a total staff of one-hundred-and-forty at Headquarters, owing to a sudden financial crisis. Only four of the hundred-and-one dismissed turned against the party; the others remained entirely loyal. Those who stayed firm were headed by Raven Thomson and those who deserted were headed by William Joyce. He was not a man to mind losing a job, but he was intensely vain; a quite common foible in very small men, as Bacon shows in his essay on the diminutive. It was a shock to his vanity that I retained chief organisers like Francis-Hawkins and dropped him.

Joyce did his best to create a revolt in the party, which I overcame without difficulty. He was expelled and founded a new party. Beginning with about sixty, mostly dissidents from our movement, after two and a half years he finished with about twenty. He failed to shake our members whose morale was much too strong for him, and shortly before the outbreak of war he went to Germany; his attitude was fundamentally different in this test to that of our members, and the rest of the story is well known. I was more fortunate in these troubles than most leaders of new parties, whether of the left, right or centre. The whole leadership of the Communist Party melted away after the disaster of 1905; in the *Lessons of October*, Trotsky claims that he and Lenin were the only survivors of the leadership in 1917. Hitler shot seventy of his previously most trusted assistants on June 30, 1934, and Mussolini, not long before his arrival in power, was near to resignation on account of divisions within the party. My companions, with no compulsion and in face of long adversity, remained loyal.

Lloyd George was right when he said our movement was a phenomenon, and it was due entirely to an idea which prevailed against the economic trend. We advanced by force of the spirit alone, and with a rapidity which threw the old world into a panic of special legislation. The defeat of violence and the failure of misrepresentation were followed by a new law of suppression. It was suggested that a triumphant 'private army' might become a danger to the State. We were assailed by special Acts of Parliament. Has any other political party in Britain experienced, let alone survived, two special measures passed by Parliament for its suppression? If not, we must bear alone the burden of this dubious honour.

The first measure was the Public Order Act, the second was the special order 18B(1A) passed with the approval of Parliament but without our knowledge, when in 1940 the normal form of law had been suspended, including the traditional and long-vaunted Habeas Corpus Act, which now maintains British freedom only when it is not in danger. The Public Order Act was passed in October 1936. Its main provision was to make illegal the wearing of uniform for political purposes and thus to bring to an end what was called a 'private army'. Happily, these Conservative gentlemen often shoot behind the bird, despite much practice. The black shirt had fulfilled its practical purpose, and the chief loss was sentimental, for men rightly love a symbol of their struggle and sacrifice together. Sacrifice was the essence of our movement and the making of it.

The second object of the Public Order Act was to prevent us maintaining order at our outdoor meetings, though we were still allowed to steward our indoor meetings with our own members. The result was that the indoor meetings continued in complete order, but the outdoor meetings sometimes became shambles. The responsibility for keeping order in the open air was placed on the police alone. An early effect was to put me in hospital for a week in Liverpool in October 1937. The cause was simple and easily foreseeable. Our members surrounded the platform in the usual way at a meeting I was to address. The reds massed for a militant counter-demonstration, which our members could quickly have seen off as usual under the previous law. A large force of police was present to maintain order under the newly made law. They placed a strong force in a ring between our members and the reds, and pressed our people against the platform. The result was to bring the platform within easy range of red missiles, and to prevent our members moving among the reds to stop them being thrown. On arrival, I was informed that the previous speaker had been knocked out by a brick, and a barrage of considerable variety was crashing on the platform with such profusion that it was clear no speaker could long survive. In fact, I was hit by a piece of metal on the left side of my forehead within two minutes of mounting the platform. The surgeon who operated in the Liverpool hospital informed me that an inch farther back it would have killed me. The police action was due not to malice but to inexperience. They had no idea how to handle the situation, and had only the simple intent of preventing the two sides fighting. The minor matter of the speaker possibly being killed had been overlooked. However, they did their best to provide some remedy by prosecuting a young man who was alleged to have thrown the missile. Two plain-clothes officers gave evidence that they saw him with the object in his hand, saw him throw it, and watched its flight until it hit my head. The case against the young man was dismissed.

The second effect was that the removal of the black shirt also removed the discipline of our movement. When our young men were in uniform we were able to enforce our rule against even heckling at the meetings of opponents, and, of course, against any form of violence. With the removal of the uniform and the consequent anonymity it was difficult to enforce the rule among men and women made angry by a sense of political injustice, which further inflamed their indignation against the disgraceful failure of the old parties to remedy economic conditions. They had been the victims of violence and persecution in the days which followed Olympia, and they remembered it. Consequently, disorder then occurred for the first time at Labour meetings, and in the streets. It was difficult to obtain evidence after the removal of the uniform, but if the facts were clear my rule was simple. A man would be expelled for seeking out opponents and attacking them, or for any form of aggression or bullying, but certainly not for defending himself against attack on the streets, to which our men and women were still subject when alone or in small parties. In fact, any disorder from our side was almost always the work of non-members, camp-followers to whom my sanctions could not apply. The general uproar which followed the passing of the Public Order Act combined with the clear possibility of electoral defeat to make Labour leaders feel that the air of East London had become less healthy; Mr. Attlee left Limehouse, and Mr. Morrison left Hackney for constituencies in other parts of London.

I appealed for order and free speech for my opponents, although I am unaware that they ever did the same for me. What occurred in East London was much exaggerated, and Labour leaders were not responsible for the earlier disorders of some of their supporters, any more than I was responsible for the later disorder of some of my supporters. It is true that I had then considerable influence in East London, because for years I had spoken at the great meetings and led the marches which finally swung its people to our side. It is also true that this influence in the period of our strength did something to save those who had sown the wind at Olympia from reaping the full force of the whirlwind.

The results of our efforts in East London led to an electoral triumph, which incidentally revealed the falsity of the allegations against us. We polled an average of nearly 19 per cent throughout the area in the London County Council elections of March 1937; 23 per cent in Bethnal Green, 19 per cent in Limehouse, and 14 per cent in Shoreditch. At that time this was a house-holders' vote, because even young married couples living with their parents in that overcrowded area had not got the municipal vote. The young were then almost solidly with us, but had not the right to vote, except at parlia-mentary elections; our 19 per cent was a vote of the old. If a general election had been held at that time on the parliamentary register, including the young vote, we should certainly have won. Yet some of our opponents contend that we should never have presented ourselves in East London, for bogus reasons I will later analyse. Claiming to be democrats, they would have disenfranchised the East London electorate.

Fair-minded men may reply to all this: yes, you had every right to express your opinions, and it was intolerable that free speech should be brought to an end in Britain by an organised minority under control which was at least dubious, but it was also intolerable that you should prance around at the head of a 'private army' and the old parties were quite right to stop it by Act of Parliament. To this I reply—agreed—provided they then kept order themselves. No one could be more strongly than I in accord with the proposi-tion that the State alone under elected majority should govern; but govern it must, or it forfeits respect and authority.

The 'private army' was born of a situation in which order at public meetings and free speech in Britain had ceased to exist. The only period in which free speech at open meetings for the opponents of communism existed in Britain during my lifetime was while the 'private army' also existed, and for a brief subsequent period. The State has never yet done anything effective about free speech, which for any new movement relying on public meetings still does not exist; its suppression since the war has been more complete than in any previous period.

It is true that television has radically altered the whole position: public meetings in the old style are now outdated. Their only purpose is to enable established party leaders to posture in becoming attitudes before the tele-vision cameras. One night such a personality can say what he has to say to the whole nation in a quiet face-to-face talk in the studio. The next night he can advertise to the world his toleration; his warm humane character can be paraded before the whole people by forbidding his stewards to eject a few interrupters at one of his rare public meetings. It does not matter to him if his audience cannot hear a word he has to say; he can address the world the night before or the night after in the calm of the studio, and the purpose of the public meeting is better secured by advertising his kindly forbearance than his oratorical inadequacy. It was different in my days of public meetings: I had to be heard or politically cease to exist, and at no time since 1934 have

I had the facilities of the BBC. If today the State denies a man the means to secure free speech for himself, it has the duty itself in one form or another to maintain his right of free speech.

The patriotism, courage, idealism and dedication of the blackshirt movement alone protected our cause in the thirties from organised violence. Those who control the old world combined in an effort to destroy the spirit of these young men, and at least succeeded in producing a supreme profusion of the opposite type. Do they now feel it is keeping really fine for them?—or are some of them beginning to wonder whether they would like a change? For my part, I am proud of having organised and led a movement which stopped Red violence and restored free speech to Britain, and if I were ever faced again with anarchy or a communist conspiracy which sought to ruin my country, I would be prepared under the law with other methods in other circumstances to do it again.

The speech which moved the blackshirts and an audience of eight thousand people in the Albert Hall on a March evening in 1935 would echo as strangely to some contemporary ears as words from another planet, but I believe that in the wider context and greater possibility of Europe—in a society free from the violence which then assailed us—a revival and extension of this same first instinct of patriotism will find a higher expression and further mission.

'We count it a privilege to live in an age when England demands that great things shall be done, a privilege to be of the generation which learns to say what can we give instead of what can we take. For thus our generation learns there are greater things than slothful ease; greater things than safety; more terrible things than death.

'This shall be the epic generation which scales again the heights of time and history to see once more the immortal lights—the lights of sacrifice and high endeavour summoning through ordeal the soul of humanity to the sublime and the eternal. The alternatives of our age are heroism or oblivion. There are no lesser paths in the history of great nations. Can we, therefore, doubt which path to choose?

'Let us tonight at this great meeting give the answer. Hold high the head of England; lift strong the voice of Empire. Let us to Europe and to the world proclaim that the heart of this great people is undaunted and invincible. This flag still challenges the winds of destiny. This flame still burns. This glory shall not die. The soul of Empire is alive, and England again dares to be great.'

17
The Ideology of Fascism
Science and Caesarism

IDEAS in a void have never appealed to me; action must follow thought or political life is meaningless. The charge is sometimes made against me that my approach was at once too intellectual and too rough, too highbrow and too popular, a confusion between the study and the street. According to this theory I fell between two stools, and my leadership was consequently misconceived. It is a criticism which shows a misunderstanding of reality in modern politics. Anyone who cannot see the essential connection between thought and action as a concerted whole is unfit for the crude and yet subtle business of real politics in the twentieth century. It is not only necessary to have ideas but also to get them accepted and implemented. I have described the results of this attempt within the old parties, and have reached the point in this story where we went beyond their world in a direct appeal to the mass of the people. Then descended upon us the whole weight of the system in the organised smother, the denial of all means of expression and publicity; also the ineluctable force of organised violence, which sought to deprive us of our only remaining means of persuasion, the spoken word at the public meeting. In retrospect I put again the key question: what were we to do, go home and call it a day?

It is precisely at this point that intellect must finally decide whether to retire into the ivory tower or to enter the street with all that this entails. Intellect, to be effective, must now unite with will[1]; otherwise the idea remains in the void. The 'thought–deed man' described in *The Alternative* was the need of the hour. It is not an attractive phrase, and I am not in love with it myself, but it expresses concisely the prime necessity of the modern world: men who can

[1] *Seinen Willen will nun der Geist, seine Welt gewinnt sich der Welt verlorene.*

both think and act. So far from thought and action being antithetical—as the criticism of combining economic policies with the blackshirt movement suggested—they are essential complements in a creative whole; their union is indispensable, vital to a new birth.

In the light of contemporary experience this is undeniable. Communism today commands half the world. It rests on a combination of Marxian thinking and communist party action. If the idea had just rested behind the whiskers would anything more have happened? It was in fact carried forward to the conquest of half the globe by the most brutal, ruthless and unscrupulous methods of action humanity has known; methods which, for reasons given, I believe will in the end be destructive of the idea, but certainly embodying action in extreme degree.

The superficial question may be raised whether the idea really had any relation to this kind of action, since not one in a hundred of Communist Party members understands Marxism, and not one in a million in the countries adhering to that creed has ever read Marx. Why then should this abstruse and far from popular doctrine have anything to do with the achievement at all? It is a superficial question, but it is difficult to answer without a psychological treatise which delves to the roots of human nature. In short reply, no movement of the human mind and spirit goes far unless it is inspired by an idea which, for better or worse, is a reality. It may be as obscure and contorted as Marxian economic theory or as clear and simple as the Christian doctrine of love, but it must be a reality in the sense that it appeals to some deep feeling in human nature. When thought is obscure it must be translated into feeling to be effective. It is understood by an élite, and if it is a real and powerful idea it develops in them a certain attitude to life. This attitude is communicated to others who may not be familiar with the detail of the thinking, and it then becomes the feeling of the mass. A decisive idea thus transmuted into mass feeling can cause the birth of a new civilisation. Without such an idea, action is in the void, and without action the idea also rests in the void.

This truth has been well understood and applied in practical affairs by men who would appear the least likely to grasp it. For this reason, Stalin, amid all the brutalities of his actions, still tolerated and even encouraged the intellectuals, who must often have maddened him for much the same reasons which led Plato so unexpectedly to suggest the exclusion of poets from the Republic. Mao clearly felt the same necessity in encouraging both 'a hundred blooms' of the intellect and the development of the Red Guards. Lenin, who more than any other Russian communist leader, except possibly his close associate Trotsky, combined in himself the qualities of reflection and of action, undoubtedly recognised the same synthesis as a prerequisite of any movement of humanity to a new form, though it was less evident in his conduct during the turmoil of his period.

Fascism too derived much from its intellectual antecedents and by no means only from the relatively modern sources usually ascribed to it such as Sorel, Pareto, Proudhon, Nietzsche, and earlier English writers and men of action like Hobbes, Strafford, Bolingbroke, and later Carlyle. Some years ago Dr. Popper brought the industry and erudition of central Europe to London University and in his book, *The Open Society and its Enemies*, virtually denounced every outstanding thinker from Plato to Hegel as a fascist: I gladly accepted the gift, and expressed my appreciation for this confirmation of what I had long suspected.[1]

Marxism was the negative of the nineteenth century, and yet communism required this intellectual background for any enduring success; more is needed than a bundle of grievances. *A fortiori*, the power of intellect and imagination will be necessary to the European creed which will be the positive of the twentieth century. During the long years since the war I have given my main energies to this necessity.

Time was too short for fascism to burgeon into a new culture which would later come to flower in a new civilisation. Indeed, the organic nature of fascism precluded a new culture in the sense of any sharp break with the past, because in essence it preserved and restored classic European values. I had already done the thinking which had produced a series of practical proposals to meet the immediate danger and long-term needs of my country; the urgency was then to implement them in practical action. It was not therefore just barbarism when at this stage I said that the men who can think are not enough, and I must go out to find the men who can feel, and do. It was recognition of a truth beyond the intellectuals with whom I was associated, and it deeply offended them precisely because it was beyond them. It is essential to surpass this antithesis of intellect and feeling in a synthesis which embraces both at a new level of thought and action.

When my original intellectual associates fell away in the shock of action which resisted organised violence, it was suggested that thereafter I was surrounded by stupid brutes who were conveniently classified as thugs. In fact, new intellectuals emerged from the study under the impact of those events, who at least equalled in mind and certainly surpassed in character those who had departed. In my company were some who would have added stature to any Cabinet and adorned any university. Their names were not well known because the smother was then operative to prevent their fame when they emerged, and threat to livelihood inhibited the open appearance of others. Our movement in these conditions became ever more like the iceberg with the main weight below the surface.

[1] A recent book by John Harrison, *The Reactionaries* (Gollancz, 1966), apparently ascribed fascist tendencies to the following writers: Yeats, T. S. Eliot, Ezra Pound, Wyndham Lewis and D. H. Lawrence. In this case the title and the theme were a contradiction in terms, because writers cannot both be fascists and reactionaries. A movement of the Right has nothing to do with fascism, which can be described as revolutionary but not as reactionary.

The vilely libelled mass of our members were the very flower of the English people. They were men and women with the vision to see the doom coming to the values and position of their country and with the will and courage to resist it. Most of them were certainly men of feeling and of action rather than of the study, the type of the soldier rather than of the scholar, giving precedence to sword over gown, but it is such men who, in union with creative thinkers, build all movements of reality. In the rapid advance of our movement there was little time for academic sterilities, and even too little time, admittedly, for the serious discussion which is necessary to the advance of thought and development of policy. In that period time was always too short, and everything was too hurried; disabilities which subsequent experience repaired. I remember one of our best men, who after a spectacular R.A.F. career proved to have an extraordinary capacity for street leadership, saying to me: 'I have read little you have ever written because my work keeps me too busy, and I have heard little you have ever said, because at the meetings I am always looking round for the next Red who might have to go out, but—I feel with you'—and his regard was a tribute to the capacity for translating new thought and morality into feeling which can hold and inspire men with a dedicated passion. In the same way, I was always pleased beyond any other praise at the end of a speech when some fine old Englishman would come up to me and say: 'You have been saying what I felt all my life'. He meant that the speech had touched some deep chord in the eternal being of England.

This will no doubt be regarded as absurd by some who are called intellectuals and who possess every qualification for that title except an intellect. Yet this is not sentiment, or worse; it is reality, the force which moves men. Leadership should be equally at home in the study of economics, in the homes of the poorest during moments of sorrow or happiness, in the merry scenes of English pubs and in the philosophic debates of universities. It must be interwoven with English and now with European life, both understanding and creative, both appreciative of the present and aspiring to new heights. Our action and also our thinking were continually developing. Even in the turmoil of pre-war politics fresh thought was added to the original economic concepts born within the Labour Party, but because fascism was so much a national creed, the new ideological development had little relation to contemporary thinking in the movements of the Continent.

Contrast has been the essence of my life, and it is good, provided it is expressed in two poles of an harmonious whole serving the same overriding purpose rather than in the discords of a split personality. I have given some account of the action in my fascist period which won the right to express at public meetings economic policies devised while I was still a member of the Labour Party. Now I must give some account of ideas in a quite different sphere of thought, which added ideology to the economics of my Labour Party days. These ideas seem to me crude and unsatisfactory in comparison with my thinking and writing since the Second World War and the enforced withdrawal into reading and reflection which it entailed for me. Nevertheless, it is difficult to contend in the light of my speech and writing in the thirties that fascism had no ideological background, though our English approach had not much to do with the main stream of fascist thought abroad. The derivation of this thinking is European, but it emphasises the English character of fascism in Britain because it is so remote from what fascist movements on the Continent were thinking or saying at that time, and in certain vital respects directly contradicted the continental approach to the same subjects.

My first speech with this theme was delivered in March 1933, at a choice of venue which in retrospect may seem curious—the English-Speaking Union, which was founded to promote Anglo-American friendship. After a conventional opening I said:

'Our opponents allege that fascism has no historic background or philosophy, and it is my task this afternoon to suggest that fascism has roots deep in history and has been sustained by some of the finest flights of the speculative mind. . . . So far it is to some extent true that the fascist philosophy has not assumed a very concrete and definite form, but you must remember that the fascist faith has only been in existence little more than ten years: it is a growth of the last decade. Already, however, its philosophic background is capable of some formulation, and that has happened in a far shorter space of time than a corresponding development in any other great political faith of history. Just as the fascist movement itself, in several great countries, has advanced towards power at a phenomenal speed, so the fascist faith and philosophy as a permanent conception, an attitude to life, has advanced far more quickly than did the philosophies of the older faiths. Take liberalism: a very long interval elapsed between the writings of such men as Voltaire and Rousseau, and the final formation of the liberal creed in the hands of English statesmen at the end of the eighteenth and the beginning of the nineteenth century.

In fact, these great political movements and psychological upheavals only very slowly crystallised into a definite system of thought, as well as a system of action; and in the fascist case it is probably rather soon to expect at the end of ten years that it should have assumed a concrete, crystallised form.'

This, of course, was true, and fascism then had only six years left before the turmoil of the Second World War which cut short its life. It is clearly too much to hope that any doctrine born as an explosion of action in a time of national crisis can develop a complete philosophy in so short a space of time. The speech continued:

'Nevertheless, I believe that fascist philosophy can be expressed in intelligible terms, and while it makes an entirely novel contribution to the thought of this age, it can yet be shown to derive both its origin and its historic support from the established thought of the past. In the first instance, I suggest that most philosophies of action are derived from a synthesis of cultural conflicts in a previous period. Where, in an age of culture, of thought, of abstract speculation, you find two great cultures in sharp antithesis, you usually find, in the following age of action, some synthesis in practice between those two sharp antitheses which leads to a practical creed of action. This conception may seem to you to suggest, to some extent, a Spenglerian approach.'

Why in this context did I refer to a Spenglerian approach?—for the concept of two antitheses leading to a synthesis is clearly Hegelian; perhaps I thought that the spectre of Hegel would be too alarming for the English-Speaking Union. Goethe remarked that since Germans found him so difficult, he must be impossible for foreigners. Referring to Spengler, I continued:

'It is quite true that the great German philosopher has probably done more than any other to paint in the broad background of fascist thought. Not very much more than that. And possibly he is inhibited from coming nearer to the subject by his innate pessimism, which, in its turn, I would humbly suggest to you arises from his entire ignorance of modern science and mechanical development. If you look through the Spenglerian spectacles, you are bound to come to a conclusion of extreme pessimism because they obscure the factor which for the first time places in the hands of man the ability entirely to eliminate the poverty problem. And I believe it is our German philosopher's misunderstanding of this immense new factor which leads him to his pessimistic conclusion. Nevertheless, that in no way invalidates his tremendous contribution to world thought.'

Before returning to Spengler and other concepts of philosophy I had some practical remarks to deliver on the fascist attitude to life:

'We demand from all our people an over-riding conception of public service. In his public life, a man must behave himself as a fit member of the State, in his every action he must conform to the welfare of the nation. On the other hand, he receives from the State in return, a complete liberty to live and to develop as an individual. And in our morality—and I think possibly I can claim that it is the only public morality in which private practice altogether coincides with public protestation— ... the one single test of any moral question is whether it impedes or destroys in any way the power of the individual to serve the State. He must answer the questions: "Does this action injure the nation? Does it injure other members of the nation? Does it injure my own ability to serve the nation?" And if the answer is clear on all those questions, the individual has absolute liberty to do as he will; and that confers upon the individual by far the greatest measure of freedom under the State which any system . . . or any religious authority has ever conferred.

'The fascist principle is private freedom and public service. That imposes upon us, in our public life, and in our attitude towards other men, a certain discipline and a certain restraint; but in our public life alone; and I should argue very strongly indeed that the only way to have private freedom was by a public organisation which brought some order out of the economic chaos which exists in the world today, and that such public organisation can only be secured by the methods of authority and of discipline which are inherent in fascism.

'Here we are brought at once into collision with the fundamental tenets of socialism and liberalism. Socialism differs, of course, sharply from liberalism in its conception of economic organisation; but in philosophy I think there are few socialists or liberals who would disagree that they really have a common origin if we go back far enough in the Voltaire–Rousseau attitude of life; and above all the latter. Rousseau, in our view, either made a big mistake, or was much misunderstood. Rousseau said: Equality. We reply, if you mean equality of opportunity, yes; if you mean equality of man, no. That is an absurdity. I believe personally that if he is properly read, Rousseau meant equality of opportunity. Equality of opportunity is a fundamental thing. Let those rule who are fitted to rule. Let no man rule because his grandfather proved himself fitted to rule. It was a revolt against privilege, an affirmation that the man of talent and of capacity should be the man to conduct the affairs of a great nation.

'But that doctrine was seized upon by his later disciples as meaning the equality of man, that all men were equal. From that construction arises the whole fallacy, as we see it. It is a manifest and clear absurdity. One man, in mind and physique, differs immensely from another. It is not a question, as socialists often say, of moral or spiritual equality. That is a totally different thing. Morally and spiritually, the man who sweeps the floor of a big business may be vastly superior to the manager of that business. But the question is, which man is fitted to do which job. What is the proper function that he has to perform? Some people are good at one thing and some at another. Certainly we eliminate altogether the social class conception from fascism, because that rests upon the chance of heredity; but we do say that certain people are fitted by nature to do certain things, and others are not. And once you adopt that basis of thought, you challenge the whole conception of democracy.'

This must be one of the last occasions when I used the term democracy in what seems the perjorative sense, no doubt in reaction to the experience of government through which I had recently passed. It was my habit during only a brief period, for it soon seemed to me clear that democracy in its true sense —government of the people, by the people, for the people, as an expression of the natural, healthy will of the people when free from the deception of financial politics—was exactly what we wanted. It was the perversion of democracy and not democracy itself which we condemned; what I subsequently called financial democracy, and in my denunciation of the system I always used that phrase, arguing that the power of money within the prevailing system invariably prevented the fulfilment of the people's will which was the essence of true democracy. In this context I was aiming in particular at the replacement of the geographical by an occupational franchise, the vote according to occupation, craft or profession rather than according to residence; an informed vote. I still think it is a preferable system, but I no longer advocate it, as we have more urgent things to do, and with certain reforms the present system can be made to work effectively.

After establishing a case against chaotic egalitarianism, I argued in favour of complete equality of opportunity, the career open to talent: 'When a man has proved himself, he may rise to the greatest position in the land, and our whole educational system must be so devised'. Then came a return to Spengler and the main themes: my preoccupation with Caesarism in history and with science in the modern age. It was Spengler's profound understanding of Caesarism which first attracted me to him, but his appreciation of modern science was shallow, indeed scanty. The union of a Caesarian movement with science seemed to me at once the prime requirement of the modern age and the answer to the ultimate fatality predicted by Spengler.

First came an analysis of Caesarism in history and of the inevitable differences of form in the modern world:

'Now you may say, and say perhaps with some truth, that these doctrines have been heard before, that this was the basis of Bonapartism, or to go back still further to its origin, was the basis of Caesarism.

'It is, of course, true that fascism has an historic relation to Caesarism, but the modern world differs profoundly from the forms and conditions of the ancient world. Modern organisation is too vast and too complex to rest on any individual alone, however gifted. Modern Caesarism, like all things modern, is collective. The will and talent of the individual alone is replaced by the will and ability of the disciplined thousands who comprise a fascist movement. Every blackshirt is an individual cell of a collective Caesarism. The organised will of devoted masses, subject to a voluntary discipline, and inspired by the passionate ideal of national survival, replaces the will to power and a higher order of the individual superman. Nevertheless, this collective Caesarism, armed with the weapons of modern science, stands in the same historic relationship as ancient Caesarism to reaction on the one hand and to anarchy on the other. Caesarism stood against Spartacism on the one hand and the Patrician Senate on the other. That position is as old as the history of the last two thousand years. But they lacked, in those days, the opportunities for constructive achievement which are present today, and the only lesson that we can derive from the previous evidence of this doctrine is simply this; that whenever the world under the influence of Spartacus drifted to complete collapse and chaos, it was always what Spengler called the "fact-men" who extracted the world from the resultant chaos and gave mankind very often centuries of peace and of order in a new system and a new stability.

'It was done ... by recognising certain fundamental facts of politics and of philosophy. Again, you have a certain wedding of two seemingly conflicting doctrines. We are often accused of taking something from the Right and something from the Left. Well, it is a very sensible thing to borrow from other faiths; to discard what is bad and keep what is good; and directly you get away from the old parliamentary mind, you of course see the wisdom of any such course. And fascism does, of course, take something from the Right and something from the Left, and to it adds new facts to meet the modern age. In this new synthesis of fascism, coming rather nearer to our immediate situation, we find that we take the great principle of stability supported by authority, by order, by discipline, which has been the attribute of the Right, and we marry it to the principle of progress, of dynamic change, which we take from the Left. Conservatism ... believes in stability and supports it by its belief in order: but where Conservatism has always failed in the modern world is in its inability to perceive that stability can only be achieved through progress: that a stand-pat resistance to change precipitates the revolutionary situation which Conservatism most fears. On the other hand, the Left has always failed to realise, thanks to its Rousseau complex, that the only way to get progress is to adopt the executive instruments by which alone change is made possible.'

I was at this point weaving into fascist ideology my long-sustained synthesis of order and progress.

'... You can only have stability if you are prepared to carry through orderly changes, because to remain stable you must adapt yourselves to the new facts of the new age. On the other hand, you can only have the progress which the Left desires if you adopt the executive instruments of progress. . . .

'Again you will say: "This is once more Caesarism or Bonapartism. . . . The basic principles remain the same; and, therefore, while your fascist movement may perform the purpose which Caesarism has performed before, may bring order out of chaos which the conflict between Spartacus and reaction has evoked, may for a few years or a few centuries give great peace to the world, it yet carries within itself its own decay, and does not really achieve what we believe to be necessary." '

It was at this point that my thinking began to differ sharply from the attitude of the national socialist movement in Spengler's country of origin, for it appeared that intellectually the leaders saw the force of his argument but found no answer to it. Their propagandists felt that it was not an attractive doctrine to say to their members from the mass of the people: struggle, sacrifice and give your all to make a few men Caesars, to secure a last, glorious blossoming of a civilisation, and then eternal night. So they saluted Spengler in private, but silenced him in their public doctrine; pessimism and revolution are contradictions in terms. We, on the contrary, saw his thesis as the premise to the modern argument, and we summoned the mighty spirit of modern science to provide the answer. Caesarism and science together could evolve Faustian man; a civilisation which could renew its youth in a persisting dynamism, as I described it in my later writing.

The speech continued:

'I believe the answer to that case, which is the only really valid case, is that always before the factor of modern science was lacking. You have now got a completely new factor. If you can introduce into your system of government a new efficiency—and everyone admits that such movements when they come to power are at least efficient: if you can bring to government for even a few years an executive power and an efficiency which gets things done, you can release . . . the imprisoned genius of science to perform the task which it has to perform in the modern world. Whatever our divergent views on the structure of the State and economics may be, I think we must all agree that it would be possible, by sane organisation of the world, with the power of modern science and of industry to produce, to solve once and for all the poverty problem, and to abolish . . . the worst attributes of disease and suffering from the world. Therefore, if it is possible to have an efficient form of government, you have available for such a system, for the first time in history, an instrument by which the face of the earth might be changed for all time. Once the essential has been done, once modern science and technique have been released and have performed their task, once you have changed your political and philosophic system from a transitory and political to a permanent and technical basis, there will be no more need of the politics and of the controversies which distract the world today. The problem of poverty will be solved, the major problems will be banished, as they can be, and as everybody knows they can be, if modern science is properly mobilised. Then mankind will be liberated for the things in life which really matter.

'Therefore, while it is perhaps true that certain of these phenomena in the eternal recurrences of history have been seen in the world before, and seen with great benefit to mankind, yet never before have the great executive movements possessed the opportunity to complete their task which modern science and invention now confer upon them.

'At a moment of great world crisis, a crisis which in the end will inevitably deepen, a movement emerges from a historic background which makes its emergence inevitable, carrying certain traditional attributes derived from a very glorious past, but facing the facts of today armed with the instruments which only this age has ever conferred upon mankind. By this new and wonderful coincidence of instrument and of event the problems of this age can be overcome, and the future can be assured in a progressive stability. Possibly this is the last great world wave of the immortal, the eternally recurring Caesarian movement; but with the aid of science, and with the inspiration of the modern mind, this wave shall carry humanity to the farther shore.

'Then, at long last, Caesarism, the mightiest emanation of the human spirit in high endeavour toward enduring achievement, will have performed its world mission in the struggle of the ages, and will have fulfilled its historic destiny. A humanity released from poverty and from many of the horrors and afflictions of disease to the enjoyment of a world re-born through science, will still need a fascist movement transformed to the purpose of a new and nobler order of mankind; but you will need no more the strange and disturbing men who in days of struggle and of danger and in nights of darkness and of labour, have forged the instrument of steel by which the world shall pass to higher things.'

In retrospect, I see at this point the merit of this speech: the union of Caesarism and modern science which could be the decisive fact of history, a final union of will with thought in a limitless achievement. After this lapse of time it still seems to me a very considerable thesis—now reinforced by the subsequent development of science—that for the first time executive men could find the means to do something truly great and enduring. The union of a revolutionary movement, which is a modern Caesarism, with the force of modern science could be nothing less than this. The genius of science imprisoned by the dull mediocrity of politics which could not realise its potential would be released for a world transforming task. The new men of politics in relation to science would transcend even the relationship of the men of the renaissance to art and a new world could be born of this union.

The speech in conclusion expressed the belief that fascism itself would eventually pass to make way for a higher order of mankind. Beyond the 'fact men' of Caesarism could already be discerned 'a new form, shadowy, as yet obscure, visible in outline only, but still a higher form' (as I wrote later) 'the will to power and the will to beauty in the mystical union which is all achieving'.[1]

It is, of course, possible to comment on the speech of 1933 that all this was just a diffuse and romantic way of saying: if you bring together executive men with modern science in an efficient system of government, you will get things done. In the present day I have some intellectual sympathy with the contemporary preference for short, flat, clear statement, but the method belongs to this humdrum period when action is not yet generally felt to be essential. If you want to move men to do great things in a great way, you must set plain facts in the perspective of history and illumine them with a sense of destiny.

I returned to some of the same themes five years later in *Tomorrow We Live*; in the last chapter I described briefly the situation of Britain as I saw it in relation to other civilisations which had succumbed to the forces now threatening us:

'British Union emerges from the welter of parties and the chaos of the system to meet an emergency no less menacing than 1914, because it is not so sudden or so universally apparent. British Union summons our people to no less an effort in no less a spirit. Gone in the demand of that hour was the clamour of faction, and the strife of section, that a great nation might unite to win salvation. A brotherhood of the British was born that in the strength of union was invincible and irresistible. Today the nation faces a foe more dangerous because he dwells within, and a situation no less grave because to all it is not yet visible. We have been divided, and we have been conquered, because by division of the British alone we can be conquered. Class against class, faction against faction, party against party, interest against interest, man against man, and brother against brother has been the tactic of the warfare by which the British in the modern age, for the first time in their history, have been subdued. We have been defeated, too, at a moment in our history when the world was at our feet, because the heritage won for us by the heroism of our fathers affords to the genius of modern science and the new and unprecedented triumph of the human mind an opportunity of material achievement leading, through the gift of economic freedom, to a higher spiritual civilisation than mankind, in the long story of the human race, has yet witnessed.

Can we recapture the union of 1914 and that rapturous dedication of the individual to a cause that transcends self and faction, or are we doomed to go down with the Empires of history in the chaos of usury and sectional greed? That is the question of the hour for which every factor and symptom of the current situation presses decision. Is it now possible by a supreme

[1] In an essay on Bernard Shaw's centenary, March 1956, Sanctuary Press.

effort of the British spirit and the human will to arrest what, in the light of all past history, would appear to be the course of destiny itself? For we have reached the period, by every indication available to the intellect, at which each civilisation and Empire of the past has begun to traverse that downward path to the dust and ashes from which their glory never returned. Every fatal symptom of the past is present in the modern situation, from the uprooting of the people's contact with the soil to the development of usury and the rule of money power, accompanied by social decadence and vice that flaunts in the face of civilisation the doctrine of defeat and decline.'

These tendencies in contemporary life, which were the subject of daily comment in our speeches at mass public meetings and were the theme of our policies seeking to reverse them, were interrupted by the war; the British showed that they were indeed still capable of the effort I had asked them to make, though for very different purposes. But a revival of the national will for the brief period of war is not enough, and the evils we combated in the thirties have now returned with renewed force in a general situation of national weakness much aggravated by war. This analysis brought me in the conclusion of this book inevitably to Spengler:

'Above the European scene towers in menace Spengler's colossal contribution to modern thought, which taught our new generation that a limit is set to the course of civilisations and Empires, and that the course that once is run is for ever closed. Every indication of decadence and decline which he observed as a precursor of the downfall of a civilisation is apparent in the scene, and from all history he deduced the sombre conclusion that the effort of "Faustian" man to renew his youth, and to recapture the dawn of a civilisation, must ever fail. History is on the side of the great philosopher, and every sign of the period with fatal recurrence supports his view. His massive pessimism, supported by impressive armoury of fact, rises in challenge and in menace to our generation and our age. We take up that challenge with the radiant optimism born of man's achievements in the new realm of science, that the philosopher understood less well than history, and born, above all, of our undying belief in the invincible spirit of that final product of the ages—the modern man. We salute our great antagonist, from whose great warning we have learnt so much, but we reject utterly the fatality of his conclusion. We believe that modern man, with the new genius of modern science within him and the inspiration of the modern spirit to guide him, can find the answer to the historic fatality.'

Before returning to the theme of Spengler I summarised two objects of our continual attack, which were only related to Spengler in that he too was determinist in attitude. There were really three doctrines of determinism at that time, Marx, Freud and Spengler; all in some aspects rejected by our belief in a Faustian revival of the human will. Spengler at least recognised the possibility of a temporary reply to his own determinism—'. . . when money is celebrating its last victories, . . . and the Caesarism that is to succeed approaches with calm, firm tread . . .'—while I went further and affirmed that with the aid of modern technics a final answer could find permanent expression in a 'persisting dynamism'.

I referred to the determinism of Marx and Freud:

'The doctrines of modern disintegration are classic in form, and pervade the political parties, which fade from a flaccid and universal "liberalism" into the sheer disruption and corruption of socialism serving usury. The doctrinaires of the immediate past come to the aid of political defeatism with the negation of manhood and self-will, and the scientific formulation of surrender as a faith. In the sphere of economics Marx portrays humanity as the helpless victim of material circumstance, and in the sphere of psychology Freud assists the doctrine of human defeatism with the teaching that self-will and self-help are no longer of any avail, and that man is equally the helpless toy of childish and even pre-natal influence. Marx's "materialist conception of history" tells us that man has been moved by no higher instinct than the urge of his stomach, and Freud supports this teaching of man's spiritual futility with the lesson that man can never escape from the squalid misadventures of childhood. . . . This predestination of materialism has proved in practice even more destructive of the human will and spirit than the old and discredited "predestination of the soul". It has paralysed the intellectual world into the acceptance of surrender to circumstance as an article of faith.

'To these destructive doctrines of material defeatism our renaissant creed returns a determined answer. To Marx we say it is true that if we observe the motive of a donkey in jumping a ditch, we may discern a desire to consume a particularly luxuriant thistle that grows on the other side. On the other hand, if we observe a man jumping a ditch, we may legitimately conclude that he possesses a different and possibly a higher motive. To Freud we reply that, if indeed man has no determination of his own will beyond the idle chances of childhood, then every escape from heredity and environment, not only of genius but of every determined spirit in history, is but a figment of historic imagination. In answer to the fatalistic defeatism of the "intellectual" world our creed summons not only the whole of history as a witness to the power and motive force of the human spirit, but every evidence and tendency of recent science.'

Some of my contemporaries were excessively preoccupied with Marx and Freud, John Strachey particularly so, and I remember teasing him with the observation: 'You are governed above the waist by Marx, below the waist by Freud, but no part of you by Strachey'; he was a good-humoured fellow. Some of these references to Marx and Freud—who at least were serious people worthy of serious study—have something of the flippancy of Disraeli's intervention in the Darwinian controversy at Oxford: 'The question is whether man is descended from angel or ape; I am on the side of the angels'. I should have more now to say on these subjects, but truth is not necessarily lacking from pithy expression.

At the end of *Tomorrow We Live* I returned to the answer politics and science could together give to the doom which threatened yet another civilisation:

'So man emerges for the final struggle of the ages, the supreme and conscious master of his fate, to surmount the destiny that has reduced former civilisations to oblivion. He advances to the final ordeal armed with weapons of the modern mind that were lacking to any previous generation in the crisis of a civilisation. The wonders of our new science afford him not only the means with which to conquer material environment, in the ability to wrest wealth in abundance from nature, but in the final unfolding of the scientific revelation probably also the means of controlling even the physical rhythm of a civilisation. Man for the first time carries to the crisis of his fate weapons with which he may conquer even destiny. But one compelling necessity remains, that he shall win within himself the will to struggle and to conquer. Our creed and our movement instil in man the heroic attitude to life, because he needs heroism. Our new Britons require the virility of the Elizabethan combined with the intellect and method of the modern technician. The age demands the radiance of the dawn to infuse the wonder of maturity. We need heroism not just for war, which is a mere stupidity, but heroism to sustain us through man's sublime attempt to wrestle with nature and to strive with destiny.'

This way of writing is very different from the flat statements of contemporary fashion by writers whose only discernible ambition is to make the world as dull as themselves, precisely because it aimed at expressing the inspiration of men with a dynamic purpose who were determined to play a decisive part at a turning-point in history; style can reflect both vitality and fatigue, and I prefer the former if it retains clarity. What really interested me in Spengler was his realisation that at certain points in history the fact-men, supported by popular but realistic movements, always emerged to arrest the decline of a civilisation. This aspect of Caesarism had fascinated me long before I read Spengler, and the possibilities of modern science had equally engaged me over a long period. It seemed clear to me that this conjunction was the instrument which had never before been available to the architects of state, and it could give the new fact-men at last the means to build a civilisation which could endure when they and their revolutionary impulse had passed. The modern age therefore presented a possibility which the world had never known before, and this could transmute the massive pessimism of Spengler's theory into an enduring and achieving optimism.

Spengler also gave new impulses to my thinking because he accentuated the sense of impending disaster if effective action were not taken. His theory was foreign to Britain and rejected by German government for reasons already described. His approach to history later became familiar to the British in the outstanding contribution of Arnold Toynbee, who acknowledged his debt to Spengler but added much in his 'challenge and response' theory with the picture of civilisations which had achieved renaissance by vigorous responses to the challenge of disaster, even without the aid of modern science. For my purpose this reinforced the view that the doom of our civilisation—a looming menace not only in economics but in national psychology, as it seemed to me —could be met and overcome by the will of a determined movement to national renaissance. Finally, Toynbee appeared to me, like Spengler, to drift from his challenging and indeed inspiring premises to another but almost equally lame conclusion; nevertheless, his contributions both to history and to the possible revival of the human spirit were important.

Six months after my speech to the English-Speaking Union, in the autumn of 1933, I met a remarkable man who then joined the party and became one of my most valuable colleagues. This was Raven Thomson, who in 1932 had published a book of exceptional interest on Spengler which I read when we came together. His approach differed from mine because his conclusion was as pessimistic as Spengler's, and his concept of the immediate future seemed to me an almost ant-heap collectivism. I had said in my E.S.U. speech that modern Caesarism would inevitably have a collective character, but his collective ideas seemed to go much too far in eliminating individual influence. The reason certainly was that at the time he wrote the book he was a communist. When he joined our movement we had many discussions and his collectivism began to admit a considerable place for individual influence, while his pessimism gradually changed to the most determined optimism I have ever encountered. Whether this metamorphosis was due to his contact with me, or to a blow he received on the head from a brick at one of his first appearances as a speaker for the party was often the subject of genial enquiry when he first appeared in a black shirt at the bar of the spacious 'barracks' which we acquired about that time in King's Road.

This exceptional thinker emerged from the study at the age of nearly forty to become a man of action and one of the finest fighters for our cause we ever knew. Intellectually Raven Thomson towered above the men I had known in the Labour Cabinet of 1929, and in firmness of character he seemed in an altogether different category to most of the contemporary politicians. Despite his academic background, he developed an exuberant enthusiasm for the work of the party and became one of its most effective speakers, as well as an outstanding writer. For years he edited the party paper, and was more than a match in controversy for the few challengers he encountered from the other side. Yet this honest man and devoted patriot, together with his companions of the blackshirt, was subjected to every insult in the catalogue of calumny which begins with the word 'thug'. This abuse, as vile as it was silly, came from every corner-boy of the intellect simply because he was associated with me in an effort of national renaissance. His offence was that he dared to choose that hard path in preference to his previous happy life, in the seclusion of his library and the company of his family. He died young, and we his friends will always feel that the prison years and the decline of his country combined to curtail a life which would have been of brilliant service to the nation. His colleague, Neil Francis-Hawkins, our chief organiser before the war, a man of outstanding character and ability, also died young for similar reasons. I shall mention no other blackshirts by name because this would be invidious among so many splendid men and women; these two may rest as the monument of those who died and the inspiration of those who live.

The Corporate State is scarcely an appropriate subject for inclusion in an ideological study of fascism because it is essentially a system for the economic organisation, but it contains a concept of the state which enters the sphere of ideology. The original corporate thinking belongs to Mussolini, and in England its chief protagonist was Raven Thomson. My own effort was then on the lines of my thinking in the Birmingham proposals and in my resignation speech, which seemed to me to offer a more direct and thorough solution of the prevailing economic problems. Throughout my subsequent life my ideas evolved much more in the direction suggested by that thinking than in the tradition of the Corporate State.

What attracted me in the ideological aspect of the Corporate State was a government strong enough to keep the ring for the producer and to protect the interests of the consumer. Just as the centralised authority of the Tudor kings protected the citizens from the depredations of the robber barons, who had previously held all private life and enterprise up to ransom, so at this stage of society would the corporate system protect and promote a genuine private enterprise in face of the large industrial combines and concentrations of financial power. In *The Greater Britain* (1932), I wrote that government or the corporate system would 'lay down the limits within which individuals and interests may operate. Those limits are the welfare of the nation—not, when all is said, a very unreasonable criterion. Within these limits, all activity is encouraged; individual enterprise and the making of profit are not only permitted but encouraged, so long as that enterprise enriches rather than damages by its activity the nation as a whole.'

Defining the Corporate State I wrote: 'In psychology it is based on teamwork; in organisation it is the rationalised State. . . . It is this machinery of central direction which the Corporate State is designed to supply . . . it envisages, as its name implies, a nation organised as the human body. Every part fulfils its function as a member of the whole, performing its separate task, and yet, by performing it, contributing to the welfare of the whole. The whole body is generally directed by the central driving brain of government without which no body and system of society can operate.'

I related the corporate machinery suggested to my previous ideas in government and to other English thinking: 'The idea of a National Council was, I believe, first advanced in my speech of resignation from the Labour Government in May 1930. The idea has since been developed by Sir Arthur Salter [a distinguished Civil Servant, at one time head of the Civil Service] and other writers. A body of this kind stands or falls by the effectiveness of the underlying organisation. It must not consist of casual delegates from unconnected bodies, meeting occasionally for *ad hoc* consultation. The machinery must be permanently functioning and interwoven with the whole industrial and commercial fabric of the nation.'

There are many ideas of the corporate system which can make valuable contribution to the present situation. For instance, some of the policies of Mussolini's Corporate State were in certain respects practically indistinguishable from co-partnership, which had previously been advocated in England by Lord Robert Cecil and myself, and in recent times has been rediscovered by the young Liberals. Quaint indeed are the divergencies caused by muddled thinking and obscure terminology in the course of controversial politics.

My criticism of the corporate system in the light of experience and further thought is that it was too bureaucratic and insufficiently dynamic; in fact, I felt this at the time, as the different form of my writings shows. The elaborate organisation could maintain equilibrium, but did not secure sufficiently the progress which is not only humanly desirable but essential in a world driven forward by science. I wrote in *The Greater Britain* that 'industrial organisations will certainly not be confined merely to the settlement of questions of wages and of hours. They will be called upon to assist, by regular consultation, in the general economic policy of the nation.' Yet the idea of organisation was over-emphasised and the direction of organisation was insufficiently considered, and this was my view of the Italian concept as well as the writings of Raven Thomson, as I told him at the time.

It is at this point that I consider my post-war thinking concerning the wage-price mechanism far surpasses my thinking within the Labour Party and also within the fascist movement. The concept of the wage-price mechanism is less bureaucratic and more dynamic; with far less detailed interference, it maintains a continuous momentum in the achievement of the ever-higher standards of life which are essential to absorb the production of modern science. It has the conscious direction and defined objectives which the

Corporate State to a large extent lacked. Therefore in my opinion the wage-price mechanism surpasses the Corporate State in economics as effectively as the doctrine of higher forms transcends my thinking of the thirties in the ideological sphere.

Two valuable ideas remain from the corporate period. The first is the State strong enough to keep the ring for producer and consumer in face of the large combinations of industrial and financial power; also—always inherent in my thinking—not only strong enough to hold the ring for science, but wise enough to make the support of science a first priority of the State. The second is the State regarded as an organic being which represents the past, the present and the future of a civilisation, an entity which asks the individual to recognise what he owes to those who preceded him and to posterity; an idea of the State as trustee for the whole course of a people and not merely as the servant of transient whim and fashion which may destroy what sacrifice and heroism have created.

Thus we return to the determination to achieve national renaissance in the thirties, rising in phoenix form from the flames of the explosion against conditions humanly intolerable and scientifically unnecessary, which seemed to us an expression of brutality and stupidity. Men and women simply felt that Britain had been great and should be great again, greater still. We owed it to the country we loved and to the mind, will and spirit of the English which derived from three thousand years of European history. I tried at the end of *The Greater Britain* to express this dedication in language combining the real and the ideal:

'In a situation of so many and such diverse contingencies nobody can dogmatise upon the future. We cannot say with certainty when catastrophe will come, nor whether it will take the form of a sharp crisis or of a steady decline to the status of a second-rate power. All that we can say with certainty is that Britain cannot muddle on much longer without catastrophe, or the loss of her position in the world. Against either contingency it is our duty to arouse the nation. To meet either the normal situation of political action, or the abnormal situation of catastrophe, it is our duty to organise. Therefore, while the principles for which we fight can be clearly described in a comprehensive system of politics, of economics and of life, it would be folly to describe precisely in advance the road by which we shall attain them. A great man of action once observed: "No man goes very far who knows exactly where he is going", and the same observation applies with some force to modern movements of reality in the changing situations of today.

'We ask those who join us to march with us in a great and hazardous adventure. We ask them to be prepared to sacrifice all, but to do so for no small and unworthy ends. We ask them to dedicate their lives to building in this country a movement of the modern age, which by its British expression shall transcend, as often before in our history, every precursor of the Continent in conception and in constructive achievement.

'We ask them to re-write the greatest pages of British history by finding for the spirit of their age its highest mission in these islands. Neither to our friends nor to the country do we make any promises; not without struggle and ordeal will the future be won. Those who march with us will certainly face abuse, misunderstanding, bitter animosity, and possibly the ferocity of struggle and of danger. In return, we can only offer to them the deep belief that they are fighting that a great land may live.'

18

Jewish Opposition
Finance and
Administration
Libel Actions

Anti-semitism was not our policy, for I never attacked the Jews as a people.
I never attacked any man on account of race or religion, and I never shall.
A movement which believed in a great future for Britain's world-wide
Empire with its large variety of races and creeds could never be 'racialist'.
Nevertheless, it is said sometimes that our success, so remarkable in the
absence of economic crisis, was due in part to anti-semitic feeling. On the
contrary, it can be shown in hard fact that the Jewish question had nothing
to do with our progress. It is suggested that antipathy to the Jews accounted
at least in some degree for our average vote of nearly 19 per cent in East
London in March 1937,[1] three months after the passing of the Public Order
Act. Yet the density of the Jewish population was more pronounced in parts
of Leeds or Manchester where we polled no more than our average throughout
the country. Our relatively quicker progress at this time in East London was
due to our physical proximity, which enabled me and other speakers there to
make an intensive and considerable effort; to the execrable housing conditions
and high unemployment; and to the lively and vital character of the people
of East London.

That population of East London has now been dispersed over a wide area,
for after our electoral success a real effort was made at last to rehouse these
people; our members naturally claim that this would never have happened if
our vote had not rocked the old parties to the foundations of their complacency. The fact that it was housing conditions which primarily stirred the
people of East London and swung them to our side was proved by our most

[1] Bethnal Green, 23 per cent; Limehouse, 19 per cent; Shoreditch, 14 per cent.

sensational vote of all, after the war in 1955 at a by-election in the small Moorfields Ward of East London. The ruling Labour Party polled 49 per cent; we polled 33 per cent and beat the Conservatives, who had 16 per cent, by over two to one; the odd 2 per cent went to an Independent. The housing conditions of the people of Moorfields at that time were almost the worst I ever saw in England, but after this vote they were quickly remedied. During the election neither we, the electors nor anyone else ever mentioned the Jewish question, which was of no interest to anyone. The coloured immigration question had not yet arisen, and still does not exist in that area because few coloured people live there. It was housing alone which roused the people and converted them to our cause; a striking symptom of how quickly typical English people can change their politics when living conditions become really bad, whether they are caused by housing, unemployment or any other reason. Moorfields was a microcosm of a national possibility.

Anti-semites in East London or elsewhere in England at any time are in a small minority. What happened in the thirties was altogether different; a quarrel arose about a definite subject for clearly discernible reasons. There is not the slightest doubt that some Jews began it in Britain, and I do not blame them in the prevailing circumstances. I understand their reasons for attacking us, while believing they were profoundly mistaken and strongly condemning some of the methods employed. Their fellow Jews were being persecuted in Germany because the National Socialist Party under Hitler's leadership was anti-semitic, and gave violent expression to this feeling, not only in word but to some extent also in deed even before the war. Jews naturally knew what was happening there, and observed the points of similarity between our movement and the National Socialist and Fascist parties on the Continent without noting the far more numerous points of difference in policy and attitude. It is comprehensible that they were in a state of considerable alarm and liable to jump to unjustified conclusions.

This is no doubt the reason that Jews from East London and elsewhere were so prominent in the attack on us at Olympia, before I had ever dealt with the subject of the Jews, a topic which had no place whatever in our party policy. Even a witness so impartial as the ex-editor of the *Daily Herald*, Hamilton Fyfe, described his observation of Olympia as follows: 'I am not likely to be suspected of any sympathy with fascism. . . . Therefore I feel free to say how unwise—and even unfair—it was to organise interruption at the Olympia meeting. It was organised; that is certain. I saw in Oxford Street, in the early evening, bands of young men, mostly Jews, on their way to the meeting. Every few minutes they shouted in unison some slogan I could not catch. They were clearly in a fighting mood—and they got what they wanted. . . .'

I would ask the reader particularly to note that the Olympia meeting was on June 8, 1934, and that I attacked certain Jewish interests for the first time four months later at a meeting in the Albert Hall on October 28, 1934; exactly two years after our movement was founded. Not only had I rarely before even mentioned Jews, but any member attacking the Jews—or indulging in any crack-pot utterance, as we regarded such speeches, on subjects with which we were in no way concerned—had been expelled from our disciplined movement, which had clear proposals for political and economic reform. We had Jewish members, and a celebrated Jewish athlete had been a New Party candidate in Whitechapel in the 1931 election. There was no shadow of suspicion that we were an anti-semitic movement when Jews attacked our Olympia meeting; and when others were responsible for many similar assaults upon our members their reasons could only have been the groundless fear that we would go in the same direction as the National Socialist Party in Germany.

This created a serious situation, to which I referred for the first time at the Albert Hall meeting in October 1934 in the following terms:

'I have been asked to enumerate the ways in which the Jews have assailed fascism and I will. In the first place, they have physically assaulted us. And that can be proved. It is not a matter merely of our own observations. It is a matter of proof. Sixty-four people have been convicted in the courts of this country of attacks on fascists or fascist meetings since June last, and thirty-two—exactly 50%—are Jews. Now, the Jews make up 0·6% of the whole population, yet they are guilty of 50% of the attacks upon fascists. And that we can prove from the law courts of this country. Now the second point is this: we can prove, and we have publicly stated, case after case of victimisation of fascists by Jewish employers—men and women dismissed for no better reason than that they were blackshirts.'

I made it absolutely clear in this same speech that we were not an anti-semitic movement in the following terms:

'From the very outset we have preserved the principle of no racial or religious persecution. And we will never have persecution on racial or religious grounds in the British Empire, because our Empire is composed of numerous races, a great conglomeration of the races of the earth bound together in a mighty unity; and any suggestion of racial or religious discrimination strikes a blow at the conception of the British Empire. For this reason we have always rigorously refused to entertain even a suggestion of racial or religious persecution. And today we do not attack Jews on racial or religious grounds. We take up the challenge that they have thrown down, because they fight against fascism, and against Britain.'

After dealing in some detail with complaints of our members on account of physical assault and victimisation, but emphasising that despite these events we were not anti-semitic and by reason of our whole policy could never be so, I came to the gravamen of my charge in the quarrel which had arisen on a specific subject:

'The organised power of Jewry, in a racial interest, has consistently striven for the last eighteen months and more to foster the policy of war. . . . From every platform and paper which they control, directly or indirectly, they have striven for the past eighteen months to arouse in this country the feelings and the passions of war with a nation with whom we made peace in 1918. . . . We fought Germany once in our British quarrel. We shall not fight Germany again in a Jewish quarrel.'

According to the report, the meeting was held up at this point for several minutes by the cheering.

This statement and the whole speech had nothing whatever to do with anti-semitism: I was concerned solely with the main passion of my life, the prevention of war. I would have attacked any man, whoever he was, if I thought he was trying to involve the British people in any war which did not threaten the life or touch the vital interests of Britain. I believed strongly in the principle summarised in our slogan—Britons fight for Britain only—and I believe in it today, with the addition that my patriotism now extends to the whole of Europe. I was ready then to attack any man, Gentile, Jew, Englishman, Eskimo or Hottentot, who injured the interests of Britain, and I felt the greatest injury of all was to drag us into unnecessary war. I would today with equal vigour attack any man who injured the interests of Europe, and I still believe the worst injury is to involve Europe in an unnecessary war. Every principle of my policy in this respect, before, during and since the war has been the same, and has been sustained throughout with consistency and determination.

The point may be made that my attitude and policy were narrow and selfishly nationalistic, that it was our duty to interfere everywhere and fight anywhere where anyone was getting a bad time; this is now the fashionable viewpoint and it is arguable, but it raises an altogether different principle to anti-semitism. Is it wrong to refuse to fight except where the vital interests of our own people are at stake? Should we always fight to save anyone who is being persecuted? This principle in the present world would involve us in perpetual war, if universally applied and not merely confined to cases where political prejudice is involved.

My opponents should not confuse this question with anti-semitism, or they will find themselves in deep water. Disraeli was the original protagonist of the view that we should not run around the world looking for any quarrel we could get into on behalf of a persecuted minority. He opposed Gladstone's attempt to drag us into war with Turkey on behalf of the Bulgarians on precisely the grounds of principle which I am now stating. In fact, until very recently this was classic Conservative doctrine; one of the principles I borrowed from the Right at the same time as borrowing social progress from the Left, before adding much more I believed to be necessary in the final synthesis of our policy. Conservatism in its weary pilgrimage a couple of paces behind Left-wing thought or emotion has now forgotten the principles it acquired from Disraeli. Tories flap into any quarrel going, whether or not they have the arms to fight, and even the dames of the Primrose League forget their hero's sage advice to keep out of unnecessary trouble. If in still honouring this principle we lay a primrose on the hallowed memory, do not let us then be accused of anti-semitism.

When it came to the question of world war the matter became deadly serious, and each side held its opinion and principle with passionate conviction. The Jews naturally wanted to aid their fellows who were being persecuted in Germany. I naturally wanted to save the lives of young Englishmen and to prevent unnecessary war—despite any minority being persecuted anywhere—which was my whole life's principle; so it came to a head-on clash. In my view it became the business of these Jews to make a war and my business to stop the war. That was the whole reason of the quarrel. If I had been a Jew, or if many Englishmen had been suffering persecution in Germany, I might possibly have felt and acted as they did, but as an English soldier from the First World War I had dedicated myself to the maintenance of peace; never another war except to save the life of Britain.

Therefore, we came to a fierce quarrel which is now over. Never even at the height of controversy did I say anything nearly so offensive about Jews as, for instance, Aneurin Bevan said about his Conservative compatriots.[1] Never at any time did I or our movement attack Jews on account of race or religion; never, therefore, were we anti-semitic. The principle of never attacking Jews on account of race or religion was maintained throughout our policy statements in East London and in our whole policy everywhere. It is also quite untrue that we organised provocative marches and meetings in Jewish areas. Never once during this period did I enter Whitechapel, which has a Jewish majority. It will scarcely be contended that we should have denied ourselves access to areas of East London with large majorities of English people where our vote averaged 19 per cent.

At the height of the quarrel I reaffirmed this position in *Tomorrow We Live*:

'We do not attack Jews on account of their religion; our principle is complete religious toleration, and we certainly do not wish to persecute them on account of their race, for we dedicate ourselves to service of an Empire which contains many different races and any suggestion of racial persecution

[1] He said, at Manchester, they were 'lower than vermin', *Daily Mail*, July 5, 1948.

would be detrimental to the Empire we serve. Our quarrel with the Jewish interests is that they have set the interests of their co-racialists at home and abroad above the interest of the British state.

'An outstanding example of this conduct is the persistent attempt of many Jewish interests to provoke the world disaster of another war between Britain and Germany, not this time in any British quarrel, but purely in a Jewish quarrel.'

That bitter quarrel is now over and I sometimes wonder whether the Jews will fall into the error of carrying the bitterness of the past to the point of inhibiting the present and endangering the future. It is not an English characteristic, for of the English in their moments of genius can be said with truth what Rosebery said of Napoleon: 'To him it was always today, there never was a yesterday'. I have utterly condemned atrocities committed on the Jews in Germany, horrors which could never have happened on anything approaching that scale in time of peace; for these Jews lost their lives as a direct result of war, just as did all the twenty-five million Europeans who died. We will regard these terrible matters and other atrocities of war in detail. At this point I may state simply the traditional English view that vengeance breeds vengeance, and that at some point the past should be buried. In *The Alternative* (1947) I wrote: 'Revenge will follow vengeance until some generation is found great enough to disrupt the circle of fatality, and to break "the bondage of the gods" '.

The clash with some Jewish interests on the specific question of the coming war complicated the work of our movement in several ways and gave me much trouble. It was not only that we were up against some powerful elements in the world of finance and industry, as well as skilfully led meeting and street attacks, but this situation tended to attract to our party a minority of members who were simply a nuisance. It took some time and trouble to get rid of them; some of them were even around for a brief period after the war. If you are in a fight for a clear reason—a temporary fight which will end with the cause of it—you tend to be joined or supported by people who hate your opponent for quite different, permanent reasons of their own, and will do anything which they can to challenge him. In this case they were the men who wanted to get into any fight with a Jew whatever the reason; the hard core of hard-boiled anti-semites, to whom our struggle to avert the war presented an opportunity to get into an altogether larger affair, a bigger and better fight.

In general principle I make no apology for having accepted the support of some such men in a struggle Jews began. If Britain for war purposes could later accept alliance with Soviet Russia—after all its crimes—it would have been folly for me to refuse the support of fellow-countrymen who in normal times would differ from me in policy and character. Certainly foolish, abusive and violent things were said and written on both sides when tempers were up in a bitter controversy. Party journals were in other hands, because I was often absent from London, and I do not accept responsibility without effective authority. Nevertheless, it will be found that I soon eliminated these men from the party, if after due warning they persisted in attitudes and utterances contrary to party policy.

These are the people who believe in a world conspiracy run by the Jews, which always seems to me the most complete nonsense. The basic reason for my disbelief in any such possibility is simply that from long experience I know men are not nearly clever or determined enough to organise anything of the kind. Anyone who knows how difficult it is to keep a secret among three men—particularly if they are married—knows how absurd is the idea of a world-wide secret conspiracy consciously controlling all mankind by its financial power; in real, clear analysis these deep plots are seldom anything more sinister than the usual vast muddle.

A man of some ability joined our party after the war who was possessed of this belief in extreme degree and in a very rationalised form; I was soon rid of him. During his brief sojourn among us, he encountered a young Italian, a man in the mid-thirties, of lucid and powerful intellect, who happened to be staying with me in London, and like most Italians had no feeling about Jews one way or the other and little experience of them. After their discussion, the Italian said to me with a logic at once simple and conclusive: 'If the Jews were as clever as that, they would be gods; and men are not gods'. Yet I have known men, honest but stupid, who really believed that all-powerful Jews possess the world and that any opposition to their desires on any point is hopeless; immediately after the war the instinct of these cases was to find the nearest rabbit-hole and to hide in it, which is the logic of their nonsense.

James de Rothschild once put to me a view of the opposite extreme. I first met him in Deauville just after the First World War, when I was there to play polo and he to play golf; he lost his eye on the golf links through an accidental shot of a French duke, a relation of his. He was a remarkable and likeable man, who was first a French deputy, and later by a strange metamorphosis became an English M.P. Finally, he was a considerable benefactor to our nation by leaving it his fine property at Waddesdon and a magnificent collection of pictures and French furniture. During the clash of the thirties I met him one day by chance and he addressed to me some pointed and impressive remarks: 'Never believe the Jews are capable of acting together—we have tried to organise them for generations—they are an anarchic people, anarchic'; and he walked off, shaking his head, his monocle firmly in his eye and his immense top hat swinging in his hand. It was the last time I saw him, and his statement seemed to me at least nearer truth than the fevered vision of the anti-semite.

Any people with the quick, volatile intelligence of the Jews tends to be difficult to organise for any concerted purpose; we can observe the same trouble in some Latins. Moreover, the chief Jews have for centuries been occupied in the operations of finance to which in early days they were largely confined, and this is generally a highly individual business, dependent on speed and initiative rather than massive co-operation. The recent renewal of their power to work together in more primitive conditions after a return to the soil in the state of Israel is of wide general interest, because it confounds one of the main Spenglerian themes which I always disputed but have not the space further to pursue.

The Jews as a people have not usually shown so much aptitude for politics, and in this sphere they tend to be rather clumsy, so far as it is possible to generalise about any gifted people. They produced in politics in the last century three men of genius, and therefore '*hors de classe*', or race—Lassalle, Disraeli and Trotsky—to compare with the glittering army of European statesmen who were in the same category. I met in official circles the formidable Rathenau when he represented Germany on a financial mission in Britain; also, of course, Mond and Samuel in the House of Commons; men of commanding capacity, but not among the really great. If Jews with abilities approaching the divine are running the world, where are they? The simple answer is, they do not exist.

All the same, when you are in a fight with the Jews for any reason, they can give you a lot of trouble. Like everyone else, they are capable of collective action when they feel themselves—in my case wrongly, but in Hitler's case rightly—collectively threatened. For instance, when Lord Rothermere was supporting me, they took him out at the point of the economic gun. He was quite frank in explaining that he pulled out on account of his advertisers, and the firms in question were under Jewish influence. This was confirmed in recent years by Randolph Churchill: 'I have seen the *Daily Mail* abandon the support of Sir Oswald Mosley in the thirties under the pressure of Jewish advertisers' (*Spectator*, December 27, 1963). Lord Rothermere withdrew from our support in July 1934, and later letters were published between us on the 20th of that month. This event and the Jewish attack on us at Olympia on June 7, 1934, described by Hamilton Fyfe, occurred well in advance of the first occasion that I ever raised the subject, at my Albert Hall meeting on October 23, 1934. In assessing blame for this quarrel it is well to be quite clear on the chronology.

I had known Lord Rothermere for quite a long time and was always on good terms with him, but for this reason our political association was brief. He began our overt companionship in his abrupt, impulsive way. A genuine patriot, he was concerned with the way things were going and had over the years discussed the situation with Lloyd George, Churchill, myself and others. He was a great business executive, dynamic in all his dealings, and he passionately wanted to get something done for England. He observed with ever growing interest the progress of the blackshirt movement, and finally his action was characteristic. I had not seen him for some time, and he was at

Monte Carlo when he suddenly sent me a telegram affirming his support. Then the headlines came pelting like a thunder-storm: 'Hurrah for the Blackshirts' was the theme. He returned, and the pace began to quicken; a new aeroplane was built on his initiative and given the name of one of our slogans: Britain First. Nothing was too large or too small for use in Lord Rothermere's drive to support our movement. The *Daily Mail* organised a beauty competition for women blackshirts. He was staggered not to receive a single entry, and I was embarrassed to explain that these were serious young women dedicated to the cause of their country rather than aspirants to the Gaiety Theatre chorus.

He was a financial genius, but a political innocent, and unwilling to accept advice on subjects of which he knew little or nothing. If he had given me any indication of what he was going to do, had returned from Monte Carlo and consulted me before his sudden plunge, things might have been different. I would naturally have suggested a more discreet discussion of this phenomenon, a rather hostile enquiry in the first instance, asking what the blackshirt movement was all about, followed by some reports of my speeches which would offer a gradual explanation and would appear to convert the *Daily Mail* at the same time as the public in a reasonable and convincing process. But this was not the method of Lord Rothermere; the business executive with a hunch believed in putting things through in a hurry. Politics however are a subtle business, more like flying an early aeroplane with fine hands than just stoking up the steam in a railway engine.

Lord Rothermere helped in other ways than with newspaper support. In the matter of funds it seems a sound and honourable rule only to mention those who so openly supported us that everyone would assume they assisted us in this way. In fact, Lord Rothermere did not give much money directly, and what he gave he insisted on handing to me personally as a gift to the party. From the start, I tried hard to dissociate myself from these affairs, and soon had something written into our constitution which removed me from all direct contact with the financial side of the party; it seemed to me that a leader had quite enough to do without these preoccupations, and in principle it was better to be rid of them.

Nevertheless, some people insisted on dealing with me directly. At the beginning of the New Party, Lord Nuffield was our chief backer and he told so many people that it became widely known. He was introduced to me by Wyndham Portal,[1] who went so far as to appear on our platform at the Ashton-under-Lyne by-election, and was well known in a wide circle to be associated with us and to be engaged in raising money for the New Party. Wyndham Portal was a particularly fine character who made his mark in several spheres. During the First World War he commanded with much

[1] Created Viscount Portal, 1945; Parliamentary Secretary to Ministry of Supply, 1940–42; Minister of Works, 1942–44.

distinction the Household Cavalry dismounted brigade when they were used for trench warfare. Afterwards he was a conspicuous case of the soldier who makes good in business; starting with his family concern, which printed notes for the Bank of England, he developed wide and successful business interests. I did not know him until after the war, as he was in another division of cavalry corps and, of course, very senior to me. I met him soon after my resignation from the Government, and he threw all his drive and energy into raising funds for the New Party from a number of prominent business men, including Lord Nuffield.

My dealings with Lord Nuffield were protracted; they began in the days when Oliver Stanley was still associated with me, though he soon fell out of these discussions, as he was always a little too sensitive for such matters. I had practically given up hope of any help from the motor magnate, as nothing seemed ever to come of our talks, when I suddenly received a telegram inviting me to lunch with him at Huntercombe golf course club-house, which he was reputed to have bought after some difficulty about becoming a member, in the same manner that Otto Kahn was said to have acquired an opera house in America.

We lunched alone, and as usual the conversation roamed widely over general political questions. Like Lord Rothermere, he was a genuine and ardent patriot, but he was even less versed in the technique of politics, a business genius who seemed to be rather lost outside his own sphere. His success rested on an extraordinary and inventive flair for mechanical processes—visual and manual rather than theoretical—and a remarkable capacity for picking men, particularly business executives. Political conversation with him tended consequently to be tedious, as the only real contribution he could make was through the power of his money, and this point seemed never likely to be reached. However, ennui flew out of the window when at the end of lunch he pulled a cheque from his pocket and handed it to me across the table; it was for £50,000. He said he had been studying me for a long time—the object of the seemingly pointless conversations were now clear—had developed full confidence in me and had decided to back me. Then came one of those white-light observations which reveal a whole career; in this case the long and dusty road from the little bicycle shop to the motor empire. 'Don't think, my boy, that money like this grows on gooseberry bushes. The first ten thousand took me a lot of getting.' I bet it did, I thought, and was deeply touched. He was a good and honest man, as well as a business genius; a combination which can occur.

Lord Rothermere entered this picture at a later stage than Lord Nuffield, Wyndham Portal and the original New Party backers, although he had known me longer than any of them. It was the combination of blackshirt success and our strong advocacy of national rearmament in what appeared to him a period of flabby surrender on all fronts which attracted him, rather than our social policies, of which he seemed to be almost unaware. He was delighted, for example, when I said in an Albert Hall speech: 'Stand by our friends, and stand up to our enemies'.

Lord Rothermere gave generously, but not on the scale of Lord Nuffield. Then he came to me one day with an extraordinary proposition. He prefaced his proposal with the statement that he had made two large fortunes, in newspapers and in the Newfoundland pulp business, and with my help would make a third, which would be the largest of the three. He had undertaken a close study of the tobacco trade and had found that distribution was the chief question; the combines had tied shops, as the brewers had tied houses. The manufacture of cigarettes was relatively easy, if the question of distribution could be solved; and that was where I came in. He had checked up through his associate, Ward Price, and other friends who were then much in my company, and understood that the movement had about four hundred large and active branches in Great Britain. If these vigorous young men would act as distributors, he would share the profits fifty-fifty, half to himself as producer and half to our movement as distributor. It was clear to him that the deal would have to be announced in order to secure the co-operation of our people, but he was quite willing to face that situation.

I warmly welcomed his proposal, for a straightforward business deal seemed to me the best and cleanest way to raise large funds, and I was sure our people would co-operate with enthusiasm in a proposition offering such benefit to the party. So off he went like a steam-engine to get everything moving; within a few days he had ordered £70,000 worth of machinery and had secured the services of one of the chief experts of the combine on the production side, with a long contract for a large and guaranteed salary. Things were moving, and we were shortly going into business in a big way. Then came a sudden message that he could not proceed, and had decided to sell all the machinery for what it would fetch. I went to see him in a hotel he frequented, and found him in a relatively modest apartment, an imposing figure of monumental form lying flat on his back on a narrow brass bedstead; it seemed an incongruous setting for one of the richest men in the world.

Lord Rothermere explained that he was in trouble with certain advertisers, who had not liked his support of the blackshirts, and in company with many other people had now heard of the tobacco business and liked it still less. This was war, and I reacted strongly. The card to play with Rothermere was always his brother Northcliffe, whom I had never met but who was a legend for his audacity and dynamism. I said: 'Do you know what Northcliffe would have done? He would have said, "One more word from you, and the *Daily Mail* placards tomorrow will carry the words: 'Jews threaten British press' "; you will have no further trouble'. The long struggle fluctuated, but I lost. He felt that I was asking him to risk too much, not only for himself, but for others who depended on him. He was a patriot and an outstanding personality, but without the exceptional character necessary to take a strong line towards the end of a successful life, which might have led to a political dog-fight. In my view, the matter could have been quite reasonably settled if he had stood firm.

These Jewish interests took this action in the mistaken belief that their life and interest were threatened. Any group of men who feel this will naturally do their utmost to resist. This is no evidence of occult Jewish power, simply the determination to fight by men who in this case had the means to do it, which I had not. The whole affair was as simple as that, there was nothing obscure or mysterious about it. When it comes to the subtle use of men in the employment of power I have known Englishmen more skilful than most Jews, and who have even used Jews for the purpose. For instance, Sir William Tyrrell, the brilliant professional diplomat who was ambassador in Paris during my youth and from whom I learnt so much, would use my friend Charles Mendl, who was a Jew, like Svengali used Trilby. It was the ambassador who had the brains and he used this likeable Jew with his universal contacts and wide friendships like a conduit pipe between himself and French life, through which he received information and executed his own manoeuvres. What matters in this world are brains and character, and they can be found in all the great peoples. I do not blame the Jews for using any power they had in what they believed to be a battle. What is blameworthy and foolish is to go on fighting when the battle is over, for that can renew the whole circle of fatality which should now be at an end.

The Rothermere experience had two effects on me; the first to suggest that despite all my preoccupations, money might be made for politics in business, and the second to make me more than ever reluctant to be dependent for political finance on the caprices of the rich. This feeling was reinforced by an encounter with Lady Houston, the widow of a shipping millionaire; the affair has already in part been published, so I am at liberty to give the details. She was a patriot of the Right, who had not the slightest idea what our policies were about, but with a vague sentiment in favour of the revival of English manhood. For instance, she most generously financed an expedition for the flight over Everest by one of the Douglas-Hamiltons.

I did not know her, but suddenly received an invitation to meet her on her yacht in Southampton when I was speaking somewhere in the neighbourhood. The old lady received me in bed in her state cabin—it was a curious habit of these magnates to do such business in bed—and indicated that she desired to support me. The interview was easy and we left with the firm understanding that she would. Afterwards she apparently wrote a cheque for £100,000 which she was about to send me, but changed her mind and tore it up. Someone had written a paragraph in *Action*, or some other journal connected with us, to the effect that she was a vain and silly old woman; maybe she was, but it was sillier still to say so. These things were liable to happen when I was constantly touring the country and speaking at least four times a week, because I often did not see a line of what was being written in our weekly press.

By then I had had more than enough of the whims of the rich, and we were constantly short of money. From first to last I gave about £100,000 of my own money to our movement in the thirties. This was to me a heavy burden because I was never as rich as I was supposed to be, but I have always retained sufficient of my inheritance to render me entirely independent. Too many tears should not be shed for this sacrifice of £100,000 as, with relative leisure for a short time after the war and opportunity to make money, I soon got most of it back again in transactions so normal, indeed banal, that they are not worth recounting. Others in the thirties made comparable sacrifices and things were always kept going; sometimes with much difficulty and with many ups and downs.

The problem was only to finance our headquarters, as our branches had always to be entirely self-supporting from the subscriptions and donations of local members without any help from us; in most periods H.Q. used to call on them for money by taxing a percentage of their takings. Some branches were relatively rich, with local businessmen forming clubs and circles for their support. Industrialists and merchants of more moderate stature than the Nuffields, Rothermeres and Houstons used also to support our headquarters. Large luncheons were organised at restaurants like the Criterion for this purpose, at which I used to speak. A club entirely independent of us was also formed, at which I met similar gatherings, sometimes with felicitous and lucrative results. My experiences at that time were diverse.

An event occurred toward the mid-thirties which reminded me of the possibility of making money for political purposes, first suggested to me by my experience with Lord Rothermere. I found fascinating the possibility of leading a movement with a revolutionary idea to power, while at the same time making the necessary money in business without financial dependence on anyone; this achievement would be unique in history, but what a labour to undertake. The opportunity came quite by chance, as many big occasions do. A young member of the movement approached me who had a business opening in his locality, and I saw at once the full possibilities which were not apparent to him. We started simply as two individuals, without any connection with the party; though I intended, of course, to use the proceeds entirely for the movement. From this relatively limited base I built in a few years a large concern which was only frustrated by the arrival of war. After the war others did in different ways what I had been doing, but all doors of that kind were then closed to me for a long period. It was a great enterprise and I shall always be proud of my part in an attempt without precedent. Some day far hence the full story may possibly be told; but not at present, or by me, for this would infringe my rule of never mentioning names and persons who were not known to have any dealings with me. They were Englishmen engaged in legitimate business and it would be wrong now to tell the story. In addition to speaking at least four times a week all the year round, except for one month's holiday, and also organising our movement, I was engaged for several years in the building of a big business.

Meantime, while our branches were self-supporting, a number of people were always busy collecting for our headquarters. Their guide lines were to receive subscriptions from any British people within the Empire, provided no strings were attached. It seemed a just principle that funds should be raised for a movement within the sphere in which it operates; our principal interest was then the British Empire. It is true that all my life—as my very early speeches show—I felt myself an European, and that as a movement we were greatly interested in keeping peace between Europeans and also in the gradual development of some common aims in European policies. It would therefore have been quite legitimate in my view to raise money, also on the condition that no strings were attached, from other Europeans; certainly the charge of the movement raising money in this way and on these conditions would not have worried me in the least. We should merely have been in the same position as so many members of the Second International, not to mention the Third.

Suggestions were sometimes made that we received money from abroad, and were always met by the direct challenge to produce evidence; with no response. Finally, in the House of Commons Mr. R. R. Stokes—well known as a Minister in Labour governments—made the following statement during the war:

'In connection with the British Union, I must say a word about the chief protagonist of that organisation, Sir Oswald Mosley. I think it should be said, although I am not a sympathiser in any way with their point of view or their activities. He appeared before the Advisory Committee, and the Committee invited his solicitors to help them in discovering whether or not any foreign money was coming into the organisation of the British Union. After a most exhaustive search, in which all the banks joined, the Committee and solicitors had to admit that no foreign money of any kind whatsoever was coming into that organisation.'—*Hansard*, December 10, 1940, vol. 367, col. 839.

After the war the Home Secretary, Mr. Chuter Ede, prefaced a reference to me in the House of Commons on June 6, 1946, with the curious observation for a Minister in a supposedly judicial position: 'I can only hope this will be an instructive foreword to the book he proposes to publish'. The book in question was called *My Answer* (1946); it was a defence of my wartime position, coupled with an exposure of the methods used to suppress our opinions and a psychological analysis of the Labour Party, which is still quite entertaining reading. His allegation in effect was that letters had been found among Mussolini's papers which purported to show that I had accepted funds from Italy on behalf of British Union in the years 1934 and 1935. I challenged him next day to produce the evidence, adding that 'evidence on any subject could now be available at a penny a packet' in alleged archives. Referring to events before the war and propaganda against the fascist powers, I said it was not 'long since phrases about the "lie factories" of Europe were current and popular, while the discovery of "revealing documents" was made the subject of universal merriment'; and concluded that in the post-war circumstances 'the hilarity of most people is but little diminished if the factories change hands'.

I went on to quote from Lord Snowden's autobiography, which cited a communiqué of Lloyd George's government attacking George Lansbury when he was Editor of the *Daily Herald*—some years before he became elected leader of the Labour Party—and I then dealt with the *Daily Herald's* refutation of Lord Snowden and denial of the government's communiqué, together with their statement that £75,000 in part composed of Russian diamonds had been 'returned to the donors of the Communist International'. A profound, unwonted silence then enveloped the Home Secretary and other spokesmen of the Labour Party. It was all quite fun even in this period of my unpopularity, particularly as for reasons given it would not have worried me in the least if the charge were proved to be true. The pundits of Labour were throwing their stones from a very fragile glasshouse, and my own long-established and well-founded independence in financial matters gave me a particular invulnerability to such attack.

It would be a pity to leave this subject without some reference to the position of Sir Stafford Cripps, when Chancellor of the Exchequer; I always thought that he and George Lansbury were personally among the most conspicuously honest of Labour leaders. The *Daily Telegraph* reported on November 26, 1948, that: 'Gifts and loans of money, totalling at least £5,000, have been sent by the British Labour Party and individual trade unions in this country to the French Socialist Party and the Confédération Générale du Travail Force Ouvrière'. This journal further reported a week later that Sir Stafford Cripps, Chancellor of the Exchequer, had stated in the House: 'The transfer of money abroad by individuals or organisations for political purposes would be approved by the Treasury if for the purpose of "strengthening the democratic forces in any country" '. Finally, the *Evening News* reported on December 7 that Sir Stafford Cripps, in answer to further questions on the matter, had replied: 'I accept full responsibility for the decisions of the Treasury'. It would appear that what is sauce for the goose should also be sauce for the gander, but error these days is less easily allowed to the masculine gender.

Finally, it would also be inappropriate and forgetful to leave the topic without some reference to the more serious record of prominent conservatives in 1914. The left-wing journal *Tribune*, in an unanswered attack on men at one time most respected in the Conservative Party, reviewed on June 30, 1967, a book on the Ulster rising and stated: 'The third Home Rule Bill . . . had passed through all stages of Parliament by July 1914. Unable to stop it, either by argument or voting strength, Carson, the Unionist leader, contacted the German Government for help. And the Germans, at that moment planning war in Europe, obligingly sent a shipload of arms for an Ulster rising'. We can at least acquit the Conservatives of joining in the snivelling hypocrisy of the attacks upon us for alleged financial dealings in 1934 and 1935.

Our opponents often attack us with charges which are contradictory and therefore self-destructive. On the one hand, they suggested in the period in question that we were financed by fascism abroad: on the other, they alleged that these fascist leaders were planning some attack on the British Empire. Leaders such as Mussolini would indeed have been starry-eyed philanthropists if they had held such sinister designs against the British Empire and yet financed the only movement in Britain which was standing for its rearmament, and agitating continuously, publicly and furiously to that end. Throughout these years we alone among the parties stood for the rearmament of our country, when Labour on principle was opposing it and Baldwin was not risking the loss of an election by advocating it. In reality, fascist and national socialist leaders everywhere were quite content to let us get on with our business, which was preserving and developing the British Empire, if we would let them get on with their business, which took them in a totally different direction to the British Empire and our vital interests.

Personally, I had quite enough to do in the development and propaganda of the movement's policies in the thirties and in rebutting on the platform, in debate and in the law courts the continual attacks upon us. The tale of our law suits in the thirties has still to be told and in retrospect is quite entertaining. The apprehension that my 'private army' might be a menace to the State had already been dealt with in the law courts, when the Public Order Act was introduced in 1936 to suppress it. The *Star* on February 25, 1933, in a leading article entitled, 'Is it Progress?' said: 'Sir Oswald Mosley warned Mr. Maxton that he and the fascists would be ready to take over government with the aid of machine-guns when the moment arrived. Mr. Tom Mann was recently thrown into prison on the mere suspicion that he might say something ten times less provocative than Sir Oswald's words'. The article referred to a public debate I had against James Maxton with Lloyd George in the chair. I sued the *Star* for libel, and the case was heard five months after the Olympia meeting in November 1934 before the Lord Chief Justice, Lord Hewart and a jury. Sir Patrick Hastings was my counsel.

The Times report stated: 'Sir Oswald Mosley, giving evidence, said that at the meeting in question he expressed the view that the Independent Labour Party were stirring up in the country a violent feeling which would be taken advantage of by the communists, who believed in violence, and that later on Mr. Maxton and other peace lovers would make way for communists who believed in violence. He used the words contained in the transcript of the shorthand notes of his secretary.'

The cross-examining counsel on behalf of the *Star* was Mr. Norman Birkett, who was chairman of the committee dealing with the various categories of 18B detainees during the war, and was afterwards well known as a judge, in particular at the Nuremberg trial.

Passages in *The Times* report ran as follows:

'Cross-examined on his speech at the meeting of February 24, 1933, Sir Oswald denied that British Fascists were training as a military organisation in the proper sense of that term.

"If," said Sir Oswald Mosley, "it is suggested that we indulge in military training, in the sense of the use of arms, the suggestion is untrue. We are on a military basis to the extent alone that we are a disciplined movement."

Have you got fascist machine-guns?—Certainly not.

Have you got armoured cars?—No.

Sir Oswald said that he only advocated the use of machine-guns in a situation in which it would be legitimate to use them—namely, to save the Crown and the State on the occasion of a communist uprising. That was a moment when any loyal citizen would be justified in using force to protect the State from anarchy.

Was the purpose of this speech to show that, when the moment comes, the fascist doctrine will be imposed on the nation?—Nothing of the sort. That was not suggested in any shape or form. I have never suggested that fascist doctrine will be imposed on the nation. It will come in only one way—by the will of the people at a General Election.

Sir Oswald Mosley agreed that he described the old political parties as the Old Gang.

The Lord Chief Justice—That is not altogether a new term. (Laughter.)

Mr. Birkett (to the witness)—Is it your view that there is no organised party except fascism in this country which could deal with the present situation? —Certainly I do, otherwise I should not lead the very unpleasant life which I do live by advocating fascism.

Who are you to take machine-guns into the street and shoot people?—No more and no less than any other British citizen who sees the State in danger of being overthrown by an anarchist rising.

You are organising to meet that?—Only to the extent to which we can do so legally in a time of peace. We do not possess machine-guns, because it is illegal to have them.

Your expressed doctrines and the failure of the "Old Gang" would not allow you to contemplate power being handed back to them after a revolution had been dealt with? It must be fascism?—After such a situation it would rest with his Majesty the King, and with him alone, to invite someone to form a Government, and fascism would loyally abide by the decision of his Majesty. I might hope that our party would be invited to power, but, if we are not, we should await the next General Election and try to obtain power then.

Asked whether the fascists had aeroplanes, Sir Oswald Mosley said that they had none. The possession of armoured cars by the fascists was a myth which had been exploded by the Home Secretary in the House of Commons. "A few young fascists learned to fly," he added, "and the Press immediately said that we were forming a Fascist Air Force."

He thought that Mussolini and Hitler had saved their countries, but he had no desire to emulate their methods in this country. He had never said that fascists would obtain power by force. That was a different thing from saying that they would obtain power after force had had to be used. Fascists were ready to meet force used against the State by force, but not by force to obtain the reins of Government.

It is new for a leader of a political party in this country to say: "I will be the judge when the guns are to shoot"?—Lord Carson said things far worse than that when he was a leader at the Bar. (Laughter.)

Sir Oswald Mosley agreed that one local branch of the fascist movement at one time formed a flying club and held "air rallies".

What earthly assistance to a political movement is an air rally?—Anything which promotes manly sport greatly helps a movement like ours. The Junior Imperial League has whist drives. We have air rallies, football matches, and boxing contests.

There is a great deal of difference between a whist drive and an air rally? —Yes, all the difference between conservatism and the fascist movement. (Laughter.)

Supposing a communist government was in power with the consent of the King, would you still oppose it with guns?—You might ask what would happen if the King enacted the law of Herod and ordered every first-born in the land to be killed. The question is so hypothetical as to be absurd.

Can you answer it?—You cannot answer questions which are by their very nature absurd.

If the Communist Party were returned to power by the country and its leader was invited by the King to form a government, would you resist it?— By then the communists would be as mild as Mr. Ramsay MacDonald is now, compared to what he used to be. (Laughter.)

In no circumstances, continued Sir Oswald, would he use fascist machine-guns against a constitutionally elected government in power on the invitation of the King.

Asked whether fascists had not often been in conflict with the "Reds", Sir Oswald said: "Yes, when they have attacked us. We have never interfered with the meetings of our opponents, but when our meetings are violently attacked, we resist attack. If people try to shout down speakers at our meetings fascists are sent to throw them out with their bare hands and nothing more."

Do you not issue rubber truncheons to your forces?—Rubber truncheons are not issued to our forces, and the carrying of any weapon is absolutely forbidden in fascism. Only once, in a very heavy fight at Manchester, rubber truncheons were used, after our men had been slashed with razors for weeks. Subsequently I forbade these weapons being used.'

The Times report then concluded as follows: 'The Lord Chief Justice, in summing-up, said that the defendants had deliberately put in the pleadings what every lawyer knew to be the very dangerous plea of justification. They had chosen to say that the words complained of were true in substance and in fact, but when they came to deliver particulars of justification they were unable to state what were the words used by Sir Oswald Mosley in his speech.

'Did not the words complained of mean that, if Mr. Tom Mann has been thrown into prison, how much more should the Government take steps to throw Sir Oswald Mosley into prison? Was the article, as had been suggested, a plea for toleration? Or was not the inactivity of the Government in connection with Sir Oswald Mosley contrasted with its activity in the far less serious case of Tom Mann? Was it not a taunt to the authorities for not prosecuting Sir Oswald Mosley?

'The jury would have to decide whether in his speech Sir Oswald Mosley used the words which he was said to have used. Whatever the jury might think of his opinions, did he seem to them to be a public man of no little courage, no little candour, and no little ability? He had stated in evidence what he had said in his speech and his secretary had produced her shorthand notes to support him. He had been cross-examined for a long time, but had anything come of it?

'On the material before the jury, was it possible for them to say that the words in the first part of the "leaderette" were true? If, however, they were true, it was admitted that the second paragraph of the "leaderette" constituted fair comment.

'Dealing with the meaning of the alleged libel, his Lordship asked the jury whether there could be any doubt that the words imputed to Sir Oswald Mosley a criminal offence.

'They might think that Sir Patrick Hastings was right when he said that it was an undefended case and that the suggestion that a farthing damages should be awarded was adding insult to injury. They must remember the terrible power of the modern printing press by which any matter could be distributed a hundred-thousandfold.

'The jury returned a verdict in favour of Sir Oswald Mosley, assessing the damages at £5,000.'

Our fight against communism in the thirties got us into further trouble; to be precise two more lawsuits, as well as a special Act of Parliament. One lawsuit was a comedy staged in the salubrious spa of Worthing-on-Sea. We did not think it so funny when we stood in the dock faced with possible penalties of two years in jail if things went wrong. With half a dozen companions I was charged with riotous assembly. We had gone, all unwitting of coming events, to hold a meeting in a hall we had hired on the seafront, which was a large tin tabernacle of flimsy construction. During the peaceful meeting with a packed and orderly audience the tin sides resounded with an orchestra of noise under the impact of sticks and stones. However, I was audible throughout the meeting, and at the end the audience left without molestation. The noise however redoubled when following my usual habit I addressed the blackshirts, who had assembled from all over the neighbourhood and were supplemented by a few from London who were experienced in the organisation of large meetings. I left the hall first, closely followed by the massed blackshirts. We were rushed, and I hit the first assailant on the jaw; it was ungenerous of him afterwards to sue me for assault[1] when he had waited for it all evening and notified his ardent desire on the tin sides of our tabernacle.

A free-for-all then ensued with no police visible. The Reds had arrived in coaches from far away, but after protracted debate left in some disorder. We too were then preparing to depart, when we were informed that our local H.Q., about half a mile away, was being beleaguered with a number of women members inside. The besieging Reds were surprised to see us enter from each end of the street where this house was situated, and again they got the worst of it. When all was clear we went home without remonstrance, and with scant appearance from the local police force.

We thought no more about it, and in the long interval which followed held many good and orderly meetings in places where we would have expected far more trouble than at Worthing. Then came summonses for riotous assembly, and after several days' hearing in the Magistrates' court in Worthing we were sent for trial to Lewes Assizes. The opposing counsel was Mr. John Flowers, K.C.; it was rumoured that lawyers sometimes marked briefs 'no flowers by request', but he was a fine old English type, well known and popular in the whole area for his long and distinguished membership of the Sussex County cricket team. Pat Hastings again acted for us, and before my appearance in the witness-box whispered in my ear: 'If you score too freely off the Sussex slow bowler this case is lost'. There were a few hilarious moments when, in his effort to show the concerted action which is essential to the proof of riotous

---

[1] On this occasion, as previously, after the fight in the Rag Market, Birmingham (Chapter 3) before the Stipendary, I was acquitted.

assembly, Mr. Flowers asked me if we had not come to Worthing intending to hang together, and I got out of the Hastings hand sufficiently to make appropriate reply. However, the proceedings had begun to dissolve after Hastings' cross-examination of the Chief Constable, who said he had been present at the events on the night of the meeting in plain clothes. Long before the normal end the jury notified the judge, Mr. Justice Branson, that they desired to hear no more, and he expressed his complete agreement in dismissing the case. This performance in two courts cost us £3,000, even in those days. Process of law in England can be a very odd thing.

A second action for libel, technically a slander, showed another strange aspect of British law. Mr. Marchbank, Secretary of the National Union of Railwaymen, read at a public meeting a document purporting to be signed by me, which instructed the blackshirts to arm. I knew well, of course, that no such document existed, and at once issued a writ for slander. Pat Hastings again appeared for me and under cross-examination Mr. Marchbanks gradually admitted that he possessed no document bearing my signature. Under further relentless cross-examination the fact emerged that the document in question consisted of notes compiled by Mr. Marchbanks himself on information supplied to him by a man with a certain record who had been expelled from our movement. The information was whispered to Pat Hastings, who said: 'I have a passionate desire to see this gentleman in the witness-box'.

These facts were proved up to the hilt, and we appeared to have an even stronger case than in the *Star* libel action. The other side then put into the box several women who gave their own account of the fight at Manchester with rubber truncheons, which had already been mentioned in the *Star* action; after this I had given orders that no weapons should ever be carried by members, as I then explained. The emotional story of these partisans—recounted without mention of the previous Red use of razors—clearly impressed the jury, which Pat Hastings had already observed contained some determined opponents. Usually so effective, on this occasion Hastings made a mistake in calling no rebutting evidence. He took the line that the case was in the bag and that a long-ago fight in Manchester had nothing in the world to do with the now clearly proved fact that I had never signed a document giving orders to blackshirts to arm. However, emotion without answer was stronger than the facts, and we were awarded a farthing damages in a case which was even stronger than the action in which we obtained damages of £5,000.

I too had made the mistake of taking the proceedings too jovially. The opposing K.C. was the able but choleric Mr. Pritt, well known as a left-wing M.P. He pressed me concerning some points on which I had taken legal advice, notably—if I remember rightly—the position of members of the forces under military law, if they were also members of the movement. Finding himself frustrated in this line, he asked with heavy sarcasm whether I never moved without a K.C. at my elbow, and I replied that I saw no reason why this advantage should be enjoyed by the Communist Party alone. This observation for some reason threw eminent counsel into a transport of indignation. Not long afterwards I had to speak at a private dinner at which members of various parties were present, and I complained that our movement was never really discussed in the Press, nor elsewhere. Mr. Pritt rose and remarked that in his circles little else was ever discussed. I was surprised. A happy feature of these lawsuits was renewing acquaintance with the gay and brilliant Pat Hastings. In our days together in the Labour Party he equally enlivened some dull evenings with his adroit teasing of Beatrice Webb.

I long ago came to the conclusion that a libel suit with a political subject in British courts under existing law is a costly and incalculable game of roulette. The outcome depends entirely on the jury, which finds disassociation from political feelings almost impossible, particularly when the matter has been discussed in the newspapers. It is possible, of course, to have an impartial jury, but you are more likely to find a jury of partisans on one side or the other. In that event, mathematically, you are unlikely to have even one juror on your side until your party polls an average of over eight per cent throughout the country. Even if most of the jury mean to be impartial, one experienced and determined politician in such cases will either pull the rest round or keep them there till all is blue. Political libel suits under the present law are a farcical gamble in which the litigant risks ruinous expense. Nevertheless, if libel goes too far it is sometimes necessary to take a lucky dip.

The sooner the law is changed and cheapened the better, and the obvious reform is to do away with juries in such cases and to give a judge the sole responsibility. Apart from the justly renowned integrity of the British judiciary, the judge will be aware that the whole Bar will be watching an action of such interest, and he will be careful only to give a verdict justified by the facts before a profession which is quick to detect a faulty judgment. There is also the possibility of appeal to courts with some of the finest intellectual standards in the world. The remedy is simple and obvious, but even to get the simple and obvious done in Britain can take a long time. Hence many of the troubles of our country.

19
Hitler and Mussolini
Conversations and
Impressions
The Abdication

MUSSOLINI and Hitler were interested in our movement, not because our policies were similar—the aims of these intensely national movements in each country were widely divergent—but because we were strongly opposed to communism, and unlikely to quarrel with any European country which had no intention of challenging British interests. Therefore, my experience of meeting these leaders can possibly convey a unique impression because it is the view of an Englishman with whom they felt it possible to get on reasonably well, at least on a basis of live and let live. I met Mussolini about half a dozen times between 1932 and the last occasion in 1936. It was convenient to see him once a year as I usually had my month's holiday in Italy somewhere in the neighbourhood of Naples.

The British Embassy, conducted with skill and grace by Sir Ronald and Lady Sybil Graham, arranged my first interview with Mussolini, who was on good terms with them. This was not because they shared his opinions but because they took the traditional view that it was the business of an ambassador to be polite, to understand the opinion of the country to which he was accredited and to transmit a clear appreciation of its attitude to his own government; the epoch of the dull, rude clerk parading his native prejudice in foreign capitals, or of the drunken dilettante on the communist fringe, had not yet arrived. Harold Nicolson, always an ornament of the great tradition in British diplomacy, went independently to Rome when I was there in January 1932. He continued his journey without me to Berlin, where he recorded in his diary that Hitler 'had missed the bus'.[1] He met neither leader, and his

[1] Nicolson, *Diaries*, January 22, 1932.

many gifts did not supply him with an inkling of what it was all about.

Mussolini, as is well known, received his guests in an enormous room at the Palazzo Venezia, and I never saw him anywhere else. On my entry he would rise behind his large writing-table at the other end of the room and give the fascist salute, which I returned; he would then come round the desk and advance some way to meet me—halting before the last few paces and throwing back his head in his characteristic gesture as he extended his hand—thus sparing his guest some of the long and solitary march to the chair in front of the table. Some people apparently found this ritual embarrassing, possibly because they were caught by the dilemma whether to return the salute, bow or just stare; there have been various accounts of these interviews, some of them quite entertaining. We used to talk in French, which he spoke well, and conversation was always easy until one fatal day when he announced with pride on my arrival that he had learnt English; after that I understood little he said. Apparently he had lessons from some old English governess, and I shall have the sympathy of my compatriots who have experienced conversation with an Italian who speaks English really badly.

Our talks ranged widely over politics and certain spheres of literature; he was erudite, particularly in the background of such authors as Nietzsche and Sorel. He expressed the warmest regard for the English people, his desire to work in peace and harmony with them, and his deep sympathy for our movement. I liked him, and found him easy to get on with. This was not always the experience of his colleagues, as I learnt on arriving in Rome at the time of the murder of Dollfuss. Mussolini was then contemplating war with Germany after the arrival in power of the National Socialist Party, which he held responsible for these events in Austria; they were supporting their own party in that German country, while Mussolini favoured Chancellor Dollfuss and Prince Stahremberg, who was running a local fascist movement. When I arrived, Mussolini was in such a rage that none of his associates dared approach him on the subject, and some of them suggested that in my interview I should try to cool him off. I made the attempt, and he took it very well; at first a hard stare of the glittering eyes, and then a most reasonable and realistic discussion. They were right in thinking that he would accept more from the outsider. This incident was an interesting commentary on the alleged fascist international, which was non-existent to a degree that even threatened world peace. It is true that these two leaders at a later stage came closer together; the antipathy of the Western world to both may have been a more potent influence than their mutual attraction.

Some of Mussolini's closest colleagues also told me that in ordinary life they found him awkward, stilted, cold and unapproachable. An extreme instance of this was an invitation to one of them—after the performance of some conspicuous service—to have dinner with him at a villa on the sea where he no doubt desired to express his appreciation. After desultory conversation during dinner, he played the violin to his guest throughout the evening without any reference to the major subject; apparently this was his only means of expressing the warmth of his feelings to an old colleague. In any social contact he seemed very inhibited; whether through a natural shyness or reluctance to abandon even for a moment the dignity of the leader it is difficult to say.

My own impression of him was different; the flash of the large dark eyes when he was excited could be surprising, but the posture vanished directly you knew him well. It seemed to me that he assumed it deliberately in public, not through vanity or emotion but with a cold purpose of producing a certain impression. He was speaking to Italians, and he gave them what he thought suitable and what he judged they wanted. Here he differed sharply from some of our Anglo-Saxon politicians; he may sometimes have deceived others, but he never deceived himself. This was a refreshing aspect of a remarkable character, reflected also in his buoyant humour. He never expressed himself to me in those terms, but I always sensed after one of his histrionic efforts an attitude equivalent to—a dig in the ribs, and that got 'em. It would be unjust to suggest that he was insincere—he was a passionate patriot with a profound sense of his mission as an Italian and to some extent as an European—but he was not taken in by his own performances. With so many politicians the contrary is the case; they are completely engrossed in their own performance and moved by nothing else. With Mussolini demagogy was not an end, but a means to an end which he clearly understood.

His humour was simple and direct; it had almost a barrack-room savour. He said to me on arrival one day: 'Do you know who sat in that chair yesterday?—The Chief Rabbi of Italy. Do you know what he said to me?—We Jews rise on top of you Gentiles like oil on water.—The effrontery of him. Do you know what happened last night?—he dropped dead.' Mussolini slapped his big thigh and roared with laughter. He was in no way anti-semitic —I understood that the Rabbi's death was entirely due to natural causes—but he had a peculiar sense of fun, a lively appreciation of life's ups and downs. Anti-semitism or any form of racialism is quite unknown among Italians, but Mussolini had an acute sense of the contrasts of life, of the 'mutability of human fortune, the whirligig of fate', as Asquith used to call it. The incident may give a rather brutal impression as baldly recorded, but this effect at the time was mitigated by the sense that he felt these sudden reversals of fortune could equally affect any other mortal at any moment, including himself, in a sad prescience of things to come. He seemed to me completely cool and realistic in his calculations; his mistakes, for example his entry into the war, were made for reasons which were at least discernible.

I should say that his morality consisted chiefly in advancing the interests of his country and in a general sense of serving the renaissance of European man. I should much doubt from my observation of him that he was guilty of the relatively few crimes imputed to him, such as the murder of Matteotti, for he would certainly have regarded it as a stupidity, a crime in which the risk and discredit far outweighed any possible advantage. Mussolini was ruthless, but not a fool. 'Never take an unnecessary risk,' said Caesar. Yet the record of men even in the highest category of achievement has on occasions been stained without purpose by impulse of sheer, brutal passion; as witness the fate of Vercingetorix or the duc d'Enghien.

Mussolini at that time was obviously having a good deal of trouble with some of his old companions. He said to me one day: 'Après la révolution il se pose toujours la question des révolutionnaires'. Caesar solved the problem by putting the legionaries on the land; Mussolini began to do something of the same kind in the Pontine Marshes and in Libya, and before the war he had this situation well under control. It was his habit with forethought and decision to keep a grip on even trivial detail; when I stood beside him at one of his blackshirt parades he mounted on a foot-stool previously placed in the box of the saluting base, which made him several inches taller than me in the photograph instead of the reverse. His detailed grasp of larger affairs in the last period of his power seems in some measure to have deserted him; partly as the result of increased pressure in the stress of war and partly because of the faulty method of over-centralisation when few colleagues are trusted.

What will be the final verdict of history on this remarkable figure who for a period so greatly inspired such a profoundly gifted people? His constructive achievements certainly contain some lessons for the future. Chief among them was the Corporate State, whose study in detail is available to all; its mechanism for industrial conciliation could be used with or without its compulsive aspects. The chief achievement of this organisation was the labour charter which abolished the chattel concept of labour, and prevented those who had served an industry well being thrown on the scrap-heap when no longer wanted. The abolition of 'wage slavery' had long been in every socialist programme, but that overdue reform was left to the Corporate State.

The elaborate mechanism of the Corporate State, like all other machines, could be used well or badly for human purposes. Men with a powerful motor-car at their disposal can use it to win a race, to expedite their daily business, or to drive it at speed into a brick wall or over a cliff. At best, the Corporate State provided a means not only to regulate relations in industry, but to secure an equable distribution of its profits. I have indicated that my criticism was and is that it tended to begin and end with machinery. It is not enough in the age of modern science to establish a machine which ensures stability, or even fair distribution. The machine must be directed and controlled by men with a clear view of the changes, the new possibilities that science has brought, and with the vision to devise new policies to meet them. The theory of the Corporate State organised as a human body was a moving idea, but I felt it should then come alive and advance with modern science and economics toward constructive and creative policies. It seemed to me too much a piece of machinery, an automatic stabiliser rather than a motive force.

I could find nothing in Italian fascism comparable with the policies I devised in my period in government or in the previous Birmingham proposals. These policies, which we recommended throughout Britain in the seven years of our fascist movement from 1932 to 1939, were ideas of an entirely different order of thought and action. I feel quite simply that they went far beyond the policies of either the Italians or the Germans at that time and had nothing at all to do with them. This may be regarded as insular or personal prejudice, but I am confident that anyone studying impartially our ideas in Britain and comparing them with those of the Continent will not only find very little relation between them, but will be constrained to admit that our policies were far more creative. The similarity between us and the continental movements began and ended with the need to fight for ideas to be heard at all, and this common experience of the Red assault gave us a certain mutual sympathy. In the end the head is more important than the fist, but this was seldom recognised at the time.

Then and since we hear much more of young fascists giving castor oil to Reds, than of the constructive thinking in the Corporate State. We never hear a word, of course, about the previous crimes of the communists, such as holding the heads of living men in steel furnaces until they were burnt off; proof of these atrocities was to be seen at an exhibition in Rome which I examined in detail in the early thirties. We hear much of the thousands detained by Mussolini in the Lipari islands, where they suffered a justly condemned imprisonment. We hear less of the millions slaughtered in the slave camps of Stalin, who became the admired ally of British Government and the toast of its leaders. These were rough times and Mussolini was a rough man, but a squalid assassin he was not. He was ruthless, amoral, brutal when fighting the brutality of the bestial Red gangs of Italy—all those things —but a patriot, a brave man who served what he saw to be great ends. He was too a man of some vision and some sense of beauty, whose epitaph might be expressed in his own words recommending certain qualities which his life and character incarnated:

Youth is beautiful, because it has clear eyes with which to regard and to reflect the vast and tumultous panorama of the world.
Youth is beautiful because it has a fearless heart that dreads not death.

My relations with Mussolini were terminated by an incident characteristic of Italian-German relations at that time. Three years after Cimmie's death in May 1933, I married again in October 1936. Diana was living in a remote country house at Wootton in Staffordshire. At that time I was often menaced by threats of assassination and violence of every kind, and it was therefore out of the question to leave a woman known to be married to me alone in the deep country; unless the house was strongly guarded, which we felt would be both expensive and ridiculous, and, worse still, would make us a constant prey to sensational journalism. The only way out of the dilemma was, at any rate for the time being, to keep the marriage secret. The question arose how this was to be done. In England, impossible; abroad, at any embassy?—We might as well tell the town crier. Was there then any country where under the law the marriage would be legal in England and where it could be kept secret? The only answer appeared to be Germany, where by a reciprocal arrangement English nationals could be married by a German registrar instead of at the embassy, as is necessary elsewhere.

Frau Goebbels, who was a friend of Diana's, helped to arrange the marriage, and after the ceremony she gave a luncheon for us at her villa near Wannsee. Hitler was a guest. From this incident arose the rumours that Hitler had been my best man, while in fact this duty was performed by an English ex-officer of the 10th Hussars who accompanied me. I recalled later that it does not necessarily follow that heads of state are best men at weddings if they pay the compliment of being present; the kings of England and Belgium had honoured my first marriage by their presence, but no one at the time was fool enough to make such a suggestion. Exceptional nonsense emerges when it is armed by political malice.

This event ruptured my relations with Mussolini because the Italians had some news of it, and relations between the two regimes at that time were none too happy. They were not quite certain about the marriage, because on my next visit to Rome an interview was arranged with Mussolini in the afternoon by his bureau in the ordinary way. However, on the morning of that day, his son-in-law, Count Ciano, then Foreign Secretary, asked to see me. In the course of a long and courteous interview he suddenly asked me the abrupt question whether I had been in Berlin on the day in question. I replied curtly that I had, without further explanation. It had been my intention to tell Mussolini of the marriage in the afternoon, but not to tell Ciano, whose discretion I did not entirely trust.

Early in the afternoon a message arrived that Mussolini was ill and could not see me. I left Rome, not to return until after the war, and I never saw him again. Clearly, my normal relations with him would easily have been restored if I had gone back to Rome a year or two later, because he and Hitler were then on good terms. But for the last three years before the war I never left England at all; I was held fast by the growth of our movement and the ever increasing intensity of our campaign. My scanty holidays were spent at Wootton in my native Staffordshire. There was a poignant moment after the war when in Italy I received a message from one of Mussolini's intimates who had been with him in the last days of his life, that he had regarded as one of his mistakes being divided from me by the intervention of Ciano. He apparently always told his associates that he believed in my star; poor man, he also believed in his own.

The fact that we had been married in Berlin made a certain amount of trouble for me in England, not when I first announced it at the birth of our son Alexander in 1938, but later on. Perhaps it should be reckoned among my mistakes, though it was not a reasonable calculation in 1936 that war would come because England would guarantee Poland and Germany would invade it. In any case, I was prepared to do anything to prevent a war by maintaining good relations between English and Germans, provided it was compatible with my duty to my own country. I will not, when charged with this error, follow Bernard Shaw in claiming that the only mistakes I ever make are to underestimate the stupidity of other people; he never could believe they could do anything so foolish, but in his sad experience they always did. However, I would not have believed in 1936 that we should have been so foolish as to fight about the Polish Corridor, instead of letting the Germans go to a possible clash with Russia, which, if it happened, would have smashed world communism, pointed Germany in the opposite direction to us, and kept its vital energies busy for at least a generation while we had ample time to take any precautions which might prove necessary; nor that the Germans would be so foolish—after getting already nearly everything they wanted—as to risk a war with the whole world against them in order immediately to establish their last position in Danzig and the Polish Corridor, when a short pause, used in a more adroit fashion, could so easily have secured this. I did not reckon on the degree of obstinate stupidity on both sides, and such conduct did not seem to be calculable by a rational mind; since then I have learned not to underestimate the follies of mankind.

These larger affairs really belong to the politics of the 1939 war. We are at present engaged with my meetings and conversations with these historic figures in the thirties, and my impressions of them at that time. My first meeting with Hitler was in April 1935, and was privately arranged without any publicity at all. This was not difficult, as Ribbentrop and others had been in London and in touch with us even before he came to power, and I think it was the Ribbentrop bureau which organised the meeting. Hitler gave a luncheon for me in his flat in Munich, where a large company assembled, including Frau Winifred Wagner, the brilliant English wife of the composer's son Siegfried, whom I met there for the first time, and whose friendship I have esteemed ever since; in recent years some of our happiest moments have been spent with her in the garden of Wagner's house at Bayreuth during the opera festival.

An interview with Hitler was exactly the opposite to a first encounter with Mussolini. There was no element of posture. At Munich in April 1935 we talked for an hour before lunch at this first meeting. He entered the small room in his flat quite simply; we sat down and talked with the aid of an interpreter, for I could speak no German until I learnt it during the enforced retirement of my war years. At first, Hitler was almost inert in his chair, pale, seemingly exhausted. He came suddenly to life when I said that war between Britain and Germany would be a terrible disaster, and used the simile of two splendid young men fighting each other until they both fall exhausted and bleeding to the ground, when the jackals of the world would mount triumphant on their bodies. His face flushed and he launched with much vigour into some of his main themes, but in the normal manner of any politician moved by strong convictions. The hypnotic manner was entirely absent; perhaps I was an unsuitable subject; in any case, he made no attempt whatever to produce any effect of that kind. He was simple, and treated me throughout the occasion with a gentle, almost feminine charm. Naturally, it was much easier for me to deal with him than for some politicians, because in the international issues under discussion we had nothing to quarrel about. The men with whom we quarrel in life are those who want the same thing as we do, with consequent clash of interest; Hitler and I pursued different paths.

My ideas for maintaining and developing the British Empire in no way conflicted with what he wanted for the Germans. He did not desire war with Russia, because his aims were limited to the union of the German peoples in Europe, but he wanted assurances from England and Western Europe that they would not jump on his back in the event of a clash between Germany and Russia, would not intervene against him during a life and death struggle with communism. If I had been responsible for British Government I would certainly have granted this wish because, while I detest all war, I certainly thought war between national socialism and communism a lesser evil than war between Britain and Germany. In return, he would have been ready to offer all possible guarantees for the support of the British Empire, which I would not have required because we were then still strong enough to look after ourselves, and that would always have been the case in any government with which I was connected. He not only expressed the warmest admiration for the British people, but said he considered Germany, as the leading land power, and Britain, as the leading naval power, to be complementary and beneficent forces, who together could become two pillars supporting world stability, peace and order. In my view, it was at least true that there was no point on the entire globe at which British and German interests clashed.

Let it not be understood from this that in real politics I would ever take anything at its face value or trust anyone in international affairs. No one has the right to risk the life of his country on what men say, or on his personal beliefs, instincts or hunches. Strive for the best, but prepare for the worst. I had for years been conducting a strenuous campaign for the rearmament of Britain. In power, I would have sought any kind of defensive alliance with France and America, or with anyone else, in case, after expansion in the east, Hitler turned round and attacked us.

I should have taken every precaution, but I do not believe he would have done anything of the kind. Apart from the fact that the Germans would have bitten off as much as they could chew for at least a generation in a successful drive east, an attack on the west, to anyone who knew anything of the subject, was contrary to the whole history and psychology of the National Socialist Party. You cannot spend a lifetime pointing a mass movement of the people in one direction, and then suddenly say: 'About turn, I really meant the opposite to what I have been saying all the time'. Some minor practitioners of the political art are now discovering the truth of this elementary fact. Hitler had said again and again that he wanted the union of the Germans and living room in the east, not the take over of crowded areas in the west. The idea of conducting our large multi-racial Empire was also entirely contrary to national socialist ideas for the proper employment of German energy. To attempt any of these things would have been to stand Nazi doctrines on their heads. It is true that all this was exactly the opposite of our British ideas, derived from the long Imperial experience, and it was precisely this difference which gave us the best chance of peace; the Germans wanted something quite different.

I would lose no time during such a discussion in dialectical exercise or moral sermonising to prove our ideas were the best. A statesman should never contravene the vulnerable foibles of his opposite number; rather they can be the means of getting what he wants, he should use them. The judo throw is one of the arts of politics; let the other man go his way, but rather faster and further than he meant to. Some pert little governess of the Eden school would spend the afternoon trying to convert such a man to her particular point of view in a fit of moral indignation. I would rather say: we have no major issue to quarrel about, because we want entirely different things. But at the same time, I should keep my powder dry; nothing is certain in the world of international politics.

My two interviews with Hitler in April 1935 and October 1936 were easy, because there was no clash of interest. He seemed to me a calm, cool customer, certainly ruthless, but in no way neurotic. I remember remarking afterwards: if it be true he bites the carpet, he knows to a millimetre how far his tooth is going. I understand he sometimes flew into considerable rages, apparently to impress those around him and to get things done; a process of dynamism. I prefer the opposite technique in history, which can be exercised when such devotion has been inspired by leadership that a Caesar has only to look sad, and address his old companions as citizens instead of soldiers, in order to reduce a mutiny to tears. These things are questions not only of taste but of method inherent in character.

Hitler impressed me at that time as in no way insane, and this view was reinforced by his private appearance in small parties he gave when Diana and her sister were present. She described him as an extraordinarily gifted mimic, who could mime as well as any actor before a discreet audience. Imitating himself in the days when he used to smoke, rolling cigarettes, licking the sticky paper in all the busy paraphenalia of the old-time continental smoker, he stopped short saying, you cannot do that sort of thing if you are supposed to be a dictator. It is a small point, but paranoiacs do not make fun of themselves. On another occasion he imitated Mussolini being presented with a sword by the Arabs, flashing it out of the scabbard and brandishing it to heaven; then he said: 'I am no good at all that, I would just say to my adjutant, "Here, Schaub, hang on to this" '.

Such private occasions with relatively few people present revealed unexpected qualities, particularly if Goebbels was there as well. Diana was very fond of Frau Goebbels, who, with her husband, was often at dinner with Hitler. Goebbels, distinguished in public by his qualities as an orator and master of mass propaganda, had in private life an almost exaggerated sense of humour which, surprisingly, Hitler shared; it was one of the bonds between them. They also had in common a love of music.

Hitler was a great talker, and lost a good deal of time in nocturnal discussions, sitting up late after supper talking to his staff or to guests, who found his conversation enthralling; in this respect at least he resembled Churchill. The habit apparently began when he could not sleep after speeches, and it no doubt contributed to his ultimate and premature exhaustion. Nothing is harder for an orator than to relax and sleep after such an occasion. Without the use of drugs, or alcohol, to which Hitler was averse, it requires not only a conscious act of will but an endocrine system capable of braking as well as accelerating, which he apparently did not possess. At interviews, conferences or on these occasions, he must have met most of the élite of Germany, but the only conspicuous absentees from these encounters appear to have been the German scientists who were working on various aspects of nuclear fission; an incredible omission which may well have changed the destiny of the world, for he failed to grasp that the first duty of statesmen in the modern age is to discover, know well, understand and support the men of science.

Diana used to stay sometimes with her sister who had taken a flat in Munich, with encouragement from me as I was naturally interested to hear more of developments in that country and of these personalities. When she was in Munich or in Berlin Hitler would always invite them to luncheon or dinner, and they were introduced to his whole circle. Unity's suicide at the outbreak of war had a clear, simple, tragic cause; she loved England, her home and her country, but had developed a great love of Germany. War between these countries was to her the supreme disaster; she walked into the 'English Garden' in Munich and shot herself. The gauleiter of the area, who was a friend, had her followed, suspecting she might do herself some injury; she was picked up and hurried to hospital. German surgeons saved her life, but were unable to extract the bullet from her head. Hitler caused her to be sent home through Switzerland, but the English surgeons could do no more. She partly recovered, but was never again the same person; nine years later, the bullet moved and she died.

Hitler had solemnly introduced me to Unity Mitford at the luncheon he gave me in April 1935, as he was unaware that we knew each other; in fact, I had first met her at her coming-out ball in London, given three years before by Diana. At Hitler's luncheon she was a girl of twenty, young, ingenuous, full of enthusiasm, in a way stage-struck by the glamour and panoply of the national socialist movement and the mass admiration of Hitler. It was quite untrue that she had any kind of a love affair with him. The only woman we ever heard of in connection with Hitler in this period was Eva Braun, whom he finally married. He effected her introduction to Diana and Unity in a highly individual fashion by giving them places next to each other in his reserved seats at the Nuremberg Parteitag.

He invited them to the Olympic Games of 1936, held in Berlin; I might have been a participant but for an odd chance. The following year, 1937, I represented Britain for the last time in international fencing as a member of the British team in the world championship at Paris, having twice been runner-up in the British epée championships during previous years. I did not become a candidate for the British team in the Olympic Games in the previous year for a quaint reason. It was decided that the British team in the traditional march past should not give the Olympic salute, which had been invented by the Greeks more than two thousand years before Hitler or Mussolini were born, and consequently long before anyone thought of calling it the fascist salute. As the French and nearly every other team decided to give the salute, it seemed on the one hand invidious that I should refrain, and on the other that it would show a lack of the team spirit appropriate to the occasion if I had been the only member of the British team to give it. So discretion became the better part of sportsmanship.

It was the habit of Hitler to convey to me his view of events through Diana. The last time was at Bayreuth a month before the outbreak of war, when he invited her to his box at the opera. She found him in a state of extreme depression. He said that he thought England would persist in its attitude over Danzig and this made war inevitable. The idea that he did not think England would fight was always a complete illusion. He regarded the coming war between England and Germany as the supreme tragedy of history, but he could not abandon Germans placed under Polish rule by the treaty of Versailles. European disaster of every kind would ensue. He added that I would almost certainly be assassinated, as Jaurès had been in France when war came in 1914. He had always a strong historic sense and my position of political opposition to the war seemed to him similar to that of the French statesman.

The occasion I remember best in these sporadic discussions of the years when Hitler gave me his views through Diana was at an earlier point in 1937. I had published in England a long essay entitled 'The World Alternative', which gave in detail my ideas of an European policy for maintaining world peace. It was then published in Germany, rather to my surprise, as I had made no such suggestion, and attracted considerable attention when it appeared in *Geopolitik*, a magazine conducted by an outstanding editor, Herr Haushofer. It never occurred to me to send it to Hitler or to raise the question with any German; rather slow of me, in fact. Diana was in Berlin soon after the essay's publication, and was invited to luncheon at the Reichskanzlerei. She was shown into a room where she was alone, and shortly afterwards Hitler entered. He was holding in his hand *Geopolitik*, and began by saying in the whimsical fashion of one of his moods: 'You know they say I never read anything'. Then giving her the magazine: 'You may examine me on any part of this article, because I have read every line of it'. He added: '*Es ist fabelhaft*'. My readers will be aware that this word in German does not mean the stuff of which fables are made, but rather denotes an excellence in the subject and an agreement with its contents. Well, there is the story for what it is worth. At any rate, it indicates that Hitler would not have turned down flat any such policy from our side. Whether the whole thing was a trick to mask a design for world domination will be considered in detail in the next chapter. In any case that would have made no difference to me, as for years I had advocated the rearmament of Britain against any contingency, and with the system of Western alliances I envisaged could have frustrated that plan if it had ever existed. Try for the best but prepare for the worst is with me a first principle.

The word Jew was never mentioned in my discussions with Hitler. I never raised it because I do not believe in interfering in the internal affairs of other countries, and certainly I do not believe in risking war because some particular minority is being treated badly elsewhere. Disraeli resisted on the same ground of principle Gladstone's demands for war because the Turks were treating the Bulgarians badly; far worse than the Jews were treated in Germany before the war. If in the modern world we adopt the principle of fighting everywhere that someone is having a bad time, we shall never have a day without war. The duty of statesmen is not to look for trouble, but to prevent a world explosion. There seemed no reason to me why the particular Jewish case should be an exception to this rule. I publicly condemned the treatment of the Jews in Germany before the war, but did not make it into an issue which might have caused war between our two countries. I stood for peace as the first interest of my country and of mankind.

It is true that people were in prison and concentration camps in Germany before the war, as some of us were in prison and concentration camps in England without charge or trial during the war, and I am prepared to believe they were badly treated, though I had no proof of it. The only account I had at first hand of those conditions was from General Fuller—architect of the

British tank arm in the First World War—soon after he became a member of our party. He was doing a tour of Germany, map in hand, and suddenly said to his companions, who were high officials of the National Socialist Party: I see we are near Dachau, I want to visit it. They went straight there and toured the camp without warning. He saw prisoners, but no evidence in those pre-war days of any ill-treatment, beyond the usual rough jail standards. It was only in the war that mass murder was let loose, and it was only in the war that it could have run riot in deadly secret.

Some would say that it should have been possible to see from Hitler's whole character that he would in the end commit atrocities. They would conclude that because he was an anti-semite he was bound finally to massacre Jews on an enormous scale. Surely a plain example from everyday life shows this view is unmitigated nonsense. Many people want to be rid of a man's company without wanting to murder him: many have such desires, but few commit murder. If someone says to you, I cannot stand so-and-so, and never want to see him again, you do not ring up the police and call on them to prevent a murder. The suggestion that Hitler's final, mad and criminal acts should have been foreseen before the war is not merely wisdom after the event, but a dishonest attempt to creat prejudice for political purposes.

What then happened in the end? How did this man come to be responsible for one of the most execrable crimes in all history? For to kill prisoners in cold blood, whether Jew, Gentile or any other human being, is a vile crime. It is inhuman, it is unsoldierly and therefore un-German. Hitler must in the end bear the responsibility for it, which is shared only by a few close associates and executioners who obeyed their orders. It was emphasised in the war crimes trials that the secret of the mass murder of Jews was so carefully kept that men were not executed for refusing to kill Jews, but only for talking about it. How, then, can it possibly be contended that the mass of the S.S.—German patriots who gave their all for what they believed was the renaissance of their country and the defence of its life—should be blamed for crimes of which they could not possibly know anything?

I know fine soldiers and airmen—some of the best in the world—who were dedicated National Socialists, but had not the least idea these crimes were being committed; in fact, at the end of the war they did not believe it until they were presented with overwhelming evidence; I personally did not believe it at first when I returned to the world, for the same reason—that it appeared incredible. How did it happen?—The question points to one of the tragic mysteries of history, but the fact remains. It in no way affects the enormity of the crime whether 12,000,000 Jews were killed, as was alleged at Nuremberg, or 6,000,000, as stated later, or far less, as many Germans claim; the killing of any defenceless prisoners, in cold blood without charge or trial, is a hideous crime. It is obviously true that it could not have happened if the process of war had not hidden crime both from the Germans themselves and from the moral judgment of mankind. If war had been avoided, the lives of 6,000,000 Jews would have been saved, as well as the lives of 20,000,000 other Europeans. Horrors of that magnitude cannot possibly be perpetrated in time of peace. Most people go rather mad in war, and Hitler in this respect went very mad. There are no restraints to crime or madness in war, either internal or external, which are comparable with the restraints of peace.

Since they were first proved, I have utterly condemned these crimes, and have summarised my view as follows: Hitler in the final period had no sense of moral law or of the limitations of the will. He tried to inflict on a whole people a cataclysm of nature; he usurped a higher function than that of man. Everything can be taken into account without excuse for this deed; the agony of defeat, his fixed belief that the Jews were responsible for the war, the fact that Germans were dying and starving and that Jews suspected of relentless enmity to the state had to be guarded and fed. None of these terrible things justify a breach of the supreme moral law which is reflected in the simple instinct of brave men, that you cannot kill helpless prisoners in your power who, as individuals, have committed no crime. Morality and the nature of manhood combine to forbid it. The motive for such crime may be remote from the crude concept of current propaganda. Yet whether it be hubris, or in simpler modern language, a monstrous vanity, it is deeply wrong.

I have often contrasted the character of Hitler with the natures of the supreme men of history: he suffered in extreme degree from what the classic Greeks called hubris; the belief that man can usurp the place of the gods in complete determination of his own fate and that of others. The supreme exponents of the art of action have known better. Julius Caesar exerted the utmost qualities of will and energy to a point where it could truly be said that everything possible had been done; but he then never for a moment lost the sense that after the ultimate effort of man the outcome must rest with the power which some call God, and others fate, or destiny. It was this restraining sense of the final realism which gave him his calm, sad resolution to achieve by the complete dedication and expenditure of himself everything humanly possible—more in the sphere of action than any other man has ever achieved —without a trace of the self-deception and hysteria which some outstanding men in face of great events find as necessary as small men find alcohol in the minor excitements of everyday life.

In lesser degree the same quality is discernible in Napoleon's admirably balanced sense of destiny and realism, in Bismarck's subtle but massive purpose, which secured the widest measure of union yet achieved during so short a period within the modern world. All these men, in their different ways, and by the diverse standards of their various epochs, were, in present terminology, very tough, but we cannot conceive any of them in the modern age ordering or allowing what occurred during the war in the German concentration camps, even if only a fraction of the record be true. This inhibition may be ascribed to moral sense or merely to their realism, the sense of what is possible.

The character of Hitler can be analysed in the same way in a totally different sphere. The same quality emerged at the end of the war in the sacrifice of young German lives when it was clear the war was lost. These children running out to meet a stream of irresistible fire erected an enduring monument to German heroism, but not to the leadership which ordered or permitted it. This had neither immediate nor ultimate purpose. It was surely vanity again: the world ends with one man's will; '*après moi le déluge*'. The part of a true immortal was at the moment rather to prepare the future. Hitler's duty was then to lose himself but to save his idea. The only thing that should have mattered to him was to preserve and to transmit whatever truth he possessed for the judgment of posterity. He should in his moral terms have committed suicide long before, directly it was clear the war was irretrievably lost; again, vanity, fantasy, the belief in miracles which accompanies this character in disaster, as it did Wallenstein in Schiller's great drama, inhibited that calm, objective realism which never deserts the supreme man. As it was, he prolonged his own life for a few weeks as a last exhibition of ineffective will, but tarnished his idea and jeopardised the future by the wanton deed of the concentration camps and the useless sacrifice of German youth. If he had gone a little sooner, leaving his idea and his fame inviolate, he might have been among those who, in the German proverb, must succumb in life in order to achieve an immortality in the minds and hearts of men.

It would have been a serious day for his enemies if he had left such a legend behind him. As it is, mankind is left with the question how such things can be prevented from ever occurring again? I have already postulated that action can be too dearly bought; a system which permits and promotes action is clearly necessary in any age where it is the only alternative to catastrophe, but we cannot accord such powers to individuals who may go mad. It may be madness, or just the Samson act of an exaggerated sense of will which pulls down the temple of humanity in the moment of its own eclipse; the border-line is obscure. There are many underlying reasons, and, unfortunately, many similar experiences in earlier history. Stalin's exaggerated suspicions resulted in the assassination of most of his closest associates, and together with other communist leaders he was responsible for the cold-blooded murder of millions of his countrymen even in time of peace. There is not a shadow of doubt that even the peace-time massacres of communism vastly exceeded the war-time slaughter of national socialism. Stalin and Hitler were both primarily responsible, and the evidence suggests that by any normal standard they were both mad in the final phase. How did it occur? At what point came the break into madness of minds which previously appeared sane? The answer belongs to the psychology of history, and should be studied with previous cases of criminal insanity in the seats of power. Some of the great literature of the world has been concerned with this transition from sanity to madness in such men, and with the reasons of extreme strain, exaggerated ambition, sense of universal betrayal ill or well founded, or final paranoiac suspicions which caused it.

We are concerned in practical politics with the simple lesson that these things must be prevented. This is another reason why the urgently necessary action of this period must be subject to full parliamentary control. I personally never departed very far from this principle, and I am now more than ever convinced it must be supported. Complete European union will also be a final and decisive safeguard against a recurrence of such events. I do not only mean that Europeans will then no longer fight each other, but also that it is incredible all Europe will ever accord such power to one man; often I have expressed the view that Europe can only be conducted by an *équipe* of equals whose diverse qualities will at least maintain a balance of sanity. The future will devise better means of preventing these disasters, but we have to work quickly with the means which exist. We must prevent these things.

Were there any means in the given circumstances and in the face of contemporary personalities and power alignments by which war could have been avoided? Would it have made any difference if I had remained in the Labour Party and become its leader? It seems now to be generally recognised that I should have had this opportunity if I had remained within the old party system.[1] Could I have prevented war in this position, by persuading Parliament? It is a bitter question, because if the answer is 'yes', I should feel a life-long remorse; but I must face it dispassionately and objectively. Could I

---

[1] 'Capable of becoming either Conservative or Labour Prime Minister.'—R. H. S. Crossman (*New Statesman*, October 27, 1961.)

'Mosley is the only man I have ever known who could have been the leader of either the Conservative or Labour Party . . . he might have been a very great Prime Minister . . .'—Lord Boothby (BBC broadcast, November 10, 1965).

'He is the only living Englishman who could perfectly well have been either Conservative or Labour Prime Minister.'—Malcolm Muggeridge (*Observer*, October 2, 1966).

'He was the only English politician who might easily have become Prime Minister as Conservative, Liberal or Socialist.'—Harold Nicolson (quoted in *New Statesman*, April 12, 1968).

'Tipped as future Prime Minister by . . . courage, drive and ideas.'—Hugh Trevor-Roper (*Sunday Times*, October 8, 1961).

'Great talents and great strength of character'—Harold Macmillan (*Winds of Change*, vol. 1, 1966).

'Almost everyone expected that, because of his popularity, he would replace Ramsay MacDonald—Emanuel Shinwell (*Daily Express*, April 16, 1952).

'How wide across all parties was the fascination which Mosley exercised.'—Michael Foot (*Tribune*, October 4, 1966).

'He was now the hero of the rank and file and was looked on by many as the future leader of the party . . .'—D. C. Somervell (*British Politics*, Andrew Dakers Ltd., 1950).

'Every prophet fixed on Sir Oswald as the next party leader.'—John Scanlon (*Decline and Fall of the Labour Party*).

Again I hope the reader will forgive these personal references for reasons stated in Chapter 10.

have affected the issue of the Abdication, and would this have had any bearing on the matter of war? Certainly I was strongly opposed to war, and to the forcing of the King off the throne. Certainly the King had the clear sense to desire peace, as well as the feeling for social justice which reinforced the drive of the inner circle to get rid of him.

It is true in this sphere that all is well that ends well, since the King has his private happiness and the functions of the Crown have been admirably performed by his successors, King George VI and the present Queen Elizabeth II. Yet there is something symbolic of all their failure in the stiff absurdity of the English ruling class at that time, when they rejected any form of marriage with an American of beauty, intelligence, charm and character which would have been a link between two divergent outlooks in different civilisations, only later through their further and greater follies to make their country a circling satellite of the American system, while they extended the begging bowl to the controlling planet and trembled at the thought of leaving its orbit. Was not this honourable and natural alliance in that day preferable to the pathetic and disgraceful dependence of this day?

If the pre-war situation had been handled quite differently—as it certainly would have been if I had had anything to do with it—would it have made any difference? I would not claim that if I had been the leader of the Labour Party we might have won the Election of 1935, as that would be a vain and egotistical assumption; though at that time a mere competition in dullness between Baldwin and Attlee resulted almost inevitably in the victory of the former. Baldwin's influence would in any case have been very powerful; behind him was certainly the full authority of the Church and ruling clique, the whole weight of the established order. Yet I should at any rate have been in a stronger position, within the Labour Party, to have some influence on events. For instance, it was not possible for me to see a constitutional King while he was on the throne and I was in a position of revolutionary challenge to the existing system; consequently, I never saw King Edward in that period and only knew him before and after.

Even had it been possible by some combination within the system with Churchill, Beaverbrook and others to prevent the Abdication—and that was very doubtful in the prevailing set-up—how would this have affected the larger issue of war? Supposing the whole thing had been played quite differently, with the help of other influences within the Establishment; say by getting Goering over to put up one of his characteristic performances in a public relations exercise, not very different from the manner in which Khrushchev disarmed British hostility? The character of Goering presented the unique combination of a hero who for great purpose was prepared to play the clown. That this wearer of the German V.C.—the Order '*pour le Mérite*' devised by Frederick the Great—was a hero in the First World War is beyond doubt. He was selected by the Luftwaffe to succeed their fallen hero

Richthofen, who had killed our hero in the greatest individual air duel of all time; it would have been no use then telling the few remaining airmen of my generation that Goering was not a hero, and in these circumstances our voices would have carried some weight.

Goering would have been far more at home than most foreigners in all the varied social and sporting occasions of English life, the ex-service clubs and institutions above all, but also the horse show, the football final, the pub, and even the drawing-room. He was capable of putting on any form of democratic, indeed demagogic performance; he would laugh at himself in a way which would make particular appeal to the English people if translated into our national terms by sensitive intelligence. An instance of this capacity was provided each year at the Nuremberg Rally, at which I was never personally present, but of which I had detailed accounts. As the Hermann Goering Division of the S.A. approached the saluting base the whole crowd would chant, 'Hermann, Hermann'; and a large and portly form would be seen at the head of the division, not only raising his arm in the salute but doing the goose step at the same time. It was his annual turn, and the crowd laughed and cheered till they 'rolled in the aisles'. Such a man would have gone down well in England; even better than Khrushchev.

Would any technique, any device within the established order have availed in the prevention of war? Could we have met destiny head-on, and have frustrated it with the petty manoeuvres which were all the existing system and prevailing sentiment would have allowed? I think not. We were up against a tragic momentum of history. All that 'patience is exhausted' stuff on their side was a fatality; the first rule of real politics is that the patience of statesmen must never be exhausted, and if they have any such sentiment, it is the last thing they should express. The English ruling class or clique were as offended by all that in Hitler as they were by the sabre-rattling of the Kaiser; in their narrow, arrogant, insular fashion, they detested to the point of phobia the whole show-off business, as they would term it. It was a prime error, for it excited their fears and furies, instead of allaying them while Hitler achieved his objectives with the minimum possible fuss.

Against Germany were not only the rigid probities and petulant emotions of the ruling class, but also the savage vendetta of a Labour movement which saw similar men and institutions swept into oblivion by national socialism; both reinforced by a world money power which felt its prevailing dominion threatened. On their side was a new proletarian hubris with an egocentric vehemence which thought destiny its toy; on our side was the old aristocratic vanity mingling in mistaken rectitude not only with the prim stupidity of bourgeois obstinacy but also with the hysteria of the frightened Left; so what hope had peace? The answer of my considered judgment, for what it is worth, is that no force on earth within the system could have prevented the hell-bent drive to war. If I had tried to ride the Gadarene plunge I would just have gone with it into the abyss and have forfeited the European honour of facing it and at least attempting to resist. My own descent would have been right royally cushioned, but that would have made no difference to the fall of the nation from the greatest power on earth to the pitiful, clinging dependence of the American satellite. *Quem perdere vult Deus dementat prius,* but he sometimes gives the English another chance.

20
Why I Opposed the War

'I HAVE not become the King's first minister in order to preside over the liquidation of the British Empire,' said Mr. Churchill at the Mansion House on November 10, 1942. Yet this is exactly what happened as a direct result of his policy. What has long been obvious is now generally acknowledged. His steadfast supporter, the *Daily Mail*, wrote on July 20, 1967, that the British Empire was now gone, 'not by conquest or defeat in the field but through the sheer effort of victory, through the erosion of power and the onset of the ideas and ideals for which we fought'.

Mr. Churchill also made clear that it was only an unforeseen accident which saved Britain from a worse fate: 'There is a widespread feeling that but for American nuclear superiority Europe would already have been reduced to satellite status: that the iron curtain would have reached the Atlantic and the Channel' (*The Times*, March 2, 1955). When Britain declared war, nobody knew that the scientists would later invent the nuclear weapons which alone held Russian communism in check. Statesmen can only deal with the facts confronting them in any given situation.

The declaration of war in 1939 risked three consequences: the disaster of defeat, the triumph of communism, the loss of the British Empire despite victory. The only power which could in no circumstances benefit from that war was Great Britain. The complete disaster of defeat was averted by the heroism of the British people, the European triumph of Russian communism was partially averted by the scientists, and the loss of the Empire and reduction of Britain to the position of an American satellite remain the only clear results of the Second World War. We escaped entire destruction, but much of Europe did not. Evil was the inevitable result of entry into that war, and we are fortunate to live only with the least of the possible evils.

This situation is chiefly due to mistaken policy. It is demonstrably incorrect to assert that our situation is due to 'the prodigious blood-letting . . . which leads to the loss of possessions,' [1] though this is often said. My generation suffered nearly three times the deaths in the First War that our next generation suffered in the second catastrophe of mankind. Yet Britain lost no possessions after the First World War, and could still claim with some justice to be the greatest power on earth. The Germans are reckoned to have lost 2,850,000 in the Second World War, and in addition are separated from a large part of their homelands; otherwise in every respect, except the possession of nuclear weapons, their position remains as strong as at any time in their history. The catastrophe of Britain is due to the mistaken policy our rulers pursued, and to the deadly poison of some of their ideas.

To write this is almost as difficult as it was to take the bitter, truly agonising decision in time of war to oppose the opinion and policy which was supported by the vast majority of my fellow countrymen. Yet it is as much my duty now as it was then, and it would be cowardice to avoid it. Nothing is more unpopular than to oppose a war, and it can be almost as unpopular after the war to say it should not have been fought. But unless we can beseech this generation, in the words of Cromwell, 'to believe it possible that you may be mistaken,' error can follow error until Britain enters the eternal night.

It is particularly hard and bitter to say to a fine people who have made a superb effort, that a war fought ostensibly to preserve the liberties of European peoples was not only in vain, but that their self-sacrifice has left our own country in a far worse position than ever before. Yet this is much the same experience as we had after the First World War, when we were told that we were fighting to 'make the world safe for democracy', and to make Britain 'a land fit for heroes to live in'. For those of our generation who survived, the results in terms of democracy were soon plain: communism in Russia, fascism in Italy, and national socialism in Germany. The results for the heroes, who were promised all at the end of their war effort, were equally plain: the unemployment queue and the slums. Bitter indeed was the question: was it for this that a million died?

Yet I always felt deeply that from this experience something immense was gained. It proved the greatness of Britain and the heroism of its people; not only that, for on the fiery anvil of that ordeal the character of the war generation was forged. Similarly, the magnificent response of the British people to the challenge of the last war evoked these same qualities, and they have by no means been lost for ever in the lassitude and dissolution which followed. Vital forces born of two wars can still inspire the tasks of construction, in erecting an enduring monument of peace. The finest qualities

[1] *Daily Mail,* July 20, 1967.

of men are often evoked by the bitter trials of history, and they will not always be misused or lost.

Men who suffered much in one war or the other—or in one way or another in both—thereby acquired the character to meet further tests of destiny; these tests will recur, there is no escape from them. They will be made harder by the vast errors of policy which preceded and followed the last war. To meet them we should be united by the future, not divided by the past. I fully accept that it was possible in this now remote period for honourable men to hold the opposite belief sincerely and with passionate conviction; I ask only in return for it to be recognised that it was equally possible to hold my minority opinion honourably and with deep conviction.

Before I give my reasons for believing that the last war was an immense mistake, I should answer the question whether it could possibly have been avoided. Policies can only be judged effectively by their results, and it is not difficult to show that this war was disastrous to Britain; but to convince, I must show that an alternative policy had a reasonable chance of avoiding the catastrophe.

The policy for which I stood before the last war was to make Britain so strongly armed that it need not fear attack from any quarter, to develop the British Empire, and not to intervene in any foreign quarrel which did not affect British interests. It may be convenient here to record my advocacy of the rearming of Britain over a long period before the war.

From the day our movement was formed I pressed for the rearmament of our country. On October 1, 1932, I wrote: 'The arrival of the air factor altered fundamentally the position of these islands, and the consequences of that factor have never yet been realised by the older generation of politicians. We will immediately raise the air strength of Britain to the level of the strongest power in Europe.' [1]

I was naturally preoccupied with the air arm in which I had served, but also advocated the modernising and mechanising of the army. For instance: 'We will immediately mobilise every resource of the nation to give us an air force equal in strength to the strongest in Europe. We will modernise and mechanise our army, and at the end of that process our army will cost less, but will be the most modern effective striking-force in the world.' (June 15, 1934.) I also advocated a national defence loan for three purposes: 'To give Britain immediate air strength. To modernise and mechanise our army. To put the fleet in proper condition to defend our trade routes.' (July 12, 1934.)

Our agitation for rearmament continued ceaselessly in these years from every platform and in all our publications. I denounced the Conservative Party on October 15, 1938, for their failure to rearm in the following terms: 'The state of our national defence has alarmed the Tory Party. The state of these defences is a national scandal and disgrace. The Tory Party is, therefore,

[1] *The Greater Britain*, October 1932.

right to be alarmed; and having been in power for the last seven years, they should be ashamed.' In an article at the same time I stated a fact which seemed to me obvious and was afterwards proved to be true: 'Modern wars are won by airmen and mechanics, not by masses of barrack-square infantry'.

Action was then a journal supporting British Union. In it on October 15, 1938, it was stated: '*Action* disagrees with Mr. Churchill on nearly every subject under the sun, and particularly in recent years for his foreign policy. But we agree with his indictment of the gross neglect of British defences. British Union pressed rearmament on the government long before they began it, and long before even Mr. Churchill advocated it. . . . Britain should be in a position to defend herself against the attack of any nation in the world.'

What was the attitude of the parties at that time to the defence of our country, the parties which later put us in jail on the pretence that we might be a danger to the State? They neglected the defences of our country while we struggled to secure its proper armament. Mr. Baldwin said in the House of Commons: 'I put before the whole House my own views with an appalling frankness. From 1933 I and my friends were all very worried about what was happening in Europe. You will remember at that time the disarmament conference was sitting in Geneva, and there was probably a stronger pacifist feeling running through this country than at any time since the war. I am speaking of 1933 and 1934. You will remember the election at Fulham in the autumn of 1933, when a seat which the National Government held was lost by about 7,000 votes on no issue but the pacifist, and that the National Government candidate, who made a most guarded reference to the question of defence, was mobbed for it. That was the feeling in the country in 1933. My position as the leader of a great party was not altogether a comfortable one. I asked myself what chance was there within the next year or two of that feeling being so changed that the country would give a mandate for rearmament. Supposing I had gone to the country, and said that Germany was rearming, and that we must rearm—does anybody think that this pacific democracy would have rallied to that cry at that moment? I cannot think of anything that would have made the loss of the election from my point of view more certain.' [1]

Baldwin risked the loss of his country in war rather than risk the loss of his party in an election. In foreign and defence policy he played politics with the life of Britain through his squalid electoral calculations; in his home policy he bequeathed to the next generation our present industrial structure through his lazy timidity which sought to avoid trouble at all costs. The doom of defeat was averted despite Baldwin, but the nemesis of the Baldwin epoch still haunts our country. It appears that the Conservative leadership still cherishes his memory.

[1] *The Times*, November 13, 1936.

For me it is difficult to write fairly on the subject of Mr. Baldwin, because I have a particular antipathy to the type of Englishman who successfully stakes a claim for exceptional honesty by a continual parade of simple virtues which in truth are at striking variance to the slowly revealed facts. In my experience honesty in British politics is often in inverse ratio to the pretensions of its claimants. For instance, over a long period Winston Churchill and F. E. Smith were held by their contemporaries to be unprincipled adventurers, while Baldwin was always accepted at his face value. Yet whatever can be thought or said of the characters and policies of Churchill and Smith, they always openly declared their principles and stood for them courageously, while Baldwin not only concealed his aims but retreated from them in a shuffling opportunism of personal and party expediency. Britain pays dearly for the transient success of these types in our politics. The fine old dockers' M.P., James Sexton, laid down an instructive and occasionally valid rule for the political neophyte: 'Whenever someone calls me comrade, I always put my hand on my watch'.

Meantime, we carried on the fight for rearmament from every platform in face of all the 'mobbing'; at any rate it did not take us long to stop that nonsense of the militant pacifists. Much of the 'mobbing' came from supporters of the Labour Party, which was voting in the House of Commons against the defence estimates while some of its rank and file were conducting the pacifist agitation in the country which so frightened Mr. Baldwin. Their pacifist principles however in no way deterred many of them from conducting a furious agitation against Germany, of which the only logical outcome was war.

Was it unfair on our platform battle of that time to say: 'All wars are good to the Socialist Party on three conditions: the first, that the war should be in the interest of the Soviets and not in the interest of Britain; the second, that our troops have no arms with which to fight; and the third, that socialist leaders are not included among the troops'. (June 26, 1936.) My punches were not pulled in attacking the policy of war without arms: 'Labour is the party of war without preparation. Labour is the party which makes trouble and leaves others to do the fighting.' 'To seek war is a crime: to seek war without the means of war is more than crime, it is madness.'

Our first demand was therefore that Britain should be rearmed and strong enough to meet any attack, no matter whence it came. We eschewed entry into foreign quarrels, but were determined to guard our own country and Empire. Our popular slogans of the period were 'Mind Britain's Business' and 'Britons fight for Britain only'. However, this basic policy of developing the British Empire and allowing nothing to distract us from this primary purpose did not isolate us from world affairs or inhibit the development of great policies. We had our contribution to make, and it was at least clearly stated. It is possible to put your own country first and yet to play a large part in world politics; modern experience certainly proves this to be possible, but unfortunately the experience is not British.

The union of Europe was the subject of my passionate advocacy in foreign policy. This was in no way incompatible with our imperial policy. Let us be absolutely clear as to our basic principles of policy at that time. National sovereignty was completely preserved, separate national armament was to be maintained with British strength equal to any in the world; the Empire was to be developed as a political and economic entity with strong measures against the introduction of sweated competition, and war was only to be fought in the defence of the Empire or in resistance to any vital threat to its interest. But it was quite compatible with this position to have a common foreign policy within Europe in relation to the rest of the world, and commercial arrangements with the rest of Europe would have followed inevitably. What I was then advocating was almost exactly similar to the present development of European union on the basis of a rigorous conservation of national sovereignty. For this reason my supporters claim that I was at least ten years ahead of any other advocate of European union.

After the war, of course, I went much farther in declaring the principle of Europe a Nation in 1948, but the speeches now in question were delivered in 1936. I said on February 21, 1936: 'Our generation was sacrificed to bring to an end the balance of power which divided European civilisation into two armed and hostile camps. The avowed purpose of the League of Nations was to consecrate that sacrifice in a new world system. . . . Again our generation is challenged to save the ideal of which the old men cheat us once again. Shall Europe be divided or unite?' Then on June 25 in the same year: 'What then is the alternative to the present League of Nations? The only alternative is the union of Europe, as opposed to the division of Europe under the old balance of power which now wears the tattered label League of Nations. The union of Europe was the determination of the war generation at the end of the war, and the hope that the League of Nations would achieve that idea alone led to its support. Meantime, with cant of League and peace, the financial democrats divide Europe in their vendetta, which jeopardises the peace of the world, while they neglect the first duty of any government in the present situation, which is to arm Britain with the utmost speed against any contingency and threat. In the confusion and collapse of British foreign policy but one alternative emerges, and that is the union of Europe, which alone can rest on a bloc of the great powers, united in common interest and inspired by a new world ideal.'

The League of Nations, which in my youth I had so ardently supported as a new instrument of world peace, had failed for reasons of personal weakness in statesmanship already noted, and by this time had been turned into an instrument of the balance of power which from historic experience I regarded as an inevitable prelude to war. The balance of power had always brought war, and now it had returned with the Axis powers in one scale and the League powers in the other; a perversion of every high aspiration of the war generation. It seemed clear to me that the only escape from the coming fatality was the union of Europe in much the same terms and to much the same degree as are now being sought thirty years later.

It will of course be replied that any form of union in Europe was impossible with the statesmen in power in Germany and Italy, and to that I have already made some answer. We should have worked with them in common European politics and interests which they declared they too desired to serve, so long as that proved possible, and I personally believe it would have been possible because our interests were complementary rather than conflicting. But if it proved impossible we should have been in a strong and safe position, our national sovereignty fully preserved and our armaments equal to any in the world. If things had gone well we could have developed both the British Empire and a gradual European union. If things had gone badly we should have been in a far stronger position than when the old parties took us into war without even attempting an alternative policy. It was indeed a strange idea to make certain of war today without arms, in case we had to fight a war tomorrow with arms. Strive for peace but prepare for war, was then the course of sense and patriotism.

Was there at that time a comprehensive world policy available which could have averted war? My essay 'The World Alternative' (1937) advancing a policy which in my view could avoid war, was published in England and also in the German review *Geopolitik*: I have already described its reception in Germany. It began with the 'idea which animated the post-war generation', in my description of 'the union of Europe in a system of public law and order which broadly applied to international affairs the law and sanctions of law commonly employed within each nation in the maintenance of domestic order and justice. The analogy clearly is subject to necessary modification by the exigencies of national sovereignty, for the men who had just fought to save the British Empire rightly would not tolerate the future of that Empire being decided by any international tribunal which might be dominated by representatives of South American republics. For despite the reiterated attempts of the international school to fetter the great with the chains of the small, the essence of national sovereignty was preserved in the original covenant of the League of Nations.'

It then contended that the League of Nations had been turned into the balance of power which had always brought war: 'The world, in fact, is divided into two camps of the possessors and the dispossessed . . . in one camp are Britain, France and the Soviets; in the other camp by inevitable gravitation of common circumstances are Germany and Italy; and to that camp by analagous folly is being added Japan. With the return of the balance of power we witness the return of the arms race and the concomit-

ant Press agitation which inflames the mind and spirit of Europe to fresh
fatality.'

I analysed the circumstances in which Europe had arrived at this situation
and how the original idea of the League had been destroyed. America had
defected, six other nations had been allowed to defy the League with impunity—Japan, Turkey, Poland, Lithuania, Bolivia and Paraguay—the
departure of Germany had been made inevitable because a Treaty had been
forced upon it 'not only unjust in its inception but subsequently violated on
repeated occasions to their own advantages by those who had dictated it'.
The process was then completed by driving Italy out of the League and into
the other camp by the application of sanctions. I quoted Sir Edward Grigg,
Governor of Kenya Colony, to the effect that Abyssinia had for years past
raided not only Italian but British territory for slaves, and had committed
definite acts of war without one finger being lifted by Geneva or the British
Government. Yet when Italy took 'precisely the same measures to suppress
these evils as had been taken at every stage of the honourable building of the
British Empire', action had been taken against her, although 'six nations had
already with complete impunity violated the covenant of the League. . . .
From this ultimate folly arises the final recurrence of world fatality in the
re-emergence of the balance of power.'

The indictment of the old party policy did not stop there. 'A feeble British
Government taking the lead in an unjust cause,' and hard pressed to find
support, had sought the assistance of the Soviets at Geneva against Italy.
'From this European alignment arises the subservience of British to Soviet
policy in the East, for Britain cannot use the Soviets in Europe without in
turn being used by the Soviets in the Orient. . . . If Russia is to join with
Britain in the iron ring round Germany and Italy, then Britain must join
with Russia in the iron ring round Japan, not only in contravention of her
own interests but in jeopardy of world peace.'

This long, critical analysis of old party policy has been much abbreviated
here, as it was only a prelude to the development of a constructive policy. I
continued that in searching for a solution 'we must return to the fundamental
conception of European union which animated the war generation'. My
advice was 'to proceed by the inductive method from the particular to the
general rather than by the deductive method from the general to the particular
which has previously failed—as the generalisations of vision without realism
invariably fail. For in 1918 and the years that followed, all paid lip-service to
the general idea of European and world union, but all ignored the fact that
such union could only rest upon the particular ability of each nation to live
and to prosper within a European system that rested upon justice and
economic reality.' I therefore began with 'an enquiry into the factors which
divided the individual nations, and in particular into the factors which
inhibit peaceful and friendly relations between Great Britain and other

great nations. Having established the particular of possible friendship between Great Britain and other nations we shall proceed to the general idea of European union built on the firm foundation of justice and economic reality.'

This enquiry began logically with the relations of Britain and Germany which constituted the chief potential threat to peace. The difference between Germany under the Kaiser and under national socialism was considered. The Kaiser's Germany was conducted by a 'financial democratic imperialism' which operated 'from the basis of an export capitalist system' and 'expressed itself naturally in terms of a vast colonial Empire and concomitant navies which clashed at every turn with British Empire'. (It is a curious omission that in the whole of this essay I made no reference to the naval agreement of 1935, which restricted the German navy to a third of the British; this greatly reinforced my argument.) The Germany of national socialism was profoundly different because 'less than any great nation today her philosophy leads her to think in terms of limitless colonial Empire which to the Nazi mind suggests loss of vital energy, dissipation of wealth and the fear of detrimental admixture of races. Her national objective lies in the union of the Germanic peoples of Europe in a consolidated rather than diffused economic system which permits her with security to pursue her racial ideals. In fact, in the profound differences of national objective between the British Empire and the new Germany rests the main hope of peace between them. Our world mission is the maintenance and development of the heritage of the Empire, in which our race has displayed peculiar genius not only without fear of racial detriment but with the sure knowledge that in this arduous duty the finest and toughest character-istics of the English are developed, and that the smallest contribution which an effective British Empire can make is the preservation of peace over one quarter of the earth's surface for one quarter of the earth's population. The world mission of Germany in Nazi eyes is the union and development of the German peoples within a European system to which that union brings a new and durable stability. Thus, so far from the objective of the British Empire clashing with the objective of the new Germany, the two objectives in terms of world stability and peace are complementary.'

However, for 'Germany to live in peace and to pursue its national objective of the wealth and happiness of its own people' it was necessary for it 'to possess an adequate supply of raw materials and full outlet for expanding population'. 'The only fundamental question outstanding between Germany and Britain is the problem of the German colonies now held by Britain under mandate from the League of Nations. On principle, the writer would not concede to any nation one inch of British territory,' but 'the German colonies have been to Britain little but a burden and an expense' and 'could be to Germany an outlet and an opportunity': I would therefore have returned them as part of a general peace settlement.

This section of the argument concluded: 'The return of the colonies together with any additional facilities for access to raw materials, easily accorded in a world faced with a glut rather than a poverty problem in raw material production, could firmly secure the postulate of national socialist policy in the shape of an economic basis to German national life. . . . Such measures would not only remove all possible cause of friction between Britain and Germany, but could also eliminate the possibility of German explosion in Europe by the provision of means for her peaceful expansion.'

Let it not for one moment be deduced from this section of the plan and part of the argument that I was ever in favour of the permanent maintenance of the old colonial system, for long before any suggestion of the present black troubles I proposed policies to bring that system to an end, and even presented a choice of methods for the purpose. I was never a racialist because I was never in favour of the domination of one people by another. To look after your own people no more denotes hostility to other peoples than to look after your own family.

It may be objected that the introduction of the Germans in any form and for any purpose to Africa would inevitably have led to the permanent subjection of black to white. On the contrary, the Germans of that period had not the least interest in anything of the kind. All they were concerned with was access to raw materials adequate to afford an economic basis to their autarchic economy, and this was quite compatible with the evolution in Africa of a different system to the old colonialism. The real, vital interest of the Germans was union with their own people in Europe. They were among the nations least likely to oppose an orderly transition to a new system in Africa which gave a fair deal to both white and black, but they might have shared my opinion that it should be a carefully planned and implemented building of a new system within a reasonable period of time, and not a precipitate retreat through fatigue and inertia, with the appearance of a bully turned weakling, leaving chaos behind his rout.

I went on to deal with the security of France, always a major consideration of my political thinking, and argued that 'the best guarantee of French security is the satisfaction of Germany' by the measures I had suggested. Hitler had enquired 'why he should seek to possess French territory with a population of 270 to the kilometre while he still was faced with at least the remnants of the unemployment problem in Germany', and this was in accord with the whole German attitude. I concluded this section of the argument as follows: 'The only policy which can logically produce another explosion on the western frontiers of Germany is the denial of expansion; not only on her eastern frontiers but in her limited though necessary and natural colonial ambitions. Yet financial democratic policy could not be more perfectly designed to promote that explosion than by the dual policy of denying

Germany colonial outlet and of circumscribing her in the East by a menacing democratic-Soviet alliance.'

Pursuing this same line of thought, I contended that in the occupation of Abyssinia 'Italy now has not only an outlet for her population but profitable access to raw materials', and that she should be left in undisturbed possession of this acquisition. The essay was at some pains to controvert any suggestion that Italy from this position could be any menace to the vital interests of the British Empire. 'A glance at a child's map of the world would show' that a hostile Italy could be 'a much greater menace to British trade routes from the base of Sicily than from any base in Abyssinia'. Furthermore, 'Italy will have enough to do in the development of Abyssinia for some generations'. In relation to Egypt and the Sudan, why should 'Italy abandon the development of the territories she already possesses in order to indulge in a savage fight with the greatest naval power in the world for extra territories which provide not greater but lesser sustenance? . . . Even his worst enemy does not describe the leader of Italy as a fool.' Rather, Italy's every interest was 'to join with the British Empire to maintain the stability and peace of the Eastern Mediterranean and of North Africa'.

I dealt next with the suspicion of 'an intention which does not in fact exist, to prosecute the expansion of a fascist and national socialist Europe at the expense of Russia . . . the solution here suggested is not the partition of Russia, not merely because it is the first interest of Europe and should be the first objective of British policy to keep the peace, but also because the solution of the European problem in terms both economic and political is possible on the lines already indicated without any offensive action against Russia'. I suggested that 'Russia should be told to mind her own business and to leave Europe and Western civilisation alone to manage their own affairs', and concluded that it rested with 'Russia herself to decide whether by withdrawal from incessant aggression and effort to promote communist revolution she will live at peace with her neighbours'. Russia might be persuaded to become a good neighbour by the consideration that otherwise she could find herself between the 'crackers of united Europe in the West and Japan in the East'.

On the question of Japan, I observed again: 'British Government, having used Soviet power in Europe, was in turn used by the Soviets in the East,' and added, 'once we are freed from the Soviet entanglement we need no longer oppose the natural expansion of Japan in northern China where she seeks an outlet for her surplus goods and population'. This is certainly not a policy I would recommend today, but at that time chaos reigned in China, to which any form of order and peace was preferable. I have in the present period quite different proposals for affording Japan a full life. At that time and in the circumstances of the period I was suggesting in the East exactly the same basic principle of building peace: satisfaction of the primary needs of all the great powers. British statesmen dealing with the Soviets at that time most conveniently forgot that Japan was not only an old friend but a traditional and remaining ally. It was strongly in our interest to give Japan such an outlet because she could then accept exclusion from our home, Indian and colonial markets. Thereby we served both peace and Britain's vital trading interests, and would frustrate the Soviet policy of promoting 'in the anarchy of northern China a breeding-ground for oriental communism'.

I concluded the argument in relation to Japan: 'The decision that she should be encouraged in northern China is reinforced by the fact that pressure in the Pacific menacing Australia and New Zealand would thereby be relieved, and America, too, becomes an interested party in that settlement not only in southern China but also by the lifting of the menace to the Philippines and relief from the general pressure on her Pacific interests'. I asked 'those who speak of the Yellow Peril' to 'explain how that peril can be surmounted by a policy of dividing and enfeebling European civilisation in the interests of Soviet policy? In the alternative, we can envisage the conception of European union extending to embrace and to combine with American policy in regions which closely affect the interests of that continent. In the final synthesis, white civilisation can discover a comprehensive policy which rests on the reality of mutual interests. . . .'

The essence of the policy was that we should 'build upon the basic fact of economic settlement and justice for individual nations'. My argument in particular was that this would not endanger the safety of Britain and France, but would secure it. This was a feasible policy whatever system of government prevailed in the individual nations, for national sovereignty was rigorously preserved. I believed, of course, passionately in the dynamic and creative influence of a new spiritual impulse which I had already striven to describe, but the four-power bloc of Britain, France, Germany and Italy was quite possible without any similarity of political system, if we had agreed in mutual interest on this common policy in foreign affairs. A common spiritual purpose is desirable but not essential if certain limited practical aims are held together. A renaissance can work wonders, but a hard-headed business deal too can get results. It still seems to me that in cold, realistic terms this policy could have maintained the peace of the world.

This political thinking will of course be rejected out of hand by all who prefer world war to the slightest deviation from their favourite ideologies or pet notions, however disastrous they have now been proved in practice. From my experience of contemporary hysteria their objection is likely to take three main forms: the policy is immoral, because it would have reduced the risk of war by satisfying three more great powers by exactly the same process which had satisfied Britain and France for over a century; Hitler would have turned the idea down flat, because his ambition was much more inordinate than this modest plan; even if he had accepted it, this would merely have been a trick to gain time for attainment of his real objective, which is alleged to have been world domination.

Let us examine the first question of immorality, with the preliminary observation that all things are relative in the real world. Was this policy more immoral than a war which killed twenty-five million Europeans? Was it more immoral than a war which killed 286,000 Americans and 1,506,000 Japanese? Was it more immoral than Hiroshima, the incineration of a whole population after the war was virtually over in a world still suffering the mania of war passion? Was it more immoral than the cold-blooded killing of prisoners in German concentration camps on a vast scale? Was it more immoral than burning alive with phosphorous bombs in the open town of Dresden a civilian population which included some of our own men who were war prisoners? None of these things could have happened without the Second World War. Were they not immoral? Were they less immoral than giving Germany, Italy and Japan an outlet and opportunity to develop a peaceful life in regions remote from any possibility of a clash with Britain or any other European power?

Was the Second World War preferable to having Germany in her old colonies pending a new and permanent settlement of the colonial question giving a fair deal to all, rather than to retreat through chaos to the present condition of Africa? Will ideological fervour go so far as to affirm this? Was the present *status quo* in that continent worth 25,000,000 European dead and the division and bondage of our own continent? In any case, a united European policy, inevitably inspired in this particular by British experience and outlook, would undoubtedly in time have evolved a reasonable settlement in these regions, which would have combined opportunity for the creative genius of the Europeans with the right of others to a full life in their own development. There is more than room for all in Africa, and the German presence, in co-operation with British experience, would have been another and powerful factor in a sane and orderly evolution.

Was it really worth sowing more seeds of another war by keeping Italy out of Abyssinia and Japan out of Manchuria? Was the financial and industrial exploitation of southern China, until it was thrown inevitably as a present to communism, absolutely necessary? Was it really so desirable to frustrate Japan's immense capacity for organisation in an orderly development of northern China, which would have given it an outlet and peaceful occupation for generations? In short, was the operation of handing all China over to a militant communism really worth the sacrifice of Europe in the Second World War? How far can madness push the values of bedlam? If this be morality, the world is upside down. The sum total of all these policies together undoubtedly produced the war, and a comprehensive alternative was certainly available which had at least a reasonable chance of preserving peace.

At this point arises the second objection, that the Axis powers and Hitler in particular would have turned down proposals which were inadequate to satisfy their ambitions, and that the strain to the moral susceptibilities of Western statesmanship would therefore have been in vain. He would certainly not have turned these ideas down flat, for I have already described his reaction after a detailed study of them. In international affairs nothing should be taken at its face value and verbal protestations must be measured against the real interests involved. Subject to that reservation, and to the strenuous rearmament of our country in any event, my own estimate is that an attempt to settle outstanding differences between Britain, France and Germany and to secure the peace of Western Europe would have succeeded on some such basis. I am not so confident that the further attempt of this policy to prevent a bloody clash between Germany and Russia would have succeeded, for in my interviews with him in 1935 and 1936 Hitler appeared to regard such an encounter between national socialism in Germany and communism in Russia as quite possible; not probable, so far as he was concerned, because he desired only the union of the Germans. He knew from our interviews, as well as from my writing in *Geopolitik*, that I desired to avoid this clash and to keep the peace, but that for my part I would not intervene against Germany if it occurred; there was therefore no point in trying to deceive me on this subject. What was interesting was the apparent enthusiasm with which he greeted the proposed accord in Western Europe, and his agreement with my essay's general vision of a world settlement. Some will regard the whole thing as a trick, but in that event it was a singularly pointless trick.

Thus we return to the main argument; everything that Hitler did was a subterfuge to mask his real design, which was world domination. He meant to do on an enormous scale what modern statesmen do on a petty scale; to belie in office everything said in opposition, double-cross party members and make party programmes look like a confidence trick, reduce politics to the level of a game played with three cards in a bar. The first answer, of course, is simply that anything of the kind would not have worked; it does not work even on a small scale directly the situation becomes serious, and it certainly would not have worked on a great scale in the conditions facing Germany in 1939.

I summarised the task which would at that time have confronted any country aiming at world domination in *The Alternative* (1947): 'Then it was not a question of dropping something on the chief cities of a dissenting country which in course of seconds could wipe their effective civilisation from the face of the earth. Conquest entailed the occupation of countries in considerable force, and the problem of 1939 must always be regarded in these terms. So it may be asked, can anyone in his senses have contemplated the German grenadier perpetually marching in pursuit of eternally dissident underground movements over every great space of the earth from the steppes of Russia to the prairies of the Americas, across the deserts of the Sahara or the Gobi until at length his devoted figure was chasing some nonconforming Lama in the remotest fastnesses of Tibet? For, in the conditions of that day, this must have been the exhausting destiny of the German soldier if his leaders had cherished the idea of world dominion, and had achieved the considerable initial success of overthrowing by force of arms the established government of every great country in the world. German troops must have occupied the entire earth and the whole manhood of Germany would have spent their lives and vital energies in incessant guerrilla fighting.'

Yet it will still be said: Hitler was not in his senses, he was already mad, and he would have tried it. In that case, how long would he have lasted with a German General Staff which had to prepare this gigantic enterprise, and with a German people which had accepted with enthusiasm the opposite idea: that salvation lay in the union of the Germans and the development of their fatherland, and mixing with alien peoples involved disaster? Any attempt by Hitler even to prepare anything of that kind would have been the quickest way to get rid of him. If he had even begun seriously to organise such an undertaking, which must have been clear in its design from the start to a great many people, let alone to launch it, he would not have lasted five minutes. In reality, everything he did was well calculated to secure the enthusiastic support of the German people, and the acquiescence of the General Staff, and it had these results. Otherwise, the German people would never have persisted through unparalleled sacrifices to resist the world in arms for six years to the last ounce of their energy and the last drop of their blood.

In *The Alternative*, after a detailed examination of this fantasy, I asked: 'Is it then very extraordinary to believe that the German leadership preferred the entirely rational concept of German manhood staying at home to build their own country and living space, once sufficient resources were at their disposal to create a civilisation which was independent of world anarchy? In fact, their whole doctrine exaggerated that possibility according to prevailing British standards. The Nazi Party concentrated on the idea of bringing all Germans living in Europe together in a homogeneous bloc within a geographically united living space.'

The giving of a guarantee to Poland by the British Government cut clean across the German drive east to unite their separated populations. It is true that if Hitler had played his hand with more patience and skill the whole situation might have been avoided. On the other hand, our British Government's guarantee to Poland was simply asking for war. If we had lost a war, and as a result Lancashire had been divided from Yorkshire by a corridor accorded to a foreign power in a peace treaty universally agreed to be monstrous, how should we have liked it if the *status quo* had been guaranteed by Germany under threat of war? Would the British people have put up with it? What conceivable interest of our people lay in this guarantee to the inflated claims of Poland? What motive had we in Poland, except the passion of the parties to stop Germany at all cost by encircling it on all fronts? I repeat the question: was not this policy simply asking for war?

The Polish guarantee came at the end of a long, fuddled, fumbling movement towards the encirclement of Germany on its eastern front; it was fatal. Not only did it obviously convince Hitler that war was inevitable, but it altered the whole strategic and political position of Britain. So long as it was a question of defending Britain and western Europe, we could look after ourselves. Directly we opposed in principle and commitment German eastern expansion, we depended on others. This objective could only be achieved by the frustration of Germany to the point of its destruction, and for this the forces of Britain and France were plainly inadequate. For this purpose Britain must call in America and Russia as soon as possible, and that meant the future of Britain and of Europe would pass into other hands. Alone we could stop Germany defeating us, but we could not alone defeat Germany.

The policy of making Britain's air force equal to any in the world, which I had advocated from 1932, would undoubtedly have saved our country from any possibility of invasion. If the Germans with their numerically far superior force could not cross the Channel in face of the heroic band of Spitfire pilots in 1940, what hope had they of defeating us if our air defences had been not betrayed but fortified to the point of equality? It is not just pride in the air arm in which I previously served which inspires the conviction that a British air force with an equal chance cannot be defeated. It is proved by what it did without an equal chance, and this confidence is sustained by the rare combination of physical and traditional qualities which give the English a singular aptitude for air combat.

Not only would a British air force equal to the Germans have ensured the safety of these islands, it would also have been a powerful factor in the event of a German invasion of France. If our joint defence had been further strengthened by the 'modernised and mechanised' army which I advocated, France too might have been defended without intervention external to Europe. Certainly this would have been the case if a clear-cut, decisive British foreign policy had shown France that we could not intervene in eastern Europe, but together would plan a massive defence in case we had any trouble in the west. France was dragged with reluctance into our eastern adventures, and would have been only too willing to concentrate effectively and realistically on the true basis of all French policy, which is the maintenance inviolate of France.

The contrary policy of neglecting our defences while making an explosion in the west inevitable by the eastern encirclement of Germany, entailed also the defeat and occupation of France. This meant in turn the intervention, as soon as British government or war development could secure it, of the outside powers of America and Russia. This in turn meant the ultimate division and occupation of Europe by these external powers. The sequence of fatality began with the decision to oppose the eastern expansion of Germany by powers which had neglected their own defences to the point where they were not in a proper position even to defend themselves. It is always an error when confronted by a strong opponent just to enquire where he wants to move and then to run around the world to stop him doing it. If this dangerous fantasy is accompanied by the belief that you can do it without arms adequate to defend even yourself, it approaches certifiable insanity. Yet in a series of passionate spasms rather than in considered policy, British government approached this position in the years before 1939 and rendered their hysteria contagious to others.

The extraordinary series of internal political intrigues and external manoeuvres in foreign affairs by which British government shuffled and stumbled to this untenable position, under every emotional impulse except the clear interest of Britain, have now been described with clarity by authoritative history. I had no part in these things, for I had long ago come to the clear decision that we must be ready to defend the West but not to intervene in the East. I am convinced now, as I was then, that this policy could have maintained the peace of Britain and of France, and have secured inviolate the whole territory of the British Empire. Britain could have been armed to resist a Germany weakened by the long eastern struggle, if it had been mad enough subsequently to attack in the west, and we should have had ample time to warn allies actual and potential, like France and America, and to persuade them to enter into mutual arrangements of well-prepared defence. At the worst, this policy affirmed the clear principle of plain sense, that it is better to fight tomorrow with arms than to fight today without arms.

The policy which made inevitable the entry into Europe of external powers not only divided Europe but liquidated the British Empire. Churchill certainly did not desire the break-up of the Empire, but Roosevelt undoubtedly did. We might reasonably have anticipated that our western ally would join us in resistance to communism, but he was more interested in some vague pursuit of hazy liberal principles to see the end of our Empire; and Roosevelt towards the end of the war was in a stronger position to implement his desires than was Churchill. This phenomenon might have been a surprise to a reasonable man who did not know Roosevelt well, or was unfamiliar with the confusion of the American liberal mind, but that anyone should have been under any delusion concerning Stalin is truly astonishing. Was it assumed that men would abandon every principle to which they had held fast on the long, hard march from Siberia to the Kremlin just because they had accepted some help from Britain to avoid defeat in the Second World War and had enjoyed a few banquets in the company of Winston Churchill?

Yet these illusions were described in Churchill's own books and speeches; also the bitter aftermath: 'It is no exaggeration or compliment of a florid kind when I say we regard Marshal Stalin's life as most precious to the lives and hopes of us all. . . . We feel that we have a friend whom we can trust. . . .' [1] 'So I filled a small size claret glass of brandy for him and another for myself. I looked at him significantly. We both drained our glasses at a stroke and gazed approvingly at one another.' [2] The morning-after came at Sir Winston's speech at the Blackpool Conference of October 1954: 'Stalin was for many years dictator of Russia, and the more I have studied his career, the more I am shocked by the terrible mistakes he made and the utter ruthlessness he showed to men and masses with whom he acted. When Hitler had been destroyed, Stalin made himself our principal object of dread. After our joint victory became certain, his conduct divided the world again. He seemed to be carried away by the dream of world domination. He actually reduced a third of Europe to a Soviet satellite condition under compulsory communism.' So the rulers of Britain met their nightmare of a bid for world domination in the end, and from the quarter whence, on the whole record, it should always have been expected.

Meantime, we not only suffered the physical division of Europe by the triumphant outside powers, but were also assailed throughout the Empire by the political principles which had been used for the defeat of Germany. Extreme doctrines of American liberalism were combined with the subversive propaganda of Russian communism and were spread by the British Government through every medium of world opinion. Not only were we so physically exhausted by the effort of war that it became difficult to maintain our position, but the whole moral position of the British Empire was undermined by the political explosives we had employed against Germany.

It is true that many changes must have come in due course, but in a considered and orderly fashion and not through the indiscriminate blasting of an improvised demolition squad. We were well and truly hoist with our own petard; the chief example of self-destruction in all history. The heirs and beneficiaries we had introduced to the scene were ready and willing to take over; America appropriated straight away the world-wide trading and financial position of Britain, and Russia prepared in its own fashion for the ultimate take-over of our Imperial trusteeship by the preliminary employment of American liberalism. Their action in Europe was even more direct: Europe was divided into two satellite powers, with Britain attached to America as the only alternative to death under Russia.

A reply may be made to all this by the good and pious, who are ever ready to sacrifice the interests of their country and their continent in response to the latest message they have received over their private telephone to heaven. They have to admit that we have lost much, but urge that it was in pursuit of a moral duty. May we begin to examine this claim with a simple question: is morality a one-way street? Does moral conscience only work if Germany is the opponent, but never when Russia is?

[1] *Triumph and Tragedy* (Macmillan, 1954), p. 315.
[2] *Ibid.*, p. 579.

This leads to further questions which start from the premise that policies can finally be judged only by their results, by a comparison of the declared objective with the end achievement. What were our war aims, and what were the results? We set out to save and liberate Poland and all other small countries from the German oppressor. I gave a summary of the post-war situation while Sir Winston Churchill was Prime Minister in August 1954, and which still seems to me mostly valid: 'Europe divided and ruined; the enslavement of eastern Germany, Austria, Hungary, Czechoslovakia, Bulgaria and the Baltic states, added to the encouragement and subsequent betrayal of Poland; the phosphorus bomb during the war, and the atom bomb after the war was effectively over; Nuremberg and the peace of vengeance, which poisons Europe for a generation; all not for the greater glory but to the destruction of the British Empire'.

That situation for the most part still prevails without a finger having been lifted in the interval by Britain or America to liberate those whose freedom we guaranteed. Can they answer the indictment? 'The war was fought to prevent Germans joining with Germans; Danzig was a German city and the Polish Corridor had been regarded for twenty years as the greatest scandal in an iniquitous treaty by every opinion in Europe and America that was worth recording. The result of a war fought in the name of freedom was to subject ten non-Russian peoples to the Soviets, at least seven of them not even Slavonic peoples.'

Are we to be told that we fought for a moral principle, but after the war were too weak to implement it? It is now admitted that we were never in a position to honour our guarantee, not even when we signed the treaty with Poland against Germany. Does morality then consist in undertaking commitments we cannot possibly meet, in signing cheques we know will be dishonoured? At any rate, we tried, we went to war—comes the reply—it was ineffective to save Poland, but we did our best. We answer again: Do you only try when it is a question of a war with Germany, and never when the question is a war with Russia? What are the influences or fantasies which determine this disparate morality? To what a quagmire of humbug, confusion and disaster are we led by this will o' the wisp of prejudice and passion masquerading as morality.

These metaphysicians of morality in foreign affairs will have a hard task to defend their thesis when the clouds of war have finally lifted and a new generation demands clear answers. They will eventually find it still more difficult to defend their case in face of my argument at that time, which is now coming right home to the British people in the further development of this situation since 1954: 'The rise everywhere of the disruptive Left, is, of course, not just the consequence of Russian victory, but a devil directly inspired and controlled by a vigorous and triumphant Soviet policy. The result is already the break-up of everything for which Churchill once stood. A good thing—some may say—it was out-of-date and bound to go. It is true that the old order must pass and give way to new forms, but it should yield only to some new form of order, in accord with coherent ideas. The flinging of primitive populations to anarchy in the service of communism is a process which neither Churchill nor any sane man of other opinion can approve. Yet this has been the result of England's weakness and of Europe's prostration.'

This indictment of the men who had ruled Britain for the whole of my political life and whom I had opposed in vain for so many years, continued in the bitterness of this vast catastrophe to stress that in my youth they had 'founded the British Empire the mightiest and wealthiest power on earth. We possessed between a fifth and a quarter of the globe; we maintained a two-power naval standard which made us twice as strong as any other country in our vital defence sphere; our industries were so vigorous, and our position was so influential, that our exports steadily exceeded our imports and commanded the international markets of that trading system; the resulting favourable balance provided us with at least four thousand million pounds' [1] worth of foreign possessions, on which interest was paid as an annual tribute which could considerably have raised the English standard of life; our Empire contained extensive mineral and raw material supplies, which only awaited direction, energy and a fraction of our great resources for development; the diverse manpower and the wealth which the British Empire then possessed could have moulded from that superb heritage the highest level of material well-being and the finest form of civilisation the world had yet seen. One thousand years of genius and heroism created it—the genius of inspired leadership and the heroism of a great people. . . .'

The British Empire is now liquidated as a direct result of war. I continued in 1954: 'The American navy controls the sea and British ships are commanded by American admirals for defence of our homeland. . . . American aeroplanes with their atom bombs also occupy England to save the English people from the same Soviet power . . . the Dominions are protected by special arrangements with America from which Britain is excluded; our old favourable balance of trade is lost and, instead, a precarious and temporary equilibrium trembles on the brink of catastrophe whenever the lightest breeze blows from across the Atlantic; our old foreign investments are nearly all gone and the very few remaining are in pawn to the Exchange Control as security against the next crisis; the resources which could have developed the Empire are scattered by the winds of war; the manpower of the colonial Empire, which would once have joined so willingly in a great development of mutual benefit, is also gone or is seething with unrest beneath the weakening grasp of the wavering giant. The British Empire has lost confidence in itself and has gained confidence in nothing else, neither hope nor idea. England —the land of genius, of daring, of energy, of eternal leadership and creative

[1] Values of 1939.

inspiration—stands humbly hat in hand to beg the support of its American children, and mumbles tired excuses as it shuffles out of Empire, Europe, leadership and history.'

A few men in the seats of power had ruled Britain throughout my political life. I opposed their policies from start to finish and invariably advanced constructive alternatives. When I contrasted the Britain they inherited from their forebears with the Britain they bequeathed to their successors, was I unfair to write: 'Has so much greatness ever before been brought so low by the errors of so few men, without defeat of its people in war?'

Should I now adjust the facts or admit the injustice of this attack? The only substantial changes in facts since 1954 appear to be the large restoration of our foreign investments position by the efforts of British industry and finance, and a belated change in the direction of our government's shuffle, under stress of necessity, towards Europe instead of away from it. Otherwise, any survey of the scene since this summary was written can only note the accentuation and acceleration of every tendency then observed; certainly the further dissolution of the British Empire. It is true that order and the affluent society still prevail on the knife-edge of our precarious economy within the main nations of the West. But everywhere else disintegration degenerates into anarchy as the direct consequence of the principle and the ally which we embraced in the war. We were certainly aided in our victory by the Soviet fighting on our side, and now we pay the price. When we entered the war, our rulers did not even know on which side the Soviet Government would fight, for it had just signed a treaty with Germany. Russian entry on the other side would almost certainly have brought the final disaster of defeat.

The result of this war could only be tragedy: in the event we lost the Empire and suffered only the partial triumph of Russian communism, because we were saved from its universal victory by the unforeseen and unforeseeable invention of the H-bomb by the scientists. I maintain the validity of the alternative policy: rearmament of Britain to the point of equality in the air with any power in the world, coupled with a strong fleet and a mechanised army which could have struck directly on the Continent in defence of France; this strength to be combined with a clear, firm foreign policy which renounced all intervention in eastern Europe and confined our interests to the British Empire and western Europe. I am still convinced this policy was right, but willingly concede that others can honourably hold the opposite opinion. The outbreak of war lies nearly thirty years behind us, and the subsequent years of peace have brought new problems, new policies, new weapons, new powers and new possibilities of immense creation or limitless catastrophe. It is folly for Europeans to be divided in face of a new world by the bitterness of a faraway quarrel. The coming situation may rather require the union of all men who have at least proved their integrity by the service of truth as they see it.

21

Action at Outbreak of War Imprisonment Under 18B

Lloyd George had strenuously opposed a war in which Britain was involved, before he led and organised victory in the First World War. By his opposition to the Boer War he incurred extreme unpopularity and caused the circulation of such legendary episodes as his escape from Birmingham Town Hall disguised in a policeman's uniform, for long afterwards the subject of Conservative caricature. He issued at the time a defence of his attitude in the following words: 'Is every politician who opposes a war during its progress of necessity a traitor? If so, Chatham was a traitor and Burke and Fox especially; and in later times Cobden and Bright and even Mr. Chamberlain [Joseph], all these were traitors.' No one was incautious enough to call me a traitor for my opposition to the Second World War, except a Norfolk M.P., by name Sir Thomas Cook. It says much for the British judicial system that I was able to sue him for slander while held in prison under Regulation 18B; he published a handsome apology and paid damages when advised he had not a leg to stand on.

Lloyd George was referring to a well-known fact of English history, that it was regarded as a proper and patriotic habit for politicians to speak out if they believed a war to be a mistake. The Labour Party could not logically deny this right, because Ramsay MacDonald had led the opposition to the First World War. This position was reaffirmed at the time of the Suez crisis in 1956 by Mr. Douglas Jay, later President of the Board of Trade in a Labour Government: 'Don't let's forget that Chatham, Charles James Fox, Gladstone and Lloyd George all carried out full-blooded political campaigns against what they judged to be unjust wars waged by Tory Governments. It is an honourable British tradition to oppose such wars.' Why then were the Labour Party so strongly in favour of silencing me in the Second World War with a special regulation to permit imprisonment without trial?

A prominent member of the party supplied some answer. Hugh Ross-Williamson, the author and playwright, wrote[1]: 'At the Bournemouth Conference of the Labour Party in 1940 one of the main subjects of conversation which I heard at "unofficial" talks was whether or not some Labour leaders had made the arrest and imprisonment of Mosley a condition of their entering the Government. The general feeling was that they had (or, at least, that they ought to) and, though the matter is, obviously, incapable of proof, it is still accepted by many of us as the real reason for 18B.' A week later he wrote: '. . . May I be permitted to make an addendum to last week's letter on a matter of fact. At the time of writing I had not, unfortunately, access to *Hansard*, and was loth to trust my memory in the matter of dates. The Amendment to Regulation 18B which made possible the arrest of Mosley was made on the evening of May 22nd, 1940 (*Hansard*, May 23, 1940). This was the second sitting-day after Labour joined the Government, and four days after the close of the Bournemouth Conference of the Labour Party.'[1] Would we have been imprisoned if some Labour leaders had not made it a condition of entering the government? Would we have been released, when all the facts had been examined if political pressure had not been exercised? Mr. Churchill said to Lord Moran (November 30, 1943): 'The government may go out over Mosley. Bevin is kicking.' Earlier Mr. Churchill wrote to Mr. Morrison: 'In the case of Mosley and his wife there is much pressure from the Left, in the case of Pandit Nehru from the Right' (*Second World War*, vol. II, Appendix A).

May I now ask the reader to consider what anyone in my position should have done, believing, as I did, the war to be a profound and possibly disastrous error; a difficult process, I know, for anyone who thinks my view quite wrong. But, given that belief, what could or should be done about it? We could, of course, after expressing our view, have shut up and volunteered for war service. That was easy for me, as I was in origin a regular soldier, and I could have applied to rejoin my regiment. This would have denied all opportunity to the British people of expressing their will to secure a negotiated peace, if they so desired. The war must then continue to a point which I knew must be a disaster to our country. There was a real chance to get a negotiated peace during what was called the phoney war of 1939-40, before the fighting in the West began, and it seemed to me right that some voice should be raised in favour of that course and that the people should have a chance to support it if they wished.

It was emphasised on all sides that the expression of opinion was absolutely free in Britain, in fact that we were fighting to maintain these basic freedoms. In such a situation it seemed to me cowardice to be silent just because

[1] *Truth*, July 17 and 24, 1942.

expressing my opinion would make me unpopular. We were told again and again that in Britain everyone had the right to say what he thought, and in these circumstances a politician who shrank from speaking out might save his own skin, but would fail in his duty to the country.

If I personally had been responsible for government in time of war, the universal call-up to the country's service from the very outset would have been the method employed. I think it right, and it would have been done. If a government had so acted and told me, as a regular soldier in original profession, that I was recalled to my regiment, I should not have said another word but would have rejoined and obeyed orders. Directly I became a soldier again I should naturally have followed implicitly the discipline and tradition of my service. But this clear-cut procedure which prevails in all European countries does not suit the happy confusion of our political mind. It is shocking to say: the country is at war; obey orders or suffer the penalty of indiscipline. We British leave such crudities to the Europeans, and say on the contrary: democracy as usual, discussion is free for all, say what you will; but if you take our freedom seriously, we will clap you in jail under some sly regulation passed in secret session when Habeas Corpus has been suspended in a moment of popular passion. Habeas Corpus—the cornerstone of British liberty—is always there, except when it is needed.

Before my readers judge whether our conduct was right or wrong in the difficult situation in which we were placed, and whether the Government was wise or fair in its treatment of us—fairness possibly cannot be expected in war, but wisdom is still required of governments—I must tell exactly what we did on the outbreak of war. The reasons for the hard decision to oppose the war have already been described, and need not be repeated. The political dilemma it imposed on us was to be completely loyal to our country while we gave its people the opportunity to express their will for a negotiated peace if they so desired.

We decided at once to issue certain instructions to our members, while at the same time arranging an intensive campaign of public meetings in favour of peace. The instructions issued on the outbreak of war read as follows: 'To our members my message is plain and clear. Our country is involved in war. Therefore I ask you to do nothing to injure our country, or to help any other power. Our members should do what the law requires of them, and if they are members of any of the forces or services of the Crown, they should obey their orders, and, in particular, obey the rules of their service. . . . We have said a hundred times that if the life of Britain were threatened we would fight again. . . .' (September 1, 1939).

This line was pursued consistently, for instance: '(1) We want peace and do our outmost to persuade the British people to declare their will for peace. (2) We are determined by every means in our power to ensure that the life and safety of Britain shall be preserved by proper defences until that peace can be made' (March 14, 1940).

We conducted a campaign in favour of a negotiated peace throughout the country at some of the largest and most enthusiastic public meetings I have ever addressed. This was a surprise to me, for MacDonald had often related his experiences in opposing the First World War and described the violent break-up of his meetings and the universal unpopularity he incurred. I was expecting the same reception of our campaign, but at that time we were still in the phoney war period and the atmosphere was totally different to the beginning of the first war. I remembered well the surging enthusiasm of the London crowds for war in 1914, but nothing of the kind was apparent in 1939. On the contrary, large crowds not only listened, but cheered our demands for negotiated peace, which in our requirement would leave every inch of British territory intact. However, two by-elections at which we tested opinion in improvised campaigns resulted in very small votes: the overwhelming majority of the people was undoubtedly in favour of the war.

Our principles led us to declare that if British soil were ever invaded we would immediately stop our peace campaign and fight the enemy. This was, of course, our firm intention, and I knew our resolve would be followed by all our members. After the collapse of the Low Countries and on the eve of the invasion of France, we issued the following statement: 'According to the Press, stories concerning the invasion of Britain are being circulated. . . . In such an event every member of British Union would be at the disposal of the nation. Every one of us would resist the foreign invader with all that is in us. However rotten the existing government, and however much we detested its policies, we would throw ourselves into the effort of a united nation until the foreigner was driven from our soil. In such a situation no doubt exists concerning the attitude of British Union' (May 9, 1940). A fortnight after these words were published we were arrested.

It may be objected that our attitude was impractical because if we were going to fight effectively we should have undergone some preliminary training instead of occupying ourselves with a speaking campaign, and there is some force in this point. I felt personally that I should be at least as effective as most of those who had enjoyed the advantage of Home Guard training then to be seen in remarkable progress throughout the countryside. I had reached marksman standard in the army and kept up practice afterwards with a nice collection of weapons which I still possessed; also I had my old uniform, which would still fit me. So I felt no personal dilemma in this respect. As for our members, the mass of our young membership was in the forces by May 1940, as we encouraged those of military age to join, while the peace campaign was mostly conducted by men who had fought in the first war, with the assistance of relatively few young men who were specialists in the organisation of meetings and general propaganda.

These older men, without any exception known to me, were in the same situation of being experienced soldiers of the first war. When we were finally imprisoned, every medal given for gallantry in the British army was being worn in the prison yard at Brixton, except the V.C. One of our members had won the Victoria Cross, but even that government had not the effrontery to arrest him. At the time of our imprisonment we reckoned that four out of five of our district leaders—usually men in the early thirties—were in the forces, and very few of them were ever detained. The authorities, of course, knew perfectly well they were not the kind of men that propaganda represented them to be.

Those who were eventually arrested were mostly the older men of the previous war who had conducted the peace campaign, and their wives. The regulation under which we were arrested, 18B (1A), gave the Home Secretary power to detain members of an organisation if 'the persons in control of the organisation have or have had associations with persons concerned in the government of, or sympathies with the system of government of, any Power with which his Majesty is at war'. I remember one member who was a farmer in Wales and had never left his home county, where he joined in the peace campaign, saying he thought it a bit odd that he should be imprisoned on the grounds that I had met Hitler three years before the war. I replied that it was odder still that not only I but my supporters should be imprisoned on these grounds when Mr. Chamberlain and many other Englishmen had met Hitler long after I had. On the same principle, presumably, if it had been a case of war with America, every member of our movement could have been imprisoned because I had been on a fishing trip with Roosevelt some years before.

The real reasons were subsequently revealed in the House of Commons (December 10, 1940) without challenge from any quarter, by Mr. R. R. Stokes, M.P., afterwards a Minister in a Labour Government:

'After sixteen hours cross-examination in the private committees to consider 18B cases, Mr. Norman Birkett indulged in this conversation with Sir Oswald Mosley, which I think ought to be quoted and put on record, whatever one's feelings. Sir Oswald Mosley said to Mr. Birkett:

"There appear to be two grounds for detaining us—
(1) A suggestion that we are traitors who would take up arms and fight with the Germans if they landed, and
(2) that our propaganda undermines the civilian morale."
Mr. Birkett replied: "Speaking for myself, you can entirely dismiss the first suggestion."
Sir Oswald Mosley: "Then I can only assume that we have been detained because of our campaign in favour of a negotiated peace."
Mr. Norman Birkett: "Yes, Sir Oswald, that is the case." '[1]

[1] *Hansard*, December 10, 1940.

An 18B Advisory Committee was set up by the Government to examine cases of people imprisoned under the regulation without charge or trial. Lord Jowitt, the Lord Chancellor, stressed this point in the House of Lords on December 11, 1946: 'Let us be fair to those people who were imprisoned under Order 18B, and let us remember that they have never been accused of any crime; not only have they not been convicted of a crime, but they have not been accused of a crime. That should be remembered in all fairness to them.' William Jowitt was an old personal friend, who had been Attorney-General in the Government of 1929, when I was Chancellor of the Duchy of Lancaster and at work on the unemployment problem. He gave me much support in the struggle within the Government prior to my resignation. During our imprisonment in the war he saw Oswald Hickson, the able and courageous Liberal lawyer who acted for us in our early days in prison, and was interested in our position. 'Cannot he bend a little?' asked Jowitt. 'He does not know how,' replied Hickson. It is perhaps one of my faults that I am rather too rigid in what I regard as matters of principle, but I try to be more amenable than most people in minor matters and believe myself to be exceptionally flexible in method.

Mr. Norman Birkett, K.C., was Chairman of the committee constituted to advise the Home Secretary whether 18B detainees should be released or not; the decision rested with the Home Secretary. By a curious coincidence, Norman Birkett had been the leading counsel who appeared for the other side in my libel action against the *Star*, and Herbert Morrison, Home Secretary during most of our detention, was the Labour leader who found it advisable to leave his constituency in East London for a safer haven in face of our gathering strength in the 1930s. The 18B Advisory Committee appeared to have been supplied with odd scraps of information mostly derived from the tapping of telephones. It is an interesting commentary on the administration of the Home Office or the veracity of politicians that during the period this process was at its height the Home Secretary, Sir John Simon, firmly denied that it was ever done.

On a later occasion Sir John Simon denounced with fervour over the radio the outrage of the Germans in arresting and detaining without trial Pastor Niemoeller, after he had been acquitted of charges in the German courts. 18B detainees were at that time allowed a wireless set, and listening to the news was the wife of an admiral; she had suffered exactly the same experience of being detained under Regulation 18B after being acquitted of charges in the English courts. As she left the court after her acquittal, she was immediately re-arrested and taken back to Holloway, where she had been on remand.

My wife too experienced the results of a bugged telephone or room microphone after my arrest and shortly before her own arrest, but it should in fairness be stated that this occurred in time of war. She made some joke in the gay and insouciante Mitford fashion to Lady Downe, which was duly eavesdropped and thrown at her in the Advisory committee. The elderly and distinguished Viscountess Downe was not herself arrested, though she was an ardent member of our movement. When she joined in the thirties, she went to see her lifelong friend Queen Mary at Sandringham, and said to her: 'Ma'am, I feel I should tell you that I have joined the blackshirts'. She received the truly royal reply: 'Is that wise, Dorothy, is that wise?' Our mutual friend Henry Williamson, the author, who had a farm in Norfolk, told me that he was with Lady Downe during the war when she was visited by a Royal chaplain who had a message from the King that she would be glad to hear, after examination of all the facts, that my complete loyalty had been established. She died some time later after a valuable and courageous life which carried her from the leadership of Conservative women in Norfolk to the dangers and vicissitudes of the blackshirt movement.

The stories of flat-footed absurdity in the information supplied to the 18B Advisory Committee are endless, and will surely be recounted one day in detail by other people. They underline once again the necessity for cross-examination in open court of all narks, spies, informers, keyhole peepers and the rest of the pestilential tribe who seek to pay off old scores when fate gives them the chance. My favourite tale is worth recounting, for it is a typical example of the trivial and the nonsensical. After several months' imprisonment without question, a blackshirt came before the committee; he afterwards gave conspicuous service both to medicine and the Church. His hobby then was beekeeping and he kept a diary to remind him of work to be done. One entry read: 'Get rid of English queen, and substitute Italian', and it was solemnly read and considered during his interrogation by the Advisory Committee. He was subsequently released; they had apparently nothing against him except his opinions and this ominous intent, but it was enough to get him a good stretch. So we could continue through the infinite absurdity of mean men who get their chance at last to exercise their prejudice and their silliness. It was not quite so amusing when you were in jail and every kind of story was being circulated against you outside, without any chance to reply, except my one slander action, which was not widely reported.

I was arrested on May 23, 1940, together with all the leading men of our movement, and Diana was arrested some six weeks later on June 29. The only suggestion made against her from official quarters was that she had in all things supported and sustained her husband; an offence of which the wives of some statesmen are most conspicuously free. We had spent the evening of May 22 in my house at Denham, and left the children there on the afternoon of the 23rd to motor the twenty-odd miles to our flat in Dolphin Square. I was surprised to see obvious plain-clothes police outside the front door; ingenuously, it had not occurred to me that I might be arrested. Getting out of the car, I recognised among them detectives whom I knew because it was their job to attend meetings where there was any chance of disorder. They informed me I was to be arrested and I accompanied them to the flat which was swarming with police. They were all most courteous throughout, and after collecting a few things I parted from Diana and went with some of them in a car to Brixton. There I found a large number of our people had already been imprisoned. Altogether some 800 of our members were detained, and were roughly divided, according to what the authorities believed to be their status in our movement, between Brixton Prison and the concentration camp at Ascot, which was later moved to the Isle of Man. Some of the northerners were thrown into jail at Liverpool, where conditions were the worst of all.

At Brixton we were kept in F Wing, which had been condemned as unfit for use. I was put in No. 1 cell and found to my mild surprise that my next-door cell companion was a Negro. Some whimsical jackass in office probably thought it would annoy me, but on the contrary I found him a charming and cultured man. I understood that he was alleged to have played in the Berlin Philharmonic Orchestra before the war and was arrested on account of the peculiarity of this occupation at that time for a coloured man; the facts of his case were never fully revealed to me, but he certainly knew a lot about music and I enjoyed his company and this mutual interest. Otherwise, I was surrounded by familiar faces and the most variegated collection of bed-bugs I had ever encountered since the First War. Captain Ramsay, the Conservative M.P. for Peebles, was in the same wing. An ex-Guards officer, he also had a considerable experience of that war, and agreed that the bugs were more plentiful than in any billet we had ever enjoyed, except in some deep dug-outs at one place just behind the front line, where both we and the Guards had been on different occasions; I think it was called Vermelles. The old familiar tramping of the massed battalions began directly we lay down to sleep.

Nearly all the men in our wing were members of our movement, except for some Germans and Italians who had been naturalised British, and a few members of the 'Right Club', to which Ramsay belonged. He and some of his friends were in jail for an odd reason, if reason it can be called. Some official in the American Embassy had revealed correspondence between Churchill and Roosevelt to outsiders, and was later sentenced and imprisoned for having done it; a woman of a well-known family of foreign origin was also sentenced to a long term in prison in connection with this business. Captain Ramsay had certainly committed no offence, or he would have been charged. So far as I could make out, he had been informed of this matter, and as an M.P. thought it was his duty to investigate the affair and communicate the facts to his leader, Mr. Chamberlain. The abrupt change of government during this process resulted in him being thrown immediately into jail. If his course had been bolder and he had stood up and attacked Churchill, then First Lord of the Admiralty, in the House of Commons, it would have been more difficult to silence him, but he probably thought in time of war this was an unpatriotic act.

In fact, it always seemed to me that in this respect he had nothing to attack Mr. Churchill about, and that the whole thing was a mare's nest. Churchill as First Lord had a perfect right to correspond with the President of the United States. It could even be argued that once we were in the wretched business of war it was the duty of all ministers to seek help where they could get it and allies where they could find them. Churchill had probably told Chamberlain all about it, and, if he had not, at worst it was a breach of etiquette. Yet the members of this right-wing group thought they were on to something of world-shaking importance, and some of them sacrificed themselves in the cause of a revelation devoid of meaning or purpose as far as Britain was concerned. In America, of course, the publication of such correspondence might have been a sensation to an electorate whose President was then stamping the country with pledges to its mothers to keep their boys out of war.

A distinguished Admiral was imprisoned with us, together with his wife, but neither of them had anything to do with this group or with our party. Admiral Sir Barry Domvile, ex-chief of Naval Intelligence, was imprisoned because before the war he had run an organisation for the promotion of Anglo-German friendship called the Link. He wrote an amusing book on his experiences entitled *From Admiral to Cabin Boy*; a sentiment of life's vicissitudes, which at that time a number of us in varying degree felt we shared.

Apart from the extra amenity of the bugs, we had the normal conditions of remand prisoners in jail, which are, of course, different in several particulars from the treatment of convicted men. The prison staff on the whole were a fine lot, mostly ex-servicemen; one warder had been a sergeant in my regiment. The prison governor, Captain Clayton, a much-wounded soldier of the first war, was a fair and honourable man, and so was the chief warder, Watson. Our particularly disagreeable jail experiences were in no way due to them. They had nowhere else to put us, except the condemned wing, and orders had been given from above that this was to be our accommodation. We were there under war conditions with a shortage of staff, and at first there appeared to be a lively apprehension concerning the possible conduct of this considerable company of men, who were accustomed to act together in a disciplined movement. It was rumoured that at first the prison was surrounded by troops at night; I do not know if this was true. In pursuance of our principle to do nothing to impede the war effort of the nation, I at once instructed our members to behave with complete propriety, which they did. Any anxiety then abated and by the staff we were always well treated.

Official instructions were given in the early days that for security or other reasons we were to be locked in our cells twenty-one hours out of the twenty-four, and only let out for one hour's exercise in the morning and afternoon and other necessary routines. This suited me reasonably well, for we were allowed books and I spent the whole time reading. There was complete silence and the considerable number of our people who also enjoyed reading found this monastic existence relatively tolerable. Paradoxically, the trouble began when the cell doors were unlocked, and my readers would have some difficulty in guessing what it was. When conditions were relaxed the curse of prison was noise.

I had to take action altogether against my interests, for I heard that a number of people were being very adversely affected by this seclusion. The Italians were particularly stricken, for they are a happy people who like a gregarious life and a merry din. It was clearly in the interests of the many to press for the doors of cells to be opened except at night, and to give every assurance of orderly conduct in this event. My request was eventually granted, and the cell doors were opened; all hell then broke loose. Imagine trying to read amid a genial babble of Mediterranean voices in an enormous room which echoes exactly like a swimming bath; it needed some concentration, to put it mildly. The final nightmare was permission to bring in a ping-pong table, when the echoing seashell of the building resounded with the music of ping and pong and Latin laughter. The subsequent discomfort of being locked in cells while bombs were falling round the prison was nothing to it. Then too I was able to perform some small service of reassurance, for I was credibly informed that some simple types among the warders felt safe in the cell below mine because they believed that those careful and skilful fellows, the Germans, would never pinpoint a bomb on me.

A strange and disquieting incident occurred during this period in Brixton Prison, which contained a certain bitter irony all too typical of the times. A member of our movement came to see me privately in my cell, and informed me that he had been certified by outside doctors as a leper. I had known him for a long time in the work of the party, and had no reason to doubt his word. The poor man was in a natural state of distress and not very coherent, but I understood that before his imprisonment at least one doctor had certified him as a leper; there was apparently some doubt about a second doctor's certificate, which in his opinion would render him liable to compulsory treatment and segregation. He was very concerned in case the prison authorities should find out about this and have him put away in still more unpleasant conditions. His story was supported by obvious evidence of some skin disease.

This put me in a considerable difficulty, but it seemed to me that my duty was clear and I explained it to him. I would do everything possible to protect him and his interest, but he could not possibly remain among the other prisoners. He agreed that I should go straight to the governor and deal with the whole matter. The affair was reported to the Home Office for their action, which in my recollection was not very prompt; the case of suspected leprosy remained among his fellow prisoners for some days. He was then removed to the prison hospital, where he was kept for a considerable period in distant view of all of us. He then suddenly reappeared in F Wing and mingled freely as before with his fellow prisoners, informing me that he had been frequently examined by doctors but knew nothing definite. I asked to see the governor again and to be informed on behalf of all prisoners in contact with the man. The reply from the Home Office was curious and equivocal. In the opinion of their doctors or the specialists they had consulted, the disease would not be contagious at this stage in the event of this man being a leper. He then remained among us for a long time, but was eventually and happily cleared of all suspicion of having contracted this terrible and infectious disease.

I agreed throughout that the affair should be kept from all but a very few people, as it was the sort of thing liable to cause panic in a prison. Living through a long period with this uncertainty was probably the most disagreeable of the prison experiences. Yet even this sinister event was relieved and enlivened by the glorious absurdity of our national capacity for humbug, which can be an endearing idiosyncrasy in normal times as a simple self-protection from the facts of life, but in times of war can assume monumental and grotesque proportions. About this time occurred the incident of the *Altmark*. Some readers may remember that a German ship operating under difficult conditions kept a prisoner who was a leper with other prisoners. Our Press rang with this sadistic brutality of the Germans, and it would seem a justified denunciation, even if it be harder to keep prisoners apart in a ship than in a prison. The newspapers were blissfully ignorant that exactly the same thing was done in a British prison with the knowledge and by the order of higher authority, without any excuse which was apparent to me. However, all was well that ended well. The victim was cured of his skin complaint and his mind was free from the suspicion that he might be suffering from this horrible disease, while the nerves of a few of us survived yet another of those tests which fortify us to support with equanimity life's vicissitudes.

Diana's imprisonment in Holloway, six weeks after my arrest, separated us entirely for some eight months, after which we were allowed once a month to visit our wives in that prison. We used to pass with strong escorts through the massive gates of Brixton Prison to be greeted on the adjoining wall with the widely advertised injunction: 'Lend to defend the right to be free'. By that time Diana was better treated than when she was first arrested. She was carted off to prison when our son Max was eleven weeks old, and she was still nursing him. She was asked if she wanted to take him with her into prison, as some women prisoners had taken their newly born babies with them. Our elder son Alexander was only nineteen months old and she was only allowed to take one of them with her, so they would be separated; also the prison was liable to be bombed at any time. She had to decide quickly and said she preferred not to take either baby; in my view rightly. In her delicate condition as a nursing mother suddenly taken from her child, she was put in a dirty cell with the floor swimming in water; there was no bed and only a thin mattress on the filthy, wet floor.

The treatment of the women was disgraceful, and should not be so lightly forgotten as were our male experiences. One section of the Press celebrated her arrest with the banner headline: 'Lady Mosley arrested at last'. Another suggested that she was having a delightful time with wine flowing like water; this pleasantry resulted in a libel action which she won. Again the British judicial system maintained the fine tradition of still offering this facility to inmates of the Government's jails. However, an impression was left on the public mind which was epitomised by the bus conductor who in halting opposite Holloway used to direct his passengers: 'This way for Lady Mosley's suite'.

After eighteen months of our respective imprisonments in Brixton and Holloway it was decided that married couples should be imprisoned together. Diana's brother, Tom Mitford, had lunched just previously in Downing Street, and suggested it. Although he had been a member of our movement, he was clearly regarded as too efficient an adjutant of his territorial battalion for any action to be taken against him. He was later killed in Burma; a tragic loss, for he was the only son among six daughters and had much ability and charm. Mr. Churchill had apparently on several occasions intervened on behalf of detainees, and conditions at that time were much better in prisons and concentration camps. A disused wing of Holloway, remote from the rest of the prison, was set aside for the married couples. The massive building had certainly a grim aspect, but our life there was much happier. We were allowed to cook our own food: Diana was very competent because in earlier days she and her youngest sister had had cookery lessons in which I occasionally joined. (When the sauces curdled they screamed so much that the teacher remarked she was glad that all six sisters were not there.) We had also some small plots in the adjoining yard where I could grow vegetables, and my early agricultural experience came in handy. There were, of course, male guards on the gate, but we usually saw wardresses, who in our experience were agreeable to deal with. At this point we were well treated, and on occasion prison rules were waived. For instance, my son Nicholas was in training with the Rifle Brigade at Winchester before going to the war and he was allowed to visit us frequently when on leave. He was permitted to stay talking long into the night; being smuggled out through some side gate in oblivion of the letter of the law; all this was in striking contrast to earlier treatment.

My visitors in prison, apart from relations, were a diverse company whose solicitude I much appreciated. The first was my old I.L.P. comrade and later opponent, James Maxton; he came to see me in a gesture of characteristic courage and generosity. Bob Boothby came from the Conservative ranks in old friendship and in his usual stalwart maintenance of his strong and independent character, which faced a political clamour at that time and persisted unruffled during the later adoration of his television days. Walter Monckton came more than once with wise and friendly advice which then and later was of much value. Mr. Churchill apparently did not approve this activity, for he accosted Walter one day with the sardonic enquiry, 'Still a prison visitor?' Harold Nicolson came in another courageous act of friendship, but to my subsequent regret I refused to see him because I was incensed by his broadcast of the night before, which seemed to me to fall below his usual high standard of intellect and integrity.

Diana's companionship was a great happiness to me in the last two years of imprisonment, just as her courage in the very rough conditions of her previous imprisonment apart from me in the first eighteen months had been a comfort to my anxiety. She showed throughout not only courage but gaiety, which I found in the first war is one of the main attributes of our English people in adversity; her humour never left her. After telling me one day about the treatment of the women in the early days by one or two old harpies in a company of wardresses, who were on the whole good people, she remarked that she yet felt she had an advantage over them: 'It was still lovely to wake up in the morning and feel one was lovely *one*'. I wickedly recounted this tale later to the merriment of family circles, and needless to say it went straight into one of Nancy Mitford's books.

Yet it was not amusing for a woman to be treated like that and in addition to be separated from all her children: our newly born babies and her elder two boys, Jonathan and Desmond Guinness, by her former marriage with Lord Moyne. They too survived entirely in temperament and character the vicissitudes of this period, and remained always devoted to their mother and my good friends. Above all, Diana retained unbroken not only her gaiety and courage but her sense of beauty. Her love of music, her ability even with simplicity to make every house beautiful were unimpaired, and in sight-seeing anywhere in the world she remains the best of companions for reasons I always explain to the children and others; a detail of beauty on such occasion is revealed to those huge eyes, continuously swivelling, which is not available to normal vision. The foundation of all these blessings are her good nature, high intelligence and firm character. We follow the good marriage rule that she runs the house and I run the business, which in my case is politics, but her view on many subjects is worth having.

After three and a half years of prison my old complaint of phlebitis returned in an aggravated form owing to the inactive life I had to lead. It had happened first in 1928 when I was young, and they put me to bed for six weeks with the traditional treatment until the blood clots in my legs disappeared. The complaint returned a few years later and I was again advised that I must go to bed. I replied that I had two pressing engagements; the first to speak in the Albert Hall, and the second to represent Britain in the European fencing championship at Lausanne. My doctors gravely intimated that I might conceivably survive the Albert Hall, but had not a hope of living through Lausanne. However, I spoke in the Albert Hall, and fenced from soon after dawn to near midnight in the heavy protective clothing under a temperature approaching ninety degrees in the shade. The performance was not so bold as it may appear, because I had then made contact with that remarkable man Mr. Arthur Dickson-Wright, chief surgeon at St. Mary's Hospital, whose method was to bind the legs of his patients with Elastoplast to stop the clots moving and then to encourage them to exercise in order to keep the blood circulating rapidly. This is no doubt a most amateur account of the medical process, but Dickson-Wright cured me of phlebitis.

This illness returned in prison in a severe form, and was believed to be endangering my life. It ceased when I left prison twenty-four years ago and I have never had a trace of it since. The reason is that I have a slow pulse, which is fine for athletics but fatal for prison. My pulse has a normal rate of 64, about 48 at rest, which gives me staying power in athletics and endurance in life; it is a quite familiar phenomenon among athletes, and it has undoubtedly helped me to withstand the general strain of my life. The only real drawback of this condition is that you cannot stand inactivity. The constitution is designed by nature to support stress; it clogs, rusts, and ceases to work in desuetude. The long lethargy of prison life brought the phlebitis back with a vengeance, and reduced my general condition to the point of losing four stone in weight; some highly qualified and experienced doctors thought that my life was in danger. After a protracted convulsion of inner circles—I do not know exactly what went on, but a lot did—we were released. Maybe the death of a political prisoner in jail was regarded as a bad advertisement for democracy, and always among my opponents were some men who were both honourable and humane.

Our release produced a great uproar. The communists ran a big campaign, and we became the subject of debate in and out of Parliament. Our release was announced on the wireless two days before we left the prison, and the Press and the cinema companies erected a kind of scaffolding outside the main gate of the prison on which they kept a day and night guard of photographers. However, the prison authorities were more than a match for them on this ground and smuggled us out before dawn through the murderers' gate, quite unnoticed; experience sometimes has value. The Press then pursued us in cars and besieged the house to which we travelled for several days.

Every sort of person was interviewed with the question whether we should be released or not, and one girl reporter met a tartar in Bernard Shaw: 'Would you think it too strong to say that the Home Secretary's decision, whether taken individually or in concert with others, is calculated to cause alarm and despondency among the masses of the people who responded to his exhortation to "go to it"?' she asked him. 'I do not think it a strong proposition at all,' replied Shaw. 'It makes me suspect that you are mentally defective. I think this Mosley panic shameful. What sort of people are they who can be frightened out of their wits by single men?—Even if Mosley were in rude health, it was high time to release him with apologies for having let him frighten us into scrapping the Habeas Corpus Act.—Mr. Morrison has not justified the outrageous conditions—the gag in Mosley's mouth and the seven-mile leg-iron. We are still afraid to let Mosley defend himself and we have produced the ridiculous situation in which we may buy Hitler's *Mein Kampf* in any bookshop in Britain, but may not buy ten lines written by Mosley. The whole affair has become too silly for words. Good evening.'

Apart from this agitation, my release in November 1943 was naturally for us a happy occasion and soon became a merry business, for British officialdom quickly staged one of its brightest pantomimes. We were asked before leaving where we wanted to go, and presented a short list of friends and relations we knew were willing to receive us; my house at Denham was requisitioned by the army, and London, where we had a small flat, was forbidden to us. From the list the Home Office carefully chose Wing-Commander Jackson, who was then married to my sister-in-law, Pamela Mitford, and had been a friend of mine from old days, which he has always remained. We arrived under escort at their house in Oxfordshire in company with a detective, who had to live with us, as we were still under house arrest. My brother-in-law immediately obtained leave from the Air Force to spend a few days with us, and my mother-in-law, Lady Redesdale, with her youngest daughter Deborah, came to join the party. The loyalty of that superb character Lady Redesdale during these hard times, like that of my own mother, was one of our mainstays, and Diana's youngest sister in these personal affairs was equally steadfast.

It was indeed a convivial gathering on that first evening, which lasted far into the night until the weakness of my illness produced the complete exhaustion of a long sleep. All was happy for a few days and we continued to live in peace after the return of Derek Jackson to his unit and the departure of our other relations to their cottage at Swinbrook, which was not far away. We were left alone with Pamela, to whom we were devoted, and the detective, who was most agreeable to us. After a few days, the Press siege was called off and we were able to walk in the garden without trouble. Then suddenly full drama exploded into this quiet country retreat. The Chief Constable of Oxford with accompanying cohorts arrived with orders that we must leave at once. For it transpired that the Home Office had inadvertently directed us into the inner sanctum of the Air Ministry's secrets.

Long afterwards we learned that Derek Jackson was then engaged in some experiments which resulted in inventions to baffle German aircraft; there is a good deal about it in Sir Winston Churchill's memoirs. In addition to gaining the D.F.C. and A.F.C. for active service flying, he was a physicist of the first order; an almost unique and in time of war invaluable combination. His scientific knowledge, which later led him to one of Oxford's chairs as a professor of physics, was, of course, a very recondite subject for a layman. With the worst will in the world on all sides he would have had a hard job to explain to me what it was all about, and with even more evil intent, I should have had an even harder job under close house arrest in Oxfordshire to communicate the stuff to anyone else. However, thought is the chief absentee from the official mind at such moments, and at the sound of the reveille in the Air Ministry the Home Office fell into a fine old flap.

It was a question of finding somewhere to sleep, and it was not easy, as Lady Redesdale had no room in her cottage, and any other possibility was far away. Finally, we went to the Shaven Crown Hotel at Shipton-under-Wychwood, which happened at the time to be empty and also had room for the children. All this was at once reported in the Press, which had been active throughout, and the Communist Party, with time on its hands in other people's wars, at once canvassed the villagers to petition for our return to jail. Despite the belief freely expressed in private and Government circles that we would be lynched if we were released among the British people, the Communist Party, we were credibly informed, failed to obtain a single signature among the regular villagers. We were treated throughout this period of adversity in the English countryside not only with toleration but with kindness and even with friendship. It was indeed a moving and healing experience to find the real people of England exactly the same as I remembered in my long and intimate experience of them, during my country childhood, my army days in peace and war, and my political friendships in the kindly homes of the workers in all the diverse industries of our land. Their fair and firm attitude was particularly remarkable in that we had throughout been the object of a hostile Press and continuous political agitation, which was not confined to the communists. When in subsequent years it was sometimes alleged that I was an object of hatred among the British people, I could truly reply that we never found a trace of it outside the square mile comprising Westminster, Whitehall and Fleet Street, where the tale was first invented and then assiduously propagated.

My chief concern at that time was my companions still left in jail and concentration camps. Most of them had been released and conditions by then were certainly improved, but a number remained. I felt they were having a worse time than I was. Some of them were held until the end of the war eighteen months later, and this, of course, worried me more than anything else. Happily, only one other married couple was still detained in Holloway with us when we were released, and by a strange coincidence the Home Office discovered that they were no longer a menace to the State on exactly the same day as we were freed and they too were released.

This close companion of my last months in Holloway was a remarkable man and a fine character. He had won the Distinguished Service Order and the Military Cross in the first war, and was detained simply because he was an active and enthusiastic member of our movement. He had the sardonic humour of the experienced soldier, and it always amused him that he was held in jail by order of a dear fellow who had spent the previous war dodging round an apple orchard; the Minister had suffered apparently from an eye disability as well as a conscience.

Very few of our people showed any bitterness at that time towards their numerous and diverse oppressors, and this attitude was often the source of wonder to our friends. Although I wrote once: 'Revenge is the hallmark of small minds', such an elevated sentiment is easier when you are again breathing fresh air than when a fat chap is sitting on your face. Nevertheless, even during the worst period of our early days in jail, the men with me took all their adversity with the same gay, good humour I remembered in the trenches of the First World War, where indeed most of them had lived through their first experience of hardship. We harboured no bitterness toward the politicians whose spite we felt had jailed us, but perhaps it should be admitted that this was not entirely magnaminity. The truth is that men only feel bitter towards those for whom they have some respect.

My own feeling was simple and was perhaps derived from my early agri-cultural experience, which brings one close to nature: if through error or a sense of duty you take too big a risk and have a fall into the manure heap, every little runt in life's farmyard will take the chance to stamp his small hoof in your face; it is the way of nature. The experience is instructive but not embittering, because it is all too natural. The redeeming happiness is that the higher intellects and finer spirits do not participate, even though they may disapprove your opinion, and in some cases they assist in your adversity.

Some public advantage may be derived from my small personal experiences, which can be briefly summarised: arrested without charge or trial and held in prison or house arrest for five years under an order passed the night before you were arrested, and of which you were not even aware; order is retrospective because it enables you to be imprisoned for something perfectly legal at the time you did it, namely seeing a foreigner over three years before; wife similarly held in jail on grounds she had supported and sustained husband; older children removed from care on motion of the Official Solicitor by order of a court of law, despite your opposition, and handed to a guardian you disapproved; younger children at most formative age allowed occasionally to visit mother in prison and dragged away crying at the end of the visit by wardresses; banking accounts frozen, though not stolen, as happened some-times abroad; safe deposit in bank opened on order signed by unknown lieutenant-colonel; house requisitioned and ransacked; held in silence without right of reply for years while vilest falsehoods are privily circulated about you. This may happen to any Englishman under our present constitutional law at a time of popular excitement, if a rogue government has a pliant majority in Parliament. The preservation of the basic liberties thus easily violated in England are enshrined in the constitutional law of most civilised countries. When we talk so much of liberty, is it not time that English liberties were truly secured?

There is much talk of democracy and the power of the people in the vote. When did they vote for this kind of thing? Such treatment of the individual was not an issue presented by Mr. Baldwin to the electorate at the previous election in 1935, when he slunk to victory with careful avoidance of the rearmament question. To throw Magna Carta, the Bill of Rights and Habeas Corpus on the scrap-heap was not the programme of the winning party or of the opposition. It is time that the British people considered a cast-iron provision in constitutional law to preserve the elementary basis of individual liberty. Perhaps I am the right man to suggest it.

22
Personal Life after the War

John bright's advice to those in political trouble was: 'Say it again, but be ruder the second time;' advice which in our circumstances at the end of the war seemed to me sound. Mr. Churchill observed to mutual friends that we adopted an attitude of defiance. I had no regret for my stand against the war, only regret for the destruction of Europe and the danger to Britain which I had foreseen. At this point we begin to enter the modern period, my life and action since the war. I was determined to begin as soon as possible the political action which I had throughout resolved to resume directly I was free, but it may be of interest first to describe our personal life and some of the adventures we undertook to secure our complete freedom.

At the end of the war our restrictions within England were lifted and we were able to move from our house and small agricultural holding at Crux Easton, Hampshire, to an eleven-hundred acre farm I had recently bought at Crowood, near Ramsbury in Wiltshire. Nine hundred acres of the farmland were in hand and the farming of it was a considerable undertaking, but I entered into this health-restoring task with zest. After our experience, it was good to put our roots back into the soil. This was different from the farming of my youth, because in place of the strong grazing of my Staffordshire homeland we had light to medium land which could only be developed into good grass by the modern ley system. We ran a mixed farm of arable and dairy cattle. The expert staff of our hereditary farming in Staffordshire had been gathered over generations and continued from father to son; a large family which had long since been dispersed. I was now dependent on the help of a few good local people who had worked formerly on the farm, and on the kindly assistance of the war agricultural committee. In addition to my long absence from the business, I was a novice to arable farming; and, as always, I was in too much of a hurry. Here I learned the useful lesson that Nature cannot be forced beyond her measured and stately pace.

We were in a strange land remote from the hereditary roots of either Mosleys or Mitfords, but we benefited again from the friendly and tolerant attitude of the real people of England; they may differ politically, but they take others as they find them in private life. We also had some old friends in the neighbourhood who made our life agreeable, such as Lord Berners, a gifted musician, endowed with the liveliest of wits, who lived at Faringdon; Mrs. Reginald Fellowes—whom I had known long since as Princesse de Broglie in Paris—lived at Donnington, near Newbury, where she was distinguished in England, as in Paris, as a beauty and hostess of exquisite manners which were barbed with a legendary *mechanceté* to people she found boring, but illumined by an affectionate and enduring loyalty to all her friends; John Betjeman and his wife Penelope, who had inherited strength of character from her father, my old divisional commander Field-Marshal Sir Philip Chetwode, lived near Wantage, and were among our most agreeable neighbours. Subsequent enquiry by journalists whether we had suffered social ostracism after the war remained something of a mystery to me, for I had not noticed it. Reflecting on this deep question, we concluded that perhaps we had been saved from the dullards whose company in our previous life it had not always been easy to avoid; sweet can be the uses of ostracism, for evasive action in the countryside is sometimes difficult without being rude.

My love, my passion for Europe consumed me with desire for the mainland directly the war was over. Owing to my constant preoccupation with English politics before the war and my consequent public meeting campaign without intermission, I had not left our island since 1936, except for one short visit to Paris in 1938. Yet at the end of the war in 1945 another four years were to elapse before we could travel to Europe. In retrospect this is strange, for the action of the Labour Government at that time not only violated every principle for which they professed to have been fighting the war, subsequently stated in the Charter of the United Nations and the concomitant instruments which British Government later signed, but also casually tossed on the scrapheap the basic principles of our own Magna Carta, the Bill of Rights and other sacred institutions long enshrined in British constitutional usage. Magna Carta ordained that any British subject might leave the country without let or hindrance. Yet we discovered that in accordance with more recent practice sly bureaucrats and tricky politicians found a way round British basic law, without exposing themselves to an action in the courts, at that time. The simple device was to deny a passport, and to say in effect: you are as free as air to leave the country, although without this document no country will receive you, and what is more no ship or airline will carry you.

We were refused passports, and despite the best efforts of personal friends and eminent politicians—notably our old friend Brendan Bracken—the refusal of the Labour Government persisted; most Conservatives, to do them justice, were dead against this denial of elementary liberty, and so of course were the Liberals. Another old friend, Hugh Sherwood—for years a Liberal Whip in the House of Commons and later Treasurer of the party—raised the matter in the House of Lords, to which he had been elevated for his part in wartime at the Air Ministry. He received the strange reply that the Government wanted to retain some control over us, long after the final abolition of all the wartime controls over individuals accorded to government by parliament. Brixton and Holloway were enlarged to become an island prison, without enactment of parliament or authority of established law. The withholding of a passport was one more trick for getting round the liberty whose alleged maintenance had cost our country so much.

However, there was one way out of the island prison: buy a yacht. It was a liberty no more available to all than the freedom to sleep in the Ritz instead of on the Embankment. But a little money worked, as so often in our land of the free. Once more, without this aid from my forebears, the dull devils might have got me down for another long spell. It was an expensive business at the time, but in the end it did not cost me much, as I sold the boat for a fair price directly its purpose was fulfilled. It is only right to admit that we found this enforced exercise of seamanship quite enjoyable, and even pursued our government-directed employment one year longer than was necessary.

The way out of the island prison was the yacht—because our physical detention would have involved the government in serious legal action—but the question still arose whether we could land in any other country; it seemed unlikely at best that we could get beyond the confines of any port we put into. However, we were determined at all costs to assert our freedom— it is a wonderful sensation when you have been imprisoned a long time to feel that you can turn a ship in any direction and sail anywhere across the free seas of the world—and we had an idea that we might make quite a happy landing in Spain. So we pored over maps and charts taking us through the Channel and across the Bay of Biscay. We took two experienced seamen with us, as my sea experience was confined to feeling ill in a troop-ship or cross-Channel steamer, and my sea hazards had so far been no more arduous than the swimming-pool of an Atlantic liner. However, we were all set to go, Diana and I, our two small children, our equally inexperienced butler, and the two sailors.

The boat, a sixty-ton fifty-fifty power-and-sail ketch, was moored in Southampton, and our plans were by no means concealed. Curiously enough, on the eve of our departure, we were given our passports; we were really free at last in the summer of 1949, four years after the end of the war. Strangely moves the mind of Whitehall in unfathomable and impenetrable mystery, but on this occasion I have some reason to believe that it was not the depths of the official world which were being stirred but only the muddy puddle of politics. Perhaps some politicians felt that the government would have looked foolish if we sailed despite the ban, and they may have surmised that we would be well received in some quarters. Anyhow, freedom came across at last with quite a good grace. I had not been obliged to 'lend to defend the right to be free', only to buy to defend the right to be free, a yacht.

It is difficult in any analysis of this strange event to discern any serious motive except pure spite. What did they fear? They had nuclear weapons, and I had only the voice and pen of Mosley. It is flattering to imagine that my physical presence would have transformed the world situation, but plainly illusory, even by Whitehall standards. If I had made a nuisance of myself and broken any of the new laws in any country, I should simply have been put in jail, and Whitehall would have been delighted. In any case, by stopping me travelling they could only suppress the voice and not the pen. They had no means of preventing my writings circulating in Europe, and in fact they were being published freely in all countries except France, which to me was always the land apart from politics. Even before I was free to leave England, publications were appearing in Europe with principles and slogans —such as 'Europe a Nation'—first declared by me in post-war speeches in East London. If they feared the impact of my ideas, they could not stop it.

However, we were free at last, and in early June we left Southampton and set off down the Channel. It was pretty rough and we were all ill for the last time, because that ten-hour buffeting cured us for good of this tiresome complaint; it was no good going on being sick on this small boat for the whole of the voyage. After a night spent struggling up the Channel and round Finisterre, we arrived off Brest around dawn, but fog reduced visibility to a few yards and we had no means of entry. Luckily, after an hour or two we met a fishing-boat which guided us into port. We landed on French soil.

The whole landscape seemed still to be flat from war bombardment; hardly a house was standing. No one appeared to be bothering much about passports, and we had a genial seafarers' welcome. We lunched early in a battered tin hut which was a seamen's bistro; it seemed three star to us. I walked a little through the remnants of the city where I had come to France for the first time thirty-six years before to learn the language, and it seemed the sea had given life back to me. In the emotion of being on French soil again, even in the desolation of these forlorn surroundings, I was moved to say to this moment of reunion with Europe—'*Verweile doch, du bist so schön*', the desperate but ecstatic apostrophe addressed to the transient moment of beauty by the immortal whose thought not only linked Germany and France but encompassed and ennobled our whole continent—I felt all Europe was

there to greet me, the past, the present and the future; the mood was *exalté*.
I awoke standing strangely amid the ruins, and went back to the sea.

We crossed the Bay of Biscay, which on this occasion was not quite so
fierce as its reputation, and put into Bordeaux, which entailed a long and slow
trip up the tawny waters of the Gironde. There we encountered the full
glories of France in the magnificent eighteenth-century architecture; and I
must add, the Basque cooking. Neither of us had ever been in Bordeaux;
we felt we were at last really beyond the confines of Brixton and Holloway
when we entered that temple of the classic French cuisine, the Chapon Fin,
now, miserable to relate, defunct. Alexander and Max, then aged ten and
nine, sat rather disconsolately through the unaccustomed though superlative
repast, but Max brightened a little toward the end and observed in his current
Wiltshire accent: 'This is almost as good as them plain ices you get down the
village'. He had not been a year at the Bar in later life before he developed as
nice a taste in food as any old bencher; perhaps Christchurch had assisted to
sophisticate Wiltshire. I trust he always remembers the classic and paternal
principle: 'Moderation in all things, especially in moderation'.

The journey continued along the northern coast of Spain with the boys
becoming much too bold now they had recovered from their initial sea-
sickness. They were running around the deck with bare feet in every sort of
weather and we had some anxiety that a roll of the boat or a wave washing
across might put them into the sea, but with the adaptability of children
they had almost become experienced seamen by the time we reached Corunna,
our first port of call in Spain. Neither of us had ever before been in Spain,
which we thus met for the first time at this point of Sir John Moore's last
stand.

We continued from Corunna to our next port, Lisbon, our first experience
of this lovely eighteenth-century city. Once more we had a little trouble with
fog on arriving in the Tagus. Visibility was almost nil, and it seemed that
large ships were bearing down on us from all sides with their imposing
warnings, which we could only answer with our small hooter. Our experienced
seamen made little of it, and we got into port near the renaissance monastery
of Belém, which celebrated the early Portuguese voyages of discovery.

After a brief sightseeing, we continued our journey and ran into our first
rough sea off the southern coast of Portugal on our way to Tangier. It was a
real storm and our boat adopted many strange and disturbing positions, but
stood up to the racket splendidly. It had been built for a first owner who
had an island on the Atlantic side of Ireland, and wanted a ship which would
resist the ocean gales. With our two capable sailors we were quite safe,
though we were far from feeling it.

We next achieved our first main objective, which was a visit to the interior
of Spain, for which we had made some arrangement in advance. We knew
few people there, but my stand against the war was well known and approved

by many in that country, who thought this division of Europe a tragedy. We crossed from Tangier to Gibraltar, where we left the boat with crew and children, all happy to be back with fish and chips.

From Gibraltar we took the train to Madrid, where we made new friends who were a source of happiness to us in subsequent years. Chief among them were the Serrano Suñers, whom we had not known before but who welcomed us with warm hospitality. He had recently been Foreign Minister of Spain, and she was the sister of General Franco's wife. He combined high intelligence with a bright gaiety of nature and firmness of character which had survived many sorrows and vicissitudes of the Civil War, and she united outstanding beauty and charm with an exquisite sweetness and gentleness of disposition. Soon after our arrival, they gave us a fascinating introduction to Spanish life. Ramón Serrano Suñer said that he would come at 11 p.m. to our hotel to fetch us for dinner. We thought it was rather late, but manfully sustained the wait without a preliminary snack. When he arrived he said that the dinner was at their house in the country, and we wondered how long the journey would take.

However, all mundane things were forgotten when, on the way, we arrived at the Escurial which he had caused to be opened around midnight. We stood alone in the awe of that sombre splendour. The purpose of the visit was to stand for a few moments by the tomb of José Antonio Primo de Rivera, founder of the Falange. I had seen him only once, when in the thirties he had visited me in London at our headquarters in Chelsea. He had made a deep impression on me, and his assassination seemed to me always one of the saddest of the individual tragedies of Europe. I was deeply moved as we stood beside the sepulchre of this young and glittering presence I remembered so vividly, and was reminded of the initial line of Macaulay's memorable tribute to Byron: 'When the grave closed over the thirty-seventh year of so much sorrow, so much glory'.

We continued our journey in a subdued mood to Suñer's country house in the hills near Madrid. There we found a brilliant and lively throng ready for dinner at an incredibly late hour by English standards, and their gaiety and good humour gradually dispersed the dark reveries of the Escurial. There were some twenty guests, among them the niece of our hostess, General Franco's beautiful daughter, who was just engaged to be married and had come with her fiancé; time flies, they now have a large family. The party lasted into the early hours of the morning and was the prelude to a number of happy occasions when the cares of our war years were dissolved in the warmth, charm and distinction of Spanish hospitality. We were just getting used to their late afternoon lunches and near-midnight dinner parties, when the time came to leave; I remember one lady saying to me at what was called a morning gathering that she must hurry home as it was after three o'clock and her parents, like all old people, wanted to lunch early.

Meantime, our boat had sailed with the boys through the relative calm of the Mediterranean to meet us in the Balearic Isles. We went by train to Valencia and on by boat to Majorca on one of the hottest journeys of our lives. These isles are a paradise now familiar to many of our countrymen, but we were there before their development and the arrival of the cinema world. At a small seaside house near Formentor, Filippo Anfuso and his lovely Hungarian wife were living; her remarkable firmness and resolution of character had done much to save his life in the final turmoil of the war. He was a professional diplomat who had been loyal to the last in his duty as the final Foreign Secretary of Mussolini's government. For this he was condemned to death and was therefore in exile at the time we met him. He was later amnestied and promptly elected as a deputy to the Italian parliament for his native Sicily; popular favour in a slight change of circumstance often now acclaims those who have recently evaded the assassin. His premature death three years ago from a heart attack while speaking in the Italian Chamber was another loss to Europe of a fine character and brilliant personality; the stress of the years had taken toll.

We left the enchanted islands with reluctance, but were soon recompensed by renewed contact with France; the first point was the little seaside town of Cassis, with a good small harbour. There we met Diana's sister, Nancy Mitford, who was staying in a neighbouring house. The merry screams of the reunited sisters could well have echoed through the short six kilometres to Marseilles, where the large majority were far from being of my political opinion. We then kidnapped the husband of Nancy's hostess, whom I had known long ago, and took him along the coast to St. Tropez, where he found himself very much at home. On the Island of Porquerolles between Marseilles and Cannes we had the joy of meeting a number of friends. The familiar Newbury figure of our country neighbour, Mrs. Reginald Fellowes, was anchored next to us in a magnificent yacht which appeared more likely to be the product of her American mother's Singer sewing-machine millions—she always crossed herself when she saw one of their numerous advertisements—than of English agriculture, in which her speciality was black sheep. Gaston Bergery, in my youth the rising parliamentary hope of the French Radical Party, was there with his American wife, Bettina, whom I remembered from earlier years in Paris for her droll wit in French, American, or an intermediate language of her own, as well as for the exquisite distinction of her appearance. With them in Porquerolles we met for the first time the Marquis and Marquise de Pomereu, whose Louis XIII château at Daubeuf in Normandy, shooting-parties and ingeniously varied guests, have combined for years with the charm of their own company to add to the felicity of our French life. By the time we had passed along the French Mediterranean coast to the Italian frontier, old friends had encompassed us like rose petals in a summer breeze, and the dark years had fallen from us.

Soon over the Italian frontier, we arrived at Portofino, where I had spent my first honeymoon, twenty-nine years before, in the mediaeval fortress on the hill; a poignancy of memory. The fishing village was apparently unaltered, the painted shutters of the pretty little houses seemed still to protect peasant interiors from the mid-day sun, but I was told that they now usually concealed the sumptuous dwellings of millionaires from Milan. Happily in Italy the rich usually have the taste not to spoil the art of the poor. Everything outwardly was just the same, and past and present happiness blended.

At Cannes we had taken on board Hugh Cruddas, a friend of happy companionship in the circle of Gerald Berners at Faringdon. At Portofino we met a friend of his, Lord Bridport, an English sailor who as a collateral descendant of Nelson had inherited the estates in Sicily and the Italian dukedom of Bronté. I understood that he was just what he appeared to be, a staid supporter of the Conservative Party, but sinister rumours were soon reputed to have reached the ears of nervous diplomats in the British Embassy in Rome. We were apparently supposed to have been seen and heard together arm-in-arm on the Piazza of Portofino singing 'Giovinezza'. Needless to say, there was not a word of truth in the tale; those were jumpy days for diplomats.

It was at Portofino that we met Oberto Doria, who took us a short way along the coast to visit the tombs of his ancestors in the romantic San Frutuoso, which can only be approached from the sea, so that in mediaeval times it could never be violated; the family had often contributed legendary figures to the Genoese past. Later we stayed with him at Torrioni, near Pinerolo, the Italian cavalry school. His occupation was the rearing of race-horses to which the exceptional grass of the neighbourhood was remarkably suitable. The pasture was irrigated by cold, clear water from the Italian Alps, and the result was an extraordinary beauty of landscape combining blue Italian skies with grass of Irish green. Old and new Italian friends have made an enduring paradise for us in that enchanted land, whenever the hard exigencies of our lives permitted the time.

The children had been left in the south of France to return with friends to England by train, and we continued alone in the boat with the crew to Rome. Although this tour was intended to be entirely non-political—a relaxation after hard years—I was a little doubtful what would happen in Rome, where such big changes had taken place since I had last been there in a more conspicuous fashion. However, we were received everywhere with the warmest friendship whenever I was recognised. I have always loved the Italian people and agree with a wise French friend who paraphrases Voltaire's aphorism on another subject: if the Italians did not exist, we should have to invent them.

At Rome we began our return journey and set sail again for France, with a resolution to return to Italy, which in our new life as in our old was often gloriously fulfilled. At Cannes we left the boat for the winter, promising ourselves at least a short holiday in the following year before disposing of a possession which in my life occupied too much time as well as being expensive. Having endured so much from the follies of British government, we felt we might at least profit a little from their last absurdity in directing us to this strange but agreeable occupation by the denial of our passports. Beckoning to us now was the exciting prospect of the first journey through France for thirteen years along the once familiar road, the national seven.

Diana's youngest sister Deborah met us in Cannes and brought us back in her car. We decided on a gastronomic tour, as we had with us an excellent guide-book of much earlier days entitled: *Où Déjeunerons-nous?* It was written in lyrical French prose which was almost transmuted to pure poesy on arrival at 'the temples of French gastronomy', and was dedicated to a gentleman whose magnificent stomach had tested these four thousand addresses for the benefit of posterity, but in the end had succumbed, a martyr to the cause.

We had a few well-proven test runs in the vicinity of Cannes and finally settled on the eve of our departure to dine at one of the fine old classic restaurants of that city. Debo insisted on paying for one in three of these occasions as she was now a married woman of some years standing, but looked so young in her diaphanous summer clothing that no one would have believed it. Waiters observed me dining magnificently in the company of Diana, then at the height of her extraordinary beauty, and of this lovely child, enchanting and also seemingly enchanted, for to their astonishment she finally pulled a large wad of notes out of her pocket and paid the immense bill. An old waiter whispered in my ear: '*C'est monsieur qui a la chance*'. He turned out to be a friend of long ago, well content to see my fortunes thus superbly restored. We returned along that road, more golden in our eyes than the one to Samarkand, back to England and politics. I had for a space taken Schiller's advice which is appropriate to an earlier period of life— '*Bleibe die Blumen dem blühenden Lenze, scheine das Schöne und flechte dich Kränze*'—and felt it was allowed for a little after so much; but I then all too soon remembered the concluding line: '*Aber dem männlichen Alter ziemts einem ernsteren Gott zu dienen*'. After this brief interlude, life must again become deadly serious.

Why not be a little more tactful and give an English quotation to describe your feelings at this point?—asked a good friend and most helpful adviser on reading my manuscript. The answer introduces a subject which to me is very interesting. Various themes are best considered in different languages, and personally I know nothing in literature which expresses that particular sentiment quite so exquisitely as the lines of the German poet. After the war I returned to Europe with my French improved and was able for the first time to speak German; extensive reading in the prison years had revealed to me a whole new literature. Consequently, during the European journey I was moved by diverse experiences to think and feel in all three languages; new dimensions of the mind had been opened to me and with the stimulus of these continually changing surroundings, often in scenery and architecture of rare beauty, the new capacity brought a supreme happiness.

Years later, I was with friends in a crowded French restaurant of our particular affection, and, in the relaxed mood of an atmosphere engendered by some of the best things of life, was talking in a rather expansive fashion. My theme was that for those endowed with the blessing of the three main European languages, a new idea might with benefit first be discussed in German, a language as rich as the sunrays glinting among the shadows of the Urwälder, those deep forests, mysterious, imaginative and creative; then lit by the full sunshine of the luminous English, which enables all thought to be presented by its masters with a clarity in some respects unique; then reduced to a lapidary precision by the exquisite sculpture of French, which for good reason is used in treaty and on other occasions when thought and language must be exact. At this point in these discursive observations a figure rose at a neighbouring table, bowed, extended his hand, smiled, shook hands and resumed his seat and his repast without a word spoken. It was not so much the square aspect, suggesting a certain combination of erudition and geniality, as the action which immediately determined his origin and background.

Superficially it may seem that the different way of thinking in the three main languages of Europe must lead to irreconcilable differences of character. Certainly it enriches life when we attain sufficient competence to be able to think in all three, because changing from one to the other can induce an entirely different mood and we see the world with new eyes. Yet the actual experience, which is available to anyone who takes the trouble, discounts an impression that difference of language inevitably produces discord; on the contrary, it can evoke in the thinking of the individual a greater harmony, and this new music of the mind everywhere awaits the European when we have evolved from our present relative infancy to the maturity of the continental future.

From the European journey we returned to farming in Wiltshire and were happy in the sense of roots again in native soil. Yet I had the feeling that the wind of their politics was blowing the soil away from these roots. I farmed in Wiltshire from 1945 until 1951 and it was difficult enough in combination with my resumed activity in English politics directly after the war; it became impossible when frequent European journeys were added after 1949. Close attention to farming in England and to European politics was incompatible, and it was no good deluding myself that I could do two entirely different things at once. The Wiltshire house and farm were sold in 1951 with regret, because we were much attached both to the neighbourhood and the occupation. The question then arose how to combine my political activities in England with the decision to become a European, and what base to establish for this purpose. My over-riding purpose in leaving England in 1951 was to make myself a European, and after seventeen years I can say with confidence that purpose is achieved. It seemed to me essential that some Englishman with a political background should become a European by spending most of his life in Europe, a decision which has given me an experience of Europe unique in British politics.

Ireland was chosen as my base for two main reasons; my old friendships in that country dating as far back as my political campaign on the Irish question in 1920, and my desire to be free of time wasted in combating what then appeared to me as the dull spite, the petty obstruction of the British official world; in retrospect I realise that a good many others were suffering at that time from these minor troubles, but I was naturally not a particular favourite of the bureaucrats, who then had much power of intervention and control in individual lives. Again it was the sentiment of evading a nuisance rather than bitterness which made me move; I felt it better to put myself beyond reach of the troglodytes who impeded my liberty. Above all, I was determined to win the freedom to become a European.

Apart from minor but time-consuming friction with the official world, I was involved before my departure from England in three lawsuits which had nothing to do with the libel courts where I have always so far won the final action. These lawsuits resulted in two losses and one win. Paradoxically, the more important of the losses was a substantial advantage to me. Some difficulty occurred in the printing of my newsletter. I took action in the Chancery Division alleging conspiracy to prevent its production and to impede my legitimate business. After protracted argument, the learned judge decided that there was no concerted action, just a matter of spontaneous combustion on a local and limited scale. However, it was made clear that any concerted action of this kind would be a very serious matter under English law, and this much fortified my position in the future. I was free to circulate my opinions within the limited means at my disposal.

The second loss had at least the charm of simplicity. It concerned a fiscal matter at an elementary level, and in conclusion eminent counsel turned to me with the friendly advice that he would have won the case for anyone in the country except me. I was not interested to take the matter further, as I was thinking already of a larger and more decisive move. The reader may now begin to think that involvement in all these lawsuits indicates a persecution complex after our unpleasant experiences. I was of course much on my guard against any such development after reading during my prison years the main books on psychology in the two languages chiefly concerned. It will however be clear that two of these lawsuits were necessary to save my publishing and farming businesses which were under attack, while the third action, just mentioned, had the simple motive of trying to prevent the loss of a considerable sum of money.

The third case was a triumphant victory which culminated in a roaring farce. At Crux Easton we went in for pig fattening on quite a large scale. We did well with our pigs on their usual noxious diet of the post-war period until suddenly they began to wilt away before our eyes. Despite the heavy and hitherto successful feeding, they got thinner every day. I was naturally in every sense much concerned with the fate of these poor animals, and found at last full exercise in farming for those disturbing, dynamic qualities of which politicians had so much complained. In my efforts to find a cure I called in no less than nine vets in a short space of time; the ninth found both the small parasite responsible and the remedy. Thereafter the pigs rapidly recovered their pristine health and blooming condition.

Fate in official shape struck first; I was served with a swine-fever notice, quickly followed by a foot-and-mouth notice, and then by a summons for starving and consequently ill-treating the pigs. I was incensed. The remedy had been found and we were going ahead with the treatment, but I said nothing. Instead, I went to London to see a good friend, the foremost physician Dr. Geoffrey Evans, who had treated me at the time of my release from prison. He told me that a pig's stomach most closely resembled the human; I became an expert on pigs' stomachs. The case was soon heard. I spent the whole morning cross-examining the official evidence on pigs' stomachs without disclosing an inkling of the defence. To my consternation, just before lunch, the magistrates unanimously and heartily dismissed the case. I was a free man; great was my indignation. Vehemently I protested that I wanted the case to continue so that I could call my evidence; I wanted to make the other side look a proper Charlie. The magistrates, however, decided they had heard more than enough, and apparently some hilarity still prevails in legal circles at the tale of the defendant who so vigorously resisted his own acquittal.

For many reasons large and small it was better to move, and we established what was technically called a main residence in Ireland, and a secondary residence in France, which later became our only home. After the requisite break in English residence, I had the right to spend up to ninety days in England, which were adequate to the meetings and conferences it was necessary to hold. Our first house in Ireland was at Clonfert in County Galway and almost in the exact centre of the country; our house in France was at Orsay in the Chevreuse valley, some twenty kilometres from Paris. It is a small house of exquisite beauty which was built by the architect Vignon, who also designed the Madeleine. He followed the style of Palladio, who added to the perfection of Greek architecture an elevation which nobly displays it. My passion for Hellenism is there consummated at every waking hour. Only one small difficulty arises. The little masterpiece was built to celebrate the victory of General Moreau at Hohenlinden, and was consequently named in 1800, Le Temple de la Gloire; a title consecrated by time, which could not be changed without vandalism. Yet I sometimes feel a slight embarrassment when asked for my address by an Englishman, in simply replying 'the Temple of Glory'; and on occasions I sense a polite restraint of the sentiment: he was always a little 'exalté', and now is right round the bend.

It was originally enacted by Queen Elizabeth I that Clonfert should be the centre of Irish culture, and it gave us an agreeable sense of fulfilling the great and learned Queen's desires to feel that even belatedly her edict was at length implemented. On our arrival, this repository of traditional wisdom consisted of a few small-holdings on the banks of the river Shannon, and so it remained, with our grateful acceptance of the solitude of our surroundings and the friendship of our neighbours. Our own house was rambling and romantic rather than beautiful, and redolent of the usual legends of Cromwellian misbehaviour. At the far end of a short lawn, almost within a stone's throw of our house, was Clonfert Cathedral, a fine example of Norman architecture with early Irish influence, and flanking one of the finest yew avenues I have ever seen even in that country of beautiful trees. Monastic life in the neighbourhood had gone back to very early times, and was centred a few miles away on Clonmacnoise with its seven churches of legendary fame and the contemporary beauty of its curious ruins beside the Shannon.

We moved into Clonfert in 1952, but just before Christmas 1954 our time there came to an end prematurely in another of the fire tragedies which have haunted our family. I was alone in the house, as Diana had gone to London to see her father, except for our elder son Alexander, then aged sixteen. a French cook, and a French chauffeur. My habit was to sleep on the ground floor in the library, where I often worked late, Alexander was on the second floor, the cook and the chauffeur on the third. In the middle of the night I was awakened by Alexander, who had found the room next to his was on fire; the origin of the fire was ultimately traced to the kitchen chimney which contained inflammable resin from the centuries-old burning of wood. It was clear to me at once that the fire had too firm a hold to be checked by anything except the fire brigade, which was fourteen miles away at Ballinasloe. The first thing was to get the cook down from the top floor, the next to send the Frenchman in the car for the fire brigade, as we had no telephone, and finally to save the family pictures, which remained after the previous fire at Rolleston in the middle of the last century.

The picture work went apace with much help from Alexander, and without undue risk except for a light shower of tiles from the roof, as the fire was moving slowly. We had left the French cook sitting peacefully if not happily on the lawn, in the dark and bitter December night, but suddenly heard her cry for help from the window of her third floor room where she had returned to rescue her forgotten savings. The staircase was now cut by the fire, and we had no means of reaching her. We laid on the lawn a heap of clothes which had been thrown from the window, and I wrapped the ends of

a blanket round the wrists of Alexander and held the other ends myself. It
was a drop of about thirty feet from the third floor and I urged her to jump
into the blanket held above the heap of clothes. The lady resisted all
blandishments until the flames were almost singeing her; then she jumped,
the whole considerable bulk of her.

The blanket broke her tumble and the clothes well cushioned her bump.
She rolled off the heap of clothes with the momentum of her fall, over and
over like a barrel across the lawn. She then lay still; we were relieved to find
her breathing heavily, but gently groaning: *'Je meurs, je meurs.'* Feeling her
ankle in the search for broken bones, I enquired: *'Où mourrez vous?'* without
response. My enquiry proceeded up her shinbone to her knee; with a wild
scream she leapt to her feet and ran across the lawn into the adjoining wood,
beyond pursuit and beyond all danger. We tried to continue the work of
picture saving, but by then the dining-room was a furnace and we lost
several old favourites.

At this point, for the benefit of posterity, I should impart a secret of medical
art for the amateur practitioner. I had learnt this trick long ago in an accident
of youthful experience. Two young soldiers were driving at speed from
Dublin to the Curragh in a very old car that I had bought for a song, reputed
to be the original four-cylinder Rolls Royce that carried Charlie Rolls to
victory in a race round the Isle of Man. It had been made roadworthy again
by hands more skilled than mine, and I knew the only way to keep it going at
all was to drive it flat out, as in the take-off of the early aeroplanes I had
recently been piloting. The old car came round a bend in the road bellowing
like a bull and must have been an alarming apparition to an Irish lady riding
in the opposite direction a bicycle heavily laden with all her shopping baskets.
We were each on our correct side of the road, but the sight and uproar of the
approaching monster caused her to wobble across the road to meet us head-on.
The car struck the front wheel of the bicycle and tossed her as the bull does
the toreador. She was personally quite unscathed by any contact with the car,
and happily made a good two-point landing down the road behind us on a
well-sprung under-carriage.

We got out with much trepidation for her safety; she was lying still, but
breathing heavily. I said to my companion: the first thing is to find if any
bones are broken. I felt her ankle, her shin, her knee; at this point with a
loud scream she jumped to her feet and ran down the road. The experience
cost me £50 in the currency of the period, a modest sum in all the circumstances, and it was well worth it, once the emotions of the lady were assuaged,
for it stood me in further and valuable stead. Like my other experiences it
is modestly offered for the warning and advantage of the coming generation.

The fire brigade eventually reached Clonfert, and the Irish are magnificent
on these occasions. They checked the fire before it reached the end wing,
where some of our favourite pictures were hung, but the old house remained

a sad, uninhabitable shell. I knew that some of Diana's favourite drawings, by modern artists like Tchelichev, were in a drawer I could not find, that much of her favourite furniture was burnt, and that the whole business would be a severe shock to her. So we left the cook with kindly neighbours and in the small hours I motored to Dublin with Alexander, who had behaved splendidly throughout, to meet Diana at the airport and break the news before she heard it from others; it was lucky that she was due back that day. The aircraft landed and she came across the tarmac waving and smiling happily as she saw us on the roof of the building awaiting her arrival. Then came to me a strange sense, heavy with the sorrow of things: for once we were in the sad position of the fates of classic tragedy, aware of what is coming to happy mortals who themselves are unconscious of a destiny often far more bitter than the news we had to impart. We went down, and told her what had happened; she took the loss of her treasures with her usual courage. The consolation was that no one suffered any physical injury, except the sense of shock from which our good-natured cook quickly recovered.

Our home in Ireland no longer existed, so we looked around for another roof to cover what was left of us. Luckily, we soon found a delightful house in a simple Regency style overlooking the Blackwater river, for a very moderate price. It was twenty miles north of Cork and about fifteen miles from Lismore, where Diana's sister Deborah went each early spring to a particularly beautiful garden and some excellent salmon fishing. We had a few hundred yards of fishing quite adequate for my occasional and sporadic use of the sport. There is an advantage in fishing of only moderate quality, because you feel no compulsion to have any ghillie assistance or to keep at it in the concentrated professional manner. I used to fish for a bit, then sit down and think or write. For this the surroundings were ideal, because the house was on a little cliff above the river facing south. The cliff was wooded with the perpetual green of the southern Irish climate, and there was room to walk between it and the river and to fish or reflect in the genial winter sunshine in an atmosphere so mild that I remember, in this favoured spot, Riviera sunshine on Christmas Day. The only awkward moment was the hooking of a fish, because the sides of the river at this point were steep and scrambling down to gaff him was quite difficult with my lame leg. However, I managed it often enough to maintain the pleasurable excitement. The only drawback of the agreeable existence in this house was that we soon became too busy to go there enough to enjoy it and to warrant the expense. So we finally sold it in 1963 and established ourselves in France.

Distance now means nothing for all practical purposes, because I can telephone by dial an office in London from Paris as easily and quickly as from London, and, living near an airport, I can get from door to door in little more than half the time it takes to travel by road to London from my Staffordshire homeland. Why did I go to France rather than to any other country?

A meeting at Birmingham Town Hall in 1956.

Debating in the Cambridge Union. The author's speeches in the Oxford and Cambridge Unions after the war were the subject of much comment: Sir Oswald Mosley received 'an ovation from a packed house in the Oxford Union last night' (*News Chronicle*, May 20, 1960). 'Mosley positively radiated sanity' (*Isis*, May 25, 1960). 'It would be a cliché to say that Sir Oswald Mosley's is the most fascinating career of any British politician in this century' (*Cherwell*, October 25, 1961).

Among friends in an East London pub.
The author with Oswald Pirow.

The author with East London friends after a meeting.

Below left With some of the audience after an orderly meeting in Trafalgar Square, which he held every year until 1962. Trafalgar Square was then forbidden to him. *Below right* Walking to an ordinary open-air meeting.

The author today, aged seventy-one.

The Mosley's home near Paris.   European journey.

I suppose the first answer is that it has always been my *pays du bonheur* since I arrived in France to fight as a young airman and trench soldier. I have spent most holidays there whenever I have not been in jail or suffering other political impediment. It is for me always a country of happy memory, warm friendship and congenial life, where I am free from politics. In France I read, think, write, see people but never touch internal politics; that would be as impolite as a guest challenging a host to a controversial argument in his own house. I now feel equally at home in England, France or Germany; in a sense all Europe is my home. In seventeen years of living in Europe, following a lifetime of visits, in the rigours of war and in the felicity of peace, I have become fully and completely a European. It seems to me entirely natural to live in France.

23
The Post-War European Idea

Directly the war was over and I was free to move anywhere in Britain I began the organisation of a political movement. The first action after resuming contact with my friends was the organisation of book clubs, which was followed by the issue of a newsletter in November 1946. Union Movement was formally constituted on February 8, 1948, when fifty-one separate organisations or groups came together and invited me to start again. As the name implies, the aim of Union Movement was to promote this wider union of Europe. We desired first a union of the British people to transcend party differences as a vital preliminary to the union of Europe. A few extracts from my writings and speeches during this period give the keynotes of a campaign which continued through the next fourteen years in public meetings which were large, orderly and continually growing in size and enthusiasm. The circumstances which then brought public meetings in Britain effectively to an end will later be examined in some detail.

As soon as I was free to speak after the war, I returned to the theme of the union of Europe and linked it with the startling development of science during the war, which reinforced my long-standing belief that it should be the main preoccupation of statesmanship. For instance: 'The union of Europe becomes not merely a dream or a desire but a necessity. The union of Europe is no new conception, the only novelty is its present necessity. . . . We must realise that science has rendered any pre-war policy entirely irrelevant in the new age. The idea I now advance is as far beyond both fascism and democracy of 1939 as the jet-propelled airplane is beyond the nineteenth-century steam-engine. The movement of science since 1939 compels a commensurate development in political thinking. Politics must bring in the new world of science to redress the balance of the old world of Europe. The union of Europe is now necessary to the survival of every nation in this continent. The new science presents at once the best opportunity and the worst danger of all history. It has destroyed for ever the island immunity of Britain and compelled the organisation of life in wider areas. It has accelerated evolution, and imposed union with our kindred of Europe if we are to survive. It is in the interest of America to have a partner rather than a pensioner. It is in the interest of the world for a power to arise which can render hopeless the Russian design for the subjection of Europe to communism. We shall thus combine in an enduring union the undying tradition of Europe and the profound revolution of modern science. From that union will be born a civilisation of continuing creation and ever unfolding beauty that will withstand the tests of time' (November 15, 1946).

An essay entitled 'The Extension of Patriotism, The Idea of Kinship' (January 1947) took this thinking further: 'We love our countries, but we must extend that love; the ideal and the practical alike now compel it. The extension of patriotism: that is the necessity and that is the hope. The new patriotism will extend to embrace all of like kind, but will not destroy the values of its kind by seeking the unnatural mingling of the old internationalism.'

Any suggestion that in urging the creation of Europe I was becoming anti-American was refuted by a further phase of the argument in this essay: 'Yet the idea of kinship carries us far beyond Europe; there are kindred of ours in both Americas. Their spiritual life is also ultimately based on nearly three millenia of European history and culture. In the deep realities and further ideals of this age all nature impels them in their final test to feel and think as we do.'

At the same time I was re-thinking the social problem in relation to past experience. The following extract briefly summarises a long process: 'Already the thought and the act of the future take shape. We reconcile the old conflicts and begin to achieve, today in thought and tomorrow in deed, the union of authority with liberty, action with thought, decision with discussion, power with responsibility, vigour with duty, strength with kindness, and service of the people with the attainment of ever higher forms of life' (March 1, 1950).

Between my early post-war speeches relating the urgent need for the union of Europe to the new compulsion of science, and this summary of a social attitude evolved from experience and new thought, two events decisive for my future were the publication in 1947 of *The Alternative*, an extensive account of my new thinking, and my declaration in favour of Europe a Nation during a speech in East London in 1948. *The Alternative* reoriented the whole course of my policy, and the phrase Europe a Nation—afterwards used so extensively in continental thinking and publication—was then uttered for the first time.

In addition to the usual papers supporting the party, we ourselves produced between 1953 and 1959 a monthly magazine called *The European*, in which I advanced these ideas in an analysis signed 'European'. Half of the journal was literary, and contributors wrote from various viewpoints. Diana was the editor; she successfully held together a diverse team and wrote admirably herself.

I did my utmost to spread my ideas throughout Britain, and later throughout Europe with the exception of France. We had long ago resolved to permit ourselves one happy land where I was free from all involvement in politics. It may seem curious to some readers that many of the people who joined with me in the European idea after the war had previously been opponents of the parties with which I was supposed to be associated. In fact, my chief German collaborator of the early post-war period had been strongly opposed to the Nazi Party; he had then been a man of the army, and later of agriculture, rather than of politics.

My objective throughout was to unite as many as possible of those who were in favour of the complete union of Europe, whatever their previous opinions. When we finally arrived at agreement among various European parties at the conference of Venice in 1962, it was only a small minority who had previously been fascists or national socialists. This event was the culmination of years of work, and resulted for me in a success which perhaps was too marked, because people from other countries went home and wondered whether they were wise to have committed themselves to such advanced ideas. The very degree of the achievement created a certain reaction.

I was asked to produce a draft programme to be circulated in advance of the conference, and wrote a document defining my full Europe a Nation policy, which I had advocated ever since 1948. It was, of course, very far ahead of contemporary thinking and I did not expect all of it to be accepted, but after long discussion the programme was adopted with a few amendments, which I gladly accepted.

There was no chairman at this conference. I suggested a gathering in the spirit of the round table of Aachen or King Arthur's round table, but without King Arthur, so that ideas and their authors could prevail by power of thought and persuasion, not by virtue of any vested authority. This implemented my conviction that Europe could only be conducted by an *équipe* of equals, that any attempt to impose any man from one country on the others in a position of authority would be a fatal error. The method worked perfectly, the discussion was calm, clear, orderly, courteous and constructive. I emerged with 90 per cent of the programme which I had come to recommend, far more than I anticipated.

The following is the European Declaration agreed and signed at the Conference of Venice on March 1, 1962: 'We being Europeans conscious of the tradition which derives from classic Greece and Rome, and of a civilisation which during three thousand years has given thought, beauty, science and leadership to mankind; and feeling for each other the close relationship of a great family, whose quarrels in the past have proved the heroism of our peoples but whose division in the future would threaten the life of our continent with the same destruction which extinguished the genius of Hellas and led to the triumph of alien values, now declare with pride our European communion of blood and of spirit in the following urgent and practical proposals of our new generation which challenge present policies of division, delay and subservience to the destructive materialism of external powers before which the splendour of our history, the power of our economy, the nobility of our traditions and the inspiration of our ideals must never be surrendered:

1. That Europe a Nation shall forthwith be made a fact. This means that Europe shall have a common government for purposes of foreign policy, defence, economic policy, finance and scientific development. It does not mean Americanisation by a complete mixture of the European peoples, which is neither desirable nor possible.

2. That European government shall be elected by free vote of the whole people of Europe every four years at elections which all parties may enter. This vote shall be expressed in the election of a parliament which will have power to select the government and at any time to dismiss it by vote of censure carried by a two-thirds majority. Subject to this power of dismissal, government shall have full authority to act during its period of office in order to meet the fast-moving events of the new age of science and to carry out the will of the people as expressed by their majority vote.

3. That national parliaments in each member country of Europe a Nation shall have full power over all social and cultural problems, subject only to the overriding power of European Government in finance and its other defined spheres, in particular the duty of economic leadership.

4. That the economic leadership of government shall be exercised by means of the wage-price mechanism, first to secure similar conditions of fair competition in similar industries by payment of the same wages, salaries, pensions and fair profits as science increases the means of production for an assured market, thus securing continual equilibrium between production and consumption, eliminating slump and unemployment and progressively raising the standard of life. Capital and credit shall be made available to the under-developed regions of Europe from the surplus at present expatriated from our continent.

5. That intervention by government at the three key points of wages, prices, where monopoly conditions prevail, and the long-term purchase of agricultural and other primary products alone is necessary to create the third system of a producers' state in conditions of a free society which will be superior both to rule by finance under American capitalism and to rule by bureaucracy under communist tyranny. It is at all times our duty in the solidarity of the European

community to assist each other to combat the destruction of European life and values from without and from within by the overt and covert attack of communism.

6. That industries already nationalised will be better conducted by workers' ownership or syndicalism than by state bureaucracy, but the system of the wage-price mechanism will, in full development, make irrelevant the question of the ownership of industry by reason of the decisive economic leadership of elected government, and will bring such prosperity that workers will have no interest in controversies which belong to the nineteenth century.

7. With the creation of Europe a Nation as a third power strong enough to maintain peace, a primary object of the European government will be to secure the immediate and simultaneous withdrawal of both Russian and American forces from the occupied territories and military bases of Europe. Europe must be as strongly armed as America or Russia until mutual disarmament can be secured by the initiative of an European leadership which will have no reason to fear economic problems caused by disarmament, as has capitalist America, nor to desire the force of arms for purposes of imperialist aggression as does communist Russia.

8. The emergence of Europe as a third great power will bring to an end the political and military power of UNO, because these three great powers will then be able to deal directly and effectively with each other. The peace of the world can best be maintained by direct and continuous contact between these three great powers which represent reality instead of illusion and hypocrisy. The production of nuclear weapons will be confined to these three great powers until mutual disarmament can be secured.

9. Colonialism shall be brought to an end. A way will be found to maintain or to create in Africa states under government of non-European but African origin amounting to about two-thirds of the continent, and other states under government by peoples of European and Afrikaaner origin amounting to about one-third. In non-European territory, any European who chose to remain should stay without a vote or political rights. He would be in the same position as any resident in another country, subject to the maintenance of basic human rights within their own communities, by reciprocal arrangement between European and non-European territories. Conversely, any non-European remaining in European territory would have neither vote nor political rights, subject to the maintenance of the same basic human rights. Multi-racial government breaks down everywhere in face of the non-European demand for one man one vote which they learnt from the West, and becomes a squalid swindle of loaded franchises to postpone the day of surrender rather than to solve the problem. Better by far is the clean settlement of clear division. Europe must everywhere decide what it will hold and what it will relinquish. The Europeans in union will have the power of decision. Today they lack only the will. We will hold what is vital to the life of Europe, and we will in all

circumstances be true to our fellow-Europeans, particularly where they are now threatened in African territory.

10. The space of a fully united Europe including the lands to be liberated by American and Russian withdrawal, the British Dominions and other European overseas territories, and approximately one-third of Africa is a just requirement for the full life of the Europeans in a producer and consumer system which shall be free of usury and capitalism, of anarchy and communism. Within the wide region of our nation the genius of modern science shall join with the culture of three millenia to attain ever higher forms of European life which shall continue to be the inspiration of mankind.'

The original draft was clearer, notably in point 4, requiring initially similar basic conditions, later to be increased as science increased production. Work was done rapidly in German, and in French, which the Italians understood.

This document was so far ahead of contemporary thinking that it was a surprise to many people, particularly as some of the signatories were supposed to be ardent nationalists. Some of the participants in the conference were in sentiment passionately involved on different sides of the bitter dispute then raging in the Tyrol. It was therefore to many still more surprising that they should together have signed the following addendum to the European Declaration: 'On the occasion of coming together to decide and publish a European Declaration, the Conference resolved to do its utmost to end the fratricidal struggle between European patriots in the Tyrol where present difficulties will be terminated automatically by the constitution of a common European Government and economic system which will guarantee freedom of movement, language and opinion. We appeal to all Europeans to cease at once violence to each other and to work together to create our Europe with the utmost speed rather than to lose lives and energies in quarrels which will disappear with the divisions of the present states in the future Europe. The Conference therefore invites the two parties to come together and to discuss a settlement, and offers its mediation for this purpose.'

The Conference provided striking evidence of what can be done when Europeans are gathered round the conference table even when some of the participants are fiercely divided in sentiment and interest on particular questions. If these questions can be lifted out of a small context into a great design all things become possible. This achievement provided some evidence in support of my long-sustained contention on the making of Europe: great things can only be done in a great way.

The Conference went further than signing the Declaration, and in addition agreed the following points:

'The Conference decided as soon as possible to constitute a Bureau de Liaison between the national parties of Europe who have accepted a united policy, Fourth of March, 1962. The Conference further resolved that the representatives of the parties should henceforth meet every two months to maintain liaison. The Conference recommended the parties represented, and all other parties which may adhere to the declaration, to change their party names to The National Party of Europe. The British, Belgian and German representatives expressed their intention at once to ask their parties to make this change of name.

'The Conference further expressed the hope that the parties represented would as soon as possible go beyond the already accepted principle of common policy and regular liaison, to accept the principle of central direction. This means that equal representatives of the parties will meet regularly at a round table and will direct in principle common action of the parties which will be carried out in detail by the parties in their respective countries.'

This was certainly more than I expected to get, the success of the Conference from my point of view was complete. The prospect was open for a National Party of Europe to which men of all opinions could adhere, provided they were agreed on the one decisive point of making Europe a Nation. Differences of opinion on other subjects could be left until this overriding purpose was achieved. Afterwards debate could be resumed on other subjects and, if necessary, new party alignments could be formed.

It is normal after a success which exceeds expectation to encounter a period of reaction and frustration. We did not at this stage get beyond a series of meetings to establish the liaison decided by the Conference. They were good meetings and consolidated agreement, but they did not take the matter further to establish a permanent organisation in the Bureau de Liaison on which depended the subsequent central direction and eventual constitution of a National Party of Europe. The basic difficulty was that we had not the means to follow it up; finance was lacking. There is never much money in the affluent society still prevailing throughout Europe for large designs of change. Money without vision is quite content with things as they are. Before extreme crisis there is always more money available for something mediocre, limited and obsolete like a return to the old nationalism, and the pull of money is strong because nothing effective can be done without it.

Lack of resources prevented the immediate achievement of the next stage, and in the consequent period of delay many things happened. Hopes of an early making of Europe receded for several reasons. The British Government not only missed every opportunity to take the initiative in Europe after the war, but still maintained an attitude which impeded any early hope of effective union. All existing European governments were certainly opposed to any union so complete as we advocated. Meantime, German hopes in particular of any redress of their grievances through the union of Europe became more and more bitterly frustrated. The most ardent Europeans were to be found among the Germans in the early post-war period, but the destruction of many hopes and the continually increasing sense of insult, humiliation and repression among many of them awakened again in some degree a sense of the old nationalism. The Conference of Venice was for the time being the last hope of merging the old patriotisms in a wider patriotism of Europe.

Germans had seen some prospect of the reunion of their country within the union of Europe. This reunion is for them naturally an overriding desire, as strong as our feeling would be if England were divided at the Trent and the northern or southern section was occupied by a foreign power. There was a serious hope that their disaster would be overcome by the union of Europe, neither by war nor turmoil, or even by the strength of demand for justice from so great a power, but rather by the assurance to be given to Russia and the world that a Germany truly integrated into a reasonable and contented Europe would no longer be a menace to anyone. The failure of this European policy reduced to the vanishing point all hope of a natural and pacific reunion of Germany within Europe. The hope too of ceasing to become a pariah power and of regaining normal, great power status within the greater Europe was also banished. When reason is assassinated, unreason enters. Nationalism, however forlorn its prospects in the new conditions, is born again.

The treatment of individuals too contributed much to the revival of nationalism. The men involved in the revival of nationalism were by no means all ex-national socialists. On the contrary, many of the leading figures had been strong opponents of that party, and the majority of the rank and file were too young to have had any involvement. At an earlier stage young Germans fresh from the army, and particularly from the S.S. regiments, were passionately European and entirely supported my advanced European ideas. I had heard from many of them long before I was free to travel, and had an insight into what they were then thinking which is perhaps almost unique. I know that it was only the long and bitter story of suppression and persecution which drove many of them back to the old nationalism. Particularly resented was the treatment of soldiers whose only crime was to obey orders. Some of these men were doomed from the start; if they did not obey when the order was given, they were shot on the spot by existing authority, and if they did obey they were subsequently executed by the victorious allies. Post-war persecution was even extended in less degree to men who could not conceivably be connected with any crime.

Such treatment may be illustrated by the conspicuous case of a post-war friend of mine who was a soldier and airman completely free from any suspicion of any crime. Hans Ulrich Rudel was the supreme German hero of the last war. He won every medal the air force had to give and a special decoration had then to be invented for him. He destroyed five hundred Russian tanks with his own machine, and also a Soviet battleship. After losing a leg, he flew again, was shot down behind the Russian lines and escaped. It was an epic of heroism, but owing to the post-war boycott even his autobiography could not be properly circulated in his own country to obtain the large sale it would normally have achieved. It must surely be a case unique in history that such a national hero should thus be without honour in his own country immediately after a war. Consequently, the story of his air exploits in the war could only be published effectively in Britain and France. My small publishing house brought out the book in Britain and sold an astonishing number of hardback copies before it went into a paper edition. Group Captain Bader, D.S.O., D.F.C., the English air ace—whom I did not know—wrote the preface as a tribute to Rudel; Bader too, in the best tradition of the air, exerted himself to secure medical treatment and a wooden leg for Rudel when he was a prisoner-of-war. Clostermann, the French air ace and later a Gaullist deputy, wrote the preface to the French edition.

Was this really the world that British authority wished to create in Germany after the war, a society in which brave men could be so treated because they would not recant an opinion or bow to the victor? British and American authority at that time had a considerable responsibility for the creation of this general atmosphere, and in course of time persistence in revenge produced a strong and inevitable reaction. It was contrary to the whole British tradition of magnaminity in victory, as I have always understood it, and was an act of folly and of mean spite which now brings a nemesis that will take time and effort to exorcise. Personally I was against the whole vile and squalid business, as I then regarded it, and after mature reflection still regard it. Rudel, for instance, had been entirely innocent of any offence except an heroic war record in defence of his country, and the refusal to recant previous opinion which became irrelevant in his adherence to the post-war European idea. If such a man could be so treated, it is not difficult to conceive the treatment and the consequent sentiment of men less well known and protected by reputation. After the war we had a unique opportunity to bring together brave men who had fought for their countries in the union of Europe and in a wider patriotism. Not only was this frustrated; men were persecuted for the crime of patriotism and for no other reason in their past record. If the past lives again in any degree, the fault lies with the policy for which the British Government was primarily responsible.

Union was achieved in sentiment, but for the time being persecution and repression impeded it in fact. Delay was imposed on us after the achievement of Venice not only by material limitations. Disillusionment and bitterness then ensued in the frustration of European hopes and in particular in the treatment of many Germans who had committed no crime. This affected in various ways all Europeans who strove to transcend the past and to achieve union. The protagonists of Venice were then thrown back into nationalism, and in some cases of the lesser groups into a wild futility. This was frustration, but not defeat. Nothing great is ever realised in one short, sharp effort. Supreme ideas come in like the tide of the sea. A wave reaches up the beach, and then recedes. Succeeding waves for a time do not reach so far. Yet in the end a wave goes farther still as the tide comes in, the force of Nature is within it. Nothing in the end can prevent the victory of the Europeans, who will come from all countries and from all parties to the final achievement. The work of Venice was done, and nothing can alter or reduce the reality of that fact. What has been done will one day be done again, on a broader front and in a greater way.

For me therefore Venice remains a massive achievement. It is idle ever to suppose that after so big an advance everything will go quite smoothly ahead; that is the way neither of nature nor of politics. Setbacks, delays, frustrations are bound to occur, and must in due course by continued effort be surmounted. What matters is that we proved it was possible to bring together men from the most diverse standpoints and with the strongest national sentiments in an European policy as complete and wholehearted as Europe a Nation. Crisis and the final bankruptcy of lesser ideas will bring us back to that position with many new participants drawn from various parties who today lag far behind the advanced idea. We were as usual in action before our time, but we proved that all is possible when time is ripe.

I did not win a position of freedom to express my opinions in Europe without some opposition, but I never encountered the savage spite which I have experienced from certain quarters in my own country, which fortunately are by no means typical of the British people. Any difficulty I have met on the Continent has usually been instigated by British officials who are supposed to be charged with the duty of assisting rather than attacking British subjects. It was certainly their action which led to my legal clash with Dr. Adenauer, for which he finally made handsome and indeed generous amends.

In the case of those who had never been fascists or national socialists there could be no overt objection to my method of accepting or establishing contact with men of all previous opinions provided they seemed to me to be genuine, wholehearted Europeans, but any man approaching me from the circles of those previous parties or administrations at once created a furore to which I was quite indifferent if he appeared to me to be a good European. A highly intelligent German in this category saw clearly at the end of the war that the only hope for all the Europeans was the making of Europe. However, his most normal and legitimate entry into politics produced a convulsion of acute hysteria in the British occupation authority, because at the end of the war he had occupied a conspicuous position in the propaganda ministry. He was too young to have played much part in previous events, and nothing in the way of war crimes or any misconduct except doing his duty as an official of his country could possibly be urged against him. In fact, no move was made against him until he was in contact with me. Then the whole fury of the British occupation authority descended upon him and the German government was ultimately dragged into the matter.

The British authorities were playing a happy game of ducks and drakes with the basic principles of British justice, starting with Habeas Corpus; these officials had been so accustomed during the war to making all that old-fashioned stuff look silly at their will and fancy. However, on this occasion they were to learn their error. When this German was arrested in January 1953 by the British authorities and assailed with a shower of ridiculous charges, I introduced to the scene Mr. Lane, of the English solicitors' firm of Marsh and Ferriman, who acted for me during and since the war. He had shown much character and ability in a stand for prime principles of British law in the Second War, after serving as a soldier in the First and being involved in Mr. Churchill's post-war frolic at Archangel. He briefed Mr. Scott Henderson, K.C., the Recorder of Hastings. Sir Ivone Kirkpatrick of the Foreign Office and his supporters then quickly learnt that British law still existed even within the arbitrary dictatorship of the occupation authority. The prisoner had been held incommunicado in violation of every principle of British justice, but was now quickly produced in court when the British solicitor and counsel appeared in Germany. The next phase was in the German courts, though it appeared possible that British official inspiration had something to do with the matter. In the end, all charges against this German were quashed in the German High Court, and he went free; he had done nothing whatever except express his political opinions openly and publicly.

While the matter was by our standards still *sub judice*, however, Dr. Adenauer weighed in with a curious contribution. He suggested in a world Press conference that the German was guilty of treason against the German state, and shocking to relate, the 'Ausländer' Mosley was at the back of the business. Then occurred an unprecedented event in contemporary German experience, for the 'Ausländer' in question went straight to Germany and demanded the institution of libel proceedings against the German Chancellor in the German courts. It was at first tactfully suggested to me that it was not the habit to bring libel actions against chancellors, particularly for foreigners. I persisted, and the matter went forward with honourable and capable assistance from German lawyers.

The action was about to come into court, when another surprising event occurred. Chancellor Adenauer suddenly came across with a handsome apology, published to the world. He had not used the words ascribed to him and there had been a misunderstanding, there was no suggestion against me, and finally the charges against the German had been quashed in the German High Court: '*Es ist daher bedauerlich*', it is therefore regrettable that Sir Oswald Mosley should have suffered any inconvenience in the matter. This seemed to me a fair and generous gesture, and I met it appropriately in a Press conference in Bonn. Thus democracy came to Germany under unexpected auspices.

It seems to me a fair reading of the facts that British officials were directly responsible for this whole trouble. They had no love for me because for years I had attacked their policies in my own country in terms which were vehement but proved finally to be an understatement, when the full facts came to light about the true character and long-concealed record of some of the favourite sons of the British Foreign Office. In addition, I had publicly denounced from the start the proceedings at Nuremberg and still more the pursuit of vengeance against a whole people. Retroactive law is always to me an outrage. This device by which any political opponent can be murdered at any time became doubly an outrage when judges were drawn from the Russian communist power, which had been guilty of crimes even worse, much worse in time of peace than any which could be charged against any German in time of war. When men commit crimes like the murder of helpless prisoners, they can be charged and dealt with under ordinary law. Any man thus guilty in any position should have been so treated at once, whether high or low. The creation of special, retroactive law and the pursuit of vengeance over the life-time of a generation can poison the whole European future. From the start and throughout I attacked this policy and its authors.

I became still more unpopular in Foreign Office circles when I was later praised for seeking European reconciliation. A successful German publisher wrote of me: 'Happy memories from a sad period are particularly unforget-table—and among them for us Germans, is the fact that since 1945 Sir Oswald Mosley had been the first, and for a long time was the only Englishman, who spoke and wrote, in his own country, passionately and with clear vision for us Germans, without any regard to the burning hatred he thereby evoked. His great book, *The Alternative*, published in 1947, is one of the most courageous and far-seeing books in the English language; it is one of those books to which one constantly returns, and is never laid aside without the greatest admiration for the mind of a statesman who points the way to a new future for Europe. The watchword Europe a Nation which later gave our review its name; was here formulated as a policy for the first time. This fact alone makes Oswald Mosley a prophetic phenomenon and directing spirit in the otherwise confused thinking of our time. . . . A character, whose destiny with others of this kind may be that greatness which only future generations can fully recognise.'[1]

It was an offence to the British official world that I should thus be addressed by the people whom they were trying to persecute, and their spite long pursued me in a trivial and often comical fashion. A ridiculous incident is worth recording which normally would merit no notice, because it is typical of this attitude and practice. Years later a British official was in very free circulation in a German city; his exact position was obscure to me, but he was undoubtedly and openly in the employment of the British Government. He had apparently the habit of attempting to ingratiate himself in a social way with the Germans by the difficult and always rather ludicrous process for an Englishman of behaving in a manner more German than the Germans. This

---

[1] *Nation Europa*, May 1954. Again I hope the reader will forgive my publication of these personal references for reasons given in Chapter 10.

worthy of the English establishment approached a friend of mine at a party, presumably because he was prominent in the industrial and social life of Germany, and said after much circumlocution: 'Why waste time with Mosley, who politically is a dead man?' This did not go well, as he was met with the reply: 'Why then do you waste time in trying to kill a man already dead?'

After further preamble, he launched another attack: 'Anyhow, you know that Mosley is a Jew'. This was all related to me with much merriment at a subsequent gathering where everyone was well aware of my ancestry and antecedents. What is the man like?—I asked—and one of the ladies replied with general assent: '*Ein ekelhafter kleiner Spion*'. Once again love's labour appeared to be lost. This man's salary was paid by the taxpayers; a curious employment for public funds, and it seemed to me a strange idea after all had been said and done, that the British government's cause could be advanced by a play on supposed German anti-semitism, which in that circle did not exist. Did this kind of thing make me bitter? Not at all; if you have long been the professional recipient of custard pies from the principal clowns of the political circus, with every opportunity to throw them back carefully removed, you are not annoyed by the antics of the chap who sweeps up the dirt in the corner.

The fight for freedom to express my opinions on the continent of Europe continued; nothing else was involved except this liberty which was one of the freedoms for which the allies claimed to have fought the war and was after-wards consecrated in the instruments of the United Nations which were signed by these and other powers. The next mile-stone in this arduous journey to liberty was a libel action in Italy against the communist paper *Unità*, which followed closely on the conference at Venice, whose outcome had apparently alarmed and enraged it. This was the most powerful communist journal in Europe supporting the strongest Communist Party. I was told this party had not been successfully challenged in the law courts on the Continent since the war. Nevertheless, I brought an action for criminal libel; they were con-demned and fined in the first court in front of three judges, and their con-viction was upheld by five judges in the court of appeal. The suggestion of the newspaper was that I was the British Hitler, and was responsible for political crimes. The court found that I could not be called the British Hitler, and pressed the other side closely on the point of political crimes. It was then admitted that there was not a shred of evidence to support this allegation, but it was contended that such was my personality and character that I must be the *fons et origo* of political crimes in general. It was not surprising that the judges rejected this defence, and to the considerable indignation of the communists present, they went down with a bump.

The next lawsuit of note was in Germany in October 1964 against the *Stuttgarter Nachrichten*. In the course of a long general attack on me it made a suggestion which had already been dealt with in the English courts. The beginning of the story was a small anti-semitic society founded around the year 1920 by a veterinary surgeon called Arnold Leese, with the name Imperial Fascist League. After languishing in obscurity for nearly half a century without any increase in the handful of members with which they began, and despite a change of name to the National Socialist Movement after the war, it received some continental publicity which suggested that the leader of the group at that time, a Mr. Colin Jordan, had something to do with me. In the course of some interlocutory proceedings in the appeal court on October 9, 1962, Lord Denning made it quite clear that on the evidence presented this was not the case. The quite unfounded suggestion that this group had something to do with me, however, continued until I proceeded in the German courts against the *Stuttgarter Nachrichten*, which, on learning the facts, apologised, paid costs and thus made honourable amends.

It has often been the habit of my opponents to give obscure people publicity and then to fasten them on to me. The method was even more marked before the war, when little societies of all kinds used to abound and odd people I had never heard of were alleged to be in some way my associates. Directly you are in unorthodox politics every freak—and there is always a plentiful supply in my native land—is ascribed to you, sometimes in innocence but more often in *malice propense*. Caricature is after all one of the oldest and most effective weapons in English politics. It may take the form of a clever, denigratory drawing, or even more effectively of a man made up to look like you in some respects walking down the street and behaving in a ridiculous fashion. There was quite a bit of that kind of thing before the war, but since then the usual supply of crackpots has seemed to me to have no motive except their own folly.

Law actions on the Continent were necessary not only in my own defence but to enable my ideas to be freely discussed throughout Europe by serious people in a manner worthy of real politics. They certainly have been so discussed, analysed, and often I gratefully acknowledge acclaimed by people whose opinion I deeply value. It may be asked why I tried to advance European policy in this way instead of seeking to support Mr. Churchill in the efforts of his Fulton and Zurich speeches to promote European union. The answer is two-fold; firstly, the policy then suggested was roughly the policy I had proposed in 1937 in *The World Alternative*, which I felt was outdated and surpassed, and someone must point the way to a far more complete and advanced policy for Europe; secondly, while I thought Mr. Churchill was sincere in this new impulse, I did not believe these utterances represented the view of the Tory Party, and my view was soon proved correct, for the future conservative Prime Minister, Mr. Eden, said of Britain's entry into Europe: 'This is something which we know in our bones we cannot do' (January 19, 1952), and the Conservative Party was thrown into precipitate retreat from the policy Mr. Churchill had proposed to them.[1] Labour, of course, was always a non-starter for the union of Europe until the threatened collapse of their nineteenth-century system and the fatigue of America with the purposeless orbit of its neo-socialist satellite impelled them toward the outer darkness of Europe which they had so long feared and so consistently rejected.

My idea was Europe a Nation, first stated in East London in 1948, for years advocated by me in my own country and subsequently discussed and widely supported in Europe. All I have ever asked is the freedom to advocate this idea openly and publicly and to invite men of all parties and past opinions to support it. I believe that nothing but a clear, great and decisive idea can surmount the past and make Europe. For this freedom to discuss ideas I was prepared to fight to the end. I wrote long ago: first comes the idea, the rest will follow. My ideas were conceived in the service of Europe, and many of them have certainly won a far wider measure of acceptance today than when they were first advanced. Much more remains to be done, and in Europe as in Britain I strive for the acceptance of ideas which I hope will first win the assent and later the enthusiasm of the peoples, when they feel the necessity for new politics and learn to love a new vision.

[1] Another account of Mr. Churchill's own attitude was published in *The Times* on September 23, 1967 under the heading: Churchill's 'Non' to Europe: 'Professor Meyer Burstein, 41, a former consultant to the United States Defence Department, who is here to take up the first chair of the Economics and Finance of Investment at Warwick University, blames Sir Winston Churchill for Britain's lack of rapport with Europe. "After the war he developed this close relationship with America in order to maintain Britain's position as a major power," says Burstein, who hastens to add that he is a great admirer of Churchill. "In his second term as Prime Minister he was invited to join Europe, but declined." '

24
North Kensington
Later Renewal of
Communist Violence

I SHALL now describe how a sudden renewal of violence, in conjunction with the government's attitude and action, effectively brought to an end the large and orderly public meetings which I addressed throughout Britain during fourteen years, from 1948 to 1962. Even before the post-war foundation of the party in February 1948, during the period of book clubs and conferences, we held some public meetings which were successful and undisturbed; in the fifties they were the largest then being held in the country and often very enthusiastic. The only trouble of any kind I remember was one boy being put out of Birmingham Town Hall for throwing a firework. Television was already taking its toll of the old English habit of public meetings, and even the main party leaders were finding it difficult to get audiences, but our meetings continued to fill some of the largest halls in the country.[1] The policies we were advocating will be described, but there is not much more to relate during a long period, because of the tranquility of the whole experience. Also my picture of the post-war years is deliberately foreshortened in order to avoid too much entry into contemporary controversy, which is not the purpose of this book.

The main event in these years was my candidature at North Kensington in the election of 1959. Our local branches had fought local elections on their own initiative throughout the post-war years, but this was our first parliamentary fight. It was what Mr. Asquith described as a 'dark and difficult adventure' before his successful by-election at Paisley, but the background of my political enterprise on this occasion made it a good deal darker and

[1] e.g., Free Trade Hall Manchester, and Birmingham Town Hall.

more difficult than any normal election. We had given warning ever since 1952 that the Government's policy of permitting unlimited coloured immigration was a grave error which would inevitably cause trouble; in fact, it gratuitously imported into Britain difficulties already evident in America. There had been considerable white versus black riots in North Kensington during the previous summer of 1958, and feeling on this matter was still smouldering. I thought that someone should give this electorate the opportunity to express legally and peacefully by their votes what they felt about the issues involved, and clearly I had the best chance to establish these difficult conditions and get a fair verdict. Yet I knew that my entry would be misrepresented as an attempt to exploit the situation, and that the excitement of my arrival might be alleged to have caused further violence if anything of the kind should occur. It was a difficult decision to take, but I felt it my duty to stand and to face the problem. Otherwise history might well record that the British people had never been given a chance to express their opinion on the acute question of coloured immigration.

We had one local branch covering South and North Kensington, where there had never been any trouble until the sudden riots, in which our people took no part except to hold meetings asking for calm and order. My first act in the election address was to reiterate our appeal to settle the issue by votes and not by violence, and I asserted my whole personal influence to secure order, and fair, peaceful discussion. The result at least in this respect was a success, for after all the previous disorder there was no trouble of any kind in this election, and from that date to this there has been no revival of mass violence in North Kensington. This was a surprise to many people. Even the usually sensible Sir Patrick Spens, Conservative M.P. for the next constituency of South Kensington, said: 'It is absolutely certain that there will be more trouble in the area if Sir Oswald Mosley persists in the views he expressed in his recent speech in Kensington'; which, of course, advocated the end of immigration. He was proved wrong, and I admit it required some effort to keep things in the control of reason. The meetings were the largest open-air gatherings I have ever addressed since the war, and the development of the campaign produced an extraordinary mass enthusiasm. I had one indoor meeting to launch the campaign in the large hall of the local municipal baths, which was packed. An outside questioner asked me why I had come to North Kensington, and the whole audience shouted: 'Because we asked him'.

The wider issues involved will be considered later in discussing the African question and the complex of black and white interests, but the main principles on which we fought this election can be briefly stated. I stood on the general policy of the party covering British, European and world issues which was summarised in more detail than is usual in an election address, but our attitude on the question of coloured immigration was made clear beyond a shadow of doubt. This was not a racialist policy, for I held to my principles already described of opposing any form of racialism in a multi-racial Empire. Our Empire was gone before 1959, and it was already clear to me that much of the new Commonwealth would not last long and that the future of Britain now lay in Europe. Nevertheless, hostility to other peoples or the domination for any purpose of one people by another—in my reiterated definition the sole reason on which a charge of 'racialism' can rest—remained as alien as ever to my beliefs and policy.

The principles of racialism had nothing whatever to do with the issue in North Kensington. The injury to our people in suddenly importing to already disgracefully overcrowded areas a large population with an altogether different standard and way of life would have been just as grave if it had been Eskimos or angels instead of Negroes. For nearly two generations the repeated pledge to rebuild the slums and to house our people properly had been broken. Without lifting a finger to fulfil the forty-year-old promise the Government piled a new population on top of people already suffering from an acute housing shortage and widespread slum conditions. The state of housing in much of North Kensington was already monstrous before the new influx.

British people and Jamaican immigrants were equally the victims of these conditions. The Jamaicans had already been hard hit by British government policy in their own country through the breach of binding undertakings to buy their sugar, which had resulted in widespread unemployment and mass hunger. These poor people were driven to Britain by the lash of starvation, and their arrival created inevitably a still more acute housing shortage, coupled with the threat of unemployment to British people if the competition for jobs became more acute in industrial crisis. A situation which was bound to make trouble was created by the deliberate policy of British government, and has resulted in a series of new laws ineffectively attempting to remedy or mitigate the error.

Much damage had already been done, but not nearly so much as was to follow from continuing and increasing immigration. My proposal was simply to repatriate immigrants to their homeland with fares paid and to fulfil the Government's pledge to buy sugar from Jamaica by long-term and large-scale contracts, which together with other measures, such as bauxite production, would have restored that island to prosperity.[1] The overwhelming majority of these people would have been only too glad to go home in these conditions. I held a Press conference after the election, sitting between an Indian and a Negro who had won the D.F.C. in the war and had wide contacts and experience in the coloured community. He stated that most of the people he knew would be delighted to return home for as little as two-thirds of the

---

[1] It was always made clear that no coloured people with roots in the country—e.g., who had been here before the Second World War—would be in any way concerned; also that students would be welcome as they always had been. The problem was a sudden, large influx of recent immigrants as a result of such errors as reducing sugar purchases from Jamaica and buying from Cuba.

wages they were getting in Britain, if they could find employment in their own country. This problem was economic and social, not racial.

It is true that it was complicated and aggravated by a different way and standard of life. If you are living in badly over-crowded conditions, it irritates you to have a lot more people dumped on top of you, and it annoys you still more in these circumstances of compulsory intimacy if they live in an altogether different way. Add to this the inevitable arrival under cover of a mass immigration of gangsters and vice peddlars seeking a larger and more affluent market than they had in their own island and finding it in a confined area of Britain; you then have every ingredient of trouble gratuitously imported. North Kensington quickly became alive with rackets, white and black, touching chiefly accommodation and what some regard as amusement. The Government appeared either entirely impotent or quite unwilling to deal with the resultant situation. They apparently feared that any attempt to cope with the problem of immigration might have adverse reactions on their general Commonwealth policy, a policy I considered equally mistaken.

It appeared to me right in my election fight to give the British people as a whole some idea of what was happening in this area—even half a mile away up the hill in the same constituency, they had no idea—as well as giving its inhabitants the chance to vote for another policy. If the policy of the old parties were followed further it seemed to me that in Britain would be all the ingredients of a tragedy. Coming events in America were already casting their shadow. The Americans had inherited their problem, but British government deliberately created our problem. This seemed to me in long-term policy to be raving insanity. The situation was aggravated in Britain by the low payment of skilled people like doctors and nurses which drove them abroad or out of the profession, while still lower paid substitutes were provided by immigrants whose services were urgently required in their own countries. The brain drain derived from the anarchic economic policy of the old parties, who for years had rejected Government intervention in favour of the highly skilled, so long advocated in my post-war policy of using the wage-price mechanism. The main parties were almost equally responsible for this whole complex of muddle and weakness, and once again it rested on me to oppose what I felt to be a vast error.

It needed both skill and resolution to get through an election fight in these conditions just after serious rioting in the neighbourhood, and to do it with the fixed determination to prevent any form of disorder or violence. I was, of course, extremely careful to treat both black and white with equal fairness, going even beyond my usual practice in courtesy to a black questioner. I entered their houses and talked to their leaders when invited; some of them were men of considerable intelligence. It seemed to me, incidentally, that this experience might be valuable in possible later dealings with the problem of black and white relations in a far larger sphere; it certainly gave me an insight into psychological questions I could never otherwise have acquired.

My relations with the white electorate apparently went from strength to strength. Not only were the open-air meetings enthusiastic, but on all sides I was received with the warmest friendship. The canvass was a winning canvass, if I ever saw one. It is true that the process of election canvass was reputed to have become much less reliable since the war and the far-off days when I used to make the winding-up speech for Labour at most by-elections; after the eve of the poll rally I had been able in the company of the skilled election agents to calculate from the canvass returns with a tiny margin of error what the result next day would be. It was true also that such fantastic legends had been spread concerning the alleged ferocity of our party members before the war that electors might have been chary of giving an adverse reply to our canvassers, but the number of women among them, including Diana, and my habit of walking alone or with one other man or woman through the constituency quickly dissipated most of this nonsense. Nevertheless, when everything was taken into account, it looked all over like a winning fight. More significant than any canvass to the experienced eye was the reception from the children who swarmed in the streets on polling day and greeted us with a favour as extreme as the disfavour they showed to our opponents. Electors may conceal the truth from canvassers but not from their own children in the free and intimate life of North Kensington. We looked like being in by thousands. It was therefore one of the chief surprises of my life when we polled only eight per cent of the votes recorded.

I was determined if possible to find out what had happened, and sufficient irregularities had occurred to get an election petition on its legs. It was admittedly to some extent what the lawyers call a fishing expedition, but I had to make a start. As usual in the English courts during recent years, I took the case myself, and as usual was treated with the utmost fairness and courtesy by the judges. Nothing of much substance came to light, and we got nowhere. The rules of British electoral procedure had been sufficiently fulfilled, and the rest was a matter of criticising the system and not of securing any redress from the law courts. As everyone is aware who knows anything of our electoral system, we are far from the method employed in some of the more suspicious Latin countries, where representatives of all parties remain within view of the ballot boxes throughout the poll, not to see how anyone votes but to ensure there is no substitution of boxes, and at the close of poll accompany the precious receptacles on the ceremonial drive to the place of the count with the hands of all party representatives firmly resting on the boxes in case anyone is around who is a good enough conjuror to make votes disappear. This procedure may seem exaggerated to the English tradition, but I would suggest there is room to tighten up the electoral procedure at present laid down by our law.

The election remains a mystery to me, but I do not accept the view of many of my friends that the result was necessarily incorrect. There is another explanation for the disparity between appearance and fact, between all the overt evidence to the experienced eye of a winning election and the decision of the ballot boxes. In fact, the contrary explanation coincides with the analysis I have already made of the movement of mass opinion, both historic and actual. An electorate never moves decisively except under severe economic pressure, which is nearly always unemployment.

There is no doubt from the reception we got in North Kensington that the sympathy of the people was with us, that they liked my policy and me, but they were practically all enjoying full employment and the high and increasing wages of the affluent society. Most of them, too, had either personal or childhood memories of unemployment, the misery and mass starvation of the thirties. They might be very angry at the conditions gratuitously imposed upon them by the old parties through sudden mass immigration, but they would think twice before upsetting the apple-cart of the affluent society. The thought that dad was on the dole and any mischance occasioned by a vote might put the elector there, could be a stronger influence on polling day than the new social habits of the neighbourhood, however remote from reality was the apprehension. A glance at the television set and car on hire purchase, and indignation would cool at the thought of possibly losing them through the uncertainty of some big change. Keep your fingers crossed and do not move until you have to, is a natural reaction of any electorate which, in newly comfortable condition, has bitter memory of the recent past.

The father of a fine young man who later was an enthusiast in our cause in another constituency said to me soon after this period: 'He is earning £50 a week now, but when I was on the dole I had to bring that boy up on two bob a week'. Most people think twice before they risk change, and I do not blame them; it is only relatively few who in the stress and preoccupation of their daily lives can look ahead and see what is coming. This issue in North Kensington must remain for the present uncertain. The area at that time combined the conflicting factors of the affluent society with the people's irritation at sudden mass immigration and the concomitant complications of some of the most highly organised gangsterism yet seen in Britain, later revealed in certain aspects by public enquiry, but at that time rampant under the nose of supine authority.

After the North Kensington election our meetings continued to be large, orderly and enthusiastic. There was in this respect no repercussion of any kind from this contest. It was not until nearly three years later, in 1962, that the whole situation changed abruptly, and the reasons were not far to seek. In March of that year we had the conference in Venice, which perturbed the Italian Communist Party sufficiently to be the occasion of the attack on me which resulted in my successful lawsuit against the paper *Unità*. Clearly this conference had sent a shock-wave through the closely knit framework of the European communist parties.

Something even more significant to their apprehension happened two months later in the local elections in Britain. Test fights were made throughout the country in the most diverse possible places and conditions, on the initiative of our local branches and with their own personnel and resources; the result was to give Union Movement candidates a national average vote of 5·5 per cent, which on the proportional system of the Continent at a parliamentary election would have given us some thirty seats in the House of Commons. It is true that new parties tend to poll slightly more in local elections than in parliamentary constituencies at a general election, nevertheless this would seem a significant event to the political expertise of the Communist Party. Unlike the vote for new parties in the proportional system of the Continent, this vote could not possibly have the practical result of securing any representation. It was a demonstration by people willing to throw away their vote without any practical effect, as a mark of their feelings; a vote of dedicated enthusiasts.

Violent disorders at our meetings all over Britain in July 1962 followed the conference in Venice on March 1, and the local elections of May; this was clearly something more than a coincidence. After fourteen years of orderly meetings, we were back in the situation of the thirties before we overcame red violence, with the difference that we were now prevented by law from keeping order at our outdoor meetings, which are the normal activity of summer. Was it spontaneous combustion all over Britain ignited by the suddenly awakened indignation of honest burghers after fourteen years of slumber? Were communists or fellow-travellers as innocent as the Church Lads' Brigade of the sudden revival of disorder at the very moment of our first considerable successes since the war? The reader can judge.

The highly trained but always anonymous specialists in street tactics, who have sympathy but usually no overt connection with the Communist Party, were moved to action at this point by quite clear reasons. They did not interfere during the fourteen years of successful meetings because they thought we should get nowhere in the conditions of the affluent society and were therefore no immediate menace to them; they had the bitter memory of their attacks upon us before the war, which had not only been heavily defeated but in their view of politics had actually stimulated the growth of our movement. There is nothing so disastrous for them as a challenge which fails. Yet things were different after the war, because the Public Order Act prevented our self-defence. When they found to their surprise we were making progress they felt that some risk must be taken to stop it: violence began again; they can turn it on and off like a hot-water tap.

Two clashes are worth considering. We organised a march and meeting in Manchester, which we had often done before in peace and order during the preceding years. My part was to lead the march and to address the meeting. On the assembly of the march we were heavily attacked, and in the course of the fight I went down for the first time in my experience of such occasions. My fall was not due to being knocked down, but to tripping over a kerbstone in the course of the mêlée. We re-formed and marched for nearly two miles, fighting all the way. I then made the speech I had come to deliver. The behaviour of the Manchester police was magnificent throughout. Their numbers were inadequate to stop us being attacked (by assailants who in some cases had been brought from as far afield as Glasgow) but they were determined to allow the march and meeting to go through; and they did.

The second occasion was a meeting at Ridley Road, Dalston, East London, where I and other speakers had frequently addressed large gatherings in perfect peace and order ever since the war. East London in the thirties and even at the beginning of the war was one of the places where I was well known as a speaker and on the best of terms with the local population, whether they agreed with me or not. In innumerable meetings before and since the war I had never previously met disorder of any kind in East London. This time, however, a reception committee was awaiting me from far afield. On arrival at the meeting I found to my surprise that the police had placed two green buses across the path to the platform, and that I must walk alone through a narrow aperture between them to reach it. My supporters were thus prevented from accompanying me. Directly I emerged from this passage I was set upon by a group of men standing near the platform and knocked to the ground, with some of them falling on top of me in their eagerness to get blow or kick in first. I then saved myself from serious injury by holding one of them closely on top of me and rolling from side to side with this protection from blows which were imminent with weapons as well as with fists and boots.

This remarkable incident was described by the Press in the following terms: 'Sir Oswald and his supporters marched through a police cordon to the lorry from which he was to speak. As he walked between two police buses, a section of the crowd surged forward and Sir Oswald was knocked to the ground. He lashed out at his attackers and quickly got to his feet, to reach the microphone. . . . He stood under a hail of coins, oranges and other missiles, until Police Superintendent — climbed on to the lorry, took the microphone from him and told him the meeting had to end.' (*Daily Telegraph*, August 1, 1962.)

'Sir Oswald Mosley was knocked down, punched and trampled on in the battle of Ridley Road, in London's East End, last night. Jewish ex-servicemen, posing as his supporters, infiltrated the cordon of two hundred foot police and fifteen mounted police guarding the meeting-place in Dalston. When Sir Oswald, sixty-five year old leader of Union Movement, appeared from a side road, he was knocked down in a sudden mêlée.' (*Daily Mail*, August 1, 1962.)

'Sir Oswald Mosley was jumped on and beaten to the ground as soon as he arrived to speak at a meeting last night. He rolled in the roadway, lashing out at his attackers. As police stopped the fight, Sir Oswald directed a well-aimed blow at the chin of a hefty spectator. His son Max, aged 22, was among fifty-four people arrested. Police held him when he went to his father's aid.' (*Daily Sketch*, August 1, 1962.)

The treatment of my son Max, who with other supporters came to my assistance, was one of the most curious incidents of the day. Subsequent court proceedings were reported in the Press as follows: 'Max Mosley, twenty-two, Sir Oswald Mosley's son, was cleared at Old Street yesterday of threatening behaviour at a meeting at Dalston on Tuesday when his father was knocked down and kicked. "It was not only my right, but my duty to go to his aid," he said. Superintendent — said in evidence: "I saw Max Mosley engaged in a fierce fight with members of the crowd. I pulled him away and restrained him". Max Mosley said that when he and his father arrived they were rushed and attacked. He pushed a man down and tried to reach his father, who was on the ground struggling. "I cannot be expected to stand idly and watch a gang of roughs kick my father while he is struggling with assailants on the ground," he added.' (*Daily Telegraph*, August 2, 1962.)

Many of my friends then believed and still believe there was a deep-laid plot to kill me. I do not think it was anything of the kind, and have another explanation. The first question is why the police placed those two buses in that particular position with the clear object of preventing my supporters accompanying me, thus ensuring that I should arrive alone at the platform. My answer is that the news of these meetings became so hot that it could not be suppressed, and after years of boycotting completely my large and orderly meetings TV cameras turned up to record these events in films which were shown all over Europe. In the view of authority it would not have looked well if I had arrived at the platform surrounded by cheering supporters with the rest of the crowd whether hostile or friendly too far away to be recorded. Things had to be so staged that this was prevented and I arrived a lonely figure at the platform, while a few subsequent shots of hostile groups of spectators would have provided the necessary *mise en scène*. However, the best laid plans of whomever it was went badly astray, and the fun nearly went too far.

Mr. Henry Brooke, the Conservative Home Secretary, was technically responsible for the affair, as political chief, but I do not suppose he knew much about it, and subsequent questions in the House of Commons were not pressed sufficiently to cause him any embarrassment. He had at least the fairness to say in answering questions: 'The full reports I have received and studied make it clear that . . . the disorder did not result from any words uttered at the meetings by those who organised them, but from the determination of others to prevent the meetings from being held'. (*The Times*, August 3, 1962.)

A meeting of our movement I was to have addressed in Trafalgar Square during this period is worth recording because it had a most remarkable result. *The Guardian* on July 23 and 24, 1962 wrote: 'Violence was in the air even before the meeting had begun. . . . Those who had come intent to break up the meeting arrived early and packed the front of the Square. . . . Sir Oswald Mosley had addressed seven meetings in Trafalgar Square since 1959 without provoking a serious incident.' *The Daily Telegraph* reported the same meeting as follows: 'Most of the fifteen thousand people estimated to be in the Square were onlookers, and police believe that not more than one thousand people, both men and women, took part in the attack'. A notable figure was reported in the *Wolverhampton Express and Star* of July 24, 1962, as giving an account to the Home Secretary in the following terms: 'Mr. Henry Brooke has had an eye-witness account of Sunday's Mosley riots from Mr. George Wigg, Socialist M.P. for Dudley and Stourbridge, who was in Trafalgar Square throughout the trouble. Yesterday Mr. Wigg met Mr. Brooke to tell him his three conclusions: the behaviour of the police was magnificent; there was no incitement by members of the Union Movement; the trouble was caused by about three hundred—out of a crowd of several thousands—mostly young people obviously determined to break the meeting up.'

The evidence is conclusive that the trouble was caused by a small minority in a large crowd which had come to listen in the usual fair, British fashion. I had addressed meetings in Trafalgar Square ever since the war without trouble of any kind. The result of this incident was indeed strange, for the Government then banned all meetings by Union Movement in Trafalgar Square. Thus the recipe for closing down free speech in Britain is quite simple, although personally I do not propose to use it: take along a few well-organised roughs to make a row in the middle of a large and orderly meeting; the Government will then close down not the roughs but the speaker. Having passed a special Act of Parliament, curiously known as the Public Order Act, to remove our right to defend ourselves, the Government then also removed our free speech by closing meetings at the behest of any small but highly organised bunch of red hooligans.

At this point we could not speak in the open-air, and we were at the same moment denied the use of halls for indoor meetings throughout the country. The reason given was that damage might be caused to the halls by the new wave of violence which now might happen anywhere. Yet even in the heavy fighting of the thirties no damage whatever had been done in these halls, which are solid structures; even after the Public Order Act we still had the right to maintain order with our own stewards at indoor meetings and had proved ourselves just as capable of doing it after the war. The real reason was that in the interval the control of municipalities which owned the halls had changed from Conservative to Labour, and in these matters the Left is much less fair than the Right and far more disposed to use any means to deprive effective opponents of free speech. They fastened with avidity on the excuse that disorder had again been caused at our meetings by their own supporters in order to deny us the use of all halls under their control. At this stage only a single hall in the whole country remained at our disposition and I gladly pay tribute to the Conservative majority controlling Kensington Town Hall for their unique distinction of standing for free speech. The right to speak in the hall was perhaps preserved as a showpiece, to prove that free speech still existed in Britain. Needless to say, despite plenty of threats and menaces of disorder, it was perfectly easy to maintain order in that building and there was never serious disorder at my indoor meetings.

In terms of pre-war politics we have since then been completely denied free speech at both indoor and outdoor meetings. Yet in any realistic appraisal of the situation it must be admitted that by the time Government action had brought our meetings to an end, this medium had become obsolete as a means of public expression. The arrival of television for all practical purposes brought the era of public meetings to an end. On television the people can see their men close up and judge them acutely; it is more interesting than seeing a man at the distance of the platform, and their view is from the comfort of their own fireside. The advantage to the politician is that he can address as many people in one night as in several years of public meetings; the medium of the platform has become obsolete. The old parties once again shot behind the bird when they suppressed our right to public meetings.

Television poses a new question in the matter of free speech. If a denial of television time is added to the suppression of public meetings, free speech has ceased to exist. In any case, if television becomes the only effective medium, the question of free speech arises acutely if the established parties alone have access to it, and fix the whole matter among themselves. How can the new-comer, who once relied on the public meeting, ever bring his policies or his party to the notice of the public at all? This question must be answered by government if free speech is to continue in any real terms.

Government and televison authority often reply to enquiries for television time that the subject or person in question is not of public interest. Happily or unhappily, it is impossible for this reply to be made in my case, as I have been made the subject of very frequent discussion on BBC programmes. In fact, I am in the peculiar situation that anyone may discuss me on the BBC except myself. I have been the subject of frequent comment and attack, but so far have always been denied the right to reply.[1] As a result of some of these

[1] As this book goes to press, I have been approached by the BBC to appear in a programme. Since the above was written I also took part in an Independent Television programme to discuss my European ideas. The presence of a prominent communist in the front row of the studio audience, with a number of supporters, produced a less serious discussion, but a lively and familiar occasion.

attacks, I brought a libel action against the BBC. The attacks continued even after the action had begun, so on February 16, 1966, I applied to the High Court for their committal for contempt of court, alleging that not only were libellous things said in a broadcast, but in the preliminary advertisement in *Radio Times*, with a circulation of 4,000,000, a photograph of me was shown and a libellous statement was attached. Lord Chief Justice Parker in his judgment, with the concurrence of Mr. Justice Sachs and Mr. Justice Widgery, made the following observations: 'May I say at once that for my part I have very considerable sympathy with this applicant. Here is a vast organisation which has the ear of the whole public who can, within the law of libel, give free expression to their views, and yet the object of those views is wholly incapable of presenting his case in the same form of medium. It is perfectly clear that the respondents will not have him on their programme. I am not criticising them for that, but it does disclose a curious system whereby someone who has the ear of the whole nation can say things and the unfortunate subject has no means of answering back in the same medium.'

My application, however, was turned down, because in the words of the Lord Chief Justice: 'I am not satisfied that there is really any genuine intention on the part of this applicant ever to bring the action to trial. He has been perfectly open about the matter, both in the action itself and in these proceedings. His whole object has been to obtain a platform, if I may use that term, on which he can answer the allegations which have been made against him, and preferably a platform in one of the respondents' programmes.' The Lord Chief Justice, of course, was perfectly correct in his appraisal of the situation. I was not at all interested in the libel action or the obtaining of damages, but was simply using it as an attempt to obtain the right of reply. I do not mind in the least what the BBC or anyone else says about me, if I have the right of reply. I am ready at any time to meet their best men face to face on television, and can answer every word they have ever said against me; the people can then judge.

The champions of the BBC have never yet faced me in public debate. The last time they even allowed me to speak on radio was after the Olympia meeting in 1934. I was told it was to be a debate with a well-known journalist, but when I arrived he was not present, so I made my statement and left. He was, however, kept in reserve in another room to comment on what I had said, without facing me. The method of the BBC has been to avoid confrontation, to attack, to deny reply; they can evade the consequences by sheer weight of money, which in the end is the money of the licence payers. Private individuals are in no position to challenge corporations with these resources at the costs prevailing in our courts. I was advised that this action might cost at least £30,000. The result would depend—as I knew from experience—on the spin of a coin, the composition of a jury. Not only that, it seemed to me that over the long term continual and unanswered attacks must have conditioned almost any jury in their favour and against me. The cost was beyond any normal pocket, and the risk was beyond any sane man's calculations. This is the system I was up against, and in these conditions I am not asking for justice from the English courts. It is a sad and bitter thing for an Englishman to say that I have twice recently obtained justice in European courts, where the procedure is relatively cheap and expeditious, and the issue is decided by judges and not by juries, but the absence of these conditions in the English courts makes it impossible for me there to fight a public corporation such as the BBC, which is supplied with £64 million per annum of the licence payers' money.

I have had to fight many law actions, and in recent times have always put my cases in person. I am not by nature litigious, but go through with the time-wasting business when it is the only way to obtain redress. The litigant in this country can be sure of fair treatment from the higher ranges of the judiciary, and it is the only place he can be sure of it. I do not like the business, because it means so much hanging about in the precincts of the courts and attention to all the pettyfogging detail of their procedure. Yet I admit the actual clash of argument is stimulating and even enjoyable; it is one of the finest of intellectual exercises. Encouraged by the courtesy and often by the kindly compliments of judges, I have on occasion been tempted to go to the Bar, but have always been restrained by the feeling that my time was meant for other things. So the courts remain to me a last resort, also a memory of good argument and, at the high level, a fair deal.

In these conditions of complete suppression of all effective means of political expression, we might well have asked ourselves how we could continue at all, how we could exist politically or our opinions be known to anyone. Naturally, the handicap is enormous, but there is a final answer to the problem. It is the party. I described what I mean in my book *Europe: Faith and Plan* (1958): 'The party can be the greatest influence in the modern world, for good or evil. The organised political party—or movement as it is usually called, when it represents an idea which is fundamental, and a party method which is serious—can be a greater influence in the State than even the Press, radio, television, cinema or any other of the multiple instruments of the established interest and the money power. This has always been the case in relatively modern times. The party must, of course, represent a clear and decisive idea of the period, an idea which the people want because its time has come. The party must also have a real national organisation, which should aim at covering every street and village in the country. Then the party is paramount. . . . To be effective in this decisive sense the party must be a party of men and women dedicated to an idea, which continually functions in promotion of that idea; a real political movement is more akin to a religious order than a social organisation.'

I described the work of the party as follows: 'The party which really

serves the people and is, therefore, organised to that end, should be represented by a single, responsible individual in every street of the great cities
and in every village of the countryside. That person should be there to serve
the people, to help them in need, to assist and to advise. . . . Such a party
would be a movement of continually available service to the people; it would
be of the people and with the people, and interwoven with their daily life.
The influence of such a party would naturally be very great, but nobody
could possibly believe it was an oppressive influence. Any individual in any
street could tell a party worker he never wanted to see him again, and the
whole electorate could convey the same sharp message to the party as a whole
at an election. And the attitude of the party worker would be the same as the
position of the party as a whole in electoral adversity; a willingness to retire
temporarily in a period of national fatigue, but a certainty of return in the
moment of need and action. A party should be a movement of service, but
also of leadership; a companion to the people, ever at hand to help, but also a
leader on paths which lead upward to new and unproven heights. It should be
the duty of a party to look ahead, think ahead, feel ahead, live ahead. . . .
Such a movement should seek always to be in the vanguard of the human
march, a leader in all adventures of the mind and spirit.'

The evidence available, that in time of crisis such a party could prevail over
the massive array of State and money power controlling all the instruments
for forming public opinion, is first the power of the existing party machines,
and the influence they wield in the canvass. Their intermittent organisations
only function at election time, apart from their paid agents and a few devoted
officials, but everyone who has been up against them knows how effective
they are. *A fortiori*, a permanently functioning organisation of dedicated men
and women interwoven with the life of the people and trusted by them because
of the continuous service they render, could wield an enduring influence.
Another point is that even the present inadequate electoral machines of the
established parties have to a large extent often defeated the opinion-forming
power of the money machine. The Labour Party has never had anything like
the Press at the disposal of the Conservative Party, but even in the days when
the Press was the only organ for forming opinion, Labour often won. The
political machine defeated the Press. I have never checked to see if it is
entirely correct, but I was brought up on the political legend that in the 1906
election the Conservatives had every newspaper in Scotland on their side,
but the Liberals won every seat.

Television is now possibly a more powerful political force than the Press,
yet it cuts both ways, it both advertises and reveals. A smooth personality
providing a comfortable and successful emblem of the affluent society may
become a disaster when things go wrong, and the people suddenly require a
completely different image. Nothing could be so stable and enduringly
effective as the pervading influence of a party which makes always available to

the people in their daily lives trusted friends who speak for the local party. Yet in practice all this is easier said than done, because the genius of the English people is improvisation under the spur of crisis rather than organisation before the necessity becomes evident. The English can do such things much quicker than most people, but they need stimulus. The most we can hope for before crisis is to get enough work done by volunteers to make most people aware of an idea worthy of allegiance. First comes the idea—always.

How far had you got with the aim of creating a party when you withdrew to write the book, the reader may justly enquire? My answer is, further than I could have expected in the absence of a national crisis. I have already given reasons produced from historic experience and statistical analysis to show that a new party can never become effective as a mass movement winning power before crisis comes. Until then, a new movement can only be a powerhouse for new ideas. Union Movement has been not so much a party as an apostle of national renaissance. The work has been done by dedicated men and women throughout the country with the character to endure through any adversity. They have made it possible for new ideas to live, and as a result many people are aware that other policies exist and that they can turn to them in time of crisis. During conditions of the affluent society this is the limit of the achievement. Serious ideas and serious men are not taken seriously until the times become serious. Then things happen very quickly.

Branches on their own initiative fight local elections, and the party occasionally intervenes in parliamentary elections. In this way ideas can be brought before the people, but, of course, there can be no hope of success until these ideas are needed. Nevertheless, results are interesting. In the General Election of 1966 I polled 4·6 per cent of the vote recorded in a prosperous constituency where there was no particular issue, like coloured immigration. The average vote of our few candidates was 3·78 per cent. Parliamentary general elections tend to give a new movement a lower vote than local elections or parliamentary by-elections, for the obvious reason that graver issues are involved; throwing away a vote as a demonstration is then a more serious matter.

What did our votes mean in terms of political reality? Our average vote of 3·78 per cent exceeded by nearly 1 per cent the percentage swing between the two main parties of 2·7 per cent. Our voters are not floaters, they go for us at all costs. It used to be said that the Bonapartist army knew what they fought for, and loved what they knew. It may with justice be said of our voters that they know what they vote for and love what they know. They have not only seen and heard us, but have withstood for years the storm of abuse from the powerful organs of opinion. This vote also considerably exceeds votes achieved in normal conditions on the Continent by new parties which in crisis have obtained power very quickly. For instance, the National Socialist

Party in Germany obtained only 2·8 per cent of the votes recorded in 1928, but won power with over 40 per cent five years later in conditions of widespread unemployment and national crisis. Our vote of 3·8 per cent in 1966 thus exceeded their vote of 1928, and our average vote in local elections nearly doubled it. The proportional representation of the Continent made these small votes effective in obtaining members of parliament, while our English system made a vote for us a pure demonstration without practical effect.

We have been faced with the handicap of our voting system as well as the absence of crisis. The only test vote in anything approaching the crisis conditions which have prevailed in other countries was in the microcosm of the small ward of Moorfields, East London, in 1955 when a few typically English people became really enraged by execrable housing conditions. Again, this small event illustrates a large fact: party allegiances can dissolve under stress, and people will then vote for real change.[1] The established order has little idea how quickly a modern electorate can change when conditions become really bad in a situation of crisis. It is an illusion to believe that in a time of continuing crisis a new party cannot be created to win power by votes of the people. We have proved before that it is possible, and could make it a fact in the graver crisis of the future.

Nevertheless, I remain more than ever convinced that the English way is preferable, a consensus of a whole people for national action in peace such as we have known so far only in time of war. I withdrew from party warfare when I began to write this book, and Union Movement has since been conducted by a Directory of five members; they continue vigorously to advocate new policies throughout the country. I detached myself from party politics in order to advocate a policy and action which is beyond party. If this again proves impossible, a new party may have to be created drawn from every vital element in our people; it would include those who have given loyal service to the old parties, but who may turn from them in disillusionment, and my friends throughout the country will make a contribution which the future will at least prove disinterested. In such a crisis the boundaries of party will disappear and men and women will come together in new alignments. Before this possibility is even discussed, everything should be done to secure a consensus, a temporary union of the whole people for national action as in time of war; when crisis is overcome normal party and political life can be resumed.

It is not my habit to keep options open; I always have a clear order of priorities. My desire through most of my political life has been a union of the nation for the reconstruction of the national life which I believe to be a vital necessity. This consensus of the nation is much the most desirable thing,

---

[1] In May 1968, Union Movement obtained a 20 per cent vote in Bethnal Green without the special conditions which produced the 33 per cent vote in Moorfields.

because it unites and does not divide. I tried for it long ago, and only turned to other methods when the attempt failed in the conditions of that time. If it is impossible to achieve for great and necessary purposes a union of everything vital to the nation, drawn from politics, the business world, the trade unions, the universities, the Civil Service, the fighting services, a true consensus of our people—then something else must be tried. If it be impossible to unite, the division of conflict must be risked. Then a new, grass-root movement of the people must come from the still-living earth in the final test of crisis to win by its passionate dedication a majority of the people to give it power. National union made possible by the particular instinct of the British genius in adversity is preferable, but division and strife, with all the bitterness which should be avoidable, is better than acquiescence in decline and death.

My order of priority therefore is perfectly clear, there is no difficulty of choice or option. In the event of a national consensus to save the nation, our movement would be a dedicated service to the people, and I hope a source of inspiration for new ideas in the continuing search for ever higher forms of existence. If all attempts to secure union and action finally fail, and the nation we know and love is dying before our eyes, then again we should not shrink from the final test. A new party would then arise from the whole people and draw together the best, both from old parties and from the initiators of new ideas. New policies and new forms will arise from the ashes of the past but the character of our people will in the end secure that England lives.

25
Policies for Present and Future

Part One

AFTER the war my policies were deliberately in advance of the time, and I did not for a moment deceive myself that they could all immediately be implemented. The reader at this stage of the story may be willing to credit me with a residue of realism behind all my intransigence; in the end there must always be a considerable element of compromise to get practical things done. Moreover, in my experience of British politics there have always been several ways of doing what was necessary. The trouble so far has been the resistance to getting anything done in time. These policies therefore are a sign of direction, not a final encampment. At this point it was indicated that someone should try to see a glimpse of light through the surrounding gloom of passion and confusion.

My key policies were Europe a Nation, the use of the wage-price mechanism first by British government and ultimately by European government, and of course always the linking of science with an effective machine of government. It may be convenient in a review of these ideas to consider external policy before the home policy, on whose success all else depends. I was the first to use the phrase Europe a Nation,[1] in 1948, and it was preceded by my advocacy of an 'extension of patriotism' (1946). I wrote in *Europe: Faith and Plan* (1958): 'Europe a Nation is an idea which anyone can understand. It is simple, but should not on that account be rejected; most decisive, root ideas are simple. Ask any child: what is a nation? He will probably reply,

[1] Chancellor Kiesinger, of Germany, was reported on November 6, 1967, as saying: 'General de Gaulle's Europe des Patries is a good idea, because we are not yet ready for Europe a Nation'. (German radio.)

"a nation has a government!"' This is the right answer, for a nation consists of a people or of peoples who have decided to have the same government. I believed and I still believe this is the way in which Europe will be made; no lesser idea will arouse the enthusiasm of the peoples to make changes so far-reaching. Yet it is probable that neither this nor any other idea will awaken the will to bold reform until the urge of economic necessity is felt. At a moment of supreme crisis the will to Europe a Nation can arise everywhere from the soil of Europe, like a primeval fire. First must come the idea.

The tragic paradox of our existing situation is that the fear of losing our individual cultures is the main impediment to a true union of Europe, while in practice nothing less than the power of united Europe can protect and maintain our present national civilisations. Not only are the industries of our relatively impotent and divided nations taken over by the power of the dollar, but the culture of the large and the powerful tends to absorb the small and the weak. This is the inevitable penalty of being a dependent of America as the only alternative to being the victim of Russia. A union of equal peoples within Europe a Nation would save us by an adequate power of economy and defence from all necessity of dependence, and would expose us to no more imposition of each other's cultures than we can freely enjoy or reject at present.

The desire for this independence is felt in varying degree by the peoples of Europe at present; they will the end but reject the means. Independence from America or the other large external power can come only from a near equality of strength. Otherwise we can have much posture of independence, but no reality. It is impossible to deploy the policy of Europe without the means of Europe. An attempt by any of our relatively small European countries to pursue a policy for which alone the power of a united Europe is adequate must fail because the strength and substance are lacking. No man can play the part of a giant with the muscles of a pigmy. All European countries are doomed to ultimate ineffectiveness until Europe is made.

It has been to me a tragedy that my own country was for years the main impediment to the making of Europe. We have passed beyond the days when British policy tried to straddle the world between America, Europe and the Commonwealth, with an end as inevitable as it was ignoble of falling between three stools. We have evolved beyond the point when a future Prime Minister[1] could say he knew in his bones we should not enter Europe, with more than full support from the ardent obscurantism of the Labour leaders, headed in the past by their most admired Foreign Secretary, Bevin. The British Government now stands at the end of a queue of humble applicants to enter Europe. I begged my fellow countrymen to take a decision and to persist in the initiative to enter and to make Europe in 1948, nine years before the Common Market began and ten years before General de Gaulle came to

[1] Mr. Anthony Eden, January 19, 1952.

power. Even today Europe, with good reason, puts to Britain the simple but still unanswered question: 'Do you enter as Europeans or as American agents?'

I believe as a dedicated, some may say fanatical, European, there is good ground to postpone the real making of Europe until this question is clearly answered. It is true that neither France nor any other of our divided nations can play the role of Europe in the world until the power of Europe is available; consequently we are all doomed to relative impotence until Europe is made. On the other hand, to turn Europe from a collection of small American satellites into one large transatlantic satellite would make things worse rather than better. At present, it is open to France or to any other European country to offer some resistance to that process, thus preserving some national and European identity. But as mere cogs in an international machine—seeking the best and getting the worst of all worlds—Britain, France, Germany, Italy— Europe itself—could be irretrievably lost.

The full development of Europe is halted at present before the dilemma that without Britain Europe cannot entirely function, and with Britain Europe might cease to exist. The answer is for Britain to become truly European, and then to take the foot off the brake and tread on the accelerator in a hard drive for complete union. Such things have happened in our history before; the British people are sadly slow to start—no one has been more frustrated and infuriated by this characteristic than I have been—but once they begin, they can be among the foremost in speed and action.

My insistence on the making of a united and independent Europe may suggest an attitude hostile to America. On the contrary, I have a long and consistent record of advocating fidelity to our American alliance and friendship with the American people. The desire to be a man's friend but not his dependent is surely a right and proper attitude. America has more to gain from a strong partner than a weak satellite,[1] and to do it justice, it has always sought to promote rather than to hinder the union of Europe; an attitude unique in its generosity, because history shows no other example of a great power trying deliberately to create another great power. This should be remembered, together with the assistance Europe received in days of adversity, when we no longer require either American assistance or protection.

Our alliances should be for purposes of mutual defence and not for the sharing or support of unnecessary adventures.[2] If the soil or vital interests of Europe or America were assailed by the communist powers, we should rally immediately to each other's support without question, but neither Britain nor Europe should be dragged at the heels of American adventures in regions remote as southern Asia, which are in no way our business, and this should be made crystal-clear. It is desirable and possible that the making of a great

---

[1] First issue of *Mosley News Letter*, November 15, 1946.
[2] Speech, March 15, 1965.

European power will enable the restraining hand of a strong and experienced friend to replace the helpless bleep of the accompanying satellite.

When European power is fully developed the American presence in Europe will be unnecessary, and this will facilitate the achievement of many objectives of European policy. Inevitably, the emergence of Europe as a great power will create a third force[1] in the world. I have always been an ardent protagonist of that idea. This does not mean that we would then desert America in face of aggression, or refuse common arrangements to meet that contingency, but that Europe as a great power should deliberately try to hold the balance of the world, and our vast experience in foreign affairs will enable us to do it, once power reinforces knowledge. We have deeper roots in historical experience and far wider and more tested contacts than America, and they can be of service to us both when we exchange the position of a camp follower for that of a colleague.

Spheres of influence

I have long suggested a division of the world into three main spheres of influence[2] to replace the make-believe of a world force in the present United Nations, which by reason of its inherent divisions can never function effectively. Keep the United Nations by all means as a debating assembly and a point where cultures can meet, animosities be mollified and personal friendships formed; clear, strong debate in public and good, friendly manners in private can do much to clarify confusion and overcome hostility. But reality can never be built on illusion, and it is a patent absurdity to believe that anything effective can be done by the United Nations when it comes to action.

The realities in terms of action are the great powers, and it is a humbug to pretend anything else; the facts survive either illusion or deceit. Two real powers exist in the world, America and Russia, and this result of the last war will prevail until the emergence of a third power in united Europe and possibly of a fourth in China. The danger of a new war will also continue until the strength as well as the wisdom of Europe can hold the balance of the world. That is why, since the war, as before it, I have stood for the strong armament of Britain and as soon as possible of a united Europe, unless and until we can achieve that most desirable objective, universal disarmament. The most likely means of obtaining disarmament is through the continual drive of dynamic policies from a united Europe; until then we must arm, because in an armed world European strength is the only alternative to servitude under America or death under communism.

My position in the wider sphere of European and world politics today is the same as in the limited region of national policy before the war. I believe

---

[1] This is the subtitle to author's *The European Situation* (1950).
[2] First mentioned in a speech on December 11, 1950, when the phrase 'Hold Europe, leave Asia' was also used for first time.

Europe should be armed, but not looking for trouble in affairs which are none of our business. Above all, we should avoid the elementary stupidity of enquiring where the strong opponent wishes to move and then running around the world to stop him doing it. That is the surest way to produce an explosion, and world war with nuclear weapons is not a remediable error.

This principle applies even more to China than to Russia, which in terms of geography, though not of political ambition, is a satisfied power; its policies will be advanced through the communist parties rather than nuclear weapons. China, on the other hand, is circumscribed with off-shore islands occupied by alien power, while its natural extension in the direction of related peoples to obtain a balance between agriculture and industrial development is thwarted by military intervention in South-East Asia. China already begins to arrive as the fourth power, since the long years in which I have advocated the division of the world into three spheres of influence. Fate presented the West with the unforeseeable good fortune of a deep split between the communist powers, but as usual we have thrown away the bounty of chance in the egregious folly of Asian war instead of seeking agreement on defined spheres of influence.

I was entirely wrong in the matter of the Russian-Chinese split; others foresaw it and I did not. Russian and Chinese leaders had all been educated in the same staff college or, to vary the metaphor, belonged to the same college of cardinals. Whether this redoubtable organisation, deeply rooted in over a century of common struggle, be regarded as a military or ecclesiastical establishment it seemed to me incredible that any differences they had in private should be reflected in a public split. A tried and tested general staff does not divide on the morning of a battle whatever differences may have occurred in the council chamber, and a college of cardinals does not extend private debate to the outside world when dogma is decided and a pope elected. In holding this view I both illustrated the limitations of a military education and vastly overrated the mutual loyalties of communism and the efficacy of the communist apparat. Germans who had been prisoners of war in Russia, or had since travelled through Russia and much of China as businessmen, told me the split was bound to happen, and they were right. Stronger than the communist faith or the bonds of long comradeship was the tradition of centuries of struggle on one of the longest frontiers in the world. We may in this context vary Disraeli's reprehensible dictum in his life of Lord George Bentinck by saying at least: territory, all is territory.

I will not plead the Shavian excuse that I was in error only because I could not believe the degree of other people's stupidity. But this moral collapse of communism, which may well have saved a Western world in apparent process of disintegration, seemed to me inconceivable. As usual, the countervailing imbecility was ready on the other side to rally the day for communism; I failed again in a position then remote either from the information or responsibility of office to foresee the full measure of an event which in my previous experience of government would have been incredible. Never did I think when I sat in the War Department of the Foreign Office at the end of the First World War, surrounded by occasionally limited but always able and honest Englishmen, that the Foreign Office in a few years' time would nurture a nest of spies and traitors who would jeopardise the Western world, because responsible statesmen in charge of the department were unable to see what was going on beneath their eyes, in spite of every warning and premonitory symptom. I did not belong to the parties whose Foreign Secretaries promoted such men or to the decadent society which nourished and protected them, and I cannot imagine myself in charge of a department where such things were happening without my knowledge.

My original suggestion to secure natural spheres of influence for three power blocs in a realistic equilibrium was the linking of North with South America; of Europe, home and overseas, with Africa; of the Soviet powers with Asia.[1] This logical arrangement is complicated by the split in the Soviet camp. It is primarily the Soviet's business, but a broker so experienced as Britain should never refuse his good offices if required in the interests of world peace and his own well-being. Whether this unexpected development really offers the prospect of a return in some form of the Russian peoples to Europe, where they belong, cannot yet be seen with certainty, but it is most ardently to be desired; the attempt to promote it is one of the merits of French policy. Will the pull of relationship in the end be stronger than the pull of creed?—Is a synthesis of European policies attainable to the extent of making European union possible throughout our continent? These will rank among the vital questions of history which challenge future statesmanship.

Nothing in real life, of course, is quite so simple as logical, geographical and political divisions. There must be many natural and inevitable overlaps in such clear-cut arrangement, many complications. For instance, most of South America would much rather be connected with Europe than with North America, and this has so far only been prevented by the relative poverty and division of Europe. A desirable development is that the two civilisations should meet in South America; initially a combination of American money and European culture, if American friends will forgive such a practical view. We should seek together to perform in that region the disinterested service which American intervention in Europe has always declared to be its objective: the ultimate creation in South America of a new great power united with us by ties of kinship, culture and traditional friendship.

Similarly in any sane order of the world the spheres of European and Soviet influence could meet in the Arab countries for what should be a constructive task. There is no reason why this desirable relationship should not be reached once a basis of live and let live in our respective spheres is firmly established as the only alternative to an entirely destructive world war. I have always

[1] Speech, December 11, 1950.

advocated in dealing with the Soviets a dual method of private negotiation,[1] as long as it worked in any particular problem, and of public debate if and when the point of frustration is reached. Public debate has its uses even in diplomacy, particularly in dealing with the Soviets. They are sensitive to being shown in a bad light before world opinion, because they rely on their communist parties in all countries for the advance of their cause now force is eliminated by the arrival of nuclear weapons. When they are unreasonable—for instance, in such matters as disarmament—they should be shown in public to be obstructive of the cause of peace; then communist parties will lose the debate in every pub, café, bistro of the political world and the communist cause will suffer the universal set-back which the Soviet leaders most dislike. The method is to get as far as you can with them in private, but to put the pressure on in public when you are held up. The reason that this technique is not more often employed is either that Western statesmanship feels itself inadequate to public debate, or that Western diplomacy still fears the public failure of any private negotiation will be disastrous. This apprehension dates from the days when the breakdown of negotiations usually preluded war, but is obsolete in a period when war is inhibited by the fear of nuclear weapons.

The Soviets have shown themselves again and again particularly susceptible to world opinion and far more skilful in its exploitation by adroit propaganda. They have even learned in recent years to choose their moment carefully before committing any particularly bestial atrocities. It was not until a diversion was caused in 1956 by the inept intervention of the British Government at Suez that the Soviets committed their last overt crime on a large scale in the savage repression of the Hungarian people. The attention of world opinion was effectively deflected by the costly inanity at Suez from the reality of Budapest; an adventure of no real interest to Britain and Europe enabled the sacrifice of an heroic European people.

Suez was not a British interest which justified war; it had ceased to be the 'life-line of Empire' since we had given the Empire away at the other end of the line, and the Suez Canal in the event of war could be closed any afternoon by a single nuclear weapon from any source. The military mind is often imprisoned within the conditions defined by the last creative genius in its sphere. Bonaparte reckoned correctly in his time that the Middle East was the key to the world, but nuclear weapons brought to an end the epoch in which this thought was valid. Yet British statesmen, whose forebears had frustrated him in this region, remained, by a curious paradox, imprisoned within the circle of his thinking as effectively as a chicken held fast by a chalk line on the floor. In time of peace the Canal is open, and in time of war with the Arabs or anyone else the Canal is closed. The answer in modern terms is to rely with proper preparation on the Cape route in all contingencies, and to cultivate good relations with the Arabs for normal times. The British Government

[1] Speech, November 24, 1956.

responded to this reality by picking a quarrel with South Africa and throwing the Arabs as a present to the Soviets by the successive performances at Suez and Aqaba. I opposed this policy throughout[1] with the addendum upon the Suez affair: don't start—but if you must start, don't stop.

It was a tragedy thus to throw away the fruits of years of long and successful work by men like Lawrence and Glubb, and this wasteful failure must be ascribed to the inability to think out policy clearly in terms of British interest and European reality. British statesmen at this point were not only incapable of thinking as Europeans, but also of thinking as modern Britons. Following my own injunction to think, feel, act as Europeans, in *Europe: Faith and Plan* (1958), I approached the whole complex of this question from the standpoint of an European. I contended that in modern terms support for the French position in Algeria was far more important than pursuit of our own past through the irrelevance of Suez. A reasonable settlement backed by the strength of united Europe in northern Africa could have secured us a safe bridgehead to Africa,[2] where lay enormous possibilities for the whole European future. History moves on beyond all blunders and creates new situations. A united Europe could have secured oil and a bridgehead to Africa, while retaining close friendship with the Arab world; instead, our division and weakness lost the essentials, and later Britain quarrelled with the Arabs about inessentials. These are errors that can be repaired, and European friendship with the Arab peoples will be restored.

We could also have secured our British position within Europe by thinking and acting as Europeans. The failure of Europe at that time to unite lost us an opportunity both to save Africa from subsequent events and to promote the union of Europe. A fraction of the energy directed to the disastrous folly of Suez would not only have saved many of our own interests in particular and those of humanity in general, but also would have forged in a common loyalty the links of the European community. The division and acrimony of this period would never have arisen.

The failure to think, feel and act as Europeans has brought trouble and immense loss. The statesmen of Europe never sat round a table and decided together what to hold and what to relinquish in the interests of Europe as a whole. This could have been done without any abrogation of the jealously guarded national sovereignties, if anything approaching a true European spirit had existed. There was no cause for rivalry in the Middle East, once we had decided together where and how we could ensure the oil supplies for all Europe; a wide choice, since there were alternatives as far apart as the Sahara and Canada; only the will to common action was entirely lacking. Except for oil supplies which could at worst, or possibly best, be secured elsewhere, our only interest in the Middle East was to prevent a conflagration. Writing in

[1] In September 1956 and on June 15, 1967.
[2] *The European*, June 1953.

August 1958, I said that it was the common duty of Europe to prevent the massacre or ill-treatment of a million and a half Jews if that contingency arose, or of any other comparable community of any people, if it lay within the power of united Europe within its own sphere of influence to prevent a catastrophe both inhuman and dangerous to peace. Again history has moved on and reversed this risk; the Arabs now appear the more likely victims, but the same principles apply. The dual method of private negotiation with the latent alternative of public debate would again in that region secure the assent of the Soviets to a humane policy, for they could not be placed in the pillory of publicly willing the atrocious events which remain possible.

A united Europe could have kept the peace in that sphere or in any other vital to our interest, and a reasonable settlement of outstanding problems would have followed inevitably from the strength of union and the wisdom of Europe in its exercise. Similarly, an effective alternative could have been devised to piecemeal defeat in detail throughout our previous imperial possessions, an orderly retreat or a firm stand where vital interests were involved. Again and again I have urged Europeans to decide where they will stand firmly together, instead of taking pleasure in each other's discomfiture while complacently attending their own downfall. The world was at our feet, but the will was lacking.

Even with the dominant American power it does not appear that a common long-term plan of action has ever been seriously considered to cover the whole globe in detail. Have Americans and Europeans ever sat down together and worked out a comprehensive plan of the positions we should hold and those we should relinquish? Have we ever got beyond wondering what the Soviets wanted to do, with the sole idea of getting there first to stop them doing it? Our attitude to Soviet policy has been no more scientific than that of the old woman who leans over the stairs and cries: 'Children, whatever you are doing, stop it'. We are repeating the classic blunder of circumventing the strong opponent on all fronts to stop him moving in any direction: the most certain formula for world explosion.

Hold Europe, leave Asia—Power of guerrillas
My own policy throughout has been clear: Hold Europe, leave Asia.[1] It rests on the simple, realistic premise that we can hold Europe but cannot hold Asia, for reasons long foreseen and now in course of being proved true. Would you then abandon India?—a question arises which is bitter to an Englishman. My answer is that I would not fight for India or any Asian country, if that is what is meant by abandoning them; we simply cannot fight for everyone, everywhere. We must make it clear where we will intervene by force of arms, and where we will not. My definition of the sphere we should thus defend is Europe, its overseas territories and communications, the British Dominions,

[1] Speech, December 11, 1950.

our vital interests in Africa, and America to honour a mutual guarantee if it were attacked in its homeland; nowhere else.

If we face this question realistically, the practical effect of giving a guarantee to defend India by force of arms is to take an unnecessary risk of world war. The invasion of India by Russian or Chinese armies is an unlikely event, but if it occurred, would the British people be disposed to honour a guarantee to hold India in the only way it could be defended, with nuclear weapons? We should be faced either with another humiliating withdrawal which dishonoured our pledged word or with a world nuclear war. However, the communist powers have other and better means of taking India or any other Asian country than by an open act of military aggression. Why risk your neck climbing a tall tree to get an apple which can be shaken down into your hands? The communist method in Asia is to use the technique of which they are past masters, a combination of political agitation with street and village violence. Will America or Britain use nuclear weapons to overthrow an elected communist government in Delhi? If not, they should stop talking nonsense about nuclear guarantees, and start assisting the Indians to develop the political techniques which can meet and defeat the communists on their own ground. We have done it, and we can do it again in Europe, but in Asia it must be done by Asians; not by European bombs, but by Asian wit and will.

America and Europe are only now learning in the hard way the elementary facts of modern political struggle. It is above all a battle of ideas and, as I pointed out long ago, it is impossible to enter that struggle effectively without an idea. I contended in *The European Situation* (1950) that these issues in the future would be decided not by regular military forces but by political guerrillas fighting for an idea. The man who won the battle would be half soldier and half politician because his primary objective must be winning the support of the civilian population. He would emerge from the dark to strike and then retire to the protecting shadows; the sympathy and sustenance of the civilian population would ensure his victory. It was what happened in elementary form during my experience of the Irish guerilla fighting, and the memory remained with me as a useful lesson years later in considering larger spheres. The resistance of guerillas to the strength of America in Vietnam has proved the ability of such a method to baffle regular armies even when supported by a completely dominant air force.[1] This American tragedy proves to the hilt the case I have urged since 1950; it will now remain for united Europe to repair

---

[1] 'The enemy is everywhere and nowhere. . . . There is some bitter truth in the image of the tiger being unable to catch the mosquito . . . phase two—guerrilla warfare.' —Henry Brandon in *Sunday Times*, October 22, 1967.

'The American giant is tragically unable—however willing—to succeed in guerrilla warfare, except at a price in destruction which makes no sense.'—Peregrine Worsthorne, *Sunday Telegraph*, February 25, 1968.

the damage, and in the meantime to do what it can to extricate a friend with the minimum possible loss from a situation he should never have entered.

Nuclear paralysis

The new guerrilla technique, baffling even the overwhelming power of America, was easily foreseeable, and was described in detail in my *European Situation* (1950). It can and will be applied with far more effect in ever wider regions if we continue simply to rely on the orthodox military tradition. The soldier alone is insufficient, he must be preceded and accompanied by a political idea and those skilled in its use. The day of the man who is half soldier and half politician has arrived. This fact begins to be understood in jungle warfare as a result of the American experience in Vietnam, but the further and more important fact does not yet appear to be grasped: urbanised guerrilla warfare can be decisive in future war between great or lesser powers. The political soldier who wins the support of the civilian population, and who is armed with the new light weapons science will provide, can defeat even great powers armed with nuclear weapons which cannot be used against an enemy interwoven with normal city life. It will then certainly be found that to win a war which is basically a war of ideas it is necessary first to have an idea. This main thesis of *The European Situation* was developed within the ambience of a general situation which I described as the age of the paralysed giants, meaning that the deterrent of nuclear weapons would be so great that it would inhibit full-scale war.

I wrote: 'It has often been said that wars would end because they would become too dangerous. That prophecy has never yet proved true. It would be a delusion of optimism to believe that it is now true. But it is possible, and even probable, that wars in the old style will now end for this reason. What state will declare war, or attack and destroy another state, if it also is certain to be destroyed? A fight in which both participants are certain to be killed is unlikely to take place. Has the world reached this point? From the evidence it appears to be so. It seems that any concentration of industry or life itself can now be destroyed by any state which has the technical means to produce sufficient hydrogen bombs and to ensure their delivery. The protection even of space and the power of dispersal begins to disappear in face of such weapons. The life of any modern state, or even of a substantial community, becomes impossible under this attack.

'Do these weapons, therefore, encourage such attack? On the contrary, a weapon which can destroy everything may be a deterrent, but it is not a winner of wars. The attacker may destroy his opponent, but the counter-blow can still be delivered, and he himself will be destroyed. At present this is the only answer, but it is effective. The Soviets cannot impose communism on the rest of the world with this weapon, even if they can obtain it. They can only make the rest of the world a desert. That is why wars between states in the old style may come to an end. Neither of the great power groups will dare to move because that would mean death to both. We are reaching the period of the paralysed giants.'

Three and a half years after I published this view Sir Winston Churchill said in the House of Commons on November 3, 1953: 'It may be that the annihilating character of new weapons may bring an utterly unforeseeable security to mankind. When the advance of destructive weapons enables everyone to kill everyone else, no one will want to kill anyone at all.' Three years later, on May 21, 1956, Mr. Walter Lippmann wrote in the *New York Herald Tribune*: 'Thanks to Churchill's genius, the West was ahead of the Soviets in realising the political consequences of the second military revolution, that of the hydrogen bomb. This second revolution has led us to the acknowledgment at the summit meeting in Geneva that the great nuclear powers themselves are in military stalemate and that they cannot contemplate war as an instrument of their policies.'

How much can be saved if facts are recognised sooner?

Britain should not tour the Far East with nuclear guarantees or equivocal evasions, but give a clear definition of its own position and suggest constructive policies designed to secure a new equilibrium. China is a fact in the Far East and its natural sphere of influence is among related peoples in south-east Asia. What matters is to prevent it going any further by force of arms; the idea of communism we should always be ready to match with a better and a stronger idea. Once spheres of influence are established and maintained, if necessary by the power of arms, the future can be decided by a battle of ideas reinforced by the success or weakened by the failure of political systems within the respective spheres of influence, and rightly so.

The balance to China—non-proliferation

Where force is necessary to prevent agression it should be effective action natural to the region, not a remote intervention from alien power. Asian affairs should be settled by Asians, and European or American influence should be confined to assisting such developments by wise and helpful policy. A natural balance to Chinese influence in Asia would be a combination between India and Japan. The energy and executive ability of Japan would be a support to India, and the Indian potential market would be a challenge and an outlet to the constructive capacities of Japan. All the influence of Western diplomacy should be devoted to promoting such developments. Instead of tramping around with much trumpeting of Western morality, which usually ends in the pathetic squeak of precipitate retreat, we should strive for some practical solution on a sound and durable regional basis, maintained and inspired by Asian ideas.

A sphere of mutual economy and defence could peaceably, but in the event of danger effectively, encircle China and south-east Asia from Japan to India, and could include in its circumference many of the Pacific islands and inter-mediate lands, without any intervention in the legitimate interests of China on the mainland of Asia and without any clash, unless that country strove to pass beyond its natural sphere by force of arms. A combination of Japan with the Philippines, Indonesia and Malaysia could provide a market with a population almost as large as the European Common Market, and the further connection for these purposes with India would bring together a population as large as that of China. If the emergence of an Indian-Japanese combination proved possible, the attraction of that vast economic and power potential might induce Pakistan to overcome differences with India and to join it as an alternative to an alignment with the Moslem world. Until we can secure universal disarma-ment the Western powers should certainly consider assisting a combination of India and Japan to acquire nuclear weapons. The non-proliferation of nuclear weapons might move from abortive discussion to a practical achievement if, on the basis of a general settlement of spheres of influence, the possession of these weapons could be confined to a five-power bloc: America, Europe, Russia, China, India-Japan. This is in my view a preferable arrangement to guarantees by Western powers which the East may suspect will not be honoured, and can bring world war if they are implemented. There are many fascinating possibilities for a dynamic diplomacy which seeks a realistic peace in place of a moral posturing which masks the imposition of alien systems.

Having established the principle that intervention in Asia by force of arms is not our business and ends inevitably in a frustration costly of both blood and treasure, we should use our influence to secure peace—but not hand out guarantees which can involve us in war. Asians must assume their own responsibilities, and this will be the making of their civilisation. It is our task to defend Australia, but not south-east Asia.

Australia and the Dominions

The theory is that we can only defend Australia by holding south-east Asia, and that in any case our economic system requires supplies from that region. As for the economic question, I know of no material from south-east Asia which cannot be developed in Africa, and I can see no good reason why we should risk a war to obtain things which we can get within our natural sphere of influence. The larger question whether Australia can be defended without bases in south-east Asia is even more easily answered. The proper place to defend Australia is in Australia,[1] where, if nuclear weapons are suitably disposed, no force from Asia can traverse the intervening sea and invade in face of such fire-power. It would indeed be a forlorn enterprise.

The reinforcement of our position by nuclear submarines based on Australia

---

[1] The author advocated this course on March 15, 1965. Mr. Walter Lippmann followed two and a half years later with a suggestion for withdrawal to Australia in the *New York Herald Tribune*, October 23, 1967.

is certainly desirable, but it is dubious whether we require any screen of bases in front of Australia. When the only serious risk of attack comes from nuclear weapons it would appear that the dispersed bases made possible in a great land mass are preferable to bases concentrated in the confined spaces of islands, within range of the attackers; but intermediate island bases between Britain and Australia would of course be necessary for purposes of supply.

Close friendship and at least a working arrangement between Europe and South Africa is important to the whole network of defence between that country and Australia. Now that folly has presented the whole Suez area to the influence of communism, all communication with the Indian-Pacific oceans depends on South Africa, and the wisdom of those who foresaw this inevitable development and maintained the necessary relationships is justified up to the hilt. These are questions of detail in which we should not be lost, but I challenge a clear answer to the proposition that the right place to defend Australia is from Australia.

While we have continually risked lives and spent money in regions remote from our true interests, we have so far been notable absentees from arrangements to defend the Dominions. The reasons are again that so large an enterprise as the defence of these great countries is beyond the individual strength of Britain, now a relatively small and isolated country. It is possible to adopt largely meaningless postures for the purpose of satisfying the nostalgia of the imperial tradition in smaller positions which are obsolete or of little importance and therefore require no large effort of defence, but the heavy burden of defending Australia or Canada is beyond us without the aid of fellow Europeans, while our moral inhibitions have stimulated the South Africans to replace our assistance with their own strength. Britain, which rejected the united power of the European community, is thus reduced to watching the defence of our own Dominions pass to America, with the inevitable result of their absorption into the American system.

The task of reuniting the Dominions with Britain requires a great policy. Economics is the basis of all, and we have neither the capital for their development nor the market for their outlet. Again we are driven by facts to turn to united Europe. The marriage of Britain and the Dominions to Europe could be an enormous advantage to the European future. Great Europe is the natural market for the Dominions today, and the Dominions are the natural living space of Europe tomorrow. At once comes the myopic objection: the trouble in Europe already is a surplus of foodstuffs, and any complete union of the Dominions with Europe would pile surplus on surplus and make confusion worse confounded. This of course is quite true of small policies, but not of great designs. If we raise our sights to a larger and further target we can turn an economic difficulty into an immense political advantage. There is no reason why united Europe should not carry on a combined budget the quite supportable charge of a large surplus of foodstuffs deliberately created by maximum production both in Europe and the Dominions. That surplus could be used both as an act of charity and as a weapon in real policy. We have talked about feeding the hungry; in this way it could be done. Such a policy would give both Europe and the Dominions the strong roots of a healthy and prosperous agriculture, bring new hope to the hungry of the world, and provide Europe with the means so to influence Asian and African policies that the creed and intrigue of communism would be swept from the map. For reasons already suggested, I would advocate also the inclusion in these arrangements of territories in southern Africa under European government. When Britain at last decided on great policies, it should ask the Queen of England to go, together with the President of France, to invite Canada to enter the European community. I reiterate that Europe can only be made, and great things can only be done, in a great way.

Frontiers, armaments and lost lands

A plague of relatively small problems will always bedevil Europe and inhibit its development until we face the future together in Europe a Nation. I have never for a moment deceived myself that Europe will readily summon this resolution until small policies have failed, but many symptoms indicate that this point may now be reached before long. Humanity only steels itself for a hard effort in case of necessity, and until then is always well content to drift along with any makeshift arrangement which can work for the moment. The decisive factor in the making of Europe will be economic in the modern age, because it will be found that nothing short of a European community with its own government can overcome the imminent economic problems.

Other questions menace the harmony of Europe and postulate the same solution even before the economic question becomes acute. There is really no acceptable settlement of the problem of frontiers within Europe, until frontiers within Europe cease to exist. While the boundary marks of the old national states still stand they will be disputed with increasing acrimony, and they can only vanish within Europe a Nation. Major questions of economic policy, mutual defence and foreign policy, should be the duty of a European government subject to a European parliament. Inhibiting memories, rivalries and animosities would then gradually disappear. Questions closely affecting the daily lives of the people should be dealt with by regional parliaments. We need devolution throughout Europe, and should begin at once with Scotland and Wales. Dialogue of central and regional government, and of both with the people, should be frequent. I long ago suggested: 'Government should always know what the people are thinking, and the people should always know what government is doing'.

Shall I again be met at this point with the long-exposed fallacy that we should lose our national cultures and individualities? Previous unions of peoples within the national states of existing Europe did not turn Englishmen into Scotsmen, Bavarians into Prussians, Normans into Marseillais, or Sicilians into Lombards. On the contrary, all present evidence indicates that the only way of avoiding a universal amalgam in the melting-pot of an American or Soviet civilisation is to make Europe so strong that it has the power as well as the will to guard and preserve its vital, precious, individual roots.

Not only will frontier questions between European peoples prove insoluble until Europe a Nation is a fact, but it will also be found that nations with long military traditions will never permanently accept the armament position of second-rate powers. The question of nuclear weapons within Europe will not be settled until we are so merged together that we cannot use them against each other, and this once again postulates a common government within Europe a Nation. Otherwise we shall have continuing and increasing friction between leading European powers on the subject of armaments until universal disarmament is achieved; unfortunately, an ideal still remote.

Closely related to the question of frontiers and armaments is the vital question of the return of Europe's lost lands. Frontier questions between these nations and the fear of arms in the hands of Germans are the main inhibiting factors. The only solution is the end of frontiers and the complete merging of German military strength with Europe as a whole: again, Europe a Nation. There will be no final peace and ease in Europe until the union of Germany is achieved and other lost European lands are free. The problem is soluble once the questions of frontiers and armaments are realistically settled. Fourteen times[1] in the period of Khruschev the Russians offered to withdraw from Europe, if America would likewise withdraw. The offers were ignored because the small and divided European powers feared to live in face of Russia without the support of American occupation. Fear was the begetter both of military dependence and ultimate economic servitude. Again and again in these years I pressed that these offers should be seriously considered, together with the related policies which alone can translate possibilities into achievement. Europe a Nation has the sole chance of regaining the lost lands, because it can eventually eliminate European fears and Russian fears by the strength of Europe deployed in a wise and conciliatory diplomacy, which will combine the physical impossibility of an individual German attack with further guarantees such as no military installations in liberated lands.

Balance of payments in Europe

These three questions of frontiers, armaments and the return of the lost lands are difficult enough to settle—in fact insoluble in the long run—without the full constitution of the European community with European government. Yet the economic problem in the present situation presents an even greater difficulty, which is already becoming evident. The fog of economic debate is now pierced by one clear fact, to which I have drawn attention for years, but

[1] November 1956–September 1960.

it has long been ignored as politely and firmly as the presence of the Devil in
the Holy of Holies. This fact is indeed blinding in its unanswerable simplicity:
it is impossible for everyone to have a favourable balance of payments at the
same time. All nations cannot simultaneously sell more than they buy; this
simple fact would not elude a child in an elementary school, but its studious
avoidance in current economic debate is at the root of our difficulty in finding
a solution. First one nation then another is in trouble, because all cannot
together attain this beatitude of the system, a favourable balance of payments.
At regular intervals each country must restrict credit, deflate and create
depression in order to put itself again in surplus on external account. This
means that the country in question can again sell more than others on world
markets, and consequently pushes some other country into deficit with compulsion to adopt the same measures. Countries only get a favourable balance
of trade by mounting on the backs of others and pushing them by successful
competition into the deep waters of deficit, an adverse balance of trade. These
countries in turn deflate and accept artificial depression in order to scramble
back to solvency on the backs of others. This is an extreme over-simplification
of the economic problem, but it is useful to state these realities because they
go to the root of the matter, which will not be settled until we transcend the
narrow nationalisms.

The entry of Britain into the Common Market will not solve our balance
of payments problem, and the same problem in other countries will not be
settled until Europe is as complete a community as the component countries
are today. It will not then be a question of Britain having an adverse balance
of payments and France and Germany having a surplus, or vice versa, but only
a question of whether a firm in Manchester can or cannot compete successfully
with a similar firm in Lyons or Hamburg. We shall no more have balance of
payments problems within Europe than we have balance of payments
problems between Yorkshire and Lancashire today. A common currency will
follow naturally from any such arrangement. Until Europe is thus integrated
it will be found that these problems are insoluble and will cause continually
increasing friction until we end in a major crisis.

The bankers' dream is of course theoretically possible with all countries
accepting the dictatorship of international finance to keep their trade in near
balance, and with temporary deficits serviced by the banks until the correction
of compulsory deflation has worked. In what the bankers conceive to be an
entirely rational world, the carrot of loan and the stick of credit restriction
would keep all trotting together in a fashion both orderly and profitable. The
trouble is that the world is not rational in this way, less so than ever today.
The completion of western industrialisation and the desire of other countries
to imitate the process both in its successes and failures, the development of
science with its enormous productive potential, and the desire of everyone to
play the big frog in the puddle at the same time, has shattered any hopes of a

return to the nineteenth-century bankers' system. It rested on the basis of poverty economics, which were easy to control, but are in extreme contrast to the plenty economics of today, which already suggest to industrialist and worker that they can be free of bankers' control in a producers' system. Bankers will eventually discover their twentieth-century role in the profitable organisation of the vast new enterprises of a scientific, producers' system. In the meantime, so far from solving the balance of payments problems for every country at the same time, the bankers have failed even to agree on a plan to secure international liquidity which is primarily their concern; several different solutions are available, but the will has been lacking to agree on any durable policy.

The matter of international liquidity and related issues, now so laboriously debated, will in the long term be found irrelevant to the fundamental question. It is highly desirable that solutions to these difficulties should be found, but the effect of success would be transient if the deeper problems are not faced. Roosevelt in the thirties temporarily solved the liquidity problem by doubling the price of gold, but the effects were exhausted within three to four years for exactly the same reasons as are still operative. Sir Stafford Cripps temporarily solved the British balance of payments problem in 1949 by a devaluation of 30 per cent, followed by the austerity of credit restrictions to prevent or rather retard a commensurate rise in internal prices, but in due course the problem returned in a form aggravated by a drug which was no remedy; it will return yet more speedily after the devaluation of 14 per cent in 1967. There are certain fundamental questions to which I have long drawn attention which will return in a more acute form than ever when the artificial effects of war and armament booms are eliminated or even reduced. Before we approach these larger questions and the solutions I have proposed, it may be well briefly to consider the policies by which Europe is now aggravating problems which are already difficult enough.

Exploitation of cheap labour

We British in particular can draw full warning from our past against the errors which all Europe is now committing. It is not a matter of theory but of fact that the chief industries of Britain were ruined in the twenties and thirties by the exploitation of cheap labour in undercutting competition, not only on world markets but by import of their goods to our own market. The experience of the cotton industry of Lancashire and the woollen industry of Yorkshire is evidence of what can occur when advanced countries export machinery to countries where finance can exploit labour with lower wages to compete disastrously against them. The uncontrolled competition developed by a greedy and anarchic capitalism within the Empire from India and Hong Kong, and without from China and Japan, was responsible for the ruin of Britain's main industries in its primary effect, and for the throwing of China to communism by the ruthless brutality of the exploitation in its secondary effect.

Britain was saved from the full consequences of these errors, against which I warned at the time, not by the wisdom of statesmanship but by the genius of science. The diversification of our industries through the new inventions of science saved us as clearly in the economic sphere as the development of nuclear weapons saved us in the military sphere. No one could have foreseen either event with certainty at that time; it is the task of statesmanship to deal with facts as they are, not to entrust the destinies of great peoples to the vagaries of chance or the luck of other people's inventions. Our scientists and technicians are singularly gifted and we can rely upon them to keep us in the forefront of the nations if we do not treat them so badly that we drive them abroad, but we cannot be sure that every time and in every sphere their talents will provide at exactly the right moment a life-raft for politicians drowning in the sea of their own follies.

The lessons of this experience have not been learnt either by Britain or by Europe, now busily engaged in including within its economic community the same possibility for the exploitation of backward labour by finance to provide a cheap internal competition in many of the relatively new industries which have recently been developed. This tendency is maturing slowly in the particular conditions prevailing since the war, because finance has had so many profitable distractions from the process which previously made vast fortunes in the East at the expense of the West, but the opportunity is still present in Africa and it will undoubtedly be exploited if nothing is done about it.

The three phases of industrial development which I concluded were inevitable in my early observations of Detroit and Pittsburgh are still a valid forecast, and are liable to occur in a world of free and intensifying competition. We have already passed the period of the classic economics when skilled labour in competition was sure to defeat the unskilled, and are progressing into the period of rationalised industry and simplified mechanical processes which enabled India to beat Lancashire in the cotton business. I long ago observed in Detroit that the elementary individual tasks of the conveyor belt could ensure the victory of unskilled labour, even in the motor industry. We are in the phase of rationalised industry which is eminently suited to the exploitation of cheap African labour under the supervision of relatively few white surveyors, and it will inevitably occur if nothing is done about it because it can be so immensely profitable.

The third phase, suggested to me long ago by my observation of tendencies in Pittsburgh, lies in general much further ahead; the development of almost fully automatic machinery in which relatively few highly skilled men work machines, or even supervise them. At that point the triumph of advanced labour will return, and the world will be presented with a quite exceptional problem if in the interval millions of Africans have been drawn from the soil to the factories and are eventually thrown into unemployment because their exploitation is no longer profitable. All looking too far ahead, all too fantastic, will come the usual reply; and again I answer that we have suffered enough from not looking far enough ahead, and that worse is to come.

Africa and South Africa

My approach to the African question is from an economic and social and not from a racial standpoint. Racialism has really nothing whatever to do with this matter. I have always stood against the exploitation of the old colonialism, the placing of one people on top of another on grounds of alleged superiority or inferiority, which is the only rational definition of racialism and which I reject.

The present nonsense of what is called racialism has nothing to do with the serious African problems, which are economic and social. If in the same economic community you mix people of completely different stages of development, you get economic exploitation disastrous alike to the advanced and the backward, and a grave social problem with bitter resentments. I may possibly claim foresight for having devised a policy to meet these difficulties in 1948 when they were not so clearly apparent. It was called the Mosley-Pirow proposals, because my collaborator was generous enough to give it this name, although he had far more knowledge of the subject and did most of the work. Oswald Pirow was at that time a distinguished member of the South African Bar; he had previously been Minister of Defence in 1939 and had occupied several posts in the South African Government, but resigned at the outbreak of war for the natural reason that he was of German origin. He had a brilliant intellect and firm character; his premature death was a loss to his country and to European thought.

These proposals in broad principle divided the whole of Africa between white and black governments. What has since occurred in a welter of confusion, bloodshed, chaos and atrocity, was suggested in a clear, calm, ordered plan. Black government in this policy received roughly two-thirds of Africa south of the Sahara, and the rest was to be held clearly and firmly by white governments where substantial and deeply rooted European populations existed. Rhodesia was naturally included in the definition of territory under white government, and the danger of a clash with British people would have been eliminated by a comprehensive plan which gave a fair deal to all. The basis of this policy was that Africa is an empty continent with a population of twenty to the square mile as compared with two hundred in Europe—and we should therefore legislate for the future rather than the *status quo* which could not endure.

If the claim of Europeans to any part of Africa be disputed, we should inform those whose passions blind them to history that Europeans arrived in Southern Africa three centuries ago in 1652, long before the present black tribes drove down from the north to encounter the whites six hundred miles north of Cape Town at the decisive battle of the Great Fish River in 1770. The only original inhabitants of Southern Africa were the Hottentots or Bushmen, who were scrupulously preserved and looked after in white territory by the Christian Europeans, but in black territory disappeared even more completely than the Red Indians in America.

On every ground of history, geography and moral right the Europeans have a proper place in Africa, and on the even stronger ground of existing facts it was clear that they will either continue to govern in regions where they have lived and ruled for centuries or will die to the last man in defence of their homeland. Practical statesmanship therefore had the task of finding workable solutions to historic and existing facts, and the division of Africa between white and black governments was our answer in 1948. That policy was rejected on principle by the British Government, but since then more than water has flowed under the bridges and soaked into the tragic soil of Africa.

Separate development or apartheid on a big scale right through Africa could then have been secured by a decisive initiative from Britain, and would have averted many past tragedies and many present difficulties. The emotions of the present had not yet been engendered. The destruction of the beautifully varied tapestry of nature's design had not yet been made an article of faith by those whose deep desire is to make the world as grey as themselves; they seek to turn a complex into a religion. It was still possible for an Archbishop of Canterbury to say: 'If it were entire separation . . . two separate countries, with separate cultures and customs and governments, there would be much to be said for it' (*The Times*, April 22, 1953). There was still time for the wind of reason rather than of chaos to bring change to Africa. The British Government preferred to import the present situation to Africa, and the American problem to Britain, in pursuit of some of the strangest aberrations which have ever bemused the thinking and distorted the morality of a generation whose sense of guilt, derived from an ancestral past, inhibits calm consideration and solution of the present.

It is necessary to face facts as they are. The present form of government in South Africa will not be overthrown except by armed intervention of a major power, and this will not occur because neither America nor Russia can afford to have the other in possession of that territory, and the South Africans have the science, the arms and the will to inflict on an invader terrible losses in a larger war than the modern world dares to contemplate. Present tendencies will therefore continue in South Africa, with the end result that white labour with modern machinery will ultimately replace the present black labour in the existing main centres of South Africa, while the Bantustans now being inaugurated will develop their own industries with black labour at a different stage of development. In this phase the logical outcome is for the white area to be linked with the European community and for the black labour to be linked with the economic community of black Africa; like with like in economic terms can reduce many difficulties.

This is an apartheid which does not perpetuate but effectively brings to an end the old colonialism. There is so much confusion over terms like apartheid, partly just muddle and partly deliberate misunderstanding or misrepresentation. I have stood throughout for a 'genuine apartheid', a real separation of the two peoples into two nations which enjoy equal opportunity and status: 'not the bogus apartheid seeking to keep the Negro within white territory but segregated into black ghettoes, which are reserves of sweated labour living in wretched conditions'.[1]

Meantime, white and black are living in the same economic community in South Africa; but even in these conditions an extraordinary effort of state enterprise has transformed housing conditions and left many European performances far behind. A start has been made with the organisation of a genuine apartheid in which white and black can have an equal chance. Personally, I have urged within South Africa the principle of equal pay for equal work, because it is right that the same reward should go to the same skill when white and black are still working in the same industries. I believe this reform will soon be completed, and will give to South Africa both fair conditions and a rapidly expanding market until the ultimate goal of two completely different economic communities is reached.

The rest of Africa presents a much more difficult problem because governments are weak and often corrupt. Finance capital is free to move in for the exploitation of cheap labour, which is unprotected either by government or trade union organisation. A helpless, illiterate mass can be uprooted from the village to become the fodder of the factory. They will be sweated under the charge of a few white supervisors. The goods will eventually dislocate the European market to which these countries often have free entry. It is nonsense to talk of racialism when the problem is so clearly in origin economic. The point is emphasised by evidence that the same thing can happen in lesser degree within Europe itself, if nothing is done to organise effectively within a common market.

The coming labour crisis in Europe

A fair basis of competition is essential within a common market. Otherwise, sooner or later there will be both a tendency for mass migration of labour from the low-paid areas to regions where higher wages are paid, and an inclination of capital to move into the more primitive parts of Europe to exploit cheap labour. Migration is to some extent already occurring, with social effects which can be disruptive in a less buoyant market for labour. The movement of capital to the backward areas is at present largely inhibited by the almost complete absence of basic facilities in these parts of Europe, such as power

[1] The Mosley-Pirow proposals, April 1948.

from coal, water or electricity, but capital may itself overcome these difficulties in time if differential wage rates become a permanent feature of European life, with opportunity to exploit the less well paid.

The clear line of solution is to approach as rapidly as possible the principle of the same rate for the same job throughout Europe, and for state capital investment to provide basic facilities in the backward areas, which will enable their development with fair and equal labour conditions. The novel idea may at some time be realised by the rulers of Europe, that it is at least equally moral and desirable to provide capital investment for the poorer parts of Italy, Spain or Scotland as for the darker parts of Africa. Not only the fantasies of existing thinking stand in the way, but also the prevailing root objection to regarding Europe as anything but a collection of competitive sovereign states.

Part Two

The crisis we face at home

How far we are from any sane regulation of European affairs is well illustrated by the furious resistance even within Britain itself to any State intervention in the question of wages and prices, which is clearly a prerequisite both to any solution of our own economic problems today and to the later establishment of a fair basis of competition within the larger European community which Britain now thinks of entering. What appears to me a major error will probably continue so long as the complacency of the affluent society endures, until we have a real crisis; then things can change almost overnight.

The leading authorities of the present system in Britain, America and Europe believe that nothing of the kind will occur, though their complacency begins to be shaken. I remain convinced that crisis in a form fairly similar to that of the thirties can recur, even in an aggravated degree. We are told that all the pre-war tendencies have been overcome by new devices, that the built-in stabilisers of a more expert handling of credit and taxation—all too easy to understand, for we were advocating these measures thirty years ago— coupled with new arrangements for international liquidity, will prevent a return of economic crisis. Opposition to this opinion is regarded as a legacy from the thinking of the thirties. Thus we are in deep disagreement at the key point, and at last approach the answer to my old question: is Keynes enough? The pundits of the present system reply yes, for in America they have brilliantly and hitherto successfully applied the doctrines of Keynes. I reply no, for the reasons I gave long ago, which have been reinforced and increased not only by my subsequent thinking but by the long-term trend of events.

Before we approach the deeper question—is Keynes enough?—it is well shortly to regard a matter in which Keynes more than thirty years ago was still seeing further than our present rulers, or any representatives of the three old parties of the British state. I have already mentioned Keynes's articles on national self-sufficiency in July 1933, when he approached the economics which I advocated on my resignation from the Government. The exaggeration of the classic free-trade doctrine expressed in the export theory of the Labour Government in 1929 and of its successor the National Government, seemed to him then an error. He approached sympathetically questions raised directly in my resignation speech in May 1930: 'We must always, of course, export sufficient to buy our essential foodstuffs and raw materials, but we need not export enough to build up a favourable trade balance for foreign investment ... or to pay for the import of so many manufactured luxury articles as today come into the country. We have to get away from the belief that the only criterion of British prosperity is how many goods we can send abroad for foreigners to consume.' Keynes then recognised the inevitable difficulties of our export trade inflated to this abnormal extent[1] and suggested a change of position, which was not far from the policy of 'controlled imports' advocated in my resignation speech.

The concept of controlled imports coupled with the floating exchange rate which was inherent in my policy from the Birmingham proposals in 1925 to my resignation in 1930 is the exact opposite of the present method of all main parties of the state, but is much nearer to the views of Keynes. I wrote after the war in 1954[2]: 'It is the control of imports and not the control of exchanges that is the key ... it is the movement of goods in and out of countries which matters in terms of economic reality, not the movement of money ... the rate of exchange can move freely—look after itself—provided the economy is protected by complete import control'. A floating exchange rate can automatically check excessive imports, as I argued in my speech recommending the Birmingham proposals, and this could render import controls redundant. Yet, to develop the full efficacy of the policy I would prefer to combine a floating exchange rate with carefully selective import controls.

Present parties have not even reached the point of fully implementing the principles of Keynes, and are therefore remote from even confronting the further question: is Keynes enough? My own answer is that the problem of the thirties will not be finally overcome until we deal with its fundamental conditions; this has certainly not yet been done, and even Keynesian principles

[1] 'Quotas on such imports, which have been in force since 1939, were finally removed, 1958–59. As a result, the total of such imported manufactures has risen by the staggering amount of over £1,500,000,000, from £977,000,000 in 1958 to over £2,500,000,000 in 1967, a rise of 150 per cent.'—Douglas Jay, *Financial Times*, February 5, 1968.

[2] The Coming Crisis: *The European*, November 1954.

are inadequate to this eventual task. Cyclical fluctuations can be and have been ironed out by the Keynesian monetary and fiscal methods. Yet the permanent tendency to crisis of the present system has not been averted but only postponed by temporary and entirely artificial measures which cannot be permanently employed. In addition to the Keynesian technique the Western world in recent years has experienced two minor wars, the armament race and the space race to absorb production surplus to normal market demand, and even a temporary check to the progress of these amenities has been hailed with Press headlines, 'Peace scare on Wall Street'.

Nothing has been done to meet the permanent drive of the system toward crisis; the general tendency of Western capitalism under the urge of continual scientific and technical invention to produce far more than the purchasing power or even the volition of the people can consume, and the particular tendency of Britain's top-heavy island economy to find difficulty in exporting over thirty per cent of its total production[1] to world markets in conditions of intensive and increasing competition. When the highly paid technocrats of America in the twenties explained to me in detail the productive potential of America even in that period, it became clear that in the long run something more would be needed to utilise that vast power than normal market arrangements, even with the addition of Keynesian monetary techniques. What has occurred since has not diminished but greatly increased the necessity for far-reaching policies, but the gravity of the need has been masked and therefore in the end aggravated by the altogether abnormal demand caused by the unparalleled destruction of the Second World War and its continuing aftermath in minor wars and armament rivalries, which any relaxation of world tension can at any time bring to an end; the economic deluge will descend when the war clouds are dissipated.

When things are going well it is a human tendency to believe that no change will ever come. 'Nothing can happen' becomes the fixed belief of a prosperous complacency, but all history is a record of the contrary; things happen, and often the least expected. This time there is little excuse for such myopia, because the symptoms are becoming increasingly plain. Despite large armaments and small wars the tendency to over-produce in relation to normal market demand becomes more and more apparent in America, and the distortion of the natural mechanism of production and market by measures necessary to maintain the artificial situation of cold or warm war tends finally to aggravate the disequilibrium. Britain in particular reels from minor crisis to crisis because we find difficulty in selling abroad a larger proportion of our

---

[1] 'That means foreign trade. For you, it is a convenience, for us an absolute necessity. Your trade is only seven per cent of your gross national product, whereas ours is thirty-two per cent of our comparable figures.' (Speech in New York by Harold Macmillan, June 24, 1962.)

According to Monsieur Aron, America's imports and exports amount to only four per cent of her national production. Le Figaro, January 4, 1968.

total production than any other Western country, and the genius of British managers and technicians will labour increasingly under the overwhelming handicap of having to sell so much in conditions becoming continually more impossible. Major crisis will supersede minor crisis in Britain when any considerable decline of world demand leads to dumping by the industrial giants below production costs; this is always possible to a big country with a large home market, and with a relatively minor margin of export trade, but not for a country which needs to export nearly a third of its total production in order to live under the present system at all. The politicians will then have to do more than exhort some of the most efficient industries in the world to become more efficient; it will be necessary by a great change of policy to create the conditions in which British industry can operate.

There is an increasing tendency for politicians to blame their own failures on British industry, until we approach the final absurdity of fussy excursions from Whitehall to teach the experienced managers of British industry their business. This is a fundamental misconception of government, for it is the duty of politicians to create the conditions in which industry can be conducted, not to instruct the managers of industry in the detailed conduct of businesses in which they are experts and the politicians entirely ignorant, a process which adds effrontery to incompetence. British industry is confronted with the necessity of selling more than any other country from the basis of a very small home market. In the least world crisis of demand it will face not only dumping below production costs from countries then obliged to do this and much better placed to do it, but also dumping from the developing communist industrial power with the deliberate intent to break the industrial system of the West; and, in the long run, the exploitation of cheap labour supplied with similar machines by a profit-seeking finance in the backward countries, for whose development British industry is *inter alia* more heavily taxed than industry in any other nation. The duty of politicians is to find a solution to these problems, not to play the universal aunt in teaching Britain's expert industrialists the details of businesses which they were busy mastering while the politicians were equally busy acquiring their inadequate standards of oratory.

The wage-price mechanism and the principle of reward

It is the principal paradox of this period that the only sphere of our economic system in which government intervention is urgently necessary is also the only point at which action of the State is now effectively inhibited. It is in the region of wages and prices that we really require the continual economic leadership of government, but in our prevailing trade structure any such suggestion has come to be regarded as impious. Eleven years before the possibility of an incomes policy was first mentioned by the British Government[1] I suggested State action through what I described as the wage-price mechanism; I devoted a chapter to the subject in *Europe: Faith and Plan* (1958), and returned to it in *Right or Wrong?* (1961). Through use by government of the wage-price mechanism the conditions could be created within which industry could operate, and then it could be trusted in free competition to look after itself with the minimum of bureaucratic interference. This guiding principle I now more than ever strenuously maintain. Neither our British problem in the short term, nor our European problem in the long term, will ever be solved without it.

To avoid overwhelming difficulty even within an European economy we shall be obliged in the end to secure the payment of the same rate for the job throughout comparable industries. On that fair basis of competition, the freer industry is, the better. As science increases the means to produce with mass production methods for this immense market it will more than ever be necessary to equate production and consumption by systematically and evenly increasing wages, salaries and fair profit to provide the market which industry will otherwise lack; and this can only be done by the economic leadership of a central authority within an economy largely insulated from the world costing system and the fluctuations of external market prices. It will not be enough to have a common market, it will also be necessary to have organisation within it if production for adequate demand and a fair basis for competition is to be secured. Everything necessary can be done by the instrument of the wage-price mechanism, and the action of government can virtually be limited to these two points. Even control of prices will only be necessary if monopoly exploits its position; otherwise, in a viable economic community prices can be left to the free play of competition.

The flexible instrument of the wage-price mechanism can secure many objectives which are becoming essential. Not only can it systematically equate production and consumption and thus overcome the basic dilemma of the thirties, which threatens to return directly war and near-war conditions and other abnormalities of the present period cease. It can also maintain a proper balance between wage, salary, profit and investment, for if you have power to influence the two former factors you automatically affect the two latter.[2] Within this equilibrium it can secure some redistribution of reward, which is vital if modern society is not to be increasingly divorced from every dynamic principle of industrial development.

The brain-drain menaces the well-being of Britain today and of Europe tomorrow, and if proper incentive is not restored to ability the drain may be

[1] *The European*, October 1955.

[2] To talk about incomes policy rather than the wage-price mechanism indicates a lack of clarity, because profit is determined by the rate of wage, when free competition determines price. The State need only interfene in prices when monopoly eliminates competition. Rent and fixed-interest charges can be dealt with by fiscal measures, or control when necessary.

followed by something like a stop of supply. It is against every principle by which the industrial revolution of the West has reached its present point of phenomenal development, and against every principle by which man has scaled the heights of evolutionary nature, that high reward should not go to high ability and energy. Yet society is becoming so arranged that the differential award between much skill and little skill is tending more and more to disappear. The reason is that power rests with the massed battalions in the industrial dog-fight by which wage questions are settled, and in that struggle all factors seem to be considered except the maintenance and promotion of exceptional ability. Nothing can remedy this condition, which drifts ever more clearly toward disaster, except the direct intervention of government in determining the basic principles of reward for effort.

Not only outstanding ability, not only the scientists and gifted technicians whose attraction and maintenance should be the first charge on any economic community, are drowning in the present industrial chaos. Any body of men is neglected, however essential, unless they are organised in a big battalion to prevail in the industrial struggle. A mass of the lowest-paid workers for no good reason draw a wage far lower than the main body of their fellow workers, and despite continual discussion of the problem the trade unions have so far failed to do anything about it. It is the top and the bottom of the scale that suffer most.

Agriculture has never yet secured recognition of its basic importance to a healthy community, and it never will be properly treated until the principle of economic leadership by government through the wage-price mechanism is firmly established. When mass production for the large and assured market of Europe is developed, and still more when automation for such a market has immensely increased the power to produce, a far larger pool of wealth will give a rare opportunity to increase the reward and the amenities of the countryman, thus fortifying the equilibrium of the State without any impairment of the purchasing power of the industrial worker. Others who are not organised in big battalions should likewise at this point, and indeed before, directly benefit from government leadership through the wage-price mechanism; the civil service, the police, the fighting services and above all the doctors, nurses and health services on which the whole structure of the State depends, and the pensioners, the old and the infirm.

No equilibrium of an economic community can be established, and no durable equation between production and consumption can be maintained, until government operates what should be the prime function of the State in the modern age: economic leadership through the wage-price mechanism. It will surely be regarded in future as one of the most extraordinary illusions of this period that government has the right and the duty to interfere everywhere in industry except at the two points which matter; wages and prices.

Setting aside the pretentious absurdity of government claiming to teach industry its detailed business, which is simply a mask for fundamental ineffectiveness, what is the function of government in the modern world if it does not give economic leadership in the key questions of wages and prices? Is it just to keep the peace at home and abroad, until the collapse of the economic system risks disorder at home and impels us toward war abroad? Is it just to levy taxes to maintain a growing and largely purposeless bureaucracy, and to hand out money to local authorities? Surely these principles derive from the stage-coach age, for every pressing problem of the modern period is economic. In real terms, government has little function except to talk and posture, if economic leadership is excluded, if intervention in wages and prices is prohibited.

Reward: a cure for the English disease

Even within the limited spheres allowed to government by the dominant forces of the present system, politicians fear any action which can remedy the malady known as the English disease. There will be no health in England until we establish the principle that it does not matter what a man is paid if he is worth it. This means quite simply that he creates more than he earns. If this principle is applied, there will be no more brain-drain, and even without a major revision of the economic system this could be achieved through a reform of the fiscal system. There is no reason why payment by results should not be extended to our methods of taxation. When a firm largely increases its production, particularly in present conditions in the export trade, the chief executives should be rewarded by a corresponding reduction in their taxation. It does not matter in the least if such a man's taxation is reduced to vanishing-point, provided his efforts have increased the wealth of the nation by more than the reward he receives. If British industry has not yet the wisdom to give good young executives an interest in the equity of the firm in American fashion, a remission of their taxation in return for productive achievement can make them free men and give them fresh creative power by enabling them to save and to acquire their own capital.

These revolutionary reforms are necessary to restore the normal working of nature and to cure the English disease. Exactly the same principle should be applied to scientists and technicians. When they can show that an invention or initiative has increased the national wealth, they should be rewarded by a corresponding reduction in their taxation even before any industrial reorganisation has given them the incentive they deserve. I can see no reason why the same principle should not be extended to the factory floor, and initiative resulting in an increase of production rewarded by reduction of personal taxation. These are instruments available to government in the ordinary fiscal system without awaiting an industrial show-down. The government has only to summon the courage to face and to eradicate the crippling egalitarianism of the English disease.

For years I have urged a large transfer of the fiscal burden from direct to indirect taxation.[1] In the old days of poverty economics there was a right and proper prejudice against indirect taxation, which was often a shifting of the burden from the rich to the poor when there was nothing like enough to go round. If this cannot today be described as thinking of the stage-coach age, it can certainly be called thinking of the railway age, for it dates from the period when Gladstone changed Pitt's system of indirect taxation into the direct levy of the present income-tax method, and since then no one has done any really new fiscal thinking. Circumstances are entirely changed in a society which is, at least temporarily, affluent. Certainly, the basic necessities of life—food, clothing and housing—should be free from all tax, but indirect taxation graduated to the luxury element should replace the direct levy which falls on the thrifty and the spendthrift alike.[2] The standards of luxury will of course change as economic prosperity increases and stability is assured, but the principle of taxing spending rather than earning could and should endure.

Unemployment, public works, the trade unions

The other sphere in which the government must give a decisive lead is in the organisation of public works on a great scale. In an island or even a continental economy overheating, with the result of inflation, can occur in a condition of full employment. On the other hand, to maintain a large pool of unemployment is inhuman and disastrous to the general morale. The answer to this dilemma of the present system is to avoid overheating and inflation by the restraints of credit policy, while taking up the consequent slack of unemployment in public works. No man should be unemployed, and work should be available to all on a reasonable standard of life in a large public works programme, but there should be sufficient differential to provide incentive to return as soon as possible to normal employment; re-training and re-deployment of labour schemes should always accompany a public works system.

Public works should now be in active preparation in all Western countries to replace in due time the distortions of the economy of the Western world, which are initially caused by the semi-wartime basis of America. When peace finally breaks out, we should be ready with the constructive works of peace to replace the destructive works of America's small wars and the concomitant arms race. The world inflationary movement, resting largely on America's deficit financing of its wars and arms, can at any time come abruptly to an end, either through peace or the objections of other nations to this financial process. So far, armament race and minor wars have taken up the slack of unemploy-

---

[1] *The European*, October and November 1954.
[2] The A.V.T. system is administratively simpler, but I see no reason why the luxury tax should not be added in defined categories of articles.

ment which would normally represent the difference between modern industrial potential and effective market demand. This has only been done by distorting the economy and aggravating the eventual problem of peace. To maintain full employment in a real period of peace only two methods are available—inflation, or public works on a great scale. We have already seen the results of inflation in an overheated economy leading to over-full employment, and wages chasing prices in a vicious spiral whose end must be a crash.

The only alternative is a stable price level maintained by a strong credit policy, with the resultant unemployment taken up in public works. The economic effect of public works in dealing with unemployment can be the same as the armament boom, without the disastrous exaggeration of deficit financing. Yet the difference in national, or I hope continental, well-being can be vital. The public works of peace can be integrated in general economic policy and can serve it rather than distort it. State action can prepare the way in works too large for private enterprise, and can thus assist rather than impede it. Such public works of peace in terms of unemployment policy can replace abnormal armament demand, can build rather than damage the economy, can benefit the nation and reduce the menace to mankind.

In theory there is no insuperable difficulty confronting a massive transfer of production from the destructive purposes of war, or the distortions of near-war, to the constructive and beneficent purposes of peace. Indeed it is now emphasised in America that great social programmes, like the rebuilding of the slums which are largely responsible for their racial problem, only await the release of resources by the outbreak of peace. In practice, however, the present system and its operators find much more difficulty in doing things in a big way in peace than in war; money is more readily available for madness than for sanity. It remains to be seen whether the vast works necessary, either to take up the slack of production consequent on peace, or to meet the social problem, can be produced by the present system and its personnel. Is it possible without some change in the structure of government and prevailing statesmanship? Will the transfer begin and end with the substitution of a temporary euphoria on Wall Street for the previous slumps on 'peace scares'? The fundamental dilemma of the system is that any continuance of the arms race in all the spheres which science is now revealing will be too great a strain for any economy to withstand, while even the partial cessation of the race will create a need for public works on so great a scale that present political thinking and action will never face it. Certainly, intelligent expenditure on developing the scientific revolution for the further and beneficent purposes of humanity could at this stage rapidly replace the organised idiocy of the arms race. Will this be done by men who appear to be scarcely aware of what is happening? The early future can summon both new ways and new men.

These problems can be overcome, and with them will be banished the haunting fear of unemployment. There is no such waste of wealth and the human spirit as unemployment. It is avoidable, and in a continental economy easily avoidable; it is simply a question of the mechanics of economics which mind and will can master. When demand flags, the market falters and unemployment follows, but we should remember there is no 'natural' limit to demand; the only limitation is the failure of our intelligence and will. It sounded fantastic long ago in the House of Commons when a wise Labour leader of clear mind and calm character, J. R. Clynes, said there is no limit to real demand until every street in our cities looks like the front of the Doge's Palace at Venice; and not even then. He was quite right, there is no limit to demand, only to our power to produce, and then to organise distribution. Certainly, there is no limit to demand while the slums disgrace our main cities and young married couples have to live with their parents for lack of accommodation. For years I have urged a national housing programme like an operation of war[1]; the phrase was picked up and used long after as what is called a gimmick in contemporary politics; yet nothing was done about it. I meant it, and it can be done. It entails cutting right through the whole rigmarole of present local authority procedure and building houses by the same methods as shells, airplanes and mulberry harbours were produced, in time of war. The restrictions of the present system and the timidity of politicians alone impede it; these inhibitions must be overcome.

It will be apparent to the reader that many of the policies I have so long advocated clash with present thinking and with vested interest. Particularly the direct intervention of government in questions of wages and prices is resisted in the mistaken belief that it threatens the position of the trade unions. When eleven years after my initial suggestion one of the ablest intellects in a Labour Government began to see 'new patterns' of economic policy in the possible intervention of government in wages and prices, a precipitate retreat followed in face of trade union opposition; the present hesitant application of any such policy is entirely negative; never positive in a readjustment of all rewards.[2] Trade union traditions in bitter memory of the past tend to slow the pace of the fast to that of the slow; dark shadows of unemployment and the unprotected worker still haunt the bright prospects of a scientific age. Not only my advocacy for the past eleven years of economic leadership by government through the wage-price mechanism, but also my still longer insistence on

[1] *Mosley News Letter*, November 1946.
[2] I wrote on October 1, 1966: 'There is all the difference in the world between our positive policy and the government's negative policy. Their temporary freeze of wages and prices will leave things worse than ever when it thaws. We need a positive and permanent wages policy. Scientists, doctors and others of the highest skill should get more, so should the lowest-paid workers who are sweated without protection. But until production increases considerably some of the stronger arms should be checked which have grabbed the most through money power or trade union power. Government elected by the whole people must lead the economy and stop the chaos. Government must decide—lead—act.'

payment by results in all spheres and ranks of industry[1] and my new proposals
for the provision of incentive through the fiscal system, are liable to collide at
present not with reason but with industrial atavism.

Reduction of government expenditure

Yet I am no enemy of trade unionism, never have been and never will be.
On the contrary, I can see an even bigger part for it in the modern world; for
instance in securing a better method of administration. Reduction of wasteful
expenditure is essential if our economy is not to founder in a sea of all-
engulfing taxation. Present bureaucracy in the necessary and desirable welfare
state should be largely replaced by the administration of trade unions and
employers' federations, and much of the operation of the welfare state should
be made genuinely contributory. People should no longer be mulcted to pay
for benefits they do not want, but only charged for the benefits they desire.
Such a system would immediately bring to an end the blatant scandal of
present practices. Large economies in this sphere can be added to the considerable saving effected by cutting down unnecessary external commitments
through policies already described. Further general economies can be secured
either by the attachment to each department of a watchdog responsible to
higher authority, or by the rationing of departments. Taxation must be
drastically reduced by the cutting of expenditure as well as transferred from
the direct to the indirect method. Nothing is more important to our present
situation than the strenuous reduction of inflated expenditure and the elimination of waste. There is no doubt that swollen government expenditure coupled
with a lax credit policy is the prime cause of inflation. Trade unions are blamed
because wages are continually chasing a rise of price caused by government
policy. Their members do not suffer so much as people with fixed incomes, or
as many highly skilled people who have no trade union to look after them.
Yet all workers, and the whole nation, suffer in some degree from inflation and
the continual rise of prices. Government expenditure must be severely reduced
until greater production for the larger market of Europe will enable us to pay
for many desirable things we cannot now afford. The present burden will
eventually be lifted by the larger turnover available for taxation through this
increase of production and of real wealth. It will be easier to secure agreement
for the policies of expansion than for those of contraction. Trade unionism can
then play not a lesser but a larger part in the developments which greater
policies make possible.

A world of many new possibilities presents trade unionism with an invitation
and a challenge to move from the present to the future. There is no limit to
trade union activity except taking over the government of the country; yet
when they forbid government to intervene in questions of wages and prices

[1] Productivity agreements go some way to meeting this demand, but rewards should
follow and not precede increases in productivity; performance not promise.

this is precisely what they are doing. The function of government in the modern world must be chiefly economic, and the main question in modern economics is the matter of wages and prices. If government cannot enter this sphere of wages and prices it ceases to be a government. If trade unionism stops a government doing the job which the people have elected it to do, a showdown in the end is inevitable and will have to be faced. The will to face such a sad situation should always be present, though I hope and believe it can be avoided, with the aid of clear thought and good will.

Law and order

Government's duty to give economic leadership in the modern age is becoming as clear as its duty to maintain law and order. Failure to play a decisive part in economic affairs can even lead to failure in its first task of maintaining order. When the government is proving so inadequate in this respect even within the affluent society, a grave question can arise in economic conditions more conducive to disorder. In dealing with any such issue I must bear in mind the long time it has taken me to live down my old reputation for being too tough, but I think many reasonable people will agree with the proposals I have now to make for the maintenance of law and order which even today shows signs of breaking down. The first principle is to have a large enough police force, properly paid and treated. Both in the size of our police force and in the treatment of their members we compare badly with some other European countries. The proper payment of scientists and police should be the first charge on the State, for even the survival of the nation can depend upon them. The second principle I advocate is the constitution of a national police force in addition to the local police forces. The local police with their regional roots give admirable and indispensable service. Yet to meet mobile threats to law in the modern age we need something more than a system devised to deal with highwaymen on horseback. It is rightly said that the certainty of detection is the best prevention of crime, though I would add that we must be tougher with violent crime than present political opinion would permit. To govern we must have a proper and modern machine of government and to prevent and defeat crime we must have a modern machine of law and order. This means a national police force, and as our people awake in crisis we shall get it.

Crisis and the way into Europe

The very severity of the coming crisis will bring a new clarity and sense to a people whose finest qualities are always shown in emergency. It may be thought that I desire this economic crisis to come, because I originally staked my political life on the belief that it would occur in the end. Yet I gave my whole life to the effort of ending the grinding misery of poverty in my generation, and cannot therefore wish to see even a temporary interruption of the affluent society for the present generation. Probably the more advanced measures I believe to be ultimately necessary—notably Europe a Nation—will not be accepted until the necessity arises with the stimulus of crisis. Yet I have rebutted the suggestion I desire this to occur; it is no more true of me than of the doctor who diagnoses the need for an operation. It is my duty to state my opinion that more drastic measures will be necessary, but I still may hope to be proved wrong in the view that so serious a crisis will happen. It would mean a hard, tough time for all of us. No one but a fool will choose the hard way if easier means are available. As for my personal position, I may be forgiven the claim at this stage of my life to have been proved right so often by subsequent events that I can now well afford with some content to be proved wrong in this particular respect. Like everyone else, I would rather continue in a happy life than have the barren satisfaction of being proved right by adversity.

Nevertheless, it is clearly my duty to warn that we may come in the end to a supreme national crisis, for the basic reason that this island will not be able indefinitely to export nearly a third of its total production in face of all the factors already discussed. Our long delay in entering Europe and the missing of so many opportunities gives us no easy escape from this situation. We shall certainly find the door of Europe closed to us until we can produce real evidence that we enter as good Europeans and not as American agents, and we may even then find considerable reluctance to open the doors of institutions which have learnt to get along quite well without us. We could have led to almost any conclusion in 1948, when I first said Europe a Nation—France and Germany were then divided and both looking to Britain for a new inspiration —now we stand instead at the end of the queue.

It is possible that the result of so many errors and this long neglect of action may finally produce such a crisis that Britain must live for a short time on a siege economy, a system very close to that employed in time of war. The period must be limited and the operation clearly defined. I am convinced that our people would support such an effort as in time of war, if they understood it was necessary both to get Britain on its feet again and to secure its entry into Europe. The end would be not destruction, but construction of the highest standard of life and the finest civilisation we have ever known. In a grave crisis all purchasing power may have to be frozen above the level necessary to give everyone just an adequate standard of life; wages, profit, interest, rent and everything else, while we sell the large surplus of our production thus created on foreign markets, not only to pay for our essential imports but also to achieve our objective. In this event we should be such a nuisance to other trading countries that a good many doors would be open before long rather than allow the process to continue. Britain can, if necessary, operate effectively not by political withdrawal but by economic dynamism, and our impact on world markets could then be considerable. One thing is clear: Britain will go into Europe when this nation is awake and means to go there. We belong there and no power on earth can stop us; also when we are truly Europeans we shall be welcome. Naturally we do not want to do anything harmful to others, but we should take vigorous action if necessary, rather than have Britain go under. Strong will in leadership evoking the strong will latent in the British people could in a relatively short time transform the European and world situation. Our great people should always be gentler and more patient than other peoples in trying to obtain our necessary ends by persuasion, but should be firmest of all when gentleness will not work; when will, strength, vigour are the need of the hour.

Re-organising the machine of government

It remains as true today as when I made my resignation speech in 1930 that we cannot solve the economic, or any other problem without first making an adequate machinery of government; this still remains to be done. That was the occasion on which a power house of government was first suggested. The reader may recall that I proposed an organisation operating directly under the Prime Minister and the head of the Civil Service, served on the one hand by a research and economic advisory department and on the other by an executive machine composed of twelve higher officials. I would suggest that this organisation should be largely staffed from the Treasury because its officials are the ablest in any department of the government. They are attacked today because their duties are negative rather than positive, restrictive rather than dynamic: also they are always overworked. Officials drawn from the Treasury should be used in the creative machine of government, where their exceptional abilities could be of paramount importance, and the watch-dog functions of their department should be largely taken over by other officials attached to each department in a judicial rather than a normal official capacity.[1] This would secure the far more persistent drive to secure economy, the elimination of all forms of waste, which has long been necessary. The officials in the Prime Minister's department should, of course, be joined in the central administration by outsiders from the business world, universities and trade unions, as in America and other countries.

I have added in recent years the proposal that a consolidated Ministry of Science and Technology should be constituted, linked directly with the Prime Minister's department. This would implement my long reiterated desire that 'statesmen should live and work with scientists as the Medicis lived and worked with artists'. Thus alone can we secure a continual dynamic drive of government to implement the scientific revolution. The work of this depart-

[1] See *Tomorrow We Live* (1938); *The Alternative* (1947); *The Problem of Power: Government of Tomorrow*, published in *The European*, July 1955.

ment would not be continual interference, but to lead, to initiate and to do things which business cannot do. We should even take risks which business will not take. Ever since my first period of office I have insisted that a vital function of government is to carry the new invention from the initial stages through to the capital market, and at last it appears some moves are being made in this direction. If some of the best scientific brains of the country were employed for this task by executive government the wins would much more than carry the losses.

I have fully developed this theory in recent years, but in origin it dates back to my long-held view that the State should be a pioneer and not a parasite,[1] a creator of new enterprise and not a nationaliser of obsolete industries, a leader and not a wet nurse holding the baby for a failing capitalism. Let the experts of industry conduct their own business with full incentive and reward for their efforts, but let the government assist them by undertaking tasks too big for industry, and in the sphere of science taking risks which the future alone can justify. Set industry free, but let government lead.

Restore Britain's health—enter Europe

We need a government of national consensus for a limited period to secure a defined objective. The object is to restore Britain's health, and to enter Europe. This method of government can and will end by natural process when its purpose is achieved and the community enters a wider sphere. Such a government, by reason of its own character and the temporary nature of the situation it is designed to meet, must finish when its task is done. I have made this proposal for years past, and summarised it again on August 1, 1966, a year ahead of the last crisis and the demand for action which it evoked: 'We need today a government of national union, drawn from all that is best and most vital in the nation. It should be strong government, but subject always to the will of the people. It should be elected by their votes, and liable to dismissal by the parliamentary majority. In any case such a government should go when its job is done, because we should then be ready to enter Europe. The life of such a government would thus be definitely limited. The task of such a government is to make Britain strong and fit again. We must press the wind and water out of our national life. Then all reward must be related directly to effort and productivity. Government must be given power not just to talk but to act.' I have stressed that this government of national consensus should be subject to full parliamentary control, but accorded by Parliament the power to act until it incurs a vote of censure. It should be a government of national consensus drawn from politics, the civil service, the business world, the trade unions, the universities and the fighting services. Then at last we may get the dynamism in government which our desperate situation requires, the drive to a future even greater than Britain's past.

[1] 'Analysis' in *The European*, July 1958.

The ideal which guides my life

Since the war I have stressed altogether five main objectives. The true union of Europe; the union of government with science; the power of government to act rapidly and decisively, subject to parliamentary control; the effective leadership of government to solve the economic problem by use of the wage-price mechanism at the two key-points of the modern industrial world; and a clearly defined purpose for a movement of humanity to ever higher forms.[1]

It is strange that in this last sphere of almost abstract thought my ideas have more attracted some of the young minds I value than my practical proposals in economics and politics. The reason is perhaps that people seek the ideal rather than the practical during a period in which such action is not felt to be necessary. This is encouraging for an ultimate future, in which through science the world can become free from the gnawing anxiety of material things and can turn to thinking which elevates and to beauty which inspires, but the hard fact is that many practical problems and menacing dangers must first be faced and overcome.

The thesis of higher forms was preceded by a fundamental challenge to the widely accepted claim of the communists that history is on their side. On the contrary, they are permanent prisoners of a transient phase in the human advance which modern science has rendered entirely obsolete. Not only is the primitive brutality of their method only possible in a backward country, but their whole thinking is only applicable to a primitive community. Both their economic thinking and their materialist conception of history belong exclusively to the nineteenth century. This thinking, still imprisoned in a temporary limitation, we challenge with thinking derived from the whole of European history and from the yet longer trend revealed by modern science. We challenge the idea of the nineteenth century with the idea of the twentieth century.

Communism is still held fast by the long obsolete doctrine of its origin, precisely because it is a material creed which recognises nothing beyond such motives and the urge to satisfy such needs. Yet modern man has surpassed that condition as surely as the jet aircraft in action has overcome the natural law of gravity which Newton discovered. The same urge of man's spiritual nature served by his continually developing science can inspire him to ever greater achievement and raise him to ever further heights.

The challenge to communist materialism was stated as follows in *Europe: Faith and Plan*: 'What then, is the purpose of it all? Is it just material achievement? Will the whole urge be satisfied when everyone has plenty to eat and drink, every possible assurance against sickness and old age, a house, a television set, and a long seaside holiday each year? What other end can a communist civilisation hold in prospect except this, which modern science can so easily satisfy within the next few years? If you begin with the belief that all

[1] *Europe: Faith and Plan*, 1958.

history can be interpreted only in material terms, and that any spiritual purpose is a trick and a delusion, which has the simple object of distracting the workers from their material aim of improving their conditions—the only reality—what end can there be even after every conceivable success, except the satisfaction of further material desires? When all the basic needs and wants are sated by the output of the new science, what further aim can there be but the devising of ever more fantastic amusements to titillate material appetites? If Soviet civilisation achieves its furthest ambitions, is the end to be sputnik races round the stars to relieve the tedium of being a communist?

'Communism is a limited creed, and its limitations are inevitable. If the original impulse is envy, malice, and hatred against someone who has something you have not got, you are inevitably limited by the whole impulse to which you owe the origin of your faith and movement. That initial emotion may be well founded, may be based on justice, on indignation against the vile treatment of the workers in the early days of the industrial revolution. But if you hold that creed, you carry within yourself your own prison walls, because any escape from that origin seems to lead towards the hated shape of the man who once had something you had not got; anything above or beyond yourself is bad. In reality, he may be far from being a higher form; he may be a most decadent product of an easy living which he was incapable of using even for self-development, an ignoble example of missed opportunity. But if the first impulse be envy and hatred of him, you are inhibited from any movement beyond yourself for fear of becoming like him, the man who had something which you had not got.

'Thus your ideal becomes not something beyond yourself, still less beyond anything which now exists, but rather, the petrified, fossilised shape of that section of the community which was most oppressed, suffering and limited by every material circumstance in the middle of the nineteenth century. The real urge is then to drag everything down toward the lowest level of life, rather than the attempt to raise everything towards the highest level of life which has yet been attained, and finally to move beyond even that. In all things this system of values seeks what is low instead of what is high.

'So communism has no longer any deep appeal to the sane, sensible mass of the European workers who, in entire contradiction of Marxian belief in their increasing "immiseration", have moved by the effort of their own trade unions and by political action to at least a partial participation in the plenty which the new science is beginning to bring, and towards a way of living and an outlook in which they do not recognise themselves at all as the miserable and oppressed figures of communism's original workers.

'The ideal is no longer the martyred form of the oppressed, but the beginning of a higher form. Men are beginning not to look down, but to look up. And it is precisely at this point that a new way of political thinking can give definite shape to what many are beginning to feel is a new forward urge of humanity. It becomes an impulse of nature itself directly man is free from the stifling oppression of dire, primitive need.

'The ideal of creating a higher form on earth can now rise before men with the power of a spiritual purpose, which is not simply a philosophic abstraction but a concrete expression of a deep human desire. All men want their children to live better than they have lived, just as they have tried by their own exertions to lift themselves beyond the level of their fathers whose affection and sacrifice often gave them the chance to do it. This is a right and natural urge in mankind, and, when fully understood, becomes a spiritual purpose.'

This purpose I described as the doctrine of higher forms. The idea of a continual movement of humanity from the amoeba to modern man and on to ever higher forms has interested me since my prison days, when I first became acutely aware of the relationship between modern science and Greek philosophy. Perhaps it is the very simplicity of the thesis which gives it strength; mankind moving from the primitive beginning which modern science reveals to the present stage of evolution and continuing in this long ascent to heights beyond our present vision, if the urge of nature and the purpose of life are to be fulfilled. While simple to the point of the obvious, in detailed analysis it is the exact opposite of prevailing values. Most great impulses of life are in essence simple, however complex their origin. An idea may be derived from three thousand years of European thought and action, and yet be stated in a way that all men can understand.

My thinking on this subject was finally reduced to the extreme of simplicity in the conclusion of *Europe, Faith and Plan*: 'To believe that the purpose of life is a movement from lower to higher forms is to record an observable fact. If we reject that fact, we reject every finding of modern science, as well as the evidence of our own eyes. . . . It is necessary to believe that this is the purpose of life, because we can observe that this is the way the world works, whether we believe in divine purpose or not.[1] And once we believe this is the way the world works, and deduce from the long record that it is the only way it can work, this becomes a purpose because it is the only means by which the world is likely to work in future. If the purpose fails, the world fails.

The purpose so far has achieved the most incredible results—incredible to anyone who had been told in advance what was going to happen—by working from the most primitive life forms to the relative heights of present human development. Purpose becomes, therefore, quite clearly in the light of modern knowledge a movement from lower to higher forms. And if purpose in this way has moved so far and achieved so much, it is only reasonable to assume that it will so continue if it continues at all; if the world lasts. Therefore, if we desire to sustain human existence, if we believe in mankind's origin which science now makes clear, and in his destiny which a continuance of the same

---

[1] The same chapter maintains that this secular belief in no way conflicts with the beliefs of the main churches or conflicts with their work, which should be sustained.

progress makes possible, we must desire to aid rather than to impede the discernible purpose. That means we should serve the purpose which moves from lower to higher forms; this becomes our creed of life. Our life is dedicated to the purpose.

'In practical terms this surely indicates that we should not tell men to be content with themselves as they are, but should urge them to strive to become something beyond themselves. . . . To assure men that we have no need to surpass ourselves, and thereby to imply that men are perfect, is surely the extreme of arrogant presumption. It is also a most dangerous folly, because it is rapidly becoming clear that if mankind's moral nature and spiritual stature cannot increase more commensurately with his material achievements, we risk the death of the world. . . .

'We must learn to live, as well as to do. We must restore harmony with life, and recognise the purpose in life. Man has released the forces of nature just as he has become separated from nature; this is a mortal danger, and is reflected in the neurosis of the age. We cannot stay just where we are; it is an uneasy, perilous and impossible situation. Man must either reach beyond his present self, or fail; and if he fails this time, the failure is final. That is the basic difference between this age and all previous periods. It was never before possible for this failure of men to bring the world to an end.

'It is not only a reasonable aim to strive for a higher form among men; it is a creed with the strength of a religious conviction. It is not only a plain necessity of the new age of science which the genius of man's mind has brought; it is in accordance with the long process of nature within which we may read the purpose of the world. And it is no small and selfish aim, for we work not only for ourselves but for a time to come. The long striving of our lives can not only save our present civilisation, but can also enable others more fully to realise and to enjoy the great beauty of this world, not only in peace and happiness, but in an ever unfolding wisdom and rising consciousness of the mission of man.'

The doctrine of higher forms may have appealed to some in a generation acutely aware of the divorce between religion and science because it was an attempted synthesis of these two impulses of the human movement. I went so far as to say that higher forms could have the force of a science and a religion, in the secular sense, since it derived both from the evolutionary process first recognised in the last century, and from the philosophy, perhaps the mysticism, well described as the 'eternal becoming', which Hellenism first gave to Europe as an original and continuing movement still represented in the thinking, architecture and music of the main European tradition.

To simplify and synthesise are the chief gifts which clear thought can bring, and never have they been so deeply needed as in this age. A healing synthesis is required, a union of Hellenism's calm but radiant embrace of the beauty and wonder of life with the Gothic impulse of new discoveries urging man to reach beyond his presently precarious balance until sanity itself is threatened. The genius of Hellas can still give back to Europe the life equilibrium, the firm foundation from which science can grasp the stars. He who can combine within himself this sanity and this dynamism becomes thereby a higher form, and beyond him can be an ascent revealing always a further wisdom and beauty. It is a personal ideal for which all can try to live, a purpose in life.

We can thus resume the journey to further summits of the human spirit with measure and moderation won from the struggle and tribulation of these years. We may even in this time of folly and sequent adversity gain the balance of maturity which alone can make us worthy of the treasures, capable of using the miraculous endowment, and also of averting the tempestuous dangers, of modern science. We may at last acquire the adult mind, without which the world cannot survive, and learn to use with wisdom and decision the wonders of this age.

I hope that this record of my own small part in these great affairs and still greater possibilities has at least shown that I have 'the repugnance to mean and cruel dealings' which the wise old man ascribed to me so long ago, and yet have attempted by some union of mind and will to combine thought and deed; that I have stood with consistency for the construction of a worthy dwelling for humanity, and at all cost against the rage and folly of insensate and purposeless destruction; that I have followed the truth as I saw it, wherever that service led me, and have ventured to look and strive through the dark to a future that can make all worth while.

Index